D0897834

# THE SAINT AND THE CHOPPED-UP BABY

# THE SAINT AND THE CHOPPED-UP BABY

### THE CULT OF VINCENT FERRER IN MEDIEVAL AND EARLY MODERN EUROPE

### LAURA ACKERMAN SMOLLER

CORNELL UNIVERSITY PRESS
*Ithaca and London*

First published 2014 by Cornell University Press

Printed in the United States of America

Library of Congress Cataloging-in-Publication Data

Smoller, Laura Ackerman, 1960–author
   The saint and the chopped-up baby : the cult of Vincent Ferrer in medieval and early modern Europe / Laura Ackerman Smoller.
      pages cm
   Includes bibliographical references and index.
   ISBN 978-0-8014-5217-8 (cloth : alk. paper)
   1. Vincent Ferrer, Saint, approximately 1350–1419—Cult—Europe—History. 2. Christian hagiography—History—To 1500. I. Title.
   BX4700.V7S66   2014
   282.092—dc23        2013024750

Cornell University Press strives to use environmentally responsible suppliers and materials to the fullest extent possible in the publishing of its books. Such materials include vegetable-based, low-VOC inks and acid-free papers that are recycled, totally chlorine-free, or partly composed of nonwood fibers. For further information, visit our website at www.cornellpress.cornell.edu.

Cloth printing        10 9 8 7 6 5 4 3 2 1

*For Bruce*

# CONTENTS

# ILLUSTRATIONS

# ACKNOWLEDGMENTS

This book began modestly, as a study of the miracles reported by fifteenth-century Breton witnesses testifying on behalf of the canonization of a Dominican preacher named Vincent Ferrer. The project has grown enormously since then. In the course of its many transformations, I have encountered a great number of debts, and it is a pleasure to recall at least some of them here. No historical study could be accomplished without the help of archivists and librarians in numerous institutions. I owe a special expression of gratitude to Karen Russ and, above all, Brenda Jackson from the Ottenheimer Library at my own University of Arkansas at Little Rock, miracle workers both of them. I have received as well extraordinary kindnesses from John Rawlings at Stanford's Green Library, Eric White at SMU's Bridwell Library, William Monroe at Brown University, Jane Jackson at Providence College's Phillips Memorial Library, and Adan Benavides at the Benson Collection at the University of Texas, Austin. A fellowship from the John Simon Guggenheim Memorial Foundation, as well as summer funds from the National Endowment for the Humanities; the College of Arts, Humanities, and Social Sciences at UALR; and the Office of Research and Sponsored Programs at UALR have all helped to support the research and writing of this book. I owe profound thanks as well to the Division of Medical Humanities of the University of Arkansas for Medical Sciences, as well as to the Office of Research and Sponsored Programs at UALR, for funds to help defray the costs of publication of this book.

The true joy in scholarship is not in the solitary pursuit of knowledge but rather in sharing ideas with others, and this project would never have taken the shape it has without the generous input of friends and colleagues, in formal venues and informal conversations and e-mails. Philippe Buc, Maureen Miller, Amy Remensnyder, Lou Roberts, Ellen Neskar, and Lisa Rothrauff were all there at the beginning and helped me to discover how rich a treasure trove lay in Vincent's canonization records. Alison Frazier, Renate Blumenfeld-Kosinski, Thomas Wetzstein, Otfried Krafft, Christian Krötzl, Sari Katajala-Peltomaa, Fernando Vidal, and the late Michael Goodich have all been sources of enlightenment and good cheer, as have colleagues Moira Maguire, Kristin Dutcher Mann, and Carl Moneyhon at UALR, and Lynda

Coon at the University of Arkansas at Fayetteville. I have benefited immeasurably from the comments of those who have kindly read drafts of chapters: Maureen Miller, Bruce Venarde, Alison Frazier, Marc Forster, Kristin Dutcher Mann, Vince Vinikas, Carl Moneyhon, and the other members of the WIMPS reading group in Little Rock. Participants at workshops at Stanford University, Johns Hopkins University, the University of Pennsylvania, the University of Texas at Austin, and the University of California at Berkeley have all provided insights that shaped my thinking on Vincent Ferrer. Jorge and Maria Villegas, Héctor Schenone, Augustine Thompson, O.P., Michael Morris, O.P., Anne Pushkal, Roberto Rusconi, Igor Gorevich, and Vera Tyuleneva generously helped me to find illustrations. I owe heartfelt thanks to Philip Daileader and Robin Vose for their careful and sensitive readings of my manuscript for Cornell University Press, as well as to my editor, Peter J. Potter, who has shepherded this book on its journey to print with uncommon good sense and humor, and to Jamie Fuller, who copyedited the manuscript with admirable thoroughness. And no one could provide a better model of scholarly exchange, friendship, and generosity than has Alison Frazier. I am a different type of scholar for having known all of these people. Needless to say, the faults and flaws in my work remain all my own.

Finally, I owe my family more thanks than can adequately fit here. My parents provided me early on with a taste for the life of the mind and have continued to take delight in my intellectual pursuits, no matter how bizarre the path my own research has taken. My sister, Susan Ackerman, has been a source of inspiration, scholarly wisdom, and practical assistance, even making her own pilgrimage in search of one of my Vincent Ferrers. My sons Jason and Gabriel not only have put up with too many saintly field trips but have also, as they have grown to manhood, reminded me daily of the sense of awe and wonder at the heart of the word "miracle," as well as of the depth of the care and concern felt by those anxious parents in the past who uttered up vows to Vincent Ferrer. And the greatest thanks go to my husband, Bruce, who has been not only a reliable sounding board and critic but also a more patient and effective cheerleader than he can ever know.

# Abbreviations

**AASS**   *Acta Sanctorum: The Full-Text Database* (Cambridge: Chadwyck-Healey, 2000–).

**ADM**   Archives Départementales du Morbihan, Vannes

**BAV**   Biblioteca Apostolica Vaticana, Vatican City

**BC**   Biblioteca Casanatense, Rome

**BHL**   *Bibliotheca hagiographica latina antiquae et mediae aetatis,* 2 vols. (Brussels: Société des Bollandistes, 1900–1901); *Bibliotheca hagiographica latina antiquae et mediae aetatis, Supplementi* (Brussels: Société des Bollandistes, 1911); Henryk Fros, *Bibliotheca hagiographica latina antiquae et mediae aetatis, Novum supplementum* (Brussels: Société des Bollandistes, 1956).

**BNF**   Bibliothèque nationale de France, Paris

**FHSVF**   Pierre-Henri Fages, *Histoire de Saint Vincent Ferrier,* 2 vols. (Paris: Picard, 1901).

**FND**   Pierre-Henri Fages, *Notes et documents de l'histoire de Saint Vincent Ferrier* (Paris: Picard, 1905).

**FPC**   Pierre-Henri Fages, *Procès de la canonisation de Saint Vincent Ferrier pour faire suite à l'histoire du même saint* (Paris: Picard, 1904).

**O.P.**   Order of Preachers

**PL**   *Patrologia Latina: The Full Text Database* (Cambridge: Chadwyck-Healey, 1996).

**Procès**   Archives Départementales du Morbihan, Vannes. Procès de canonisation de saint Vincent Ferrier, MS 87 G 11.

**Proceso**   Universidad de Valencia, Biblioteca, Valencia. Proceso de la canonizacion de San Vicente Ferrer, 9 del junio 1590, G.C. 1869, M. 690.

**RVV**   Pietro Ranzano, *Vita Vincentii.* In *Acta Sanctorum: The Full-Text Database* (Cambridge: Chadwyck-Healey, 2000–), Aprilis, 1:482–512.

**WBSA**   Walberberg (Germany), Bibliothek St. Albert.

# A NOTE ON NAMES

This story of Vincent Ferrer's cult relies on sources in a variety of languages and from a number of different regions and cultures. In order to retain some of the sense of that diversity, I have kept the names of rulers in the language of their native regions (French for the dukes of Brittany, Catalan for the count-kings of Aragon, Castilian for the Trastámara rulers of Aragon and Naples). For Vincent himself, as well as for popes, I use the more common English spelling. In the case of persons who appear in the canonization inquests, I have left their names in the Latin of the records.

# Events Relevant to the Canonization of Vincent Ferrer

| | |
|---|---|
| April 5, 1419 | Death of Vincent Ferrer in Vannes |
| October 18, 1451 | Letter of Nicholas V opening the canonization process |
| January 5, 1452 | Letter appointing the Brittany subcommissioners |
| February 18, 1452 | Letter appointing the Toulouse subcommissioners |
| May 19, 1453 | Election of Martial Auribelli as master general of the Dominican order in Nantes |
| October 26, 1453 | Appointment of the Brittany procurer, Guillermus Coetmur |
| November 23, 1453 | First witnesses heard in Brittany at Saint-Guen |
| December 8, 1453 | Last Brittany testimony at Saint-Guen; beginning of subcommissioners' inquests in other parts of the duchy |
| April 7, 1454 | Ceremony closing the Brittany inquest |
| May 11, 1454 | First Toulouse testimony heard |
| May 13, 1454 | Letter appointing the Naples subcommissioners |
| June 25, 1454 | Last surviving testimony from Toulouse inquest |
| August 3, 1454 | First Naples witnesses heard |
| November 18, 1454 | Last surviving testimony from Naples inquest |
| March 25, 1455 | Death of Nicholas V |
| April 8, 1455 | Election of Calixtus III |
| June 3, 1455 | Calixtus III announces decision to canonize Vincent Ferrer |
| June 29, 1455 | Canonization ceremony for Vincent Ferrer |
| October 1, 1458 | Pius II's canonization bull for Vincent Ferrer (*Rationi congruit*) |

# THE SAINT AND THE CHOPPED-UP BABY

# PROLOGUE

# From Preacher to Saint

This is not a book about Vincent Ferrer. Rather, it is a book about *Saint* Vincent Ferrer. That is to say, it is a book about an idea: the idea that a Valencian Dominican friar named Vincent Ferrer, after his death in 1419, was sitting at the right hand of God and could thus intercede on behalf of people still on earth. With Vincent Ferrer the person I concern myself very little; indeed, there are good reasons to find the real Vincent Ferrer a somewhat unsavory character, and I am just as happy to leave him to other scholars.[1] I am not so much interested in this reality as in Vincent's representation and image: What did it mean to someone to say, "Vincent Ferrer is a saint"? What thoughts and images did people conjure up when they remembered or conceived of *Saint* Vincent Ferrer? In short, what stories did they tell about this saint?

I first encountered Vincent Ferrer—and began asking these sorts of questions—more than fifteen years ago. I was a graduate student, eager to finish a dissertation about a late medieval cardinal's use of astrology to predict the end of the world. Vincent's name presented itself as a fine specimen of a contemporary apocalyptic preacher, and I summoned from the Berkeley library Pierre-Henri Fages's monumental *Histoire de Saint Vincent Ferrier* in order to read what Vincent had to say about Antichrist. There, in the back of the second of two massive burgundy-colored tomes, were Fages's

---

1. Philip Daileader has recently completed a new biography of Vincent (forthcoming with Cornell University Press), which will be a welcome addition.

transcriptions of testimony given at three canonization inquests, fact-finding missions that stood at the first of the long judicial process that would, in 1455, result in Vincent's being inscribed—in the papal court's flowery language—in the catalog of saints.[2]

I wrote this book because I fell in love with that set of documents, particularly the large, sprawling series of three hundred and thirteen depositions taken in Brittany, where the saint is buried, in the years 1453–54. What drew me in were the stories: stories of a preacher so old and debilitated that he had to be helped to the pulpit but who became as spry and animated as a young man of thirty when he began to preach of the imminent Last Judgment and of sinners' need for repentance; stories of bizarre illnesses and mishaps—the man whose intestines hung down to his knees, the youth who expelled some sixty stones; and stories of ordinary people at the most dire moments of their lives, saved by the intercession of Vincent Ferrer. Whatever caveats scholars may raise about the way in which procedures shaped and distorted witnesses' words, I had the sense that in these stories I had come as close as I ever would to hearing the voices of ordinary people in the later Middle Ages.[3]

As I continued to read their tales, something else began to strike me. People did not tell the same story in the same way. In some cases, witnesses added seemingly inconsequential details to the same basic narrative, as in the tale of the child who asked to eat an egg on the moment of his miraculous cure from plague. But in other cases, the differences were of apparently greater import. Could all witnesses hear and understand Vincent's sermons, no matter how far away they stood and no matter what their native language? Had the recipient of a miraculous cure merely been out of his senses, or had he been possessed by demons? Had the victim really died before Vincent's intercession had resuscitated her, or had she only appeared to do so? Who, among several contenders, had in fact initiated the vow to Vincent Ferrer that brought about a miracle? Pondering these differences and their possible significance, I realized that, in the period from his death in 1419 up to his canonization in 1455, Vincent Ferrer was, in a sense, a symbol without a fixed meaning—if not quite a blank canvas, at least one on which only the broadest of outlines had been sketched and one on which different observers and narrators could put their own stamp. And I became fascinated by those contested meanings of the potential saint and by the ways in which individuals and institutions told stories about Vincent in order to make claims about themselves.

---

2. The books in question, bound together into two volumes by the Berkeley library, were FHSVF, FND, and FPC.

3. See, e.g., Lett 2008.

Still, I had assumed—perhaps because André Vauchez, ending his magisterial study of canonizations in 1431, had remarked on the greater control exercised over the cult of the saints by the fifteenth-century papacy—that once Vincent was canonized in 1455, that fluid situation would come to an end.[4] Or if canonization did not cement a fixed image of Vincent Ferrer, at the very least, that stabilization would come in the first "official" biography of the saint, composed by a Sicilian Dominican named Pietro Ranzano in the year following Vincent's canonization, at the behest of the pope and the head of the Dominican order.[5] Ranzano's *vita* (life), which portrays the saint as an effective converter of Jews and Muslims and as instrumental in healing a protracted papal schism, in fact informs modern hagiography about Vincent, epitomized in devotional cards such as one can buy in the Valencia cathedral today. But even though Vincent's canonization came in the same decade as the new medium of print that might have broadcast such an official image, Ranzano's *Life of Vincent* was not printed until the late seventeenth century. And, further, as I began to read the early *vitae* of Vincent—those from the first half-century or so following his canonization, as well as sixteenth- and seventeenth-century lives of the saint—it became apparent that there existed an almost bewildering array of portrayals of the saint in manuscript, print, and art, few of which took up Ranzano's spin on the holy preacher.

A single miracle found in the canonization inquests and highlighted by Pietro Ranzano illustrates the way in which divergent narrations of the same story helped their tellers shape an image of Vincent Ferrer that served their own individual purposes. The tale involves a crazed mother, who cuts up and cooks her own infant son, only to have the child restored through the merits of Vincent Ferrer. In testimony from the canonization inquests through the *vitae* of the late seventeenth century, narrators used the story of the chopped-up baby for their own ends, whether to illustrate the saint's intercessory powers, to validate Vincent's role in church politics, to boost claims of regional identity, or to proclaim the persistence of the age of miracles. All this attention helped assure the tale's wide depiction in art as well, where it served as an emblem of the saint's thaumaturgic abilities well into modern times. And as European missionaries brought the Christian message—and Christian saints—to the New World, the chopped-up baby continued to epitomize Vincent's miracles, while the effectiveness of his apocalyptic preaching in converting sinners, Jews, and Muslims spoke to the self-image of the friars who traveled to convert the Americas in preparation for the millennial kingdom of the saints.

---

4. Vauchez 1997, e.g., 6–7, 417, 420–21.
5. RVV (BHL no. 8657/8658).

This book, then, tells that long story of the shifting idea of *Saint* Vincent Ferrer, from his death in the fifteenth century to the threshold of the modern age, in which a more stable and consistent image of the saint emerges in the hagiography. The geographical area covered in these pages ranges from the saint's tomb in Brittany to cult centers in Spain, Italy, France, and Germany and to the Spanish colonies in the New World. My sources largely deal with memories, impressions, and representations: the canonization inquests, hagiography in both manuscript and print, liturgical sources, art, devotional materials, and the traces in those sources of rumor and word of mouth. Where possible to do so, I have tried to think about the reception of these portrayals by their audiences and how subsequent authors and artists combined bits and pieces of various representations of the saint to create their own portraits of *Saint* Vincent Ferrer.[6]

The man on whom all these texts and images centered was born in Valencia in the midst of what is often called the calamitous fourteenth century. Vincent's birth in 1350—to the notary William Ferrer and his wife, Constance Miquel—came just two years after the Black Death unleashed its devastation on Europe. His adulthood would be marked by the years of the Great Schism (1378–1414) that rent the "seamless garment of Christ" into two and then three papal obediences, and his career played itself out against a backdrop of persistent political crises: the Schism, the Hundred Years' War, rising hostility against religious minorities on the Iberian Peninsula, a change of dynasty in the Crown of Aragon that paved the way for the unification of Spain, and a host of other disturbances. Vincent himself would become embroiled in many of these events.

Vincent entered the Dominican order in the convent in Valencia in the winter of 1367, taking his vows the following February. In accordance with the Friars Preachers' commitment to education—St. Dominic had begun the order with the goal of converting, by learned preaching and example, Cathar heretics in the south of France—Vincent was sent to further his studies in Barcelona, Lérida, and eventually Toulouse, acquiring expertise in logic, philosophy, theology, and the Hebrew language. Returning to Valencia in 1378, he briefly served as prior of the city's Dominican convent. He acquired a reputation as a teacher, preacher, and peacemaker, accepting the chair in theology at the Valencia cathedral (1385), intervening in family

---

6. In conceiving this book, I have drawn upon the scholarly notion of "lived religion," investigating what people *do* with religious ideas to shape the worlds they make for themselves, as well as how religious idioms and practices are formed in turn by those worlds. The notion of lived religion invites scholars to look at even the artifacts of high ecclesiastical culture (such as a saint's *vita*) as part of this shaping of meaning. See, e.g., Orsi 2003. Some scholars have objected to the term "hagiography" as implying a specific genre of writing (see A. Taylor 2013 for a sense of the debate). I use the word here simply as shorthand for "writings about saints."

feuds in the town, and receiving subsidies from the *jurados* (the city's leading men) for the needs of prostitutes converted by his efforts.[7] He also became close to the ruling house in Aragon, serving as confessor for the wives of Joan I (r. 1387–96) and Martí I (r. 1396–1410). When, after Martí's death, the crown of Aragon was disputed among several rival claimants, Vincent was one of the nine judges selected to adjudicate the matter in the so-called Compromise of Caspe of 1412. But the largest influence on Vincent's career would be his close ties to an Aragonese churchman named Pedro de Luna, whom he first met when the latter was serving as cardinal-legate for the Avignon pope Clement VII and who succeeded Clement on the papal throne as Benedict XIII.

With the September 20, 1378, election of Clement VII as pope by the same cardinals who had several months earlier voted for the now-despised Urban VI, European Christendom was riven by papal schism. In response, the Aragonese king Pere III (Pedro IV of Aragon, r. 1336–87) adopted a politically shrewd position of neutrality on the topic. In an effort to rally to his Avignon obedience the crown of Aragon (along with the other as yet undeclared kingdoms of the Iberian Peninsula), Clement VII sent Pedro de Luna to the region as his legate. There in Valencia, the gifted young Dominican prior caught his eye, and Vincent spent three years accompanying Cardinal de Luna on his embassy. When Pedro de Luna's efforts were unable to persuade Pere to put Aragon in the Avignon papacy's camp, Vincent wrote and dedicated to the king a long treatise *On the Present-Day Schism* (*De moderno ecclesie scismate*) in which he argued vigorously for the legitimacy of Clement's papacy.[8] But only with Pere's death in 1387 did his son, Joan I, declare Aragon's adherence to the Avignon obedience. Still, Pedro de Luna remembered the talents and friendship of his countryman, and after becoming the Avignon pope Benedict XIII in 1394, he called Vincent to his side, where the celebrated friar served the pope as confessor, chaplain, and, perhaps, master of the sacred palace.

Although Vincent remained convinced of the legitimacy of Benedict's election, he deplored the schism in the church, which, as he wrote at the end of his treatise *On the Present-Day Schism,* appeared to mark the imminence of the time of Antichrist and the end of the world.[9] No fan of letting a church council sit in judgment over the vicar of Christ on earth, Vincent instead hoped that the competing popes would simultaneously resign, paving the way to a new canonical election of a single, universally recognized pope. The wily Benedict kept dangling that promise but never delivered on it, to what

---

7. Niederlender 1986–88, 7:248.

8. Hodel 2008. Benedict XIII kept a copy in his portable library, ibid., 14; see also Valois (1896–1902) 1967, 1:221–23.

9. Hodel 2008, 113–17.

must have been Vincent's intense frustration. In 1398, after the French subtraction of obedience from Benedict left Avignon in a state of siege, Vincent
quit the papal palace. Then, according to his own account in a 1412 letter
to Benedict, as he lay ill with a fever, Christ appeared to him with the saints
Francis and Dominic, healed him, and sent him forth to preach repentance
prior to the Last Judgment.[10] The following year, Vincent departed Avignon
with the title of legate *a latere Christi* (exempting him from local supervision)
for a preaching tour that took him throughout most of western Europe—
at least the parts loyal to Avignon—until his death in 1419 in the city of
Vannes in Brittany.[11]

Although he was disgusted and disheartened by the Schism, as well as
by Benedict XIII's obstinacy, Vincent continued to maintain in sermons
and in writing that the Avignon papacy was the legitimate line even as
late as 1413, on the eve of the Council of Constance that would eventually bring the division to an end.[12] On several occasions (1408 in Genoa,
probably 1414 in Morella, and 1415 in Perpignan), Vincent attempted
to persuade Benedict to resign the papal throne in the name of church
unity. At last in Perpignan—where negotiations between the king of Aragon, the German emperor, representatives from the Council of Constance,
and Benedict had come to naught, and after yet another miraculous cure
from illness—Vincent publicly broke with Benedict, first denouncing his
intransigence (though still admitting his legitimacy) in a sermon and then,
on January 6, 1416, proclaiming Aragon's withdrawal of obedience from
the Avignon pontiff.[13] Deprived of his last support, Benedict XIII fled to
a retreat in Peñiscola, from which distance he was solemnly deposed by
vote of the Council of Constance, paving the way for the election of Pope
Martin V in November 1417. Vincent, for his final year and a half, had the
pleasure of urging audiences at his sermons to obey the new head of the
now unified church.

Although the Schism dominated most of Vincent's adult years, clearly
the role he most relished personally was that of preacher. As legate *a latere
Christi* he traveled on foot and later on a humble donkey, celebrating Mass

---

10. *Epistola Fratris Vincentii de tempore Antichristi et fine mundi,* in FND, 213–24.

11. Legate *a latere Christi:* Hodel 2008, 226; FND, 97.

12. See, most recently, Hodel 2008, 228–31. Cf. Blumenfeld-Kosinski 2006, 78–81, who
suggests that the 1398 vision marked a "change in his attitude," namely, the end of "overtly political
activism" linked to Benedict XIII and of proclaiming, as a preacher, who the true pope was (80).
José M. Garganta also implies as much: Garganta and Forcada 1956, 68. See also Brettle 1924,
44–69, esp. 62, who argues that Vincent's change of heart about Benedict came between 1412 and
1415. According to Noël Valois, Vincent was convinced of Benedict's legitimacy even in 1416.
Valois (1896–1902) 1967, 4:348; similarly, Garganta and Forcada 1956, 78n8.

13. Bertucci 1969, 12:1171–72; Niederlender 1986–88, 7:252; FHSVF, 2:101–5; Garganta and
Forcada 1956, 68–80.

daily and then preaching for as long as three hours before admiring crowds. Vincent's goal as a preacher was conversion: of sinners to penitents, of heretics to orthodox Christians, and of non-Christians to the Christian fold. Contemporaries admired Vincent for bringing tens of thousands of Jews and Muslims—as hagiographers reckoned—to the font of baptism. So, too, did pious authors from the fifteenth through the early twentieth centuries. But for many modern authors, Vincent's preaching, particularly to Iberian Jews, has proven to be a sticking point. Most scholars refrain from directly implicating Vincent Ferrer in the horrendous pogroms of 1391, and some authors stress that his goal of converting Jews was not the same as that espoused by other preachers, such as Ferrán Martínez de Ecija, whose violent rhetoric inspired the 1391 pogroms in Seville.[14] Still, Vincent's harsh words against Jews in sermons and treatises earned him the opprobrium of contemporary Jews and have frequently resulted in modern critics' assigning him a critical role in the rising antisemitism of late medieval Spain.[15]

Contemporaries in the fifteenth century (or at least some of them) appear to have been far more troubled by the apocalyptic content of Vincent's preaching than by his denunciations of Muslims and Jews. Although some modern scholars dispute the characterization of Vincent's preaching as completely dominated by eschatological themes, the saint's moving descriptions of the impending torments of Antichrist—"He will tear away from you one member after another, not all at once, but continuing over a long time," he once warned his listeners[16]—clearly helped to bring his audiences to "despise earthly things and to love heavenly ones," as Pius II would note in his 1458 bull of canonization, a sentiment echoed by countless other authors.[17] Among the signs of those changed lives were the bands of flagellant penitents who followed Vincent from town to town, publicly "disciplining" themselves in nightly processions wherever the saint preached. Still, at least one observer, the moralist Jean Gerson, was disturbed by the appearance of these groups and specifically linked their behaviors to the preaching of the imminent Last Judgment.[18] And others, too, must have murmured against the friar's pointed sermons, for the saint felt compelled to send a letter to

---

14. E.g., Bisson 1986, 175; Toldrà 2004, 157–73; Ruiz 2007, 157.

15. E.g., Jewish sources quoted by FHSVF, 1:70 and 334; Netanyahu 1995, 183–202; Bisson 1986, 167; Nirenberg 2002, 1081–83; and Esponera Cerdán 2008, 223–64.

16. Sermon from 1404, quoted in Smoller 1994, 95, translating from Brettle 1924, 179.

17. Although Fages asserts that 70 percent of Vincent's sermons dealt with the Last Judgment, some later scholars have disputed the notion that the Apocalypse dominated his preaching. See Huerga 1994, vol. 16, cols. 819–20; Niederlender 1986–88, 7:253. See also Rusconi 1979, 219–23. The bull of canonization (Pius II's *Rationi congruit,* October 1, 1458) can be found in *Bullarum diplomatum* 1857–72, 5:144–49 (remarks on apocalyptic preaching, 147).

18. See chapter 4 and Smoller 1994, 116–17.

Benedict XIII in 1412 in defense, as hagiographer Pietro Ranzano would later write, against the charge of "disseminat[ing] novel doctrines."[19]

The novelties to which Ranzano alludes are not entirely apparent in the letter to Benedict. There Vincent laid out "four conclusions about Antichrist and the end of the world [that] I am accustomed to preaching in my sermons."[20] Most of what Vincent concluded here was completely standard biblical exegesis, although with some additional proofs incorporated into his argumentation. Thus, for example, in defense of his fourth conclusion ("That the time of Antichrist and the end of the world will be soon, and very soon, and in an extremely short time"), Vincent described (in the third person) his own 1398 vision, in which Christ sent him forth to preach "for the conversion and correction of men before the advent of Antichrist," adding, if perhaps a bit immodestly, that many observers believed the friar so commissioned by Christ to be the angel of Revelation 14, who warns of the impending day of judgment.[21] Neither the description of his vision nor even the claim to have been the angel of the apocalypse appears to have been problematic to fifteenth-century audiences, however. Indeed, for artists after Vincent's canonization, the angel's admonition became an emblem for the new saint: "Timete Deum et date illi honorem, quia venit hora iudicii eius. [Fear God and give him honor, for the hour of his judgment is at hand]" (Rev. 14:7; my translation). In a manner perhaps more bothersome to some contemporary observers, however, Vincent also mentioned a number of other visions that had been related to him, visions that all pointed to the terrifying fact that Antichrist was at the time of writing already nine years old.[22] Thus, not simply had the preacher violated the oft-cited injunction against naming a specific time for the end ("It is not for you to know the times or moments, which the Father hath put in his own power" [Acts 1:7, Douay-Rheims Version]), but also, by the time Vincent was canonized some forty-three years later, his pronouncement about Antichrist was patently wrong, for the fiend had failed to materialize.[23]

For later devotees, Vincent's apocalyptic preaching could serve as a source of both pride and embarrassment. On the one hand, his forceful sermons, linked to a divinely inspired mission, did propel listeners to change their lives and repent of their sins, as Pius II's bull of canonization observed. On the other hand, for readers of Vincent's 1412 letter to Benedict XIII—and the letter circulated widely in manuscript—there remained the increasingly

19. RVV, 1:492.
20. FND, 213–24 (quotation, 213).
21. Ibid., 220–21.
22. Ibid., 222. See also Smoller 1994, 94–95.
23. On the "uncertainty principle" of Acts 1, see Lerner 1976, 103.

apparent fact that the saint had been wrong.[24] Later hagiographers, particularly in the early years after Vincent's canonization, would sometimes scramble to explain away the fact that Antichrist had never revealed himself, while fifteenth-century forgers simply invented new, not yet fulfilled apocalyptic prophecies for the beloved saint.[25] Still, by and large, observers respected Vincent as the stern angel of the apocalypse whose fiery sermons brought sinners to penance and Jews and Muslims to the baptismal font. Whatever the actual focus of most of Vincent's preaching, what his hearers remembered and later biographers chose to emphasize were his vigorous warnings that God's judgment was at hand.

The charismatic power of Vincent's sermons and humble life were abundantly apparent in his final mission, to the duchy of Brittany in 1418–19. Even thirty-five years later, witnesses at the Brittany canonization inquest recalled the striking image of the old, feeble friar, who walked with a cane and supported by companions, who became so animated and sprightly while preaching that, when he came down from the pulpit, "it seemed he was not the same person who had preached."[26] They testified to the effectiveness of Vincent's sermons: blasphemy and gambling ceased; those who never had known how could now say the Pater Noster and the Ave Maria and make the sign of the cross. And above all, they recalled Vincent's asceticism and his kindness. He never ate meat until his final illness, when at the bishop's command he took some broth made from meat. He never slept in a bed but instead lay on a hard pallet on the floor. He greeted others humbly, with a bow and with kind words. He was solicitous of the well-being of the poor ass that carried the preacher's books, intervening when one of his followers began to beat and berate the beast, which had fallen into a ditch.[27] Rumors fed on Vincent's reputation as a living saint: voyeurs who spied on his chamber at night saw him bathed in an ethereal light, although no fires or candles were lit.[28] When crowds flocked around him in the hopes of a miracle, the man of God patiently made the sign of the cross over them, laid his hands

---

24. List of extant manuscripts, Kaeppeli and Panella 1970–93, 4:463–64. See also Rusconi 1990, 216.

25. E.g., *De fine mundi,* of which the earliest manuscript appears to be 1470 and which was often printed in Germany in the late fifteenth and early sixteenth centuries. Brettle 1924, 157–67.

26. Testimony of Petrus Floc'h, as translated by me in Head 2000, 785; original Latin in *Procès,* witness 8; FPC, 27: "Videbatur quod non esset ille qui predicaverat." When I quote from the canonization processes, my quotations are always from the manuscripts (*Procès* for the Brittany inquest, *Proceso* for the Toulouse and Naples inquests). The Brittany manuscript (*Procès*) is not foliated, and in general I give witness numbers in lieu of folio citations; I supply folio numbers for the Valencia manuscript (*Proceso*). I also cite the page number in Fages's edition for the convenience of the reader. Fages altered and abbreviated the testimony, however, so his edition is not reliable.

27. Testimony of Brittany witness Henricus du Val (*Procès,* witness 3; FPC, 13–14).

28. Bathed in light: e.g., testimony of Brittany witnesses Perrina de Bazvalen (*Procès,* witness 7; FPC, 25); Egidius Maletaille (*Procès,* witness 39; FPC, 76).

on them, and prayed, often uttering the words of the Gospel ("They shall lay their hands upon the sick, and they shall recover." [Mark 16:18]) or a simple litany ("May Jesus, Mary's son, savior of the world and Lord, be merciful to you.").[29] According to witnesses, miracles inevitably followed.

At length, worn out by his labors, Vincent fell ill with a lingering fever; the duchess of Brittany's litter conveyed him to the home of a man named Dreulin in Vannes. It was just before Easter, already a moment of intense liturgical drama. Attended by fellow clergy, the duchess, and her ladies, Vincent patiently bore his final sufferings and prepared his soul for death, the name of Jesus ever at his lips. He received the Eucharist and extreme unction from Johannes Collet, vicar of the Cathédrale Saint-Pierre in Vannes, and slipped into a state of unconsciousness. Finally, after the vicar had read the Passion narrative from the four Gospels and had recited the seven penitential psalms, on the afternoon of April 5, 1419, Vincent breathed his last. Witnesses, already moved by the preacher's exemplary Christian death, marveled as two or three white butterflies fluttered through the chamber window, just as the holy friar's soul exited his body.[30] For the next several days, until Vincent was buried in the Vannes cathedral, crowds flocked to see and reverently touch the dead man's body, which never exuded the slightest bad smell—a sure sign of sanctity.[31] Thirty-five years later in 1455, on the Feast of Saints Peter and Paul (June 29), Pope Calixtus III, another native of Aragon, solemnly pronounced Vincent's canonization. The holy preacher from Valencia had at last become *Saint* Vincent Ferrer.

The specific type of juridical process that resulted in Calixtus's proclamation has long caught the attention of historians.[32] The canonization process grew out of the tightening of papal control over local churches in the course of the high Middle Ages, crystallizing in the thirteenth century into an extended procedure that involved petition to the papal court, the order to open local fact-finding inquests (*inquisitiones in partibus*), and several levels of evaluation of the testimony generated at those inquests before a final recommendation to the pope by the College of Cardinals. (This process was

---

29. E.g., testimony of Brittany witness Gaufridus Bertrandi (*Procès,* witness 21; FPC, 52): "Et ipse testis vidit eum sepius manus pluribus ex ipsis apponere et signum crucis facere. Et audivit eum dum manus imponeret dicendi Super egros manus imponet et bene habebunt"; and Toulouse witness Jacobus Ysalgueri (*Proceso,* fol. 181v; FPC, 292, witness 4): "dicens praeterea Jesus Marie filius salus mundi et dominus sit tibi clemens et propitius dicentemque alias orationes iuxta talium infirmorum infirmitatem."

30. Account drawn largely from the testimony of Brittany witnesses Prigentius Ploevigner (*Procès,* witness 2; FPC, 9), Henricus du Val (*Procès,* witness 3; FPC, 14), Perrinus Hervei (*Procès,* witness 4; FPC, 16), Oliverius le Bourdiec (*Procès,* witness 6; FPC, 20–21), and Perrina de Bazvalen (*Procès,* witness 7; FPC, 23–24).

31. Testimony of Brittany witness Dominus Yvo Gluidic (*Procès,* witness 1; FPC, 7).

32. Starting with Toynbee 1929.

changed for the early modern period with the 1588 creation of the Congregation of Sacred Rites and with reforms instituted by Urban VIII in 1634; since 1969 canonization has been under the purview of the Congregation for the Causes of Saints.)[33] Since the early 1980s, a rich body of scholarship on medieval saints and canonizations has taken as a starting point the magisterial study of the French historian André Vauchez, whose *Sainthood in the Later Middle Ages* (originally published in French in 1981) surveyed seventy-one canonization processes carried out between 1185 and 1431. Aside from clarifying the various stages of the process, Vauchez subjected his voluminous sources to quantitative analysis, from which he drew a number of more general conclusions about sainthood and miracles in late medieval Europe. He noted a tendency toward ever-tighter restriction of the appellation "saint," with fewer processes opened and fewer canonizations granted over the course of the years studied.[34] He pointed to a "feminization of sanctity" in the later Middle Ages, with increasing numbers of women receiving canonization in the fourteenth century.[35] And, relying on this evidence, he drew a distinction between northern and southern models of sanctity. He found that northern Europeans preferred high-ranking individuals, often victims of a violent death, who were primarily seen as sources of miraculous favors, while those in Mediterranean regions picked out ascetics whose lives appeared to be an imitation of Christ, and who were mainly viewed as models for a holy life.[36]

For Vauchez, the fifteenth century marked a real change in canonization and a clear stopping point for his study. Not simply was there a hiatus between 1418 and 1445, during which period no saints were canonized and no new causes were initiated, but also, when the papal curia reopened what Vauchez calls the "saint factory," the process was of a vastly different nature. At local inquests, the role of witnesses was reduced to one of simple assent to a schema put to them, while on a broader level, as Vauchez puts it, "the Roman Church resumed control of the cult of saints and gradually imposed a new discipline which paid much less heed to popular conceptions."[37] Faced with an ecclesiastical hierarchy "[i]ncreasingly hostile to popular religiosity," Vauchez argues, European Christendom in the later Middle Ages settled into a situation in which the church officially recognized a few, possessed of heroic virtue, as true saints, while at the popular level a variety of

---

33. See Katajala-Peltomaa 2010 (overview of scholarship on medieval canonizations) and Woodward 1996 (postmedieval canonization process).

34. Vauchez 1997, 61–63.

35. Ibid., 267–69.

36. Ibid., 217–18. But cf. critical comments in reviews of Lehmijoki-Gardner 1998, Bynum 1999, and Herlihy 1984, and my own musings in Smoller 2004a.

37. Vauchez 1997, 6–7 (quotation, 7).

unofficial and unrecognized local cults flourished. The trial of Joan of Arc, which pitted the spiritualized notion of sainthood shared by an elite clerical minority against "a sainthood lived and recognized by simple people," epitomized this growing divide.[38] Although the church of the early fifteenth century, weakened by schism, struggles between popes and church councils, and the growth of the Hussite heresy in Bohemia, was unable to impose this stricter notion of sainthood on the body of the faithful, by the middle of the fifteenth century, Vauchez implies, the situation had changed.

The first saint canonized after the early fifteenth-century pause was the Observant Franciscan preacher Bernardino of Siena (1380–1444), in 1450. The next saint proclaimed by the papacy was Vincent Ferrer. His process, opened in 1451, thus affords an excellent opportunity to test Vauchez's hypothesis about the increasing curial control of the canonization process in the second half of the fifteenth century. The first half of this book, in fact, based on the canonization records in Vincent's case, seeks to demonstrate the considerable leeway still left for local ecclesiastical and political leaders to shape the process—and the resultant portrait of the potential saint that emerged from it.[39] Furthermore, as a close reading of the testimony from the canonization inquests will reveal, individual witnesses played a far greater role in the proceedings than mere assent to a predetermined script. Rather, individuals crafted narratives of the putative saint and their encounters with him in such a way as to make their own claims about their social and spiritual worth.

Vauchez's massive tome inspired a wave of studies of canonization processes, whether for the details such records could provide about lay spirituality, everyday life, gender, the experiences of women and children, and notions of sanctity or for the insight the study of individual causes could bring to the understanding of the canonization process in the later Middle Ages.[40] Together, these works amply demonstrate what rich and engaging historical sources canonization records have proven to be. But few scholars have extended their research beyond the moment of canonization, as if the papal ceremony marks somehow the end of the story. Those historians who have peeked beyond the process of canonization, however, have shown the situation to be more complex. Donald Prudlo demonstrates, for example, that the cult of the Dominican preacher Peter Martyr (Peter of Verona, ca. 1205–52, canonized 1253) came to focus on the martyred friar's role as *inquisitor* only toward the end of the thirteenth century, just as the Dominican

---

38. Ibid., 139–40, 417, 539 (quotations, 417, 539).

39. As Letizia Pellegrini has argued, the more rigid control of canonizations in the fifteenth century did not extend to the local inquests but rather manifested itself in a stricter management of the curial phase of the process. Pellegrini 2004, 316, 323.

40. See Katajala-Peltomaa 2010.

order came to see the office of inquisitor as central to the friars' mission.[41] Cecelia Gaposhkin, after a brief consideration of the canonization process for Louis IX of France, focuses on the portrayal of Saint Louis in early liturgical offices (the prayers recited at fixed hours by priests, religious, and clerics), brilliantly showing the way in which different contexts produced varying images of the saint.[42] And Gerald Parsons, although he devotes only a few pages to the medieval cult of Catherine of Siena, effectively catalogs Catherine's transformations from *la santa senese* (the Sienese saint) to patroness and symbol of a newly unified Italy, of an aggressively nationalistic fascist state, and finally of a transnational Europe.[43]

In the second half of this book, I extend the insights gained from these sorts of long-term studies of saints' cults to examine the meaning of *Saint* Vincent Ferrer from the time of his canonization down to the dawn of the modern era. Artworks, sermons, liturgical offices, and hagiography reveal a plethora of differing Vincent Ferrers produced for a variety of contexts, occasions, and audiences. All too often, fenced in by the disciplinary or temporal boundaries by which we define ourselves as scholars, we grasp only one of these images. In the pages that follow, however, the saint of the canonization process stands next to the saint of the hagiography, the saint of the iconography, and the saint of the liturgy; the fifteenth-century Vincent Ferrer jostles with the multiple Vincents of later centuries. This all-embracing, long-ranging view will, I hope, reveal in the cult of the saints a complexity sometimes obscured by a narrower focus solely on one type of source or on a single time period.

In Vincent's case, even as the image of the saint slowly began to stabilize in the late seventeenth century *vitae,* what evidence there is of popular practices suggests that individuals continued to understand, invoke, and tell stories about the sacred on their own terms. The goal of the fifteenth-century

---

41. Prudlo 2008, 100–102. Prudlo offers a tantalizingly brief epilogue tracing Peter's cult from the late fourteenth century through the saint's removal from the liturgical calendar in 1969. On the Dominican order's own view of its inquisitorial office, see Ames 2009.

42. Gaposhkin 2008. While Louis's kingship is virtually absent in the canonization process, Gaposhkin argues (24–25), the office performed at the royal Sainte-Chapelle stressed Louis's role as a king similar to those in the Old Testament (100–116). The Cistercians' office for Louis's feast depicted him as a contemplative ascetic (125–36), whereas the Franciscans portrayed him as a second Francis, embodying the order's ideals (156–59).

43. Parsons 2008. Although Parsons devotes only a brief chapter (15–42) to tracing Catherine's cult from her death in 1380 to the mid-nineteenth century, his remarks hint at a more complexly evolving image than the label "la santa senese" that he applies to the Catherine of this era. Still, the stress in the chapter is on Catherine's role as vehicle for Sienese civic religion (e.g., ibid., 13). Also worthy of mention here is Eugene Rice's study of the cult of Saint Jerome. Although Jerome's cult extends back long before the beginnings of papal canonization, Rice nicely demonstrates his appropriation by humanist scholars as one of their own (Rice 1985, 84–93) and then by Counter-Reformation Catholic apologists to defend traditional doctrine and practices (ibid., 144–58).

popes to control more tightly the process of canonization and the resultant understanding of sainthood proved nearly as elusive in the sixteenth and seventeenth centuries as it would be in the later Middle Ages. Although a text like Ranzano's *Life* could lay out an officially sanctioned image of the newly canonized saint, getting other hagiographers to adopt that portrait—much less individual believers to buy into it—was a difficult task indeed.

The chapters that follow trace the image—or rather, images—of Vincent Ferrer from his last days into the early eighteenth century, from his final resting place in Vannes to Spanish colonies in the New World. The first three chapters focus on the years leading up to Vincent's 1455 canonization, in which a variety of interested parties, as well as individual Christians, sought to impose their own meanings on the potential saint. Chapter 1 outlines the interests of the powerful backers whose support—and purse strings—would be crucial in securing Vincent's canonization: the dukes of Brittany, the rulers of the crown of Aragon, and Vincent's own Dominican order. In both Brittany and Aragon, the saintly Vincent would be appropriated as a symbol of legitimacy by dynasties of relatively recent origin, while Dominicans looked to the popular preacher's canonization to get a leg up on rival orders, particularly the Franciscans. Chapter 2 examines the legal proceedings that resulted in Vincent's 1455 canonization. The three surviving inquests held in Brittany, Toulouse, and Naples reveal the differing ways in which local organizers attempted to shape the image of Vincent Ferrer, both to present the curia with a canonizable candidate for sainthood and to fan popular devotion to the hoped-for saint. In chapter 3 I shift my attention to the experience of those testifying at the canonization inquests. Although some scholars have insisted that the entire process was set up to produce a portrait orchestrated by the procurers who ran the inquests,[44] I argue instead that the inquest functioned more like a hub of communications, in which witnesses could both learn what was expected in their testimony and shape their narratives in such a way as to further their own claims of social and spiritual worth.

The book's second half follows the effort to create and stabilize an image of the now *Saint* Vincent Ferrer along lines dictated by the papal curia and the Dominican leadership. Chapter 4 examines in detail Pietro Ranzano's biography of Vincent Ferrer. Whitewashing potential blemishes on the new Dominican saint's reputation, Ranzano portrayed Vincent as an effective converter of souls and healer of the Schism, seizing upon the miraculous restoration of a baby chopped up and cooked by its mother as an emblem of the preacher's ability to make whole what was once in pieces. Chapter 5 traces the various portrayals of Vincent Ferrer in text and in art produced

---

44. E.g., Lett 2008.

between the time of Ranzano's *vita* and the early sixteenth century. Unable to establish a single, stable image of the newly canonized Vincent Ferrer, Ranzano did, however, succeed in popularizing the miracle of the chopped-up baby, which became a virtual emblem of the new saint and a near universal in early hagiography. Chapter 6 looks at depictions of Vincent Ferrer in a Christendom divided between Catholic and Protestant. Early modern Catholic authors and artists appropriated Vincent not simply to affirm the continuing power of saints and miracles in the face of Protestant challenges but also to bolster regional identities in response to the growing power of national monarchies. Only in the late seventeenth century did hagiographers begin consistently to adopt Ranzano's spin on the Dominican saint, however. Finally, an epilogue follows Vincent's cult with missionaries to Spain's New World colonies, where a winged Vincent appeared primarily as angel of the apocalypse and source of supernatural succor.

Those who study the saints frequently turn to the *Acta Sanctorum,* the massive collection of saints' lives and hagiographical dossiers begun by the Bollandists in the seventeenth century and still not complete. Its sixty-eight folio volumes (or now, more conveniently, the online *Acta Sanctorum Database*), arranged according to the liturgical calendar and compiled with a critical acumen that earned the immediate praise of contemporaries, continue to be the starting (and sometimes ending) point for much scholarly research into medieval sanctity. When in 1675 the Bollandists' researches reached the saints with feast days on April 5, it was Ranzano's *vita* that they chose to represent the life of Vincent Ferrer. In some respects they were right. Ranzano's was, after all, the official life commissioned by the pope upon Vincent's 1455 canonization. But even if Ranzano's became—in part thanks to the Bollandists—the predominant vision of Saint Vincent Ferrer, his was only one voice in a long, multifaceted conversation about the saint, one that has stretched across many centuries and covered many miles. This book seeks to restore the voices of that conversation in all its complexity. Rather than portray a definitive portrait of one among the scores of saints in the Bollandists' many volumes, I hope to present in this one volume the multiple meanings and facets of *Saint* Vincent Ferrer.

# CHAPTER 1

# The Situation

Vincent came to the duchy that would be his final resting place early in 1418, entering the Breton ducal city of Nantes on February 5.[1] We do not know the full details of his arrival. Certainly there was some version of the procession that formed each time Vincent entered a new town: the celebrated preacher, now quite old and debilitated, riding Christ-like on his humble and beloved donkey, wearing the black-and-white habit of the Order of Preachers;[2] the crowds who traveled with him, from the young clerics who took children aside during Vincent's daily Mass and sermons to teach them the elements of the faith to the pious lay and religious who abandoned everything to follow him for a week, a month, or years;[3] local clergy and notables who journeyed outside the city walls to

---

1. Nantes was not yet a clear capital for the duchy of Brittany; the three most important cities for the Breton dukes were Rennes (where ducal coronations occurred), Vannes (site of the Chambre des Comptes), and Nantes. See Jones 2003b, 264–67; Kerhervé 1996, 63–78. The procession greeting Vincent's arrival in Nantes is described by the Brittany witness Eudo David (*Procès,* witness 296; FPC, 245–46) and briefly mentioned by Fr. Johannes Mahe, O.P. (*Procès,* witness 245; FPC, 209).

2. Henricus du Val (*Procès,* witness 3; FPC, 13–14) tells of Vincent's concern for the donkey when, while carrying the preacher's books, it tumbled into a ditch and one of his followers began beating the beast and telling it to get up in the name of the devil. The Carthusian friar Johannes Placentis explains that Vincent had gotten an infirmity in one leg that necessitated his going about on the donkey (*parvam asinam*) (*Procès,* witness 295; FPC, 243).

3. For example, Eudo David (*Procès,* witness 296; FPC, 246), Fernandus, bishop of Telesia (*Proceso,* fol. 282v; FPC, 420, Naples witness 9), and Robertus Juno (*Procès,* witness 241; FPC, 204). Less spectacularly, Alieta, wife of Perrotus Alanou, followed Vincent from Vannes to the town of Josselin (*Procès,* witness 10; FPC, 37).

meet Vincent's retinue; and crowds of curious onlookers who had heard of the saintly man's advent or who came simply out of curiosity. It seems that Vincent was no longer joined by the band of self-flagellating penitents who had accompanied him throughout southern France and whose activities had made such an impression that, years later, witnesses in Toulouse remembered their cries, their hymns, and the bloody chunks of flesh that adhered to their dirty garments.[4] No matter. It was a spectacle nonetheless.

For later memory, however, as well as in the display of pageantry that was so crucial to the fabric of life in late medieval Brittany, Vincent's real and important advent was that in Vannes, the favorite city of the reigning duke, on March 5 of the same year.[5] Of this entry we have abundant records in the testimony gathered thirty-five years later at the canonization inquest that took place largely in and around that city. Following only very loosely the now-traditional division of an inquest into the life and merits and inquest into miracles, the procurers who were the impresarios of the Brittany inquest gathered 313 persons to testify on Vincent's behalf. They summoned a parade of witnesses who put Vincent's time in Vannes—both his initial entry into the city in 1418 and his return for his final illness and death in April 1419—at the center of the tale they were telling. And in both those crucial episodes in Vannes, the Breton duke, Jean V, and his wife, Jeanne de France, played starring roles.

In life and in death Vincent became an important symbol for the powerful in Brittany. If a saint, whether living or dead, meant different things to different people, it is clear that for Jean V and his successors in the Montfort line of dukes, Vincent Ferrer represented an opportunity to lend their dynasty an aura of sacred authority. Their close association with the saint bolstered the Breton dukes' assertions of equality with or at least independence from their nominal overlords, the kings of France, and it helped answer lingering doubts about the legitimacy of their rule, questions that stretched back to the bitter civil war fought in the duchy from 1341 to 1364. Hints of other political uses of Vincent's sanctity also emerge from the canonization inquests: his importance to the new ruling house of his native Aragon, his canonization as a ready and rapid Dominican answer to the 1450 canonization of Bernardino of Siena of the rival Franciscan order, and the attempt to use Vincent's canonization to smooth over tensions between competing religious groups in the duchy of Brittany. While a holy person might receive veneration and a local cult without important backers, it took this sort of political will—and the strong arms and deep purses of powerful lay and religious supporters—to see a case through to canonization.

---

4. Flagellants' garments: Fr. Petrus de Pelafiga (*Proceso,* fol. 232v; FPC, 376, Toulouse witness 33).
5. Favorite city: Kerhervé 1996, 72.

## Vincent Ferrer and the Dukes of Brittany

From the very first, Vincent Ferrer's mission in Brittany was closely linked to the ducal family. He came to Brittany at the invitation of Duke Jean V. As the knight Henricus du Val remembered, Jean, having heard of Vincent's fame, "sent a certain messenger from his servants" to ask the preacher to come to Brittany.[6] That messenger was one Johannes Bernier, who told the panel at the canonization inquest that Jean V had sent him out on three different occasions—to Le Puy, Berry, and Tours—bearing letters for the celebrated Dominican. When he at last caught up with Vincent, Johannes had "humbly asked him to deign to come to Brittany in order to instruct [the duke] and the people of his fatherland in the Christian faith," a request the preacher just as graciously heeded.[7] At least one witness who had been in Nantes during Vincent's time there recalled that the duke and duchess, along with other notables, had attended all of Vincent's sermons in the city.[8]

Duke Jean was also conspicuously present to greet his guest on his arrival in Vannes. Vincent approached the city from the east. The priest Oliverius le Bourdiec remembered, as a member of the cathedral choir, being part of the procession that met Vincent as he arrived on the road from the little hamlet of Theix, two leagues from Vannes. Oliverius and the rest of the greeting party went as far as the chapel of St. Catherine in the suburb of St. Patern beyond the city walls, not far from the present-day Hôtel du Departé-ment, near the edge of the Étang du Duc.[9] The duke was present, Oliverius remembered, as were Bishop Aumauric and a great number of people from the city of Vannes.[10] The procession doubtless entered the city through the Porte St. Patern, just above the floral gardens and the lovely medieval *lavoirs* that one can still see at the foot of the high city walls; it then moved solemnly

---

6. *Procès,* witness 3; FPC, 13: "Misit ad querendum ipsum quemdam nuntium de servitoribus suis cuius nomen ignoscit."

7. *Procès,* witness 32; FPC, 67–68: "Humiliter ipsum rogavit quatenus accedere dignaretur ad partes Britannie pro sui et populi sue patrie in fide catholica instructione." The letters, now lost, are cataloged as nos. 1272, 1273, and 1274 in Blanchard 1890, ser. vol. 5 [2]:227.

8. Symon Maydo (*Procès,* witness 9; FPC, 31).

9. *Procès,* witness 6; FPC, 18. Some witnesses said the procession met Vincent at the chapel of St. Lawrence: e.g., Dominus Yvo Gluidic (*Procès,* witness 1; FPC, 4); Petrus Floc'h (*Procès,* witness 8; FPC, 26); and Symon Maydo (*Procès,* witness 9; FPC, 31). The chapel of St. Catherine appears in the suburb of St. Patern on a map of fifteenth-century Vannes in Leguay 1975, between 116 and 117. He lists no chapel of St. Lawrence in the suburbs of Vannes, but perhaps the procession in fact went farther than the suburb of St. Patern.

10. Aumauric de la Motte became bishop of Vannes in 1409 and was transferred to the bishopric of St.-Malo in 1432: Tresvaux 1839, 163. Some witnesses do not specifically mention the presence of the duke but refer to large numbers of "nobles"—e.g., Petrus Floc'h (*Procès,* witness 8; FPC, 26), Bonadius de Colledou (*Procès,* witness 19; FPC, 49)—or simply to a procession of clergy and citizens or "the people"—e.g., Symon Maydo (*Procès,* witness 9; FPC, 31), Alieta, wife of Perrotus Alanou) (*Procès,* witness 10; FPC, 35), and Michael Maceot (*Procès,* witness 30; FPC, 64).

uphill along the narrow street whose edge just touches the northern wall of the cathedral whose nave would shelter Vincent's tomb. If this procession was like the one that greeted Vincent in Toulouse, the aged Dominican made his way to the cathedral, where he knelt and prayed before the main altar and then rose to turn and bless the crowd.[11] At least one witness, one of the seaside town's many sailors, believed Vincent had made such a stop at the Cathédrale Saint-Pierre; another simply was not sure.[12] In Toulouse, Vincent had moved on to the Dominican convent, where he stayed during his time in the city. With no Dominican house in Vannes, he was lodged not far from the duke's residence in the home of one Robin le Scarb, "between the Franciscan convent and the [duke's] castle l'Hermine," as witnesses recalled.[13]

For residents of Vannes who were old enough to recall Jean V's accession to the dukedom, the procession that greeted Vincent Ferrer may well have reminded them of the new duke's own joyous entry into Vannes after his coronation. Jean's advent into Vannes may not have been quite as elaborate as the ceremonies that had surrounded his coronation in Rennes on March 22, 1401, but the processions in Rennes would have been the model for the duke's joyous entries into other important cities in the duchy. Like the ceremony that greeted Vincent Ferrer, the coronation procession began outside the city walls and entered the city at the gate closest to the cathedral, where the duke swore the first of several oaths. The procession then moved on to the cathedral, where an overnight vigil preceded the coronation and investiture proper. After the duke's coronation, the procession exited the cathedral, circled its walls, and reentered the church, where the new duke left an offering at the main altar. Finally, the group left the cathedral and enjoyed a sumptuous banquet.[14] While it is highly unlikely that the ascetic Vincent partook of more than the sparsest of suppers that March day in 1418, other elements of the procession were remarkably similar to a ducal entry. Indeed, since the days of the declining Roman Empire, clerics and laypeople had honored the saints and their relics with ceremonies based on those held for an emperor's *adventus,* or solemn entry into a town.[15]

The next morning Vincent celebrated Mass and preached at the Place des Lices (the plaza where jousts were held), just next to the duke's castle of l'Hermine. It was and still is the largest open space in the old walled town,

11. Bernardus de Rosergio, archbishop of Toulouse (*Proceso,* fol. 173r; FPC, 278–79, Toulouse witness 1).

12. Rinaldus Madec (*Procès,* witness 87; FPC, 120): "Credit ipsum M. V. intrasse ecclesiam Venetensem in dicto ingressu dicte civitatis." Cf. Petrus Floc'h (*Procès,* witness 8; FPC, 26): "Nescit si fuit tunc ad ecclesiam cathedralem vel non."

13. E.g., Petrus Floc'h (*Procès,* witness 8; FPC, 26); also Alieta, wife of Perrotus Alanou (*Procès,* witness 10; FPC, 35).

14. Jones 2003b, 263–66.

15. Brown 1981, 98–99; see also Gecser 2010, 153.

larger by far than the little square in front of the Cathédrale Saint-Pierre, a space so small that, sitting at one of the cafés facing the west portal, I have to tip my head back to see the cathedral's mismatched towers. Today, on Wednesdays and Saturdays, the Place des Lices is filled with all the sounds, smells, and colors of a bustling French market, where vegetable and fish vendors hawk their wares next to stalls whose owners serve up steaming plates of fragrant, saffron-hued paella. That March morning, it was another Valencian import who provided the spectacle of color and sound in the Place des Lices.

Vincent delivered his sermons from an elevated platform constructed at the command of Duke Jean V and Bishop Aumauric.[16] It was decorated with colored linens, perhaps like those ordered in midcentury in Nantes to cover the mouth of hell that featured in a local mystery play.[17] It may be that Jean had flying the ermine, the black-and-white ensign representing the ermine's fur that the Montfort dukes took as their coat of arms; heraldic crests appear behind the pulpit in Sano di Pietro's 1441 painting of Bernardino of Siena preaching in the Campo in Siena. No matter if the banners were not there. Nestled in the shadows of l'Hermine, Jean and his duchess were prominent members of the audience, as many witnesses remembered well thirty-five years later.[18] Like other celebrated preachers of his day (Bernardino of Siena, John of Capestrano), Vincent separated the men and women in the audience with a long, thick cord, as if the approach of spring might suggest diversions other than the day's sermon.[19] Did all of the town's five thousand inhabitants turn out to hear the celebrated preacher? Maybe not, but witnesses recalled great crowds, from Vannes as well as from villages for several leagues around.[20]

---

16. Dominus Yvo Gluidic (*Procès,* witness 1; FPC, 4).

17. Archives municipales de Nantes, CC 244 (Le Compte Pierre Leflo miseur de la ville de Nantes, 1454–57), fol. 167v: "Au Pyllays pour une vii me estam vert et dore pour la goulle denfer. vi s. vi d." (This mouth of hell, which took at least three days to construct, must have been some sight: other expenditures included fire to come out of its nostrils and oxtails to decorate the head. Fols. 167v–168v.)

18. E.g., Yvo Gluidic (*Procès,* witness 1; FPC, 4) and Prigentius Ploevigner (*Procès,* witness 2; FPC, 9), who recalled that the duke had gone to Normandy with Vincent; also Henricus du Val (witness 3), Perrinus Hervei, alias Grasset (witness 4), Symon Maydo (witness 9), Herveus Maydo (witness 18), Michael Maceot (witness 30), Petrus Colin (witness 31), Johannes Bernier (witness 32), Petrus de Bonabri (witness 33), Eudo Bugant (witness 34), Alina, wife of Egidius Maletaille (witness 40), and Robertus Juno (witness 241, who recalled the duke's presence at sermons in Dinan).

19. According to Michael Maceot (*Procès,* witness 30; FPC, 64): "Durantibus hujusmodi predicacionibus segregari fecit viros a mulieribus et inter ipsos unam apponi grossam et longuam [*sic*] cordam." Similarly, Johannes Rolandi (*Procès,* witness 13; FPC, 41); Alanus de Cressoles (*Procès* witness 20; FPC, 51); and Petrus de Bonabri (*Procès* witness 33; FPC, 70). Men and women separated at sermons of John of Capestrano: Gecser 2010, 157.

20. Population of Vannes: Galliou and Jones 1991, 210; crowds: e.g., Prigentius Ploevigner (*Procès,* witness 2; FPC, 8); Henricus du Val (*Procès,* witness 3; FPC, 13).

The morning's service began with a sung Mass. If Vincent's *fama* had reached Vannes, those in the know may have doubly held their breath in anticipation of the rite's central moment, the elevation of the consecrated host, for the preacher was known to be so overcome at that point that he wept copious tears.[21] Christians in the later Middle Ages were taught to hold in reverence the bread that became the body of Christ in the Mass. The ringing of bells generally accompanied the moment where the priest lifted the consecrated host for worshippers to see, and one Breton witness was able, thirty-five years later, to recite for the papal commissioners the Latin antiphon that one of Vincent's assistants had taught him to say at that moment.[22] If Vincent's emotional response to the sacrament was not marvel enough, his audience also wondered at his agility in the pulpit. When he ascended the platform that was his stage, he was old and frail and needed help; as he performed Mass and preached, he seemed as vigorous as a man of thirty, as Prigentius Ploevigner put it.[23]

After Mass, the preacher began his sermon, which would last for the next three hours. Like any late medieval preacher, Vincent began with a *thema,* a biblical verse that he would explain and elaborate in a series of divisions and subdivisions.[24] Yvo Gluidic remembered that on this day, for his first sermon in Vannes, Vincent preached on the verse "Colligete que super-averunt fragmenta" (John 6:12, "Gather up the fragments that remain").[25] In this linguistically divided duchy, Vincent's own Catalan was intelligible to both Breton and French speakers, a fact that witnesses attributed to the apostolic gift of tongues.[26] No one was bored or found the sermon tedious, even youths who, presumably, would have preferred a more physical type of recreation.[27] Although audience members arrived in the wee hours of the morning to secure a prime spot near the preacher's platform, witnesses

21. E.g., Gaspar Peregrini (*Proceso,* fol. 277r; FPC, 413, Naples witness 3).

22. Petrus de Bonabri (*Procès,* witness 33; FPC, 69).

23. *Procès,* witness 2; FPC, 10. He is one of many to remark such; e.g., see also Symon Maydo (witness 9).

24. See Debby 2001, chap. 2.

25. Dominus Yvo Gluidic (*Procès,* witness 1; FPC, 4). The verse comes from the story of the miracle of the loaves and the fishes; later lives of Vincent would emphasize his miraculous multiplication of bread and wine to feed thousands of followers. Mention of the sermon's theme appears also in the testimony of Oliverius le Bourdiec (witness 6), Petrus Floc'h (witness 8), and Guillermus Conannou (witness 46).

26. E.g., Symon Maydo (*Procès,* witness 9; FPC, 31–32), who actually quizzed Breton speakers who knew neither French nor "the Aragon dialect" in which Vincent spoke yet found them able to reproduce what Vincent had said in his sermons. On what may have been understood and how, see Cassard 1996, 341–43; H. Martin 1997, 130–33; and Gecser 2003, 9–11.

27. Youths: e.g., Petrus Floc'h (*Procès,* witness 33; FPC, 69), who was a teenager at the time. Bad weather did not deter the enjoyment of Vincent's sermons, according to Oliverius le Bourdiec (*Procès,* witness 6; FPC, 19).

acknowledged that both near and far away, all heard the preacher perfectly.[28] Another miracle.

With the duke and the duchess in constant attendance, Vincent remained in the ducal city until just after Easter, at which point he embarked on a tour throughout much of the duchy and into Normandy, where he was said to have preached before the English king Henry V.[29] At length, now some seventy years old, weak and feverish, he returned to Vannes, borne in the litter of Duchess Jeanne herself, and again a procession of clergy and citizens greeted him.[30] Another Vannes notable, a certain Dreulin, provided lodging in his home just steps from the portals of the cathedral. "Johannes le Fauchour lives here now," witnesses wanted the panelists at the canonization inquest to know. Today, a little cutout metal sign points out for tourists the "Maison Saint Vincent."

Dying was a public business in the fifteenth century, particularly for one whose followers were already convinced that he was a saint. Besides the lucky Dreulin, his wife Margareta and whoever from his household may have been allowed into the chamber, local clergy, Breton notables, and members of Vincent's own Dominican order thronged to Vincent's bedside. But the duchess of Brittany was *the* constant presence in the crowded sickroom in which Vincent spent his final days, as were numerous members of her female retinue. One of these was Lady Malestroit, who must have been a relative of the long-serving chancellor of Brittany and soon-to-be bishop of Nantes, Jean de Malestroit, whose house in Vannes still stands.[31] Witnesses later recalled that it was the duchess herself who bathed the saintly corpse and wrapped Vincent's body in its shroud.[32] She also took the opportunity to procure for herself a choice relic: the saintly preacher's *cappa* (black cloak), substituting that of her own Dominican confessor in its place. Later that cloak would be a family treasure, lent out only to the closest of friends in

---

28. Arriving in the middle of the night to secure a spot: Dominus Petrus Molinis (*Proceso*, fol. 187r; FPC, 302, Toulouse witness 7), Vincentius Joannis Marcelli, O.F.M. (*Proceso*, fol. 205r–205v; FPC, 331–32, Toulouse witness 14), Joannes Regis (*Proceso*, fol. 236v–237r; FPC, 382, Toulouse witness 36), Jacobus Quintanis (*Proceso*, fol. 276v; FPC, 412, Naples witness 2).

29. Just after Easter: Yvo Gluidic (*Procès*, witness 1; FPC, 4), Oliverius le Bourdiec (*Procès*, witness 6; FPC, 19), and Alieta, wife of Perrotus Alanou (*Procès*, witness 10; FPC, 35); preaching before the king: Eudo David (*Procès*, witness 296; FPC, 246). On Vincent's journey through the duchy, see La Borderie 1900; H. Martin 1997; Cassard 1998, 2000 (esp. 199–201), and 2006.

30. Alieta, wife of Perrotus Alanou (*Procès*, witness 10; FPC, 35).

31. Jean de Malestroit was bishop of Nantes from 1419 to 1443 and chancellor of the duchy from 1408 to 1443; for a time he held the Dreulin house in which Vincent died. Cassard 1998, 339. Brittany witnesses who recall the duchess's presence include Yvo Gluidic (witness 1), Prigentius Ploevigner (witness 2), Oliverius le Bourdiec (witness 6), Perrina de Bazvalen (witness 7), Petrus Floc'h (witness 8), Alieta, wife of Perrotus Alanou (witness 10), Herveus Maydo (witness 18), Johannes Bernier (witness 32), and Thomas le Brun (witness 60).

32. E.g., Oliverius le Bourdiec (witness 6) and Perrina de Bazvalen (witness 7).

hours of dire need.[33] And although Duke Jean was not physically present in the death chamber, perhaps at least Vincent had been served well in his final days by one of the four linen kerchiefs the duke had ordered made for him in late December.[34]

While the duchess featured prominently in the scenes surrounding Vincent's deathbed, Duke Jean himself had the pivotal role in the drama's next act. Almost immediately after the preacher's death, an intense struggle broke out. The issue at stake was who would get the privilege of housing Vincent's tomb and therefore receiving the offerings of the hordes of grateful pilgrims who everyone anticipated would soon materialize. The chief contenders were three: the bishop and cathedral chapter of Vannes, Vincent's own Dominican order, and, oddly enough, the rival Franciscan friars of Vannes.[35] The bishop's reasoning was clear enough. Vincent had died in Vannes and should be buried there. The Dominicans also had a point, arguing that they deserved to bury one of their own sons. But the nearest Dominican convent in the diocese was in the town of Quimperlé, some fifteen leagues distant, and Vannes, it seems, had come to regard Vincent as her own property.[36]

The Franciscans' claim was the most threatening of all. They seem to have reckoned that Vincent was from one of the so-called mendicant orders—that is, religious who took vows but who lived in the world, not apart from it in some secluded monastery—and since theirs was the only mendicant house in Vannes proper, his body should reside with them. The Franciscans of Vannes may simply have wished to thwart any favor going to the cathedral and its chapter, with whom they were in frequent competition over the burial of even ordinary Christian souls in Vannes. But they were vigorous enough in their claims that the bishop believed it worthwhile to keep Vincent's corpse—as he had the dying man—under constant watch and to post guards between the Dreulins' house and the Franciscan convent.[37]

---

33. As attested by Perrinus Hervei, alias Grasset (witness 4), Oliverius le Bourdiec (witness 6), and Perrina de Bazvalen (witness 7). The *cappa* was lent to Perrinus Hervei when he suddenly went out of his senses. See Smoller 2006.

34. Archives municipales de Nantes, II 120 (Comptes. 1390–1493. 33 pièces. Parchement), no. 9 (Compte de l'hotel du duc, 1418–19): "A Jehan de l'Haies marchant demourant a Rennes le penultime jour de decembre l'an mil iiii c xviii pour x aulnes de toille ... pour faire xi covrechief de teste pour mon dit seigneur le duc. De liceulx couvrechieffs de teste fut baille iiii dudit Guillamus Babonn iiii de mestre Vincent Ferrier par le command de mon dit seigneur."

35. As attested, e.g., by Brittany witnesses Prigentius Ploevigner (*Procès,* witness 2; FPC, 12); Alieta, wife of Perrotus Alanou (*Procès,* witness 10; FPC, 36) (she mentions that Vincent's body had to be guarded against the Franciscans and Dominicans); and Alanus de Cressoles (*Procès,* witness 20; FPC, 51).

36. Oliverius le Bourdiec (*Procès,* witness 6; FPC, 20–21). There was also a Dominican house in Guérande, which was ten leagues or more away, but it was not in the diocese of Vannes and lay a difficult sea crossing from the town.

37. Oliverius le Bourdiec (*Procès,* witness 6; FPC, 20–21): "Dicitque quod prefatus dominus episcopus diligenter faciebat custodire dictum corpus dicti M. V. tam in infirmitate quam in morte ne sepeliretur alibi quam in ecclesia Venetensis," and later "Dicit quoque quod ... ante exitum corporis

In the end, the question of Vincent's final resting place lay in the hands of Duke Jean V, who was away in Nantes.[38] A tense several days followed while all the interested parties waited to hear the duke's pronouncements and probably gazed with some greed or envy at the crowds who thronged to view the carefully guarded Vincent lying in his coffin in the Vannes cathedral. Predictably enough, the duke ruled in favor of the cathedral of his beloved city of Vannes. The funeral took place with great pomp, although two witnesses recalled that even after Vincent's burial in the cathedral, his tomb was surmounted by large stones and surrounded by iron bars lest anyone seek to steal the body.[39] Jean's decision may not have been simply an exercise of power and prerogative. One witness recalled Vincent's telling another Dominican, in response to a question about where he wanted his tomb, that he wished to be buried "where it should please the bishop of Vannes and the duke of Brittany," a strange statement coming from a member of a religious order that prided itself on not being beholden to any secular powers.[40] It is perhaps significant that we hear this statement only from a noble lady who was a member of Duchess Jeanne's entourage.

Thirty-five years later, at the time of the canonization inquest, at least one witness claimed to have seen the hand of God behind Vincent's death and burial in the duchy. The canon lawyer Prigentius Ploevigner had heard that, when the aged preacher's retinue began to fear that he would die far from his homeland, they convinced him to start for Aragon. Mounting his faithful donkey, Vincent journeyed all through the night with his servants. As dawn broke, however, they discovered that they were in the very same place they had left. At that, Vincent told his followers that it was clear that "God wished that he should end his days there." And so, concluded our lawyer, Vincent was "miraculously returned to Brittany."[41] The source of the lawyer's tale was one Hervei, the almoner to Jean V. His source is less certain, but clearly this story of God's miraculously guiding Vincent to his deathbed in the ducal city of Vannes—in the duchess's litter, no less—is one that members of the duke's circle enjoyed telling and retelling.[42]

---

de domo tunc Dreulin nunc vero Fauchour custodiebant inter ipsam domum et conventum minorum ne minores haberent hujusmodi corpus."That Druelin's house was closed up as soon as Vincent was dead is attested by Petrus Floc'h (*Procès*, witness 8; FPC, 28, who says that iron bars and great stones were placed around the tomb after Vincent's burial) and Johannes Lavazi (*Procès*, witness 14; FPC, 43, who notes that the cathedral wanted to keep Vincent's body as a relic).

38. According to Brittany witnesses Prigentius Ploevigner (witness 2) and Oliverius le Bourdiec (witness 6).

39. As attested by Brittany witnesses Petrus Floc'h (*Procès*, witness 8; FPC, 28) and Johannes Lavazi (*Procès*, witness 14; FPC, 43).

40. Perrina de Bazvalen (*Procès*, witness 7; FPC, 23):"Interrogavit dictum M.V. ubi vellet sepeliri qui respondit *ubi placeret prelate Venetense et principi Britannie"* (emphasis in original).

41. *Procès* witness 2; FPC, 11:"Deus volebat quod inibi dies suos terminaret. Et sic in Britaniam reversus miraculose [est]."

42. The Dominicans did try to get back Vincent's body but were ultimately unsuccessful (see below, text accompanying note 114).

## The Politics of Sainthood

If Jean V and his wife took pains to establish and demonstrate close ties between themselves and the saintly Dominican, they had good political reasons to do so. First, a linkage between the ducal family and Vincent Ferrer helped to bolster the image put forth by Breton dukes in the later fourteenth and fifteenth centuries, as independent sovereigns, fully the equal of their nominal overlords, the kings of France. Breton dukes maintained their own *parlement, États,* mints, and system of taxation; from the early fourteenth century, no French king levied taxes in the duchy. Like the French king, the duke of Brittany kept an elaborate household that was the stage for the performance of all sorts of elaborate ceremonies and rituals demonstrating the ruler's power. The coronation of Jean V in 1401, in which the new duke ostentatiously had a gold circlet placed on his head, aped French royal coronations, omitting only the anointing of the new ruler from its Gallic model. The duchy's historians insisted the ceremony dated back to the ninth century, when Brittany's rulers were, so the claim went, kings in their own right. Ducal funerals, too, were rich occasions for propaganda, with Jean V laid out "en son habit royal" ("in his royal robes"), as the saying went.[43] Jean V also went so far as to seal his documents with a seal of majesty, an act one historian calls "a unique usurpation of sovereign rights by a French prince."[44] By the year of Vincent Ferrer's death, Jean had added the royal-sounding phrase "by the grace of God" to his title as duke of Brittany.[45]

In short, Jean V put forth a strong message that the Montfort dukes of Brittany were every bit the equal of the kings of France. There was just one item about which the French kings could boast that Jean could not match: having a saint in the family. There is no question that the French king Louis IX (later Saint Louis) had displayed an extraordinary piety and religiosity in his lifetime; ditto his Angevin cousin Louis of Toulouse, made a bishop at the tender age of twenty-two. But no one could deny either that French kings aggressively sought the canonization of their own family members and that they made much of their saintly kin in promoting an image of French royalty as special agents of God's will, the "most Christian kings of France."[46] The Montforts simply did not have those sorts of relatives; in fact it had been rumored that Jean de Montfort—who had claimed the ducal throne in 1341, inaugurating nearly twenty-five years of civil war—had pursued his claim with a particularly noteworthy greed.[47]

---

43. Jones 1988c, 8–11; 2003b; Galliou and Jones 1991, 237–46.
44. Jones 1988a, 121.
45. Ibid., 123.
46. See, e.g., Gaposchkin 2008; Field 2006; Bozóky 2007.
47. According to the chronicler Froissart. See Galliou and Jones 1991, 218; and Jones 1981.

True, Jean V and his predecessor, Jean IV, had done their best. They actively supported mendicant foundations in the duchy, not simply Vincent's Dominican order but also the rival Franciscans and other mendicant groups such as the Carmelites. The dukes kept, as Jean V's wife Jeanne de France did, their own confessors, generally also mendicants.[48] It was her Dominican confessor's black cloak that Jeanne had substituted for Vincent Ferrer's as she washed and laid out his corpse that April day in 1419. Each year, Jean V would send a pilgrim off to Compostela, resting place of the relics of Saint James the Apostle and one of the most important medieval pilgrimage sites. Another yearly event was a ducal offering at the tomb of the Breton Saint Yves, better known as the patron saint of lawyers, north of Vannes in the town of Tréguier. And in one of his most lavish displays of religious charity, Jean V would have his weight in gold presented to the Carmelites in Nantes in fulfillment of a vow made during a period of captivity in 1420.[49]

Still, confessors and offerings hardly made a saint. No wonder Jean V sent his messenger three times to solicit Vincent Ferrer to preach in the duchy, and no wonder that the duke and duchess made such a point of being near the holy man. After Vincent's death, Jean V himself would make at least two concerted attempts to convince Rome to open canonization proceedings on Vincent's behalf, petitioning both Pope Martin V and, after his death, Pope Eugenius IV to look into Vincent's life and merits. His efforts persuaded at least one subsequent observer to remark that no one had labored more strenuously for Vincent's canonization than the Breton duke.[50] Jean also was careful to cultivate and nourish Vincent's cult in Vannes even if he had not yet been canonized, giving thirty *livres* to have Masses said at the altar of Vincent Ferrer in 1430, as well as making a highly public yearly offering at his tomb.[51] His daughter-in-law Isabeau (wife of François I) endowed a perpetual Mass on Vincent's altar in Vannes.[52] To have a contemporary saint's relics in one's own backyard was nearly as good as having a saint in the family.

The urgency with which the Montfort family courted Vincent Ferrer was intensified by the lingering scars of the Breton War of Succession. In the years 1341–65 the duchy had been racked by a fierce civil war. When Duke Jean III

---

48. H. Martin 1975, 12, 67–8, 155; Leguay and Martin 1982, 65.

49. Jones 2003b, 259; 1988d, 378. This event is depicted in a missal from the Carmelite house in Nantes (Robert Garrett Collection, MS 40, Princeton University).

50. As related by Pietro Ranzano, the author of the first official life of the new saint, in a summary of the biography of Vincent Ferrer excerpted from book 20 of his *Annals* that he sent to fellow Dominican Giovanni da Pistoia in 1463 (BC, MS 112, fol. 61r–62r). E.g., "Omnium [i.e., of all those petitioning Martin for Vincent's canonization] tamen diligentissimus fuit Ioannes britonum dux" (fol. 61r). Ranzano's letter was edited in Termini 1916, 91–92, 96–97.

51. Masses at the altar of Vincent Ferrer: FHSVF, 2:376. Donation at Vincent's tomb: Jones 2003b, 259.

52. FHSVF, 2:376.

had died childless in 1341, the succession was disputed between his half-brother Jean de Montfort and his niece Jeanne de Penthièvre, who was married to Charles of Blois (nephew of Philippe VI of France). Jean de Montfort was essentially an outsider, but he managed to attract considerable support among the lesser knights and esquires of Brittany, perhaps because of the Penthièvre family's close ties to the French crown, a constant subject of worry in this fiercely independent duchy. On September 7, 1341, a commission appointed by King Philippe VI predictably bestowed the dukedom on Charles of Blois, driving Montfort into the waiting arms of Edward III of England. By November war had broken out. Even with Montfort's untimely death in 1345, Edward III carried on the fight (along with Montfort's wife, Jeanne de Flandres).[53] After several failed truces and attempts at negotiations, Montfort's son Jean IV at last gained the throne in 1364, when victory at the Battle of Auray left Charles of Blois dead on the battlefield.

Despite Jeanne de Penthièvre's long-awaited concession of defeat and the official recognition of the Montfortist claims by King Charles V of France after Auray, there were two potential trouble spots for the Montfort party. First, according to the terms of the Treaty of Guérande that ended the civil war, the succession would revert to the Penthièvre branch should the Montforts fail to produce a male heir. Second, there was the problem of Charles of Blois. Charles had been a great patron of the mendicant orders, lavishing his alms particularly on the Franciscans, with whom he and his wife elected to be buried.[54] His generosity to the poor and extravagant shows of piety gave him a reputation for holiness, which, if he did not deliberately cultivate, he at least enjoyed. How else to explain the large crowds who just happened to show up to watch Charles make a barefoot pilgrimage, in the snow, to the shrine of Saint Yves in Guingamp.[55] Once Charles was said to have remarked to his valet that he would have preferred a Franciscan habit to the silk and gold vestments he had to wear to please the people.[56] Upon his death at Auray Charles was found to have been wearing a hair shirt; he was said to have confessed three times on the day of the battle.[57] Rumors of his saintly

---

53. The most readable account is that in Galliou and Jones 1991, 217–29; see also Leguay and Martin 1982, 216–29; Jones 1981. Jean de Montfort had never been satisfied by the provision his father (Arthur II) had made for him. In Brittany he held only the castellany of Guérande; outside the duchy he possessed the county of Montfort (where he resided before 1341). Prior to his claim of the ducal throne, Jean engaged in a protracted dispute with his father-in-law over lands claimed on his wife's behalf.

54. Hervé Martin tabulates that 8,850 francs (*livres tournois*) were given to the Franciscans in Guingamp (seat of the Penthièvres), and 120 francs to the Franciscans for the costs of a chapter general. H. Martin 1975, 194, 279–80.

55. Jones 2003d.

56. H. Martin 1975, 187.

57. Jones 2003d, 219–20.

life and of miracles worked at his tomb in Guingamp soon circulated.[58] A pilgrimage of children from Blois and the Île-de-France "miraculously" materialized in 1364–66, and grateful Franciscans (and Penthièvres) actively promoted his cult.[59]

That Charles's saintliness was a threat to Montfort legitimacy was not at all lost on the precariously victorious Jean IV. In 1368 it came to Jean's notice that the Franciscan church in Dinan had put up a painting of Charles of Blois as duke, with the arms of Brittany, kneeling before scenes from the life of Saint Francis. Furious, Jean ordered the painting covered. The next morning, while he attended Mass in the church, the whitewashed image began to bleed from the spot where Charles had been wounded at Auray. The significance of the miracle was all too apparent to the crowd.[60]

In September 1371, pressure from the French crown, the Friars Minor, and the Penthièvres resulted in the opening of a canonization inquest in Angers. As if in response, there was a great swell of miracles in September, October, and November, the result, it has been suggested, of careful Franciscan manipulation.[61] In Avignon in 1372, Jean IV's partisans tried in vain to obstruct the proceedings, arguing unsuccessfully that a number of procedural irregularities should render the Angers testimony invalid. Jean, though a vocal objector, was soon an insignificant one, however. As part of the general Anglo-French hostilities (better known as the Hundred Years' War), he had been driven into English exile by French forces in 1373, returning to his duchy only in 1379.[62] By 1376 it seems that Pope Gregory XI was prepared to canonize Charles. Such at least is the import of a bull dated February 1376, directing the cardinals to ignore the irregularities in the Angers inquest; a letter of Christophe de Plaisance's dated September 7 reported that the common gossip in Avignon was that Gregory planned to canonize Charles immediately. One week later, however, Pope Gregory left Avignon to return the Holy See to Rome; he died the following March without having enrolled Charles of Blois in the catalog of saints.[63]

---

58. Ibid., 221; see also Vauchez 1997, 229–31.

59. H. Martin 1975, 366–71; Jones 2003d, 221. See also Plaine 1921.

60. H. Martin 1975, 409.

61. Marie, the daughter of Charles of Blois, was married to Louis of Anjou, the king's brother. On the push to canonization, see, esp., H. Martin 1975, 367–69; and Jones 2003d, 221–22. See also H. Martin 1975, 408–11, who demonstrates the Dominican support for the Montfort cause and Franciscan support for the Penthièvre side. One indication of the stakes involved is provided by the fact that Duke Jean IV had Pope Urban V condemn Franciscan sermons that proclaimed Charles to be a saint and martyr of justice.

62. Galliou and Jones 1991, 235. He returned, ironically, at the request of a band of Breton lords, clerics, and townspeople who had once been loyal to Jeanne de Penthièvre and who were more interested in preserving the duchy from absorption by France than in which family should rule it.

63. For the final stages in the 1370s, see Vauchez 1978; H. Martin 1975, 371–72; Jones 2003d, 224–28.

Although the near canonization of Charles of Blois might have seemed like old news by the time Jean V was inviting Vincent Ferrer to preach in the duchy some thirty years later, the nagging problem of the Penthièvre claims to the dukedom still remained. The grandsons of Charles of Blois were coming of age, and their mother was full of schemes to discomfit the rival duke. The nearly thirty-year-old Jean V himself had only a four-year-old son, hardly reassuring in an age of high childhood mortality.[64] The matter was far from settled. In February of 1420, scarcely a year after Vincent Ferrer's death, Jean would find himself taken prisoner by his Penthièvre cousins and would remain a captive for the next five months. The Penthièvre family would maintain its claim on the ducal throne almost as long as the duchy remained independent from France; only in 1480 did Nicole de Penthièvre renounce her rights to the duchy in return for a handsome payment from the king of France.[65]

After his death in 1442, Jean's sons and heirs, François I (r. 1442–50) and Pierre II (r. 1450–57) continued to assert the sovereignty of the Breton dukes (with varying degrees of success) and to tread the delicate line between England and France (source of a fratricidal battle among Jean V's three sons) in the climactic years of the Hundred Years' War, just as they still had to deal with their Penthièvre rivals. Despite the condemnation of two of Charles of Blois's grandsons in 1425 for the kidnapping of Jean V and the subsequent confiscation of Penthièvre lands, a third grandson was still at it in 1448. He actually managed to regain possession of the county of Penthièvre in 1450.[66] Both François and Pierre were well aware of the value of symbols, as well as careful diplomacy, in shoring up the duke's authority. François, for example, created a chivalric order, the Épi, while Pierre promoted the "secular cult" of the Nine Barons of Brittany, a parallel to the twelve peers of France.[67] Furthermore, the dukes continued to pose as patrons of the church, for example, endowing a new Carmelite foundation in Rennes in 1448.[68]

Not surprisingly, then, Jean V's sons worked hard to secure the canonization of the saintly preacher whom their father had gone to such great lengths to cultivate. In that work they were aided by the crown of Vincent's native Aragon, the cathedral chapter in Vannes (whose members were not insensitive to the value of the relics of a canonized saint), the Dominican order, and Pierre II's wife, Françoise d'Amboise. Françoise had essentially been raised by Jean V and his wife, Jeanne de France, who had been so

---

64. Knowlson 1964, 113; also Touchard 1969, 177–79.

65. Jones 2003b, 259; Leguay and Martin 1982, 237–38; Galliou and Jones 1991, 248. On the reigns of the Montfort dukes, see also Kerhervé 1987.

66. Touchard 1969, 179.

67. Galliou and Jones 1991, 245–46; see also La Borderie 1895.

68. H. Martin 1975, 68.

devoted to Vincent Ferrer in his final illness. She obviously absorbed Jeanne's attachment to the Dominican preacher and either supported or propelled her husband's efforts on behalf of Vincent's canonization.[69]

Encouraged by the 1447 election of a new pope, Nicholas V, who presumably lacked some of the many distractions of his predecessor, Pierre II began petitioning the pontiff to open canonization proceedings almost as soon as he assumed the ducal throne in 1450. By June of 1451, Pierre's henchmen were in Rome for the chapter general of the Dominican order, at which the friars agreed to urge Nicholas to "bring an end at last to this business, of which mention had been made not just once in the Roman curia."[70] Acceding to the friars' request, Nicholas promised to devote himself to the cause of Vincent's canonization. Members of the order were urged to send reports of authenticated miracles to the order's procurers.[71] To what must have been Pierre's great joy, the Dominicans scheduled their subsequent chapter general for May of 1453 in Nantes, specifically so that they could meet with the duke in person.[72] Françoise d'Amboise herself contributed to the costs of that gathering, at which the new master general of the Dominican order, Martial Auribelli, entered into conversation with the duke, his court, and other Breton nobles.[73] The result: "Putting aside all other matters, [the duke] began to think solely about the matter of the blessed Vincent."[74]

When it came to asking Rome to open canonization proceedings for Vincent Ferrer, the third time indeed had been the charm, and the pope gave ample credit to the dukes of Brittany for keeping the matter alive these many years. In a letter dated October 18, 1451, acknowledging the requests made by the Dominican order, the late Breton duke Jean V, King Juan II of Castile and León, King Alfonso V of Aragon (Alfons el Magnànim "the Magnanimous," r. 1416–58), and the current duke Pierre II, Pope Nicholas V issued orders to three of his cardinals to organize inquests into the life and miracles of the blessed Vincent Ferrer. By January of the following year, they had appointed subcommissioners to carry out four local inquests, of which the largest would be that held in Brittany from November 1453

---

69. Raised by Jean and Jeanne: FHSVF, 2:261.

70. According to Ranzano, who was present at that chapter general in Rome (BC, MS 112, fol. 62r): "Postulauit ut finis tandem fieret negocii cuius non semel in romana curia facta fuerat antea mentio."

71. Reichert 1900, 3:256. One can presume that it was this directive that prompted a 1451 inquest in Aragon in Lérida (Lleida), nearly a dozen miracles from which appear in a fifteenth-century Sicilian collection, edited (and discussed) in Pagano 2000.

72. BC, MS 112, fol. 62v.

73. FHSVF, 2:315, 322.

74. Again, according to Ranzano's narrative (BC, MS 112, fol. 62v): "Omissis ille caeteris omnibus negociis solum de beati Vincentii re coeperit cogitare." Nicholas's appointing of three cardinals to organize canonization inquests on Vincent's behalf was announced at the chapter general: Reichert 1900, 3:258.

to April 1454.[75] Although he did not testify in the canonization inquest (as Alfonso V would), Pierre II, along with the other Montfort dukes, nonetheless loomed large in the testimony from the Brittany inquest.

Even though the canonization inquest was, strictly speaking, a church matter, carried out by the clergy of Brittany under the rules of canon rather than civil law, the dividing lines between powerful nobles and powerful clerics were never so firm in practice. As the subcommissioners in charge of the Brittany inquest would later report to the three presiding cardinals, although it was Yvo de Pontsal, Bishop of Vannes, who "elegantly recited" the life, virtues, and miracles of Master Vincent Ferrer at a ceremony opening the inquest, he was assisted not simply by other Breton clergy but also by Duke Pierre II.[76] The duke also perhaps figured among the "very many nobles" who greeted the subcommissioners as they made a visit to Vincent's tomb four days later and at the ceremony held to mark the closing of the canonization inquest on April 7, 1454.[77]

The Montfort dukes featured prominently in the testimony gathered at the inquest as well. Of the first 50 of the 313 Brittany witnesses, at least 10 had some sorts of clear ties to the Montfort family, and many remembered well the devotion that Jean V and his wife had shown to Vincent Ferrer, as well as the gracious deference with which Vincent had left the decision about his final resting place in the hands of the duke and bishop. They also told stories of Vincent's miracles, tales that revealed Jean V and his sons basking in just the sort of sacred aura the Montfort dukes must have hoped this adoptive local saint could bring them.

Take, for example, the story of Perrinus Hervei, also known as Grasset (Fatty).[78] Perrinus was close to the Montforts; the notaries who took down his testimony at the canonization process identified him as a "client" (or important retainer) of Duke Pierre II.[79] At fifty-seven years of age, Perrinus had a crisp memory of Vincent Ferrer's days in Vannes and was important enough to Jean V to have been admitted to Vincent's chamber in the Dreulin house where he lay dying in April 1419. Perrinus's age and his ties

---

75. For a brief chronology of the canonization process, see Wetzstein 2004a, 382–83. The letters appointing the panel of cardinals and the subcommissioners appear in *Procès,* pp. [1]–10. (There are page numbers in a later hand at this portion of the manuscript, the eighth signature, which is misbound between witnesses 239 and 240, as it appears also in my microfilm of the MS [ADM, 1 Mi 1]). On the manuscript, see also Wetzstein 2002, 353n6. The letters also appear in *Proceso,* fol. 169v–173r, 264v–267v, and 270r–270v, and (often in abridged form) in FND, 381–85, 393–94, 407. In general, on the process of canonization, see chapter 2.

76. *Procès,* p. 13; FND, 395–96 (abridged).

77. FND, 397, 400.

78. On this miracle and the connections of witnesses to the miracle to ducal circles see Smoller 2006, esp. 155–62.

79. *Procès,* witness 4; FPC, 15.

to the ducal family were probably the factors that prompted the organizers of the canonization inquest to summon him as the fourth of the line of witnesses to present testimony about the holy preacher. There Perrinus also told the story of his miraculous cure, some twenty-eight or so years earlier, the very first miracle related in the Brittany testimony.

He was at the home of a friend, Petrus Floc'h, one Saturday morning around the time of Easter. Suddenly there came over Perrinus an illness that left him out of his mind, running about through the streets and plazas of town like a madman and leading his friends to tie him up for safety's sake. In retrospect, Perrinus's assessment of the situation was the same as that of other observers: he had been possessed by a demon. The following afternoon, his wife, friends, and neighbors made a vow to Vincent Ferrer and brought Perrinus, still bound and raving, to the preacher's tomb in the Vannes cathedral. There Perrinus quieted, slept, and awoke cured. Vincent had appeared to him in a dream, saying "My son, you will soon be in good health."[80]

The spectacular and public nature of Perrinus's infirmity, combined with his high social status, assured that the story was widely known in fifteenth-century Vannes. When he arose that Sunday afternoon, asking bystanders, "Didn't you see Master Vincent talking with me just now?" the cathedral clergy rang the bells loudly to announce the working of a new miracle.[81] Some three decades after the fact, no fewer than fourteen Brittany witnesses testified to this miracle.[82] And their testimony reinforced in two important ways the connection between the saintly preacher and the ducal family members who were Perrinus's patrons and friends. First, as Perrinus himself stressed, not simply was he placed on Vincent's tomb as he lay bound and ranting that Sunday afternoon, but also Duchess Jeanne herself sent the holy preacher's cloak—the relic she had saved from his deathbed—for Perrinus to lay under his own, troubled head.[83] In some sense, the duchess who had been so devoted to Vincent Ferrer had interceded with the saintly Dominican, who in turn had pleaded with God on Perrinus's behalf. Second,

---

80. *Procès,* witness 4; FPC, 16. Vincent's words are reported in the vernacular: "Mon fils, tu seras tantost en bon poinct" (then helpfully translated into Latin for the benefit of the curia). Petrus Floc'h (Pierre Filloche) served from 1424 to 1426, around the time of the miracle, as purveyor general for the ducal *Hôtel.* Kerhervé 1987, 1:247.

81. As related by Petrus Floc'h (*Procès,* witness 8; FPC, 30): "Numquid vidistis M.V. loquentem nunc mecum?"

82. Brittany witnesses Perrinus Hervei (witness 4), Petrus Floc'h (witness 8), Symon Maydo (witness 9), Johannes Rolandi (witness 13), Johanna, wife of Perrinus Hervei (witness 15), Johanna, widow of Johannes Damon (witness 17), Herveus Maydo (witness 18), Herveus Le Goff (witness 26), Yvo Le Houssec (witness 27), Michael Maceot (witness 30), Petrus de Bonabri (witness 33), Johannes Boayden (witness 36). Thomas le Brun (witness 60), and Silvester Stephani (witness 156).

83. *Procès,* witness 4; FPC, 16. He is described as lying, "capa [*sic*] dicti M.V. que honorifice a dicta quondam domina Ducissa custodiebatur sibi ab eadem domina transmissa, subtus caput eiusdem testis existente."

as Symon Maydo, another well-connected citizen of Vannes recalled, Perrinus had received from Vincent Ferrer not simply a cure from his infirmity but also a message. Namely, in his dream the preacher had "commanded [Perrinus] to tell the duke that he should get Master Vincent canonized."[84] While Vincent, brought close through relics like his cloak, could intercede with God on behalf of the duke's friends, the story of his command to Perrinus made it clear that the preacher also expected and needed the Breton duke to work favors for him.

Another miracle story related to the commissioners of the Brittany inquest served even more clearly to lend an aura of sacred legitimacy to Montfort rule. This tale came from the lips of a noble widow who had been a member of Duchess Jeanne's retinue during Vincent Ferrer's sojourn in Brittany. She recalled well that one day, before the duchess even realized that she was pregnant, Vincent told her that "God would bless the lord whom she was carrying [in her womb]." Making the sign of the cross over Jeanne, Vincent offered his benediction of the child, saying that the duchess would give birth to a duke.[85] Given the dates of Vincent's time in Brittany, that duke had to have been Pierre II—who was born in 1418, the year of Vincent's arrival in Brittany—and not his older brother François, who had been born in 1414. The Montforts must have felt more than the usual anxiety about producing male heirs, since their failure to do so would give the ducal crown to their rival Penthièvre cousins. While François did in fact live long enough to become duke of Brittany, he died before reaching forty. Vincent's blessing of Jeanne's womb had indeed turned into a benediction of the reigning duke of Brittany, as well as a sign of God's approval of continued Montfort rule in the duchy.

This story must have been widely repeated by Pierre II as he pushed for Vincent's canonization, for a version of the same tale shows up in the testimony of a Naples witness,[86] in Pietro Ranzano's *vita* of Vincent, and in the brief life of the saint that Ranzano compiled to help a fellow Dominican preach the cult of the newly canonized saint. According to Ranzano, Vincent had actually miraculously brought an end to an agonizing spate of stillbirths and infant deaths suffered by Jean V and Jeanne de France. As he made the sign of the cross over the duchess's womb, Vincent had prophesied not simply that Jeanne would conceive the future duke but in fact that this duke

---

84. *Procès,* witness 9; FPC, 34: "Ipse vero Perrinus replicavit se nullum malum habere asserens se vidisse M. V. et sibi allocutum fuisse ac mandasse ut diceret Duci quod ipsum M. V. canonizari faceret."

85. *Procès,* witness 7; FPC, 25: "M. V. dixit domine ducisse ignoranti tunc se esse pregnantem quod Deus benediceret illum dominum quem ipsa ducissa portabat et benedixit ei cum signo crucis et dicit [*sic*] quod ducissa peperit post ducem modernum."

86. Fernandus, bishop of Telesia (*Proceso,* fol. 283v; FPC, 422, witness 9), who has the infant baptized by Vincent himself and given the name Vincent of Brittany.

would see to it that Vincent would be placed "among the saints of Christ by the Roman Church."[87] Ranzano's narrative, which surely would have pleased Pierre had he still been alive to hear it, imbued Pierre II's reign with the aura of a holy mission. In Ranzano's account, the saint himself prophetically identifies the two great heroes of his canonization process: Nicholas V's successor, Calixtus III—the pope who would proclaim Vincent a saint—and Pierre II, the duke who worked so hard to see it happen.[88]

Once the papal subcommissioners closed the Brittany canonization inquest on April 7, 1454, Pierre II continued the push to see the affair through to its conclusion. In December 1454, he sent a Nantes cathedral canon to Rome as his ambassador in the canonization process. He returned, flush with success, the following September.[89] Meanwhile, Pierre was preparing for the long-hoped-for event. In 1455 he levied a tax in the duchy of five pennies to help pay for the cost of the canonization itself.[90] Perhaps Pierre had set his courtiers to leaf through ducal archives, where he could have gotten a good idea of the costs involved. Charles of Blois, the Montforts' old rival, had paid three thousand florins for the cost of the final stages of the canonization of the Breton Saint Yves in 1346–47.[91] The price of the near-contemporary canonization of Saint Osmund in 1457 would come to over seven hundred pounds; expenses for the ceremony alone in the 1482 canonization of Saint Bonaventure would run to twenty-seven thousand gold ducats.[92] In the end, as the eyewitness Ranzano reported, Pierre II would contribute two thousand gold pieces to pay for the canonization ceremonies, not so shabby if one considers that Alfonso V, the king of Naples as well as of Vincent's native Aragon, gave only eight hundred gold pieces.[93]

Pierre kept up the pressure on Rome to the bitter end. Even as Pope Calixtus III was announcing in a public consistory his intention to enroll Vincent in the catalog of the saints, a messenger from Brittany entered the chamber with a report of another miracle.[94] When at last Vincent's

---

87. The fuller version of the story is in the brief life (BC, MS 112, fol. 59v–60r): "Praediceret illam concaepturam parituramque filium qui patre mortuo esset et britanibus imperaturus et operam daturus ut se quoque mortuo inter christi sanctos a romana ecclesia referret: nec multis interiectis diebus uideret coniugem (prout ille praedixerat) grauatam iam esse." In the version in book 4 of the official *vita* (RVV, 1:509), Ranzano omits the prophecy but notes that Pierre spent "many thousand gold coins" toward the cause of Vincent's canonization.

88. Calixtus: BC, MS 112, fol. 53r.

89. FND, 385. Ranzano also mentions legates of the duke of Brittany: BC, MS 112, fol. 68r.

90. FHSVF, 2:320–21.

91. Vauchez 1997, 65–66.

92. Delooz 1969, 435. On the costs of canonization see also Wetzstein 2004a, 371; D. Martin 2004, 140, in which Martin quotes Vincent's brother Boniface (head of the Carthusian order) lamenting that a canonization cause can last fifteen years of great labor and expense.

93. BC, MS 112, fol. 62r–63v.

94. Ranzano: BC, MS 112, fol. 66r.

canonization was formally proclaimed in St. Peter's in Rome, Pierre II's arms were paraded throughout the city. Even if, as a mere duke, he had to acquiesce in the precedence given to the arms of Alfonso V, King of Aragon, Pierre could smile with pride that the clergy involved knew that he had paid the lion's share of the expenses. Calixtus, well aware of the duke's interest, wrote Pierre personally to inform him that the affair was at last over and to thank the "most Christian prince" for his hard work on behalf of Saint Vincent Ferrer.[95] Furthermore, the duke would have his own day in the sun the following year at the ceremonial elevation of the new saint's corpse in the Vannes cathedral.[96]

In April 1456, Alain de Coativi arrived in Vannes as papal legate to preside over the elevation of the new saint's relics. If he was the star of the several days of ceremonies to follow, the impresario of events was Pierre II. On his arrival, Alain feasted and lodged with the duke himself in Vannes. Also in town for the ceremony were sixteen bishops and archbishops, the abbots of every monastery in the duchy, the Dominican master general Martial Auribelli, and large numbers of nobles from Brittany, Anjou, Normandy, Maine, Poitou, and various regions of France and England. On April 4, as the cathedral bells were sounding for vespers, Pierre II left his castle of l'Hermine and walked the few short blocks to the cathedral, accompanied by all the duchy's nobles. His entry marked the beginning of the ceremony in the cathedral. There, together with the papal legate and the other ecclesiastical dignitaries, seated in his elevated chair in the cathedral, Pierre and his retinue heard the vespers of Saint Vincent Ferrer. Near midnight, the duke and the pope's legate returned to the cathedral, accompanied by the ecclesiastical dignitaries, Breton nobles, important citizens of Vannes, the priors of every Dominican convent in Brittany, and the Franciscan friars of Vannes. The office of matins in honor of Saint Vincent was "solemnly chanted." And at last, after the coffin was opened, the legate placed the holy bones in a coffer, carried them all the way around the cathedral, and then placed them near the high altar. The next morning, the saint's feast day proper (April 5), the papal legate celebrated Mass, during the course of which he officially announced Vincent's canonization in Latin, Breton, and French.[97] A spate of miracles ensued, as crowds thronged to the church to view Vincent's relics.

---

95. FND, 387–88.

96. BHL no. 8669. The ceremony was described in Le Grand 1901, 132–33; and in the *Acta capitulorum generalium ordinis praedicatorum* for 1456: Reichert 1900, 3:264. There is a brief mention of the ceremony written ca. 1475 in Meyer 1933, 95. See also AASS, Aprilis, 1:525–26; FND, 415–17, quoting Albert Le Grand.

97. Le Grand 1901, 133. There is also a very brief account in book 4 of the early sixteenth-century chronicle of Alain Bouchart, *Grandes croniques de Bretaigne* 1986, 2:369. The Breton Alain de Coativi had replaced Alfonso de Borja as a commissioner in the canonization process upon the latter's elevation to the papal throne as Calixtus III.

At last, the holy corpse was settled into a new, more sumptuous, and carefully locked sepulchre. Two of the coffer's three keys went to the papal legate and the bishop of Vannes, but the third went to Duke Pierre II.[98] Most wonderful of all, Pierre was allowed a relic: one of Vincent's fingers.[99] All in all, it must have been a most satisfactory week for the Montfort family.

The ducal family continued to stress its ties to the new saint in books of hours produced for the private use of family members. In these precious devotional items, we see the Montforts as they wished to see themselves: as most Christian rulers in the manner of the royal house of France or the other great noble families, such as the dukes of Burgundy, on whose court Jean V had modeled his own. So, for example, Vincent's portrait appears in Pierre II's own book of hours, today preserved at the Bibliothèque nationale de France in Paris. His is the fourth in a series of twenty-eight saints' portraits (suffrages), just following that of the Franciscan preacher Bernardino of Siena, canonized in 1450.[100] Vincent also appears in the calendar of a breviary evidently belonging to Pierre's wife, with an indication that there were nine lessons celebrated in his honor on April 5.[101] And a lovely portrait of Saint Vincent Ferrer graces the pages of the exquisite little book of hours belonging to Isabeau d'Ecosse, Pierre's sister-in-law and widow of Duke François II.[102]

All in all, the ducal family's courting of Vincent Ferrer, together with their strenuous work for his canonization, seems to have had the desired effect. Through their association with the pious Dominican, the Montforts found the saint who could compete with the memory of Charles of Blois. Whereas Jean IV could, at best, stall the canonization proceedings of his defunct rival in the 1370s, Pierre II in 1455 could parade the arms of Brittany at the canonization of the Montforts' "own" saint. True, those witnesses at the 1453–54 inquest who were close to ducal circles were also those who remembered best that Duke Jean and Duchess Jeanne had lavished devotion on the holy preacher. Books of hours depicting the new saint in company with kneeling Montforts were probably seen only by the ducal family and their own clergy, servants, and intimates. But those groups were the Montforts' most important audience in the game of political propaganda; the peasants, the artisans, the sailors, and the fisherman of Brittany would heed the local lord, as they had always done. And no one could deny that the saint's relics lay in the cathedral in Vannes, an arrow's shot away from the castle of l'Hermine and a mere stone's throw from the chancellor's house in

---

98. Reichert 1900, 3:264, chapter general of 1456; also noted in FND, 417.

99. FND, 418.

100. BNF, MS lat. 1159, fol. 128v.

101. Bibliothèque municipale, Nantes, MS 32; Molinier 1893, 8. See also FHSVF, 2:378.

102. BNF, MS lat. 1369, p. 318. See L'Estrange 2008, esp. chap. 5, 210–15.

which so much of the important business of the duchy took place. If in 1455 the scars of the War of Succession still remained in the duchy, they were less and less visible. The body politic was healing.

## Canonization and Religious Harmony

In a similar fashion, Vincent Ferrer's advent—and final rest—in the duchy helped to ease, or at least to reconfigure, religious tensions there. The issue of Vincent's burial had stirred up enough animosity between Dominicans, Franciscans, and members of the cathedral clergy to prompt the bishop to keep his body under guard. As with any serious family quarrel, this one, too, had a long history. Since their near simultaneous inceptions at the beginning of the thirteenth century, the Order of Preachers and the Order of Friars Minor had maintained a healthy rivalry. Saints from each of the two groups jostled with one another in a contest for spiritual prestige among the orders. Although the Dominicans had no one whose popularity could come close to that of the charismatic and beloved Saint Francis, still they could boast not just about their founder but also about a modern-day martyr (Saint Peter Martyr, canonized in 1253),[103] as well as Thomas Aquinas, the "angelic doctor," canonized in 1323. The importance of having their own canonized saints helps explain why 88 of the 128 saints canonized between 993 and 1634 were members of some religious order, as well as the urgency with which the Dominican order promoted the cause of Vincent Ferrer's canonization in 1451, the year after Franciscan Bernardino of Siena received papal canonization.[104] From 1468 on, the Dominicans included in their liturgy special thanks to God, who "deigned to illuminate your church with the merits and doctrine of your saints Peter, Thomas, Vincent, and Catherine [Catherine of Siena, canonized in 1461]."[105]

Since both orders were dedicated to the principles of apostolic poverty and, in theory at least, depended on begging (hence the term "mendicant orders") and the offerings they received in their churches, they competed not simply for spiritual prestige but for their means of living as well. The mendicants thrived in cities and the highly urban atmosphere of northern Italy; in a more sparsely populated area like fifteenth-century Brittany, they were hard-pressed to find a population of adequate size to support them on top of the ordinary (or so-called secular) clergy, that is, the parish priests and their bishops. The Franciscans, all in all, were more successful than other

---

103. See now Prudlo 2008.

104. Figures: Delooz 1969, 387. Vauchez notes that the Franciscans and Dominicans had a "quasi-monopoly" of canonizations in the years after 1431. Vauchez 1997, 75–76.

105. Archives nationales, Paris, LL 1529 (Frères prêcheurs, Chapitres généraux, 1459–1518), fol. 40v.

mendicant groups in implanting themselves in the duchy, but a number of new foundations in the fourteenth century had brought in less well-known groups, like the Augustinians, Trinitarians, and Carmelites.[106] Not surprisingly, then, in medieval Brittany the mendicants viewed one another with jealous suspicion. Franciscans and Dominicans in Nantes worked together to oppose the installation of a Carmelite house there, fearing that the city did not hold enough souls to support three mendicant convents.[107]

More hostilities still flared between mendicants and secular clergy. On the one hand, by the late fourteenth century, large numbers of donations to mendicant houses had made it more and more difficult for mendicant friars to keep up the appearance of the apostolic poverty the faithful so admired. On the other hand, the patronage of the dukes and other great lords had raised the hackles of the secular clergy, particularly because mendicant preachers were fond of giving sermons in which they encouraged their audiences not to tithe to the local clergy.[108] Of fourteen new mendicant foundations in the fourteenth century, four were greeted with such opposition by the secular clergy of Brittany that it was necessary to offer them some financial compensation before the convents could be built.[109] In fourteenth-century Nantes, synods passed statutes limiting the mendicants' sway; in Vannes, Franciscans and secular clergy battled throughout the fourteenth and fifteenth centuries over parishioners who elected to be buried in the Friars Minor's cemetery instead of in their parish church. (Who would receive their funeral offerings was the main issue.)[110] Still, the advent of Vincent Ferrer in the duchy did much to raise the status (or arrogance) of mendicants in general. In 1418, perhaps emboldened by the popularity of Vincent's preaching, Dominican preachers used their Lenten sermons to attack parish priests.[111]

Vincent's burial in the Vannes cathedral did not, however, immediately smooth over rivalries between the various religious orders. Although they were doubtless comforted that the Franciscans did not win the prize of housing Vincent's tomb in their convent in Vannes, Breton Dominicans mounted

---

106. Galliou and Jones 1991, 268; Leguay and Martin 1982, 142, 299.

107. H. Martin 1975, 104.

108. Leguay and Martin 1982, 143; H. Martin 1975, 313.

109. H. Martin 1975, 139.

110. Ibid., 144. They were still at it in 1433 (ADM, 49 H 2 "AA": "Les monseigneurs de St Pierre ne peuvent faire l'office dans l'eglise des religieux contre leur consentement tam occasione sepulturae quam…"); 1476 (ADM, 49 H 2: "Accord terminé devant le seigneur evesque de Treguer entre le recteur de St. Patern et les religieux au sujet des sepultures. 26 decembre 1476," an agreement with the clergy of St. Patern after a very tense moment during the burial of Johanna de Fetiff, who had asked to be buried with the Franciscans); and 1493 (ADM 49 H 2, pièce 3: "Transaction entre le chapitre de Vannes et Religieux au subjet des sepultures").

111. H. Martin 1975, 324.

a succession of attempts to take back the preacher's corpse. In 1428, ten years after Vincent's burial in the cathedral, the Dominicans took the step of purchasing a house in Vannes.[112] They must have felt the need even more urgently after the canonization of Franciscan Bernardino of Siena in 1450, for shortly thereafter the Franciscans in Vannes had erected a chapel and altar to their new saint and were offering one hundred days of indulgence to those participating in ceremonies on his feast day and contributing to the church's renovation.[113] In the midst of the Brittany canonization inquest, in 1454, the Dominicans received papal permission to open a convent in the town in the evident hope that a house in Vannes might strengthen their case in demanding Vincent's body. When, in 1459, the pope ruled definitively in favor of the cathedral and chapter, however, the Dominicans sold the land and gave up plans for a presence in Vannes.[114]

Furthermore, both Franciscans and Dominicans were threatened by the existence of other mendicant houses, particularly the Carmelites, whom the Montfort dukes favored greatly in the early fifteenth century.[115] A miracle story from the canonization inquest gives us a glimpse at the competition for spiritual prestige among the orders. It is a tale we have encountered already: the story of the demoniac Perrinus Hervei. While Perrinus, friend of the duke and duchess, ranted and raged that Saturday afternoon in 1423 or so, his keepers' first stop was not Vincent Ferrer's tomb. In fact, as several of the Brittany witnesses to this miracle recalled, the crowd first carried Perrinus to the Carmelite house of Bondon, just about a kilometer outside the city walls.[116]

Bondon was the newest addition to the collection of churches, chapels, and religious houses in and around Vannes. It had been founded by Duke Jean V, ever eager to cultivate an air of religiosity, probably within a few years after Vincent Ferrer's advent to the duchy. And, as Hervé Martin

---

112. Ibid., 94.

113. ADM, 49 H 2 "A," April 10, 1452; also mentioned in H. Martin 1975, 363, who sees the chapel as a response to the growing cult of Vincent Ferrer.

114. H. Martin 1975, 94. Perhaps in tacit furtherance of the order's claims on the relics, Dominican Pietro Ranzano in his *vita* of Vincent Ferrer omits Vincent's demurral to the bishop of Vannes and the duke of Brittany and has the preacher instructing bystanders at his deathbed, "I entreat you that you entrust the decision about the burial of my body to the prior of the convent of my order closest to your town." RVV, 1:510.

115. H. Martin 1975, 67–70. For example, Duke Jean V's "good gift" of the chapel of Notre-Dame du Bondon to the Carmelites in 1425—see Le Mené 1895, 4–8—and the missal from the Carmelite house in Nantes that contains a depiction of Jean V having himself weighed, part of his fulfillment of a vow to give his weight in gold to the Carmelites in Nantes if he should be released from the captivity in which his Penthièvre cousins were holding him in 1420. See note 49 and accompanying text.

116. Brittany witnesses Petrus Floc'h (witness 8), Symon Maydo (witness 9), Herveus Le Goff (witness 26), and Yvo Le Houssec (witness 27); see also Smoller 2006, 152–55, 161–62.

has suggested, the duke had promised the house to the Carmelite Thomas Cornette.[117] Cornette considered himself Vincent Ferrer's successor in many ways.[118] Certainly Brother Thomas, like Vincent, must have been an extremely moving and effective preacher. On one occasion, he fired up young children, deputizing the little innocents to offer Thomas's (and God's) reprimand to their mothers for their extravagant hairstyles.[119] In the later Middle Ages, as now, fashion and hair provided observers with major evidence of the sorry state of society. Moralists blamed the fourteenth-century Black Death on the pointy-toed shoes and tight clothing favored by fashionable courtiers; women were sporting "clothes that were so tight," lamented one chronicler, "that they wore a fox tail hanging down inside their skirts at the back, to hide their arses."[120]

In a town already tingling from the effects of the spiritual revival inaugurated by Vincent Ferrer, Brother Thomas's preaching, too, appears to have caught the imagination of Vannes's citizens. That must be why Perrinus's friends first tried the services of the newest local spiritual hotshot. As Symon Maydo recalled, when Perrinus was brought to the Carmelite house in Bondon, "many followed so that they might see if a miracle would be worked through the merits of said Brother Thomas."[121] The results were disastrous. Thomas certainly knew the routine: whereas Vincent Ferrer had made the sign of the cross over the sick and lame who came to seek his blessing, murmuring the Gospel phrase, "They shall lay hands on the sick, and they shall recover" (Mark 16:18),[122] Thomas sprinkled holy water on Perrinus, hoping thereby to expel the demon who had possessed him. Instead, Perrinus became only more agitated, invoking the devil, cursing God and the saints, trying to bite Brother Thomas, and even spitting on the image of the Blessed Virgin and calling her a whore.[123] If the curious and anxious townspeople who followed Perrinus to Bondon had longed for the presence

---

117. H. Martin 1975, 68. On Thomas Cornette, see Ben-Shalom 2004, esp. 219–23; H. Martin 1988, 53–57, 173–74; and Levot (1852–57) 1971. Brittany witness Symon Maydo (*Procès,* witness 9; FPC, 34) describes "Frater Thomas, Ordinis Fratrum Carmelitarum" as being in Bondon to start a new convent: "Inchoaverat ibidem unum novum conventum dicti Ordinis."

118. Ben-Shalom 2004, 236.

119. Leguay and Martin 1982, 358; Ben-Shalom 2004, 220.

120. Anonymous monk's continuation of the Westminster chronicle, quoted in Horrox 1994, 131.

121. *Procès,* witness 9; FPC, 34: "Et multi sequebantur ut viderent si meritis dicti fratris Thome fieret miraculum et sanaretur idem Perrinus."

122. For example, as described by Michael Albiol (*Proceso,* fol. 262r; FPC, 34, Naples witness 19).

123. According to the testimony of Symon Maydo (*Procès,* witness 9; FPC, 34), at Bondon, Perrinus was seen "dyabolum invocantem continue ymaginem B. Marie spuentem et vocantem eam meretricem." Herveus Le Goff (*Procès,* witness 26; FPC, 59) described how Perrinus "nisus fuit mordere quemdam religiosum illius loci [Beate Marie Boni Doni] Ordinis Fratrum Carmelitarum fratrem Thomam nuncupatum."

of another living saint in Brother Thomas, they were disappointed in that hope. Thomas was forced to acknowledge his inability to cure Perrinus, and the glory of the cure went to Vincent Ferrer, thanks to Perrinus's slumber at his tomb and the kind loan of Vincent's *cappa* by my lady the duchess.

Miracles were, among other things, God's signs to humankind. The message Perrinus and others brought out of the experience was that God wished on that day to highlight the merits of the recently dead Vincent Ferrer. It would certainly not be the first time God and his saints had chosen to act in such a manner. A famous story from the chronicle of William of Malmesbury recalls another friendly competition between two saints. When a leper was laid between the relics of Saints Germanus and Martin—whose relics had been transported to Auxerre to keep them safe from the Vikings—only the side nearest Saint Martin was healed, as Saint Germanus graciously yielded to the visiting saint at his side.[124] Such a demonstration of Vincent's superiority was what witnesses reported before the papal commissioners in 1453–54.

And as for the four witnesses who insisted on the prior failure of Brother Thomas, the subsequent course of events had already proven them right. If Bondon's Brother Thomas was indeed Thomas Cornette, he had been burned for heresy in 1433, while the Carmelites whom the dukes had so favored were widely suspected of heterodox leanings.[125] In underscoring the site of Perrinus's healing—Vincent's tomb in the Vannes cathedral—this oft-told miracle story put the locus of spiritual power at the center of the diocesan hierarchy, in the hands of the bishop, and not with any of the competing groups of friars. Yet the fact that the saintly Dominican did repose in the cathedral assured that the chapter would work hard for (and pay for) Vincent's canonization, even as it signaled the bishop's tacit approval of the mass, open-air style of preaching favored by Dominicans, Franciscans, and Carmelites alike.

In the end, just as Vincent Ferrer's advent had helped, if only symbolically, to smooth over the scars of the duchy's War of Succession, so, too, his death and burial there, as well as his subsequent canonization, played some role in sorting out some of the religious tensions in fifteenth-century Brittany. Had a Breton cleric written a life of the newly canonized saint, he might well have emphasized Vincent's close ties to the Montfort family of dukes,

---

124. Cited in Moore 1987, 49.

125. For Thomas Cornette's heresy conviction, H. Martin 1975, 68; 1988, 174 (he places it in 1434). See also Ben-Shalom 2004, 221–23. Vaucelle 1908, 83, cites a papal letter of October 11, 1448, confirming a concession made by Martin V to Thomas Connette "condamné pour hérésie, de recevoir dans le duché de Bretagne deux endroits pour y bâtir des couvents." One issue was Thomas's repeated insistence on vociferously attacking priests for keeping mistresses, but the real reasons for his heresy conviction remain a mystery. It seems likely that Eugenius IV took him for an agent of the Council of Basel. Ben-Shalom 2004, 219–23. For the heterodox leanings of Carmelites in Brittany, Leguay and Martin 1982, 358.

as well as the way his canonization became a win-win situation for all the religious parties involved. Instead, we have only snapshots to suggest the ways in which powerful Bretons appropriated Vincent Ferrer as a symbol: the repeated memory of the duke and duchess's involvement with the saint; the numbers of Breton witnesses who could tell the story of Perrinus Hervei's cure at Vincent's tomb; the energy, time, and money that Pierre II expended to the end of seeing Vincent canonized.

Perhaps it was a sense that Vincent Ferrer's presence in Brittany had indeed brought divided parties back together that inspired the Vannes cathedral clergy to commission, for a painting of miracles displayed at Vincent's tomb, a depiction of the miraculous healing of a chopped-up baby. We can glimpse just the blurred outline of that painting through the testimony of one witness at the canonization inquest. As Guillermus Rolandi told the tale of the miraculous cure of his own daughter, he noted that he had thought to call on Vincent's intercession only after he recalled "a certain miracle of which there was mention on a certain painted tableau on Vincent's tomb."[126] That miracle was the story of the resuscitation of a baby killed by its mother; we learn from another Brittany witness the gruesome details that the mother had cut the child into two parts—through the head—and that even after the miracle, one could still see the "signs of this division."[127] While the scars doubtless still remained, Vincent Ferrer's canonization had repaired the divisions in Breton society too. Maybe that is why Bretons told and retold this story of the chopped-up baby; enough did so that travelers to the duchy remembered that one, among all Vincent's miracles, years later.[128]

## Vincent Ferrer and the Crown of Aragon

While Vincent Ferrer became a valued symbol for the powerful in Brittany, there is evidence that the saint was also important to the self-presentation of the kings of his native region of Aragon. The rulers of the confederation that was the late medieval crown of Aragon did not have an easy task. They had to balance the interests of the ancient kingdom of Aragon proper with those of the once autonomous county of Barcelona/Catalonia and the kingdom of Valencia. Each of the component regions of the crown of Aragon retained

---

126. *Procès,* witness 263; FPC, 222: "Testis reducens ad memoriam quoddam miraculum de quo fuit mentio in quadam tabula depicta existente supra sepulcrum dicti M. V. videlicet quod Deus resuscitavit quemdam infantulum quem eius mater occiderat ad preces M. V. recommandavit et vovit dictam filiam suam M. V."

127. Oliva de Coatsal (*Procès,* witness 73; FPC, 110): "Fuerat a matre per caput in duas partes abscissus et divisus et signum huius divisionis in capite ipsius infantis apparebat."

128. That is, two unnamed witnesses from the Naples inquest (*Proceso,* fol. 257v–258r and 260r–260v; FPC, 438–39 and 411–12, Naples witnesses 16 and 18).

its own identity, language, customs, institutions, and capital city; kings of Aragon were technically only counts of Barcelona.[129] Further, the rulers of Aragon in the fourteenth and fifteenth centuries fought to establish and maintain control over Majorca, Sicily, Sardinia, and eventually Naples. Moreover, like the dukes of Brittany, they had to navigate through the troubled, shifting waters of European ecclesiastical and secular politics in the age of schism, church councils, and the Hundred Years' War.

Furthermore, like the duchy of Brittany, during the lifetime of Vincent Ferrer the region went through a bitter succession crisis that brought a new ruling family to the throne of Aragon. As did the Breton Montfort dukes, the Trastámara dynasty in Aragon looked to the saintly Dominican preacher as an important source of legitimacy as the family, which had ruled Castile since 1369, now came to dominate Aragon as well. Although the Trastámaras would eventually usher in Spain's Golden Age with the marriage of the cousins Fernando II (Ferdinand) and Isabella in 1469, the family's initial accession to the throne of Aragon was far from obvious. The year 1410 saw the death of Martí I (the Humane, r. 1396–1410), ending the dynasty that had originally united Aragon and Catalonia under a single crown. Each of several rival candidates began to put forth the claim that he was the rightful successor to the defunct Martí; for two long years the region was plunged into a period of factionalism and disorder as powerful families took advantage of the interregnum to rekindle old rivalries.[130]

The chaos came to an end in June 1412, when, at the suggestion of the Avignon pope Benedict XIII (himself an Aragon native), a commission of nine God-fearing men from Aragon, Catalonia, and Valencia met to elect a king. Among the nine were Vincent Ferrer and his brother, the Carthusian monk Boniface. Like his sometime patron Pope Benedict, Vincent supported the claims of the Trastámaran candidate, and the end result of the Compromise of Caspe, as it is called, was the installation of Fernando I ("de Antequera"), uncle and regent of Juan II of Castile and father of Alfonso V, as king of Aragon.[131] The family remained beholden. Fernando stayed loyal to Benedict XIII well beyond the endurance of other supporters of the Avignon papacy. His eventual break with Benedict XIII did not come until January 1416, when it became apparent that the stubborn pontiff would neither resign nor acquiesce in the judgment of the Council of Constance

---

129. Ruiz 2007, 3–4; O'Callaghan 1975, 225. Other good English-language introductions to the region's history include Bisson 1986; Reilly 1993; and, for Vincent's own religious order, Vose 2009.

130. Ruiz 2007, 77, 101–2; Bisson 1986, 131–35; O'Callaghan 1975, 543; Ryder 1990, 14–16.

131. For Vincent's role in the Compromise of Caspe, see Garganta and Forcada 1956, 57–67; Toldrà 2004, 163–72. Toldrà details the way in which interpretations of Vincent's role in the compromise have been tied up with Catalan and Spanish nationalism; on this latter point, see also Bisson 1986, 135–36.

convened to end the Schism. Fernando and his son continued to display their devotion to Vincent Ferrer.

It was Fernando's son, Alfonso V, who contributed eight hundred gold pieces to the costs of Vincent's canonization, whose banners were borne through the streets of Rome the day of the ceremony, and who himself testified at the Naples canonization inquest. Alfonso had inherited from his father the crowns of Sicily and Sardinia as well as that of Aragon, and he devoted a considerable amount of energy to the management of his overseas possessions, never setting foot on the Iberian Peninsula from 1432 on. Further, his adoption as heir by Queen Joanna II of Naples in 1421—and again in 1433—put him in line to succeed her as ruler of Naples, a position he finally took up in 1443. Naples remained the seat of Alfonso's government and permanent residence through to his death in 1458.[132] Both his relocation to Naples and the family's devotion to Vincent Ferrer must be the reasons that a canonization inquest—chock-full of witnesses from the kingdom of Aragon—took place in Naples but not in Vincent's natal city of Valencia.[133] Like Duke Pierre II of Brittany, Alfonso must have loomed large in the background of the canonization inquest.

With only twenty-four witnesses, the Naples inquest was much smaller than its Breton counterpart. It survives today in an imperfect sixteenth-century manuscript copy.[134] Nonetheless, it is still possible to glimpse through the testimony the importance of Vincent Ferrer to the ruling house of Aragon, an impression underscored by surviving letters in the royal archives in Barcelona.[135] In addition to the testimony of Alfonso V himself, the lineup of witnesses included the king's personal physician, his Dominican confessor, and a member of his immediate household.[136] The king's confessor, the esteemed bishop of Majorca, recalled Vincent's role in choosing Alfonso's father as successor to King Martí at Caspe.[137] Several witnesses also mentioned Vincent's seemingly miraculous role in pacifying feuds in the kingdom, including the bitter strife between two powerful Valencian families.[138]

---

132. On Alfonso's reign, see Ryder 1990; Bentley 1987, esp., 7–20; Abulafia 2004, 218–21; Ruiz 2007, 102–7; Bisson 1986, 143–57.

133. Of the twenty-four witnesses in Naples, twenty-one have clear roots in Valencia, Catalonia, or Aragon.

134. *Proceso.* A second copy of the MS, Valencia, OP "Catalinas," MS in quarto, incipit—"Liber sive transumptus processus Beatificationis et Canonizationis santi Vincentii Ferrarii, Ordinis B. Dominici, Valentie orti"—was listed as lost in 1936. Robles Sierra 1984, 401.

135. See Martinez Ferrando and Solsona Climent 1953.

136. That is, Jacobus Quintanis (*Proceso,* fol. 276r–276v; FPC, 412–13, Naples witness 2); Joannes, bishop of Majorca (*Proceso,* fol. 290r–292v; FPC, 431–35, Naples witness 14); and Innocentius de Cubellis (*Proceso,* fol. 278r–278v; FPC, 414–15, Naples witness 4).

137. Joannes, bishop of Majorca (*Proceso,* fol. 290r–290v; FPC, 431–32, Naples witness 14).

138. Jacobus Quintanis (Fages's witness 2), Gaspar Peregrini (Fages's witness 3), Bernardus Catalanus de Pratz (Fages's witness 8), Ludovicus Cardona (Fages's witness 11), two unnamed witnesses

They may well have been thinking of the period of disorder between Martí's death and the Compromise of Caspe. Another Naples witness recalled that Vincent had been the confessor of Queen Yolande, wife of Joan I of Aragon (r. 1387–95), the great-uncle of Alfonso V.[139] Friar Bartolomeus of Aragon further testified to the devotion in which King Martí had held Vincent. Like Duke Jean V in Vannes, Martí had honored Vincent in his advent to Barcelona by joining the procession that went out to meet the preacher beyond the city gates.[140]

Just as in the Brittany inquest, miracle stories helped to underscore the ties between ruling family and holy man. Whereas the duchess of Brittany, through her loan of Vincent's cloak, had participated in the miraculous cure of Perrinus Hervei, so, too, the king of Aragon shared in the healing of a crippled man in Lérida. The Catalan noble Bernardus de Pratz recalled the events well. Vincent had been in the midst of a sermon outside the Dominican church in the town. King Fernando, to whom Vincent had given the nod at Caspe, was there, and he must have been seated in a prime location just in front of the celebrated preacher's platform, for when Vincent noticed a badly crippled man a long way off, he said to Fernando, "Send two of your trustworthy knights to see if this man is debilitated and can't get around." As the king's men began to lead the man to Vincent's pulpit, however, the holy man made the sign of the cross at him, and "at once the cripple lifted himself and began to walk on his own feet without the assistance of his hands."[141] Now if the point of the story was simply to demonstrate Vincent's ability to work miracles, it was not necessary to mention the presence or the assistance of King Fernando and his knights. Nor, if other witnesses are to be believed, was this tale the only example of a spectacular healing at one of Vincent's public sermons. But surely this particular miracle tale, which gave the first Trastámara king of Aragon a role as coparticipant in the cure, must have pleased Alfonso V by closely associating his family with the miracles of Vincent Ferrer.

There were other stories about Vincent that were not quite as flattering to the rulers of Aragon, but we hear them only from witnesses in Brittany and Toulouse. Somehow these tales do not surface in the Naples

---

(Fages's witnesses 16 and 18), Michael Albiol (Fages's witness 19), and Antonius Roca (Fages's witness 20).

139. Gaspar Peregrini (*Proceso,* fol. 277v; FPC, 413, Naples witness 3).

140. *Proceso,* fol. 263v; FPC, 446–47, Naples witness 22, adding "sicut judei fecerunt Christo in die palmorum."

141. Bernardus Catalanus de Pratz, principatus Catalonie (*Proceso,* fol. 281r; FPC, 88, Naples witness 8): "Mitatis duos ex militibus viris ad ipsum dignos fide ad videndum si est debilitatus membris et non potest ambulari nisi per terram....[A]spexerunt Magistrum Vincentium a longinquo facientem crucem versus infirmum, et subito infirmum ipsum levari et ambulare suis pedibus sine manuum adiutoris tanquam si esset sanus."

testimony. Alfonso V's own confessor, the bishop of Majorca, was one of the three subcommissioners in charge of the Naples inquest as well as a witness therein. He must have had a role in selecting and shaping the testimony that emerged as witnesses assembled in the archbishop's palace in Naples, passing over tales that did not appeal. At any rate, we hear only from the Brittany testimony of a woman named Perrina de Bazvalen, an intimate of Duchess Jeanne's, that (as she heard it told) once in Aragon the late king had entered into Master Vincent's chamber at night while the holy man knelt in prayer. Although the king had not uttered a single word, Vincent later reprimanded him for the intrusion, saying that he had "greatly annoyed him."[142] And, despite the fact that several Naples witnesses recalled the presence of Vincent, King Fernando, and Alfonso at Perpignan in 1416, only from the Toulouse witness Petrus Andrea de Fulcovisu do we learn that there Vincent had sternly upbraided Queen Margarida de Prades, widow of King Martí, because her husband had given such support to Pope Benedict XIII. The poor woman not only was moved to tears but also joined a nunnery not far from Barcelona.[143] In the fact that these tales were not told in Naples we see perhaps as clearly as in the stories that *were* narrated there the importance of Vincent Ferrer as a source of sacred legitimacy for the Trastámaras of Aragon.

Certainly Alfonso V made his presence felt in the lead-up to Vincent's canonization. He joined in the 1451 petition to Pope Nicholas V that resulted in the opening of the canonization process, and when Calixtus III succeeded Nicholas in 1455, to his note of congratulations to his fellow countryman, Alfonso added yet another request to see Vincent canonized.[144] Alfonso continued to display his devotion to the holy preacher after Calixtus proclaimed him a saint in June 1455.[145] Our eyewitness to the canonization, Pietro Ranzano, noted Alfonso's contribution of eight hundred gold pieces to the costs of canonization, as well as the fact that his arms were carried through the streets of Rome on the day when Vincent's canonization was proclaimed.[146] Ranzano is also our source for the story of Vincent's foretelling that the then Alfonso de Borja (Borgia) would become pope and would enroll Vincent in the catalog of saints. It was Borja, now Pope

---

142. Perrina de Bazvalen, widow of Yvo du Beizit (*Procès,* witness 7; FPC, 25): "Et postea quod dictus M. V. dixit regi ipsum alloquenti quod multum gravaverat eum."

143. Petrus Andrea de Fulcovisu (*Proceso,* fol. 197v; FPC, 318, Toulouse witness 12). Margarida de Prades was Martí's second wife, following María de Luna (kinswoman to Pope Benedict XIII). Margarida's letter to her uncle, the bishop of Majorca (Luis de Prades), is in Martinez Ferrando and Solsona Climent 1953, 105–6 (doc. no. 66).

144. Martinez Ferrando and Solsana Climent 1953, 22, 130–32 (doc. no. 81: letter from Alfonso V to Calixtus III, April 28, 1455). He also had written to Nicholas V on October 6, 1450, supplicating the pope for Vincent's canonization.

145. BC, MS 112, fol. 62r.

146. BC, MS 112, fol. 62v (eight hundred gold pieces), 67r (Alfonso's arms).

Calixtus III, together with the Dominican master general Martial Auribelli, who commissioned Ranzano to write the first official *vita* of the new saint, a task Ranzano carried out in Sicily, close to the watchful eye of Alfonso V.[147] When, after King Alfonso's death in 1458 the rule of the kingdom of Sicily and Naples went to his illegitimate son, Ferrante, the son continued to honor the memory of Vincent Ferrer. Ferrante's devotion to the saint is suggested by the appearance of his wife, Isabella of Chiaramonte, and children in the posture of kneeling donors on an altarpiece of Vincent Ferrer painted for the Dominican church of San Pietro Martire in Naples, probably around 1460.[148] In 1465, Isabella would be buried in that same church. And in 1475, Ferrante would appoint Vincent's biographer Ranzano as tutor to his own son Giovanni. When Giovanni earned a cardinal's hat two short years later, Ranzano briefly became a member of his household.[149]

The tenacity with which the Trastámara family sought to associate them-selves with Vincent Ferrer spoke to a conception of political power, like that of the Montfort dukes of Brittany, that was closely tied to a notion of the ruler as a steward of the Christian faith.[150] For the rulers of Aragon, that image of the Christian monarch would reach its apogee in later generations, particularly in the reign of Fernando II (1479–1516) and his wife, Isabella, whose 1469 marriage would unite Aragon and Castile to produce modern Spain. Dubbed by Pope Alexander VI "the Catholic kings," Fernando and Isabella would pursue a policy of religious purification, expelling Jews from their kingdom as they completed the centuries-long reconquest of Muslim territories on the Iberian Peninsula. For the rulers of Aragon in the first half of the century, however, lesser goals would do: the conversion of large num-bers of Jews and Muslims to the Christian faith. And in that task, as witness after witness testified at Naples, the miraculous preaching of Vincent Ferrer was the key.

And so it was that, as Pietro Ranzano saw, there came to Rome that June day in 1455 Dominicans from all regions, together with the master general of the order and the Breton ambassadors Pierre II had sent there. They all formed part of the "great crowd of both sexes" who paraded to St. Peter's behind banners bearing the arms of Alfonso V of Aragon

---

147. Ranzano tells us about Vincent's prophecy to Calixtus in BC, MS 112, fol. 53r; for the commission from Auribelli and Calixtus, 53v.

148. Colantonio, Vincent Ferrer altarpiece, Museo Nazionale di Capodimonte, Naples (for-merly at San Pietro Martire); reproduction, Kaftal 1965, figures 1316, 1317, 1319, 1322, 1325, 1330, 1331, 1333, 1336, 1337; Limentani Virdis 2001, 349–52.

149. Termini 1916, 90; Barilaro 1977–78, 75, 88; Figliuolo 1997, 111–13, 115–18. Pietro Ranzano's time in Hungary was also linked to the requests of Ferrante's family: Beatrice (Ferrante's son by Isabella) was wife to Kings Matthias Corvinus and Ladislaus II of Hungary. On Ferrante's reign, see Bentley 1987, 21–34.

150. Ruiz 2007, 132–35.

and Pierre II of Brittany and the arrayed ranks of the Dominican order. The basilica itself shone with the light of nearly two thousand candles; in Ranzano's eyes, "it looked like a sky full of stars."[151] Calixtus III proclaimed Vincent a saint; letters went out to Pierre II.[152] Thus, as Ranzano would write, "the divine business was completed, and with it, at last was finished the matter on which the fathers of the Order of Preachers had worked for so long."[153] He might well have included the Montfort dukes of Brittany and the Trastámara kings of Aragon in that statement. It took a lot of grease to move the wheels of papal bureaucracy and a lot of gold to fund petitions, inquests, and ceremonies. Canonization was primarily for the powerful and their friends.

There were indeed sound political reasons behind the push to canonize Vincent Ferrer. The dukes of Brittany and various players on the duchy's religious scene stood to gain much from the Dominican preacher's canonization. The Order of Preachers craved the canonization of one of their own to answer the enrollment of the popular preacher Bernardino of Siena in the catalog of saints in 1450. The Trastámara rulers of Aragon looked to Vincent as the divine source of the legitimacy of their dynasty, as well as a person who could further their image as most Christian kings. The will and the means were there to see the affair through the long, tedious process of canonization. As we shall see in chapter 2, evidence also suggests that at least some of these actors made a significant effort to fan popular devotion to the departed holy man even as they attempted to shape the stages of the process of canonization. Force could lead the horse to water, but it took more subtle measures to make the horse of popular *fama* drink.

On the other hand, the stories told by witnesses at the canonization inquests reveal that their presence at the inquest was due to more than pressure from above. To see Vincent canonized and, above all, to have the chance to tell their own stories were goals for which each witness had his or her own sound personal reasons as well, as we shall see in chapter 3. In the end, Vincent's canonization succeeded because these social and political forces coincided and not simply because the powerful were able to impose their will upon a docile herd.

---

151. BC, MS 112, fol. 66v–67r.
152. For the letter to Pierre II, see text accompanying note 95.
153. BC, MS 112, fol. 68r.

# CHAPTER 2

# The Process of Canonization

Like any other candidate for sainthood in the later Middle Ages, Vincent Ferrer was the object of a lengthy canonization process (or *processus,* in the Latin of the papal curia), which was essentially a judicial trial. Because canonization involved a *process* and did not consist in a single act or declaration by the pope, a number of players were involved, each of whom was able to put, in however small a way, his or her own spin on it. While the basic steps of that process had remained fixed since the late thirteenth century, even in the mid-fifteenth century there was no standardized form or procedure for carrying out those steps.[1] Particularly at the local level, the so-called inquests *in partibus* (local fact-finding inquests) were shaped by the prelates delegated to the task by the papal curia and by the procurers (or organizers) appointed by local clergy or secular leaders to organize, supervise, and in general see the matter through to completion. Here on the ground, the procurers and the clerics who ran the inquest *in partibus* had extraordinary leeway in shaping the picture of the proposed saint that would eventually be presented to the pope and College of Cardinals. In Vincent Ferrer's case, four such inquests gathered information about the proposed saint. The organizers of these inquests carried out their tasks in decidedly different ways. Records survive from three of the four,

---

1. See Vauchez 1997, 40–57; Kleinberg 1989; Delooz 1969, 28–36; Krötzl 1998, esp. 120; 1999; Toynbee 1929; Kemp 1948; Goodich 1995, esp. 7–17; Wetzstein 1999, 42–58; 2004a, esp. 354–499; Klaniczay 2004; Lett 2008; Katajala-Peltomaa 2009.

offering an excellent view of how various approaches led to differing portraits of the same man.

If the primary purpose of the local canonization inquest was to gather a body of reliable evidence about the putative saint's life and miracles, it also had a second, unspoken, function that could not have escaped the notice of its organizers. As records from the Brittany inquest into Vincent Ferrer's sanctity reveal, the inquest could also serve as public spectacle. Vincent's case is unusual in that the organizers included a meticulous description of the ceremonial aspects of the proceedings as part of the records they prepared to forward to Rome.[2] In the tableau of ritualized gatherings and processions that surrounded the opening and closing of the inquest, its organizers and participants both portrayed the case for Vincent's sanctity in pageant and encapsulated the steps of the canonization process in visual form. And these ceremonies were merely a foretaste of the hoped-for goal: the moment when the pope would proclaim publicly that Vincent Ferrer was a saint. An eyewitness account of the pageantry surrounding Vincent's canonization in 1455 is one of the rare descriptions of such ceremonies we possess from the later Middle Ages.[3] The papal canonization ceremony, too, offered a living tableau of Vincent Ferrer's sanctity, complete with dramatic interruptions of divine intercession. And Vincent's promoters, like corporate sponsors of modern-day sporting events, got to associate their names publicly with the new saint's. From beginning to end, the canonization process both generated the legal case for the candidate's sainthood and advertised his holy reputation (or *fama sanctitatis*) to an admiring audience.

And at every step of the way, the participants in the process had the opportunity to shape its content. Postulators like Duke Pierre II of Brittany, Juan II of Castile and León, and Alfonso V of Aragon, and the procurers who were often their agents hoped to present as strong a case as possible for the candidate's canonization, arranging witnesses and questions to that end. One of the most striking aspects of the Vincent Ferrer process is the way in which the various parties interested in his canonization each tried to mold the proceedings in their own way. As contemporaries were well aware, human agents (and the hand of God) could have a profound impact on the judicial process that was canonization. And, as participants in the stages of the process also knew very well, the audience for the canonization process was not simply the papal curia but the entire body of the faithful.

---

2. This description is the most detailed of the few surviving examples cited in Wetzstein 2004a, 408–9.

3. On the ceremony, Dykmans 1985, 4:276–88; and Schimmelpfennig 2004.

## The Stages of the Process

As with other canonization processes before the late fifteenth century, Vincent Ferrer's *processus* opened with a letter from the pope on October 18, 1451.[4] In this letter, lovingly preserved (complete with its papal seal, or *bulla*) by the cathedral chapter in Vannes, Pope Nicholas V appointed a commission of three cardinals, whom he charged, either in person or through whatever deputies they might appoint, with the task of "receiving diligent information and separating out the truth" about the life and miracles of Master Vincent Ferrer. Once they had gathered their information, the three cardinals—Georgius, bishop of Preneste; Alfonsus, Cardinal of the Four Crowned Martyrs (Alfonso Borja, later Pope Calixtus III); and Johannes, Cardinal of Sant Angelo—were to pass on the materials to the curia to be reviewed in a secret consistory. Nicholas reminded the cardinals that "among other weighty matters that are acted on at the Apostolic See, this is the weightiest." Accordingly, any deputies to whom the cardinals entrusted their charge were to swear an oath to have "only God and the truth before their eyes" and to proceed "with all care and diligence."[5]

As Nicholas had foreseen, the cardinals indeed chose to delegate, appointing subcommissioners to carry out four inquests *in partibus:* in Brittany, Toulouse, Naples, and Avignon. (The Avignon inquest, unfortunately, is now lost, but presumably it aimed to establish Vincent's efforts to end the Schism and to authenticate the vision that propelled his preaching tour.) The earliest of these letters of appointment went out on January 5, 1452, addressed to the Breton bishops of Dol and St. Malo, the abbots of the monasteries of St. Jacut and Buzay, and unspecified "officials" of the cathedrals of Nantes and Vannes. Carried out by Radulphus, bishop of Dol; Guillermus, abbot of St. Jacut; and Johannes du Bot, an archdeacon in Nantes and canon in the Vannes cathedral, the Brittany inquest did not begin hearing witnesses until November 1453, nearly two and a half years after Nicholas V had first indicated his intention to open canonization proceedings on behalf of the saintly Dominican whose body reposed in the Vannes cathedral.[6]

---

4. See Wetzstein 2004a, 354–71, 376–77, and 382.

5. Nicholas's letter with its seal as preserved by the cathedral chapter in Vannes is found in ADM, 1 Mi 293 (Reliques de Saint Vincent Ferrier, 1ère liasse, no. 4; the film reproduces documents held by the cathedral in Vannes); the letter was also reproduced in *Procès,* pp. 2–3 (these numbered pages are part of the misbound signature 8, which is bound between witnesses 239 and 240 of the inquest); and in the opening matter of the Toulouse inquest in *Proceso,* fol. 265r–266r, and of the Naples inquest at ibid., fol. 270r–271r; FPC, 381–82.

6. Letters of subdelegation: Brittany: *Procès,* pp. 4–10; FPC, 382–85; Toulouse: *Proceso,* fol. 264v–267v; Naples, *Proceso,* fol. 271r–272v. The term "official" (*officialis*) referred to a person who performed the function of a notary and who sealed contracts for church courts. Jones 2003c, 776.

Evidence from Brittany indicates that the promoters of Vincent's cause in the duchy made good use of the delay in order to stir up enthusiasm about the holy preacher's sanctity so as to make as strong a case as possible at the canonization inquest. If one reads the Brittany testimony carefully, it appears that the Vannes cathedral clergy and members of the Dominican order in Brittany had probably been engaged in such a public relations campaign since the accession of Pope Nicholas V in 1447 gave new life to hopes for Vincent's canonization. Indeed, a number of witnesses at the 1453–54 Brittany canonization inquest would observe that pilgrimages to Vincent's tomb, so numerous in the years immediately following his death in 1419, had died down thereafter but had picked up in the last several years.[7] If that increase in foot traffic to the Vannes cathedral had a cause, it no doubt lay in the efforts that interested clergy were making on Vincent's behalf in those years.

Breton promoters of Vincent's canonization appear to have employed several tactics to increase his *fama sanctitatis,* to foster pilgrimages to his tomb in Vannes, and to encourage an eagerness to testify at the anticipated canonization inquest. Some of these efforts had begun almost as soon as the holy man died, such as the altar erected at Vincent's tomb within two years after his burial.[8] From the first, too, the priests in Vannes rang the cathedral bells as soon as they learned of a new miracle worked by Vincent's intercession, just as, according to witnesses, they had done after Perrinus Hervei was freed from demonic possession.[9] As was not infrequently the custom at pilgrimage sites, a priest in the Vannes cathedral also recorded pilgrims' tales of Vincent's miracles in a little book. A certain master Salomon Periou had personally delivered that book to Pope Martin V (1417–31), doubtless accompanying an initial request that the pontiff open canonization proceedings in Vincent's case.[10] Such an early canonization was not to be, but it is clear that the promoters of Vincent's case redoubled their efforts in the years leading up to the 1453 opening of the Brittany inquest.[11]

---

7. E.g., Petrus Floc'h (*Procès,* witness 8; FPC, 30). For efforts to fan a cult around the same time in nearby Angers, see Matz 1991. An even longer delay before the opening of the Toulouse and Naples inquests may well have afforded interested parties there the opportunity to stir up support as well, but the records are less extensive. Still in the Toulouse testimony, there is a mention of an altar to Vincent Ferrer in Prouille: *Proceso,* fol. 192r; FPC, 309 (Johannes Massa, witness 9). The Naples articles asked about miracles "ubi altaria ad prefati Beatissimi memoriam sunt constructa" (*Proceso,* fol. 275r; FPC, 410, art. 26).

8. According to Brittany witness Johanna, wife of Oliverius Kaerscab (*Procès,* witness 165; FPC, 165).

9. For example, Petrus Floc'h and Symon Maydo (Brittany witnesses 8 and 9). See chapter 1; Smoller 2011a, 781; and 2006, 149–76.

10. Testimony of Oliverius le Bourdiec (*Procès,* witness 6; FPC, 22). The book is also mentioned by Yvo Gluidic, Johannes Jegoti, and Guillotus le Mareschal (Brittany witnesses 1, 28, and 89). See also Smoller 2011a, 781–83.

11. It is tempting to view in this light the ducal edicts against blasphemy issued in the year after Vincent's death and again in the year in which Nicholas would open the canonization process,

Several incidental details in the Brittany testimony suggest ways in which backers of Vincent's canonization attempted to fan his *fama sanctitatis* in preparation for the inquest. So, for example, after a lapse of a number of years, the clergy at the Vannes cathedral once again began to record grateful pilgrims' tales of Vincent's miracles. The new book was the work of a priest named Yvo Natal. At the time he testified at the canonization inquest, Father Yvo had been recording miracles in the cathedral for four years. In that time he had written down so many stories ("faithfully [writing] the miracles told him according to the pilgrims' narrations") that he could not number them.[12]

But the situation had not always been thus. "Six years ago," he explained, "very few came to said tomb; nor were the miracles recorded that were publicized there, but afterwards there was a great wave [of pilgrims], which grows larger from day to day."[13] What exactly Father Yvo meant by "publicizing" the miracles is not entirely clear, but another witness's testimony suggests that it was also something relatively new in the Vannes cathedral. A woman named Johanna, in telling the story of the miraculous cure of her nursling Johannes Maydo some five years previously, noted that she, along with little Johannes's mother, had carried the infant to Vincent's tomb to leave the saint a little wax baby and cradle. "But," Johanna insisted, "this miracle was not publicized then, because at that time miracles were not being publicized."[14] As late as 1448 or 1449, no one was recording Vincent's miracles.

As Johanna's subsequent testimony makes clear, however, almost as soon as Pope Nicholas V initiated the canonization process, Vincent's miracles— and their publication—became an important matter in Vannes. Like several other Brittany witnesses, Johanna expressed the belief that a miracle worked by Vincent's intercession would not stick unless its beneficiaries publicized it. So when little Johannes got sick again in the summer before the opening

---

mentioned in Leveleux 2001, 361 (October 8, 1420) and 363 (May 25, 1451). Since witnesses frequently mentioned how blasphemy had ceased after Vincent's sermons, it would be nice to be able to show that this reform had persisted.

12. *Procès*, witness 239; FPC, 198: "Fideliter scripserat sibi miracula recitata secundum concurrentium recitationem."

13. Ibid.: "Dicit quod ante sex annos de tempore suo pauci concurrebant ad dictum sepulcrum nec scribebantur miracula que ibi publicabantur. Sed ex post fuit ibi magnus concursus qui de die in diem magis augmentatur."

14. Johanna, wife of Johannes Baut (*Procès*, witness 38; FPC, 74–75): "Non tamen tunc fuit huiusmodi miraculum publicatum quia illo tempore non publicabantur miracula." The infant's father, Herveus Maydo, lord of Treduday, was an important man in the duchy's finances (once serving as treasurer) and had been among the lucky group admitted to Vincent's death chamber, according to his own testimony (*Procès*, witness 18; FPC, 47) and that of his brother Symon (*Procès*, witness 9; FPC, 32). Herveus saw distinguished service in the duchy's financial administration under the wing of the Breton duke Jean V's son François. Kerhervé 1987, 1:227, 252, 281, 290, 353; 2:767. He surely must have been close to the ducal party promoting Vincent's canonization.

of the Brittany inquest, the Maydo family knew instantly what was wrong. As the father said, "The child could not get well because that miracle had not been publicized at Master Vincent's tomb."[15] As soon as the boy had recovered some strength, the parents had Johanna carry him to Vincent Ferrer's tomb, where, as Johanna noted, "*then* it was publicized...that he had been healed by the intercession of said Master Vincent."[16] Perhaps the notion that one had to publicize a miracle was the product of clerical sug-gestion; certainly the "requirement" that a miracle be publicized assured a steady advertising of Vincent's intercessory powers.

It would be wonderful to know exactly what such an advertisement looked and sounded like. Probably publication involved a ringing of the cathedral bells and, by this time, a recitation of the miracle story for Father Yvo Natal to write down in his little book. Perhaps the cathedral choristers sang a "Te Deum Laudamus," as described in many miracle tales.[17] Little Johannes must have been alternately terrified and delighted at the rush of sound and the attention of the crowd. Most important, the cathedral clergy would have acquired, with the miracle's publication, yet one more tale of Vincent Ferrer's intercession: more fodder for the canonization dossier and another testimonial to use as they promoted the wonder-working tomb housed under their own roof.

For the Vannes cathedral clergy did make an effort to broadcast Vincent's miracles. Never mind that the papal curia was pushing the notion that saints were more to be imitated than solicited for supernatural help.[18] Let Vincent receive the seal of canonization, and then he could be an example. In the meantime, there were cardinals to impress and that stream of coins, candles, and wax offerings to collect. The tales in Father Yvo's little book furnished the script for public recitation of Vincent's miracles on Sundays and at other special occasions when even bigger crowds flocked to the Vannes

---

15. Testimony of Herveus Maydo (*Procès,* witness 18; FPC, 49): "Quia illud miraculum non fuerat publicatum ad sepulcrum dicti M. V. predictus infans non poterat se bene habere ymo vide-batur languere."

16. Johanna, wife of Johannes Baut (*Procès,* witness 38; FPC, 74–75): "Et tunc fuit in presencia testis publicatum quod ad intercessionem dicti M. V. sanatus esset" (emphasis in text added). See also testimony of Margareta, wife of Johannes de Cressoles, and Johanna, wife of Johannes Aufray (Brittany witnesses 65 and 69; FPC, 102–03, 106). Johanna's case is particularly illustrative. After she declined out of shyness to publicize her miraculous cure from apoplexy and blindness, her infirmity returned until she recalled that she had not publicized the miracle. She went to the cathedral, con-fessed to a priest, again invoked the intercession of Vincent Ferrer, and was cured, at which point she did publicize the miracle, and the cure persisted.

17. E.g., Bartlett 2004, 11, 109; Finucane 1997, 129; Lett 2008, 20–22 (one resident of Tolentino suspected the friars in the church housing the tomb of Nicolas of Tolentino of ringing the bells falsely to make people think Nicolas was working miracles).

18. Vauchez 1997, e.g., 6–7, 417, 420–21; Pellegrini 2004, 322.

cathedral.[19] Several witnesses recalled hearing about Vincent's miracles and seeing the many ex-voto offerings at his tomb when they attended a sale of indulgences in Vannes cathedral within the past year.[20] One Brittany witness mentioned that he had learned about one of Vincent's miracles from a painting at the holy preacher's tomb.[21] As all these witnesses' tales confirm, the Vannes cathedral clergy's advertising worked. For each told how the example of other miracles worked by Vincent's intercession had inspired him or her to invoke the saint, resulting in yet another miracle to be publicized in Vannes.

The promoters of Vincent's canonization also benefited from the fortuitous presence of a plague epidemic in Brittany around the time of the inquest.[22] Word soon enough had it that Vincent Ferrer's intercession could protect against the plague. The disease was terrifying and devastating. When Johannes de Quelen's fiancée, Ysabellis, developed a bubo (*struma*) in her groin, "it was feared that she would die, because all who have and who have had such a *strumam* in the parish were dead and had died." Johannes would have well known the disease's course. He had lost his first wife, eight children, and two serving maids to the pestilence—all in the space of a mere week. Now his only resort was a vow to Vincent Ferrer, at which Ysabellis "vomited forth said infirmity from her mouth and was entirely healthy." [23] In a world with few reliable remedies, Bretons grasped at that straw of hope. Several parishes organized processions to Vincent's tomb, after which, as witnesses asserted, plague abated among their inhabitants.[24] Anxious parents invoked Vincent's protection for their entire households.[25] Other witnesses noted the holy preacher's reputation for curing plague victims as the decisive factor leading them to make a vow to Vincent Ferrer.[26]

---

19. Yvo Gluidic (*Procès*, witness 1; FPC, 7) and Johannes Jegoti (*Procès*, witness 28; FPC, 62) confirm that the book was the source of the recitation of the miracles, for which Yvo Gluidic also used the term "publicize" ("Audivit...miracula in dicta ecclesia publicari"). Other witnesses who recalled hearing miracles include Alanus Philippot (*Procès*, witness 5; FPC, 18) and Johanna, wife of Johannes Baut (*Procès*, witness 38; FPC, 75).

20. E.g., Johanna, wife of Guillermus Bourdon (*Procès*, witness 58; FPC, 97) and Ludovica, widow of Johannes Durant (*Procès*, witness 54; FPC, 94).

21. Guillermus Rollandi (*Procès*, witness 263; FPC, 222).

22. Biraben mentions plague in Nantes in 1444–46, in Angers in 1448–50, and in the Vannetais in 1452–53. Biraben 1975–76, 1:121, 2:379–80.

23. Testimony of Johannes de Quelen (*Procès*, witness 262; FPC, 221): "Sperabatur ipsam mori quia omnes habentes et qui habuerant talem strumam in parrochia predicta erant mortui et moriebantur.... Ipsa Ysabellis... evomuit dictam infirmitatem per os suum et fuit omnino sana."

24. According to Fr. Johannes Le Bonner (*Procès*, witness 72; FPC, 108), Guillermus Terronin (*Procès*, witness 102; FPC, 132), Yvo Marec (*Procès*, witness 103; FPC, 132), and Oliverius Connan (*Procès*, witness 128; FPC, 146).

25. E.g., Johannes Sanzterre (*Procès*, witness 114; FPC, 139) and Johannes Danyon (*Procès*, witness 121; FPC, 142).

26. E.g., Johanna, wife of Johannes Germanus (*Procès*, witness 78; FPC, 113–14).

Rumor had it, in fact, that plague would not leave the duchy until Vincent received papal canonization. As Alanus de Cressoles testified, "He heard...many people murmuring and saying that the plague was still raging because Master Vincent was not [yet] canonized."[27] This rumor may well have had its source with Brittany's Dominicans or other parties interested in Vincent's canonization. If so, it would not be the first time the duchy's mendicant friars had "worked" plague epidemics for their own benefit.[28] And the strategy of linking Vincent's canonization to the end of the plague appears to have had some effect. Two witnesses testifying about miraculous cures from plague included, among the votive offerings they promised to Vincent Ferrer, money to help with the costs of his canonization.[29] Other witnesses, on their own initiative, went to considerable trouble to come testify at the Brittany inquest. The peasant Johannes Pauli, "leaving everything and at his own expense, came here so that he could testify...[despite] the distance...of fifteen leagues...and the winter weather."[30]

Having succeeded in heightening Vincent's *fama* in the duchy, the promoters of his canonization were ready for the opening of the local inquest. The first step here, as was common in late medieval canonization inquests, was the appointment of a procurer (*procurator*), who both organized the local inquest and served as the representative of the promoters of Vincent's cause during hearings.[31] In Brittany, the Vannes cathedral chapter appointed one of their own as procurer, Guillermus Coetmur, in a letter dated October 26, 1453. Guillermus's appointment came just more than two years after Nicholas V opened the Vincent process and nearly ten months after the commission of three cardinals had written their letter of delegation regarding the Brittany inquest. Guillermus was charged with carrying out whatever was necessary to further the cause of Vincent's canonization, including the exhibiting and procuring of witnesses and other proofs of his sanctity.[32] Although the

---

27. *Procès*, witness 20; FPC, 52: "Audivit etiam quamplures murmurantes et dicentes quod presens pestis durabat ex eo quod dictus M. V. non canonizabatur." Similarly, Herveus Maydo (*Procès*, witness 18; FPC, 48).

28. H. Martin 1975, 365; Leguay and Martin 1982, 366 (implicating the Dominicans). It is possible also that the rumor originated in ducal circles, since one of the witnesses to the rumor, Herveus Maydo, was very close to the Montfort family.

29. Perrotus an Louarn (*Procès*, witness 226; FPC, 191) and Thomas Jegat (*Procès*, witness 232; FPC, 193).

30. Testimony of Johannes Pauli (*Procès*, witness 110; FPC, 136): "Et modo audiens nos esse hic pro inquesta miraculorum statim postpositis omnibus et propriis expensis venit hic ut premissa deponeret...obstante distancia dicti loci de Corleyo per quindecim leucas a civitate Venetensi et tempore hyemali."

31. Wetzstein 2004a, 393, 397.

32. The letter of appointment, like Nicholas's commission and the three cardinals' letter of delegation, is included in the narrative report that accompanies the Brittany inquest (a narrative composed by the three subcommissioners): *Procès*, pp. 20–21; FND, 390–91.

author of Guillermus's letter of appointment was the cathedral chapter, as Radulphus, bishop of Dol, made apparent, the procurer was viewed as acting on the part of the duke of Brittany, the bishop of Vannes, and the cathedral chapter.[33]

The procurer's first official act, and the opening of the inquest *in partibus* proper, was to present to the Brittany subcommissioners the papal letter appointing the commission of three cardinals along with the cardinals' letter of subdelegation. Guillermus must have made these presentations in person, and the subcommissioners in their report commented on the cords and seal that hung from the pope's letter and guaranteed its authenticity. The presentations took place over a series of days, from October 31 through November 3, 1453. At last, the Brittany subcommissioners agreed to meet with Guillermus on November 15 in the town of Malestroit, some forty kilometers from the still plague-infested Vannes. Arriving late in the day, they put off their business until the next morning. On November 16, the subcommissioners, procurer, and other notables participated in a grand ceremony in the church of St. Giles, and on the following day the sub-commissioners formally accepted their charge and swore an oath to fulfill their duties faithfully, diligently, and truthfully. By November 20, plague had abated enough that they felt safe in visiting Vannes; there another ceremony greeted them as they inspected the holy man's tomb.[34]

The actual work of the inquest began on the following day, November 21, 1453, in the priory of Saint-Guen one kilometer north of Vannes. Forming the original commission of inquiry were Radulphus, bishop of Dol (who seems to have been in charge of the inquest); Guillermus, abbot of St. Jacut; Johannes du Bot, the official from Vannes cathedral; and Johannes, bishop of St. Malo (who would soon excuse himself from most of the proceed-ings). Also present were Yvo de Pontsal, the bishop of Vannes, and the pro-curer Guillermus Coetmur. As the subcommissioners would later report to the three cardinals in charge of the canonization, first Guillermus Coetmur appeared before them and presented them with a copy of his appointment as procurer. Next the commissioners swore an oath faithfully and truthfully to carry out their task, as did the notaries whom they had appointed both to serve as scribes and to make from the testimony a "public instrument" to be sent to Rome.[35]

With those preliminaries over, finally the commissioners began hear-ing testimony, and by the end of the day on November 23, they had taken the depositions of the first five witnesses (some dozen folios in the manu-script). At that point, the bishop of St. Malo excused himself, saying that

33. *Procès,* p. 8; FND, 394.
34. *Procès,* pp. 16–19; FND, 397–99.
35. *Procès,* pp. 19–22; FND, 391–92.

"various matters" made it so that "he could not stay any longer."[36] From November 23 until December 8, 1453, the remaining three commissioners examined another 234 witnesses from Vannes and the regions nearby. At that point, the shortness of the days, the winter weather, the upcoming Christmas holiday—and possibly some degree of burnout—prompted the commissioners to recess for several weeks. They had examined their 79th witness on (or perhaps shortly after) December 2, meaning that they must have heard the testimony of on average around two dozen witnesses *per day* in the last week of their work at Saint-Guen.[37] Afterward the commissioners agreed that they would separately examine witnesses in various other regions of Brittany until after Candlemas (Feast of the Purification, February 2, 1454), at which time they would reconvene in the cathedral in Vannes.[38] During the winter interim, the bishop of Dol and abbot of St. Jacut heard the testimony of 22 witnesses in the diocese of Dol and the town of Dinan, while Johannes du Bot examined another fifty-two witnesses in and around Vannes, as well as in the region around Nantes. As usual, notaries transcribed and authenticated the testimony.[39]

At last, Bishop Radulphus and Johannes du Bot met up again in the Vannes cathedral in early April, where they spent several days observing the action around Vincent's tomb.[40] Abbot Guillermus had sent word to Radulphus that he was gravely ill and unable to see the commission's work through to its completion.[41] It would be nice to think that Radulphus and Johannes had made a special effort to be in Vannes to commemorate the

---

36. *Procès,* p. 22; FND, 392. A note after the testimony of Alanus Philippot (Brittany witness 5) also indicates the bishop of St. Malo's departure.

37. Johannes Cire (*Procès,* witness 79; FPC, 114) describes losing a number of costly gold and silver coins and cups on "die sabbati ultimo preterito primam instantis mensis decembris," which he found the next day. He then made a trip of thanksgiving to Vincent's tomb, from whence he must have been sent to the commissioners in Saint-Guen, perhaps on the same day (December 2) but certainly not much later than December 3, since the commissioners still heard another 160 witnesses after him before recessing on December 8.

38. All this information is found in the letter to the cardinals dated December 8, 1453, written from the priory of Saint-Guen: *Procès,* pp. 19–23, at pp. 22–23; FND, 392–393 (Fages's transcription of the letter starts on p. 391).

39. As indications in the inquest records make clear, the bishop of Dol and abbot of St. Jacut, assisted by the notary Radulphus de Rocha Calida (who was from Dol), heard witnesses 240–42 in the parish of Plumaugat in the diocese of St. Malo, on December 15, 1453 (not, as Fages has it, September 15 [FPC, 204]). They examined witnesses 243–61 in Dinan between March 11 and March 15, 1454. The subcommissioners mentioned their separate inquests in the letter dated April 7, 1454, written at the close of the inquest: *Procès,* p. 24; FND, 393. Meanwhile, Johannes du Bot, assisted by the notaries Guillermus de la Houlle and Johannes Anglici, heard witnesses 262–313 in Vannes, Rothon, Nantes, Fégréac, Questelbertz, and Guerrand from January 3 [?] through February 23, 1454. On the role of notaries, see Krötzl 1998; Wetzstein 2004a, 411–14 (making extensive use of Vincent's process); and Lett 2009. See also Jones 2003c.

40. *Procès,* p. 24; FND, 400.

41. *Procès,* p. 24, FND, 393.

day of Vincent's death, April 5 (which would become the saint's feast day). There would have been no special office or liturgical celebration for the holy preacher yet—not until after his canonization would Pietro Ranzano compose the first office of Vincent Ferrer—but after hearing so many tales of Vincent's saintly life and his miraculous intercession, perhaps the commissioners were moved to hear a Mass celebrated in his honor.

There was, however, a special celebration prepared for them on Sunday, April 7, when a grand procession met the commissioners and escorted them into the cathedral. There they heard Mass as well as an exhortation by the bishop of Vannes. Radulphus and Johannes must have been torn. On the one hand, as Bishop Yvo signaled for them, "the miracles of Blessed Vincent had continually increased" throughout the period of the Brittany inquest. In confirmation of this statement, the good bishop had "an infinite number of witnesses ready to be examined" should the commissioners choose to do so, as if a quick glimpse at the huge number of wax ex-votos at Vincent's tomb would not have been sufficient to substantiate the bishop's words. On the other hand, the weary pair—together with their notaries, the procurer, and the promoters of Vincent's canonization—was eager to forward the dossier on to the cardinals in Rome so that the holy father might indeed proceed to canonize Master Vincent. As the organizers of the grand procession of the morning must have known in advance, Radulphus and Johannes decided finally to end their labors, deeming it "superfluous to examine any more" witnesses. The three notaries were on the spot, turning out a narrative of the day's events and adding their seals of attestation to the document.[42] The Brittany inquest was over.

Held in close proximity to Vincent Ferrer's wonder-working tomb, the Brittany inquest would prove to be the longest and most extensive of the four inquests *in partibus* that resulted from Nicholas V's initiation of the canonization process. About the Avignon inquest we know only what the bull of canonization states: that the cardinals delegated the task to the bishops of Vaison and Uzès (*Utricensis*) in Dauphiné, as well as to the official from Avignon and the dean of the church of St. Peter in Avignon, and that they examined eighteen witnesses in Avignon and neighboring regions.[43] Historians will probably never know exactly who testified and when they did so, for the canonization inquests had disappeared from Rome as early as

---

42. *Procès*, pp. 24–28; FND, 400–2. Quotations: "Miracula Beati Vincencii continue crebrescebant. Testesque infinitos ad huc [Bishop Yvo] dicebat habere paratos ad examinandum" (*Procès*, p. 24; FND, 400); "reputantes supervacuum plures examinare" (*Procès*, p. 26; FND, 401).

43. *Bullarum diplomatum* 1857–72, 5:147–48. The published bull's *Utricensis* (Utrecht) is clearly not right. Fages supplies the more plausible identification of Uzès (*Ucetia*) (FPC, 270). The Breton Alain de Coativi (Coëtivi), titular cardinal of Santa Prassede at the time of the inquests, had been bishop of Uzès in 1442–45. The bull's number of 18 witnesses may not be entirely reliable, since the bull cites a figure of 310, not the actual 313, witnesses for the Brittany inquest.

the mid-sixteenth century, when Hieronimus Domenicus Valentinus went looking for them, and they were presumably lost in the sack of Rome in 1527. But a copy had survived in Palermo, it turned out, containing the incomplete text of the Brittany, Toulouse, and Naples inquests. Hearing of the Palermo manuscript, in 1577 the Valencian Dominican Luis Bertrán arranged to have a transcription made, which is now lost. The Dominican Vicente Justiniano Antist utilized this Valencian manuscript in composing a biography of the saint, eventually copying out his own exemplar, which is the sole surviving version of the Toulouse and Naples inquests. The original Palermo manuscript was in bad shape and the folios were out of order, Antist explained, because the locals had the habit of taking a quire or even the entire codex to place on the sick in order to hasten Vincent's intercession.[44]

Thanks to Antist's labors, however, we do have partial versions at least of the inquests held in Toulouse and Naples, both of which took place after the closing of the Brittany inquest. Fortunately, that ragged Palermo exemplar contained most of the Toulouse inquest, despite Antist's frequent pitiful annotations that "here much is missing" ("hic deerant multa"). Apart from some obvious deficiencies in the introductory letters, Antist's manuscript includes testimony from forty-three of the forty-eight Toulouse witnesses indicated in the bull of canonization.[45] In a letter of delegation dated February 18, 1452, the commission of three cardinals entrusted that inquest to Bernardus, the archbishop of Toulouse; Eustachius, the bishop of Mirepoix; and their officials, along with the dean of the church of St. Stephen in Toulouse.[46] As so often is the case in human affairs, the good archbishop and bishop found a way to pass much of that duty along to an underling.

Most of the work in Toulouse fell to Joannes Arnaldi, canon and archdeacon in the cathedral there, who issued summons to and heard the testimony of the great majority of the forty-three witnesses whose depositions survive

---

44. Antist's 1590 copy of the manuscript survives in *Proceso.* Valentinus's unsuccessful attempt to locate the complete canonization records was recorded in the now-lost copy ordered by Luis Bertrán (see chapter 1, note 134), as quoted in FPC, 267–68. The use of the Palermo manuscript as a relic is described in an inscription by Antist dated June 9, 1590: *Proceso,* fol. 2r (FPC, 269): "Tanto in pretio a Panhormitanis habebatur ut ad aegrotos sanandos passim per domos circumferretur ac subinde tereretur: eamdem etiam reor fuisse causam quod nonnulli eius (ut vulgo appellantur) quaterni, et dissuti fuerint et praepostere ordinati." Antist believed that the Palermo manuscript had been made at the command of the Dominican master general (from 1481 to 1483) Salvo Cassetta. It may also represent the manuscript referred to in a 1674 letter. Barilaro 1977–78, 102.

45. *Bullarum diplomatum* 1857–72, 5:148.

46. *Proceso,* fol. 264v–267v; the remainder of the initial letters appear in *Proceso,* fol. 267v–269r; FPC, 399–404. It would seem Toulouse was chosen as a site for an inquest because of its importance to the Dominican order as locus of Dominic's original religious foundations (in nearby Prouille in 1206 and in Toulouse in 1214), as well as because of Vincent's extensive preaching there during Lent in 1416.

in Antist's copy.[47] Joannes's relation dated May 10, 1454, indicates that he planned to summon and examine witnesses, starting the very next day, in the absence of the Archbishop Bernardus and Bishop Eustachius.[48] Working largely in the cathedral in Toulouse, with a short stint in the Dominican female house of Prouille southeast of the city, Johannes heard testimony from May 11 through at least June 25, 1454. As in Brittany, skilled notaries helped him in his task.[49]

The inquest that took place in Naples between August and November 1454 is the shortest and most incomplete of the three for which records survive. Antist's manuscript reproduces the depositions (or often fragments of depositions) of twenty-four witnesses; the bull of canonization indicated that there had originally been twenty-eight Naples witnesses.[50] The cardinals charged with fulfilling the canonization process delegated this inquest to Arnaldus, the patriarch of Alexandria; Reynaldus, the archbishop of Naples; and Joannes, the bishop of Majorca. The charge went out rather late in the game; the cardinals' letter of delegation is dated May 13, 1454 (that is, a month after the completion of the Brittany inquest).[51] Perhaps the curia was responding to urgent lobbying by Martial Auribelli, the head of the Dominican order (who had an important role in this inquest), and the king of Aragon (who testified in this inquest). At any rate, the three subcommissioners officially received the cardinals' letter and accepted their charge less than two weeks later, on May 24, 1454.[52]

Although the records are incomplete, it is possible to make out some of the details about this inquest. As was the case in Toulouse, the hard work of the inquest flowed down the ecclesiastical hierarchy. Of the twenty-one depositions for which a questioner is indicated, the patriarch of Alexandria heard two, the archbishop of Naples eight, and the mere bishop of Majorca

---

47. Of the testimony that indicates which of the commissioners heard it, only the first witness, the subcommissioner Bernardus, archbishop of Toulouse, was not heard by Johannes Arnaldi. Bernardus delivered his deposition to his fellow subcommissioner Eustachius, bishop of Mirepoix, nearly a month before any other witness testified: *Proceso,* fol. 176v; FPC, 278. The archbishop delegated his part of the work to Johannes in a letter dated February 13, 1454: *Proceso,* fol. 265r; FPC, 402. In the manuscript, following this letter (fol. 265v), Antist indicates that letters from the bishop of Mirepoix were missing in his exemplar.

48. *Proceso,* fol. 170r–170v; FPC, 275–76 (with omissions).

49. The latest witness for which we have the testimony is Guillermus Portas, heard on June 25, 1454 (*Proceso,* fol. 242v; FPC 392, witness 41). The records of depositions taken at Pouille are perhaps incomplete, since at least three witnesses were issued summons for which no record of their testimony exists (Guillermus de Mondicort, Fr. Enardus Bosqueti alias Ronselli, and Fr. Joannes Befas): *Proceso,* fol. 172v. The notaries assigned to the inquest were Robertus Assolenti and Bertrandus Barbeti: *Proceso,* fol. 268r; FPC, 400.

50. *Bullarum diplomatum* 1857–72, 5:148.

51. *Proceso,* fol. 271r–271v; FPC, 407 (short excerpt).

52. *Proceso,* fol. 272v–273r.

eleven. It appears that Martial Auribelli, master general of the Dominican order, acted as procurer in the Naples inquest. Although there is no letter of appointment like the one naming Guillermus Coetmur in Brittany, Auribelli made the formal presentation of the letter of delegation to the subcommissioners (the procurer's job in the Brittany inquest). In addition, he was the initiator of the order of summons of witnesses, and he supplied the articles of interrogation to be used in questioning them.[53]

If he was indeed the procurer for the inquest, Auribelli may well have drawn up the witness list, including specifications about the specific articles to which each witness was to offer testimony. Many of the depositions include remarks such as the following indication from the testimony of one Bartholomeus Perilta: "He was examined by us about the twenty-sixth article, skipping over the others as the procurer wished."[54] Somebody in charge had a clear sense of protocol, for the questioning began in early August with Alfonso, king of Aragon and Naples, and Joannes, bishop of Majorca.[55] All the witnesses gave their testimony in Naples itself, always before only one of the subcommissioners and a notary. Unlike the Brittany or Toulouse inquest, there was no excursion to hear testimony in some more remote location. The witnesses were summoned, testified on the articles they were asked about, and that was that. The subcommissioners heard their final witness in the middle of November 1454. The first phase of the process was over.

After the completion of each of the four canonization inquests, the subcommissioners forwarded a copy of the testimony, together with prefatory letters and the attestations and seals of their notaries, to the three cardinals in Rome commissioned by Nicholas V. Full details of what happened in Vincent's case beyond that moment are not clear; as is unfortunately not uncommon with late medieval canonization processes, the records of the curial end of the proceedings are lost.[56] Still, the bull of canonization, as well as a brief resume written by Pietro Ranzano,

---

53. *Proceso,* fol. 272v (presentation of the letters), 273r–273v (summoning of witnesses and articles of interrogation) (also in FPC, 407–8).

54. *Proceso,* fol. 276r; FPC, 411, witness 1: "et per nos super xxvi° articulo obmissis aliis de voluntate producentis...interrogatus."

55. Antist's copy is out of order, perhaps because of the condition of his exemplar; witnesses who testified between September and November 1454 appear before witnesses testifying between August 3, 1454 (Joannes, bishop of Majorca) and September 7, 1454. Alfonso's testimony, incomplete and missing a date, appears in the manuscript between a deposition dated November 18, 1454 (that of Petrus Julius de Valencia, Fages's witness 13) and Bishop Joannes's testimony of August 3, 1454 (he is Fages's witness 14). Fages, for reasons not at all clear to me, prints Alfonso's deposition last (as witness 24). It seems highly likely that Alfonso testified *before* the bishop, perhaps as the first witness, rather than at the inquest's end.

56. As noted in Wetzstein 2004b.

Vincent's first biographer, fills in some of the drama, if not the behind-the-scenes reality.[57]

Some four months after the closing of the Naples inquest, the death of Pope Nicholas V (on March 25, 1455) complicated matters slightly, especially when, on April 8, the College of Cardinals named as his successor Alfonso de Borja, Cardinal of the Four Crowned Saints and one of the three commissioners overseeing Vincent Ferrer's canonization process. As the bull of canonization makes clear, Alfonso (now Pope Calixtus III) could not also continue as a member of the commission and therefore appointed another cardinal (Alanus, titular of Santa Prassede—that is, Alain de Coativi) to take his place. So it was that the two remaining members of the original commission, together with Alanus, made their report to their former colleague in two secret consistories, deeming the case about Vincent's "faith, excellence of life, labors, chaste morals, strenuous acts, humility and simplicity, and miracles" to have been "legitimately proven."[58] At last, as the bull of canonization relates, with the consent of the College of Cardinals, Calixtus proceeded to Vincent's canonization, holding two public consistories in which were made known contents of the testimony from the local inquests. On June 3, Calixtus announced to assembled cardinals and other prelates his intention to canonize Vincent on the Feast of Saints Peter and Paul (June 29).[59]

Ranzano, whom Calixtus would commission to write the first official *vita* of the new saint, adds some sense of the personal and political drama involved in this canonization. For apart from the biography he wrote at the pope's command, Ranzano also wrote about Vincent Ferrer's life and canonization as current events in the long historical work he composed called the *Annals*. From that work he excerpted, in great haste, the sections dealing with Vincent and sent them to fellow Dominican Giovanni da Pistoia to help him preach about the new saint. According to Ranzano's account, there was a considerable amount of behind-the-scenes work to be done in Rome. In particular, Martial Auribelli "took up almost infinite labors" during the time the cardinals were scrutinizing the materials gathered from the inquests. Ranzano's descriptions of Auribelli's actions make him sound like a cross between a careful lawyer and a skilled lobbyist. Without revealing anything more specific, Ranzano ("who was for a while a companion in his labors") simply notes that Auribelli "excluded all that could be adversaries [to the canonization]" and "omitted nothing that appeared to be useful for

---

57. *Bullarum diplomatum* 1857–72, 5:148–49; Ranzano in BC, MS 112, fol. 51r–68r, with partial edition in Termini 1916, 91–92 (prefatory letter to Giovanni da Pistoia), 96–97 ("Dalla *Canonizzazione di San Vincenzo*").

58. *Bullarum diplomatum* 1857–72, 5:148.

59. Ibid.

such a difficult business."[60] The efforts of Martial Auribelli and representatives of the duke of Brittany notwithstanding, it was the Almighty himself,
according to Ranzano, who had arranged the circumstances of Vincent's
canonization.

In Ranzano's narration the important thing about Calixtus was not his
service as a member of the canonization commission appointed by Nicholas
V. Rather, the pontiff was first and foremost Alfonso de Borja, a promising
young Valencian cleric, whose talents attracted the attention of the king of
Aragon and, it turned out, Vincent Ferrer. As Ranzano tells it here, the
king used his influence to secure for Alfonso first the bishopric of Valencia
and then a cardinal's hat. But Alfonso, not satisfied, kept on telling people
he would be pope one day. By the time Nicholas V died in the spring of
1455, Alfonso was more than seventy and "ridiculous, delirious, and aged,"
in the opinion of some Roman observers. Those same scoffers, according
to Ranzano, were stupefied at Alfonso's election as Pope Calixtus III, which
proved true his repeated insistence for so many years that he would one
day head the Roman Church. The new pope explained that when he was
a youth, Vincent Ferrer had prophesied to him that after the holy preacher's death Alfonso "would be above all mortals" and, as pope, would place
Vincent "among the saints of Christ."[61]

In Ranzano's view, God indeed had arranged matters "before he created
the world" so that none other than Calixtus III would canonize Vincent
Ferrer.[62] Martin V, the pope at the time of Vincent's death, was persuaded
of the worthiness of his cause but was distracted by other pressing matters.
Ditto for Eugenius IV, who also wished to see Vincent made a saint but
was instead forced to flee Rome for his own safety. And Nicholas V, who
had initiated the canonization process, found himself "in bad health" at the
very time when he and his cardinals should have begun scrutinizing the
material from the canonization inquests. After an interval of four months
(that is, from roughly the end of November 1454 to late March 1455), "he
departed this life." Master General Martial Auribelli, Ranzano as his assistant,
and representatives of the other promoters of Vincent's sanctity were "so
shaken that there was not one of them who did not lose all hope of seeing

60. BC, MS 112, fol. 52, 63v–64r. Quotations, fol. 63v ("Dum harum rerum perscrutationi dare-
tur opera Martialis fere infinitos suscepit labores") and 64r ("Cuncta quae aduersari potuerunt exclu-
sit. Denique nihil unquam praetermisit: quod uisum sit tam arduo negocio conducere…ego…fuit
aliquando suorum laborum comes").

61. Ibid., fol. 52v–53v; quotations, fol. 53r ("Ridiculum eum deliriumque senem / ridiculas et &
eius futurae rei praedictiones esse affirmabant"), 53r ("mortalium omnium ego eminentissimus
essem"), and 53v ("Cum igitur nunc quod ille futurum praedixerat factum iam in me dei munere
uideam quod a me pontifice maximo in se implendum uaticinatus est. Est ergo mea sententia ut
tantus uir inter christi sanctos a me quom primum fieri poterit referatur.")

62. Ibid., fol. 64r–64v: "Deus ad hoc ipsum antequam mundus conderetur elegerat."

this matter brought to a conclusion." But God had simply prepared the way for Calixtus to act.[63]

Even after the new pope had made his intentions clear to canonize Vincent, inspiring "tears of joy" in Auribelli and his fellow postulators, there were still anxious moments.[64] It was the very day that Calixtus had set to publicly announce his intention to enroll Vincent in the catalog of the saints, one of the two public consistories mentioned in the bull of canonization.[65] A large crowd had assembled outside the pope's residence in anticipation of his appearance. Suddenly a Roman nobleman named Andreas de Sancta Cruce, who was there to make a speech in Vincent's praise, "was taken by a sudden syncope and fell to the ground, half dead." People rushed to the spot, where it became apparent that Andreas was either dead or in the process of dying. The crowd became divided. Some said it was an act of God, "who by no means wished...that a man be enrolled among the saints who did not appear to be worthy of such glory." Others, among whom Ranzano counted himself, believed God had allowed Andreas's attack in order "that there might be shown through a miracle how great were Vincent's merits."[66]

On the threshold of Vincent's canonization it seemed that God might once again thwart the hopes of his supporters. Auribelli, Ranzano, and the Brittany legates "did not know how to contain our tears." The pope emerged, and a procession began. Ranzano, his fellow Dominicans, and the representatives from Brittany "implored God's help with most intent minds" and commended themselves "to blessed Vincent's merits." Perhaps Calixtus wondered why the Dominican friars, who should be so joyful at this occasion, were advancing "with sighing and tears." But they were not to be disappointed this time. Just as the pope reached his decorated seat, Andreas sprang to his feet and delivered a lengthy and admirable oration in praise of Vincent Ferrer.[67]

---

63. Ibid.; quotations, fol. 64r ("Pontifex in aduersam ualitudinem: qua interiecto quatuor mensium interuallo / e uita discessit. Quam ob rem tum legatorum tum Martialis animus ita est labefactus. Ut nemo eorum fuerit: qui non omnino absoluendi negocii spem omnem amiserit").

64. Ibid., fol. 54r.

65. *Bullarum diplomatum* 1857–72, 5:148; on the octave after the pope's public announcement, Ranzano has Calixtus putting the matter before his clergy and, hearing their decision, determining to canonize Vincent on the Feast of Saints Peter and Paul (June 29): BC, MS 112, fol. 65v.

66. BC, MS 112, fol. 64r: "Andreas cognomento de sancta cruce uir Romanus nobilis iure consultus / qui eo in loco erat in uincentii laudem orationem habiturus sincopi repente correptus in terram semianimis concidit...Erant qui dicerent id dei iudicio factum: qui nequaquam pati pro summa iusticia uoluit ut referretur inter sanctos uir qui non uideretur tanta gloria dignus. Plerique in quorum numero ipse fui / arbitrati sunt eo fuisse id dei benignitate permissum: ut ostenderetur specioso aliquo miraculo quam magna Vincentii merita fuerint."

67. Ibid., fol. 65r–65v; quotations, fol. 65r ("Lachrimas continere nequiuinus [*sic*]...dei auxilium intentissimis mentibus implorauimus: nosque beati Vincentii meritis commendauimus: eum precantes:...Sic nobis cum gemitu lachrimisque precantibus non defuit diuina benignitas.")

Ranzano's narration is a little coy here. Andreas de Sancta Cruce was not just a Roman nobleman who happened to be present and was prepared to sing Vincent's praises. He was, in fact, the procurer appointed by the postulators seeking Vincent's canonization, whose job it was to smooth the process through the bureaucracy of the Roman curia. Such curial procurers—there were two or three in some canonization processes—were expected to be intimately familiar with the procedures and customs used in the papal court. Andreas, an advocate of the consistory court, was well suited to the task, not simply by his noble Roman birth and knowledge of the law but also by having served as the procurer representing the bishop and chapter of Salisbury in the canonization process of Osmund of Salisbury in 1452. He evidently knew his way around the curial machinery, for he advised the local procurers from Salisbury to mention in their petition that the people of Salisbury wanted the bishop to translate Osmund's relics so as to allow for his public veneration as a saint even without papal canonization. He noted that this information would prod the pope, who would be fearful of losing English obedience.[68] He must also have anticipated the impact of his fainting spell and subsequent recovery in Vincent's case.

Still, if the healing of Andreas was not proof enough of God's will, the events of the day of the canonization itself provided further ammunition for Ranzano. On the appointed day, the Feast of Saints Peter and Paul, "it pleased God to show the pontiff not to have spoken from empty counsel."[69] Just after the pope had heard from 176 bishops their opinion that nothing should impede Vincent's canonization, a messenger arrived from Brittany with news of a fresh miracle worked in Vannes. The messenger's letter told how a woman named Margarita, who had lost her eyesight for nine months, had had her vision restored at Vincent's tomb on April 20 just past. Reading the letter, the pope said that the decision to canonize Vincent must be pleasing to God, who had arranged that the letter would arrive "at this moment especially" as proof of all that had been said about the holy preacher's sanctity. Decreed Calixtus, "We will not make a mistake if we enroll such a man in the catalog of saints."[70] In Ranzano's eyes, not simply Vincent's life but his canonization

---

68. Andreas presented the request of Juan of Castile and León, Alfonso of Aragon, and Pierre II of Brittany to open the canonization process, according to Nicholas V's letter of October 18, 1451 (*Procès*, pp. 2–3; FND, 381). See also Malden 1901, xxiv–xxv, 106–7, 108–10; Harvey 1993, 117; Wetzstein 2004a, 362–67 (who notes that Andreas de Sancta Cruce had been one of Vincent's followers).

69. BC, MS 112, fol. 65v: "Placuit deo ostendere non inani consilio pontificem in beati Vincentii gloriam quae iam narraui decreuisse."

70. BC, MS 112, fol. 66v: "Placuit rerum omnium autori deo: ut he litterae hac potissimum hora nobis redderentur…Nihil fallemur si tantum uirum catalogo sanctorum ascripserimus." Ranzano describes three additional miracles out of numerous ones that occurred at the occasion of Vincent's canonization in Rome (fol. 67r–68r).

as well bore the marks of the miraculous hand of God. Canonization may well have been an established juridical process, but to observers and in actual practice, human actions and the divine will could have an enormous impact on the outcome of that process.

## Different Places, Different Procedures

While Vincent's canonization thus followed the same basic general steps as any other late medieval canonization, moving from commission to local inquests to a final adjudication and ceremony in Rome, actual procedure varied greatly in the three local inquests whose records still survive. Where the Brittany inquest was large, expansive in scope, and yet carefully attended by its presiding subcommissioners, the Toulouse and Naples inquests were small, much more tightly scripted, and followed less closely by the entire panel of subcommissioners. Once again, people and places mattered, as a loosely defined process was translated into actuality. The portraits of Vincent Ferrer that emerged from these three inquests varied with the personnel involved, the number and character of the witnesses, and, possibly, regional conceptions of sanctity.[71]

The structure and format of the Brittany inquest lay largely in the hands of Guillermus Coetmur. As procurer, Guillermus was empowered to summon and gather witnesses, acts, letters, instruments, and any other manner of proof necessary for the canonization and generally to take charge of the matter and follow it through to its conclusion.[72] A canon in the Vannes cathedral, Guillermus acted officially on behalf of the cathedral chapter, as his letter of appointment acknowledged.[73] But the procurer was also, more generally, the advocate and representative of those promoting the canonization of the putative saint. In that broader role, Guillermus also must have received some instructions, advice, or support from the Breton duke, Pierre II, who had already taken the trouble to meet with the chapter general of the Dominican order in Nantes in 1453 to begin planning for the canonization inquest. It probably went without saying that the bishop and cathedral chapter would also be happy for the inquest to stress Vincent's miracles, which had already provided such a lucrative source of offerings in wax and coin. As the priest Oliverius le Bourdiec noted, the candles and wax ex-votos left at Vincent's tomb had already been put to good use in the service of the cathedral.[74]

Perhaps not surprisingly, then, the Brittany inquest entrusted to Guillermus Coetmur was structured in such a way as, on the one hand, to stress the close

---

71. I draw here on Smoller 2004a.
72. *Procès,* pp. 20–21; FND, 390–91. The letter is dated October 26, 1453.
73. *Procès,* p. 20; FND, 391.
74. *Procès,* witness 6; FPC, 22.

relations between Vincent and the ducal family and, on the other hand, to demonstrate as vehemently as possible the miracles worked by the holy man's intercession. The first of these goals appears to have been met largely through Coetmur's stacking of a number of high-status witnesses near the beginning of the inquest. More than half of the first forty witnesses heard in Brittany, for example, were marked by noble birth, important civil office, or clerical status. Many of these initial witnesses described the ties between Vincent and the Montfort family, such as the presence of the duchess at his death in Vannes and her role in preparing the saintly corpse for burial.[75] The majority of them offered testimony about the holy man's life, although most also mentioned Vincent's miracles. Significantly, the first miracle mentioned in the Brittany testimony was the one worked on the person of Perrinus Hervei, client of Duke Pierre II, a miracle about which another eleven of those initial witnesses offered testimony.[76]

The organizers of the Brittany inquest were able to satisfy the desire to accentuate Vincent's miraculous intercession by leaving the witness list and the instructions for questioning the witnesses as wide open as possible. Not simply did Guillermus Coetmur and the Bishop of Vannes (who apparently also summoned witnesses) call significantly more witnesses than did their counterparts in Naples, Toulouse, or Avignon, but they also kept to a campaign of actively recruiting even more witnesses, adding names to the roster during the course of the inquest itself.[77] Thus there was the post-Christmas excursion of the bishop of Dol and the abbot of St. Jacut to hear witnesses in Dinan and the diocese of Dol, along with the canon Johannes du Bot's examination of additional witnesses in Vannes and in the region of Nantes. The bishop and Guillermus must also have been on the watch for more testimony about miracles, for their colleagues in the Vannes cathedral were apparently soliciting witnesses from the numbers of pilgrims offering their thanks at Vincent's tomb. Several Brittany witnesses specifically mentioned being sent to testify by the cathedral clergy after leaving their thanksgiving offerings.[78] A number of others made their depositions on the same day on which they had made a pilgrimage to Vincent's tomb in fulfillment of a vow.[79] As noted above, in Brittany the word was out about

---

75. See Smoller 2004a, 294, 301–3.

76. See chapter 1 and also Smoller 2006.

77. That Guillermus Coetmur and the bishop of Vannes summoned the witnesses is attested in *Procès*, pp. 21–22; FND, 392.

78. E.g., Ludovica, widow of Johannes Durant (*Procès*, witness 54; FPC, 94) and Johannes Rocheland (*Procès*, witness 75; FPC, 112).

79. E.g., Johannes de Dieux (*Procès*, witness 278; FPC, 230), Petrus an Neuezic (*Procès*, witness 279; FPC, 13), Eonetus Johelle (*Procès*, witness 285; FPC, 234), and Petrus Thome (*Procès*, witness 286; FPC, 235).

the canonization inquest, but, just in case, the Vannes canons were keeping their eyes and ears open.

The loose format apparent in the Brittany subcommissioners' questioning of witnesses may also have worked to generate a large body of testimony about Vincent's miracles. Although the subcommissioners reported having examined witnesses according to the "form" provided them by the cardinals in Rome, it is clear from the testimony that they were not working from a specific list of articles of interrogation.[80] By "form," they must have meant what scholars refer to as the *forma interrogatorii,* that is, a list of questions designed to help the papal curia decide on the reliability of the testimony offered, for they mention soliciting the witnesses' names, cognomens, and "qualities." The subcommissioners had likely also received as part of that form instructions for asking about the circumstances of alleged miracles, such the length and severity of an illness (in the case of a cure), the form and method of the invocation, and any medical help sought on the patient's behalf.[81] Their records indicate that the panelists stopped witnesses to ask such questions as "How did you know the child was dead?" or "Did he consult any doctors?"[82] Such phrases suggest that the subcommissioners (or their notaries) were familiar with the *forma interrogatorii* specified in other canonizations.

Although the Brittany subcommissioners were perhaps in possession of a *forma interrogatorii,* they clearly did not work from a specific set of articles of interrogation, such as those procurers prepared in other canonization inquests. No question in any of the Brittany depositions makes reference to a numbered article (*articulus*), nor is a list of articles of interrogation included with the documentation and letters the Brittany subcommissioners prepared for the Roman curia. In omitting articles of interrogation, the procurer may have been following a regional tradition, for there were no such articles in the canonization inquests for Saint Yves, held in Brittany, and for the Breton ducal contender Charles of Blois, held in nearby Angers.[83] Nonetheless, the subcommissioners appear to have had some rough sketch of what to ask witnesses, for many early witnesses responded to prompts about their first knowledge of Vincent, his arrival in Brittany, his sermons and their effects, his gift of tongues, his various virtues (such as sobriety, humility, chastity, patience, and peacefulness), his exemplary Christian death, the devotion at

---

80. As the subcommissioners reported, the witnesses were examined "secreto et ad partem...juxta formam nobis datam." *Procès,* p. 22; FND, 392.

81. For examples of such *forma,* see Vauchez 1997, 50; Goodich 1995, 7; Krötzl 1998, 128. The *forma interrogatorii* typically were found in the papal letters opening the process but not in Vincent's case.

82. E.g., Alanus de Cressoles (*Procès,* witness 20; FPC, 52), in testifying to the cure of his broken leg, "interrogatus si habuit medicinam." See Smoller 1997.

83. Smoller 1997, 337; Toynbee 1929, 168.

his tomb, and his miracles.[84] None of these topics, save perhaps the question about the gift of tongues, was clearly specific to Vincent Ferrer alone but rather sketched out a generic picture of sanctity. The final heading (*de miraculis*) was nothing more than an open invitation to the witness to share *anything* he or she considered miraculous (including, evidently, the cure of a sick ox and the death of a suffering child).[85] Many a tale in the Brittany testimony begins, "Questioned about miracles, the witness said that..."

In examining witnesses on such broad topics, the subcommissioners may have been guided by the brief—and also rather generic—*vita* of Vincent recited to them by Bishop Yvo of Vannes during the initial ceremony in Malestroit. The good bishop, too, touched briefly on Vincent's "holy life,...honest conversation,...fruitful and efficacious preaching,...many labors, chaste morals, strenuous acts,...and operation of miracles."[86] He made specific mention of Vincent's gift of tongues, as well as the fact that those both near and far heard and understood the sermons, calling the subcommissioners' attention as well to the way in which Vincent's preaching had brought about a reformation of morals in the duchy that lasted until the present.[87] If this short *vita* did provide the commissioners some direction in examining witnesses, the inquest still remained relatively free-form in comparison with other late medieval canonizations, in which a preinquest *vita* prepared by the promoters of the canonization served as the basis for sometimes very specific articles of interrogation.[88]

The open style of questioning used for the Brittany witnesses, together with the inclusive nature of the witness list, proved an ideal combination for generating testimony about miracles. Rare was the Breton witness who did not tell at least one miracle story. With the cathedral clergy directing grateful pilgrims to go find the subcommissioners, these add-on witnesses brought with them an abundance of tales of Vincent's intercession. The procurer Guillermus, Bishop Yvo, and whoever else might have been involved in summoning witnesses appear to have been happy to have the evidence so stacked. More than half of the Brittany witnesses were forty or younger, not old enough to have any reliable memories of the preacher who had come to their duchy some thirty-five years previously. Between two-thirds and three-quarters of them, in fact, offered no evidence whatsoever about Vincent's

---

84. This list of questions is compiled from the testimony of the first four Brittany witnesses, but they were not all asked about the same topics or in the same order.

85. Ox's cure: Johannes Hoarmen (*Procès,* witness 178; FPC, 171); child's death, Henricus Carne (*Procès,* witness 97; FPC, 128).

86. *Procès,* p. 13; FND, 396: "reverendi magistri Vincencii de Ferrariis...religiosam et sanctam vitam conversacionem honestam...fructuosam et efficacem predicacionem...ipsiusque labores multos ac mores castos ac in ecclesia dei et fide catholica strenuos actos ac operacionem miraculorum."

87. Ibid.

88. Smoller 1997, 337; Vauchez 1997, 49.

life and testified only about miracles.[89] While the ecclesiastical authorities in fifteenth-century Rome might have preferred the faithful more to imitate than to invoke the saints, in the testimony from the Brittany inquest, Vincent Ferrer was much more a source of supernatural power than he was a role model. That implication must have pleased the keepers of his tomb in Vannes.

The Toulouse and Naples inquests offer a major contrast in both procedure and the resultant image of the saint. Not only were these two inquests smaller in scope than the Brittany inquest, but they also involved a more focused control of the witnesses and their testimony. The Toulouse subcommissioners (meaning mainly Johannes Arnaldi, who alone heard the majority of the witnesses) worked from a list of seven articles of interrogation, which are listed in full in two of the depositions.[90] By and large, these articles addressed the same broad topics with which the Brittany commissioners concerned themselves: Vincent's excellent life, chaste morals, fruitful preaching, patience in adversity, observance of the rules of the Dominican order, and many miracles, worked both in his lifetime and posthumously. Only one of the seven was specific to Vincent, and that was a question "about the solemn, devout penitence and public flagellation" that the preacher had inspired in audiences.[91] It is not clear who prepared the questions, for the records do not indicate the name of a procurer. If the serving of the letters of subdelegation was the procurer's work, as it was in Brittany, then a high-ranking Toulouse Dominican named Hugo Nigri acted as procurer in

---

89. Ninety-six point five percent of Breton witnesses testified to at least one miracle. Smoller 2004a, 295. By my count, 90 Breton witnesses offered some testimony about Vincent's life, whereas 223 (71%) testified exclusively about miracles. Thomas Wetzstein has a slightly different breakdown (82 on life and miracles; 231 on miracles only): Wetzstein 2002, 355–56. See also Vauchez 1997, 500.

90. Whether they were included in the prefatory matter is not clear, since all that survives is Antist's sixteenth-century manuscript copy, based ultimately on the damaged Palermo exemplar. In that front matter the subcommissioners did include a list of all witnesses and a record of the summons of each witness (appearing before any of the testimony in Antist's manuscript, at *Proceso*, fol. 170v–172r), and it is not inconceivable that the list of articles appeared there in the original also. The full list of articles appears in the testimony of Alricus de Ruppe (*Proceso*, fol. 194v; FPC, 313, witness 11) and Joannes Hugonis (*Proceso*, fol. 228r–228v; he is Fages's witness 29, but Fages omits the heads) and is embedded in other testimony (e.g., that of the first witness, Bernardus de Rosergio, the archbishop of Toulouse). In the testimony of Alricus de Ruppe (*Proceso*, fol. 194v; FPC, 313), we learn that he had seen and read the articles ("quibus quidem capitibus per ipsum testem visis ac per lectis, idem testis loquens deposuit super illis"). In other cases the articles were read out to witnesses, sometimes translated into the vernacular (Krötzl 1998, 134–35).

91. Testimony of Alricus de Ruppe (*Proceso*, fol. 194v; FPC, 313): "De solemni devota penitentia et disciplinis publice per singula loca civitates provinciasque castra oppida que multis annis peregrinando ad laudem et honorem Dei et continue predicando ad salutem animarum Christi fidelium personaliter visitavit idem Magister Vincentius per suam solemnem et fructuosam penitentiam et predicationem edivulgatam et continuatam." Not all of the witnesses testified about each of the seven heads, and some also seemed to respond to a question about *fama*.

Toulouse, possibly with the assistance of the prior of the local Dominican house, Johannes Bosigne, and two other Dominican theologians.[92]

If Hugo Nigri did act as procurer in the Toulouse inquest, then the witness list reflects well the tastes and prejudices of a man like Nigri, who, according to his own testimony in the inquest, was priest, professor, dean of the faculty of theology of the University of Toulouse, inquisitor for the kingdom of France, confessor to the pope, and councilor to the king of France.[93] Clearly someone in Toulouse hoped to impress the pope by lining up high-status clerics and holders of university degrees to testify on behalf of Vincent Ferrer. Nearly two-thirds of the Toulouse witnesses were members of the clergy, the majority of whom held some sort of higher office. Nearly half of the witnesses possessed university degrees. And even though Johannes Arnaldi and his notaries heard witnesses at the female religious house of Prouille, not a single woman's voice appears in the Toulouse testimony. That Nigri (or whoever compiled the witness list) did indeed have a sense of what would fly in Rome is confirmed in the bull of canonization. There Pius II notes approvingly that among those who testified on Vincent's behalf were "numerous Cardinals of the Holy Roman Church, many bishops and prelates of churches, the aforesaid King of Aragon, and many other noble members of the laity, and many other bachelors, doctors, masters, and licentiates in law, the liberal arts, and theology."[94]

If the Brittany inquest acted as a dragnet for miracle tales, the format adopted in Toulouse generated a dossier more focused on Vincent's holy life. True, there were miracles in Toulouse. Almost two-thirds of the witnesses testified about them, but the sort of personal testimonial that the Vannes clergy so actively sought is rare indeed in the Toulouse inquest. Indeed only two Toulouse witnesses were actual beneficiaries of Vincent's intercession.[95] And if Guillermus Coetmur and Bishop Yvo of Vannes were happy to solicit the testimony of many witnesses too young to remember Vincent's time in Brittany, in Toulouse the preference was clearly for those who had seen Vincent in action. Of the forty-three witnesses whose depositions survive only one had no direct memories of the holy preacher. In Brittany it was the

---

92. *Proceso,* fol. 267v; FPC, 399 (mention of Hugo Nigri only serving the letters); for the full list of Johannes Bosigne, Hugo Nigri, Guiglelmus Ganberti, Petrus Ganterii, *Proceso,* fol. 169v–170r; FPC, 274.

93. *Proceso,* fol. 183v; FPC, 295, witness 6.

94. *Bullarum diplomatum* 1857–72, 5:148. Ranzano, too, was impressed by and remarked upon the witnesses' status: BC, MS 112, fol. 63r–63v. See also Smoller 2004a, 293. On the preference for high-status witnesses, see Lett 2008, 345–55; Katajala-Peltomaa 2009, 32–42, 48–53.

95. That is, the Carmelite friar Galliardus de Ruppe (*Proceso,* fol. 226v–227r; FPC, 367, witness 27[bis]), who was cured of a fever after laying his head on Vincent's tomb, and the merchant Guillelmus Petri Seuhier (*Proceso,* fol. 245v; FPC, 396–97, witness 48 [43]), who was cured of blindness after Vincent made the sign of the cross over his face.

rare witness who had no miracle tales to relate; in Toulouse it was that single exceptional witness who offered no testimony about Vincent's life.[96] Toulouse witnesses' responses were guided and shaped by the articles of interrogation, both the generic questions about Vincent's exemplary virtues and the more Vincent-specific article asking about the public penitence he had inspired. Indeed, the Toulouse testimony is full of striking, graphic descriptions of the flagellant processions that began when Vincent had preached in the region.[97] Perhaps it pleased Nigri (or whoever organized the witness list) to illustrate for the Roman curia such a vivid example of the clergy's leading the laity to penitence. While some contemporaries looked askance at Vincent's band of self-flagellating followers, tradition had it that he had composed a rule for their edification and guidance.[98]

Whereas the Toulouse testimony both illuminated Vincent's exemplary life and provided an example of the faithful imitating his virtues, the Naples inquest seems to have been geared toward portraying him as a converter of Jews and Muslims (and of lax Christians) and a healer of grave divisions. Even more scripted than the one in Toulouse, the Naples inquest focused on soliciting the testimony of a relatively small group of high-status witnesses about twenty-seven articles of interrogation. As noted above, the structure and content of the Naples inquest were the work of Martial Auribelli, who, though never specifically so named in the surviving records, performed all the duties of procurer for this inquest. As master general of the Dominican order, Auribelli was probably more familiar with the details of Vincent's cause than was any man or woman in Europe. Having met with the Breton ducal family during the order's chapter general in Nantes in 1453 and subsequently having traveled "to various parts of France, Spain, Germany, and Italy" to consult with civic and religious leaders, Auribelli also well understood the concerns of the promoters of Vincent's canonization.[99]

The articles of interrogation that Auribelli supplied for the Naples inquest must represent the picture of Vincent Ferrer that the Dominican order most wished to portray. Although they were evidently modeled on the articles drawn up for the inquests into the sanctity of the Franciscan preacher Bernardino of Siena (canonized in 1450), the Naples *articuli* sketched out a

---

96. Arnaldus de Malocasali, who acknowledged that he had never seen Vincent Ferrer preach but did testify to a miracle: *Proceso,* fol. 244v–245r; FPC 395–96, witness 42.

97. Smoller 2004a, 297.

98. Jean Gerson rebuked Vincent for not discouraging the flagellants. See Smoller 1994, 116–17. M.-M. Gorce cites two sixteenth-century editions of a rule for these flagellants attributed to Vincent Ferrer, but in the absence of any surviving exemplars, it is impossible to establish the authenticity of the text. Gorce 1923, 11.

99. As Pietro Ranzano relates (BC, MS 112, fol. 62v–63r): "Dum haec aguntur in britania Martialis ad diuersas galliarum / hispaniarum germaniae italiae partes / mira celeritate profectus [est]" (quotation, 63r).

life narrative that was clearly Vincent's while portraying him as an exemplary and idealized preacher.[100] Thus witnesses such as Bishop Joannes of Majorca, who answered questions on each of the twenty-seven articles, traced Vincent's career from his birth in Valencia (articles 1 and 2) through his death in Brittany (articles 19 and 20) and the subsequent outpouring of devotion and miracles (articles 25–27).[101] Besides demonstrating Vincent's pious and virtuous mode of life, Auribelli's articles specifically sought to elicit testimony about the holy preacher's ability to heal feuds (articles 9 and 10), convert Muslims and Jews to the Christian faith (articles 9 and 10), and bring sinful Christians, especially prostitutes, to a better life (articles 10 and 13). Alert to the still-bitter memory of the Great Schism (1378–1414), Auribelli, in article 15, aimed to demonstrate "that the aforesaid Brother Vincent most miraculously worked for the union of God's holy Church, so that many dissident princes and kingdoms in the obedience of the various popes were brought by him to union and the obedience of a single pope."[102] Miracles were not absent from Auribelli's concerns. But aside from the characterization of Vincent's efforts to heal the Schism as "miraculous," the holy man's intercessory abilities receive mention in only four of the twenty-seven articles (articles 7, 12, 25, and 26).

The general picture that emerges from the Naples testimony shows the effectiveness of Auribelli's guiding hand. As in Toulouse, the subcommissioners examined a lineup of witnesses enjoying the sort of high social status that evidently bespoke credibility. All but one of them (not coincidentally, the only woman in the group) offered testimony about Vincent's life; 60 percent of the witnesses spoke about his miracles as well.[103] Many of the witnesses testified to Vincent's extraordinary abilities to bring Jews and Muslims to the Christian faith. Several described the fruits of his activities

---

100. So Pellegrini 2004, 318–19. The articles are listed in *Proceso,* fol. 273v–275r (articles 21 and 22 are missing); FPC, 408–10. We know from the testimony of Joannes, bishop of Majorca; Joannes Alvarus de Valentia; and King Alfonso of Aragon that article 21 had something to do with Vincent's *fama* and reputation and article 22 concerned his observance of the rule of the Dominican order: *Proceso,* fol. 292r, 292v, 289v; FPC, 434, 436, 448.

101. *Proceso,* fol. 290r–292v; FPC 431–35, witness 14. Testifying on August 3, Bishop Joannes was probably the second witness questioned, after Alfonso V. Alfonso, whose testimony survives only in fragments, was probably asked about all twenty-seven articles, although he said he knew nothing about many of the articles: *Proceso,* fol. 289v; FPC, 447–48. Joannes Alvarus de Valentia who, testifying on August 7, was probably the third witness examined, answered articles 1–25 but not 26 and 27, although it is possible that the end of his deposition was missing in Antist's exemplar: *Proceso,* fol. 292v–294v; FPC, 435–37, witness 15.

102. *Proceso,* fol. 274v; FPC, 410, article 15: "Item quod prefatus frater Vincentius pro unione ecclesie sancte Dei miraculosissime operatus est adeo quod multos principes et regna in obedientiam diversorum pontificum dissidentia ad unionem et unius pontificis obedientiam reduxit."

103. The exception is Alcira Myra Rodriquez, who, testifying on October 15, was probably the fifteenth witness heard (*Proceso,* fol. 278v–279r; FPC, 415), who gave evidence only on article 12, regarding Vincent's laying on of hands (*Proceso,* fol. 274v; FPC, 409).

in a village formerly known as Vallis Puta (modern-day Vallouise) on account of the ungodliness of its inhabitants; after Vincent's advent, it was known as Vallis Pura.[104] Nearly half of the Naples witnesses attested to Vincent's role in settling disputes, including a feud of centuries' duration. Almost a third also mentioned his efforts to bring the Great Schism to an end. These latter two points come up significantly more often in the Naples testimony than they do in the inquests from Toulouse or Brittany, a fact that must owe something to the direction provided by Martial Auribelli.[105]

The three surviving inquests into Vincent Ferrer's sanctity varied significantly in their procedures and in the sorts of testimony they generated about the candidate for sainthood. Still, the smaller, more tightly controlled inquests from Toulouse and Naples resemble one another much more than they do the sprawling, open hearings from Brittany. In other words, one could make the case that the differences seen in Vincent's canonization inquests were somehow related to cultural differences between northern and southern Europe. In fact, André Vauchez, in his study of seventy-one canonization processes conducted between 1185 and 1431, has argued that northern Europe did produce different types of saints from those seen in the Mediterranean south. Mediterranean saints were doers, exemplary Christians whose ascetic lifestyle and actions in the world appeared to be an imitation of Christ. Outside the Mediterranean world, in Vauchez's typology, "a saint was first of all a dead person, or more precisely a dead body, that performed miracles."[106] Although other scholars have sometimes questioned Vauchez's model, in the case of Vincent Ferrer the Brittany inquest did stress Vincent's miracles, while the two southern inquests put the emphasis on his exemplary life.[107]

That such striking differences could appear between northern and southern testimony about the same man may lend some credence to Vauchez's distinction between Mediterranean and non-Mediterranean sanctity. In addition to the sorts of considerations suggested above—the specific interests of the Vannes cathedral chapter, the duke of Brittany, the clerical elite in Toulouse, and the head of the Dominican order—the organizers of Vincent's canonization inquests may well have had in the backs of their minds

---

104. Vincent wrote a letter to the Jean Puynoix, master general of the Dominican order, describing his work preaching against Waldensian heretics in Valpute. The letter is edited in FND, 109–111, and translated in FHSVF, 1:128–31. A new, better edition is in Hodel 2006, 200–3. The letter is preserved in a single, badly mutilated manuscript copy kept by Jean Puynoix and subsequently used as a contact relic by the faithful in Sicily. See also Paravy 1984, 1993, 1:343–55; Gorce 1924, 179–80; Cohn 1975, 38–39; Smoller 2009; and Ginzburg 1991, 302, who describe the presence of Waldensian heretics in Valpute throughout the fifteenth century (despite Vincent's preaching).

105. Smoller 2004a, 298–99.

106. Vauchez 1997, 157–218; quotation, 217.

107. See Smoller 2004a, 291, 301–8.

the sorts of saints that appealed to their own flocks.[108] Although judicial procedures dictated every step of the canonization process, the resultant product was not a transparent, "just the facts, Ma'am" narrative.[109] From the number and types of witnesses called (just which Ma'am are we talking about?) to the sorts of questions each one was asked (which facts?), the canonization inquest was the product of a series of decisions taken by the individuals entrusted with its completion. Canonization processes began and ended with the Holy See, but the pope could work only from materials generated by local personalities and interests.

## Canonization Inquest as Spectacle

While the promoters and backers of Vincent Ferrer's canonization shaped the local inquests in such a way as to produce the type of evidence they believed would hold up well in Rome, the papal curia was not the only audience for their work. The local inquest served both to authenticate and to spread the potential saint's *fama sanctitatis*. The city or town in which an inquest was held formed the backdrop for a spectacle that broadcast and publicized the holiness of the candidate for sainthood, while procurers, subcommissioners, and notaries collected proofs of his or her sanctity. In the case of Vincent Ferrer, from the ceremonies marking the opening and close of the Brittany inquest to the experience of individual witnesses in Brittany, Toulouse, and Naples, participants in the canonization inquest experienced a living tableau of Vincent's sanctity.

Ritualized ceremonies marked the opening and closing of the Brittany canonization inquest. These rituals served a number of purposes: first, to honor the putative saint; second, to honor and invoke God's aid for the papal commissioners who ran the inquest; third, to demonstrate popular devotion to Vincent (the *fama sanctitatis* required for canonization); and finally, to present in brief the case for his canonization. The ceremonies that greeted the papal subcommissioners, in fact, shared much with the processions that marked the living saint's entry into Vannes in 1418, as well as with the elevation of the dead saint's relics after his canonization in 1455. All echoed the elements of papal celebrations of the canonization of new saints.

Just as a dramatic procession had greeted Vincent Ferrer on his arrival in the Breton ducal city of Vannes in 1418, ritual and ceremony also marked

---

108. While the presence of Vincent's relics in Vannes would perhaps have generated more miracles there than in another location, it is also clear that the orchestrators of the Vannes inquest were searching for miracle stories in a way that those in Toulouse and Naples were not. Still, their emphasis on the saint's miracles could find an explanation entirely apart from regional notions of sanctity, namely, in a simple desire to keep the pilgrims coming to Vannes. Smoller 2004a, 299–301.

109. See, e.g., the skepticism expressed in Lett 2008, 259, 409, and 2009, 93–101.

the Breton inquest into his sanctity. That we know about these ceremonies at all is unusual for late medieval canonizations, and the descriptions of the Brittany ceremonies are more detailed than any others from the fifteenth century.[110] The ceremonies staged to accompany the canonization inquest of 1453–54 stand somewhere in between the processions that accompanied the famous preacher on his entry into Vannes and the elaborate ritual involving the elevation of the new saint's body in 1456. The ceremonies were planned and executed on behalf of the duke and the chapter of the Vannes cathedral, probably by Guillermus Coetmur, the indefatigable procurer for the Brittany inquest. The plague raging in Brittany in the fall of 1453 ensured that matters did not go entirely as Guillermus might have anticipated, however. The chapter had evidently hoped to open the proceedings with a grand ceremony at the site of Vincent's tomb in Vannes cathedral, but, as we have seen, that visit to the cathedral had to wait while the subcommissioners were summoned for their initial meeting in Malestroit, some forty kilometers safely down the road.[111] Under the circumstances, Guillermus did the best he could.

The subcommissioners arrived in Malestroit on November 15, 1453. The next day the four—"together with a multitude of people"—went to the parish church in Malestroit. There they were reverently greeted at the doorway by a procession consisting of Yvo de Pontsal, bishop of Vannes, together with the rector, priests, and other notable persons, accompanied by the hymn "Veni Creator Spiritus" ("Come, Creator Spirit") and the ringing of the church bells. Next, the rector of the parish church chanted the Mass of the Holy Spirit, and then the four subcommissioners were shown to honorific seats in front of the altar of the chapel of the Blessed Virgin Mary in the parish church. There they formally received their letters of delegation, and the bishop offered a brief *vita* of the proposed saint. Citing the need for mature deliberation on such an important matter, the subcommissioners set aside the following day to make their official response. On that day they agreed to take up the charge,[112] expressed their desire to personally visit Vincent's tomb in Vannes as soon as it was safe, and swore an oath in which they promised to pursue the inquest with all due diligence and care.

On the following Tuesday, November 20, 1453, the parties involved in the inquest must have felt it safe enough to venture a visit to the cathedral in Vannes. The cathedral clergy in Vannes staged an elaborate ritual, presumably the one with which they had hoped originally to greet the subcommissioners before they were forced to put together an alternative ceremony in Malestroit. Indeed, the Malestroit ceremony seems to have been a pale

---

110. See note 2.
111. *Procès*, pp. 8–16; FND, 393–97.
112. Excepting the bishop of St. Malo: *Procès*, p. 15; FND, 396.

imitation of the actions that now took place in Vannes. At the tenth hour of the day, the subcommissioners (now including the bishop of St. Malo), together with a number of nobles and notable persons, processed to the Vannes cathedral. They were met honorifically at the great portal by the bishop of Vannes in his pontifical robes, together in procession with the archdeacon, the canons, other persons attached to the cathedral, all dressed in cloaks; other local clergy; and many nobles, citizens, and people from Vannes and nearby places. The bells were ringing, the organ sounding, and a choir was again singing the hymn "Veni Creator." After the hymn, the bishop recited the collect "Deus qui corda fidelium" ("God, who has instructed the hearts of the faithful"), and the entire procession led the subcommissioners to seats of honor prepared for them in the cathedral choir. Still dressed in his pontifical robes, the bishop chanted the Mass of the Holy Spirit.[113]

The hymn, prayer, and Mass performed in this ceremony marked it out as a special event indeed. The hymn "Veni Creator Spiritus," invoking the aid of the Holy Spirit, is traditionally sung at Pentecost and on important occasions such as the election of popes, consecration of bishops, ordination of priests, and the opening of synods and councils. Its chanting here both summoned the aid of the Holy Spirit in the task set before the subcommissioners and underscored the importance and seriousness of the occasion. The collect recited by the bishop also asked for guidance from the Holy Spirit: "God, who has instructed the hearts of the faithful by the light of the Holy Spirit," goes the prayer, "grant us that we may understand rightly by the same Spirit and always rejoice in the consolation of the Spirit." Reciting the "Deus qui corda fidelium" also marked the importance of the ceremony. Like the "Veni Creator Spiritus," this collect featured among texts used at the vestment of a priest and in an early set of prayers for the attestation of relics.[114] This prayer also forms a part of the votive Mass of the Holy Spirit, also employed to invoke the aid of the Holy Spirit.[115]

Further, the hymn "Veni Creator," the prayer "Deus qui corda fidelium," and the Mass of the Holy Spirit figured in late medieval canonization ceremonies.[116] When Pope Boniface IX canonized Saint Bridget in 1391,

113. *Procès*, pp. 16–19; FND, 397–99.

114. Vestment of priest: Sicardus Cremonensis in PL, 213, col. 87; attestation of relics: "Oratio ad probandas reliquias," PL, 71, col. 1185.

115. For example, in the election of a new Carthusian prior. See Guigo I, prior Carthusiae, "De ordinatione prioris," PL, 153, col. 661. I have taken the text of the Latin *Missa de Spiritu Sancto* from *Missale Romanum* 1911, 55*–57*.

116. E.g., see the following descriptions of ceremonies: for Bridget of Sweden in 1391, Dykmans 1985, 4:235–42 (from the *Ceremonial* of Pierre Ameil) and 4:276–79, app. 2 (relation by Laurent le Romain ca. 1400, as translated into Latin in the seventeenth century); and Petrus Amelius, "De canonizatione sanctae Brigidae," PL, 78, cols. 1359–62; for Nicolas of Tolentino in 1446, "Solemnia Canonizationis" 1909, 236–37; for Bernardino of Siena in 1450, Dykmans 1985, 2:202;

for example, immediately prior to the ceremony of canonization, he heard the Mass of the Holy Spirit in his private chambers. At the public ceremony, the pontiff first asked the audience "to pray God that he should not permit [Boniface] to err" in enrolling Bridget in the catalog of saints. Next, he chanted the hymn "Veni Creator Spiritus" and then intoned the prayer "Deus qui corda fidelium." Only thereafter did Boniface pronounce Bridget's canonization.[117] By including these elements in the ceremonies at Vannes and Malestroit, the advocates of Vincent's sanctity certainly also must have aimed to invoke the aid of the Holy Spirit in this important matter. But the rituals also foreshadowed the canonization ceremony that they hoped would result from the inquest.

The Vannes ceremony continued after Mass. Again the subcommissioners were seated honorifically. Then one Johannes Maucazie, prior of the Carmelite convent of Bondon near Vannes, addressed them on behalf of the bishop, the cathedral, and the nobles and citizens of Vannes. It was a "solemn oration" in which Maucazie offered the subcommissioners many strong reasons for diligence in their appointed task, citing "various authorities and sacred scriptures." Next, the bishop of Vannes summarized the holy life, good works, and miracles of Vincent Ferrer, exhorting the subcommissioners to carry out the visit to the tomb and inquest into Vincent's life and miracles "diligently, prudently, and maturely, as fitting in a matter holy and glorious pertaining to the exaltation of the Catholic faith and the honor of the whole church." He also entreated them to give careful attention to the "wax images, crosses, coffins of the dead who (as he asserted) had been resuscitated, sudaries, and iron shackles of those liberated from prison and captivity" placed at Vincent's tomb in memory of his miracles without number.[118]

The third part of the ceremony began when the subcommissioners, together with the bishop, archdeacon, canons, priests, nobles, and citizens

---

for Catherine of Siena in 1461, Dykmans 1985, 4:280–84; for Bonaventure in 1482, Muratori 1900–[75], vol. 23, pt. 3, 95–97; and for Leopold in 1485, Muratori 1900–[75], vol. 32, pt. 1, 100–106. Also see the *ordinanda* of 1487 for the hoped-for canonization of Francesca Romana, which did not take place until 1608, Dykmans 1985, 4:285–88. See also Jacopo Stefaneschi's early fourteenth-century prescription for the canonization of a saint, Dykmans 1985, 2:458–66; Patrizi Piccolomini's order for the same in his 1488 *Ceremonial*, Dykmans 1980, 1:118–24; and Schimmelpfennig 2004.

117. Amelius, in PL, 78, cols. 1359–62. Quotation, col. 1360.

118. *Procès*, pp. 16–17; FND, 397–98: "Johannes Maucazie...solemnem oracionem fecit per quam nos ad exercicionem superius narrati operis multis et vigentibus racionibus tum allegacione diversarum auctoritatum sacre scripture incitabat" and Bishop Yvo "requisivit quatenus ad visitacionem sepulcri inquisicionem vite et miraculorum prefati magistri Vincencii...et gloriose et ad exaltacionem fidei catholice et honorem tocius ecclesie tendentis diligenter prudenter et mature procedere necnon ymagines cereas cruces feretra mortuorum ut asserebat resuscitatorum sudaria compedes ferreos a carceribus et captivitatibus liberatorum ibidem in memoriam miraculorum dicti magistri Vincencii sine numero ut subiungebat existentes cernere et de super testimonium dare curaremus."

there, proceeded to examine Vincent's tomb. Made "of saffron–colored
stone," elevated on four stone columns, and covered with a "golden cloth,"
the tomb was located within the choir of the cathedral in front of the bishop's seat and to the right of the altar. The assembled crowd (numbering
around a thousand, we are told) then swore to the subcommissioners that
Vincent's body indeed was buried at that site. Then—and it is difficult to
imagine exactly how this might have looked or sounded—"with their hands
raised toward heaven, the great altar of the cathedral, and the saints," the
crowd unanimously testified under oath about the public fame of Vincent's
sanctity, his holy and irreproachable life, and the many miracles worked at his
invocation, again directing the subcommissioners' attention to the numerous wax ex-votos left at his tomb: "many ships, wax images of bodies, heads,
eyes, hands, arms, legs, feet, and diverse other members; many sudaries, wax
breasts, crutches, and many wooden crosses and coffins from the resuscitated
dead—as they alleged." Finishing the day's ceremonies, the subcommissioners enjoined the bishop and cathedral chapter to produce witnesses and
other evidence for them to examine at the nearby priory of Saint-Guen.[119]
As we have seen, the subcommissioners began examining witnesses there on
the following day.

This opening ceremony served a number of purposes besides simply
greeting the subcommissioners and impressing them and the crowd of
onlookers with the importance of the occasion (as the singing of the "Veni
Creator Spiritus" implied). First, it presented in a dramatic tableau the stages
of the canonization process. The ceremony summarized the information that
would have been contained in the petitions leading the pope to open canonization proceedings. For example, the subcommissioners heard from the
mouth of the bishop a resume of Vincent's life and merits, as well as mention
of the multitude of miracles worked before and after his death. The bishop
reminded the subcommissioners of the contents of the papal letter initiat-
ing the canonization process. The crowd itself bore testimony to Vincent's
*fama sanctitatis.* And in their unanimous affirmation of Vincent Ferrer's sanctity, the crowd enacted, in brief and in general terms, the testimony that
would be gathered at the inquest, swearing together that Vincent had been a
holy and faithful man and an exemplary preacher and that God had worked
countless miracles through his merits. Through their very gestures—"hands
raised toward heaven, the great altar of the cathedral, and the saints"—the

---

119. *Procès,* pp. 17–19; FND, 398–99: "Ibidem unum tumulum lapideum lapidis crocei coloris
satis honorificum ostenderunt qui uno panno aureo coopertus erat...Nobisque elevatus manibus
versus celum et magnum altare dicte ecclesie ad sanctos et per sua juramenta unanimiter et con-
corditer testificate fuerunt...Que quidem vota cerea ibidem vidimus videlicet naves plures ymagines cereas corporum capitum oculorum manuum brachiorum tibiarum ac pedum et diversorum
aliorum membrorum multa sudaria mamillas cereas potencias ac quamplures cruces ligneas et aliqua
feretra a mortuis ut dicebant resuscitatorum que in tanto numero erant quod in pluribus diebus
enumerari non possent."

crowd drew into their audience (and their number) not simply the subcom-missioners but the entire church, living and dead, the court of heaven, and Christ himself in the bread and wine just consecrated on the great altar. All of heaven became witness to Vincent's sanctity in both senses of the word (that is, as observer and as giver of testimony).

Through careful attention to rank and order, the ceremony also encap-sulated earthly hierarchy, harmony, and concord. The subcommissioners, describing the ceremony with which they were greeted, placed people in orders and in hierarchies within those orders. First came the nobility: "nobles and notables" (representing the duke and secular authority) accom-panied them to the cathedral. Second came the clergy: the commission-ers were greeted by the bishop of Vannes, then his archdeacon, then the cathedral canons, then other persons attached to the cathedral, then local priests, religious, and clergy. Third came the *laboratores:* citizens and people of Vannes were waiting at the cathedral as well. By representing the entire earthly hierarchy, the ceremony carried out in the Vannes cathedral gave a foretaste of the universal cult of Vincent that its stagers hoped would result from the canonization inquest. In their liturgical elements, the events also gave a nod toward the rituals that would accompany Vincent's hoped-for canonization.

The ceremony that greeted Bishop Radulphus of Dol and the official Johannes du Bot at the inquest's closing in April 1454 contained several of the elements from the inquest's opening events. Absent were the spe-cial invocations of the aid of the Holy Spirit, but, once again, the ceremony offered a ritualized version of the testimony about Vincent's sanctity. As had happened before, a procession of clergy, nobles, and ordinary people greeted the subcommissioners as they entered the Vannes cathedral to hear Sunday Mass. Again the subcommissioners listened to speechifying. Address-ing Radulphus and Johannes in the names of the duke, the clergy, and the nobles and people of the diocese of Vannes, Bishop Yvo of Vannes noted that Vincent's miracles had grown in number throughout the time of the canonization inquest. Again the assembled crowd swore under oath, "with their hands raised towards heaven and the saints," about Vincent's holy life, miracles, and reputation. In response, the subcommissioners reassured the crowd that they intended to close the inquest and send the testimony they had gathered to the commission of cardinals appointed by Pope Nicholas V. With the witness of important members of the ducal administration and the local clergy and the attestations and seals of the three notaries who had served throughout the inquest, the ceremony—and the Brittany phase of the process—came to a noisy and very public end.[120]

---

120. Letter dated April 7, 1454: *Procès,* pp. 24–27; FND, 393, 400–402: "Dicens insuper jurans et attestans prout omnes cleri nobiles cives et populi ibidem ut prediximus processionaliter et alias

Whether these sorts of ceremonies accompanied the opening and closing of the other inquests into Vincent Ferrer's sanctity is not clear. There are no such descriptions in the records of the Toulouse and Naples inquests, but, then again, they are also absent from other late medieval canonization inquests.[121] Nor do we know details about the liturgical elements of the canonization proper in June 1455. If it was similar to the handful of other late medieval canonization ceremonies for which we have records, the ceremony included a procession, a Mass (perhaps the Mass of the Holy Spirit), a prayer that God not allow the pope to err in this canonization, the singing of the hymn "Veni Creator Spiritus," the prayer "Deus qui corda fidelium," the pronouncement of the canonization, the singing of a "Te Deum Laudamus," and the leaving of offerings.[122] Pietro Ranzano, however, as an eyewitness to the events, left a record of his impressions of the festivities.

Ranzano's account depicts a ceremony that celebrated the promoters of the canonization—those who had expended their time, energy, and money on Vincent's behalf—as much as it honored the newly named saint. A procession of around four hundred Dominicans, who had come to Rome expressly for the occasion, together with their master general and the Breton legates, sang hymns throughout the city streets, carrying the arms of King Alfonso of Aragon and Duke Pierre II of Brittany at the head of the ranks of the Dominican order. A great crowd of both sexes followed them as they made their way to the Vatican and the basilica of St. Peter. "The divine matter" occurred in the midst of St. Peter's, where a large space had been prepared. Lights were hanging everywhere; nearly two thousand candles adorned the walls. To Ranzano, "it looked like the glittering star-studded face of heaven." The banners of Pierre of Brittany, Alfonso of Aragon, and the Order of Preachers hung in the basilica. "The other things were done on that day that pertained to that solemnity," wrote Ranzano, but he did not believe it necessary to burden his correspondent with those details.[123]

In a society where much still was oral, the ritual and ceremonies attached to canonization served not simply to mark the importance of the entire process but also to convey information about the saint to a larger audience. The processions that greeted the living Vincent Ferrer, the subcommissioners in charge of the Brittany inquest, and the announcement

---

diversimode et diversis locis congregati et sepulcrum dicti M. V. devote visitantes eiusque beneficia implorantes elevatis in celum et ad sanctos manibus juravit et attestabantur."

121. See note 2.

122. See note 116.

123. BC, MS 112, fol. 66v–67r: "Res diuina a pontifice acta est in templi medio...Eratque luminum omnium talis tantusque decor: ut quaedam stellati micantisque coeli facies iuderetur...Alia praeterea facta eo die sunt: quae solennitatem in primis decuere."

of his canonization displayed to participants as well as to observers the holy Dominican's *fama sanctitatis*. The ceremonies in Brittany that so carefully included all of the earthly hierarchy demonstrated that the entire body of the faithful held Vincent in reverence; ditto the unanimous sworn testimony of the crowds in Vannes cathedral at the opening and closing of the inquest. At each ceremony, audiences heard the salient aspects of Vincent's biography, while the display of ex-votos at his tomb offered eloquent testimony to his intercessory powers. If the ceremonial aspects of the canonization process served—like stained glass in a cathedral—as books for the illiterate, teaching about Vincent's life and miracles, they also gave out equally powerful messages about who Vincent's best friends were. Observers at the Brittany ceremonies could not fail to note the connections being drawn between Vincent Ferrer, the Vannes cathedral clergy, and, most important, the ducal family. Nor could a bystander in Rome on June 29, 1455, miss the importance to this new saint of Duke Pierre II of Brittany, King Alfonso V of Aragon, and his own Order of Preachers. The ceremonies and rituals that accompanied the canonization process underscored not simply who Vincent Ferrer was but also who were the backers to whom the new saint owed favors.

In the deceptively simple language of the bull issued by Pope Pius II on October 1, 1458, his predecessor Calixtus "canonized" Vincent Ferrer. But behind that word and behind that glorious summer day in 1455 stretched a long, arduous path. Because canonization involved a lengthy judicial process, the individuals and groups most interested in promoting it were able to put their stamp on the contents of the process. Their money and staying power assured them of a role, whether in appointing the procurer who helped shape the inquest *in partibus,* sending their representatives to Rome as lobbyists during the curial phases of the process, or funding the final canonization ceremonies (and thereby procuring the right to have their banners borne throughout Rome). In the case of Vincent Ferrer, we can see the role of individuals in shaping the testimony gathered at the local inquests, particularly in the striking differences between the types of testimony generated in Brittany on the one hand and Naples and Toulouse on the other. In each case, the procurers structured an inquest that generated the sort of evidence they thought would impress the College of Cardinals while remaining alert to the interests of those who had appointed them to their task. By tracing the stages of the canonization process, we see a variety of individuals and groups each trying to put its own brand on the hoped-for saint.

Although the promoters, procurers, subcommissioners, and notaries gathered testimony about the potential saint specifically for the College of Cardinals in Rome, their work also had a local audience. Not simply were the records generated at the inquest a source of local pride and veneration, but the inquest *in partibus* became a part of lived experience in the region.[124] For participants in and observers of the ceremonies marking its opening and closing, the inquest became a celebration of the life and miracles of a holy person with ties to their hometown. The act of testifying must also have been a profound experience for witnesses. The procurers' summons and questions, as well as the contact with subcommissioners, notaries, and other witnesses, must have offered a set of portraits of the potential saint. Yet here again, on a smaller, more intimate scale, one can see the give-and-take of individuals trying to impose their own meanings on their memories of Vincent Ferrer and on the meaning of a new saint.

---

124. The records were reverently kept, as was the Brittany inquest, which remained part of the treasury of the cathedral chapter well into the twentieth century (it still belonged to the cathedral when it was microfilmed for the ADM in 1955). Wetzstein 2004a, 560–65, lists numerous local manuscript copies of canonization inquests. And, as Antist's note about his Palermo exemplar indicates, such texts could also be used as precious relics.

# CHAPTER 3

# Shaping the Narratives of the Saint

Although important studies of late medieval canonizations have clarified the major phases of the canonization process as well as the considerable differences in actual procedure from canonization to canonization, scholars have only in the last decade begun to ask about the experience of participants in a canonization inquest.[1] The sad truth is that the surviving sources make this question a difficult one to answer. The documents generated at the inquests, carefully recorded and authenticated by notaries, were legal instruments whose aim was to present and guarantee as valid the testimony gathered there. The notaries who so meticulously wrote down the witnesses' names, ages, and places of habitation were simply not interested in passing on to curious readers a novelistic description of the setting and circumstances under which those persons had offered their testimony. In what sort of chamber did witnesses testify? Who else was present, if anybody? Who sat (or stood) where? Were there witnesses waiting in an antechamber? All these details the notaries omitted to record. At the same time, however, there are cracks in the documents. In the records of

---

1. See, e.g., Goodich 2006a, 102; and Bartlett 2004, 31, 52–55, 114. More attention has been given to the experience of those conducting the canonization process. See Wetzstein 2004a, esp. 354–499; and Lett 2008, who insists that the "real" experiences of individual witnesses cannot be reconstructed from the text. Historians of heresy and inquisition have shown slightly more interest in similar questions. See, e.g., Pegg 2001, 39–44, 57–62; Arnold 2001, who, however, like Lett, tends to regard the text produced by the inquisitorial process as the only "reality" to which historians can truly have access.

the inquests held into Vincent Ferrer's sanctity, unobtrusive remarks slip in here and there.[2] Those legally unnecessary details offer tantalizing hints of what it was like to be present at a late medieval canonization inquest and exactly how those charged with its execution carried out their duties. The lived experience of the inquest could be crucial for the image of the potential saint passed on to Rome in the testimony, as well as for the reputation of the holy person that witnesses took home with them after giving their testimony. Witnesses were both sources of testimony and observers of the inquest itself, both shapers of and audience for the portrait of the potential saint being drawn there.

In the case of Vincent Ferrer, records from the three surviving canonization inquests afford a fair glimpse at the participants' experience, from the witnesses' receipt of an official summons to testify to the cast of characters present at their depositions, their swearing on oath to testify truly, and the sorts of questions that the subcommissioners asked witnesses about their veracity. The records, for example, frequently indicate the date and place at which witnesses testified. That numbers of witnesses appeared on the same day raises the possibility of their collaboration, intentional or unintentional, on the details of their testimony. In many respects, the canonization inquest represented a spider's web of communications among participants on both sides of the bench. Witnesses learned about the potential saint—and about ecclesiastical conceptions of sainthood—from their fellow witnesses as well as from the subcommissioners who prompted their testimony with their questions. But witnesses also had the opportunity, through their stories, to shape the emerging image of Vincent Ferrer and, equally important, to make claims about their own identities. Just as Vincent Ferrer was crucial to the self-representation put forth by the dukes of Brittany, the crown of Aragon, and the Dominican order, so, too, individual witnesses created, out of their encounters with the holy man, narratives that made powerful assertions about their own spiritual and social worth.

## The Physical Circumstances: Summons, Setting, and Cast

The information contained in the reports prepared for the Brittany, Toulouse, and Naples inquests into Vincent Ferrer's sanctity suggests that testifying before the papal subcommissioners was hardly a quiet, private affair. From the issuing of an official summons of witnesses to the notaries' final subscription and seal, the canonization inquest was a public event in every sense of the word. In the first place, the inquest itself began and ended with

---

2. What Carlo Ginzburg calls "the anomalies, the cracks that occasionally (albeit rarely) appear in the documentation, undermining its coherence." Ginzburg 1991, 10.

a large procession and involved the gathering of testimony in what must have been at times a rather crowded space. But canonization inquests were also public in a more technical sense. For notaries turned the witnesses' carefully translated and recorded testimony into what was dubbed a "public instrument."[3] The canonization inquest marked the moment in which private stories became a matter of public record. Evidence suggests that witnesses were well aware of the solemnity of such an occasion and that they relished the chance to have their stories—tales that must have been often rehearsed and even argued over—valorized by inclusion in such an authoritative piece of writing.

For the majority of participants in a canonization inquest—that is, the witnesses—the experience began with the receipt of a summons to appear before the papal subcommissioners. On a small scale, this summons paralleled the profusely worded and elegantly sealed letters of commission that initiated the canonization process among the panel of cardinals and their subdelegates. The notaries for the Toulouse inquest into Vincent's sanctity, Robertus Assolenti and Bertrandus Barbeti, kept a careful record of each summons that went out and included these annotations in their final report. The notaries' entries reveal that several local clerics were involved in summoning Toulouse witnesses, and it seems likely that they delivered their messages in person. While the text and exact form of the Toulouse summons orders do not survive, the notaries' report makes it clear that summoners informed witnesses that they were to appear on a certain date before the subcommissioners, specifying often the hour of vespers (sunset) or terce (9:00 a.m.) for the witness's appearance, and that they offered some sort of official "proof" of their mission. In a typical example, a priest named Guiglielmus (who did most of the summoning) reported:

> I, Guiglielmus de Cabisolis, priest [and] inhabitant of Toulouse, requisitioned by those named in the present letters, cited religious fathers Petrus de Columberio and Egidius Morelli of the Order of Preachers, found in their own persons in Toulouse, to appear on the said day at the hour of vespers before the lord official of Toulouse aforesaid [Joannes Arnaldi], to carry out the instructions contained in those letters, [my own] hand serving as authentication [*manus pro sigillo*], in the year aforesaid on the 18th day of the month of May.[4]

---

3. See Jones 2003c; Krötzl 1998; Wetzstein 2004a, 411–14 (making extensive use of the example of Vincent's process); Bartlett 2004, 106–8. On the various stages of written documents that emerged from canonization inquests, see Lett 2009.

4. *Proceso*, fol. 171r: "Ego Guiglielmus de Cabisolis presbyter Tholose habitator requisitus pro parte nominatorum in presentibus literis citavi religiosos viros fratres Petrum de Columberio et Egidium Morelli ordinis Predicatorum in propriis personis repertos Tholose comparituros dicta

While Guiglielmus's description leaves some details open to question (Was the summons carried out in person or by letter? Did Brothers Petrus and Egidius get to see the "present letters" of commission?), it is clear that witnesses in Toulouse at least received some sort of formal and legalistic notice ordering their appearance at the inquest.

A set of general instructions from Joannes Arnaldi, the Toulouse cathedral official who did most of the actual work in the inquest, adds some clarification. The original signed and sealed commission opening the Toulouse inquest was not to be trotted about town, but rather was to be kept available to show to any witness desiring to see it; alternatively, Joannes would be happy to provide a copy of the same. As for the witnesses cited, they were to appear in person before Joannes in the Toulouse cathedral "as quickly as possible" and at the very least "on the first juridical day after presentation of the summons." And, lest the witnesses fail to take seriously the order to testify, Joannes wished them to know that unless they should appear then and bring forth causes why they could not testify, they would suffer ecclesiastical censure, "as will be just and reasonable."[5]

When witnesses obeyed their summons—in Toulouse often on the same day it was presented[6]—they more than likely came to an impressive public space. In Naples, whose notaries left the clearest indications on this account, witnesses to Vincent's sanctity testified in the archbishop's palace, presumably next to the cathedral that still dominates the tangled web of narrow streets of the historic city center.[7] In Toulouse, according to Joannes's instructions, they came to the cathedral itself, the large impressive Gothic structure before which Vincent had preached to eager crowds in 1416.[8] Whether they offered their testimony inside the basilica or in some affiliated space such as the archbishop's palace or the chapter house is not clear. Only in Brittany, because of the plague raging in the duchy, were witnesses

---

die hora vesperorum coram domino officiali Tholosano retroscripto ad actus in literis contentos manus pro sigillo anno retroscripto et die decima octava mensis Maii." The list of names of witnesses appears at fol. 170v–171r, while an enumeration of each summons follows at 171r–172r.

    5. *Proceso,* fol. 170r–170v; FPC, 275–6 (with omissions): "Mandamus vobis quantocius citatis et peremptorie omnes et singulos infrascriptos et alios de quibus requiremini, ut die prima juridica post harum presentationem et aliis diebus fueritis requisiti,…intimantes eisdem citandis quod nisi tunc comparuerint et causas que obstent in contrarium allegaverint contra ipsos censura ecclesiastica et alias in hac parte per nos procedetur ut juris erit et rationis."

    6. In the Valencia manuscript, there are discrepancies between the date of summons and the date of testimony, although perhaps reflecting scribal error in copying the Palermo exemplar. Many witnesses appear on the same day on which the summons was noted, but for some the testimony is actually dated the day before the date of the reported summons (e.g., Petrus Gauterii, Fages's witness 12[bis], was summoned on June 1, 1454, but his testimony was recorded as given on May 29, 1454).

    7. For example, Joannes, bishop of Majorca, gave evidence "in prefato nostro Archiepiscopali palatio" (*Proceso,* fol. 290r; this phrase is omitted in Fages's edition).

    8. See note 5. On Vincent's stay in Toulouse, see Montagnes 1992.

asked to come to a less imposing site. Most of the Brittany witnesses were heard at the priory of Saint-Guen just outside Vannes, a dependence of the abbey of Saint-Gildas-de-Rhuys.[9] For the rest, the subcommissioners traveled to various towns throughout the duchy, and the notaries left no hint as to where they heard those witnesses.

When witnesses arrived before the panel of subcommissioners, they swore an oath before giving their testimony. In that respect, too, the experience of witnesses paralleled that of the officials charged with carrying out the canonization inquest. In the records from the Naples inquest, for example, the three subcommissioners described for the Roman curia how they had sworn to undertake their duties faithfully and diligently. Raynaldus, archbishop of Naples, and Joannes, bishop of Majorca, had sworn their oaths to the third of their company, Arnaldus, patriarch of Alexandria, placing their hands within his (*in manibus Arnaldi*) in a gesture of their fidelity. Arnald himself swore his oath "in the hands of Raynaldus,...placing his right hand on his chest, in the manner of prelates, [and] on God's holy gospels."[10] Witnesses went through a similar series of gestures in swearing to the truthfulness of their testimony. The testimony of each Naples witness, for example, includes the information that the deponent "was cited and produced and swore an oath in [i.e., with his hands between] our hands."[11] For Toulouse witnesses, the formulaic refrain has them "sworn to tell the truth about those things about which they will be interrogated."[12] Brittany witnesses were "received and sworn" on the Gospels before their testimony as well.[13]

For those witnesses who were old enough to remember Vincent Ferrer's sermons, this swearing of an oath must have been a particularly meaningful act. Vincent's crackdown on unnecessary swearing and oath taking was a constant theme in the testimony about the holy friar's preaching. According to canon law, an improperly taken oath constituted blasphemy, either through invoking the Lord's name in a nonserious matter ("I swear to God I saw him touch it!") or by including frivolous, untrue, or injurious words

---

9. See chapter 2.

10. *Proceso,* fol. 272v: "Et Arnaldus Patriarchus Alexandrini in manibus Raynaldi Archiepiscopi Neapolitani manum dexteram ad pectus more prelatorum ponendo ad Sancta Dei evangelia." On the gestures associated with oath taking, see Burrow 2004, 11–17; Schmitt 1990, 16–17, 61–62, 98–100; Arnoux 2002.

11. The recurring phrase is "testis citatus productus et in manibus nostris juratus."

12. E.g., Frater Petrus de Colomberis, "juratus deponere veritatem de his super quibus interrogabitur" (*Proceso,* fol. 176v; FPC 284, witness 2). Some variation of this phrase appears in each deposition.

13. E.g., Yvo Gluidic (*Procès,* witness 1; FPC, 3): "receptus iuratus et diligenter examinatus." See also the report by the subcommissioners (*Procès,* p. 22; FND, 392): "Testes...produxerunt quos...ad sancta dei evangelia in forma iuris de peribendo [prebendo] super contentis in dictis litteris superius insertis iuramentis...inquisivimus diligencius."

about the Creator ("By God's beard, I tell you!").[14] Vincent's sermons came down hard on such inappropriate speech, to apparent good effect. Witness after witness in Brittany noted that the duchy's inhabitants had ceased their swearing and blasphemy as a consequence of Vincent's sermons.[15] Similarly, in and around Toulouse, witnesses affirmed that after Vincent's advent "people scarcely swore by God or the saints, but just swore or in the place of swearing, they said, 'surely.'"[16] For those so attuned to the solemnity of *any* oath, the ceremony of swearing on the Gospels at the canonization inquest marked not simply the importance of the occasion but also a lesson in correct oath taking of which Master Vincent would surely have approved.

The witnesses "received and sworn" at the canonization inquests offered their testimony in a space that contained at least a few other people and often many more. At the minimum, witnesses faced at least one of the subcommissioners, at least one notary, and, for many of the witnesses, a translator.[17] The Naples inquest was probably the most intimate of the three surviving ones. According to annotations on each deposition, witnesses appeared at the archbishop's palace before a single notary and only one of the three subcommissioners in charge of the inquest. Nor was anyone else there waiting in the wings, either in the room or in a hallway or antechamber, for there was never a day during the Naples inquest on which more than one witness testified. In Toulouse, the whole affair was somewhat less quiet. True, one of the three commissioners, Joannes Arnaldi, single-handedly heard all but one of the witnesses' testimony. Yet there were several days on which a number of witnesses testified, all of them summoned to appear at the same hour.[18] In Brittany, the inquest was definitely an affair of many. The majority of the witnesses (that is, the first 239, who testified at Saint-Guen) appeared before a panel of three questioners and three notaries. Assuming that the panelists took no days off in the first stage of the process (November 21–December 8, 1453), they heard the testimony of, on average, 9 persons a day. Some days were much more crowded, however, for the 79th witness

---

14. See Leveleux 2001, 68, 78–81, 111.

15. E.g., Oliverius le Bourdiec (*Procès,* witness 6; FPC, 19) and Symon Maydo (*Procès,* witness 9; FPC, 31).

16. Jacobus Ysalgueri (*Proceso,* fol. 180v; FPC, 291, witness 4): "Et introduxit in civitate Tholose et aliis diversis locis circunstantibus, quod vix gentes jurabant per Deum nec alios sanctos sed solum jurabant, seu loco juramenti dicebant, seguramently."

17. On translators, see Krötzl 1999, 30–33; 1998, 132–36; Bartlett 2004, 106–8; Lett 2009.

18. E.g., Guillelmus Michaelis, Hugo Nigri, and Petrus Mollinus all testified on May 19, 1454 (*Proceso,* fols. 182v, 183v, 187r). According to the report by Guiglielmus de Cabisolis, the latter two were both summoned for the hour of vespers on May 19, and Guillelmus had been summoned to appear at vespers on the previous day (*Proceso,* fols. 171r–171v). At least seven witnesses were reportedly summoned for June 7, presumably at the hour of terce, which was the commission's default hour (*Proceso,* fol. 171v). Testimony of seven witnesses is recorded as having been given on June 2 (Fages's witnesses 14–20).

appeared before the panel on December 2 or 3.[19] That means that for the last week they were at Saint-Guen, the subcommissioners heard approximately 20 witnesses per day.

When witnesses did stack up, where did they wait? Did they stand and listen to the other testimony being given? Were they left to shiver outside in the December cold? Or were they shepherded into an antechamber so as to allow the testimony taken at the inquest to be "secret and apart," as the Brittany commissioners promised in their report?[20] If so, did they talk among themselves about the proceedings, the other witnesses, and their own testimony? From the surviving records, it is impossible to answer these questions with certainty. Evidence from the expansive and looser Brittany inquest, however, suggests that the taking of testimony was not as secret a matter as the commissioners made it out to be. Read carefully, the Brittany testimony gives an impression that witnesses either heard one another's testimony or otherwise had a good idea of what had already transpired in the inquest.

When the Brittany subcommissioners heard so many a day at Saint-Guen, many of those who testified must have waited their turn either in the room in which testimony was being taken or in some nearby space. Several of the depositions give the impression that at least some witnesses did hear others testify. For example, when the widow Oliva de Coatsal told the story of her son Guillermus's miraculous resuscitation some thirty-three years previously, she brought along Guillermus and his two brothers to corroborate her testimony. That they were in the room during their mother's testimony is suggested by the fact that the notaries did not list them as separate witnesses in their report, although they did record that the brothers had been "received and sworn." And the scribe noted that the brothers "testified that they had heard…about that miracle…just as their mother testified."[21] Similarly, when Katherina, the wife of Johannes Jegat, testified about the miraculous cure of her little son Bertrandus's case of plague, she brought forth the child and proudly showed him to the panelists.[22]

A slightly more problematic piece of evidence is provided by the numerous statements in the Brittany testimony that the witness under examination testified "as the preceding witness" had or as had some other named witness. It is certainly possible that such annotations represent an act of

19. Johannes Cire (*Procès,* witness 79; FPC, 114): "Deponit per suum juramentum quod die sabbati ultimo preterito prima instantis mensis decembris…[he lost some money] et omnia in crastinum…uxor cujusdam Johannis Caignart…sibi restituit. Et propterea…venit hic…ad sepulcrum ipsius M. V."

20. *Procès,* p. 22; FND, 392: "secreto et ad partem."

21. *Procès,* witness 73; FPC, 110 ("receptos et juratos"); ibid.: "Dixerunt et deposuerunt se in omnibus et per omnia de eodem miraculo et eius circumstantiis *sicut dicta eorum mater deposuit audivisse*" (emphasis added).

22. *Procès,* witness 67; FPC, 104.

shorthand on the part of the notaries, weary of writing page after page of nearly identical testimony. That appears to have been the situation, for example, in the depositions of two witnesses examined in Dinan in March 1454, Petrus Bonair and Brother Johannes Etaillet. In reporting each man's testimony, the notary indicated that the witness had testified "as [did] Robertus Juno."[23] Since Robertus Juno had testified three months earlier in Plumaugat, some twenty-seven kilometers southwest of Dinan, it is highly unlikely that the two Dinan witnesses were asserting their own conformity with his testimony.[24] Rather, it is much more plausible to assume that the annotation was the notary's.

Yet at other times, the notaries' apparent shorthand seems to reflect the witnesses' own words. So, for example, Alieta, wife of Perrotus Alanou, made note of the crowds of pilgrims at Vincent's tomb, "just as Perrotus Floc'h, the witness examined above, deposed."[25] Given that the notaries who recorded his testimony referred to Perrotus by the latinization "Petrus," it is possible that Alieta, who was only the second witness to testify after Petrus Floc'h's deposition, did in fact hear his rather detailed description of Vincent's tomb and referred her questioners back to Petrus's remarks, using a vernacular version of his name (Perrot). At any rate, Petrus was a high-ranking ducal official and must have been well known in and around Vannes.[26] Anyone wishing to add weight to his or her words would have done well to invoke the authority of Petrus Floc'h. And if the notaries really had wanted to save on ink and parchment, they could have abbreviated the testimony of Oliverius du Quirisec about the crowds visiting Vincent's tomb, for his words also echoed those of Petrus Floc'h, who had testified four places ahead of Oliverius.[27] In at least some cases, then, the evidence suggests that Brittany witnesses heard, and commented on, one another's testimony.

Examples from other canonization processes substantiate this notion. In the case of Philip of Bourges studied by Michael Goodich, for example, nearly two dozen witnesses were present throughout a three-day period

---

23. *Procès*, witnesses 243 (Petrus Bonair) and 249 (Frater Johannes Etaillet); FPC, 208, 212: "In effectu deponit ut Robertus Juno testis superius examinatus." Their testimony was heard by Radulphus, bishop of Dol, and Guillermus, abbot of St.-Jacut, and was recorded by the notary Radulphus de Rocha Calida, who took depositions in Dinan between March 11 and March 15, 1454.

24. Robertus Juno is witness 241, heard sometime between the subcommissioners' Christmas recess and March 11, 1454. The previous witness, Radulphus de Bosco Johannis (*Procès*, witness 240), and the first of three witnesses to be heard in Plumaugat, testified on December 15, 1453, and it seems likely the other two Plumaugat witnesses were heard around the same time.

25. *Procès*, witness 10; FPC, 37: "ut Perrotus Floch testis superius examinatus deposuit."

26. On Petrus Floc'h (Pierre Filloche), see Smoller 2006, 156–57; and Kerhervé 1987, 1:247.

27. *Procès*, witness 12; FPC, 40. Another example is provided by the cluster of witnesses who offered their versions of the miraculous cure of Perrinus Hervei. One, Michael Maceot (*Procès*, witness 30; FPC, 65), "deponit…ut Petrus Floch testis precedens." Many of the witnesses to this miracle had connections to one another and to the ducal court: Smoller 2006, 155–59.

of testimony, six of whom testified about a single miraculous cure from insanity.[28] As Goodich hypothesizes, the witnesses, who came from different parishes, would likely have become acquainted with one another during the three days of hearings, sharing and comparing their own stories and "reinforc[ing] their allegiance to the cult of Philip of Bourges."[29] Although testimony was supposed to be taken in secret and apart, as the promoters of Vincent Ferrer's cult well knew, the canonization inquest itself was good advertising for the nascent cult. At least one Breton witness reported that knowing that the canonization process was under way was what had prompted his wife to make a vow seeking Vincent's intercession.[30] Backers of the canonization could not have been unhappy for witnesses to talk among themselves while waiting to appear at the bench. Similarly, in a study of a miracle attributed to Thomas of Cantilupe, Robert Bartlett notes that several of the witnesses to the miracle had traveled to the inquest together and must have talked over the events, agreeing emphatically, for example, on the precise date of an event that had taken place some fifteen or sixteen years previously.[31] Indeed, modern scholars have remarked on the tendency of witnesses in canonization inquests to mimic the example of the first among them. Likewise, medieval experts in canon law cautioned against letting a witness "be informed by another and follow him."[32]

## Learning about the Saint: Vincent as New Apostle

The canonization inquest, then, functioned as a hub of communications. First, and most obviously, the questioners learned from witnesses about the potential saint, his mode of life, his deeds, and his miraculous intercession. But communications traveled in several directions. Witnesses learned, through the process of answering the subcommissioners' questions, about the potential saint as he was being packaged by the promoters of his canonization. This message was especially clear in cases in which specific articles of interrogation governed the questioning of witnesses, such as the Naples inquest into Vincent Ferrer's sanctity. But even in more loosely controlled proceedings, such as the Brittany inquest, witnesses could gather a sense of the picture of the putative saint that his promoters wanted to emerge from the inquest. For example, the testimony of the first four Brittany witnesses indicates that even without articles of interrogation, the subcommissioners were guiding witnesses through a series of topics beginning with a mention

---

28. Goodich 2006a, 102.
29. Ibid.
30. Petrus Villehorri, *Procès,* witness 259; FPC, 218.
31. Bartlett 2004, 30, 54–55.
32. Ibid., 55, citing Paul 1983, 23; and Hostiensis, as cited by Krötzl 1999, 22n16.

of their first notice of Vincent Ferrer, continuing with a discussion of his virtues and his fruitful preaching, and ending with notice of his miracles and his continuing reputation for sanctity.[33] Witnesses also must have spoken with one another. Those waiting to testify learned about the saint and about the inquest procedure, much as students make each other aware of the questions that appear on examinations and of the answers they themselves have already given. Finally, participants on both sides of the bench brought with them a lifetime of experiences and expectations that gave shape and color to their communications with one another.

In the case of Vincent Ferrer, it did not take much prodding to encourage witnesses to paint a portrait of an extraordinary preacher. They did so in ways that both echoed the words of their questioners and reflected their own understanding of charismatic preaching, gleaned from sermons, stained glass, wall paintings, or other devotional materials. Whereas Brittany witnesses were prompted to speak about Vincent's "fruitful" or "pleasing" sermons, and Toulouse witnesses were asked about Vincent's "fruitful preaching, with charity," Naples witnesses faced as many as seven highly specific questions about Vincent's preaching and its effects. The Naples articles of interrogation included questions about the crowds who followed Vincent from place to place to hear his sermons, his effectiveness in extirpating vices and implanting virtues in people's hearts, and his ability to heal feuds and convert Jews and Muslims. Naples witnesses were asked to detail Vincent's effectiveness in bringing enemies to concord and prostitutes to a better life, as well as his rigorous daily schedule of celebrating Mass and preaching. They answered questions about the prodigious knowledge of scripture apparent in Vincent's sermons and about his gift of tongues and were encouraged to see God's grace behind it all.[34]

In response to these sorts of questions, witnesses spoke of Vincent's preaching in ways that also reflected their own understanding of charismatic preaching. For example, although the suggestion does not appear in any of the questions asked at the inquests, numerous witnesses to Vincent Ferrer's preaching equated his voice, appearance, or words to those of an angel. This identification may have been prompted instead by Vincent's own self-projection. In his 1412 letter to Pope Benedict XIII, Vincent, alluding to himself in the third person, described himself as the angel in Revelation 14, sent to preach the upcoming judgment.[35] Later tradition would have it that in a

---

33. See chapter 2.

34. See, e.g., article XVII: "Item quod tanta gracia in dicendo Dei dono resplenduit ut presentibus in ejus predicatione multis millibus christianorum et in ydiomate ad dicendum differentibus omnes eum audirent sua lingua magnalia Dei loquentem" (*Proceso,* fol. 275r; FPC, 410). The complete set of articles appears in *Proceso,* fols. 273v–275r; FPC, 408–10 (abridged in places).

35. Edited in FND, 213–24; the pertinent passage is at 221.

sermon in Salamanca in 1412, Vincent had publicly declared himself to be the angel of the apocalypse. (By the sixteenth century, authors would relate that he resuscitated a dead woman just in order for her to confirm this identification.)[36] The reference in Vincent's letter was to Revelation 14:6–7: "And I saw another angel flying through the midst of heaven, having the eternal Gospel, to preach unto them that sit upon the earth and over every nation and tribe and tongue and people: [7] Saying with a loud voice: Fear the Lord and give him honor, because the hour of his judgment is at hand" (my translation, based on Douay-Rheims). In the minds of Vincent and many contemporary observers, he *was* that angel.

Clearly, Vincent's wide-ranging preaching mission, his gift of tongues, and the overtly apocalyptic content of many of his sermons reinforced the angelic parallel, and witnesses at the inquests offered numerous instances supporting the identification. So, for example, Naples witness Gaspar Peregrini (a knight and physician) noted that everyone who heard him said that Vincent was "an angel of God."[37] Several Toulouse witnesses also described Vincent's preaching as angelic in nature, with one Carmelite friar opining that, in preaching, Vincent's face appeared to be that of an angel.[38] And the Toulouse priest Joannes Regis related that during one sermon, as Vincent intoned the words, "Arise you dead and come to judgment," "his voice was so clear and loud that the hearts of the men and women who heard him were afraid and trembled." The priest, as well as others in the audience, believed "that then his voice was angelic, rather than human."[39]

If witnesses to Vincent's sermons tried to encapsulate their experiences by comparing Vincent to an angel, they also pointed to other well-known exemplars, namely, the apostles. The apostles' mission, as laid out, for example, in the risen Christ's injunction in Mark 16:15, was to go out to the four corners of the globe in order to preach and convert. Signs, such as the gift of tongues (received with the descent of the Holy Spirit at Pentecost) and the ability to cast out demons and work miracles, strengthened the apostles' work. The extent and effectiveness of their preaching was well known to

---

36. See Antist 1956, 172–73. See also FHSVF, 1:312.

37. *Proceso,* fol. 277r; FPC, 413, witness 3: "Populi eum audientes una voce proclamarent eum esse angelum Dei."

38. Galliardus de Ruppe, *Proceso,* fol. 225v; FPC, 364, witness 27[bis] ("vultum…tanquam angelicum"); similarly, Toulouse witnesses Raymundus Fabri (*Proceso,* fol. 190r; FPC, 304, witness 8) and Berengarius Alberti (*Proceso,* fol. 213v, 214v; FPC, 345, 347, witness 19).

39. *Proceso,* fol. 236v; FPC, 382, witness 36: "Et recordatur ipse testis quod una dierum, cum dictus frater Vincentius predicaret in dicta ecclesa Tholosana, et haberet dicere *Surgite mortui, et venit ad judicium* premissa proferendo vox eius fuit tam clara, tam alta, quod corda hominum & mulierum audientium timuerunt et tremuerunt. Et ipse loquens credit quod ut et plures etiam crediderunt, quod tunc sua vox fuit et erat potius angelica quam humana" (emphasis added). The phrase "Surgite mortui, et venit ad judicium" comes from a discussion of the Last Judgment in a *Regula Monachorum* sometimes attributed to Jerome: PL 30, col. 417.

late medieval audiences. According to the *Golden Legend,* a widely circulated collection of tales about the saints, Peter "converted three thousand men by his preaching on the day of Pentecost," and his mere shadow's passing was sufficient to effect miraculous healings.[40] Not surprisingly, then, Vincent Ferrer's long and far-flung evangelizing suggested parallels with the apostles. This identification was strengthened by his own report of the divine origin of his preaching mission. In the same 1412 letter to Benedict XIII, Vincent related that Christ had appeared to him in a sickbed vision and instructed him to go preach the gospel "apostolically" throughout the world. In fact, the earliest frescoes depicting Vincent Ferrer, probably from around 1429, well before his canonization, show him with the text of that authorizing letter.[41]

The most obvious and frequently mentioned parallel between Vincent Ferrer and the apostles was his ability to bridge all language barriers. Naples witnesses were specifically prompted to mention this gift of tongues and did so, as did, without similar prompts, most Toulouse and Brittany witnesses to Vincent Ferrer's preaching.[42] They also added to the apostolic gift of tongues an extraordinary ability on Vincent's part to make himself heard even at extreme distances. Both near and far away, members of his audience heard and understood him perfectly, as a Breton woman named Alieta Alanou testified, noting that she sometimes was near the preacher and sometimes far from him yet always heard his sermons.[43] In a dramatic illustration of the miraculous power of Vincent's voice, a Dominican friar from Toulouse related the story of a monk, forbidden by his abbot to journey the fifteen leagues to see Vincent preach in Toledo, who climbed the monastery's tower and was able to hear and write down Vincent's sermon word for word.[44] A Breton witness named Symon Maydo testified that "all the audience, both French and Breton speaking who did not know either French or [Master Vincent's Catalan], greatly profited from hearing his sermons." Symon added that he had quizzed several acquaintances who understood neither French nor "the Aragon vulgate," and "always these people in their own language, namely Breton, related to [him] what Master Vincent had said in his sermons,…whence [Symon] greatly marveled, and he believes that this happened to them by divine grace more so than by any other reason."[45]

---

40. Jacobus de Voragine 1993, 1:341.
41. Letter: FND, 220. Frescoes: Rusconi 1990, 213–18 (and figs. 1–4); see also chapter 5.
42. Naples article XVII: *Proceso,* fol. 275r; FPC, 410.
43. *Procès,* witness 10; FPC, 36.
44. Fr. Egidius Morelli (*Proceso,* fol. 179r–179v; FPC, 288–89, witness 3).
45. *Procès,* witness 9; FPC, 31–32: "Item deponit quod omnes astantes in suis missis et predicacionibus tam galici quam Britones britonizantes etiam non intelligentes eius vulgare et galicum multum proficiebant audiendo predicaciones suas.…Aliquando ipse testis a pluribus ignorantibus galicum et etiam vulgare aragonis…perquisivit quid proficiebant in dictis predicacionibus.…Continuo

A number of the witnesses who reported on Vincent's gift of tongues specifically linked him to the apostles in that context. For example, a Naples witness named Innocentius de Cubellis, a citizen of Vincent's hometown of Valencia, reported that those who heard Vincent preach said, "Truly he is an apostle, because anyone understands him in his own language."[46] An unnamed Naples witness noted that people said that Vincent "had the grace of the apostles" and the gift of tongues.[47] The Breton priest Oliverius le Bourdiec simply proclaimed, "As was commonly said by all, he was the best preacher, so that it be said that there had not been a greater doctor after Saint Paul."[48] The Toulouse witnesses Joannes Juvenis and Joannes de Avessane averred that there had been no better preacher since the apostles.[49]

But not everyone heard or understood the preacher perfectly. Small cracks in the solid mass of testimony about Vincent's gift of tongues suggest rather that those seeking to convey the experience of being present at one of his sermons looked to descriptions of the apostles for an appropriate comparison and thus emphasized (or exaggerated) Vincent's gift of tongues. This shaping of the testimony is most apparent in the Brittany inquest, where evidently no articles of interrogation prompted the witnesses to specifically mention the preacher's gift of tongues. For example, Johannes Rolandi testified that he had heard eleven of Vincent's daily celebrations of Mass and three-hour-long sermons but admitted that "in the first sermon he could not understand him well."[50] Still others acknowledged that the signs that Vincent made in his preaching helped them to comprehend his meaning. The Breton lawyer Prigentius Ploevigner noted that those who did not understand Catalan were able to retain the fruit of his sermons "with the help of the sweetness of his preaching" but also with "the signs that he made, and, as was commonly reported, divine assistance."[51] The Breton speakers whom Symon Maydo quizzed said that they "understood [Vincent] well both in

---

ipsi in vulgari suo videlicet Britonico referarunt eidem loquentem ea que ipse M. V. dixerat in suis predicacionibus quibus interfuerant....Unde ipse testis multum miratus fuit et credit quod hoc eis accidebat ex gratia divina melius quam alias."

46. *Proceso,* fol. 278r; FPC, 414–15, witness 4: "Vera est unus apostolus secundum quod unusquisque eum intelligit sua lingua loquentem magnalia Dei."

47. *Proceso,* fol. 257v; FPC, 438, witness 16: "Publice dicebatur ipsum fratrum Vincentium habuisse gratiam apostolorum."

48. *Procès,* witness 6; FPC, 19: "Erat etiam optimus predicator et dicebatur communiter et ab omnibus optimus predicator ita quod diceretur quod post beatum Paulum non fuerit maior doctor."

49. *Proceso,* fol. 217r; FPC, 351, witness 21; and *Proceso,* fol. 217v; FPC, 352, witness 22.

50. *Procès,* witness 13; FPC, 41: "In prima predicatione ipsum non poterat bene intelligere."

51. *Procès,* witness 2; FPC, 9–10: "Mediante dulcedine sermocinationis ejus ac signis que faciebat et nutu ut communiter ferebatur divino omnes fructum effectualem huiusmodi predicacionum reportabant et retinebant." For John of Capestrano's use of signs and interpreters, see Gecser 2003, 8–10.

word and with his signs."[52] Most tellingly, Alanus an Noblan, who as a young child had heard Vincent preach in Brittany, testified that he was a Breton speaker, did not understand French well, and had been a long distance from the preacher, so he had asked some other bystanders what Vincent had said and learned nothing more specific than that he had preached the Catholic faith and instructed the audience in some rudimentary practices.[53]

Furthermore, despite the miracle of the monk who climbed the tower reported by Toulousan witnesses, there were also limits to the reach of Vincent's voice. Yvo Gluidic, the first witness examined in Brittany, reported, as many would, that Vincent's entourage included a young secular cleric who instructed youth in such basics of the Christian faith as the Lord's Prayer, the Ave Maria, the Apostles' Creed, and how to make the sign of the cross. But Yvo also specified that Vincent's assistant took his young charges out of the range of Vincent's voice during the Mass and sermon, thereby acknowledging that there was in fact some place where one could not hear the preacher.[54] But for Christians steeped in tales of the apostles, Vincent's preaching truly shared in the same divine grace as did the disciples on Pentecost, when the Holy Spirit descended upon them in the form of tongues of fire, and filled with the Spirit, they began to speak in tongues. No wonder that many later portraits of the saint would depict him with tongues of flame playing about his head or in his open hand, an open allusion to his apostolic gift of tongues, as well as the actions of the Holy Spirit in inspiring his preaching.

Witnesses also described other aspects of Vincent's preaching in terms reminiscent of the deeds of the apostles. Whereas the apostles had confirmed their mission by signs and wonders, audiences at Vincent's sermons reported the crowds of possessed, sick, and crippled people who thronged the preacher afterwards seeking a miracle. As numbers of witnesses attested, Vincent would lay his hands on the afflicted person, make the sign of the cross over him or her, and then say, "They shall lay their hand upon the sick, and they shall recover" (Mark 16:18, Douay-Rheims translation).[55] Vincent's words were in fact those spoken by the risen Christ, as he sent his apostles out to preach the Gospel, describing the "signs [that] shall follow them that believe" (Mark 16:17). Not infrequently, the celebrated preacher was also called upon to cast out demons (also a sign in Mark 16:17), as reported, for example, by the Toulouse priest Petrus de Pelafiga.[56]

---

52. *Procès,* witness 9; FPC, 32: "Tam verbo qua signis suis ipsum bene intelligebant."

53. *Procès,* witness 149; FPC, 155.

54. *Procès,* witness 1; FPC, 4: "Et durante missa et predicatione eiusdem M. V. trahebat *extra auditum vocis dicti M. V.* juvenes pueros et ipsos instruebat in fide" (emphasis added).

55. E.g., Naples witness Fernandus, bishop of Telesia (*Proceso,* fol. 283v; FPC, 422, witness 9).

56. *Proceso,* fol. 233r; FPC, 377, witness 33. A woman possessed by a demon was brought to Vincent, who adjured her and sprinkled her with what he believed to be holy water. The woman, however, washed her face with the water, saying, "Oh how good this water is!" ("dicendo huius

Furthermore, the fruits of Vincent's preaching appeared to resemble the rich bounty reaped by the apostles. Witnesses reported huge numbers of Jews and Muslims converted by his preaching. For example, the knight Sanccius de la Maurella testified at Naples that in one six-month span Vincent had converted more than fifteen thousand Jews and Saracens in Castile and Aragon[57]—many more, incidentally, than Peter's three thousand on the day of Pentecost! Witnesses from Toulouse were particularly struck by the extreme penitence Vincent inspired in local populations, inducing people to take up nightly flagellant processions that in many cases persisted for years thereafter.[58] Prostitutes and their pimps were reformed, in some cases miraculously; blasphemy and swearing ceased, as witness after witness stressed.[59]

While witnesses to Vincent's preaching attempted to encapsulate its charismatic quality by comparing it to that of an angel or the apostles, they also used a wide range of references that pointed to his inspiration by the Holy Spirit. Not simply did Vincent possess the apostles' gift of tongues, but witnesses also noted in his preaching a wide range of signs of the activities of the Holy Spirit, as detailed in sermons and devotional literature. Mirk's *Festial,* for example, notes that Pentecost "ys called Whitsonday, for bycause þat þe Holy Gost as þys day broȝt wyt and wysdome ynto all Cristes dyscyples, and soo by hor prechyng aftyr ynto all Cristys pepull."[60] When witnesses made frequent reference to Vincent's wisdom, to his knowledge of the Bible by heart, or to the erudition of his sermons, their words pointed to the presence of the Holy Spirit in his mission. As the Carmelite friar Galliardus de Ruppe testified in Toulouse, not simply did Vincent have the appearance of an angel in his sermons, but also his preaching was "as if

---

verba. A tam bona es questa aygua") At those words, Vincent knew that the water had not been blessed, sent for more water, blessed it, and then again sprinkled it on the demoniac, whereupon at once the demon exited her body. Or in another instance, as reported by Naples witness Michael Albiol (*Proceso,* fol. 262r; FPC, 444, witness 19), he expelled a demon from a woman with the imposition of his hands and a simple prayer.

57. *Proceso,* fol. 279r; FPC, 416, witness 6.

58. E.g., Toulouse witness Petrus Bonaldi, bishop of Garlate (*Proceso,* fol. 208r; FPC, 336, witness 15): "Et post ipsius Magistri Vincentii recessum a Tholosa, tam dicte processiones quam etiam penitentes continuate et continuati fuerunt per multos annos." Toulouse witness Petrus Gauterii reported that among the flagellants were boys as young as four (*Proceso,* fol. 201r; FPC, 324, witness 12[bis]).

59. According to Naples witness Bernardus Catalanus de Pratz (*Proceso,* fol. 281r–281v; FPC, 419, witness 8), for example, when Vincent's preaching in Lérida (Lleida) converted all the prostitutes there, their pimps laid ambush for the holy man as he journeyed to the next town. But when Vincent made the sign of the cross over the approaching men, they laid down their arms and were converted to a better life, joining the entourage that followed Vincent in his journeys. On blasphemy, see, e.g., the testimony of Toulouse witness Fr. Hugo Nigri (*Proceso,* fol. 184v; FPC, 297–98, witness 6).

60. Mirk 1905, 159.

the Holy Spirit gave him eloquence."[61] A Toulousan canon lawyer named Joannes Hugonis told how a Franciscan master of theology had heard Vincent preach and had proclaimed that "the words he spoke were not his, but those of the Holy Spirit who was guiding [*gubernat*] him."[62] The Holy Spirit also must have hovered in the minds of the numerous witnesses who made mention of Vincent's copious tears. According to Jacobus de Voragine's discourse on Pentecost in the *Golden Legend,* for example, the Holy Spirit "generates a rain of tears."[63] Thus it was perhaps not merely a sign of Vincent's piety when witnesses like Naples physician Gaspar Peregrini noted that "in the celebration [of Mass], when he held the body of Christ in his hands, he wept greatly."[64] Vincent's tears also could have served to strengthen his identification with the apostles, in particular Peter, of whom Jacobus de Voragine writes, "He always carried a towel with which to wipe away his frequent tears."[65]

Audiences must have perceived the Holy Spirit also as the source of the ardor with which Vincent preached. Sermon literature stressed that the appearance of the Holy Spirit in the form of tongues of fire at Pentecost had brought the apostles not simply the gift of tongues but also the fire of effective preaching. As John Mirk put it, the Holy Spirit had appeared thus "for bycause þat þe apostolys and all oþyr prechours aftyr hom schuld speke brennyng wordys."[66] Jacobus de Voragine, too, in the *Golden Legend,* stressed "how necessary [the Holy Spirit] is to preachers…because he makes them speak fervently, without hesitation."[67] Echoes of the Holy Spirit's work thus probably lay behind the near unanimity with which witnesses made statements like the following testimony from Symon Maydo in Brittany: "Although [Vincent] was old and debilitated, so that it was necessary to help him to ascend the pulpit, nonetheless, when he celebrated Mass and preached, he appeared as strenuous and agile and strong as if he were thirty years old." Symon believed "this happened more through divine help than otherwise."[68]

---

61. *Proceso,* fol. 225v; FPC, 365, witness 27[bis]: "prout spiritus sanctus dabat eloqui illi."

62. *Proceso,* fol. 229r; FPC, 369, witness 29: "credatis quod verba que ipse dixit non sunt sua sed Sancti Spiritus qui eum gubernat."

63. Jacobus de Voragine 1993, 1:301, citing Ps. 147:18. Likewise, the fifteenth-century Dutch mystic Henricus de Herpf describes a "rivulet of tears" emanating from the Holy Spirit: Henricus de Herpf 1509, fol. r2 v.

64. *Proceso,* fol. 229r; FPC, 413, witness 3: "Item dicit quod in celebratione tenendo corpus Christi in manibus uberrime flebat."

65. Jacobus de Voragine 1993, 1:341.

66. Mirk 1905, 161.

67. Jacobus de Voragine 1993, 1:306.

68. *Procès,* witness 9; FPC, 32: "Item deponit quod licet ipse esset senex et debilis adeo quod oportebat sibi succurrere ad huiusmodi habitaculum ascendendendum [*sic*] nichilominus in actibus huiusmodi celebrationum et predicationum apparebat ita strenuus et agilis et fortis ac si esset etatis

The Holy Spirit also must have appeared to be at work in a miracle reported by several witnesses from Toulouse.[69] In the midst of one of Vincent's sermons, a youth perched on a high wall behind Vincent's platform had fallen asleep and appeared to be in danger of falling off, likely to his death. Although he was behind the preacher's view, Vincent stopped his sermon to issue a stern warning to "the one sleeping on the wall to wake up, lest he fall to his [death and] damnation."[70] This tale did not simply reinforce the notion that Vincent appeared to be, as one Toulouse witness put it, "inspired by the Holy Spirit…in all his acts"[71] but also served to link him again to the apostles. One of the miracles attributed to Saint Paul in the *Golden Legend* had him restoring to life a servant of the emperor Nero, who had climbed onto a windowsill to hear Paul preach, only to fall to his death. "Paul knew about this by the Spirit," we are told.[72] The story also serves to point out that not everyone found Vincent's preaching spellbinding enough to prevent him from nodding off in the midst of a three-hour sermon.[73] Like the testimony of the Breton witnesses who understood Vincent more by signs than by words—or not at all—this small crack in the solid wall of testimony about his preaching shows us the way in which witnesses framed their tales to conform to their notion of a charismatic preacher inspired by the Holy Spirit.

## Learning What Was Expected

While the canonization inquest represented a two-way conversation, with both interrogators and witnesses helping to shape its end result, the deposition chamber also became a place in which witnesses absorbed notions of sanctity and the miraculous that underlay the papal commissioners' work. Nowhere is this exchange more apparent than in the relatively free-form

---

triginta annorum tam in verbis quam gestu suis. Et credit quod hoc sibi accidebat plus nutu divino quam alias premissis attentis."

69. That is, Jacobus Ysalgueri, Galhardus Dahusti, Stephanus de Ardenta, and Joannes Regis (Fages's witnesses 4, 17, 27, and 36).

70. As reported by the knight Jacobus Ysalgueri, who opined that Vincent's outburst must have originated in "an angelic warning or divine permission." *Proceso,* fol. 181r; FPC, 291, witness 4: "Non valens videre dictum dormientem cum esset retro ipsum ex denuntiatione Angelica, aut divina permissione,…ipse Frater Vincentius alta voce interrumpens sermonem suum…dicit alta voce verba sequentia seu similia Digan en aquell dolent qui dorm sus la muralla que sesvele altrament tombera e fara son dany."

71. Galhardus Dahusti (*Proceso,* fol. 211r; FPC, 341, witness 17): "spiritu sancto in dictum patrem reverendum inspirante qui in omnibus actibus suis videbatur inspirare videre ipsius loquentis."

72. Jacobus de Voragine 1993, 1:352.

73. Indeed, as one witness to the miracle noted, "Those who saw the youth were afraid he would fall and began murmuring." Galhardus Dahusti (*Proceso,* fol. 210v; FPC, 340, witness 17): "videntes perterriti de case aliquo murmure tumultuarunt."

testimony on miracles from the Brittany inquest.[74] In truth, what exactly made an event a miracle was a subject on which Christian authors had not entirely agreed. Between the time of the church fathers and that of the great scholastic theologian Thomas Aquinas (1225–74), the very concept of "miracle" had undergone an important shift in theological writings. No longer defined by its "gee whiz!" effects, a miracle was now identified by its divine cause; any event, however extraordinary, for which a natural cause could be posited was not a miracle in this new definition. The miracle stories Brittany witnesses told at the canonization inquest show that even ordinary people were aware of the newer scholastic understanding of the miraculous, for they structured their tales in such a way as to prove that the phenomena they described defied natural explanation.

The original meaning of "miracle" (Latin, *miraculum*) was a thing to be wondered at or *admired*; the root for both words is the same Latin verb, *miror*.[75] In the eyes of the influential church father Saint Augustine, the whole of Creation was a "miracle" in that humans should feel wonder and awe at all of God's handiwork.[76] Illustrations of miracles throughout the Middle Ages and Renaissance reflected that fundamental root meaning by depicting witnesses to miracles with their hands raised in a gesture of admiration and wonder.[77] Still, the scholastic theologians of the high Middle Ages sought to define exactly what it was about a given event that made it the object of the sort of admiration and wonder implied by the epithet "miracle." In the hands of authors like Thomas Aquinas, a miracle was defined as an event that fell outside the normal pattern or capacity of nature and that, lacking a natural cause, could only be attributed to divine intervention.[78] The canonization process, in part, aimed at allowing the College of Cardinals to determine whether alleged instances of intercession by the candidate for sainthood were in fact miracles according to that definition. Specifically, at canonization inquests from the thirteenth century on, those who testified about miracles were supposed to answer a list of questions about the circumstances of the alleged miracle; other witnesses to the events; the words used to invoke the putative saint's intercession; the date, length, and severity of the illness (in the case of a cure); and possible natural explanations for the event in question.[79] It was not uncommon for witnesses at canonization inquests to name physicians, barbers, or surgeons who could confirm the nonnatural

---

74. I draw here on Smoller 1997.

75. On definitions of the miraculous, see Ward 1987, chap. 1; Goodich 1995, 4–6, 148–49; Smoller 1997, 338–39; Daston 1991.

76. Ward 1987, 3–6.

77. Bynum 2001, 41–42, 44–47, although Bynum notes (59) that in medieval texts miracles seldom evoke wonder.

78. Thomas Aquinas 2012, Ia 105, art. 7, ad 1, 2; art. 8.

79. Vauchez 1997, 50, gives a general *forma interrogatorii;* see also Goodich 1995, 159n19.

character of the cures to which they testified and for inquest panels to call upon those healers' expertise.[80]

The papal subcommissioners at the Brittany inquest into Vincent Ferrer's sanctity were careful to gather testimony that would satisfy the questions set out by the Roman curia. While witnesses testified in response to a general question "about miracles," the commissioners did not hesitate to interrupt their stories to ask for the sorts of details of interest to the cardinals in Rome.[81] The commissioners might ask a witness, for example, to name other eyewitnesses to an alleged miracle or to provide the words of the vow to Vincent that preceded his intercession. Most important, they would interrupt a tale with questions designed to rule out a natural explanation of the putative miracle, seeking to know the details of an illness cured or what medical remedies the patient might also have tried. For example, when Alanus de Cressoles testified that his broken leg had been cured after a vow to Vincent Ferrer, a question from the commissioners forced him to admit that "one skilled in medical arts had given him a plaster [cast]."[82] The butcher Yvo Le Houssec, describing his cure from a progressively debilitating illness of three years' duration, was interrupted and "asked if he had had any medicines or other remedies against this infirmity." Yvo, at least, was able to answer, "no, and that he had been cured solely at the intercession of Master Vincent."[83]

The papal commissioners also carefully quizzed witnesses who told stories of the resuscitation of a dead person, the ultimate healing that both imitated Christ's miracles and had become increasingly common in the later Middle Ages, if we are to believe miracle collections.[84] After Johanna Aufray told of the resuscitation of her neighbor Alieta's stillborn son, the commissioners asked her "how she knew that said offspring, in her estimation, was not alive." Among other signs of the infant's stillbirth, Johanna noted that "the afterbirth [*lectus suus*] by which he was nourished in his mother's womb…came out of the womb entirely along with said offspring, not in the fashion of other births."[85] When a woman named Richarda told the story of

---

80. Ziegler 1999.

81. Brittany witnesses did not respond to specific articles of interrogation, but miracle tales are generally preceded by the phrase "Interrogatus/a de miraculis." See Smoller 1997, 337–38.

82. *Procès,* witness 20; FPC, 52: "Interrogatus si habuit medicinam dicit quod unus probus in arte medicinis dedit sibi unum emplastrum."

83. *Procès,* witness 27; FPC, 61: "Interrogatus si habuerit medicinas vel alia remedia contra hujusmodi infirmitatem dicit quod non et quod solum ad intercessionem M. V. fuerit sanatus ut firmissime credit."

84. Vauchez 1997, 467–68. Still, the fifteenth-century Dominican archbishop Antoninus of Florence called the resuscitation of the dead "maximum miraculum." Antoninus Florentinus 1484, fol. CCIXv.

85. *Procès,* witness 69; FPC, 107: "Interrogata quomodo scit quod dictus partus suo videre non haberet vitam….Et dicit quod erat frigidus et lectus suus quo nutritus extiterat in ventre matris

the resuscitation of Johannes Guerre, an archer who was badly wounded in a fight with another archer, the commissioners waited until the end of her tale, then "asked if she believed that said Guerre was [really] dead." Responding in the positive, Richarda noted that "she saw him, rigid and stiff like the dead; nor did he exhale any breath from his body."[86] Nor was a presumably learned cleric exempt from such questioning. When Oliverius Bourric, rector of the parish church of Montcon and a chorister in the Vannes cathedral, told the same story, at the moment in the narrative where Guerre appeared to die, the commissioners interrupted him to ask "how he knew this." The obliging priest described how "he touched and palpated his mouth, nostrils, ears, throat, chest, and many other places in his body, and in all those places he was cold, stiff, and rigid, like the dead, of whom he had seen many."[87]

Not simply could Bretons who testified about Vincent's miracles provide answers designed to confirm the nonnatural character of the resuscitations and cures they described, but witnesses also offered these sorts of details spontaneously, without the prodding questions of the commissioners.[88] The noble widow Oliva de Coatsal's tale of her own infant son's death and resuscitation included such words of proof. After describing how the poor boy had become progressively sicker over the course of a week, she arrived at the story's nadir: "One day, around noon, he came to his death, in the witness's judgment, because he was cold, stiff, and colored like a dead person, and he did not breathe, because this witness checked in several ways, both at his mouth, as well as at his nostrils and his ears."[89] Without being asked, Oliva cataloged the signs that indicated her son was truly dead (including, evidently, the lack of breath from his ears!). The widow Ludovica, describing

---

et quem testis ipsa sic nominabat venerat totaliter cum eodem partu extra ventrem ultra modum aliorum partuum." Interestingly, the child is never described as dying. It is born as a *partus* without life, and "vita eidem partui data fuerit ad intercessionem dicti M.V." Only after the "resuscitation" does Johanna shift from calling the infant a *partus* and refer to it as a *filius*. It is possible that the infant lived (after the vow to Vincent) long enough simply to be baptized, a commonly reported miracle, on which see Finucane 1997, 42–46. As Finucane observes (43), some parents seem to have believed that the act of baptism actually created the infant's soul, which may explain Johanna's language.

86. *Procès*, witness 51; FPC, 91: "Interrogata si credit quod dictus Guerre fuerit mortuus respondet quod sic quia ipsa vidit eum in dicta domo rectum et durum ut mortuum nec exhibat hanelitus de corpore suo." Guerre, described as archer of the duke of Brittany, whose resuscitation was reported to have occurred around five years before the 1453–54 inquest, likely formed part of the militia of *francs archers* from each Breton parish originally raised by Duke Jean V in 1425 and created again in the 1440s. See Galliou and Jones 1991, 242.

87. *Procès*, witness 52; FPC, 91: "Interrogatus quomodo hoc scit dicit quia ipse testis tetigit et palpavit eum tam in ore quam naribus auribus guture pectore et multis aliis locis corporis et in omnibus erat frigidus durus et rigidus sicut mortui sunt quorum plures ipse testis vidit."

88. See Smoller 1997, 338.

89. *Procès*, witness 73; FPC, 109: "devenit uno die circa meridiem alias non recordatur judicio testis ad mortem quia fridigus rectus et coloratus ut mortuus erat nec hanelabat quia ipse testis pluribus modis tam per os quam per nares et aures hoc respexit."

her own miraculous cure after a vow made to Vincent Ferrer, was careful to note not only that physicians had diagnosed her illness as leprosy but also that she had "had recourse to several physicians" and "had received many cures and taken many curative baths, and none had benefited her in the least."[90] As if to reinforce this testimony about the supernatural character of her healing, the commissioners asked her why she believed that she had been cured through Vincent's intercession, a question Ludovica answered with the fact that "the physicians had told her that they feared that her disease was incurable."[91]

The fact that some Brittany witnesses would spontaneously offer their interlocutors precisely the sorts of confirming details others were asked to provide after being interrupted suggests that witnesses did indeed share the experience of testifying with one another. Whether from direct observation of others' testimony or from conversations snatched in a waiting room or in the narrow streets and public squares of Vannes, many Brittany witnesses understood quite well that a convincing miracle story required more than a dire problem and its happy resolution. The tale also needed to demonstrate the supernatural character of the supposedly miraculous resolution. While medieval audiences frequently heard miracle tales in sermons preached on feast days, such narratives often focused on the miracle's didactic purpose. There was no need in a sermon to prove or authenticate the miracle by reference to eyewitnesses, named beneficiaries, or details of the event's supernatural qualities. What mattered was that the saint in question had listened to the requests of the faithful and could intercede with God (or punish a doubter or blasphemer) and that his miraculous intercession worked to strengthen the faith. The new scholastic definition of the miraculous became most apparent, rather, at those moments where a miracle was put to the test, such as at a canonization inquest. For ordinary believers, that many-sided conversation that was the *inquisitio in partibus* may unwittingly have served as a classroom in which they absorbed the learned understanding of miracles and demonstrated their ability to return the correct sorts of responses.[92]

## Shaping the Narratives of the Saint: Vincent as Plague Saint

While the canonization inquest could serve as a means through which the clergy in charge suggested a portrait of the potential saint (Vincent as

---

90. Ludovica, widow of Johannes Durant, *Procès,* witness 54; FPC, 94: "Ipsa habuit propter hoc [infirmitatem] recursum ad plures medici et inter alios ad magistrum Georgium Nourri et recepit multas medelas et habuit multa balnea et nichil sibi profuerunt."

91. *Procès,* witness 54; FPC, 94: "Interrogata quare sic credit respondet quod medici dixerant sibi quod dubitabat ne sua predicta infirmitas esset incurabilis."

92. As I argue more fully in Smoller 1997.

apostolic preacher) and taught the faithful the correct meaning of the miraculous, individual witnesses could also place their own stamp on the proceedings. This fact becomes most apparent in the emergence of Vincent Ferrer as one of the major plague saints of the fifteenth and sixteenth centuries. Art historians have often been puzzled or, frankly, misled by Vincent's appearance in paintings and woodcuts in the company of well-known plague saints like Sebastian and Roch.[93] Their confusion is understandable for one who knows only the official *vita* of the saint, composed just after his canonization by fellow Dominican Pietro Ranzano. In detailing Vincent's miracles, Ranzano breathes scarcely a word about his intercession's serving to protect or cure a postulant from plague.[94] Nor was plague evidently on the minds of the Dominican promoters of Vincent's canonization. Plague does not appear in either the brief headings for questioning prepared for the Toulouse canonization inquest or the more detailed articles of interrogation supplied to the commissioners for the Naples inquest by the Dominican master general Martial Auribelli. If those articles and Ranzano's *vita* represent in some sense an "official" line, one that hoped to hold up Vincent Ferrer (or any saint) as a model for imitation, Vincent's emergence as a plague saint indicates the strength of a more popular image of saints as healers.

The notion of Vincent Ferrer as plague saint, then, comes not from Ranzano's *vita* or any prodding by the promoters of his canonization but rather from the testimony at the relatively unstructured Brittany canonization inquest. That inquest, as mentioned in chapter 2, took place against a backdrop of plague, whose ravages caused the postponing of the opening trip to the Vannes cathedral and prompted many of the miracle tales told to the papal commissioners. True, the association of Vincent Ferrer with the duchy's plague epidemic may not have originated entirely with the Breton populace. As I suggested above, the Dominican clergy and other supports of Vincent's sainthood may have been the ultimate source of the persistent rumor that, as one prominent Breton put it, "plague will not cease unless [Vincent's] canonization should succeed."[95] Nonetheless, the testimony at

---

93. E.g., Zucker 1992, esp. 187–91 (Zucker is unable to come up with a satisfactory explanation for Vincent's inclusion in the groupings with other plague saints, other than finding a passage in which Vincent writes, "I am a plague spot," 187); and Saffrey 1982, esp. 292–23. Louise Marshall reproduces a late fifteenth-century plague panel, without recognizing Vincent Ferrer as its subject (a Dominican saint with his index finger gesturing toward the heavens, a frequent attribute of Vincent). Marshall 1994, 514, fig. 12.

94. RVV, 1:511, mentions only one miraculous cure from plague (*epidimia*), that of a man in Saragossa named Joannes Zanitus, whose cure had also been related by Naples witness Joannes, bishop of Majorca (*Proceso*, fol. 291r; FPC, 432, witness 14), who gives the man's name as Joannes de Sammano (Fages renders it Salmarina).

95. Herveus Maydo (*Procès*, witness 18; FPC, 48): "Et dicit quod multi timorati credunt quod pestis non cessabit nisi procedatur ad canonizationem suam."

the inquest shows that many Bretons eagerly embraced the idea of Vincent as protector against the plague they so feared.

One may perhaps also object that the parish processions to Vincent's tomb mentioned by so many witnesses mark another instance in which the clergy (who presumably organized the processions) attempted to manipulate popular opinion.[96] Still, witnesses were sincere in their estimation that such processions had decreased the severity of plague in their villages. As the peasant Guillermus Terronin told the papal commissioners, the two processions mounted by his parish of Noyal Muzuillac, some seventeen miles from Vannes, were so effective in obtaining Vincent's intercession that whereas "then and before, plague was so raging that a hundred persons would die of plague in a week," after the processions, "it was so mitigated that scarcely a person died in a week or in two weeks."[97] In the estimation of the peasant Oliverius Connan, after his parish of Ploeandren had organized a procession to Vincent's tomb some five weeks previously, only three infants had died of the disease, as opposed to the "five, six, seven, eight, or nine cadavers a day, at least" before the procession. That number had included Oliverius's own wife and all of his children but his sixteen-year-old son Yvo, saved, just before the parish processions, by the father's tearful vow to the Virgin Mary and Vincent Ferrer.[98] Even if it was a story line suggested by a clergy perhaps too eager to see the canonization of a "local" saint, the tale of Vincent's intercession protecting an individual, a household, or even an entire village from the plague was one that many Bretons readily made their own.[99]

Take, for example, the story told by Katherina, who, together with her husband, Johannes Jegat, knew all too well the heavy hand of plague's scourge. After the death of one of their sons from plague, she informed her husband that "it was just as well if he were [also] to get enough wood for a coffin

---

96. Examples of such processions in the testimony of Fr. Johannes Le Bonner (*Procès*, witness 72; FPC, 108), Guillermus Terronin (*Procès*, witness 102; FPC, 132), Yvo Marec (*Procès*, witness 103; FPC, 132), and Oliverius Connan (*Procès*, witness 128; FPC, 146). Yvo Natalis, a member of the Vannes cathedral clergy, testified about the many processions that had taken place starting on the Feast of Saint Michael (September 29), after which plague had mitigated (*Procès*, witness 239; FPC, 198).

97. *Procès*, witness 102; FPC, 132: "tunc et per antea [pestis] vigebat in ea adeo quod in ebdomada moriebantur centum persone de peste huiusmodi vel eo circa. Et ex post dicta pestis est ibi taliter mitigata quod non moriuntur nisi aliquando in ebdomada et aliquando in duabus preter unam personam."

98. *Procès*, witness 128; FPC, 146: "postquam…tres infantes tantummodo in eadem parrochia mortui sunt et ante huiusmodi processionem quamplurimi peribant ita quod essent cadaveri in die quinque sex septem octo vel novem ad minus."

99. There are some Brittany witnesses who note that the idea for the vow that saved them or their loved ones from plague came from the priest: e.g., Alanus Guerric (*Procès*, witness 190; FPC, 177) and Johannes Guidomari (*Procès*, witness 274; FPC, 229). All in all, 90 of the 313 Brittany witnesses mentioned miracles having to do with the plague (not including descriptions of processions against the plague).

for Bertrandus," another of their children, since he was already ill, his skin marked by the signs of death witnesses called *pineures*[100] and his body rapidly becoming cold. That last motherly mixture of compassion and practicality proved too much for Katherina, however. As she told the papal commissioners, at that point she began to cry and "lamenting, say that God had taken her boy[s]—for by now they had all died of plague besides [Bertrandus] and one daughter aged, then, one week—to the number of ten." With her husband fetching the wood for two small coffins, a sick child in bed, and a week-old infant presumably at her breast, Katherina, clearly at the end of her rope, asked her husband's brother Oliverius to go to the Vannes cathedral and have a Mass said for little Bertrandus. And "before said Oliverius had gone three stones' throw from the house," Bertrandus, who had not eaten in four days, ate a little bit of egg and appeared to be better. Within a few days, he was totally cured and, nearly a year later, accompanied his proud mother to illustrate her testimony at the canonization inquest.[101] Katherina's tale offers a glimpse into the reasons why Bretons so eagerly accepted the notion of Vincent as a plague saint. Not simply did his intercession represent hope in a moment of hopelessness, but it also offered a path to the healing of Katherina's own grieving heart. When ten children had died, to be able to focus on the miracle that saved one of them was a blessing indeed, one that many Bretons readily adopted.

Although Pietro Ranzano, in his official life of the newly canonized Vincent, chose not to build a case for Vincent's power against plague, there were other early biographers of the saint who had seen the canonization inquests and who did pick up on that aspect of Vincent's career. In a short biography that formed part of his *Chronicle,* Archbishop Antoninus of Florence (d. 1459) appended a list of a dozen or so miracles worked after the saint's death. The archbishop clearly had read the Brittany canonization inquest, for he included a description of the resuscitation of the son of a certain "Perrinus" (that is, Perrinus Hervei, whose liberation from possession was the first miracle described in the inquest) after the boy's death from plague.[102] In a 1470 brief *vita* of the new saint based in part on Antoninus's work, Francesco

---

100. Red, purple, or black blotches on the skin, likely *petechiae,* a sign of sepsis.

101. *Procès,* witness 67; FPC, 104: "Dixit eidem testa quod melius esset quod portaret etiam asseres pro feretro Bertrandi .... Testis ipsa incepit clamare et lamentando dicere quod deus dimitteret sibi puerum suum cum iam omnes alii essent mortui dicta peste preter eum et unam filiam etatis illo tunc unius septimane ad numerum decem.... Et antequam dictus Oliverius frater a domo per tres jactus lapidis discessisset prefatus puer qui per antea a quatuor diebus non comederat comedit de uno ovo et apparuit melius habere et infra paucos dies post sanatus fuit et ex post usque nunc vixit et vivit prout eum nobis ostendit."

102. Antoninus Florentinus 1484, fol. CCXr. Cf. the testimony of Johanna, wife of Perrinus Hervei (*Procès,* witness 15; FPC, 44), where the infant does not in fact die but is at the point of death ("de cuius morte magis quam vita sperabatur").

Castiglione, too, offered a short list of posthumous miracles drawn from the canonization inquests. Among the eleven miracles he related from the Brittany inquest appeared the story of a Vannes man named Oliverius whose six-year-old daughter was cured of plague at Vincent's tomb.[103] Castiglione's biography and list of miracles circulated as a preface to an early edition of Vincent's sermons and therefore offered some publicity for Vincent's power to intercede against plague.

The writings of Antoninus of Florence and Francesco Castiglione, not the official biography penned by Pietro Ranzano, must have inspired the artists who portrayed Vincent among such better-known plague saints as Sebastian and Roch. Vincent appears, for example, alongside Saint Sebastian in the altarpiece, attributed to the school of Giovanni Bellini, in the Dominican basilica of Santi Giovanni e Paolo in Venice, and with Roch and Sebastian in an altarpiece executed by the workshop of Domenico Ghirlandaio for the Malatesta chapel in the church of San Domenico in Rimini. Similarly, a fifteenth-century triptych by Andrea da Murano pairs Vincent and Roch, with Sebastian and Peter Martyr flanking them, while a woodcut from Ravenna depicts the same group, now placing Vincent with Sebastian.[104] In his diary the seventeenth-century Barcelona tanner Miquel Parets recounts how his wife, preparing bravely for her own death from plague, requested that he have sung for her the Mass of Saint Vincent Ferrer.[105] This image of Vincent as having power over plague arose without the push of the most powerful and influential backers of the holy preacher's sanctity. Instead, it was a notion that gained currency in the stories told by grateful Bretons at the canonization inquest.

## Storytelling and Self-Promotion

While the testimony of earnest witnesses could shape the identity of the potential saint in ways perhaps not imagined by (or necessarily welcome to) the promoters of his canonization, the inquest also offered witnesses

---

103. Castiglione 1496, at fols. a1v–a5r. The miracle appears at fol. [a4r] and corresponds to the miraculous cure of her daughter Johanna related by Alieta, wife of Oliverius Collet (*Procès,* witness 170; FPC, 167–68); in Alieta's tale, after her husband's vow to Vincent Ferrer resulted in the girl's cure, she brought the girl to Vincent's tomb in thanksgiving, and, while Alieta knelt with her head and hand on the tomb, she felt the sepulchre move (as also noted by Castiglione, who, however, conflates the story's two moments). A modern edition of Castiglione's text from a manuscript in Florence (Biblioteca Nazionale Centrale di Firenze, Conventi Soppressi, MS J-VII-30, ff. 33–45v) can be found in Wittlin 1994, 16–27. Castiglione's list of miracles also appears in *AASS,* Aprilis, 1:510–11.

104. For a discussion of the Bellini and Ghirlandaio altarpieces, see chapter 5. Murano: Réau 1959, 3 (pt. 3): 1331; Humfrey 1988, 415, fig. 12; Zucker 1992, 188, fig. 8. Woodcut: Zucker 1992, 189; Areford 2010, 124, fig. 46. For more examples, see chapter 5.

105. Parets 1991, 68.

the opportunity to tell stories that furthered an even more personal agenda. In a still largely oral world, the act of having one's story committed to writing and signed with a notary's seal must have appeared as a tremendous affirmation. Again, this is a pattern that emerges most clearly in the relatively unguided testimony gathered at the Brittany inquest into Vincent's sanctity, and particularly in cases in which several witnesses testified to the same miracle. In some cases, telling a miracle story simply offered a way of getting at neighbors, in the way that people often have of subverting the agenda of any official bureaucracy to their own private ends.[106] Occasionally, though very rarely, a witness could use the opportunity to tell a miracle story to further a petty rivalry or grudge. For example, after Johanna Gualtier came before the Brittany subcommissioners to testify to her miraculous cure from a disease involving swelling and paralysis, a neighbor and then Johanna's former maid each stepped up to corroborate the story of the cure. But they both added that Johanna's disease had rather been a case of possession by demons. As the former maid testified, Johanna herself had "many times called on demons…and uttered other similar unclean words."[107] Clearly, Johanna's maid did not see her mistress's illness in as innocent a light as Johanna herself presented it.

For others, however, the miracle about which they testified marked a high point in a deeply spiritual life. Through a careful reading of their testimony, we can glimpse the sort of rich interior existence experienced by those persons—both lay and clerical—who attempted to lead such a life in the later Middle Ages. Two sorts of details, it appears, set the miracle stories told by those persons apart from those of their neighbors. The first was a careful attention to the liturgical calendar, meaning not simply an awareness of religious time but also a tendency to bring details of the liturgy into one's own experience of or memory of events. The second was the teller's appropriation of a fairly common understanding that a successful invocation of a saint's intercession reflected something positive about the invoker's own spiritual worth.[108]

In the Middle Ages, the agricultural calendar and the "church's time" of the liturgical year frequently provided the temporal framework upon which

---

106. See, e.g., Given 1997, esp. chap. 6.

107. The witnesses are Johanna, wife of Mathelinus Gualtier (*Procès*, witness 183; FPC, 172–73); Anthonius Roant (*Procès*, witness 184; FPC, 173–74); Ameota, widow of Luca Locquemeren (*Procès*, witness 185; FPC, 174), who added that Johanna "invocabat demones dicta durante infirmitate per sex menses dumtaxat quibus durantibus fuit inclusa"; and the maidservant Johanna, wife of Johannes Courbin (*Procès*, witness 186; FPC, 175), whose deposition noted that "multotiens ipsa Johanna vocabat demones et dicebat quod demones juxta eam erant et consimilia verba inhoneste vociferabat."

108. See, e.g., the comments about the spiritual condition of the vower in Finucane 1997, 13, 72.

individuals situated their memories of the past.[109] In fourteenth-century Brittany, for example, witnesses at canonization inquests for Saint Yves and for Charles of Blois recalled events by reference either to the seasons ("last winter," "two summers ago") or the appropriate feast day ("around last Feast of John the Baptist," "the Wednesday after Pentecost"). Numerous witnesses at the inquest for Vincent Ferrer dated the stories they told with respect to the liturgical calendar.[110] And for some of those persons, what they heard in sermons on feast days became inscribed in their memories of events happening around the same time. True, these were not just any events but the already spiritually charged miracles worked by Vincent Ferrer's intercession. For those attuned to spiritual issues, the miracle and the liturgy could blend together into a coherent whole.

For example, one of the most dramatic miracle stories to come out at the Brittany inquest was the tale of the near drowning of a youth named Johannes Gueho. Four witnesses testified to this miracle: Johannes Le Vesque, described as a married cleric, probably in minor orders; Petrus Cadier, a merchant; Thomas Tournemote, a weaver; and Margota Boudart, a *domicella,* or woman of the lesser nobility.[111] All four witnesses agreed on the basic outline of the story. The near disaster had occurred the previous year, on the vigil of the Feast of Saints Peter and Paul (that is, on June 28), when a youth called Alanus Bouic tried to teach Gueho to swim in the river near the town of Josselin. The two boys had gotten out into deep water near a mill, where they quite literally found themselves in over their heads; Bouic had swum to safety, leaving Gueho behind. When he went under for the third time, Margota Boudart and then all the bystanders called on Vincent Ferrer to intercede, at which point Gueho miraculously floated back to shore. There the anxious bystanders took him up, wrapped him in a tunic, and marveled at his rescue.

Witnesses differed on certain details of the story. For example, Johannes Le Vesque, Petrus Cadier, and Thomas Tournemote claimed that Gueho had died before the vow to Vincent Ferrer, and thus the miracle consisted in both his resuscitation and his return to shore. Margota Boudart was not sure that Gueho had died but insisted that he had been rescued from the danger of death by the saint's intercession. Johannes Le Vesque and Margota Boudart noted their surprise that no water had come out of Gueho after he was pulled from the river; the two others did not recall this detail at all.

---

109. For the notion of "church's time," see Le Goff 1980.

110. Leguay and Martin 1982, 134 (inquests for Yves and Charles of Blois). Approximately 25 percent of the Brittany witnesses at the inquest for Vincent Ferrer dated events by the liturgical calendar. See also Paul 1983, 28–31.

111. *Procès,* witnesses 41–44; FPC, 79–82. I treat this case in Smoller 1998, 440–43. On married clerics, see D'Avray 2005, 157–67.

Even more striking, however, are the differences in the witnesses' memories of what happened between the time of the vow to Vincent Ferrer and the time that Gueho recovered from his trauma. According to three of the witnesses, after the vow to Vincent Ferrer, Gueho was conveyed miraculously across the river to the bank on which all the bystanders were waiting. As Johannes Le Vesque recalled it, for example, the dead Gueho traversed the river "alone, not moving his body any more than a log would move." In Margota Boudart's memory, however, after the vow "the boy raised his hands toward heaven, then pulled them down, joined, toward his chest."[112] Margota's memory, then, pictured the revived Gueho with the upstretched hands of the resurrected dead at the Last Judgment. A fifteenth-century Book of Hours prepared for the duke of Brittany a few years after the canonization inquest portrays the Day of Judgment in just this manner.[113] Although Margota would not swear that Gueho had in fact died before his rescue, her memory supplied this interpretation for her, conflating in gesture Guerre's miraculous revival and the general resurrection of the dead on Judgment Day.

The addition of the image of Gueho's raised arms and clasped hands was not the only way in which Margota's memory of his revival differed from that of the three other witnesses. She alone of the four insisted that after the invocation of the saint, Gueho had moved through the water toward the crowd on the riverbank "[as if] he were walking on the land." And, to underscore the miraculous nature of this walking, she added that those present had told her that the water was so deep that one could not touch the bottom and walk with one's head above water.[114] According to Johannes Le Vesque and the other witnesses, Gueho had floated to shore like a log. Where, then, did Margota get the idea that Gueho appeared to be walking? The miracle's liturgical setting seems to have provided this detail. As did the other witnesses, Margota recalled that the miracle had occurred on the vigil of the Feast of Saints Peter and Paul. Her description of Gueho walking on the water recalls the Gospel story of Jesus walking on the water and Peter stepping out to meet him, sinking as his faith faltered. It is a story Margota could easily have associated with the Feast of Peter and Paul. She seems to have inscribed this image from the liturgical setting onto her memory of the miraculous rescue of the previous day.

---

112. Johannes Le Vesque (*Procès,* witness 41; FPC, 80): "Solus non movendo quoquomodo corpus suum plusquam unum lignum se moveret"; Margota Boudart (*Procès,* witness 44; FPC, 82): "Et statim voto facto dictus puer adhuc supra dictam fossam existens elevavit manus versus celum quas postmodum junctas citissime retraxit versus pectus."

113. BNF, MS lat. 1159, fol. 80r.

114. Margota Boudart (*Procès,* witness 44; FPC, 82): "Et inde per aquam venit versus terram ex transverso ripparie predicte. Et videbatur huic testi quod supra terram gradiretur nullum tamen aliud signum natandi aut movendi corpus faciebat."

The testimony of Johannes Le Vesque, the married cleric, offers another example in which the miracle's liturgical setting could shape memories of the events. Le Vesque's narration of Gueho's rescue contains a bizarre detail to which none of the other three witnesses make reference. When they boy at last reached shore, as he recalled, "even though Gueho appeared to have both his throat and his head disconnected from his body, and was the color of a dead person and had closed eyes, he began to cry out 'Jesus.'"[115] None of the other witnesses described Gueho in this manner, nor does it make sense that the head of a drowning victim would appear thus (unless he had dived headfirst into shallow water, which was not the case here). No other witness had Gueho crying out to Jesus. Rather, Le Vesque's story makes sense only if one looks again to stories told about Saints Peter and Paul. In particular, Le Vesque's tale has resonances of the story of Paul's martyrdom by beheading. As Jacobus de Voragine told it in *The Golden Legend,* "as soon as [Paul's] head bounded from his body, it intoned, in Hebrew and in a clear voice, 'Jesus Christ,' the name that had been so sweet to him in life."[116] Le Vesque's memory, it seems, wove together the stories of Paul's beheading and Gueho's drowning to produce his own moving narrative, just as Margota's memory reflected stories of Peter and the Last Judgment. Their recollections mingled spiritual images and lived experience.

It is perhaps not surprising that a minor cleric like Johannes Le Vesque could have inscribed such a highly charged spiritual moment with details drawn from the liturgical context. In Margota's testimony, however, a laywoman's memories of the miracle also appear to have drawn upon a rich reserve of spiritual images. It seems that Margota's memory of Gueho's drowning reflects the fact that she, too, sought to live a spiritual life. The gestures and actions in her description of Gueho's upstretched hands and walking on the water suggest that Margota recalled this miracle along the lines of a set of visual images drawn from spiritual meditations, Christian iconography, and the messages of the preachers.

Some indication about Margota's spirituality comes from the way in which Johannes Le Vesque described her. He calls her "a *domicella* named Margareta Boudart, aged forty or so, who was never married and who is of the highest reputation and life."[117] Women in fifteenth-century Brittany tended to marry young, and we may see deliberate choice behind the

---

115. Johannes Le Vesque (*Procès,* witness 41; FPC, 80): "Et statim post licet ille Gueho videretur habere et gutur et caput uti disligata a corpore et esset coloris mortui et haberet occulos clausos incepit clamare Jhesus."

116. Jacobus de Voragine 1993, 1:353–54.

117. Johannes Le Vesque (*Procès,* witness 41; FPC, 79–80): "una domicella nominata Margareta Boudart etatis quadraginta annorum vel circa que numquam maritata fuit et est optime reputacionis et vite."

never-married state of a forty-year-old woman of the minor nobility. The virginal status of this *domicella,* combined with Johannes's praise of her life and reputation, hints that Margota's single status reflected a dedication to a life of piety and chastity. This assumption is strengthened by her description of herself as having invoked Vincent's aid "along with certain maidens who were with her."[118] Margota may have gathered around her a company of like-minded women, along the lines of a beguinage, or community of spiritual laywomen. All the witnesses to the miracle agreed that Margota had been the first to invoke Vincent Ferrer on behalf of the drowning youth even though she was not present at the moment when Gueho got into trouble. Rather, she had been walking on a high riverbank and had been attracted only by the shouts raised by other bystanders. Of all the crowd (estimated at forty), she was the first to think to call on divine assistance.

The examples of Margota Boudart and Johannes Le Vesque suggest that for persons of a spiritual bent, the moment of a miracle was deeply charged with religious significance: a moment in which God intervened in this world, but also a moment with resonances to the liturgical season in which that miracle occurred. If God were to work a miracle through Vincent Ferrer's intercession, why should he not also at the same time pay tribute in some way to his martyrs, Peter and Paul, who were being honored on the same day? Their stories offer some indication of the richness of their religious imaginations.

This sort of layering of memories also suggests that a deeply spiritual life lay behind the testimony of another witness at the Brittany inquest. Guillermus de Liquillic, a lawyer, told the following story about his father's experience some thirty-five years previously, when Vincent Ferrer was preaching in Brittany.[119] The miracle was this: that on the night of Vincent Ferrer's death Guillermus's father awoke in the middle of the night and saw two candles miraculously burning on a chest next to the bed. Only later did he learn that the famous preacher had departed the world on that very day, and Guillermus's father and mother both assumed that the candles had been lit miraculously in honor of Vincent Ferrer.

Guillermus prefaced this story, however, with two additional pieces of information. First, his father had held an official post in the town of Dinan (that of *misor* or *miseur,* an official in charge of the town's accounts), and when Vincent Ferrer came to Dinan, the father thus was given the job of providing for the famous preacher's food, drink, and other needs. Because of his position, Guillermus's father was able to collect the residual wax left by candles burning on the altar upon which Vincent Ferrer had celebrated

---

118. Margota Boudart (*Procès,* witness 44; FPC, 82): "Ipsa cum certis puellis secum existenti-bus…puerum…vovit deo et Beate Marie ac prefato magistro Vincencio."

119. *Procès,* witness 247; FPC, 211.

Mass. This he brought home, and his wife put it in the chest next to their bed. Second, Guillermus told how "afterward," a little before the Feast of the Purification of the Blessed Virgin, his mother had looked for the wax the father had gathered from Vincent's Masses in order to make candles for the feast. (At Purification, also known as Candlemas, parishioners traditionally would bring candles in procession to be blessed and offered to the parish priest.)[120] She was, unfortunately, unable to find the wax. In his testimony, only after describing these two prefatory incidents did Guillermus relate how—"afterward, with the passage of time"—his father and mother had awakened to see the miraculously burning candles on the night of Vincent Ferrer's death.[121]

What is noteworthy about his testimony is that in Guillermus's mind, three incidents widely separated from one another in time all made up one coherent story of the miraculous candles. Vincent Ferrer was probably in Dinan in June 1418. Candlemas takes place on February 2, and the feast to which Guillermus makes mention would have to have been in early 1419. Vincent Ferrer died in April 1419. The link between these diverse moments was wax: the wax gathered from Vincent's sermons, then lost at Purification time, and at last—by implication—miraculously recovered on the night of the holy man's death. The importance of this wax, however, stems not simply from the fact that it was a relic of Vincent Ferrer but also from the resonances suggested by Guillermus's references to Candlemas.

The candles blessed at the Feast of Purification were specifically said to have healing powers; people brought additional blessed candles home after the service to be used in times of trouble.[122] Sermons preached at Candlemas included miracle stories centering on the blessed candles carried in the procession on that day. A story that features in the *Golden Legend,* for example, tells of a woman's vision of a Candlemas procession and service. A man presented the woman with a candle to offer, but the woman was unwilling to part with such a prize. After a struggle in which a messenger from the Virgin tried to wrest the candle from the woman's hand, the candle broke, and the woman came to her senses holding a broken candle half, which she kept ever after as a treasured relic.[123] Candlemas candles were special.

While the connection is not as clear as in the cases of Margota Boudart and Johannes Le Vesque, it seems that the liturgical moment of the Feast of Purification was crucial to Guillermus's understanding of this miracle.

120. On Candlemas traditions: Duffy 1992, 16–22; A. Thompson 2005, 160–61; Cameron 2010, 57.

121. *Procès,* witness 247; FPC, 211: "Ex tractu temporis post idem Johannes quadem nocte de sompno expergefactus viderat duos cereos accensos super predictam archam."

122. Duffy 1992, 15–22, esp. 16–17.

123. Jacobus de Voragine 1993, 1:150–51.

The story he appears to tell, then, is as follows. The wax that mysteriously disappeared before Candlemas in some way signified Vincent Ferrer's own donation of a blessed candle in the Virgin's honor. The miraculously burning candles that appeared in the middle of the night represented a reciprocal gift or return of the same candles (on the Virgin's part?) to honor the saint who was now with God. Since the miracle proper was simply the sudden apparition of candles lit in honor of the holy preacher's death, the fact that Guillermus included the two additional episodes that form the beginning of his tale indicates that he understood the three incidents as one. The center of this tripartite tale was Candlemas. The liturgical setting provided the full meaning that connected the three parts of the miracle story.

While a keen attention to the liturgical calendar marked the spiritual bent of the tellers of some miracle stories, for others the ability to successfully petition the saint was the signal of their higher religiosity. Miracle stories told in sermons and at canonization inquests indicate a general assumption that the saints listened to the pure, the innocent, and the holy in preference to the average sinner.[124] So, for example, when four Breton fishermen found themselves caught up in a terrible tempest and in fear that their boat would sink and they would all drown, it was not enough that they seek the intercession of Vincent Ferrer. To be absolutely sure, they turned to the youngest of their number, "figuring him to be the most innocent among them," asking him to kneel and make the first petition to Vincent Ferrer. Only afterwards did the others join in the invocation that resulted in the immediate and miraculous cessation of the storm and the sailors' rescue.[125] One witness in the Brittany inquest, Martinus Guennegou, recounted with evident pride how *he* had counseled the husband of a gravely ill woman to make a vow to Vincent Ferrer on her behalf and how the husband had entrusted Martinus himself with taking the couple's offering of five pennies to the saint's tomb. Returning two weeks later, he found the woman completely cured.[126]

That some spiritual worth was accorded to the successful invoker of a saint also becomes apparent in the Brittany story of the miraculous resuscitation

---

124. An impression witnesses could have gained as well from sermons, in which the invoker frequently appears as the real hero of a miracle tale or is described as being particularly devoted to the saint. See Smoller 1998, 435; Finucane 1997, 13, 72.

125. The story is told by two of the four fishermen: Joannes Guezou (*Procès,* witness 74; FPC, 111–12), whose son Natalis was the innocent asked to make the first vow, and Johannes Rochelart (*Procès,* witness 75; FPC 112). Both mention that Natalis was asked to make the vow. I quote the phrasing of Johannes Rochelart ("Et presens testis rogavit dictum Natalem juvenem existimans eum magis innocentem inter alios ut oraret dictum M. V. ne morentur sine confessione"), but Joannes Guezou's is very similar ("Dixit primo dicto Natali...tanquam magis innocenti deinde testi et aliis predictis ut ponerent se ad genua et voverant se dicto M. V.").

126. *Procès,* witness 210; FPC, 185–86.

of the archer Johannes Guerre, who had been wounded in a fight and died of his wounds about eight days later. Here the two men (a priest and a notary) who testified told a much different tale from that of the four women who witnessed the miracle.[127] The men recalled that the priest, who had been called to hear the dying man's confession, had invoked Vincent Ferrer's aid after an unsuccessful attempt to rouse Johannes Guerre so that he could confess and after Guerre's subsequent death. The women insisted instead that the priest had left the house in which Guerre died upon finding him unconscious and unable to confess. The women maintained that one of their number—and not the priest—had encouraged bystanders to invoke the holy preacher's aid after Guerre's death so that he might return to life and confess his sins. The miracle, as they told it, was not so much that Guerre was restored to life but that he was restored to spiritual health by being allowed to return to confess. Unlike the men, the women insisted that Guerre had been a scoundrel and blasphemer before his infirmity but that his morals were reformed thereafter. One woman noted that he had forgiven his attacker on the day after his resuscitation. Another added that he insisted that the women's prayers had saved him and that he called the women present at the bedside his "mothers," as if to underscore his rebirth as a new man.

The women thus described themselves as the prime actors in a story of physical and spiritual regeneration (their only possible rival—the priest—was absent at the crucial moment of the miracle in their version of the tale). The differences between their testimony and that of the two men suggest that the women were attempting to lay claim to the role of spiritual, holy women: both in the events surrounding the resuscitation (in which they tended the sick *and* worried about his soul) and in their telling of their memories of the miracle (in which they insisted that a woman, and not the priest, had called down the divine assistance that brought about Guerre's spiritual and physical rebirth). And in fact, some saintly women in the later Middle Ages were referred to as mothers by their male devotees. In Thomas of Cantimpré's life of Christina Mirabilis, for example, Louis, Count of Looz, who venerated Christina, "whenever he saw her...would rise and run to her and call her his mother." Catherine of Siena's followers routinely referred to her as "mamma."[128]

---

127. The witnesses are Katherina, wife of Johannes Guernezve; Margareta, daughter of Guernezve and wife of Guillermus Ruant; Johanna, wife of Radulphus Ruallani; Richarda, wife of Johannes Lefichant; Oliverius Bourdic, a priest; and Johannes Anglici [Langlais], one of the notaries for the canonization inquest (*Procès,* witnesses 48–53; FPC, 86–93). For what follows, I draw upon Smoller 1998, 443–53.

128. Thomas de Cantimpré 1986, 31. See Smoller 2005.

Like Margota Boudart, Johannes Le Vesque, and Guillermus de Liquillic, these women also appear to have remembered the miracle in an appropriate liturgical setting. The men who testified about Guerre's resuscitation both recalled, somewhat vaguely, that the miracle had happened "four or five years ago."[129] The women all were quite specific in situating the miracle on the vigil of the Feast of Saint Lawrence (that is, on August 9). One of the miracles ascribed to Saint Lawrence was that his intercession had brought a sinner back to life for long enough to do penance for his sins. This story appears in the *Golden Legend,* for example, and also features prominently in a fourteenth-century Franciscan sermon for the Feast of Saint Lawrence.[130] It is not unlikely that the four women who told the story of Johannes Guerre's resuscitation saw their invocation of Vincent Ferrer as in some way parallel to Saint Lawrence's intercession with God. Both acts resulted in the rescue of a sinner from the threat of hell. Their recollection of the miracle's liturgical setting underscores not simply their own important role in the tale but also their interpretation of the story as one of spiritual rebirth—a meaning apparently lost on the men who testified to the miracle.

Such tales suggest that the liturgical calendar could shape people's perceptions and memories of lived events in ways that demonstrate the richness of late medieval spirituality. Layers of meaning and multiple references within the liturgy encouraged this sort of spiritual free association.[131] What the testimony of these Brittany witnesses indicates is that for *certain* devout individuals in the later Middle Ages this type of creative religious thought could extend beyond the church walls to those charged moments in which God acted in their own lives. Just as the symbols used in the Mass and in the cycle of feast days were mutually reinforcing and served to convey a theologically coherent message, so, too, for such individuals God's miraculous interventions in the world were perceived as part of that larger whole in which God's time intersected with lived time. Their stories perform the same work as the histories composed by medieval clerics, which give meaning to events by tying them back to sacred history.

---

129. Oliverius Bourdic (*Procès* witness 52; FPC, 91): "iam sunt quatuor vel quinque anni"; Johannes Anglici (*Procès,* witness 53; FPC, 93): "iam sunt quinque anni vel circa."

130. Jacobus de Voragine 1993, 2:68–69; sermon: BNF, MS lat. 3303, fol. 104v–105. Here the story is told at great length, taking up one and one-half columns, as opposed to the previous four miracle stories in the sermon, which each take up a third to a half of a column. Tradition recorded in one *Passio* had it that Lawrence had the right, each Friday, to liberate one soul from the flames of purgatory and to escort him or her to heaven: Benvenuti, Giannarelli, and Baldasseroni 1998, 119–20.

131. See Duffy 1992 for examples.

To be sure these were exceptional individuals: not saints, not even priests, but clearly more pious than the ordinary mass of believers and the great majority of witnesses whose stories do not mingle miraculous event and liturgical setting. The conflation of lived experience and liturgical time in their memories points to a life of heightened spirituality. It may be that these devout persons prided themselves on their ability to see the interconnections between the manifold actions of God in this world in a way that their contemporaries did not. This realization could be one of the ways in which "super pious" lay Bretons understood the difference between themselves and ordinary believers, just as the frequent taking of Communion functioned for other lay holy persons, such as Margery Kempe. For these few persons, not only was the liturgical calendar a way of marking time, but it also gave meaning to their memories of past events. And for some observers, these super pious Christians represented just the kind of person whose invocations could most effectively reach a saint's ear. Those of a religious imagination, like Margota Boudart or even the young and "more innocent" sailor Natalis Guezou, could mediate between the ordinary Christian and the saints, just as the priest stood between his parishioners and God. Their position may have appeared particularly threatening to a priest, like the one in the tale of Johannes Guerre's resuscitation, whom witnesses could not recall being present at the vow to the saint.[132] If the clergy who were the impresarios of the canonization inquests appear to have been more interested in establishing *that* a vow to Vincent Ferrer had preceded a miracle than in inquiring exactly *who* had made that vow, their lack of interest surely was not entirely disinterested.

To see a canonization inquest merely as a site at which a manipulative clergy guided docile witnesses through a set of carefully designed leading questions is to misrepresent a much more complex and messier process. It was a conversation in which many voices spoke and were heard. To be sure, witnesses must have talked among themselves before and after testifying, and their shared experiences, along with the questions they heard, ensured that the canonization inquest was, in part at least, a place in which lay and clerical participants grasped at least some of the portrait the promoters of the potential saint's canonization were trying to shape. But witnesses also could alter or at least complicate that emerging portrait. Despite the efforts to portray Vincent Ferrer as a new apostle, there was the occasional witness to whom his gift of tongues and his miraculously powerful voice did not reach. Despite the goal of the Roman curia to promote saints as role models more than wonder workers, a virtual tide of Brittany witnesses

---

132. A point I develop at greater length in Smoller 1998, 445–46, 452–53.

testified to Vincent's miraculous power over the plague. And despite the care of the papal commissioners to inquire diligently into *Vincent's* virtues and reputation, individual witnesses managed to tell stories that were as much about their own religious identities, demonstrated through their contact with the holy. For a brief, wonderful moment, we glimpse Vincent as a symbol up for grabs, without a stable meaning or hagiographic emblem. At the moment of his canonization the official image making began. But in the canonization inquests, we experience the lived religion of the later Middle Ages as the multivoiced, sometimes raucous conversation that it was.

# CHAPTER 4

# Creating the Official Image of the Saint

With the canonization of Vincent Ferrer on June 29, 1455, the work of his promoters was far from done. True, the duke of Brittany, the Vannes cathedral clergy, the king of Aragon, and the Dominican order had convinced the pope and the College of Cardinals that the Valencian preacher was indeed a saint, but that was not enough. There still remained the important job of marketing the new product to the faithful. In sermons, liturgy, banners, sculpture, stained glass, altarpieces, woodcuts, books of hours, and hymns, Vincent Ferrer would be offered up to Christian audiences as an object of veneration and a source of divine intercession.[1] As with a television spot for a modern-day politician, Vincent's entire career would be summarized in, at most, a half-hour's sermon and, at least, a single two-dimensional image. In many late medieval canonizations, that representation was the first item produced in the course of the canonization process, in the form of a life whose contents, it was hoped, would sway the pope to open canonization proceedings as well as guide the questioning posed at the inquests *in partibus*.[2] In Vincent's case, canonization came first, and a *vita*—and hence a "packaged" portrait of the saint—came second. Huge codices of manuscript testimony about the holy Dominican needed to be collapsed into a readable and preachable form. The diverse opinions of hundreds of

---

1. Banners at the canonization ceremony: Cobianchi 2007, esp. 209, 211, 213–14, 219.

2. Vauchez 1997, 49; Wetzstein 2004a, 361; Krötzl 1998, 12; Frazier 2005, 23–24 (and 26, citing J. O'Malley 1997, 20, on length of sermons preached before the papal court). For an example of a precanonization *vita,* see Zanacchi 2010.

witnesses had to be smoothed into a single narrative and a coherent image of the newly canonized saint.

As the death of Pope Calixtus III within three years of Vincent's canonization reminds us, the generation who had firsthand knowledge of the famous preacher was rapidly declining. Accordingly, the work of creating the official image of the new saint fell not to an eyewitness to Vincent's career but rather to a young Dominican who was both very close to the events of the canonization and well trained in the humanist rhetoric so fashionable with the elites of the day: Pietro Ranzano. As Ranzano himself relates, he received the commission to write the first life of the new saint from the lips of both Martial Auribelli, the Dominican master general at whose side he had remained in those final agonizing months before Vincent's canonization, and Calixtus III himself.[3] What private instructions those two might have imparted to Ranzano along with the commission and the dossier of materials he needed to write we can never know with certainty. But by reading carefully against the grain in other contemporary accounts of Vincent Ferrer's career, we can guess the sorts of criticisms Ranzano may have felt compelled to address. His whitewashing of those blemishes to Vincent's reputation shows Ranzano's considerable narrative and rhetorical skills. In a way that must greatly have pleased his patrons, Ranzano's *Life* effectively crafted the official image of the new saint.

## Pietro Ranzano, Humanist Author of Saints' Lives

The man who created that portrait of Vincent Ferrer must have seemed ideally suited to the task. A member of the Dominican order since his teens, Pietro Ranzano was a master of theology and knew well the Christian classics and medieval scholastic authors. But he had also received an up-to-date humanist education and was celebrated for his rhetorical skills. The humanist authors of fifteenth-century Italy had many, and sometimes differing, goals, but they shared the aim of writing in the style of ancient Latin authors.[4] Trained in what they called the *studia humanitatis* (the study of human matters), the humanists stressed rhetoric, oratory, history, poetry, and ethics. They believed that such a program of education could transform

---

3. RVV (BHL no. 8657/8658); for a list of manuscripts, see Kaeppeli and Panella 1970–93, 3:254. On Ranzano, see Barilaro 1977–78; Termini 1916; Figliuolo 1997, 89–200; Zeldes 2006, 161–63; Cochrane 1981, 151, 153–54. Ranzano mentions Auribelli's command to write the *Life* in the prologue to the *vita* (RVV, 1:483). In the summary of Vincent's life sent to Giovanni da Pistoia (BC, MS 112, fol. 54r), he notes that his commission came from both Auribelli and Calixtus: "Ea delegi ego ex tam multis illis quae accurate perscripse in opere illo quatuor libris distincto quod hoc anno & *Martialis auribelli hortatu* & *Calisti pontificis iussu* de illius uita composui" (emphasis added). See also Termini 1916, 85.

4. Frazier 2005, 9–17; Zeldes 2006, 160–61.

society both by the example of virtuous and heroic figures from the past and through the power of their own rhetoric. And they often turned a critical eye to texts from the medieval past, not just bemoaning barbarisms that had crept into pristine classical Latin but also stripping away inaccuracies, anachronisms, and assertions not supported by contemporary sources. One of the most famous achievements of quattrocento humanism was Lorenzo Valla's unmasking as a forgery the Donation of Constantine, one of the textual pillars of medieval papal power.[5] This is the humanism in which Pietro Ranzano was steeped.

Ranzano was born in the Sicilian city of Palermo in 1426 or 1427, a younger son in an educated family and therefore destined for a church career. As a Sicilian, Ranzano was part of a territory belonging to the kingdom of Aragon, whose Mediterranean holdings included the Balearic Islands, Sardinia, and Malta, as well as the island of Sicily. Before young Pietro reached the age of twenty, King Alfonso V had added the kingdom of Naples to his empire as well. If his Sicilian birth put Ranzano under the jurisdiction of the king of Aragon, it also enabled him to participate in the wider culture of the peninsula. His immersion in the culture of the quattrocento, combined with his career in the church, allowed Ranzano to straddle two educational worlds: the traditional scholasticism of the medieval university and the new humanist education of the Renaissance.

Ranzano's earliest studies were in Palermo under the tutelage of the humanist Antonio Cassarino;[6] he received instruction as well at the new Dominican convent of St. Zita in Palermo from Enrico Lugardo. Next, however, came more education in the city that has come to epitomize Renaissance Italy to modern readers: Florence. After beginning university studies in Florence, the young teenager traveled with Lugardo to Perugia, where he studied for two years and during which time he got to know a number of local humanists. Returning to Florence, Ranzano completed his university studies—and firmed up humanist contacts—receiving the degrees of bachelor of arts in 1447 and master of theology in 1449.[7]

In the next five or six years, Ranzano established a series of contacts that would shape the future of his career: connections with important humanists, the court of Aragon, the Roman curia, and Martial Auribelli. Upon completing his university education, Ranzano spent a few months in Rome, during which period he befriended a number of humanists, the

5. See now Camporeale 2000; Fubini 1996; Ginzberg 1999. Valla, a friend of Ranzano's, wrote the 1440 *Oratio* on the Donation of Constantine at the request of Alfonso V, who wished to rebut papal assertions of the right to invest the King of Naples.

6. See Resta 1978.

7. Largely following Figliuolo 1997, 92–99; Barilaro 1977–78 (38) postulates that Ranzano's master of theology was obtained in Rome in 1449–50.

most important of whom was Lorenzo Valla. The ties between the two men were so close that young Pietro was among the trusted few to whom the older scholar showed drafts of his Latin translation of Thucydides before its publication.[8] In the early 1450s Ranzano also became a fixture at the court of Aragon, housed in Naples since Alfonso's taking possession of the kingdom in 1442. By 1453, Ranzano's talents had come to the notice of local Dominican leaders, and he was appointed *socius,* or companion, to the Sicilian provincial, Antonio Bellassai. In that capacity he accompanied Bellassai to the Dominican chapter general held at Nantes that year. This was the meeting at which Martial Auribelli assumed the role of Dominican master general and began to devote himself to securing Vincent Ferrer's canonization.

Ranzano would be an integral part of the final stages of that canonization process. On returning from Nantes, he evidently stopped in Rome; we find him there still (or again?) two years later, at Martial Auribelli's side, as the dossier of materials gathered on behalf of Vincent Ferrer made its way through the curia. Ranzano was already known to Pope Nicholas V, whose pontificate was marked by his patronage of Roman humanism. And after Nicholas's death in March 1455, Ranzano's talents also caught the eye of Calixtus III, who would later appoint him to the post of provincial, heading the Dominican province of Sicily. For aside from his role in assisting Auribelli, Ranzano had a long-standing reputation for his skills in rhetoric and oratory. When he was only fifteen, the curial humanist Maffeo Vegio was so impressed that he asked the younger scholar to send him anything he should write.[9] Perhaps it was because of his literary talents that Auribelli and Calixtus chose Ranzano to compose the first *vita* of Vincent Ferrer. He took up the work with gusto. At least the preface to the work was finished by the end of 1455, and the entire life was approved by the Dominican order at its chapter general in Montpellier in May 1456.[10]

In the years following the composition of the *vita* of Vincent Ferrer, Ranzano continued to distinguish himself in the Dominican order and to be a trusted part of the entourage of the Aragon court in Naples. He served twice as provincial of Sicily and was charged in 1463 with collecting tithes to fund Pope Pius II's dream of a crusade. At the death of Alfonso V in 1458, Ranzano wrote a series of elegiac verses in praise of the late king.

---

8. According to Ranzano (*Annales,* vol. 1, book 4, fol. 242), as cited by Barilaro 1977–78, 38; also noted in Figliuolo 1997, 138; Zeldes 2006, 162.

9. Figliuolo 1997, 134 (Vegio was also a writer of saints' lives: Frazier 2005, 484–90).

10. Figliuolo 1997, 101, citing Reichert 1900, 259–68; also Barilaro 1977–78, 46; Termini 1916, 85. As Barilaro notes, the *vita* is not mentioned anywhere in the acts of the chapter general; however, according to Ranzano himself, the *Life* was approved there (BC, MS 112, fol. 51v): "Verum opus [i.e., Ranzano's *vita*]...probatum iam a nostri ordinis patribus qui anno ab hinc octavo conventum aegerunt in monte pesulano."

From 1468 to 1476, he served in the court of Ferrante, Alfonso's illegitimate son and successor in Naples, as tutor to Ferrante's son Giovanni.[11] The ties between master and pupil remained strong, as did the gratitude of Giovanni's family. When Ranzano's work as tutor was over, Aragon connections secured for him the bishopric of Lucera. Ferrante retained him as one of his own confessors and in 1488 entrusted Ranzano with a delicate mission to the court of King Matthias Corvinus of Hungary, Ferrante's son-in-law. Although Matthias was not receptive to the official purpose of Ranzano's mission (Ferrante had hoped that the succession to the kingdom of Hungary might be settled in favor of Aragonese interests), he was delighted with the Sicilian humanist's talents and persuaded him to stay several years in Hungary. At Matthias's request, Ranzano composed, in 1489 and 1490, a history of the kingdom.[12]

Sometime after Matthias's death on April 6, 1490, Ranzano left Hungary and returned to his bishop's seat in Lucera, where he died in either 1492 or 1493.[13] He appears to have spent his final years revising and editing the huge work with which he had occupied himself for the previous thirty years: the *Annales omnium temporum* (*Annals of All Times*). The *Annals,* encompassing eight volumes of material, traces the geography, history, culture, and customs of the world from creation through the mid-fifteenth century.[14] For places he had visited himself, Ranzano offered eyewitness descriptions of their geography and customs, and he fleshed out his narrative with the stories of famous men and women from the regions he addressed. In addition to providing what one scholar dubs "the first complete geographic description of Italy," Ranzano's *Annals* are replete with the lives of the saints, including a brief life of Vincent Ferrer. Modeled on ancient authors like Livy, medieval scholastics like Vincent of Beauvais, and contemporary humanists like Biondo Flavio and Enea Silvio Piccolomini (Pope Pius II), the *Annals* sums up the multifaceted interests and educational paths of this Dominican humanist.[15]

11. On Ferrante's often troubled reign and his patronage of scholars, artists, and musicians, see Abulafia 2004, 220–21; 1995; Bentley 1987, 21–34.

12. Figliuolo 1997, 101–21, 132–34; Barilaro 1977–78, 55–91; Termini 1916, 88–90.

13. According to the most recent study of Ranzano, Figliuolo 1997, 123. Death in 1490: Termini 1916, 90; in 1492: Barilaro 1977–78, 92; and Zeldes 2006, 16.

14. The sole manuscript, now in the Biblioteca Comunale di Palermo, MS 3, Qq. C, fasc. 54–60, consists of only seven of the eight volumes. The original arrangement appears to have been in four large volumes. So Leandro Alberti described seeing it in the Dominican convent of St. Domenico in Palermo in 1526. At some point in the sixteenth or seventeenth century the manuscript was moved into eight volumes, with some loss of folios and complete books; volume 4 of the eight (including book 20, in which the biography of Vincent Ferrer appeared) has been missing since at least 1730. Barilaro 1977–78, 100–108; Figliuolo 1997, 199–200.

15. Figliuolo 1997, 189–98; 175.

## Ranzano's Writing on the Saints

Like many of his contemporaries, Pietro Ranzano was interested in writing—or rewriting—the lives of the saints. In addition to the *vita* of Vincent Ferrer commissioned by Calixtus III and Martial Auribelli, he also composed a briefer life of the same in his *Annals,* a set of verses about Vincent's life, an account of the 1460 martyrdom of fellow Dominican Anthony of Rivoli, a life of the early Christian martyr Barbara, and numerous short biographies in the *Annals* and his history of Hungary, as well as offices for the feasts of Saints Barbara and Vincent Ferrer. He may have been influenced or encouraged by the example of his friend Maffeo Vegio, who composed nearly a dozen lives and offices on various saints in the 1450s.[16]

Although the fact has largely been ignored by modern scholars more attuned to the secular concerns of Renaissance humanism, humanist authors produced hundreds of saints' lives, as Alison Frazier has cogently demonstrated.[17] To the humanists' minds, the saints clearly needed some help. The highly formulaic saint's life of the Middle Ages could become an object of embarrassment and contempt to readers steeped in the study of classical rhetoric. A gathering of clerics on Saint Stephen's Eve in 1518, for example, degenerated into hilarity after a reading on the life of the protomartyr as the company took turns mocking the text they had just heard.[18] Humanists who wrote about the saints worried about the often laughably poor Latin style of many traditional *vitae* and hoped to produce more elegant and more effective accounts aimed at encouraging their readers to venerate or, better yet, imitate the saints. Some humanist authors turned a critical eye to their source materials as well, but when they wrote about the early Christian martyrs (as humanists did, in great numbers), the sources were just too poor to add much in the way of precision or accuracy. For the humanist Giovanni Garzoni, the most prolific quattrocento writer on the saints and a student of Ranzano's friend Lorenzo Valla, rhetorical concerns typically outweighed issues of critical accuracy. Involved in the teaching of Dominican novices, he hoped to create by example effective preachers whose words could stir an audience's emotions.[19]

Pietro Ranzano made known some of his various goals for his writings about saints in prefaces and letters accompanying his *vitae.* In an introductory letter addressed to Martial Auribelli, Ranzano explained that he hoped that his life of Vincent Ferrer would spur people to disdain the present life

---

16. On Vegio's work: Frazier 2005, 484–90; on Ranzano's friendship with Vegio: Figliuolo 1997, 134.

17. The definitive study is now Frazier 2005; see esp. overview of general trends in chap. 1. See also D. Collins 2008; Caby 2004; Caby and Dessi 2012.

18. Frazier 2005, 291.

19. Frazier 2005, chap. 4. See also Frazier 2010.

and all its voluptuous temptations.[20] In the preface to his life of Saint Barbara, he told Filippo Perdicari, who had requested the life, that his own family had long since instilled in him a special devotion to the virgin martyr.[21] Based on that life, at the request of Filippo's brother Federico, Ranzano composed an office for the Feast of Saint Barbara, with nine readings, or *lectiones,* that summarized her life in brief.[22] Ranzano also hoped to foster the cult of Vincent Ferrer through his writings. In 1463, he sent a copy of the brief narration about Vincent from his *Annals* to fellow Dominican Giovanni da Pistoia, along with a set of verses on the saint. In a prefatory letter, Ranzano reveals that Giovanni had requested a copy of the life of Vincent in order to help spread, through his preaching, devotion to the new saint. The reason for composing the additional poem on Vincent was, as he tells Giovanni, that it would be much easier to commit to memory—and hence more helpful to the preacher—than would prose.[23] Finally, Ranzano's account of the martyrdom of Anthony of Rivoli, in the form of a letter to Pope Pius II, may well also have been intended for a larger audience; its epistolary form, as one scholar has suggested, may simply have been a nod to some early Christian *passiones* (martyrdom accounts) and its contents a reminder that the heroic age of martyrdom was not over.[24]

What did Pietro Ranzano expect to accomplish when he wrote lives of the saints? In the cases of Vincent Ferrer and Anthony of Rivoli, he surely hoped to contribute to the growth of a new cult of a recently dead hero. But that could not have been his reason for writing the life of Barbara, long since martyred and widely venerated, particularly in Ranzano's native Sicily.[25] Aside from expressing his own devotion to Saint Barbara, Ranzano must have also hoped, as with Vincent Ferrer, to spur his readers to a better life in imitation of the virtues of the saint. It seems, in fact, that Ranzano had a reputation for pushing the example of the saints as role models.

At least that is how he appeared to one contemporary. Fellow humanist Aurelio Brandolini, who also spent some time in the court of Matthias Corvinus, composed a dialogue for the aging Hungarian king to help him bear the suffering of his final illness. The dialogue features a character named Petrus Ransanus, a stand-in for Ranzano, whom Brandolini had known at Matthias's court. In an effort to bring the monarch to accept his impending

20. RVV, 1:483.

21. BC, MS 112, fol. 1r. Letter of dedication also edited in Termini 1916, 92–93. Also requesting the life were Ranzano's brother Antonio and the Sicilian lawyer Guido Crapona. Figliuolo 1997, 151.

22. BC, MS 112, fol. 38v–49r (prefatory letter at 37v–38v).

23. BC, MS 112, fol. 51r–51v; letter also edited in Termini 1916, 91–92.

24. Frazier 2005, 22 (she notes that Ranzano's passion was among the "few *vitae et passiones* written about contemporaries by eyewitnesses [that] were lauded" by early modern scholars: 318).

25. Figliuolo 1997, 152.

death, Ransanus reminds him of the saints' virtuous suffering. When the king dismisses Ransanus's arguments (preferring to hear about men with whom he can identify), Ransanus will not drop the topic, offering instead a long defense of the saints' usefulness as role models.[26] If Brandolini's Ransanus is a creditable representation of our Pietro, it seems that the latter could in fact get a little tedious in his insistence that we imitate the saints.

However varied were his motivations and commissions for writing each of the *vitae* he composed, Ranzano had a consistent stylistic goal in mind as he wrote. He wanted to reach (and move) as wide an audience as possible. As he explained to Martial Auribelli about his *Life of Vincent,* "I will employ an altogether plain style, namely, so that (since this work is to be spread among all sorts of people) the things that are narrated here might easily be understood by various people, both learned and uneducated."[27] Similarly, in the preface to his *Life of Saint Barbara,* Ranzano commented that he would try to write "using such a simple writing style that [its contents] could easily be understood, not only by learned men, but also by those who have only a little education."[28] In other words, in writing about the saints this student of humanist oratory deliberately toned his rhetoric down—for good rhetorical reasons, namely, a consideration of his audience. He also thought about his readers' likely attention span. As Ranzano told Calixtus III in the preface to book 2 of his *Life of Vincent,* he had deliberately kept his narration short and tempered the style "lest the length of the work should become tedious to those who read it."[29]

In writing about the saints, Ranzano may have been reaching, as many other humanist hagiographers did, to re-create not the ornate Latin of Cicero but rather the plainer language of the early church fathers.[30] As Augustine had remarked in his *Confessions,* when he first came to Christian scriptures as a professor of rhetoric, he found their writing style appallingly elementary.[31] Jerome's Latin translation of the Bible does read simply and clearly, and that plain, accessible style may have been in Ranzano's mind. At least he sets up a parallel between his own task in writing Vincent's *vita* and that of Jerome in writing the life of Saint Hilarion. In defense of his decision to skip over some of the details of the holy preacher's career, Ranzano quotes Jerome's lament that there was so much material about Hilarion that

26. Frazier 2005, 294–95; also see Figliuolo 1997, 144.

27. RVV, 1:483.

28. BC, MS 112, fol. 2v: "Enitar autem quo ad fieri poterit: ea in scribendo facilitate uti: ut non a doctis tantum viris sed ab eis quoque qui parum literati sunt intelligi perfacile queant ea" (also Termini 1916, 93).

29. RVV, 1:490.

30. Frazier 2005, 20.

31. Augustine of Hippo 1950, III.5 (1:112–15).

"if Homer were to take [it] up, he would either be envious or would be completely overcome."[32]

If Ranzano hoped to reach as broad as possible an audience with his saints' lives, he also wanted, like fellow humanists, to stir their emotions through the power of his words. One technique humanist hagiographers used for drawing in the reader was to invent (or reproduce) dialogue. Humanists who reworked earlier versions of martyrdom accounts, for example, put long, emotional speeches in the mouths of the martyr and his or her anxious parents.[33] For example, when the father of the determined virgin Barbara wishes to marry her to a noble husband, Ranzano gives her a speech refusing him that lasts nearly two pages, ending with the blunt assertion, "I have already betrothed myself to the author of all things, Jesus Christ, who, since he be a heavenly and immortal husband, does not defile, but protects from absolutely all impurity his spouses and all of those who consecrate themselves to him wholeheartedly."[34]

What humanist hagiographers evidently did not enjoy was recapitulating the lengthy, legalistic lists of miracles generated at canonization inquests. That humanist distaste for the unadorned style of notaries' miracle collections may explain a mystery about Pietro Ranzano's *Life of Vincent*. Ranzano states in the prologue to the *vita*, a letter sent to Martial Auribelli probably before the completion of the entire work, "I will divide this work into five books, and each book into its chapters, by which it will appear more clearly about what there will be narration."[35] The version of Ranzano's *Life* printed by the Bollandists in their enormous collection of saints' lives has in fact only four books, of which the last chronicles the saint's death, burial, and posthumous miracles.[36] And in the prologue to that fourth book, Ranzano writes, with some apparent relief, "In this book will be the completion of the work I took up."[37] At least as he came to write book 4, then, Ranzano had abandoned all plans for a fifth book. Given the theme of book 4, the only possible subject of the unwritten fifth book would have been a longer list of posthumous miracles.[38]

---

32. RVV, 1:490.

33. Frazier 2005, 196–97.

34. BC, MS 112, fol. 20r: "Me ipsa desponsaui iam autori rerum omnium iesu christo: qui cum sit celestis & immortalis sponsus: non polluit: sed ab omni prorsus inquinamento seruat sponsas suas & eos omnes: qui ei se se tota mente dicauerint." Entire speech: fol. 19r (middle)–20r (seventh line).

35. RVV, 1: 483. "Quinque libris" also appears in BAV, MS Chigi F. IV. 91, fol 1v., although in this manuscript the initial parts of book 4 are folded into book 3, so the *vita* is in only three books. The discrepancy is also noted in Barilaro 1977–78, 128.

36. RVV, 1:509.

37. Ibid.

38. In the Bollandists' version, Ranzano's book 4 contains only a chapter dealing with Vincent's time in Brittany and a listing of a small number of posthumous miracles (specifically, ten). Since there

Alison Frazier has speculated that Ranzano chose to abandon his planned fifth book on miracles because he had no taste for the sort of styleless catalog such a narration would involve.[39] Indeed, it has been suggested that Ranzano may well have composed an initial version of the *vita* in only three books with *no* treatment of posthumous miracles whatsoever. A manuscript of a similarly truncated *Life* is known to have existed in the Palermo Dominican convent of St. Zita and has been hypothesized to represent Ranzano's own copy of the original *vita*.[40] Perhaps it was only this initial version that the Dominican chapter general of 1456 approved. Even if this assumption is correct, however, Ranzano fairly soon thereafter added a section including ten of Vincent's posthumous miracles and expanding the *vita* to a fourth book. And in his book 3, devoted entirely to Vincent's *in vita* prophecies and miracles, Ranzano included the stories of eighteen prophecies and thirty-three miracles attributed to the living saint, many related at considerable length and with great dramatic style. By 1463, the *vita* consisted of four books, for when Giovanni da Pistoia requested a copy, Ranzano excused his substitution of a briefer version by explaining that the *vita* was in "*four prolix volumes*."[41] While that last book is, indeed, rather brief in the Bollandists' edition, a longer version of book four survives in a manuscript in Toulouse that has been said to represent Ranzano's own working copy of the text. Here, a number of *in vita* miracles have been transposed from book 3 in the Bollandists' redaction.[42] That the miracle tales there are largely from Aragon suggests that Ranzano chose his material with an eye to his friends and patrons, for a celebration of Vincent's miracles in the Iberian Peninsula would doubtless have pleased the Aragonese court in Naples. Humanists—even Dominican ones—were accustomed to being pens for hire.

---

is no conclusion to book 4, the Bollandists speculate that the manuscripts they worked from were missing parts.

39. Frazier 2005, 24.

40. The suggestion of Barilaro 1977–78, 128, citing Valentino Barcellona. Cf. Barcellona 1761, 94–95, who describes the Palermo manuscript as having three books. This manuscript might then be the parent of the text in BAV, MS Chigi F. IV. 91 (in three books, with the sections of book 4 dealing with Vincent's death and burial folded into book 3), and Basel, Univ. Bibl. E III 12, as well as the model for a 1490 Italian translation by Iohannes Caroli (both listed as having only three books in Kaeppeli and Panella 1970–93, 3:254).

41. BC, MS 112, fol. 51v: "Diuisum nanque in quatuor prolixa uolumina est." Also Termini 1916, 91.

42. Bibliothèque municipale, Toulouse, MS 486, which initially belonged to the Dominican convent of Toulouse, evidently a gift from Pietro Ranzano himself. See *Catalogue général des manuscrits* 1849–85, 7:viii, 293–94. The Toulouse manuscript contains a list of miracles in book 4 that extends beyond the point at which the Bollandists' text ends. They appear in the Bollandists' edition in III.5.31–42 (RVV 1:507–8). If, however, Termini 1916, 81, is correct that the neat humanist hand in fol. 49v–50v of BC MS 112 is that of Ranzano, the identification of the Toulouse manuscript as autograph is problematic, unless Ranzano employed one hand (the humanist script) for presentation copies and another (the cursive Gothic hand of the Toulouse manuscript) for his own personal drafts.

## Pietro Ranzano's Hidden Agenda

As Martial Auribelli's right-hand man in Rome during the months leading up to Vincent Ferrer's canonization, Ranzano must have been privy to all the rumors and gossip surrounding the cardinals' deliberations about Vincent's sanctity. Martial Auribelli himself had enemies, as would become apparent in 1462, when he was temporarily removed from his post as master general by Dominicans who accused him of opposing the cause of reform in the order.[43] Vincent's Breton promoters, too, continually struggled to find the most opportune way to position themselves between the rival French and English crowns; too close an alliance with the one was sure to anger the other.[44] Further, there were those who did not like the house of Aragon or, at the very least, Aragonese presence in Naples and interference in northern Italian politics.[45] And there were voices murmuring against Vincent himself.[46] That there were people in Rome opposed to Vincent's canonization Ranzano himself attests in his dramatic description of the day Pope Calixtus III announced his plan to canonize the Dominican preacher. When the Roman nobleman Andreas de Sancta Cruce was suddenly stricken with apoplexy, at least some in the crowd had insisted that it was a sign that God did not wish "that a man be enrolled among the saints who did not appear

---

43. See Hinnebusch 1965, 1:229–32; Creytens 1975; Barilaro 1977–78, 61–62.

44. See, e.g., Galliou and Jones 1991, 237–39.

45. Nicholas V, who initiated the canonization process for Vincent, had encouraged René of Anjou in his claim to the throne of Naples, as a counterpoise to Alfonso V's growing power, although he would eventually prove to be quite compliant to Alfonso's desires. Alfonso, in the years 1447–50, asserted himself against Milan, Florence, and Venice. In 1450 he allied himself with Venice against Florence and the new Sforza lord of Milan, prompting Medici supporters in Florence to refer to him as "the Catalan pest." Only through Nicholas V's insistence that Naples be included was Alfonso made part of the league formed by the Peace of Lodi in 1454. Despite Alfonso V's hopes that the former head of the royal council in Naples, Alfonso de Borja, would prove to be an even more acquiescent pope than Nicholas had been, relations with the now Pope Calixtus III soured within weeks after Calixtus's canonization of Vincent Ferrer in June 1455. Most gallingly, Calixtus III would refuse to recognize Alfonso's nomination of his bastard son Ferrante as his heir to the kingdom of Naples, as the pope had high hopes that one of his nephews might be installed in Naples instead. See, especially, Ryder 1990, 259–90; also Labalme 1996, 241; Abulafia 1995, 21; 2004, 219; and Bentley 1987, 14–19.

46. One can see this in miracles in the canonization inquests. E.g., in Brittany, a man who "murmured" against Vincent Ferrer was stricken so that "his intestines fell from his belly" (Perrina de Bazvalen, *Procès,* witness 7; FPC, 25: "Murmuraverat contra eumdem M. V. cum certis aliis in sua predicatione et ob hoc eius intestina ceciderant de ventre"). Toulouse witness Joannes de Saxis testified that after hearing Vincent Ferrer preach a sermon on Easter morning, he went to hear a second sermon in the Franciscan convent, by a famous theologian and minister of the Franciscan province of Toulouse. Without directly naming names, the Franciscan friar criticized Vincent's sermon of the morning as "apocryphal" (*apocrifa*), at which the preacher became pale, was unable to complete his sermon, and never again was seen to preach in Toulouse (*Proceso,* fol. 219v–220r; FPC, 356, witness 23).

to be worthy of such glory."[47] When Calixtus III and Martial Auribelli gave Ranzano the commission to write Vincent's life, they must also have made known to him in some way the nagging concerns they hoped the great rhetorician might smooth away into oblivion. Aragonese eyes may well have been watching over his shoulder as he sifted through his materials and began writing in Palermo. Ranzano's *vita* would have to silence the lingering voices of Vincent's detractors.

A careful reading of some contemporary writings gives an indication of the sorts of objections raised by those opposed to Vincent's canonization. True, Vincent had a pan-European reputation as a pious ascetic and inspirational preacher. The antisemitism that propelled and accompanied his celebrated mass conversions of Jews probably would not have disturbed many contemporary Christians.[48] But there were clearly distinct problems that lay in the path of Vincent's *fama sanctitatis.* The first had to do with his activities during the years of the Great Schism and in particular with his close association with the recalcitrant Avignon pope Benedict XIII, who had clung to his title unto death, long after all the nations of Europe had lined up behind the decisions of the Council of Constance, which ended the Schism. Whatever one's allegiances had been during the Schism years, Benedict's behavior during and after Constance had left him roundly disliked. Vincent had early on come out in favor of the Avignon popes in a 1380 treatise *On the Present-Day Schism* (*De moderno ecclesie scismate*) addressed to the crown of Aragon.[49] It was written less than two years after French cardinals had repudiated the election of Urban VI, electing as their pope Clement VII—who took up residence in the conveniently vacant papal palace in Avignon. And in 1395, soon after the Aragonese cardinal Pedro de Luna had succeeded Clement as Pope Benedict XIII, he called the talented young Valencian Dominican to his side to serve as his confessor, domestic chaplain, apostolic penitencer, and, according to some, master of the sacred palace.[50]

Not simply had Vincent served in the household of Benedict in Avignon, however. His Valencian origins and his writings also linked him publicly with the Avignon pontiff. Indeed, as one scholar has noted, the best known of Vincent's works in the fifteenth century was the letter he wrote

---

47. BC, MS 112, fol. 64r: "Erant qui dicerent id dei iudicio factum: qui nequaquam pati pro summa iusticia uoluit ut referretur inter sanctos uir qui non uideretur tanta gloria dignus." See chapter 2.

48. Contrast, however, the Jewish sources quoted by FHSVF 1:70 and 1:334. See, e.g., Netanyahu 1995, 183–202, for Vincent's role in conversions of Spanish Jews. On fifteenth-century Observant preaching's link with anti-Jewish activities, see Rubin 1999, 119–28.

49. See Montagnes 1980, 607–13.

50. So, e.g., Bertucci 1969–80, 12:1170. Fages (FHSVF, 1:105) says at most "maybe" on Vincent's appointment as master of the sacred palace, a position traditionally held by a Dominican friar.

to Pope Benedict XIII in 1412.[51] In that letter, as in the 1380 Schism treatise, Vincent vehemently defended the legitimacy of the Avignon papacy against its Roman rivals, a fact not lost on contemporary observers. In a fifteenth-century manuscript copy of this letter in the Bibliothèque nationale de France, a contemporary reader notes in a marginal comment: "He speaks here of Benedict [XIII], whom he calls the true vicar of Christ."[52]

That true vicar of Christ would come to disappoint his confessor, however. In the conclave following the death of Pope Clement VII in 1394, Cardinal Pedro de Luna had promised, should he be elected pope, to resign the papacy if his cardinals asked him to do so and if his Roman rival could be persuaded to do so simultaneously. Each time an opportunity arose for the two popes to follow what contemporaries called the *via cessionis* (the way of resignation), however, Benedict XIII found some excuse that would prevent his participation. At last, in 1398, frustrated by the wily Aragonese prelate's obstinacy, the kingdom of France, Avignon's largest supporter, withdrew its obedience from Benedict. Chaos ensued in the city of Avignon, as most of Benedict's cardinals decamped for the settlement of Villeneuve across the river, and the citizens of Avignon declared their support for the cardinals over the pope. On behalf of the cardinals and the city, a French mercenary troop began a seven-month siege of the papal palace. Rumors swirled through the city's streets, as Avignon and its embattled pope became entangled in the political struggles between Burgundians and Armagnacs. For the next five years, Benedict became a virtual prisoner in his palace, reduced to eating cats, rats, and sparrows.[53]

The events surrounding the subtraction of obedience must have taken their toll on Vincent. He left the papal palace for the more neutral turf of the city's Dominican convent. There he became gravely ill and, as he told Benedict in that famous letter of 1412, experienced a vision of Saints Dominic and Francis praying at the feet of Christ. In answer to their prayers, Christ came to Vincent in his bed, touched him gently on the jaw, and charged him to go forth and preach penitence in preparation for the advent of Antichrist. At once, Vincent was healed and, with Benedict's license, began what would

51. See Rusconi 1990, 216. The letter has been edited in FND, 213–24; extensive excerpts also appear in Brettle 1924, 167–72. Kaepelli and Panella 1970–93, 4:463–64, list eighteen surviving manuscripts of that letter, more than for any other single treatise of Vincent's (though not more than for collections of his sermons).

52. BNF, MS lat. 14669, fol. 142v (margin): "adverte hic de benedicto quem vocit verum xpi [Christi] vicarium." According to Fages, whose edition is based on it, this manuscript dates to 1441. FND, 213.

53. Based on the narratives in Valois (1896–1902) 1967, 3:148–87, 3:189–205; Rollo-Koster 2003, 71–74, 79–85; FHSVF, 1:103–110. See also Kaminsky 1971. For a brief overview of the Schism's course, see Blumenfeld-Kosinski 2006, 2–11. See also Rollo-Koster and Izbicki 2009.

become a twenty-year preaching mission.[54] In sermons, Vincent urged his listeners to repent of their sins and fortify themselves against future temptations, graphically and terrifyingly laying out the torments his audiences could expect at the hands of Antichrist.[55] Although he was no longer at Benedict's side, Vincent maintained his loyalty to the Avignon pontiff, even as he urged the recalcitrant pontiff to follow the *via cessionis*.[56]

Still faithful to Benedict, Vincent played no part in the Council of Pisa of 1409, organized by a number of dissenting Roman and Avignon cardinals, which deposed Benedict and his rival, Gregory XII, creating a third line of popes in western Christendom. In fact, in 1408–9, Vincent joined Benedict XIII at a gathering of the Avignon obedience in Perpignan, the Avignon pontiff's answer to the council of Pisa, where the indefatigable Dominican urged Benedict, once again, to follow the "way of renunciation." In the summer of 1414, Vincent again tried, in vain, to secure Benedict's resignation, this time in Morella, where the pontiff met with Vincent and with Fernando, king of Aragon.[57] By that fall, prelates from all three obediences were gathered in Constance to work, at last, for an end to the Schism. But not Vincent.

Although no less a personage than the University of Paris chancellor Jean Gerson would ask him to come to Constance, Vincent never appeared at the council that ended the Schism, apparently preferring to continue his vain effort to persuade Benedict XIII to resign the papal throne.[58] In his 1380 treatise *On the Present-Day Schism* Vincent had rejected the notion that a church council had the authority to depose the rival popes and substitute a single, new pontiff in their place. He appears to have kept to that view to the end.[59] True, Vincent had a major role in the negotiations that brought the German emperor Sigismund, along with a sizable delegation

---

54. FND, 220–21. Vincent describes the vision as "facta cuidam religioso." That the *quidam religiosus* (certain religious) is Vincent is, however, obvious. See also Montagnes 1988.

55. E.g., in Freiburg on March 10, 1404, Vincent told his audience, "primum omnia bona temporalia auferet a te. Item interficiet pueros et amicos in presentia parentum. Item de hora in horam, de die in diem faciet a te abscindi unum membrum post aliud, non simul et semel, sed per plura tempora continuando." Brettle 1924, 179.

56. According to M.-M. Gorce, Vincent would spend significant amounts of time with Benedict XIII only twice after 1398: once in Genoa in 1405–7 (where Benedict had taken up residence temporarily, Genoa belonging then to France) and again in 1408–9 at the council of Perpignan, where Benedict resided from 1408 to 1415: Gorce 1924, 208. See also Garganta and Forcada 1956, 69, 71; FHSVF, 1:202–4.

57. FHSVF, 2:56; Gorce 1924, 211 (the meeting is dated to 1413); Garganta and Forcada 1956, 71.

58. Gerson wrote to Vincent on June 9, 1417; an accompanying postscript by Pierre d'Ailly is dated June 21, 1417; both are edited in Gerson 1960–73, 2: 200–202; similarly, Gerson makes an appeal for Vincent's presence at Constance in his *Tractatus contra sectam flagellentium,* dated July 18, 1417, Gerson 1960–73, 10:46–51. See Smoller 1994, 116–17.

59. See Montagnes 1980; similarly, Gorce 1924, 209–10.

from the Council of Constance, to Perpignan in 1415 with the fruitless goal of obtaining Benedict's resignation.[60] And Vincent would be instrumental in bringing about the eventual withdrawal of obedience from Benedict XIII by Aragon, Castile, and Navarre in January 1416. In a letter to the famous Dominican, Gerson glowingly expressed his gratitude for the preacher's efforts on that end.[61] But Vincent's efforts were not sufficient to earn him universal praise.

For some contemporaries, Vincent's well-known allegiance to Benedict was enough to damn him. According to his early twentieth-century biographer, hermits in Lombardy once confronted the famous preacher and called him an impostor. The proof of his deceit? "That you follow the party of the evil pope who is Antichrist."[62] And the fact remains that in the widely circulated 1412 letter to Benedict Vincent had presented the Avignon papacy as the only legitimate one and viewed the Roman and Pisan obediences as clearly schismatic. There, commenting on the ten-horned beast of Daniel 7, which Vincent read as representing the now-divided Roman Empire, the preacher interpreted the tenth horn as "the Catholic people and, now, the Spanish under our lord Pope Benedict XIII, the true vicar of our Lord Jesus Christ."[63] The Pisan (French) and Roman (Italian) obediences appear as the beast's horns number eight and nine, in company with such other luminaries as heretics, Armenians, Greek Orthodox, Muslims, and Jews. This was, evidently, the opinion for which contemporaries remembered Vincent.

That Vincent's activities during the Schism years were of concern to the promoters of his canonization is apparent in the carefully controlled testimony elicited at canonization inquests held in Toulouse and, most particularly, Naples. In those inquests a portrait emerges of Vincent Ferrer as a healer of all sorts of divisions, particularly the Schism.[64] The subcommissioners at the Naples inquest had questioned witnesses on a battery of articles of interrogation that had been supplied directly by Martial Auribelli.[65] The fifteenth of those articles asked witnesses to aver that Vincent "most *miraculously* [had] worked for the union of the Holy Church of God."[66]

---

60. Gorce 1924, 215, citing testimony of G. Dalruste [*sic*].

61. Montagnes 1980, 613; Gerson 1960–73, 2:200–201.

62. Quoted in FHSVF, 1: 136 (without citation of his source; my translation). Fages evidently has, however, no contemporary source, noting only that the eighteenth-century author José Teixidor y Trilles speaks of the "diables de Lombardie." FND, 113.

63. BNF, MS lat. 14669, fol. 142v: "decima pars populi catholici et modo hyspanorum sub domino nostro papa benedicto xiii° vero vicario domini nostri Ihesu Christi." (Also FND, 221.)

64. See Smoller 2004a, 289–308.

65. See chapter 2. Articles: *Proceso*, fol. 273v–275r (articles 21 and 22 are missing); FPC, 408–10.

66. *Proceso*, fol. 274v; FPC, 410, article 15: "pro unione ecclesie sancte Dei miraculosissime operatus est" (emphasis added).

The need to gloss over Vincent's associations with Avignon is also abundantly apparent in the brief notice about his life in the *Chronicle* of fellow Dominican archbishop Antoninus of Florence, written some time between Vincent's canonization in 1455 and Antoninus's death in 1459. There Antoninus felt compelled to note that "even though this Saint Vincent spent nearly his entire career under the obedience of Benedict XIII..., and the Italians and many other nations judged him [Benedict], with his followers, to be an apostate and schismatic... in no way does this overshadow the saint's merits or diminish his sanctity." Antoninus went on to note that saintly and experienced men had supported both sides of the Schism, and thus there were legitimate doubts about who was the true pope. Anyone who had erred would be excused by nearly "invincible ignorance."[67]

If Antoninus sensed a need to explain away Vincent's long adherence to the Avignon papacy, he also bore witness to the second of the new saint's major image problems: his role as an apocalyptic preacher. For not simply did Vincent proclaim himself the angel of the apocalypse[68] and move audiences to penitence with graphic descriptions of Antichrist's upcoming torments, but he also announced the imminence of that final persecution in a most decisive manner. Like many contemporaries, Vincent viewed the Schism as a sign of the approaching reign of Antichrist, along lines laid out in 2 Thessalonians 2:3 ("For that day shall not come, except there come a falling away [*discessio*] first, and that man of sin be revealed, the son of perdition.") Following the interpretation suggested in the *glossa ordinaria,* Vincent interpreted the "falling away" as a schism in the church. He had said as much already in 1380 in his *On the Present-Day Schism,* in which he worried that the Schism would last until Antichrist's open appearance.[69] Thirty-two years later, the situation appeared even more ominous.

In the same well-known letter written to Benedict XIII in 1412, Vincent described the sources of his assurance that Antichrist in fact had already been born and was now nine years old. The very specificity of this pronouncement, which presumably Vincent had broadcast in sermons as well, appears to have raised some contemporary eyebrows.[70] The letter was apparently

---

67. Antoninus Florentinus 1484, Pars III, titulus xxiii, capitulum viii, §4, fol. CCVIII v.

68. He did so, coyly, in the 1412 letter to Benedict XIII: FND, 221. Later tradition had Vincent making that announcement in Salamanca in the same year in the context of his conversion of an entire synagogue of Jews. See Antist 1956, 172–73.

69. Montagnes 1980, 611. On Vincent's apocalyptic preaching in Toulouse, see Montagnes 1992, 341–43, who notes that the apocalpytic theme was not always dominant in his sermons.

70. Toulouse witnesses Hugo Nigri (*Proceso,* fol. 185v; FPC, 299, witness 6) and Johannes Inardi (*Proceso,* fol. 241v; FPC, 390, witness 40) both report instances in which Vincent was forced to defend apocalyptic ideas that he had preached in his sermons. In addition, a Tuscan hermit named Franciscus related that he and others living with him believed Antichrist to have been born already because Vincent Ferrer had asserted that a hermit in Lombardy had told him so. Melk, Stiftsbibliothek,

written in response to Benedict XIII's rebuking Vincent for his apocalyptic preaching. In the letter, Vincent cited private revelations made to several different people with whom he had talked; all pointed to the same date for Antichrist's birth some nine years previously. Accordingly, Vincent's sermons terrifyingly reminded his audience that the end was at hand, a fact that helps to explain the extreme degrees of penitence to which he inspired his hearers. In Gerson's treatise against flagellants, aimed at the penitential band that accompanied Vincent on his preaching travels, he recommended that any preaching about the Last Judgment should be very general, noting that each person would meet his own judgment when he died. This remark very likely was a salvo aimed against Vincent's specific insistence that Antichrist had already been born and would soon begin his reign of terror.[71]

By the time of his canonization in 1455, Vincent's statement was patently and manifestly false. As Antoninus of Florence acknowledged, it was anticipated that Antichrist—the inversion of Christ—would manifest himself at age thirty to begin a three-and-one-half-year reign of terror. Antichrist clearly had not appeared at the appointed time (i.e., 1433). After raising some doubts as to whether his hero had in fact said Antichrist was already alive with the phrase "if these are his words," Antoninus explained that Vincent's erroneous prediction was not a lie but rather an opinion, "just as it seemed to him from the testimonies of scriptures [and] according to signs given or revelations made to him or passed on to him from others, which revelations sometimes are not fully understood." Other saints and church fathers, such as Gregory the Great, had also incorrectly assumed themselves to be living near the end of time, Antoninus pointed out. As for the famous letter to Benedict in which Vincent made his pronouncement, Antoninus couched his description of it in such evasive language as to make it seem of trivial importance, saying, "There is found a certain letter of his in which he *seems to say* expressly that Antichrist is already in the world."[72]

One scholar has noted that an early (1429) fresco depicting Vincent Ferrer with text from that letter proved to be an iconographical dead end. What emerged instead was an iconography that made a generalized reference to Vincent's apocalyptic preaching (the text uttered by the angel in Revelation 14:7 and, sometimes, the saint pointing upwards to a mandorla enclosing the Christ of the Last Judgment) but nothing that would indicate Vincent's

---

Hs. 688, f. 105v: "Quendam venerabilem religiosum ordinis predicatorum / vocatum magistrum Vincencium hactenus in regno Aragonum predicantem audivi narrantem / quod dum ipse in lumbardia predicaret / ad se venit quidam in vestibus albis heremetics habitu / asserens se in lucanis montibus habitare / contestans antichristum procreo iam natum in mundo." I am grateful to Daniel Hobbins for pointing me to this anecdote, as well as for sharing with me his transcription from the manuscript and the text of his unpublished article to appear in a festschrift for John Van Engen: Hobbins 2013.

71. Letter: FND, 222. Flagellants: Gerson 1960–73, 10:46–47. See Smoller 1994, 94–95, 116–17.

72. Antoninus Florentinus 1484, *Chronicon,* fol. CCVIII v (emphasis added).

specific pronouncements about Antichrist's presence in the world.[73] The two problems with Vincent's image—his predictions about Antichrist and his role during the Schism—were in a sense linked by that 1412 letter to Benedict XIII, and while promoters of his cult could not make the letter go away, they could minimize its importance and redirect attention to other aspects of Vincent's career.

## Pietro Ranzano's Portrait of Vincent Ferrer

Such, perhaps, were the instructions that Calixtus III and Martial Auribelli whispered in Pietro Ranzano's ear as they handed him a copy of the canonization proceedings and sent him off to Palermo to write Vincent's life. Ranzano must certainly have had a copy of the canonization inquests, and a well-worn manuscript of the same could still be found in Palermo in the sixteenth century, from which derived Vicente Justiniano Antist's copy of the text. Antist assumed that this manuscript represented a copy of the canonization proceedings made for the Dominican master general Salvo Cassetta to use in writing a life of Vincent Ferrer.[74] Later scholarship by Alfred Strnad, however, has discounted the notion that Cassetta ever wrote such a *vita*.[75]

But maybe the manuscript belonged instead to Ranzano. Rather than believe, as suggested by Antist and by Strnad, that the Palermo manuscript represents a copy given to the Dominican convent by Salvo Cassetta, it seems equally plausible to believe the remark of one seventeenth-century Dominican who reported that the Palermo library possessed what was said to be the original process of canonization.[76] If it did, perhaps Martial Auribelli and Calixtus III gave Ranzano the copy of the canonization process intended for deposit in the Dominican convent of Santa Maria sopra Minerva in Rome. After all, to wait to have a copy made of the hundreds of folios of testimony from the canonization inquests would have delayed Ranzano's task considerably.[77] If Ranzano *did* take the original manuscript to Palermo with him,

---

73. Rusconi 1990, esp. 222–24, 232–33.

74. On the copying of the Palermo manuscript, see chapter 2. Cassetta: FPC, 267–69; *Proceso*, fol. 12r. On Cassetta: Foa 1978.

75. Strnad 1978. But cf. Frazier 2005, 366, and Foa 1978, both of whom, on the basis of a remark by Leandro Alberti, believe Cassetta to have written such a *vita*, now lost.

76. Strnad 1978, 540, 544; Foa 1978 also assumes the Palermo manuscript was made at Cassetta's request. In 1674, Dominican master general P. Giovanni Tommaso de Rocaberti wrote, "They tell me in the same library [of St. Domenico in Palermo] is a manuscript of the original process of canonization of Saint Vincent Ferrer, or an authentic copy" (my translation), quoted in Barilaro 1977–78, 102.

77. As Ranzano wrote to Giovanni da Pistoia, the excerpts on Vincent Ferrer from the *Annals* (some sixteen folios) had taken two days to transcribe: BC, MS 112, fol. 52r. Antist's copy of the Palermo manuscript, which is incomplete, covers around three hundred folios.

that would explain not simply the inability of Valencian Dominicans to turn up a copy in Rome in the 1570s but also the rather puzzling fact that the canonization process does not appear in a late fifteenth-century inventory of the library of Santa Maria sopra Minerva, of which surely the manuscript would have been a major treasure.[78]

Whether Ranzano had the copy intended for Santa Maria sopra Minerva or another, he clearly was working from the canonization inquests, and it was that testimony that he would mold to create an official image of Vincent Ferrer in his *vita*. There one sees the author manipulating this material in such a way as to produce a portrait of Vincent Ferrer that would silence the nagging questions contemporaries like Antoninus of Florence felt compelled to address: the concerns about Vincent's unfulfilled apocalyptic predictions and his questionable role in the Schism years. In short, Ranzano's *vita* seeks to recast Vincent Ferrer primarily as a healer of the Schism and secondarily as a converter of Jews and Muslims. His youth and his entire adult life are marked by the presence of the Holy Spirit, which informs his preaching and facilitates the conversion of so many others. Ranzano's Vincent Ferrer appears as a new apostle—not as the sometime friend of Benedict XIII and not as a failed apocalyptic prophet.[79]

Ranzano's portrayal of the saint is most notable in his treatment of Vincent's adult life in book 2, in which the humanist moves thematically rather than chronologically through the saint's career. By so doing, Ranzano can assign the most prominent position in the book (chapter 1) to Vincent's labors in healing the Great Schism. First, he skillfully deals with the issue of Vincent's ties to Benedict XIII, on the one hand downplaying what some have characterized as a genuine friendship[80] and on the other hand being careful not to so deprecate the stubborn old pontiff that he taints Vincent by association or alienates readers who were favorably disposed toward the Avignon papacy. Second, although he does not go as far as Martial Auribelli's claim in the Naples articles of interrogation that Vincent had "miraculously" healed the Schism, Ranzano does indeed magnify Vincent's role in ending the division. Third, he places in this chapter the vision that authorized Vincent's preaching mission, shearing it of any connection to its context in the wake of the 1398 French subtraction of obedience from Benedict. Finally, he deals with the issue of Vincent's apocalyptic preaching, dismissing any concerns in a manner disarmingly forthright yet at the same time subtly oblique.

---

78. Meersseman 1947.

79. As will become apparent below, my reading of Ranzano differs from that of the author of the only other major study of the *Vita Vincentii,* who argues that there is little polemical aim apparent in Ranzano's *vita.* Coakley 1980, 107–40.

80. E.g., Gorce 1924, 199.

Taking the same strategy that his fellow Dominican Antoninus of Florence would employ in his *Chronicle,* Ranzano begins the first chapter of book 2 with a markedly dispassionate description of the Great Schism. Benedict XIII, he explains, was a cardinal under Pope Clement VII, "who, as we said in the previous book, was named pope in Fundos by that part of the cardinals who withdrew from Urban VI." Even though, as Ranzano details, that double election would lead to a situation in which three popes presided over the Catholic Church, with each claiming to have been legitimately elected, he does not denounce any of the rival claimants. Rather, embracing an almost studied neutrality, Ranzano adds that how the Schism happened "is not for us to say here; it is for those to say who have written the catalog of the highest pontiffs." Instead, Ranzano simply notes that nearly all the "princes and cities" of Spain and Gaul followed Benedict.[81]

When he describes Vincent Ferrer's affiliation with Benedict XIII, Ranzano is equally careful not to make the relationship too close, particularly on Vincent's part. In Ranzano's telling, upon his election to the papacy (1394), Benedict "commanded the man of God Vincent to be summoned to him." Knowing Vincent's erudition and saintly life, Benedict chose him to be his confessor and master of the sacred palace. In Ranzano's words, however, Vincent's response sounds like that of an obedient servant and not that of either a true friend or one excited about the chance to serve in the papal household. "Lest he appear to disobey the pontiff's commands," Ranzano writes, Vincent "diligently carried out all that was imposed on him" even though "it pained him" to follow the court of a terrestrial ruler. For Ranzano, Benedict XIII's Avignon becomes a place in which Vincent applied himself to sacred readings, vigils, fasts, hymns, and prayers but not the locus of a deep, personal relationship with the pope to whom he acted as confessor.[82]

Although Ranzano takes a neutral stance about the legitimacy of any of the papal lines during the Great Schism, he does acknowledge that the situation caused many to be troubled and to try to end the division. Yet since it seemed wrong to use force to remove the three rival pontiffs, Ranzano admits, "those who wished for [union] were not able to bring it about." What to do? According to Ranzano, there had been only one clear answer: "Accordingly, many people, both prelates of the church and earthly princes, committed the whole matter to the faith of Blessed Vincent....Everyone judged that no one among mortals could be found who would complete such a matter more diligently or prudently or better."[83] It is not clear when or how this commission took place, and Ranzano is carefully vague about

---

81. RVV, 1:491.
82. Ibid.
83. Ibid.

when and where and just who the "many" and "everyone" were who entrusted the healing of the Schism to Vincent's hands.

What exactly Vincent did to end the Schism is also not entirely clear in Ranzano's narration. "First," he tells us, "the man of God went to Pope Benedict" and persuaded him to call a meeting of prelates, theologians, and lawyers to talk about what could be done. Then Vincent counseled Benedict "that it would be better to lead a life of the greatest want than that because of his earthly dignity he should sow discord among Christians." At length, Vincent urged Benedict to resign the papacy "for the peace of the church." But, as Ranzano admits, "the pope...did not want to resign." While he has Benedict gathering his prelates around him for still more talks, Ranzano places his hero in action. "But Vincent," he assured us, "meanwhile omitted nothing in order that [even] his smallest works would make for the union of the Church." Specifically, Ranzano has Vincent traveling throughout Spain and France, conferring with the German emperor Sigismund in Catalonia, King Martí of Aragon, Charles of France, and Benedict himself "so that some happy end at last might be imposed on such a dangerous matter." Ranzano implies that Vincent's negotiations were indeed fruitful. "*For that reason [itaque]*," Ranzano continues, a general council was called in the city of Constance.[84]

Ranzano's narration is, one is tempted to say, deliberately fuzzy about the timing of all these events. First, he jumps abruptly from the time of Benedict's election in 1394 to the creation of a third line of popes at Pisa in 1409. The order of his narration implies that the drafting of Vincent Ferrer to end the Schism occurred at a time when there were already three popes (after 1409), but when he details Vincent's efforts to that end, he mentions that Benedict was unwilling to resign because "he had not long been pope," clearly not the case in 1409.[85] As for Vincent's shuttling between the German emperor Sigismund (r. 1410–37), the Aragonese king Martí (r. 1395–1410), and the French king Charles VI (r. 1380–1422), Ranzano must be referring to Vincent's activities during Sigismund's 1415 embassy to Perpignan (although Martí was long dead at that point), for he stipulates that the emperor was in Catalonia at the time. At any rate, Vincent's diplomacy in 1415 could hardly be said to have caused the calling of the Council of Constance, for which invitations went out in the fall of 1413 and which opened in the fall of 1414. But by his vague chronology, Ranzano is able to imply that Vincent's voice had been the most important one in the summoning of the council.

Ranzano next discusses Vincent's vision of Christ with Saints Dominic and Francis, the vision the preacher had described in his widely known

---

84. Ibid. (emphasis added).
85. Ibid.

1412 letter to Benedict XIII and the vision that authorized Vincent's twenty-year preaching mission. Again, Ranzano plays a little loose with his chronology, for he situates Vincent's illness and vision in a time "when these things were happening in Avignon and in Constance," presumably, then, during the Council of Constance (1414–17) that he has just mentioned.[86] In Ranzano's version, Vincent's illness is brought on not by the turmoil of 1398 but by "an excessively agitated mind," ruminating anxiously on what to do about the Schism.[87] In Ranzano's telling, then, the circumstances surrounding Vincent's illness and vision have been stripped of all connection to the French subtraction of obedience from Benedict. Better simply to avoid that troubled time, it seems.

Ranzano's treatment of Vincent's vision also shows the humanist at his rhetorical best. If Vincent's own narrative hides its protagonist behind a cloak of third-person anonymity ("a certain religious"), Ranzano relishes the moment, inventing a long speech to Vincent, which he puts in the Savior's mouth. In Ranzano's version Christ instructed Vincent to "go away from Benedict's court," to evangelize all of Gaul and Spain, to preach the imminent coming of the Day of Judgment, and eventually to meet his death "in the ends of the earth." Gently touching Vincent's cheek "as if to show a sign ... to him of his singular familiarity," Christ healed the preacher and disappeared.[88] Vincent now struggled to obey both Christ and Benedict, jumping up from his bed to beg Benedict's permission to embark on his preaching mission. Benedict, however, only looked for ways to keep Vincent near him and, that failing, to detain him through offering him the bishopric of Valencia or even the position of cardinal. Vincent, however, could not be bribed or dissuaded, and eventually Benedict gave him leave to go begin his preaching mission.

At this point Ranzano meets head-on the concerns contemporaries had about Vincent's apocalyptic preaching and offers a vigorous and ingenious defense of his hero. Ranzano has already in effect defended Vincent's preaching on the end of the world by making it a specific part of the mission entrusted to him by Christ in his vision. So Vincent was merely fulfilling a divine command when "among other things that he taught, he asserted, with many reasons, that the Last Judgment was coming soon." Nonetheless, according to Ranzano, "for that reason there were many who said to the pope that Master Vincent was disseminating several novel doctrines, among which the chief was that he said the day of the Last Judgment was near in

---

86. Ibid. It may be that Ranzano has simply confused the 1398 illness and vision with Vincent's illness in Perpignan in 1415, for which he refused a physician but prophesied his recovery. See FHSVF, 2:101.

87. RVV, 1:491.

88. Ibid.

our own times." Ranzano says that Benedict, in response, sent letters to Vincent asking for an explanation.[89] Vincent's famous letter of 1412, then, becomes the obedient response of a humble cleric to a pope's request, not an indication of close ties or friendship between the two men.

In fact, Ranzano downplays the famous letter and baldly avoids the topic of Vincent's specific pronouncements about the end of the world. So when he discusses the 1412 letter to Benedict XIII, Ranzano dubs it almost dismissively a "little book [*libellus*]." And, while he notes that in this "little book" Vincent "showed with probability the Judgment to be close to our own times," Ranzano adds that neither the pope nor those who had criticized Vincent's teaching about the apocalypse "could find anything in it worthy of the least censure."[90] That Vincent had proclaimed Antichrist to be already nine years old never appears in Ranzano's treatment. Nor does the fact that Vincent's assertions had obviously, in retrospect, been wrong.

Indeed, Ranzano quickly refocuses the reader's attention on the Schism, describing the deposition of all three rival popes by the Council of Constance. Two of the popes, Gregory XII and John XXIII, thereupon gave up their positions, but, as Ranzano must admit, Benedict clung fiercely to his title. He paints a poignant picture of Vincent trying, one last time, to reason with the recalcitrant pope, urging him to heed the council's decrees, but as Ranzano tersely puts it, "his words could not persuade [Benedict]." Perhaps surprisingly, Ranzano does not take the opportunity to give Vincent credit for the withdrawal of the kingdom of Aragon from Benedict's obedience, the act for which Jean Gerson would later thank the Dominican preacher so lavishly. Rather, he prefers to keep the focus on Vincent himself, who, thwarted once more by Benedict's stubbornness, "forsook him." (The Latin word Ranzano chooses to describe Vincent's abandonment of Benedict is *discessit*, from the same root as the term used in the apocalyptic 2 Thessalonians 2:3 to describe the "falling away" preceding the arrival of Antichrist, and which Vincent and other medieval interpreters understood to mean a schism in the church.) Ending chapter 1 of book 2, Ranzano has Vincent "return[ing] to his usual activities."[91] The remainder of book 2 Ranzano devotes to detailing those activities—Vincent's travels and mode of life (chapter 2), his preaching and especially his conversion of Jews and Muslims (chapter 3), and his counsel to religious and political leaders (chapter 4). Deftly silencing Vincent's potential detractors, Ranzano in book 2 casts his protagonist primarily as a healer of schism and a converter of Muslims and Jews.

---

89. Ibid., 1:492.

90. Ibid.

91. Ibid. On late medieval readings of the *discessio* of 2 Thess. 2:3 as referring to the Great Schism, see Smoller 1994, 87, 94, 97–98, 100, 105.

## The Chopped-Up Baby Story

While Ranzano in book 2 used a deliberately vague chronology and description of Vincent's apocalyptic ideas to shield his hero from the criticisms of
some contemporaries, a yet more remarkable transformation of his source
material occurs in the hagiographer's third book, one devoted to the living
saint's prophecies and miracles. There Ranzano effects a transformation of
the inquest testimony that shows the Palermitan humanist hard at work to
create a shorthand icon for his new portrait of Vincent Ferrer. The third
book opens with two chapters on Vincent's prophetic gifts, then ends with
three chapters about miracles worked by the living saint. And in detailing
Vincent's miracles, Ranzano works a little marvel of his own. The very first
miracle that he describes, and in considerable detail, is the story of a baby,
chopped up and cooked by its mother, then reconstituted and resuscitated
by the saint's intercession. By position and length alone Ranzano establishes
a prime importance for this singularly striking miracle tale.[92] He doubtless
took the story from the canonization inquests, for versions of it appear in
the testimony from both Brittany and Naples. He took considerable liberty
with his sources, however.[93]

The earliest traces of the story of the chopped-up baby appear in the
Brittany canonization inquest, in the testimony of a noble woman named
Oliva de Coatsal, a widow of about fifty.[94] Some two or so years after Vincent's death, Oliva's own son had been resuscitated at the site of Vincent's
tomb in Vannes, only the second such miracle "publicized" in Vannes after
the saint's death, as she believed. Then, "immediately after the resuscitation
of her son," the widow told the commissioners, the parents of another infant
came to the tomb, a child—in her estimation—of some one and a half years
in age. This child, as the parents related, had been cut into two parts by his
mother, and one could still see the "sign of this division" in the child's head,

---

92. RVV, 1: 502–3. There follow tales of another infant's resurrection, the healing of a mute
woman, the healing of another mute woman, the multiplication of a small amount of food to serve
two thousand, the expulsion of several demons from people and horses, weather miracles, cures
of many sick and crippled people, and, last, the miraculous loss of voice of one who spoke against
Vincent in Toulouse. The chopped-up baby story is not only the first of these but is also among
the longest of the miracle stories in Ranzano's *vita*. My assessment is thus in contrast to the view
of Ranzano presented by Coakley 1980, 121 ("For there is little evidence in the *Vita Vincentii* that
Ransano intends to appropriate the supernatural attributes of his saint for particular ends.") and 124
("Raymond uses the miracles associated with Catherine [of Siena] as a means to a propagandistic
end....Ransano has no such apparent propagandistic intent in the *Vita Vincentii*.").

93. There is always the possibility that the missing Avignon testimony included a version more
in conformity with Ranzano's telling of the tale. The fact would remain, however, that Ranzano
chose to narrate *that* version of the story and not the one appearing in the Brittany and Naples
inquests, a posthumous miracle that served his purposes much less well, as will be made apparent below.

94. *Procès,* witness 73; FPC, 110.

presumably a seam indicating where the two halves had been fused. Why had the mother committed such a horror? According to the father, she was pregnant with another child and desired to eat meat, but the couple had none.[95] A vow made to Vincent Ferrer by the parents had resulted in the baby's resuscitation and complete healing through the saint's merits, and—presumably—the trip to Vincent's tomb to offer their prayers and thanks.

This tale obviously struck the commissioners impaneled in Brittany. They stopped Oliva to ask her several questions. *Did she know these parents?* No, nor did she know whence they had come, only that they spoke in French and not Breton. (In the fifteenth century, a north-south line divided the duchy into two parts linguistically, with the western half speaking Breton and the eastern half speaking French.) *Did she know how long the infant had remained dead and cut into two parts and how long afterward he had been carried to Vincent's tomb?* She did not know. Nor did she know anything else about the infant.[96] And there it stands: a story known through hearsay, tantalizingly bizarre, maddeningly unverifiable, but vigorously affirmed—not at all unlike a modern urban legend.[97]

By the time that Oliva related her memory to the Brittany panel some thirty years later, the case of the chopped-up baby had apparently acquired a certain notoriety in the duchy. We hear it again from a witness who testified late in the course of the inquest, a man named Guillermus Rollandi, of some thirty years of age, born presumably a year or two *after* the events Oliva de Coatsal had recalled. Guillermus was testifying about the miraculous resuscitation of his own daughter some two years previously. The girl had apparently sickened and died following an acute, grave illness, when Guillermus "recalled a certain miracle of which there was mention on a certain painted tableau on Vincent's tomb, namely, that on account of the prayers [*preces*] of Vincent Ferrer, God had resuscitated an infant whose mother had killed him." That memory prompted Guillermus to invoke Vincent's intercession on behalf of his own daughter, and she immediately returned to life.[98]

---

95. Ibid.: "Subjungit quod immediate et in instanti post resuscitationem dicti infantuli venerunt ut dicebatur parentes unius alterius infantuli etatis ut apparebat unius anni cum dimidio vel sic qui ut dicebatur fuerat a matre per caput in duas partes abscisus et divisus et signum huius divisionis in capite ipsius infantis apparebat ex eo quod illa mater pregnans ut pater dicti infantuli dicebat tunc appetebat comedere carnes quas non habebat." On the cravings of pregnant women and the real danger to the woman and fetus if such cravings were denied, see Pseudo-Albertus Magnus 1992, 141. In one case, according to Pseudo-Albertus (122), a pregnant woman greatly desired to eat her husband's testicles and fell gravely ill when her craving went unfulfilled!

96. *Procès,* witness 73; FPC, 110.

97. See, e.g., Brunvand 1989; Enders 2002.

98. *Procès,* witness 263; FPC, 222: "Et cum filia esset in tali statu donec testis reducens ad memoriam quoddam miraculum de quo fuit mentio in quadam tabula depicta existente supra sepulcrum dicte M. V. videlicet quod Deus resuscitavit quemdam infantulum quem ejus mater occiderat, ad preces dicte M. V."

The custodians of Vincent Ferrer's tomb took care to cultivate public memory of the miracle-working powers of its occupant, particularly in the years leading up to the canonization inquest. The canons rang the cathedral bells with the news of each new miracle worked by Vincent's merits, and we know from several witnesses that they carefully recorded the miracles in a little book.[99] This book was perhaps the source for the miracles depicted on the tableau to which Guillermus alluded. The important fact here is that the story of the chopped-up baby featured prominently in such a representation, perhaps because it was one of the earliest miracles so recorded or perhaps because of the striking nature of the story. The Brittany version of the story was thus intimately associated with a specific place: Vincent Ferrer's tomb in Vannes. Vincent's tomb represented the site at which the story first reached public eyes and ears, and it was also the place where others learned of the miracle. The story was a testimonial to the wonder-working shrine that was in the Vannes cathedral.

But the bizarre tale of the chopped-up baby was not just part of Brittany's memory of Vincent Ferrer. It traveled with those who visited the duchy and who knew a good story when they heard one. Thus, we encounter the tale as well in the testimony of two of the witnesses at the Naples inquest into Vincent's sanctity held in 1454. First, we hear the story from an unnamed witness who in turn had gotten the information from a monk who had traveled to Brittany to visit Vincent's tomb and had returned with "many authentic miracles in public form."[100] It is not clear what the witness meant by this phrase, but perhaps he meant to say that these narratives had been made public at the cathedral, an act that in and of itself represented a form of authentication on the part of the cathedral clergy.[101] In fact, our witness remembered only one miracle from the collection of "authentic miracles": the story of the chopped-up baby. This time the vestiges of cannibalism are missing. The mother who chops up her child is described simply as foolish (*fatua*), not as a meat-craving pregnant woman. The husband gets the credit for finding the child's two parts, joining them together, and taking them to Vincent's tomb, where the infant is revived ("which is beyond the power of nature," the eager witness notes). Our witness reports having encountered the story some forty years ago, that is, around the time of the saint's death.[102] Presumably, his story is fairly close to the "authentic public" version he had

---

99. E.g., Brittany witness Yvo Natalis (*Procès,* witness 239; FPC, 198), who testified that he had been recording miracles in a book for the last four years in the Vannes cathedral.

100. *Proceso,* fol. 257v–258r; FPC, 438–39, witness 16: "multa miracula auctentica in publica forma."

101. See Smoller 2011a, 780–83.

102. *Proceso,* fol. 257v–258r; FPC, 438–39, witness 16: "Quedam mulier fatua divisit filium suum in duas partes et veniens maritus eius reperit filium suum mortuum in duas partes divisum, cepitque ipsum et coniunxit partes ipsas et portavit ipsum ad sepulcrum B. Vincentii in summa devotione

read. The tomb in Brittany has become even more central to the miracle, for the resuscitation now takes place at the tomb itself.

A much more elaborate version of the chopped-up baby story comes from the Naples testimony of a man from Valencia who is not named but identified simply as a herald. He had spent some time in Brittany, where he "heard tell" of a man who had a demented wife. The unfortunate man instructed his wife to prepare him lunch to be ready on his return home. The woman took up their fourteen-month-old son, killed him with a sword, "dividing him through the middle," and then took one-quarter of the body—from the upper half—and cooked it. When her husband returned home for lunch, she presented him with "the said part of his son, boiled in broth and saffron, in which was apparent a hand and a certain part of the boy's body." "What have you done?" wailed the husband, with "tears and great sorrow." The wife's reply: "This is a quarter part of your son and mine: eat." At this point, according to the herald, the husband gathered up the various parts of the boy, took them to the Vannes cathedral and placed them on Vincent Ferrer's tomb. There he remained, wailing and lamenting, until nightfall, when those presiding in the cathedral gave him leave to go home. But when the father arrived home, he found his son playing "under the bed, in the manner of boys." And—a confirming detail—the quarter part of his body that had been boiled was tinted with saffron. The father, seeing this great miracle, presented his son to the cathedral to help with the service of Vincent Ferrer. Our Valencian herald added that he himself had seen the boy alive and well, still tinged with saffron, only six days later. And he added that this story was well known in Vannes and beyond.[103] When pressed to provide a date, he said that this had taken place "around the time of the Jubilee in Compostela," probably within a few years of the saint's death.[104]

By the time the Valencian herald recalls the case of the cut-up baby for the Naples inquest in 1454, the tale has been considerably embellished from

---

sperans precibus et meritis B. Vincentii filium suum resurrecturum et sanari, cuius B. Vincentii meritis omnipotens Deus suscitavit filium ipsum et sanavit quod fuit ultra vires nature et potentias."

103. *Proceso,* fol. 260r–260v; FPC, 441–42: "Testis ipse audivit dici in dicta civitate Venetensi in qua est corpus B. V. predicti eidem erat quidam habens uxorem dementem....Que mulier habens unum filium de dicto suo viro etatis quatuordecim mensium dicta mulier demens capiens gladium dictum suum filium occidit, ipsum dividens per medium et ipso interfecto et diviso ut premititur, cepit quartam partem corporis dicti filii sui ex parte superiori et eam posuit in ollam, et veniens maritus suus prefatus in prandio paravit eidem dictam quartam partem sui filii lixatam cum brodio et croco in quo apparebat manus et certa pars corporis ipsius pueri filii ipsorum coniugum. Qui videns stupefactus est cum lacrimis et maximo dolore dicens sue uxori, quid fecisti, que respondit, ista est quarta pars dicti filii tui et mei, comede....Invenit dictum filium suum ludentem subtus lectum more puerorum, tenens dictam quartam partem corporis sui tinctam de croco sufarane prout cissa fuerat....Interrogatus de tempore dixit quod tempore jubilei in Comp[ost]ella."

104. I am assuming he means the Jubilee decreed in 1423 by Martin V, that is, some four years after Vincent Ferrer's death.

the stark version encountered in the Brittany testimony of widow Oliva de Coatsal, whether through many previous retellings or through the herald's own imagination (and one must suspect the latter in part). The foolish or meat-craving pregnant wife has become more sinister and is now in fact demented. The recitation now has dialogue, homey details like the baby playing under the bed, and a recipe (boil one part baby with broth and saffron; serve). This recipe at least is more Valencian paella than *enfant à la Bretagne*. The poor infant is actually cooked and very nearly eaten. (One shudders to think what might have happened if the hand had not been visible in the stew.) There is a definite setting, the city of Vannes, and the dramatic vigil at the tomb followed by the boy's miraculous reappearance—whole and alive—at home. And the sign of the baby's division of the original Brittany tale has been replaced by the saffron-tinged quarter of his body. In the place of the parents' grateful pilgrimage to the saint's tomb, we have the father's oblation of the child to the service of Vincent Ferrer.

To these striking depositions, Pietro Ranzano applied the full powers of his humanist rhetorical training. But, in his *Life of Vincent,* Ranzano does not simply elaborate the story by adding dialogue and other gripping details, as the Valencian herald had done and as humanist hagiographers also frequently did. Rather, he makes some important changes to the miracle's setting. First of all, he shifts the time of the miracle to the saint's own lifetime, despite the fact that all four mentions of the story in the canonization inquests put it after Vincent's death. Second, he moves the miracle's location from Brittany and Vincent's tomb to a town in "that part of Gaul which is called Languedoc."[105] Third, he plays with the problem plaguing the butchering mother, who suffers now from temporary insanity, not the cravings of a pregnant woman. With these changes, Ranzano is able to create a tale that stands as icon for his portrayal of Vincent Ferrer.

According to Ranzano's *vita,* the story concerned a noble man and his beautiful and virtuous wife, who suffered from an illness that rendered her at times dangerously insane. When Vincent Ferrer came to their village, the man begged the saint to lodge in his home, and whenever Vincent was in the house, the wife suffered no intervals of dementia and the husband believed her to be cured. But one day Vincent was out of the house preaching a

---

105. RVV, 1:502. The Bollandists note that the name of the town was left blank in the manuscript from Utrecht that they used (rendering it, "in quamdam villam, quæ dicitur ___"); in the version in Vatican City, BAV, Chigi F. IV. 91 (fol. 13v), the city (*civitas*) is simply not named, but there is not an obvious blank either. The Bollandists speculate that the town's name was omitted to spare the family embarrassment (RVV, 1:504). In the version from Toulouse presumed to represent Ranzano's own copy of the work, the miracle takes place in Le Puy-en-Velay (*Anicium*). Bibliothèque municipale, Toulouse, MS 486, fol. 62v: "Cum per eam partem galliacum quam vocant anicium verbum edifficacionis beatus Vincencius seminaret devenit in quamdam villa que dicitur anicium." Vincent preached in Le Puy in October 1416: FHSVF, 2:180–83.

sermon (which the husband faithfully attended). The man had left his wife and a servant at home to prepare the saint's meal. With Vincent out of the house, however, her old fury swept over her, and she seized her infant son, cut the body into pieces, and put one part on the fire for lunch and left the other part for dinner.[106] When the sermon was over, the husband hurried home and asked his wife if she had the preacher's lunch ready. She replied, yes, that she had cooked some choice meat along with some fish and that she had set aside the rest of the meat for dinner. The husband reproached his wife because he had told her not to cook meat, which the holy man never ate. Investigating the matter further, he apprehended the truth: that the choice meat she described was their own son. Not simply grieving, the father poured forth outrage that this should be his reward for his works of piety in playing host to the famous preacher. News quickly reached Vincent, who hastened to the man's house, had the parts brought to him, and prayed over them. At once, before the admiring spectators, the body was reassembled and the infant restored to life.[107]

Ranzano's concern to reshape the memory of Vincent Ferrer is apparent, I suggest, in his highlighting (and reworking) of the tale of the chopped-up baby, describing the miracle as one effected during the saint's life on earth. A hearsay tale with no named beneficiary or witnesses, it did not adhere to late medieval standards of evidence and proof of miracles.[108] Nonetheless, Ranzano gives prime position to just this miracle in his *vita*, also featuring it in the office he composed for the Feast of Saint Vincent Ferrer, another important source of the dissemination of this story.[109] Just as the most important of Vincent's life works became, in Ranzano's *vita*, his role in healing the Schism, so, too, his most important miracle became his reassembling of the baby who, like the church, was cut into pieces.[110] The miracle's new location, somewhere in Languedoc, sanctifies a region that is much closer to Avignon (and Vincent's troublesome ties to Benedict XIII) than is Vincent's tomb in Brittany. It may not be too much of a stretch to read the sometimes demented mother of Ranzano's tale as *Mater Ecclesia,* the Mother Church, who has rent her child (the body of the faithful) into pieces (the two and then three obediences of the Great Schism).

Even though the mother is guilty of infanticide and, nearly, cannibalism, Ranzano does not condemn her, although by the time he was writing,

---

106. RVV, 1:502.

107. Ibid., 1:502–3.

108. For the rigor with which witnesses were questioned and the materials scrutinized, see Goodich 1995, 6–14; and Vauchez 1997, 35–39, 49–55, 481–98.

109. BC, MS 112, fol. 79v: "In frusta mater lacerat demens infantem proprium sed patris fletus impetrat ad vitam reddi filium."

110. This identification of the chopped-up baby with the church of the Schism years was also made by Fages in the early twentieth century. FHSVF, 2:55.

European women were being accused of infant cannibalism in conjunction with the earliest witch trials. Ranzano's mother is, rather, like *Ecclesia:* beautiful, gentle, and proper when her madness is not upon her. The still-living saint's prayers heal both infant and mother, just as Ranzano insists elsewhere in the *vita* that Vincent's labors end the division and madness in the church.[111] The frequent medieval attribution of maternal imagery to the clerical office may have helped to clarify the hagiographer's point: the temporarily insane mother represented those wrong-headed clerics whose actions had initiated and prolonged the Schism.[112]

Associations with other tales of infant dismemberment and cannibalism would have reinforced Ranzano's meaning. Ranzano's audience would have known well the story of the judgment of Solomon, in which two harlots each claimed the same child as their own. Solomon's order to divide the child in half revealed the true mother: the one who would rather see the child alive and given to her rival than dead and shared between the two. Since at least the time of Gregory the Great, commentators had identified the two quarreling mothers with *Ecclesia* and *Synagoga*.[113] The madness of the Schism years threatened to transform the church into the bad mother (*Synagoga*), who would rather see the infant perish after being divided. Again, the implication was that Vincent's prayers had healed the madness. A 1219 letter from Pope Honorius III to Irish prelates complaining of the church's slowness in implementing the reforms of the Fourth Lateran Council invokes the image of "poor women who cook their children" to castigate those prelates who dissipate and consume church properties committed to their keeping.[114] Here again, maternal cannibalism serves to express the clergy's improper stewardship of the church. Ranzano may have intended a nod as well to Saint Nicholas's miraculous restoration of the dismembered and pickled flesh of three young men. By the fourteenth and fifteenth centuries, these youths were held to be three clerics.[115] Perhaps hints of this miraculous reassembling of three clerics ("where there are two or three gathered together," Matthew 18:20) also reinforced Ranzano's implication that the healing of the chopped-up baby stood for the restoration of the church.

---

111. It is perhaps worth noting that among authors writing during the Schism, images and metaphors for the divided church tended more to include two-headed monsters, prostitutes, and adulterous spouses. See Blumenfeld-Kosinski 2006, 2007, and 2009.

112. See, e.g., Bynum 1982, esp. 110–69. I discuss such maternal imagery as applied to holy *women* in Smoller 2005.

113. *Biblia sacra* 1545, 3 Regum 3:16, *glossa ordinaria,* fol. 129v.

114. The letter appears in Mansi 1759–98, 22: cols. 1098–1100 (the relevant passage is at col. 1099). I am grateful to David Foote for pointing my attention to this passage.

115. See Ricci 1982. My thanks to Daniel Bornstein for suggesting this parallel.

## From Folklore to Hagiography

Pietro Ranzano's highlighting of the chopped-up baby's resuscitation brought to the fore a tale whose roots seem to lie as much in the world of fairy tale and urban legend as in the day-to-day events of fifteenth-century Brittany. Folklorists who study such stories theorize that urban legends become a part of our social memory because they strike some receptive nerve in society. Many of today's urban legends, for example, express a fear of the extent to which technology has become a part of the modern world, yet in their bizarreness they allow us to laugh at those fears.[116] If the tale of the chopped-up baby resembles a modern urban legend, then its circulation and currency must reveal something about the fears and concerns of the fifteenth-century Europeans who repeated it over and over, perhaps converting a story heard in childhood into a narrative of the saint's prowess. While the Valencian herald who testified in Naples brought home with him the outlines of a miracle tale, his imagination must have merged that story with folktales of child-eating ogres and sinister mothers, narratives with grabbing—and memorable—details like dialogue and saffron-tinged flesh.

In fact, the herald's telling of the story has strong echoes of other European folk and fairy tales. The serving up of a stewed child to an unsuspecting father shows up, for example, in the Grimms' tale "The Juniper Tree," versions of which have been collected by folklorists from all over Europe.[117] In the Grimms' story, an evil stepmother kills the son born to her husband's first wife to assure her own daughter's inheritance. She cooks him into a stew and serves it to the boy's father while the sister stands by crying. But after the father finishes the meal, the loyal sister gathers the boy's bones, ties them up in her scarf, and buries them under the juniper tree in the yard. Suddenly the bones are transformed into a beautiful bird, who goes around singing, "My mother, she slew me, / My father, he ate me." At length, the bird returns to the house, showers the sister and father with gifts, and drops a millstone on the evil stepmother's head, killing her. At that, the bird disappears, and the brother, alive and whole, is restored to his joyous father and sister.[118]

Closer to home, the Breton folktale "The Red Shoes" has a mother (not a stepmother) chopping up her son and making him into a stew. (Folklorists collected at least one version of this tale in Morbihan, the region in which

---

116. See, e.g., Brunvand 1989.

117. Grimm no. 47, "Von dem Machandelbaum" (Aarne-Thompson tale type 720), in Rölleke 1985, 209–17. See Bolte and Polívka (1913–32) 1963, 1:413–23; Tatar 2002, 158–71; Fentress and Wickham 1992, 62–75; Darnton 1984, 15 (French version, "Ma mère m'a tué"). See also S. Thompson 1966, nos. E 121.4.1, G 64, G 303.25.4, G 61.1, G 86, G 10ff, H 46.1, G 30ff, S 324, T 571. Paul Sébillot lists three Breton tales involving elements similar to the chopped-up baby story: Sébillot 1892, 13.

118. Quotation from the translation in Tatar 2002, 165.

Vincent's tomb in Vannes stands.)[119] As in the Valencia herald's retelling of the Vincent miracle, the recipient of the stew (in this case, the sister) recognizes her brother's head and fingers in her plate. This time, the Virgin instructs the sister to gather up the bones, then reassembles the pieces and makes of them a beautiful white pigeon (dove), who promises to fill the sister's apron with bonbons. Instead, stones rain from the sky on the heads of the mother and father, and the dove rejoices, "We are saved; my mother is damned."[120]

Motifs from the tale of the chopped-up baby can also be found in folktales, ancient mythology, and medieval saints' legends. The story of Tereus, Procne, and Philomela—known to medieval and Renaissance readers through Ovid's *Metamorphoses*—also ends with an unknowing, although cruel, father eating a baby stew prepared by the mother.[121] In a grislier variation on the theme, reported by Josephus and repeated by many medieval authors, it is the mother herself who eats half of the child she has cooked in a harrowing moment during the Roman siege of Jerusalem.[122] Resuscitation from parts is also a frequent folktale motif, such as in the Egyptian legend of Isis and Osiris, which has the goddess gathering up the scattered pieces of her brother-husband's body and restoring him to wholeness and life. Restoration of a dismembered body similarly shows up in medieval miracle stories, such as the tale of Saint Germanus of Auxerre's resuscitation of a calf cooked for him or the story in which Saint Nicholas of Bari restores life to three youths who were cut up and pickled by an evil butcher.[123] In fact, a late fifteenth-century book of hours from Brittany depicts just this scene for its portrait of Saint Nicholas, just one page before an illumination of Vincent Ferrer.[124]

Given the many narrative models of dismemberment, cannibalism, and recomposition from parts, it may well be that the story of the chopped-up

---

119. Sébillot 1880, 336–37; also mentioned in Bolte and Polívka (1913–32) 1963, 1:418. (In the Grimms' tale, one of the gifts received by the sister is a pair of red shoes.)

120. Sébillot 1880, 337. In the Breton folk tale "La Princesse Félicité," in order to revive a servant who has been killed and transformed into a statue, a father kills his son and sprinkles the statue with his blood. All that is needed to revive the son is for him to chop up the son's body and put the parts in warm water, at which the son instantly comes back to life. Sébillot 1881, 115–17. Sébillot also recounts also a Breton sailor's tale in which in exchange for favors a father is asked to cut up and deliver only one-half of his son. But when he agrees to do it, the request is rescinded. Sébillot 1882, 168–69 ( Jean de Calais).

121. Ovid 1972, 2:50–56 (VI, ll. 424–674).

122. Josephus 1981, 340–42 (VI.3.201–13); see below. Like Ovid, Josephus was a favorite among humanist readers.

123. The story of Saint Germanus appears in Jacobus de Voragine 1993, 2:29. Germanus was hosted by a swineherd, who butchered and fed the saint his only calf. After the dinner, the saint laid all the calf's bones on its hide and prayed over them, after which the calf stood up alive, whole and intact. See also Bertolotti 1991, 42–70. On Nicholas's miracle, see Ricci 1982, esp. 370–82.

124. BNF, MS lat. 1369, Heures d'Isabeau d'Écosse, duchesse de Bretagne, 316.

baby had its ultimate origin in the world of folktale, although we can never know what really happened or did not happen to that unnamed Breton family. But clearly, the folkloric character of the tale helped make it memorable and provided narrators with models for further elaboration.[125] As the story made its way through Brittany and abroad, via our Valencian traveler and others like him, tellers recalled the miracle along the lines of other tales they knew (such as folktales or *exempla*), conflating a bare-bones version of the story with other dramatic narrations to create the fleshed-out narrative that shows up in 1454 in Naples. In highlighting this miracle story, Ranzano at the very least knew that it was one that would grab his readers' attention and linger in their memories.

For those still angered over the events of the Schism, Pietro Ranzano's tale of Vincent Ferrer and the chopped-up baby may well have helped to smooth over questions about the new saint's association with Benedict XIII. But by the time of Vincent's canonization many European Christians had begun to move on, preferring a deliberate neutrality on the Schism that allowed them to focus on the problems of their own times.[126] For such an audience, the chopped-up baby story also had resonances with other more sinister themes in the air in the mid-fifteenth century. These years, after all, witnessed the crystallization of the witch stereotype. In 1449 John of Capestrano had described a sect of heretics that included women who slept with the devil and then roasted and ate the resulting children. In 1459–60, around a dozen alleged witches would be burned for similar crimes in Arras.[127] Like the stereotypical witch, the mother in this miracle tale also murdered a child to eat. As the story traveled from Brittany to Naples and to the pen of Pietro Ranzano, the mother was transformed from a meat-craving pregnant woman to one demented or insane. It was only a short step away from her being possessed by or in league with a demon. Yet none of the tale's tellers condemn the mother of the chopped-up baby. Did the miracle of the baby's resuscitation in some way speak to the fears and paranoia that inquisitors and demonologists were trying to whip up in the mid-fifteenth century? Perhaps so. Or perhaps the story of the chopped-up baby served on some deep level as the antithesis of a witch trial. If so, Ranzano's narration may have stood as an oblique answer to sorcery charges once leveled against

---

125. It has been suggested that such recurrent themes help storytellers to remember their tales. See Fentress and Wickham 1992, 62–75.

126. As I argued in Smoller 2004b. For example, Werner Rolevinck's *Fasciculus temporum,* a chronicle of world history from Creation through the year 1474, simply displays the competing popes in two parallel lines. "The most learned and reasonable men were not able to discuss to which [side] one should adhere," he says, adding that "and therefore from this Urban VI up to Martin [V], I do not know who was the pope." Rolevinck 1479, fol. h4r.

127. See N. Cohn 1975, 50–52 (John of Capestrano) and 230–32 (*Vauderie* of Arras).

Pope Benedict XIII, distancing the saint at least, if not the stubborn pope, from imputations of demonic attachments.[128]

The tale's dissemination in the later fifteenth century also coincided with a heating up of hostilities against the Jews, including a number of trials of European Jews on charges of host desecration and ritual murder.[129] Audiences immersed in a climate charged with antisemitism would doubtless have been struck by parallels between the chopped-up baby story and the cannibal incident in Josephus's history of the siege of Jerusalem. The story had wide currency in the later Middle Ages, having been repeated in the *Golden Legend* and Mirk's *Festial,* as well as by such literary stars as Dante and Boccaccio. The tale does not paint the Jews in a good light. According to Josephus's version, as the besieged Jews in Jerusalem were in the most desperate throes of starvation, a wealthy woman named Mary, from the village of Bethezub, yielding to "uncontrollable fury," took up her own infant son, roasted him, and ate one half, reasoning that it was better for the child to die than to become a Roman slave. When party chiefs smelled the roasting flesh and demanded a share, "she replied that she had kept a fine helping for them, and uncovered what was left of her child." The men slunk away in horror but not without repeating the tale, which spread rapidly throughout the city and to the Roman legionaries. According to Josephus, this crime gave the Romans their excuse "to bury this abomination of infanticide and cannibalism under the ruins of their [i.e., the Jews'] country."[130]

The version of the tale reported by the thirteenth-century Dominican Jacobus de Voragine in the widely read *Golden Legend* offers the same basic outline: the woman is "noble by birth and by riches" but is driven to despair when robbers steal the last bits of the starving mother's food. Again, she kills the child and cooks him, eats half and puts half aside for later, which she offers to robbers who rush into the house on smelling roasting meat. Again, the robbers recoil in horror. For Jacobus de Voragine, this story is clearly the high (or low) mark of a string of Jewish perfidies, the moment where at last enough is enough. For immediately after the end of the cannibal story, he writes, "*Finally,* in the second year of Vespasian's reign, Titus took Jerusalem, reduced the city to ruins, and leveled the Temple."[131]

There are striking parallels between the two tales of infant killing. Just as in the story of Mary of Bethezub, so in the Vincent Ferrer chopped-up baby miracle, there is a mother who kills and cooks her child. In both stories, the cook saves half of the meal for later, and in both tales she offers the gruesome meal to another (the husband in the Naples tale, Vincent Ferrer in Ranzano's *vita,* and the soldiers/robbers of Jerusalem in the Mary of Bethezub

128. Kieckhefer 1989, 155.

129. See Rubin 1999; Trachtenberg (1943) 1983, 109–55; Langmuir 1990, 297–305.

130. Josephus 1981, 340–42.

131. Jacobus de Voragine 1993, 1:276 (67. St. James, Apostle) (emphasis added).

story). But then the parallels break down. While Josephus's account of the siege of Jerusalem comes the closest to building some modicum of sympathy for the butchering mother, in his and other versions of the Mary of Bethezub story, the mother's inhumanity stands as an epitome of the crimes of Jews in general, as illustrated most clearly by the incident's inclusion in a fifteenth-century French mystery play, *The Vengeance of Our Lord Jesus Christ on the Jews, through Vespasian and Titus.*[132] It was a small step for the imagination to move from the infanticide of a starving mother to the ritual murder charges of the later Middle Ages.

In contrast to Mary of Bethezub, the mother who chops up her baby in the Vincent Ferrer story is never condemned by any of the tale's tellers, and Ranzano has her in fact "cured" of her madness when Vincent Ferrer is nearby. While the cooked child of Jerusalem does in fact get eaten (at least half), the half-cooked child of the Vincent miracle is recognized before the first mouthful and consequently recomposed and brought back to life. Later depictions of the miracle often portray the resurrected child on the serving platter on which he was carved. (See figure 1.) For an audience steeped in the antisemitic narratives of the later Middle Ages, the Vincent Ferrer miracle story transformed the frisson of echoes of Jewish ritual murder to the happy ending of the restored baby. Ranzano's tale hinted to readers that Vincent's vigorous conversion of Jews might have saved Christian bodies as well as Jewish souls.[133]

As the tale passed from written *vita* to visual representation, a curious feature of some of these depictions may also have served to reinforce Ranzano's double image of Vincent Ferrer as a healer of the Schism and converter of Jews. Several of the portrayals of the chopped-up baby miracle end with the baby raised, Eucharist-like, on an altar, as for example in a panel attributed to the school of Domenico Ghirlandaio in the Stibbert Museum in Florence.[134] In fact, some depictions of this miracle have striking similarities to contemporary host desecration charges, in which Jews were accused of stealing and torturing the consecrated host. In such scenarios, witnesses sometimes reported seeing hosts that bled, that appeared to become small pieces of a cut-up child, or that became infants when tossed into a pot of boiling water, much as, in fact, the chopped-up baby appears in one vivid fifteenth-century fresco.[135] (See figure 2.) Several such accusations were raised in Aragon in the late fourteenth century, and another host desecration

132. *Vengeance de Nostre Seigneur Jhesucrist sur les Juifs par Vespasien et Titus.* I am grateful to Danna Piroyansky for details about the medieval dissemination of the Mary of Bethezub story.

133. For a fascinating consideration of the cultural meaning of cannibalism, see Heng 1998, esp. 102–16. See also Rusconi 2004, 230–32.

134. Stibbert Museum, Florence, no. 834. See chapter 5.

135. The fresco, from Gubbio, is also reproduced in Kaftal 1965, fig. 1323. Cf. the painting on the cover of Rubin 1999 (and reproduced therein as figure 21, p. 160): Jaime Serra, altarpiece for the monastery of Sijena, Catalonia (ca. 1400), detail, Museum of Catalan Art, Barcelona.

**Figure 1.** Lucas de Leyde (attr.), *Saint Vincent Ferrier ressuscite un enfant mort né*, no. 1.36 (now lost). Musée du Hiéron, Paray-le-Monial. The painting seems to depict the moment of miraculous resuscitation. Vincent, with wings referring to his role as angel of the apocalypse and Pentecostal tongues of flame playing over his head, prays over the formerly chopped-up baby, who lies on a serving platter. The child's parents kneel at the saint's feet, the father still imploring, the mother now docile and cured of her insanity.

**FIGURE 2.**    O. Nelli (attr.), fresco of Vincent Ferrer, detail. San Domenico, Gubbio. Photo courtesy Jason G. Smoller. In the leftmost of the fresco's three scenes, shown here, the mother thrusts her child headfirst into a pot set over a blazing fire while an alarmed observer calls for help. In the scene to the far right of the fresco, Vincent grasps the child by the arm and raises him, whole and alive, from a basket-like serving container (presumably the one being pawed by the cat in the foreground here). The middle of the fresco has been obliterated.

trial took place in Segovia in 1412 after Vincent Ferrer had preached there the preceding winter.[136] If Vincent Ferrer's chopped-up baby did remind audiences of this alleged Jewish perfidy, then the baby's miraculous restoration may again have underscored Vincent's role as a converter of Jews. Additional parallels with the story of the judgment of Solomon, as well as

---

136. Rubin 1999, 109–15, 128.

the implication that Vincent had saved the butchering mother from being the *Synagoga* figure, may also have reinforced the ways in which Ranzano depicted Vincent's preaching toward the Jews.

Furthermore, the story's echoes of host desecration narratives may have strengthened the identification of the miracle with the healing of the Great Schism. While in Vincent's case a demented mother replaces the sinister Jews, both tales end with a miracle. For medieval Christians, the Eucharist represented the mystical body of Christ, the community of all the faithful, or, in a word, the church. The miracle of the Mass saw that body daily broken up, eaten, and yet eternally whole and living. In the Vincent miracle, a real baby becomes food, as opposed to the consecrated bread becoming a real infant Jesus, as some medieval visionaries reported seeing during the Mass. Ranzano's tale has the baby wrongfully chopped up, cooked, and reserved in part (just like the sacrament); Vincent's praying over the pieces (much as a priest says the words of consecration in the Mass) brings about the appropriate ending to this deformation of the Eucharist. Contemporaries who saw parallels with the Eucharist or with stories of alleged host desecration could do so because in Ranzano's tale the chopped-up baby stands in for the body of Christ—that is, the church rent by the Schism—made whole by the prayers of Vincent Ferrer.[137]

Like any candidate for political office or sacred dignity, Vincent Ferrer had his supporters and his detractors. The power, persistence, and wealth of his fans ensured the success of the project of seeing the famous preacher enrolled in the catalog of the saints, but the voices of Vincent's critics are still audible if one reads the sources carefully. Their objections to his sanctity centered on complaints that Vincent had openly (and wrongly) predicted the imminent appearance of Antichrist and that he had helped to prolong the Schism in the church by his long-standing loyalty to the Avignon papacy. Ranzano, in his life of Vincent Ferrer as well as in his other writings about the new saint, skillfully downplayed such blemishes to Vincent's reputation. Instead, he cast his fellow Dominican, first, as a highly effective preacher whose words converted thousands of Jews, Muslims, and hardened Christian sinners, and, second, as a healer of bitter and long-standing divisions. Vincent's announcements of the upcoming end of the world became, in Ranzano's hands, no more precise than the stern but vague warning of the angel of the apocalypse with whom the preacher identified himself: "Fear God and give him honor, for the hour of his judgment is at hand" (Rev. 14:7). And not simply the arbitrator who ended centuries-old feuds as in the

---

137. Perhaps reinforcing this equation of the chopped-up baby with the Eucharistic body of Christ (and thus the church) is the strange fact that in no narratives or depictions of the miracle story is there any mention or trace of the infant's blood. Christ's blood had its own set of religious resonances. See Bynum 2007.

**FIGURE 3.**    Illuminated initial *B* with portrait of Vincent Ferrer. Bibliothèque Municipale de Colmar, INC G 1614, fol. a 2r, Vincent Ferrer, *Sermones de tempore et de sanctis* (Cologne: Quentell, 1487). In this emblematic portrait, Vincent gestures upward toward a vision of Christ in judgment, while at his feet lies the once chopped-up baby. A clear seam runs vertically through the child's now-whole body, and the boy's left half is still tinged with the saffron in which it was boiled, according to a version of the tale related at the Naples canonization inquest.

canonization inquests, Vincent also became, in Ranzano's *vita,* a committed participant in the efforts to end the Great Schism.

Ranzano's portrait of Vincent Ferrer received reinforcement in the tale of the chopped-up baby, which served to epitomize Vincent's healing of divisions, just as the verses from Revelation stood in for the power of his preaching. In fact, early portraits sometimes combine the two: showing the saint with a Bible, announcing the upcoming judgment, the chopped-up baby at his feet. (See figure 3.) Here was an image that was both preachable and paintable.

# CHAPTER 5

# Competing Stories

*Whose Vincent Ferrer Is It Anyway?*

When Pietro Ranzano's new *Life* of Vincent
Ferrer was approved by the brothers of his order in May 1456, it did not
immediately have the effect its author and commissioners must have intended:
to stabilize an "official" image of the new saint as a healer of Schism and
converter of infidels. Rather, throughout the first half century or so after
Vincent's canonization, there were a number of competing stories told about
the saint, both in words and in pictures. The new medium of print helped to
keep these various images alive, alongside a still vigorous circulation of manuscript materials. In fact, in what would have been, for Ranzano, a frustrating
irony, his *Life* never appeared in print in its entirety until the seventeenth
century, and his fashioning of the new Dominican saint did not begin to
reliably inform subsequent portrayals of Vincent until the last decades of the
seventeenth century.[1] Still, if Ranzano did not succeed early on in imposing a
single meaning on the memory of Vincent Ferrer, his efforts did accomplish
this much in the decades following Vincent's canonization: a wide dissemination of the miraculous story of the saint and the chopped-up baby.

Fifteenth-century authors and artists in fact had more information at
their disposal than that provided by Pietro Ranzano in his *Life* and other

---

1. The first printed edition of Ranzano's complete text was that of the Bollandists in the AASS
in 1675. For a list of manuscripts, editions, and translations, see Kaeppeli and Panella 1970–93, 3:254.
A version of Ranzano's life first appeared in print—though with some omissions and rewording—
in Surius 1570–75; I have consulted Surius 1875–80, 4:172–217. On Surius, see D. Collins 2008,
133–34, and chapter 6.

writings on Vincent. Already by the 1430s, Dominicans hoping to promote Vincent's sanctity had begun publicizing the preacher's career, even as crisis prevented the papal curia from devoting its attention to the cause of canonization. A short biography of Vincent embedded in the moral treatise *Formicarius* (*The Anthill*) of the Dominican Joannes Nider, as well as a set of Italian frescoes, is testimony to this early attempt to capture the holy man's essence. After Vincent's 1455 canonization, there were also the bull of canonization and the canonization inquests, which by papal order were to be made available for public consultation in Rome at the Dominican headquarters of Santa Maria sopra Minerva. At least two early biographers of Vincent Ferrer besides Ranzano made clear use of the inquests, particularly the miracle-laden Brittany process. And there were still other sources, now lost. A collection of Vincent's miracles makes reference to an inquest held in Lérida in Aragon in 1451; some of those tales made it into Ranzano's and others' biographies. Archbishop Antoninus of Florence mentions a "letter of canonization"—most likely a missive announcing Vincent's sainthood that circulated among Dominican houses prior to the issuance of the bull of canonization in 1458—an epistle that included at least some enumeration of Vincent's miracles.[2] And there was oral tradition, with its continuing honing of stories about the new saint and accumulating of new ones, as Vincent's intercession worked fresh miracles for the faithful.

From these various sources, authors and artists pieced together their own Vincent Ferrers, at times in service of a cause—such as the promotion of Observant reforms in the Dominican Order—at times with an eye to nothing more than spinning an engaging and spiritually edifying story. And these tales and depictions stand as witness not simply to the different materials available to a late fifteenth-century hagiographer but also to the various ways in which individuals experienced the new saint. For at a layer further removed from the written and the painted, there stand the reactions of the faithful encountering Saint Vincent Ferrer, emotions and sentiments of which we have only the faintest of traces. But this much is clear: however much the Dominican order, the papacy, the crown of Aragon, and the duchy of Brittany hoped to mold the image of *Saint* Vincent Ferrer, Ranzano's *Life* offered, for the time being at least, only a suggestion of how that depiction might turn out.

## The Earliest Portraits: Dux Aymo and Johannes Nider

The first glimpses we have into a cult of Vincent Ferrer date from the second decade after his death. They do not present a consistent image of the

---

2. On the Lérida inquest and the letter of canonization referred to by Antoninus, see the appendix below.

not-yet-canonized saint but rather point to a situation in which the meaning and essential features of the holy man's life had not yet been defined. Two frescoes in a small chapel in the Italian Piedmont provide *visual* evidence of a nascent cult of Vincent Ferrer as apocalyptic preacher and wonder worker. And there is *written* testimony of devotion to the potential saint in the brief biography included by fellow Dominican Johannes Nider in his *Anthill* (ca. 1437). These early portraits, as does later hagiography, depict Vincent as a gifted preacher but do not share Pietro Ranzano's presentation of his hero as healer of the Great Schism.

The two frescoes appear in the chapel of Santa Maria Assunta in the tiny hamlet of Stella, located in the Italian Piedmont region of Pinerolo.[3] The earliest is a 1429 votive painting, which credits Vincent's intercession with healing a newborn baby.[4] Higher up, in the arch of the chapel, appears a more extensive fresco by the painter Dux Aymo, most likely dating from 1429–30. (See figure 4.) Here vignettes from the life of Vincent Ferrer intermingle with text scrolls bearing quotations from his 1412 letter to Pope Benedict XIII, the epistle describing the 1398 vision that launched the preaching tour of the holy friar's final two decades.[5] In the top of the arch is a scene of Vincent preaching, pointing meaningfully from the pulpit, while the dove of the Holy Spirit whispers in his ear. To the left, the painter has depicted Christ, Francis, and Dominic appearing to a bedridden Vincent with the command, "Go and preach throughout the world as these two did, so that you might convert [the world] before the advent of Antichrist."[6] Significantly, the portion of the letter specifically (and, in retrospect, embarrassingly) informing the pope that Antichrist is already nine years old has been omitted.[7] To the right, a large group of men and women listen to the preacher, who gestures to a large text scroll that reproduces the passage from the letter to Benedict concerning Vincent's commission to preach the imminent arrival of Antichrist. Vincent's audience includes a pope, cardinals, and a Franciscan bishop, as well as a Franciscan scribe who is taking down the text of the sermon.[8] In the background, at the foot of Vincent's high pulpit,

---

3. See Rusconi 1990; Kaftal and Bisogni 1985, cols. 660–62 (figs. 932–35); Di Macco 1979, 398–403 (reproduction, 399); Monetti 1978a, 978b; Monetti and Cifani 1985, 35–44; and Kovalevsky 2002, 199–208.

4. Vincent is depicted here without a halo (reserved for a canonized saint) but with rays emanating from his head. Kaftal and Bisogni 1985, col. 661; Rusconi 1990, 215.

5. Transcriptions in Monetti and Cifani 1985, 41–42.

6. Monetti and Cifani 1985, 41 (my translation). Also quoted in Rusconi 1990, 216–17. Cf. the letter to Benedict: FND, 220–21.

7. As also noted in Kovalevsky 2002, 205.

8. It is possible that the scribe is a nod to the fact that two Franciscans from Pinerolo were sent bearing letters to Vincent Ferrer in Fossano in 1402 or 1403, presumably to ask him to preach in Pinerolo, where records attest to Vincent's presence in 1403. FND, 114; see also FHSVF 1:140. On Vincent's time in the Piedmont, see also Monetti and Cifani 1985, 36–37.

**FIGURE 4.**  Dux Aymo (attr.), fresco cycle, detail. Chapel of Santa Maria Assunta, Stella. From Rusconi 1990. Photo by Mario Martini (Pinerolo). Vincent is shown here in the act of preaching. The dove of the Holy Spirit hovers near his right ear, providing inspiration for his words, while the saint points to a text scroll, the portion of his letter to Benedict XIII that describes the vision in which Christ enjoined Vincent to go forth and preach the imminent Last Judgment.

a demon exits the mouth of a possessed woman, who swoons into the arms of bystanders.[9]

What is the effect of these frescoes? While the 1429 votive panel presents Vincent's wonder-working powers, the fresco series highlights, first and foremost, his preaching, with the Dominican in the pulpit at the center of the composition. Second, Aymo's panels emphasize and rely heavily on the text of the 1412 letter to Benedict XIII. In so doing, the artist (or his patron) has chosen to emphasize Vincent's ties to the Avignon pope, a decision reinforced by the inclusion of a pope (surely Benedict himself) among those listening to the holy man's preaching. No great risk here, for the territory had been firmly in the Avignon camp at the time of the Schism. Further, in the first generation after the Schism's end, many adopted a cautious neutrality about the division, understanding that no one could say with certainty who had been the true pope.[10] The fact of Vincent's long loyalty to Benedict here in the Piedmont in 1429–30 was no more than that: a simple fact.

---

9. Rusconi notes that this motif is common among the iconography of other popular fifteenth-century preachers and that it points to the effectiveness of their word. Rusconi 1990, 217.

10. As I argued in Smoller 2004b; see also Howard 2005, 315.

And, as scholars have pointed out, other paintings in the chapel also indicate allegiance to the Avignon papacy, in particular a depiction of Peter of Luxembourg, the saintly young French cardinal who died in Avignon in 1387 and whose canonization was actively sought by Avignon partisans of the Schism years.[11]

If the depiction of Vincent's letter to Benedict XIII underscored his ties to the Avignon papacy, it also served to authorize both the form and the content of the holy man's preaching mission. In the portion of the letter represented on the Stella frescoes, Christ himself commands Vincent to preach throughout the world and dictates his theme, namely, to prepare people for the coming of Antichrist. This mandate is important because in the fifteenth century not just anybody could stand on a street corner and begin preaching. In an age haunted by the fear of false prophets and obsessed with demonic deception, it was crucial that a preacher—particularly an itinerant outsider who attracted large crowds and announced an impending Last Judgment—display a proper license to preach. As Vincent's contemporary the cardinal Pierre d'Ailly had put it in a treatise *On False Prophets,* "Such [preachers] must prove their mission by canonical documents, and in such a mission and the reception [of such preachers], there should be great caution and diligence."[12] Vincent's letter to Benedict XIII, in essence, stood in place of these canonical documents. As he explained to the pope, Christ's injunction was an "apostolic legation conferred on him by God." Furthermore, "divine providence had bestowed many signs [on him]…in testimony [of its] truth."[13] In acknowledgment of the divine origin of his mission, Vincent adopted the title of legate *a latere Christi* (literally, from Christ's side), in a sense bypassing earthly clerical authorization.[14]

Viewed in that light, the Stella chapel frescoes present, in a tableau from left to right, the origin, source of power, and effectiveness of Vincent's preaching. On the left, Christ significantly touches the bedridden Dominican's jaw, healing him, imparting force to his speech, and commissioning his preaching tour. In the center, the presence of the dove hovering above and to the left of Vincent's ear makes clear the source of his eloquence and doctrine in the pulpit. And at the right, the effectiveness of Vincent's inspired

---

11. Rusconi 1990, 219; Monetti and Cifani 1985, 38. On the 1390 Avignon canonization process for Peter of Luxembourg, see Vauchez 1997, 82, 307–10. Peter's canonization also was being pushed by adherents of the Avignon papacy in 1417–18, as the Schism's wounds were being healed. See also Kieckhefer 1984, 33–44.

12. Quoted in Smoller 1994, 199n74. Later, Antoninus of Florence would make a similar point, adding that in the absence of a proper commission from church authorities, only a miracle could attest that a preacher was a messenger from God. Howard 1995, 96–97, 105.

13. FND, 221.

14. For his self-identification, see Vincent's sermon on the Feast of Saint Cecilia in Hodel 2008, 226; FND, 97; Montagnes 1980, 612.

preaching receives confirmation in the liberation of the possessed woman, the attentive faces of the assembled clergy, and the diligent reporting of the Franciscan scribe. The horizontal flourishes of the text scrolls draw the viewer's eye from the head of Christ to the preacher in his pulpit and thence to the fruit of his words in the audience at his feet. In this earliest configuration of the potential saint, Vincent appears primarily as an inspired preacher of the word of God. That he fell in the Avignon camp during the Great Schism and that his pronouncements of the impending advent of Antichrist were as yet unfulfilled—so troubling to later hagiographers—were seemingly a matter of no concern to the painter or his patrons.

The biography of Vincent Ferrer in Joannes Nider's *Anthill* similarly focuses the reader's attention on Vincent's preaching career.[15] Of Vincent's early life, before the inauguration of his preaching mission in 1398, Nider says only that he was from the kingdom of Aragon, that he had been a professor of theology, and that he had for a long time served in the papal curia before beginning to disseminate the word of God. Unlike Dux Aymo and those responsible for the design of the Santa Maria Assunta frescoes, Nider is careful to present Vincent as having a *curial* mandate for his mission. He makes no mention whatsoever of Vincent's authorizing vision of Christ or, indeed, of the 1412 letter to Benedict XIII.[16] Rather, Nider unobtrusively slips in the information that Vincent had papal authorization for his mission. "He had with him several brothers of various religious orders," Nider writes, "to whom he subdelegated the apostolic authority to hear confessions that he first received from Lord Petro de Luna [Benedict XIII], and [which] after he [i.e., Petro de Luna] was deposed by the Council of Constance, he secondarily received from the same [council.]"[17] Nider thus carefully presents Vincent as having credentials from both the Avignon pope and the council that ended the Schism.

Nor is Nider's Vincent Ferrer as overtly inspired by God as is the preacher in the Stella frescoes. Without any mention of the vision of Christ, Nider does not identify a direct heavenly source for the content of Vincent's highly moving sermons. Nor does he give his readers the slightest indication that Vincent's preaching was intended to announce the imminent reign of Antichrist. Nider's Vincent Ferrer does not stand at the pulpit with the Holy Spirit whispering in his ear. Rather, for Nider, Vincent's seeming

---

15. On Nider's life of Vincent, see FND, XXXIII–XXXV; Brettle 1924, 2; and, especially, Chène 2006, 121–66 (edited version and translation at 162–66).

16. A fact noted as well by Chène 2006, 132, who evidently does not know the frescoes at Stella and says, "au moment où Nider compose son récit, la vision de Vincent ne fait donc apparemment pas encore partie de la tradition."

17. Chène 2006, 163–64 (my translation); Chène notes that in three sermons Vincent makes specific mention of this concession of the right to hear confessions granted by Benedict, asserting that Nider must have been the source for Ranzano's assertion of the same (145–46).

divine inspiration stems from discipline and rigor. "Wherever and whenever he could, he abandon[ed] himself to contemplation," Nider writes. The
word "contemplation" here had a technical sense, referring to a focused state
of prayer and inner silence believed to prepare one for ecstatic union with
God. As Catherine Chène observes, Vincent himself had written about this
sort of contemplation in his *Treatise on the Spiritual Life*. From that contemplation, in Nider's view, Vincent "seemed to drink in by divine revelation
the sense, words, and gestures that he, in a most divine manner, put forth
and displayed in his sermons."[18] For Nider, the grace apparent in Vincent's
preaching, while ultimately divine, was more directly linked to his ascetic,
contemplative practices.

In the first half of the brief biography, Nider details Vincent's mode
of life, stressing his humility, his extreme asceticism, and his predilection
for contemplation, as noted above. Catherine Chène has suggested that
this passage betrays Nider's commitment to the Observant movement
within the Dominican order. Although Vincent had died long before such
reforms came to Spanish Dominican houses, Johannes Nider had been
immersed in the Observant reform since his entry into the Dominican
order in Colmar in 1402. During the Council of Basel (1431–49), at the
same time he was collecting information about Vincent Ferrer, Nider
penned a treatise advocating abstinence from the eating of meat, a hall-
mark of certain reformed convents. Probably not coincidentally, in the
*Anthill,* Nider praises Vincent's avoidance of eating meat along with his
devotion to poverty and other ascetic practices.[19] In short, as Chène argues,
Nider co-opts Vincent as a model of the Dominican Observance so near
to his own heart. That Vincent's divine inspiration, for Nider, stems from
his austere life underscores this subtle praise of Vincent as Observant hero.

Still, Nider devotes nearly one-half of his biography to Vincent's preaching, stressing the large crowds who followed him from town to town and the
even greater numbers who gathered daily to hear him preach. As evidence
of the fruits of these sermons, Nider cites the testimony of "trustworthy"
persons with whom he spoke during the Council of Basel, who assured
him that Vincent had led "more than thirty thousand Jews and Saracens into
the bosom of the church" and had induced an "infinite" number of sinners
to true penitence. Nider also specifically notes that at the end of Vincent's

---

18. Nider quotations: ibid., 163 (my translations). On "contemplation": ibid., 140–43. The
motto of the Dominican order is "to contemplate and give to others the fruits of contemplation."
Hinnebusch 1984, 4:243.

19. Chène 2006, 137–38. She also notes that Nider praised the Dominican reformed convent
of San Domenico in Chioggia specifically for its strict abstinence from meat. This convent is the
source of another early biography of Vincent Ferrer. On the Dominican reform movement, see
Hinnebusch 1965, 1:229–33; 1984, 4:253–54; Ashley 1990, 60–61, 90–95; and on Nider and his push
for reform, Bailey 2003, esp. chap. 4–5, 75–117.

sermons, he liberated innumerable people from possession by demons, "over whom he was recognized to have had a special power from Christ." Aside from a vague reference to "miracles" worked in Brittany before Vincent's death, this detail is Nider's only mention of any supernatural powers on the part of the holy man.[20] Nider also gives some indication of how Vincent was able to convince Jews and Muslims to convert to Christianity. To the Jews, Vincent would expound upon the Old Testament, relying on his familiarity with "Hebrew doctors"; to an audience of "pagans," the holy preacher adduced the "law of nature" and other natural things leading to faith.[21] More disciplined hard work on Vincent's part.

Chène, following Sigismond Brettle, views the *Anthill* as an outline for all future hagiography of the saint.[22] Inasmuch as Nider describes the preacher's mode of living and his ability to convert sinners and nonbelievers, his biography does indeed provide one basis for most later writings about Vincent. Many authors, like Nider, will repeat the story of the preacher's refusing to ride on anything but a humble donkey. Ranzano in particular will delight in relating tales of Vincent's power over demons. And few authors will fail to note the thousands of Jews and Muslims brought to the Christian faith by Vincent's preaching. But Nider's outline does not include several elements crucial to some later hagiographers. Notably absent in the *Anthill* are the themes emphasized in the frescoes in Stella: Vincent's relationship with Benedict XIII (and more broadly, the Great Schism), his role as herald of the Last Judgment, and the miracles attributed to his intercession.

These two early portraits of Vincent Ferrer share above all a focus on the holy man's preaching. In that respect, both Dux Aymo and Johannes Nider were almost certainly relying on the living memory of those who had heard the famous Dominican's sermons. Among Nider's informants at Basel, plausibly, could have been the Dominican Raphael de Cardona, who had been a member of Vincent's band of followers.[23] There must have been persons still alive in Stella in 1429 who had witnessed Vincent's preaching in the Italian Piedmont in 1402–3. And these early depictions of Vincent's sermons ring true with the descriptions provided by witnesses at the canonization inquests of the 1450s.

---

20. Quotations: Chène 2006, 164; Chène also notes (158) that Nider in the *Anthill* displays little interest in thaumaturgic miracles attributed to any saints.

21. Ibid., 164.

22. Ibid., 160; Brettle 1924, 2. Chène also notes fascinating parallels between Nider's biography and the pat biography offered at length in the testimony of the Brittany witness Johannes Placentis, who, she suggests, may have known Nider's *vita* and used it as the basis for his remarks. Chène 2006, 134. The Carthusian Johannes Placentis was a follower of Vincent Ferrer's who also spent some time in the charterhouse of Porta Coeli in Valencia before becoming prior at the Carthusian house of Saints Donatian and Rogatian in Nantes. FHSVF, 1:144.

23. So suggests Chène 2006, 159.

These two early, brief glimpses of Vincent's cult also share a focus on his ability to cast out demons. Although exorcisms were rarely attributed to saints in the High Middle Ages, a demonstration of power over demons was an important aspect of fifteenth-century sanctity.[24] It may be that in underscoring Vincent's liberation of those possessed by demons, both Dux Aymo and Johannes Nider sought to present him as one well qualified for sainthood. Alternatively, Michael Goodich has suggested that often, in the later Middle Ages, a spectacular public liberation from possession was the miracle that inaugurated a new saint's cult.[25] So perhaps both artist and writer were trying to prime the pump of veneration of Vincent Ferrer. Or maybe, in a century fascinated by the activity of unclean spirits, both simply calculated that portraying Vincent expelling demons was a sure way to get attention for their hero. Nider's *Anthill,* after all, is best known for one of the earliest descriptions of the witches' Sabbath.[26] This interest in the demonic would be shared by Pietro Ranzano, who devotes a chapter of book 3 of his *Life of Vincent* to the liberation of demoniacs and who also details several instances in which Vincent himself encountered and triumphed over demons.[27]

Finally, both fresco and text devote considerable attention to the question of authority, although with slightly different answers to that question. Dux Aymo presents Vincent Ferrer as an inspired visionary, whose authority to preach derives directly from Jesus's mandate and whose eloquence in the pulpit comes immediately from the Holy Spirit. In a quite literal sense, in the Stella frescoes Vincent disseminates the word of God. For Johannes Nider, writing as pope and church council squared off against one another in Basel—a "rump" council in Basel would actually depose Pope Eugenius IV and elect its own pope—the proper chain of *ecclesiastical* authority appears to have been of utmost importance. In a two-page biography he takes the trouble to let his readers know that Vincent had properly delegated to the clergy in his entourage the authority to hear confessions granted to the preacher, first by the pope and subsequently by the Council of Constance. As for the divine source of Vincent's preaching, Nider emphasizes its clear link to the holy man's ascetic practices and contemplation.

In short, in these two early portraits of Vincent Ferrer, we see artist and author striving to define what there was about this clearly charismatic preacher that would also make him a saint. One solution—Dux Aymo's—was to stress the supernatural: visions, inspired speech, exorcisms, and miracles. Another course—Johannes Nider's—was to present Vincent as

---

24. Rusconi 1990, 216–17; Chène 2006, 156.

25. Goodich 2001.

26. See, most recently, Bailey 2003, esp. chap. 2, 38–48; Ostrero et al. 1999.

27. RVV, 1:487–89 (all tales of demonic temptations of or assaults on Vincent), 1:504–6. Vincent had liberated seventy demoniacs, by Ranzano's count (RVV, 1:505).

*Table 1.*    Early Lives of Vincent Ferrer

| DATE | WORK |
|---|---|
| ca. 1437 | Joannes Nider, *The Anthill (Formicarius)* |
| 1455–56 | Pietro Ranzano, *Life of Vincent Ferrer* |
| 1456–63 | Pietro Ranzano, *Annals excerpts* |
| 1456–63 | Pietro Ranzano, *Heroic Verses* |
| 1456–63 | Pietro Ranzano, *Office* |
| 1455–58 | Antoninus of Florence, in his *Chronicle* |
| After 1463 | Epitome (based on Ranzano's *Office* lessons) |
| 1466 | Johannes Meyer, in *Book about the Illustrious Men of the Order of Preachers* |
| After 1467 | Chioggia friar, *Life of Vincent Ferrer* |
| 1470 | Francesco Castiglione, *Brief Life of Vincent Ferrer* |
| 15th century (post 1455) | *Life* in Trier manuscript (based on Ranzano's *Life*) |
| 15th century (post 1455) | *Legend of Saint Vincent* from Bologna manuscript |
| Before ca. 1480 | Gabriel Barletta, sermon on Vincent Ferrer |
| 1483 | Supplement to *The Golden Legend* |
| Before 1495 | Roberto Caracciolo, sermon on Vincent Ferrer |
| ca. 1495 | Girolamo Albertucci de' Borselli, in his *Chronicle of Master Generals of the Order of Preachers* |
| 1510 | Miquel Peres, *Life* |
| 1517 | Giovanni Antonio Flamini, *Life*, in Alberti, *Concerning the Illustrious Men of the Order of Preachers* |
| 1519 | Supplement to Petrus Natalibus |
| ca. 1519 | Claudius Rota, supplement to *The Golden Legend* |

a model of discipline and obedience and thereby of Dominican Observant reform. On such obedience—although clearly of secondary importance in Nider's mind—divine favors followed: extraordinary preaching, exorcisms, and vague, unspecific miracles. Both Aymo and Nider seemingly struggled to present an answer to an implied objection about the legitimacy of Vincent's itinerant preaching. But of the other concerns that would later be so carefully negotiated by Pietro Ranzano in the official life of the newly canonized saint, we see scarcely a clue.

## Ranzano's Other "Drafts"

In fact, Pietro Ranzano himself tried several approaches to presenting Vincent Ferrer. True, in the *vita* commissioned by the pope and the Dominican master general, Ranzano took considerable pains to present Vincent more as healer of the Schism than as a partisan of the Avignon papacy, structuring his narration of the saint's mature life to highlight his labors to bring peace to the church and, as I have suggested, reworking and foregrounding the miracle of the chopped-up baby to underscore, symbolically, Vincent's ability to heal division. Ranzano also devoted some effort to defending (and tempering) his hero's teaching about the apocalypse, downplaying the 1412 letter to Benedict XIII in which—besides describing his vision of Christ and Saints Francis and Dominic—Vincent had proclaimed that Antichrist had already been born. As noted in the previous chapter, these were precisely the concerns about Vincent Ferrer that the more straightforward Antoninus of Florence would identify and meet head-on in his *Chronicle.* But in Ranzano's other writings about Vincent—the excerpt from the *Annals* he sent to Giovanni da Pistoia, the set of verses he also forwarded to Giovanni, and the *Office* he composed for the Feast of Vincent Ferrer—the Sicilian humanist experimented with other ways to answer (or ignore) contemporary critics of his hero.[28]

In the official *Life,* Ranzano stressed Vincent's efforts to end the Schism, even as he showed the saint maintaining a dutiful, if coolly polite, relationship with Benedict XIII. Yet in the brief life of Vincent excerpted from the *Annals* in 1463, Ranzano never used the word "schism" and scarcely even mentioned the division in the church. Describing Vincent's initial meeting with Benedict, Ranzano in the *Annals* stated simply, "There came to Valencia Benedictus Luna, who in Spain and France was held as pope. He was one of the three popes whom the Christian church, divided into three factions, had set over itself." (In truth, Benedict was not yet pope at the time, probably in first few years of the Schism; nor were there three popes until 1409.) Ranzano minimized the pope's association with the saint whom he made his confessor and master of the sacred palace by insisting that the latter appointment was simply "an office that Roman popes used to demand of the Order of Preachers." He compressed the time of Vincent's association with Benedict to a mere two years.[29] And when Vincent's vision of Christ precipitated

---

28. All can be found in BC, MS 112: the brief *Life* (BHL no. 8660), at fol. 52v–68r (with prefatory letter to Giovanni da Pistoia at fol. 51r–52r); the "heroic verses" (BHL no. 8662) and prefatory epistle to Giovanni da Pistoia (BHL no. 8661), at fol. 68v–71r; and the *Office* (BHL no. 8660b), at fol. 71r–80v. At the first of the manuscript, there are fragments of an opening foreword in praise of Ferrante I of Naples, son of Alfonso V. The hand for the sections on Vincent Ferrer appears to be that of Iacobus Laurentianus, who is known to have produced three deluxe manuscripts in the Aragonese royal library in Naples, two of which were dedicated to Ferrante. I am grateful to William S. Monroe for making me acquainted with examples of Laurentianus's hand and for sharing with me the text of Monroe 2008.

29. BC, MS 112, fol. 55v–56r: "Per id temporis uenit ualentiam benedictus luna qui in hispaniis atque in galiis pro pontifice maximo habebatur. Unus enim erat e tribus illis pontificibus quos Christiana ecclesia in tres divisa factiones sibi praefecerat: uti supra demonstratum est. Is supra quasi cuiquam credibile est Uincentii uirtutibus illectus uoluit ut esset & suarum confessionum auditor & palacii magister. Est enim id munus quod Romani pontifices iis qui ordinis sunt praedicatorum demandare solent. Adaegitque eum in id: ut duos annos suam curiam fuerit secutus."

his leaving Avignon, Ranzano—like Johannes Nider—was careful to note that his hero "asked of [the pope] leave by which he might carry out the duty imposed on him by Christ."[30] Vincent, in the excerpts from the *Annals,* was polite and respectful to the Avignon pope but really had not that much to do with him. Nor did he do anything toward ending the Great Schism.

In the set of verses appended to the *Annals* excerpts he had copied out for Giovanni da Pistoia, and in the *Office* for the feast of Saint Vincent Ferrer, Ranzano moved even further from the official *Life*. In the verses, which Ranzano hoped would be easier to recall in the pulpit than a lengthy prose biography, there is no longer a trace of the humanist's portrayal of Vincent as a healer of Schism.[31] In fact, the poem sent to Giovanni da Pistoia contains no mention whatsoever of the divided church. A more daring approach still appears in the *Office* that Ranzano most likely composed between 1456 and 1463.[32] There, a series of *lectiones* (readings or lessons) presented a brief biography of the saint similar to that copied from the *Annals* for Giovanni da Pistoia. Just as in the *Annals* excerpts, Ranzano introduced Vincent's patron as "Benedictus Luna, who in France and Spain was held to be pope," noting straightforwardly now that "there was then a Schism in the Christian Church."[33] Again, as in the *Annals,* Vincent's association with the Avignon pope was compressed to a short two-year span. But then Ranzano tried a startling new tactic.

In a statement that blatantly contradicts what Vincent wrote about his own sentiments, Ranzano asserted, "After having worked two years in Avignon,…it came to [Vincent] without any doubt that Benedict was not the legitimate pope." At that point, according to Ranzano, "he began to plan

---

30. BC, MS 112, fol. 56v: "Pontificem adiit eumque ordine quae christus iusserat docuit ac simul petiit ab eo ueniam quo demandatum sibi a christo legationis munus exequeretur." Also in RVV, 1:492.

31. BC, MS 112, fol. 68r–68v. The verses have also been edited in Vincent Ferrer 1496, fol. [a5] v–[a6]r; FND, V–VII; and in Termini 1915, 151–54.

32. BC, MS 112, fol. 71r–80v. On the *Office,* see Roy 1966, who demonstrates that there were at least three fifteenth-century offices composed, the first by Ranzano (at the request of Dominican master general Martial Auribelli, probably before 1463 or even 1462), the second (a revision of the first) by Auribelli (sometime after 1463), and a third Spanish office that Roy postulates predates and is a possible source for Auribelli's anthems. Auribelli's *Office* was approved by the Dominican order during his second term as master general (1465–73) and was in use until 1603. There appears to have been at least one other early office in circulation. Francisco Diago, O.P. (ca. 1562–1615) relates a miracle not in the other offices from an "ancient lectionary of the Archbishopric of Tarragona." Diago 2001, bk. 1, ch. 36, 408–9. Finally, one other possible version is described in Jordan 1992. See also "Diurnale ad usum Fratrum Praedicatorum XVe," BNF, MS lat. 1324, fol. 148r–151r, which lacks the biographical *lectiones* of Ranzano's and Auribelli's offices (a *diurnale* contains all offices but that of matins, at which the *lectiones* were recited), but does make reference to the chopped-up baby miracle (fol. 149v: "Infantulus laceratur mox matris per excidium vite alter restauratur.")

33. BC MS 112, fol. 76r: "Benedictus luna qui in galliis & hispaniis pro maximo pontifice habebatur (scisma enim tunc erat in ecclesia christiana)."

most carefully to forsake [Benedict]." After Vincent's praying earnestly to God about his predicament, Christ appeared to him and commanded him to leave Avignon and to go forth preaching in the manner of the apostles.[34] In the *Office,* then, Ranzano intensified his distancing of the saint from the widely detested Benedict XIII by placing the break much earlier in the saint's lifetime, neatly ignoring the fact that Vincent's withdrawal of support from Benedict did not come until 1416, in the face of Benedict's obstinacy toward the Council of Constance. Of Ranzano's portrayal of Vincent as healer of Schism in the official *Life,* only the faintest trace remained: the miracle of the chopped-up baby, the sole miracle described in the *Office.*[35]

These three texts also show Ranzano experimenting with various ways to present Vincent's somewhat problematic apocalyptic utterances. In the official *Life,* Ranzano had defended his hero's teaching about the end of the world by making it part of Christ's mandate in the 1398 vision, noting additionally that although detractors had complained of Vincent's "novelties," the pope had been unable to find anything worthy of reproof in his teaching on Antichrist. In the brief biography excerpted from the *Annals,* however, Ranzano declined to mention any hint of scandal about Vincent's apocalyptic preaching. Instead, he emphasized that Christ himself had charged Vincent to preach the nearness of the Last Judgment, an event that, Ranzano wrote, "the Christian religion declares is to be expected in our times altogether soon."[36] In other words, Ranzano here implied that anyone would have come to the same conclusion that Vincent did.

Perhaps Ranzano now took his cue from the bull of canonization issued by Pius II on October 1, 1458. There Vincent is introduced as an extraordinary man provided by God "to confute the errors of the Jews, Saracens, and other infidels, and to pronounce the day of the terrifying Last Judgment like another angel flying in the midst of heaven, and to evangelize those living on earth" and, again (in the same sentence), as sent specifically "to show [all people and nations] that the Day of Judgment was approaching."[37] In Pius's formulation, echoing the words of Revelation 14:6, the effectiveness of Vincent's preaching in converting Jews and Muslims and in bringing sinners to penitence stemmed from his apocalyptic message, namely, his "showing how terrible a judge to the base and unjust the Redeemer will be in that Final Judgment."[38] In like manner, Ranzano's brief biography in the *Annals*

---

34. Ibid., fol 76v: "Actis postea duobus annis apud auinionem cum absque ulla dubitatione sibi constaret benedictum non esse legitimum pontificem coepit de illo deserendo accuratius cogitare."

35. Ibid., fol. 79v: "In frustra mater lacerat demens infantem proprium sed patris fletus impetrat ad uitam reddi filium."

36. Ibid., fol. 56r–56v: "Praeter caetera tamen nunciari futuri illius iudicii diem quod expectandum proponit christiana religio esse nostris temporibus admodum propinquum."

37. *Bullarum diplomatum* 1857–72, 5:146, sec. 2.

38. Ibid., sec. 4.

depicted Vincent as announcing a vaguely imminent and ultimately terrifying judgment, a rhetorical technique that moved thousands to penitence and the true faith.

The canonization bull seems also to lie behind Ranzano's presentation of this material in the verses sent to Giovanni da Pistoia and in the *Office* for Vincent's feast day. In the poem, Ranzano again identified Vincent with the angel of Revelation 14:6–7, exclaiming, "You showed all people that Christ [is] soon to come, who will judge the world, for you are that other sublime angel whom John previously saw." But he gave no indication that Vincent's predictions of the end included any specificity about Antichrist's birth or appearance.[39] In the *Office* Ranzano was equally vague. Once more he linked Vincent with the angel of Revelation 14:6–7, a text used for the first chapter reading in the *Office*. As in the bull of canonization, Ranzano noted the rhetorical effectiveness of Vincent's apocalyptic preaching. "You fervently, clearly, with a loud voice, announced the end of the world soon to be near," he addressed the saint, "so that people might fear God."[40] And, as in the *Annals* and in the official *Life*, Ranzano indicated that the imminent Last Judgment was announced to Vincent by Christ himself.[41]

Aside from the official *Life*, Ranzano's other writings about Vincent Ferrer, then, show the Dominican humanist imagining several ways to present the new saint. True, his various biographies highlighted the saint's extraordinary preaching abilities, as did every other early description of Vincent Ferrer. Like Aymo in his Stella frescoes and Pius II in the bull of canonization, Ranzano also linked that preaching mission, and its apocalyptic content, to Vincent's 1398 vision of Christ. But when it came to the embarrassing specificity of Vincent's pronouncements about the End, Ranzano appeared torn between taking the problem head-on (as in the official *Life*) or subsuming it under a more generic depiction of Vincent as angel of the apocalypse. Dealing with Vincent's activities during the Schism years suggested to Ranzano an equally wide number of approaches, ranging from the *Life*'s portrayal of Vincent as actively involved in healing the division to the complete silence on the topic in the verses to Giovanni da Pistoia. If this one, extremely important author struggled to define what would be the essence of this new Dominican saint, it should not be surprising that the image of Vincent Ferrer would prove difficult to stabilize for many years to come.

---

39. BC, MS 112, fol. 70v: "Hinc [that is, by Christ's revelation of future things to you] cito uenturum christum qui iudicet orbem / Omnibus ostendis populis: nanque angelus alter / Ille is: sublimem quem uiderat ante ioannes."

40. BC, MS 112, fol. 71v: "Inde feruenter cito iam propinquum seculi finem fore nuntiasti ut deum gentes timeant patenter uociferando."

41. Ibid., fol. 76v.

## After Ranzano

Of the lives of Vincent Ferrer composed in the first century after his death, not all were derived from Ranzano's texts. The biographies of Vincent written by Antoninus of Florence and Francesco Castiglione appear to have been based entirely on sources other than Ranzano's *Life*, including the canonization inquests, the letter of canonization mentioned by Antoninus, and tales circulating in personal epistles.[42] Both of these texts, unlike Ranzano's, appeared in print in the fifteenth century (as did Nider's *Anthill*), Antoninus's as part of his widely circulated *Chronicle* and Castiglione's at the head of a volume of Vincent's sermons.[43] Other biographies—including works by Girolamo Albertucci de' Borselli,[44] an anonymous compiler of saints' lives,[45] and Giovanni Antonio Flamini[46]—depended directly on Ranzano's official *Life*. Still another set of lives drew upon Ranzano's alternative versions of Vincent's biography; these included the short *Epitome*, which circulated in manuscript,[47] and a revision of the *Office* (and its lessons) by

---

42. Antoninus makes one reference to *historia eius,* which may mean Ranzano's *vita,* and includes one small detail (the setting of Vincent's miraculous multiplication of bread and wine in Vic) that appears only in Ranzano, perhaps indicating his reading of the *vita,* which Antoninus then would have deliberately rejected as a model. Antoninus Florentinus 1484, fol. CCXIIIr ("historia eius") and CCIXv (Vic); cf. RVV 1:504.

43. Antoninus Florentinus 1484, Pars III, titulus xxiii, ch. viii, fol. CCVIIv–CCXr (BHL no. 8663). This is the *editio princeps.* Of seventeen editions of the *Chronicle* listed by bibliographers, ten survive: J. Walker 1933, 28, list of manuscripts and editions at 26–30; summary of the whole at 37–52; see also Howard 1995, 22. Castiglione's *Brief Life* (*Vita beati vincentii abbreviata,* BHL no. 8664) appears in Castiglione 1496, at fol. a1v–a5r. Castiglione's list of miracles also appears in AASS, Aprilis, 1:512–14. Bausi and Frazier also list two manuscripts, both in Florence. Bausi 1991, 136; Frazier 2005, 393. Curt Wittlin has edited Castiglione's text as found in Biblioteca Nazionale Centrale di Firenze, Conventi Soppressi, MS J-VII-30, fol. 33–45v. Wittlin 1994, 16–27.

44. Biblioteca Universitaria, Bologna, MS 1999, fol. 155r–160v, facsimile from P. C. Bonniwell Collection, Phillips Memorial Library, Providence College, Providence, R.I. (I am grateful to Jane Jackson for providing me with a copy of this facsimile.) On Borselli: Rabotti 1960. Albano Sorbelli says that Borselli appears to have drawn on Francesco Castiglione's life of Vincent Ferrer. Borselli's text (particularly the list of miracles), however, is much closer to Ranzano's. Frazier 2005, 393, citing Sorbelli 1922, 100.

45. Stadtbibliothek, Trier, MS 1168/470, fol. 266r–296r (BHL no. Vincentius 06). The manuscript originated in the Carthusian house of Beatenberg b. Coblenz. On the Trier manuscript: Keuffer and Kentenich (1914) 1973, 232. The Bollandists also make note of a later manuscript copy (dated between 1551 and 1650) of this text in Biblioteca Alessandrina, Rome, codex 092 (alias I.g.7.8), fol. 611–14, http://bhlms.fltr.ucl.ac.be/Nquerysaintsection.cfm?code_bhl=Vincentius06&RequestTimeout=500.

46. Edited in Alberti 1517, fol. 156v–174v. The life appears also in Flamini 1529, fol. CLXIr–CLXXXIIIIv.

47. Archivio Storico Diocesano, Novara, codex XXVII, fol. 120v–123r (BHL no. 8658d). Although this is the only manuscript for this text listed in the BHL, the text here is nearly identical to that of a brief life of Vincent in the British Library, London, MS additional 32,579, fol. 200v–204v. The *Epitome* closely follows the *Annals* excerpts, but with some additions, changes, and deletions.

Martial Auribelli.[48] Finally, several *vitae,* sermons, and brief notices brought together materials from a number of authors. Whatever his sources, however, each compiler of these early lives of Vincent Ferrer put a slightly different spin on the saint.

## Lives Independent of Ranzano's Works

The lives of Vincent by Antoninus of Florence and Francesco Castiglione, evidently composed without use of Ranzano as model, show little interest in the Sicilian Dominican's goal of depicting Vincent Ferrer as healer of Schism. Archbishop Antoninus's take on Vincent Ferrer, rather, reflected the concerns of a man whose career from the outset was devoted to the cause of Dominican reform and the task of preaching. Antoninus Pierozzi (1389–1459) became a novice in the Observant Dominican convent in Cortona in 1405. He served for a time as prior of the Dominican house of San Pietro Martire in Naples, a convent that would later house Pietro Ranzano. And in 1436—around the time Johannes Nider was writing the *Anthill*—Antoninus became involved with the new reform Dominican house of San Marco in Florence, where he also held the post of prior. For nearly a decade thereafter, Antoninus served on and off as vicar general of the Observant wing of the Dominican order in Italy before accepting the post of archbishop in Florence, which he retained until his death in 1459.[49]

As archbishop of Florence, Antoninus renovated the bishop's palace to remove traces of previous pomp, worked to reform the city's clergy, and delivered a series of popular and inspiring sermons. Contemporaries recalled that he always went about garbed in the simple dress of the Dominican habit, that he walked everywhere until ailments forced him to ride, at which point he rode a humble donkey in imitation of Christ's entry into Jerusalem.[50] In that respect, Antoninus sounds rather reminiscent of Vincent Ferrer, whose simple mount garnered Johannes Nider's praise. And it is not hard to imagine the ascetic Aragonese preacher's appeal to the ardent Antoninus. Yet, as Peter Howard has shown, Antoninus was also an immensely practical man, who knew well the world of his flock (how to adapt himself to it) and whose characteristic mode of thought and action was the sermon.[51]

All those elements are present in Antoninus's life of Vincent, composed between 1455 and 1458 for a section of the archbishop's *Chronicle*

---

48. *Breviarium secundum ordinem* 1481, fol. [B8]v–[C4]r. On the various versions of the *Office,* see note 32.

49. Biography based on Howard 1995, 2005, 2008; and J. Walker 1933, 3–17.

50. J. Walker 1933, 14.

51. Howard 1995, 28.

devoted to the history of the Dominican order.[52] The biography in fact reads like a sermon for a saint's feast day, beginning with a scriptural tag, moving through the saint's biography, and ending with a recitation of miracles. Given that Antoninus frequently incorporated his own sermons into his didactic works,[53] it seems plausible that this passage reprises a sermon he preached to celebrate the newly canonized Vincent Ferrer. If it does, then to his flock Antoninus presented Vincent as a model of Dominican reform and the order's preaching mission. Practical and patient, Antoninus also—as we have seen in the previous chapter—forthrightly acknowledged and answered the objections to Vincent's sanctity that had concerned Pietro Ranzano and of which contemporary Florentines must have been aware.

"With thy comeliness and thy beauty set out, proceed prosperously, and reign. Because of truth and meekness and justice" (Ps. 44:5).[54] So begins Antoninus's biography of Vincent Ferrer. In the ensuing prologue, commenting on the passage from the Psalms, Antoninus makes of Vincent a model of virtuous purpose ("set out"), action ("proceed prosperously"), and their reward ("reign"), all through the triple attributes of "truth and meekness and justice." Echoing the Psalm, Antoninus establishes a portrait of Vincent Ferrer as doggedly working to fulfill God's commandments through his preaching and ascetic life and receiving as reward the crown of sainthood and intercessory powers: resuscitating the dead, healing the blind, curing the sick, and "procuring bread and wine for two thousand persons."[55]

Whereas Ranzano had foregrounded Vincent's role in healing the Schism, Antoninus's focus in the biography proper was on Vincent's preaching mission (which he stretched from twenty to thirty years' duration) and his humble life.[56] Antoninus moves quickly over Vincent's youth, profession as a Dominican friar, and theological studies. While he describes the title of master of theology as a "crown," the rank of preacher was evidently dearer to Vincent.[57] In a long passage on Vincent's preaching that follows these remarks, Antoninus emphasizes his apostolic gift of tongues, conversions of twenty-five thousand Jews and "Saracens," and bringing of hardened sinners to penance. Most notably, in Lérida, Vincent had moved all the prostitutes to take up an honest life, an event that prompted their pimps to come after

---

52. Following Morçay 1913, Walker dates title XXIII to 1455–57. J. Walker 1933, 24.

53. E.g., Howard 2005, 312, 316.

54. I quote from the Douay-Rheims translation (Ps. 45:5 in the Hebrew [Masoretic] numbering).

55. Antoninus Florentinus 1484, fol. CCVIIv–CCVIIIr (quotation, CCVIIIr).

56. That is, after describing Vincent's youth up to his entry into the Dominican order, Antoninus moves to a long description of Vincent's evangelization and conversions of Jews, Muslims, and sinners. The thirty-year preaching mission appears at ibid., fol. CCVIIIr. By contrast, Ranzano, after discussing Vincent's childhood and youth in book 1, turns directly to Vincent's labors in ending the Schism to open book 2.

57. Ibid., sec. iiii, fol. CCVIIIr.

him, armed to the teeth. With evident sangfroid, Vincent observed, "These are pimps who are coming so that they can kill me." Thereupon, dismissing the band of followers eager to defend their master, he turned to the pimps and made the sign of the cross, prompting the men to kneel in penitence and to reform their lives as well.[58] Antoninus also dwells on the austerity of Vincent's life: his fasting, modesty, castigations of the flesh, and nighttime vigils. So modest was Vincent, for example, that he rarely allowed himself to see his own naked body or even bare feet,[59] and when he found himself surrounded by admiring crowds, he forbade relic seekers from plucking the hairs from the poor donkey on which he rode in his final years.[60] In emphasizing Vincent's austere life and tireless evangelizing, Antoninus makes him a model of Dominican Observance and the order's preaching mission.

And in between praising Vincent's apostolic activity and celebrating his ascetic lifestyle, Antoninus took the time—as we have seen—to patiently defend his hero against those who murmured that he had taken the wrong side in the Schism and had spoken untruthfully in announcing that Antichrist was already in the world. As Peter Howard has recently argued, Antoninus was haunted throughout his career by the fear of Schism, having experienced abundant examples himself.[61] He became a Dominican during the years in which the Great Schism split his own order, lived through the rupture between Pope Eugenius IV and the Council of Basel with its Antipope Felix V, witnessed the Council of Florence that was supposed to heal the breach between Roman and Eastern Christendom, and saw innumerable factional disputes among the citizens around him. As Howard demonstrates, Antoninus often preached against schism and factionalism, linking schism in the church to disruptions in the civic body and eventually asserting that the Great Schism had inaugurated the seventh age of history and the Last Days.[62]

Still, in discussing the crises of his own lifetime, Antoninus adopted a conciliatory tone that diminished rather than exacerbated divisions. In defending Vincent's adherence to the Avignon papacy, for example, Antoninus noted, "It is indeed an article of faith to believe that, just as there is one holy Catholic Church, so there is also a single pastor of it. But it is not an article to believe this one or that one to be [he] when several so declaim themselves."[63] Similarly, in discussing the schism between Eugenius IV and Felix V—although he certainly had no kind words for Felix—Antoninus remarked that many had followed Felix out of expedience even while

---

58. Ibid.
59. Ibid., sec. v, fol. CCVIIIv.
60. Ibid.
61. Howard 2005.
62. Ibid., 301–10.
63. Antoninus Florentinus 1484, fol. CCVIIIv. Also cited by Howard 2005, 315n10.

inwardly hating him as Antichrist.[64] As for Vincent's teaching on Antichrist, Antoninus both acknowledged a need to defend his pronouncements and praised Vincent's preaching for being so terrifying "that it might convert all to excessive terror and thus horrify sinners."[65] Antoninus's head-on rebuttals of Vincent's presumed detractors thus aimed to offer something to discordant groups, fitting well with the archbishop's larger obsession with a peaceful and harmonious society.

As noted previously, Antoninus also made abundant use of the canonization inquests and other sources to append to his life an extensive list of prophecies and miracles, both *in vita* and worked after Vincent's death.[66] To Vincent, whom Antoninus calls at times a "new apostle," the Holy Spirit had provided not simply the apostles' eloquence but also their wonder-working abilities. In detailing miracles worked during Vincent's lifetime, Antoninus mentioned several of the same miracles that had attracted the notice of Ranzano. Yet for Antoninus, Vincent's most important miracle was his multiplication of bread and wine to feed his followers. This was the only specific miracle mentioned in Antoninus's prologue, and he emphasized it again by placing it first in his section on Vincent's miracles *in vita*.[67] His subsequent list of miracles worked after Vincent's death includes a double catalog drawn both from what he refers to as the letter of canonization and from the canonization inquests.[68]

Near the end of the catalog Antoninus relates the tale of the chopped-up baby, as found in the Brittany testimony, although he cannot resist filling in some of the gaps to make the story more vivid. It is the tale of "a certain pregnant woman in the region of Brittany," who was overcome with such a craving to eat human flesh "that it seemed to her that she should die if she did not eat [some]." When her husband returned to find that she had cut their son in two and cooked half, "he was seized with as much sorrow as anyone can imagine." "All of Brittany" wondered at the miracle of the boy's restoration and at the residual thread-like "sign of the division made in the little one's body."[69] Antoninus's *Chronicle* thus gave currency to a postmortem

---

64. Howard 2005, 316.

65. Antoninus Florentinus 1484, fol. CCVIIIv.

66. The sections on prophecies and miracles take up as much printed space as do the prologue and the *vita* proper.

67. Antoninus Florentinus 1484, sec. 7, fol. CCIXv.

68. Ibid., secs. 8–9, fol. CCIXv–CCXr. Section 8 includes an initial three resuscitations and the reference to the letter of canonization mentioned before. Section 9 contains four miracle recitations, all of which can be found in the Brittany inquests, as well as a note that there were twenty-eight resuscitations of dead persons "in the processes made to inquire into his life and miracles in diverse kingdoms and sealed with their distinct marks by notaries," citing specifically the inquests in Brittany and in "Apulia" (possibly meaning the Naples inquest). Ibid., fol. CCXr.

69. Ibid., fol. CCXr.

version of the chopped-up baby miracle at odds with Ranzano's. As we will see, this doubling of the tale was the source of some later iconographical and hagiographical confusion. Still, with detailed, vivid narrations like this one, Antoninus highlighted Vincent's intercessory powers in a manner that was both eminently readable and highly preachable.[70] Embedded within a title lauding the Dominican order, Antoninus's Vincent Ferrer biography presented his subject, in short, as a new Dominic or, better yet, a new apostle, distinguished in virtues, deeds, and miracles.

In the *Brief Life of Vincent Ferrer* by Antoninus's secretary, Francesco Castiglione, there is an even greater emphasis on Vincent's miraculous intercession. Castiglione's life, written in 1470 and printed as a preface to a 1496 edition of Vincent's sermons, perhaps was intended as a sort of votive offering in the hopes that Vincent's prayers could help to restore the fortune of a family down on its luck.[71] As he makes clear in a dedicatory letter to Cardinal Jacopo Ammannati, Castiglione examined and drew upon Vincent's canonization inquests; a citation later in the life demonstrates as well that he had read Antoninus's life of Vincent.[72] On the basis of these sources Castiglione presents an extremely abbreviated biography of the holy preacher, followed by an extensive catalog of miracles that takes up nearly six times the printed space consumed by the biography proper. He narrates at great length a miracle not found in the canonization inquests (or in Ranzano's biography) about which he learned by letter from a certain aged priest named Bartolomeo in Alessandria. In this incredible story two grave sinners were spontaneously reduced to nothing but dry bones during the course of one of Vincent's sermons. Thanks to the compunction and contrition he aroused in their hearts, they suffered on earth the penalty reserved for them in their future life, "freed to eternal peace and happiness."[73] If Castiglione did indeed

---

70. It has been suggested that Antoninus's life of Vincent lay behind the brief notice about the saint in the *Nuremberg Chronicle* (although much of what is found there could also have come from the bull of canonization). Wittlin 1986, 219, 222–23.

71. On the life of Francesco Castiglione, see Bausi 1991, 112–81. Bausi speculates that Francesco's father may have suffered from having been part of an anti-Medici faction in Florence (117). He also relates a number of largely unsuccessful attempts on Francesco's part to ingratiate himself with the Medici after 1447; the *vita* of Vincent Ferrer and an account of the martyrdom of Antonio da Rivoli are each prefaced by a dedicatory letter to Cardinal Jacopo Ammannati Piccolomini, perhaps more indication of the Medici's lack of interest in Francesco (121–23). For the *vita* as ex-voto, see Frazier 2005, 38–39. As for the date of Castiglione's *Brief Life,* the assertion of J. Walker 1933, 94, that Antoninus drew upon Castiglione's biography of Vincent is not correct. Frazier follows this suggestion as a basis to posit 1459, the year of Antoninus's death, as a *terminus ante quem* for Castiglione's *vita.* Frazier 2005, 393. But Castiglione did draw on Antoninus and not vice versa, and I see no reason to reject a 1470 date for Castiglione's *vita.* Castiglione specifically cites Antoninus. Castiglione 1496, fol. a4v; cf. Antoninus Florentinus 1484, fol. CCXr.

72. Castiglione 1496, fol. a1v and a4v.

73. Ibid., fol. a4v–a5r (quotation from a5r).

hope that his *Brief Life* might bring both Vincent's intercession and the cardinal's patronage, this focus on the miraculous made good rhetorical sense.

Castiglione only nods gently in the direction of the two criticisms that Antoninus had tackled head-on. Castiglione's Vincent Ferrer is neither a wholehearted supporter of the Avignon papacy nor a key figure in the healing of the Great Schism. Thus, while he mentions that Vincent was called to Avignon by Benedict XIII, Castiglione merely states that, given the Schism in the church, Vincent often admonished Benedict to resign the papal throne. When Benedict consistently broke promises to abdicate, Vincent "left him and converted himself to preaching the word of God."[74] As for Vincent's apocalyptic pronouncements, perhaps following the example of the 1458 bull of canonization, Castiglione notes that "in all his sermons, he testified that the advent of Antichrist was soon at hand."[75] Far from presenting Vincent as a *failed* prophet whose words required some defensive explaining, Castiglione implies that this pronouncement was the source of the force and effectiveness of a preacher whom all held to be "like an angel or a new apostle of God."[76] As a modern-day apostle, then, Castiglione's Vincent Ferrer appears predominantly as holy preacher and miracle worker but not as the healer of schism Ranzano makes of him.

## Lives Utilizing Multiple Sources

A second set of Vincent biographies combines material from Pietro Ranzano's writings and from other early *vitae*. In these texts, too, we see authors ignoring Ranzano's presentation of Vincent Ferrer in favor of their own concerns. This continued shaping of one's own Vincent Ferrer is perhaps most apparent in a life composed sometime after 1467 by a friar from the reformed Dominican convent in Chioggia, a coastal town on an island in the southern part of the Venetian lagoon.[77] This flowery and almost fantastic *vita* draws upon Ranzano, Antoninus, Castiglione, and local informants to magnify the portrait of Vincent as wonder worker. The Chioggia friar both

---

74. Ibid., fol. a2r.

75. Ibid.

76. Ibid. The bull of canonization similarly links Vincent's effective preaching to his raising the specter of the imminent Last Judgment. *Bullarum diplomatum* 1857–72, 5:147.

77. *Vita Vincentii Ferrerii auctore monacho Clugiensi*, WBSA, MS 27, fol. 1–55v; Hill Monastic Manuscript Library, film no. 35,238 (BHL no. 8665). The work postdates 1467, an internal date in the manuscript. The manuscript originated in the Dominican priory of San Andrea in Faenza and contains lives of three Dominican saints/blessed ("blessed" refers to a holy person who has not yet been canonized): Vincent Ferrer, Catherine of Siena, and James Salomoni of Venice (who heard the confession of the murderer of Peter Martyr). See "Supplementum ad vitam Beati Iacobi Veneti" 1893, 367–68. That he also knew Antoninus's work is indicated by the author's retelling of a miracle of soldiers moved to extraordinary public penitence (fol. 22r–22v), which is similar to a miracle about a Lyon squire related by Antoninus but not by Castiglione or Ranzano. Antoninus Florentinus 1484, fol. CCIXv.

adds spectacular new miracles to Vincent's dossier and presents elaborated versions of more familiar ones. While the friar is not insensitive to the topics that so concerned Ranzano and Antoninus, his graceful prologue makes clear his greater interest in Vincent's preaching, peacemaking, and, primarily, miracles.

For the Chioggia friar, Vincent lived in a world marked not so much by the Great Schism as by intractable *political* strife. As he says in the prologue, "And indeed at that time not the faith of Christ but rather a profession of Guelph or Ghibelline resounded; nor did anyone glory in being a Christian, but rather either Guelph or Ghibelline."[78] Vincent was sent by God to remove such scandal. As for division in the church, the Chioggia friar acknowledges its gravity, calling it a "murky schism" that shook the church and noting that many schismatic, or at least doubtful, popes succeeded one another.[79] But he softens Ranzano's depiction of Vincent as a key agent in the Schism's end, choosing instead simply to distance his hero from the Avignon papacy. In discussing Vincent's relationship with Benedict XIII, for example, the friar stresses the uncertainty of the Schism years and even asserts that "Vincent, for a considerable time, remained undecided," all the while urging Benedict XIII to resign.[80] But upon hearing of the decisions of the Council of Constance, according to the friar, Vincent withdrew his support from Benedict and preached against him and in favor of the new pope, Martin V.[81]

As for Vincent's erroneous announcement of Antichrist's birth, the friar from Chioggia bypasses the sorts of defenses offered by Ranzano or Antoninus and instead largely ignores the matter. In the Chioggia *vita,* in fact, while Vincent's vision of Christ has Jesus commanding him to go forth and preach his word, it does not include any instruction to announce the imminent Last Judgment.[82] When the author does later mention that Vincent often warned that "the judgment [of God] is at hand" (Rev. 14.7), the friar simply notes—as had the bull of canonization—that these words were highly effective in bringing sinners to penance.[83] The Chioggia *Life* does add, however, a second vision not found in previous biographies of Vincent but seemingly

---

78. WBSA, MS 27, fol. 2r: "Et enim tunc temporis non fides Christi sed aut Gelphi aut Gibelli professio personabat nec se quisquam Christianum sed vel Gelphus sive Gibellum se esse gloriabatur."

79. Ibid., fol. 13r–13v: "Agitabatur autem tunc forte in ecclesia turbidum scisma."

80. Ibid., fol. 13v: "Inter que mala et Christi confessor vincentius aliquamdiu anceps mansit verumtamen ipsi benedicto sepius suasit ut papatui resignaret quatenus hac occasione unitas ecclesie rederetur."

81. Ibid., fol. 13v.

82. Ibid., fol. 14r: [Christ's words to Vincent] "Viriliter age vincenti quoniam verbi mei nuntium atque predicatorem [?] te esse constitui. Surge perge discure et oviculas meas pabulo vite et sapientie verbo quo te replevi diligenter refoveas."

83. Ibid., fol. 17r. "Sepissime autem ad exterrendos convertendos quod populos futuri iudicii terrores et cominationes proponebat illud apocalipsis frequenter repetens *Timete deum et date illi honorem quia venit hora iudicii eius*" (emphasis added).

modeled on the 1412 letter to Benedict XIII. This time, however, Saint Dominic appears to Vincent during an illness and instructs him to go forth and preach the coming Judgment Day. Far from acknowledging any potential problem, however, the Chioggia friar specifically praises Vincent's "prophetic spirit," which he contrasts to that of the false prophets and hypocrites who will attend the birth of Antichrist.[84]

Perhaps as part of some sort of miraculous one-upmanship, the friar of Chioggia most notably magnifies Vincent's intercessory abilities by inserting into the biography several wild tales circulating at the time. In part, these miracle stories may have been calculated to draw pilgrims specifically to the Dominican friary in Chioggia; others are unrelated to local places and offer a glimpse of the sorts of exchanges of information that lurk beneath the surface of surviving texts.[85] Whereas someone like Antoninus of Florence strove to present Vincent as a model to emulate, in the world of rumor and more casual reporting into which the Chioggia friar was also plugged, he appeared more as a supernatural superhero.

One simple example demonstrates the sort of ante-upping in which the Chioggia friar was engaged. Pietro Ranzano had related a miracle in which Vincent's intercession stabilized a shaky makeshift bridge in Tortosa, saving a crowd endangered by the structure's imminent collapse. The Chioggia friar repeats this story but then adds a second, similar but more fantastic tale not found elsewhere. Namely, one other time, when Vincent and his followers were confronted with a raging stream and no way to cross it, Vincent laid his

---

84. Ibid., fol. 23v–24r (quotation 24r): "Unde instructus diunitus [sic] prophetico spiritu nova quedam sacramenta de mundi fine et antichristo frequenter populum premonebat....Et quia multitudinem nuntiorum destinabit ante se [Antichrist] qui in ostentatione religiositatis ac ob ypocrisi in simulatam cum quamdam devotionis fidem obtinuerit sibi credentibus in ruine schandalum convertentur." The implication is that this time will come soon. Ranzano does include a scene in which Dominic appears to the young Vincent (RVV, 1:497–98), praising Vincent's virtues and telling him that he will be, in essence, a second Dominic but without the mandate to preach the Last Judgment.

85. Some of the miracle tales seem designed to plant the idea that Vincent Ferrer was working miracles for those who invoked his aid at Dominican houses, such as those related in the Chioggia friar's chapters 43 and 44. The first tells of the resuscitation of a young boy from the town of Rivolta Secca near Cremona (present-day Rivolta d'Adda, about sixteen miles east of Milan), who had fallen into a body of water and drowned, only to be resuscitated after his father made a vow to Vincent Ferrer and brought his body to a (Dominican) convent some sixteen miles distant and asked the prior also to make a similar vow and celebrate a Mass in Vincent's honor (WBSA, MS 27, fol. 52v–54r). The second, which took place in 1467 in the town of Vigevano in the diocese of Novara (also in Lombardy), concerned the death of a nobleman's son, who fell from a high tower and was resuscitated after the family took his body to the local Dominican church (fol. 54r–55r). It seems plausible that these tales were miracle stories that circulated among reformed convents. Like Choiggia, Lombardy was a center of the Dominican Observant reform. Hinnebusch 1965, 1:229. On the oral circulation of miracle tales, see Koopmans 2011.

cape on the water and made the sign of the cross over it. Instantly, the cape became "like a table under their feet," enabling their safe and dry crossing on nothing but a layer of thin cloth.[86]

Two other miracles illustrate the sorts of tales that the Chioggia friar delighted in collecting and passing on. The first, found in no previous *vita* of Vincent Ferrer, involves a Spanish man who, when given custody of his orphaned nephew, poisoned the lad in order to obtain his inheritance. Sometime later, the man attended one of Vincent's sermons, during the course of which the preacher repeatedly shouted out, "At Palermo," words that greatly troubled the man. Approached by the man for an explanation, Vincent told him, mysteriously, that he would meet his punishment in Palermo—unless he confessed his sins at once. Ignoring Vincent's warning, the man soon thereafter found himself on a ship, which, buffeted by storms at sea, made landfall at a place that turned out to be Palermo. Seeking refreshment at a local butcher shop, the man purchased the head of a lamb, from which blood immediately began pouring. Then, to his even greater dismay, the lamb's head took on the appearance of his nephew's head. Hauled before a local judge by a crowd of amazed witnesses, the man recalled Vincent's prophetic words, confessed to the murder, and was promptly beheaded.[87]

In another instance, the Chioggia friar related an equally stupendous tale about the celebration of Vincent's canonization at his burial place in Brittany. It was not enough that when Vincent's tomb was opened, the saint's body was uncorrupted and exuded a marvelous fragrance—after thirty-four years in the grave. Even more remarkably, as the participants celebrated Mass in the Vannes cathedral, Vincent's dead corpse raised itself up and knelt in reverence from the time of the elevation of the host until the priest had taken communion, at which point it lay back down as before. According to the author, the source of the story was a subdeacon who had chanted the Mass in question and who many years later became a bishop. On business in Italy, he stopped at the convent in Chioggia and there related the tale to the amazement of the brethren, swearing an oath that he had seen it all "with his own eyes."[88]

To an author like the Chioggia friar, possessing a taste for the most stupendous of miracles, Pietro Ranzano's favored tale of the chopped-up baby would certainly be appealing. Relying as he did on a variety of sources, the

---

86. WBSA, MS 27, fol. 38r (chap. 31): "Cappam super aquas extendit et facto signo crucis cum socio asendens ita sub pedibus suis quasi tabula sibstitit: quod secure in Christi nomine gurgitem illum pertransivit." Cf. RVV, 1:507.

87. WBSA, MS 27, fol. 29v–31r (the story takes the whole of chapter 25).

88. Ibid., chap. 40, fol. 50v: "Hec que nunc retulimus fratribus ipse narravit eadem propriis occulis se aspexisse iure iurando sacrarum manuum firmiter aseverando contestatis."

friar encountered the tale in both its versions, as postmortem miracle and in Ranzano's narration of a miracle worked by the living saint. The friar appears to give more credence to the former version, as related by Antoninus and Castiglione. He presents the miracle in a chapter headed "Concerning the boy marvelously resuscitated at his tomb," sandwiched between a chapter on Vincent's death and one describing his canonization by Calixtus III.[89] The story includes the now-familiar crazed wife, "who blazed with an immoderate desire to eat meat," and the unwitting husband, who returned home to find the dismembered and partially cooked child. He took the parts to Vincent's tomb, where, "with … nearly all of Brittany witness and all the people of Vannes watching," the boy's flesh "joined itself together" and the child began again to breathe.[90] Still, after completing the tale, the Chioggia friar immediately offers the alternative version, presented as "another similar to this [miracle], more illustriously … done by him while still alive." This time he relates Ranzano's story of the chopped-up baby, complete with the insane mother in Languedoc, the noble husband, and the child cut up and cooked for the holy preacher himself. For the Chioggia friar, this doubled miracle illustrated the "marvelous types of grace" granted by God to Vincent, through whose intercession "there have been furnished the desired benefits to anyone, bolstered by faith, asking for any type of health."[91]

For the friar from Chioggia, then, detailing Vincent's abundant and stupendous miracles was as important as—or even more important than—documenting his holy life or asserting, as had Ranzano, his crucial role in ending the Great Schism. More than half the folios of the manuscript *Life* are devoted to the saint's prophecies, exorcisms, and miracles. A number of these tales appear in no other source, such as the six postmortem miracles listed after the description of Vincent's canonization. And there may have been even more originally. In the sole manuscript copy, the *Life* ends abruptly in the midst of chapter 44.[92] The effect of the friar's flowery narration nonetheless was more than sufficient. If one wanted to fan devotion to the saint's

89. Ibid., fol. 47v (chap. 38, "De puero ad eius sepulcrum mirabiliter su[s]citato").

90. Ibid., fol. 47v–48r: "Ad tumulum … res miranda nimis et pene cunctis incredibilis contigit tota tamen fere contestante Britania et omni venetensi populo spectante in veritate comperta. Cuiusdam nobilis viri uxor in furorem versa comedendi carnes immoderato exarsit desiderio….Rediens igitur domum maritus … consurgens infantuli sui partes et membra colegit in unum. Et accedens ad tumulum beati vincentii … omni spectanta populo concisum infantis corpusculum super santi tumbam obtulit … miro modo se caro pueri simul compegit et reintegrato statim in pristinam formam corpusculo respirare cepit."

91. Ibid., fol. 48r–48v: "Et aliud consimile huic eum ad huc mortalem perfecisse clarius sit compertum….Si igitur manus domini ad ipsum dum in hoc vixit mortalitatis exilio numquam abreviata fuit in ingentium virtute signorum quanto magis nunc secum regnantem in presentia anpliori [sic] gratia potestatis in consimilibus mirabilibus suis … decorabit….et quibusque quarumvis sanitatum sufragia fide poscentibus optata beneficia prestabantur."

92. At the bottom of folio 54v; see also "Supplementum ad vitam Beati Iacobi Veneti" 1893, 368.

cult and particularly to encourage pilgrims to visit shrines in his honor, the Chioggia friar's *Life of Vincent* provided ample evidence.

## Lives Directly Dependent on Ranzano's Works

Even authors directly dependent on Ranzano's *vita* for their knowledge of Vincent Ferrer only occasionally followed the Sicilian humanist's concerns in portraying the new saint as healer of the Schism, converter of Muslims and Jews, and unproblematic preacher of the Last Judgment. For example, in his *Chronicle of Master Generals of the Order of Preachers* (ca. 1495), Girolamo Albertucci de' Borselli reduced Ranzano's *vita* to a telegraphic style, largely omitting those sections in which Ranzano had driven home his major polemical points. In fact, Borselli neatly sidestepped the issue of the Schism. True, he acknowledged that Vincent had been summoned to Avignon by "Petrus de Luna, who was Benedict XIII" and served the pope as confessor and master of the sacred palace. But then he simply noted—with some confusion as to chronology, perhaps stemming from Ranzano—that Vincent urged Benedict to resign "because it had been decreed in the Council of Constance [1414–17] that the power had flowed to Martin." Borselli next recounted the vision (of 1398!) that had spurred Vincent's preaching journeys, set here during a fever brought on by Vincent's agitation over how to leave Benedict's court.[93] In Borselli's not entirely lucid presentation, Vincent's leaving Benedict appears to have been motivated by a desire to obey the Council of Constance and not to have represented the culmination of long-standing efforts to end the Schism. As for the issue of Vincent's apocalyptic preaching, Borselli simply made no mention of the fact. Still, he did follow Ranzano in giving prominence to the miracle of the chopped-up baby, placing it second in his list of Vincent's miracles.[94]

If Borselli had any particular aim in his life of Vincent, it appears to have been part of a larger goal of his entire chronicle, namely, magnifying the

---

93. Biblioteca Universitaria, Bologna, MS 1999, fol. 156r: "Petrus de Luna qui fuit Benedictus 13 B Vincentium ad se recurritur [?] eumque suum confessorem et magistrum sacri pallatii constituit....Hunc Patrem Benedictum induxit B. Vin. ut papatu renuntiaret quia in concilio Constantiensi ita decretum erat et Martino erat collata potestas. In curia predicti pape existens B. Vincentius fluctuebat modo quo curiam eius deserere posset ex qua febres incurrit. Dum ergo decumberet apparuit ei Christus." The treatment is reminiscent of that in Ranzano's *Office* (BC, MS 112, fol. 76r–76v).

94. Biblioteca Universitaria, Bologna, MS 1999, fol. 157r. Borselli lists miracles before prophecies (that is, in the reverse of the order in book 3 of Ranzano's *vita*). He then picks up some material from Ranzano's book 2 before moving on to the treatment of Vincent's death as in Ranzano's book 4. Borselli declines to list any miracles postmortem. The first *in vita* miracle described by Borselli, as for Antoninus, is a tale of multiplication of bread and wine to refresh Vincent's followers. Borselli follows Antoninus's basic order of narration for the remaining miracles.

glories of his own Order of Preachers. One small detail points to Borselli's awareness of rivalries between the Dominicans and the Franciscan order, particularly in the sticky area of saints. As had Ranzano, Borselli reported that Vincent had prophesied the future glories of Bernardino of Siena (1380–1444) when the young Franciscan had stood among the crowd at one of Vincent's sermons in the Italian town of Alessandria.[95] This episode does not appear at all in the canonization inquests, and it may well represent an invented tradition meant to answer the embarrassing fact that the younger Bernardino was canonized in 1450, five years before Vincent. At any rate, like Ranzano, Borselli portrayed Vincent predicting just that event, telling the crowd that "the church will honor him before me." Then Borselli added a remark not found in Ranzano's *Life,* which clarifies the import of this tale of prophecy and demonstrates what was clearly, in his mind, the proper hierarchy among the characters involved. "Note," he wrote, "that Saint Bernardino, moved by the fame of Saint Vincent, went to Alessandria. He was not yet then famous. And when he heard [Vincent], he said, 'The things I see and hear are greater than what the report [*fama*] was about this apostle of the Lord.'"[96] Bernardino may have preceded Vincent in canonization, but in Borselli's telling, he acknowledged the Dominican to be the true master.

While Borselli largely bypassed Ranzano's portrayal of his hero as healer of the Schism and dispenser of apocalyptic orthodoxy, a cut-down version of Ranzano's *Life* found in a Trier manuscript went even further in ignoring the Sicilian humanist's concerns.[97] The copyist of the Trier manuscript largely reproduced Ranzano's text, but with significant omissions. Most glaringly, the scribe skipped those passages in which Ranzano had tried to whitewash Vincent's activities during the Great Schism or to excuse Vincent's apocalyptic preaching. The Trier *Life,* in fact, removed Vincent from *any* contemporary setting and certainly from anything that could be the least bit controversial. Sections where Ranzano had described Vincent advising rulers, converting Waldensians, and reconciling feuds were all dropped in the Trier manuscript, as were any mentions of Pope Benedict XIII and even

---

95. This prophecy appears in RVV, 1:500 and also in the excerpts from the *Annals* (BC, MS 112, fol. 59r: "Prophetico spiritu cum multa futura tum vero diui Bernardini praedicationem sanctitatisque claritatem praedixit").

96. Biblioteca Universitaria, Bologna, MS 1999, fol. 159v (roughly following the text in Ranzano's *vita*): "Dixit Hic est unus de ordine minorum qui est futurus magnus predicator et magne fame ecclesia ipsum ante mihi honorabit....Nota quod sanctus Bernardinus motus fama S. Vincentii ivit Alexandriam nundum tunc ipse famosus et cum audisset eum dixit Maiora sunt que video et que audio quam fama fama [*sic*] fuit de isto apostolo domini." Witnesses at the time of the canonization inquests were evidently aware of the rivalry between the various religious orders regarding their famous preachers. Toulouse witness Joannes Salvatoris remarked that he had heard sermons by Bernardino of Siena and several other noted orators and could attest that Vincent's sermons were better than those of the other famous preachers (*Proceso,* fol. 212v; FPC, 344, witness 18).

97. Stadtbibliothek, Trier, MS 1168/470, fol. 266r–296r (see note 45, above).

of the duke and duchess of Brittany.[98] On one telling leaf, in the course of describing Vincent's vision of Christ, the scribe drew a line through two short phrases. The first has Christ assuring Vincent, "Indeed soon will peace be returned to the church." In the second, Christ sternly instructs Vincent to announce the Last Judgment, but the scribe has stricken through the words "the time is soon to come."[99] Nothing could make more apparent than these two scribal corrections the decision of the compiler of the Trier *Life* to consistently suppress Pietro Ranzano's shaping of the image of Vincent Ferrer.

In two lives ultimately dependent on the excerpts from Ranzano's *Annals,* we also see authors turning their backs on Ranzano's depiction, in the official *vita,* of Vincent Ferrer as healer of the Schism. In the anonymous *Epitome* of Vincent's life as well as in Martial Auribelli's revision of the lessons for the *Office* of Vincent Ferrer, the pope whom the friar served is unnamed, and the word "schism" appears not at all. [100] Vincent's vision of Christ is correctly set in Avignon but without any reference to its being a papal city. True, neither author goes as far as Borselli or the compiler of the Trier manuscript in also removing Vincent's apocalyptic preaching from the record. Christ does instruct him to announce the imminence of the Last Judgment.[101] But neither Auribelli nor the *Epitome*'s author is willing to reproduce the longer defense of Vincent's apocalyptic predictions found in the official *Life*—or to take up Ranzano's portrait of Vincent as healer of the Schism.

Likewise, a brief anonymous *Legend of Saint Vincent* preserved in a fifteenth-century Bologna manuscript omits any mention of the Great Schism and

---

98. The text follows Ranzano's order of presentation exactly, with the following significant omissions (what is listed are book, chapter, and paragraph numbers of RVV): I.2.12 (Pedro de Luna and the Schism); II.1.1–3 (Schism); II.1.5–6 (apocalypse); II.1.7 (Council of Constance); II.3.13 (reconciling feuds); II.3.16–17 (counsel to royalty); II.4.21 (conversions of heretics); III.5.41 (Benedict XIII in Perpignan); IV.1.8 (duke and duchess of Brittany).

99. Stadtbibliothek, Trier, MS 1168/470, fol. 273r. The crossed-out phrases are "Cito enim erit pax ecclesie reddita," and the italicized portions of the following phrase: "volo ut populis extremi iudicii *tempus cito futurum esse* denuncies rigore."

100. *Epitome:* Archivio Storico Diocesano, Novara, codex XXVII, fol. 121r: "Postmodum vero ob ipsius Vincentii virtutes mirificas ac eximie sanctitatis nomen tandem effugere non potuit quo minus duos annos summum pontificem sequeretur essetque confessor eius et magister apostolici palatii." Similarly, Auribelli's revision of the *Office: Breviarium secundum ordinem* 1481, fol. [C1]v. Cf. Ranzano, *Annals:* BC, MS 112, fol. 55v (see note 29). Both the *Epitome* manuscripts were collections designed to be read out to groups of religious. The Novara manuscript, with 125 entries, largely saints' lives, was evidently compiled for liturgical use by the cathedral chapter. Poncelet 1925, 339–48. The British Library manuscript originated in the Dominican nunnery of St. Louis de Poissy as a nonliturgical book designed for public reading. Naughton 1995, 281, 327.

101. Archivio Storico Diocesano, Novara, codex XXVII, fol. 121r; *Breviarium secundum ordinem* 1481, fol. [C1]v. But neither of the authors follows here the *Annals* biography, in which Ranzano has Christ also commanding Vincent specifically "that he should no longer stay in the papal court" (BC, MS 112, fol. 56r: "nihilo plus in pontificis curia moraretur"). In the opening paean in the *Office,* Auribelli repeats from Ranzano's version the identification of Vincent with the angel of Revelation 14:6–7: *Breviarium secundum ordinem* 1481, fol. [B8]v. Ranzano: BC MS 112 fol. 71r–71v.

touches only lightly on Vincent's apocalyptic preaching.[102] Following the lead of the *Epitome,* on which it appears to depend, the Bologna life has Vincent unable to escape serving the (unnamed) pope for less than two years and receiving from Christ the mandate to announce the impending Judgment Day.[103] To the portrait of Vincent sketched in his source, however, the author of the Bologna *Legend* has added a listing of six miracles, two of which are drawn from Antoninus's biography and the remainder of which appear to come from the Brittany canonization inquest. The final tale in the catalog is the miracle of the chopped-up baby, following Antoninus's postmortem version of the prodigy, while the first two stories detail the resuscitations of plague victims. The presence of these particular miracles in a life evidently meant to be read out loud, perhaps to a group of clerics, demonstrates not simply the wide currency attained by Ranzano's signature miracle in literate circles but also the force of what might be said to be a more popular image of Saint Vincent Ferrer as an effective intercessor against the plague.[104] But despite the embrace of Ranzano's favored miracle in this *Legend of Saint Vincent,* the humanist's polemical spin of Vincent as healer of the Schism is again strikingly absent.

The first hagiographer to enthusiastically adopt Ranzano's portrayal of Vincent Ferrer was Giovanni Antonio Flamini, who furnished a life of Vincent for a collection of biographies of famous Dominicans published in Bologna in 1517. Leandro Alberti's *Concerning the Illustrious Men of the Order of Preachers* reflected printers' growing realization that there was a steady market for encyclopedic collections of saints' lives. The anthology's compilers, Alberti and Flamini, were educated in a humanist tradition that saw schoolboys assigned to compose vivid, dramatic paraphrases of older saints' lives—just the sorts of biographies that would sell to the reading public.[105]

---

102. Biblioteca comunale dell'Archiginnasio, Bologna, MS B 2019, fol. 49v–54r: "Incipit legenda sancti vincentii confessoris ordinis predicatorum feliciter." For a description of the manuscript, see Mazzatinti 1957, 9–10.

103. Biblioteca comunale dell'Archiginnasio, Bologna, MS B 2019, fol. 50v.

104. The miracles appear at ibid., fol. 52v–54r and take up about one-third of the text. The narrations of the resuscitations of Johannes Guerre and of the chopped-up baby are close to the language found in Antoninus's *Chronicle.* The manuscript in which the *Legend* appears contains ten homilies and saints' lives (Mazzatinti 1957, 9–10); it likely was intended to be read out loud to a group of religious.

105. Alberti 1517. Flamini's *Vita Divi Vincentii* appears at fol. 156v–174v. The life appears also in Flamini 1529, fol. CLXIr–CLXXXIIIIv. On Alberti's collection, see Frazier 2005, 217, 335–37, 323. In keeping with the classicizing trend seen in many humanist saints' lives, Flamini gives Vincent the honorific title *divus* (holy) rather than using the postclassical term *sanctus* (saint). For other instances, see D. Collins 2008, 31, 151n49. Although I am labeling Flamini the first to fully take up Ranzano's portrait of Vincent Ferrer, it is worth noting that Ranzano's *vita* had evidently led the abbot Johannes Trithemius (1462–1516) to believe that Vincent played a major role at the council that ended the Schism. Trithemius (1601) 1966, 350.

In the case of Vincent Ferrer, Flamini's models were Ranzano's official *vita* as well as the *Chronicle of Master Generals* of his fellow Bolognese, Albertucci de' Borselli.[106] Flamini closely followed Borselli for the order of narration but looked to Ranzano for more abundant detail, all the while incorporating his own flourishes of color and emotion to draw in his readers.

While Flamini's *Life* added dramatic emphasis to Ranzano's exemplar, he nonetheless faithfully reproduced his model's major themes. As in Ranzano's *vita,* for example, Flamini's Vincent Ferrer worked tirelessly to end the Schism in the church. If anything, his efforts were even more stringent than those detailed by Ranzano. At one point, Flamini invented a long, passionate speech for Vincent, in which he urged Benedict XIII to resign the papacy for the good of the church and tried desperately to get the pontiff to acquiesce in the decrees of the Council of Constance.[107] "Only the Blessed Vincent," added Flamini, "boldly spoke to him in this firm manner."[108] Similarly, Flamini followed Ranzano in defending Vincent's apocalyptic teaching, adopting wholesale Ranzano's strategies for presenting his hero. As in the official *vita,* Flamini had Christ, in a vision, commanding Vincent to preach the impending Last Judgment. Likewise, in response to charges that he was disseminating novelties about the apocalypse, Vincent wrote a *libellum,* which he sent to the pope, who could find in it nothing worthy of condemnation.[109] Finally, like Ranzano, Flamini praised, in typical flowery language, the extraordinary fruits of Vincent's preaching. "How burning his eloquence," Flamini exulted, "how powerful and efficacious," noting "not only that evil Christians moved by his oratory were impelled to abominate their former life and move to the right [path], but also many Jews and gentiles."[110]

In enumerating Vincent's miracles and prophecies, Flamini again adopted Borselli's order of presentation yet looked to Ranzano's *vita* for fuller drama and details. Thus, like Borselli, Flamini led his list of miracles with Vincent's miraculous multiplication of bread and wine for his followers. Following Ranzano, however, he specified a location (Latona, between Vic and Barcelona). Characteristically, Flamini went beyond Ranzano in adding dramatic color to the tale, increasing the number of mouths fed from two thousand to three thousand and interjecting exclamations of wonder. "Oh! Thing worthy of all amazement," Flamini gushed. "Fifteen loaves and a small amount

---

106. The order of presentation, particularly in the miracles section, makes it possible to see that Flamini was guided by Borselli's work and not just by Ranzano's *vita,* although he does not include all the material in either. In at least one other case, Flamini's source for a saint's life was also Borselli's chronicle. Sorbelli 1922, 93–94, also cited in Frazier 2005, 385.

107. The speech appears at Alberti 1517, fol. 161r–161v.

108. Ibid., fol. 161r.

109. Ibid., fol. 162r. Cf. RVV, 1:492.

110. Alberti 1517, fol. 161r.

of wine—which such a blessing converted into the best [quality]—sufficed more than enough for such a multitude."[111] Still, according to Flamini, this miracle was insignificant compared with the second miracle in his list: namely, that of the chopped-up baby (also Borselli's second miracle).[112]

Like Ranzano, Flamini relished the dramatic tale of the crazed mother and the near cannibalism of her hapless child. He realized how extraordinary a miracle was Vincent's reconstitution of the dismembered and half-cooked infant. And, again, he added his own interjections to underscore the wonder of the story. Flamini's narration of the wife's butchering and cooking of the boy, for example, began with his explaining, "*But for the greater glory of his servant,* it was done by God's permission, that, suddenly seized with her usual fury, she killed her infant son, and cooked part."[113] And, as he described how, on Vincent's prayers and to the astonishment of onlookers, the parts of the boy "were at once conjoined," Flamini interjected in parentheses, "Wondrous is God in his saints."[114] With Flamini's *Life of Vincent* one sees, in short, an author embracing both Ranzano's portrayal of Vincent Ferrer as healer of the Schism *and* Ranzano's favored miracle of dismembered parts made whole. Printed both in Alberti's anthology and in a separate volume of *Lives of Famous Fathers of the Order of Preachers,* Flamini's Vincent biography, with its vivid and eloquent Latin, helped to give currency to Pietro Ranzano's vision of the new Dominican saint—and to the tale of the chopped-up baby.

## Brief Notices in Anthologies and Sermons

Early lives of Vincent Ferrer thus show authors wrestling with their sources to present a variety of portraits of the new saint. Only Giovanni Antonio Flamini adopted completely the image of Vincent proposed in the *vita* that Pietro Ranzano penned to please his Dominican and Aragonese patrons. Still, authors found irresistible the tale that Ranzano had made Vincent's signature miracle: the story of the chopped-up baby. Similarly, if one examines the brief notices about Vincent that appear in supplements to older collections of saints' lives in the century following his canonization, the same pattern emerges. The saint stands as preacher par excellence, with the force of his sermons, in many accounts, enhanced by his warnings of the imminent Last Judgment.[115] Ranzano's portrayal of Vincent as healer of the Schism largely

---

111. Ibid., fol. 164v.

112. Ibid.

113. Ibid. (emphasis added).

114. Ibid, fol. 165r.

115. This emphasis on Vincent's apocalyptic predictions is also underscored by the popularity (particularly in German-speaking lands) in manuscript and print of a prophetic text attributed to him, *De fine mundi.* For a list of manuscripts and editions, see Brettle 1924, 157–67, who also makes a

disappears, while the chopped-up baby often remains, shorn of its emblematic meaning but highlighting Vincent's intercessory powers.

For some authors, Vincent Ferrer served mainly to exemplify the goals of the Dominican Observant movement. In 1466, for example, the Dominican reformer Johannes Meyer (1422–85) inserted a brief notice about Vincent Ferrer into his *Book about the Illustrious Men of the Order of Preachers*.[116] Heading a section devoted to "reformers and propagators of Observance," Meyer's Vincent shares more with the portrait of the saintly preacher in Johannes Nider's *Anthill* than he does with Ranzano's hero, although Meyer evidently knew Ranzano's *vita* and briefly appears to borrow language from it.[117] Most important, the Schism appears not at all in this notice. And while Meyer stresses Vincent's preaching, he breathes not a word about his apocalyptic warnings. Tellingly, however, in a biography that covers less than a single printed page, Meyer takes the time to inform his readers that Vincent followed the constitutions of the Order of Preachers wherever he happened to be, whether in a Dominican convent or not.[118]

A brief biography printed as part of a supplement to *The Golden Legend* in 1483 offers an example of an author who follows Ranzano's presentation but does not adopt Ranzano's spin on the new saint.[119] This short *vita*, based on Ranzano's *Life* and the anonymous *Epitome*,[120] highlights the extraordinary

---

convincing case that the attribution to Vincent is spurious. Cf. Reeves 1969, 171–73, who appears to accept the work as genuine and in keeping with Vincent's teaching in general. For another example of an apocalyptic prophecy attributed to Vincent (probably dating to the first years of the sixteenth century), see Britnell and Stubbs 1986, 138–39.

116. Meyer 1918, 55–56.

117. E.g., "homines in sceleribus perditos *fere quadraginta millia reduxit ad propriorum flagiciorum cognicionem et ad agendam penitenciam*" (emphasis added). Meyer 1918, 55. Cf. RVV 1:495: "Meretrices, lenones, homicidas, piratas, usurarios, Dei Sanctorumque blasphemos, & hujusmodi generis homines, in sceleribus perditos, *fere quadraginta millia reduxit ad propriorum flagitiorum cognitionem, & ad agendam publicam pænitentiam*" (emphasis added). Loë (Meyer 1918, 55n2) observes that Meyer made use of Ranzano's *vita*, which appears in the same manuscript as Meyer's *Liber*. According to Curt Wittlin, Meyer had a copy made of Ranzano's *vita* as early as 1456 or 1457 and translated the text into German, a text that appears in Bibliothèque Municipale de Colmar, MS CPC 280. Meyer also made mention of Vincent in his *Buch der Reformatio Predigerordens*. Wittlin 1986, 216–19. See also Wittlin 1987 (which contains an edited version of one excerpt); Heck 1978, 67 (who notes that the manuscript was willed to the Franciscans in Colmar in 1462). Meyer's translation of Ranzano appears also to be the text contained in Servitenkloster Innsbruck, codex I.b.29, Hill Monastic Manuscript Library no. 28950; the manuscript is dated 1509.

118. Meyer 1918, 55–56. There is another short notice about Vincent by the Dominican Heinrich Kramer, who often collaborated with Observant Dominicans, in Kramer 1501, fol. 79v. (My thanks to Tamar Herzig for bringing this work to my notice.) On the *Clippeum*, see Herzig 2006, 36–43, 54.

119. *Historiae plurimorum sanctorum* 1483, fol. 266a–267b (supplement to Jacobus de Voragine, *Legenda aurea*; BHL no. 8666).

120. That is, the author at times adopts Ranzano's text word for word (including some details not in the *Epitome*) and at other times adapts text from the *Epitome*.

circumstances around Vincent's birth, his holy life and preaching, his gifts of prophecy, and his "many miracles."[121] As in the *Epitome* and Martial Auribelli's revision of the *Office,* Vincent's service "for two years" as master of the sacred palace is noted (without any mention of the pope whom he served, Benedict XIII). Likewise, a description of Vincent's vision of Christ commanding him to go forth and preach follows this passage.[122] Still, the author makes absolutely no mention of the Schism and thus grants Vincent no role in healing the divided church. Nor does he report that Christ also instructed Vincent to announce the imminence of the Last Judgment, a detail nonetheless present in Ranzano's *vita,* the *Epitome,* and Auribelli's *Office.* The Vincent of this brief notice, although an inspired prophet and preacher, is neither healer of the Schism nor angel of the apocalypse.

Yet another abbreviated biography appears in a supplement to a catalog of saints' lives by Petrus de Natalibus (fl. 1370–1400), printed in Lyon in 1519.[123] Again, Ranzano's shaping of Vincent Ferrer is not apparent. This extremely compressed biography, most likely derived from Antoninus's *Chronicle,* lists the areas evangelized by the preacher, credits him with the conversion of twenty-five thousand Jews and Saracens, and summarizes his ascetic lifestyle.[124] The author also describes one miracle *in vita* and one of the twenty-eight resuscitations from the dead he says were worked between Vincent's death and his canonization. The former is Antoninus's feature miracle: the multiplication of bread and wine to feed two thousand followers. And the latter is the tale of the chopped-up baby, much as it appears in Antoninus's *Chronicle,* where the culprit is a pregnant mother with a desperate craving to eat human flesh.

A supplement to a 1555 edition of the *Golden Legend,* completed by Claudius Rota around 1519, again demonstrates the growing popularity of the chopped-up baby story, combined with a lack of interest in Ranzano's shaping of the image of Vincent Ferrer.[125] This brief life presents Vincent Ferrer as a pious ascetic, an inspired and singular preacher, and

---

121. *Historiae plurimorum sanctorum* 1483, fol. 267b. The author makes specific mention of the prophecies concerning Calixtus III and Bernardino of Siena but offers only a generalized catalog of miracle types.

122. *Historiae plurimorum sanctorum* 1483, fol. 266b.

123. Petrus de Natalibus 1519, fol. 242v (The Bollandists imply that this text is a variation on BHL no. 8668, listing it as a separately numbered entry under 8668.) Evidence of Vincent Ferrer's popularity in Lyon can also be found in the numbers of printers (nearly two dozen) who put out editions of his sermons in the fifteenth and sixteenth centuries. Levesque 2000.

124. The figure twenty-five thousand points to Antoninus (Castiglione lists "thousands," Ranzano has twenty-five thousand Jews and eight thousand Saracens converted, while Nider puts the figure at thirty thousand), as do the two miracles mentioned below, and the number of twenty-eight resuscitations.

125. Jacobus de Voragine 1555, fol. 174 (mismarked as 714) (BHL no. 8667). On Rota: Stadler, Heim, and Ginal 1858–82, 1:xxvi.

a worker of wonders in the form of prophecies and miracles. The first half of the entry, abridged from the anonymous *Epitome* of Ranzano's *Annals* biography, details Vincent's birth, entry into the Dominican order, sojourn in the papal court (as in the *Epitome,* Vincent "could not escape" this brief period of service), and enormously fruitful preaching mission.[126] The Schism features not at all in this brief life, although the author has retained, from the *Epitome,* the reference to Christ's enjoining Vincent to preach the impending Last Judgment.[127] The second half of the biography largely portrays Vincent as a wonder worker, detailing in particular two miracles *in vita* and two prophecies made by the saint. The first miracle, following Ranzano's official *vita,* though situated now in Toulouse, is the story of a baby boy "divided and cooked" by his "lunatic" mother. The tearful father brings the parts to Vincent, at whose prayers the child is resuscitated, "preserving the signs in his body to his death, as a sign of the miracle."[128] The second miracle tale is Antoninus's story of the pimps who came after Vincent following his conversion of their prostitutes to a better life.[129] Citing Vincent's gift of prophecy, the author also relates the tale of his predicting to the young Calixtus III his future as the pope who would canonize Vincent, as well as a second prophecy that appears to be a version of one of the wilder miracle stories narrated by the friar from Chioggia. That is, the author asserts that Vincent had prophesied "about the man who, carrying the head of his brother whom he had killed, believing it to be under cover; a calf's head predicted that he would die at the command of justice."[130]

Sermons and vernacular literature from the late fifteenth and early sixteenth century also reinforce the impression that although Ranzano succeeded in popularizing the miracle of the chopped-up baby, he largely failed in his bid to portray Vincent as the effective healer of the Great Schism. In his sermon for the feast of Vincent Ferrer, for example, the Dominican Gabriel Barletta (d. after 1480) largely employed the *vita* of his erstwhile master Antoninus of Florence, as well as that of Francesco Castiglione, to compose a portrait that highlights Vincent's roles as a virtuous preacher and miracle worker. Vincent's apocalyptic preaching and the Schism make only

---

126. Jacobus de Voragine 1555, fol. 174.

127. Ibid. The biography also includes a description of Vincent's refusal of a cardinal's hat offered him by Benedict XI (*sic*), a scene to which some early portraits of Vincent make reference by portraying him with a cardinal's hat at his feet. This episode actually falls between the *in vita* miracles and a description of the fruits of Vincent's preaching; two prophecies come next, then a brief mention of Vincent's death and burial in Vannes.

128. Ibid.

129. Ibid.

130. Ibid.

cameo appearances in Barletta's sermon.[131] He devotes more attention, in fact, to Vincent's effective intercession against the plague, remarking that, just as with Sebastian and Roch, Vincent was given patronage over plague and later noting that "when a process was made about his miracles," Vincent's intercession was found to have effected sixty-six plague cures. In the printed sermon, clearly designed as a model for subsequent preachers, Barletta depicts Vincent as an ascetic, preacher, and wonder worker but not as the decisive arbiter of peace in the church. Even still, in listing a number of miracles that proceeded from Vincent's "virtue of faith," Barletta begins with the chopped-up baby story, complete with Ranzano's setting in the region of Languedoc and during the saint's own lifetime.[132]

In a sermon by Roberto Caracciolo (ca. 1425–95), a Franciscan friar who had ties to the Aragonese court in Naples, Vincent again appears primarily as an exceptional preacher.[133] Imposing a tripartite structure on material closely drawn from Ranzano's *vita* and *Office,* Caracciolo details, first, how Vincent was "truly suited to preach the Gospel of Christ"; second, why his preaching was "singular and most excellent"; and third, the "utility" or fruits of his preaching. Caracciolo's emphasis on "review[ing] the exceptional praises of [Vincent's] preaching" does not preclude his talking about the Schism, but he makes no effort to portray Vincent as bringing the division to a close.[134] In language close to Ranzano's in the *vita,* the Franciscan recounts Vincent's early encounters with Pedro de Luna, as well as his residence in Avignon after the cardinal became Pope Benedict XIII. And while Caracciolo does mention Vincent's efforts to persuade Benedict to resign the papacy and his subsequent decision to quit the papal curia, the entire story of Vincent's time

---

131. Barletta 1521, fol. 27v–30r. On Barletta, see Alecci 1964. When Barletta mentions the Schism, the conciliatory tone found in Antoninus's *Chronicle* is missing, as is Ranzano's attempt to assign Vincent a leading role in healing the division (fol. 29r–29v). Although Barletta mentions Vincent's vision of Christ, it is accompanied not by a command to preach the Last Judgment but merely by Christ's electing Vincent "my general preacher in the west" (fol. 29r, just *before* the mention of Pedro de Luna and the Schism). When Barletta cites the passage from Revelation 14:6 often applied to Vincent (fol. 28v) he follows by comparing Vincent to an angel but not specifically to the angel of the apocalypse.

132. Ibid., fol. 28r–28v (patronage over plague); 30r (sixty-six plague cures); 28r (miracle of chopped-up baby). At the end of the printed sermon, Barletta finishes with instructions to other preachers: "Applica eas tuo modo. Dicque aliquod miraculum in fine si videbitur. Ideo magnus vocabitur etc." (fol. 30r). The sermon is sprinkled with additional tales of Vincent's miracles and prophecies. Highlighting Vincent's numerous resuscitations of the dead, Barletta adds what are evidently recent miracles known to him and not found in other *vitae:* the cure of one Creme de Mattheo, an *armiger* of Sant Angelo; the resuscitation of a three-year-old girl found dead in a well in the same place; and, during a Mass in Vincent's honor, the gradual acquisition of human shape by a formless fetus previously expelled by a Domina Marchesana in Mantua (fol. 29v).

133. Caracciolo 1490, fol. [K6]v–L3r. On Caracciolo, see Aguzzi-Barbagli 2003 and Zafarana 1976.

134. Caracciolo 1490, fol. [K6]v.

in Avignon is presented as an example of the saint's humility, as illustrated by his refusal of the cardinal's hat Benedict offered him in hopes of persuading him to remain.[135] Signally absent from the sermon, furthermore, is any mention of Vincent's authorizing vision, of Christ's mandate to warn of the impending judgment, or, indeed, of Vincent's apocalyptic preaching. It is as if this Franciscan preacher wanted to remove from the Dominican Vincent the now customary marks of divine inspiration and the identification as the angel of the apocalypse. Strikingly, although Caracciolo lists a number of miracles and prophecies—all taken from Ranzano's *vita*—signs, as he says, that confirmed Vincent's preaching, the now nearly ubiquitous miracle of the chopped-up baby is not among them.

Finally, the early Catalan *Vida* of Vincent Ferrer by Miquel Peres further illustrates the tendency of early authors to ignore Ranzano's portrayal of Vincent as healer of the Great Schism.[136] Although he knew the Latin *vita* of Ranzano, Peres's preferred sources were Antoninus's *Chronicle,* on which he based his treatment of Vincent's life, and Castiglione's *Brief Life,* on which he relied largely for his account of Vincent's miracles.[137] Although Peres closely follows Antoninus in excusing Vincent's apocalyptic preaching and pronouncements, he does not equally take up his source's defense of the holy friar's adherence to the Avignon papacy. In fact, Peres makes no mention whatsoever of the Great Schism and certainly assigns to Vincent no role in its end. Nonetheless, he does include in his catalog of miracles the tale of the chopped-up baby, in the postmortem version found in Antoninus and Castiglione. Peres's *Vida,* chock-full of emotional speeches and prayers for the faithful, emphasizes Vincent's prophetic and thaumaturgic powers, including a Latin prayer that, if devoutly recited and carried on one's person, would protect him or her against the plague.[138] Again, Ranzano's image of Vincent as healer of the Schism falls by the wayside, while the chopped-up baby remains as a sign of Vincent's miraculous intercession.

## Artistic Representations

In fifteenth-century artistic representations of the newly canonized saint, one sees a similar pattern of embracing the miracle of the chopped-up baby championed by Ranzano while ignoring his insistence on Vincent's role in healing the Schism. Of seven surviving Vincent Ferrer altarpieces

---

135. Ibid., fol. L1r–L1v. The Avignon episode begins with the refusal of the cardinalate, a vignette that appears several paragraphs *after* the discussion of Vincent's labors to end the Schism in Ranzano's *vita.*

136. Peres 2007. On Peres, see Wittlin 1994, 9–16.

137. See Wittlin 1994, 9–10.

138. Peres 2007.

with miracle cycles from before 1500, four include portrayals of the miracle of the chopped-up baby. Only two of the complete altarpieces, however, closely follow Ranzano's *vita* for the remainder of their panels, and none of the polyptychs makes any visual reference to Vincent's role in healing the Schism. Other favored themes in early paintings of Vincent include exorcisms of demoniacs, healings of the sick and crippled, and the vision of Christ that launched Vincent's preaching mission. Four of the seven altarpieces have depictions of the Annunciation, perhaps a nod to Vincent's intense devotion to the Virgin Mary. And a number of artistic representations portray Vincent as a modern-day plague saint.

Portraits of Vincent Ferrer executed after his 1455 canonization tend primarily to emphasize his apocalyptic preaching in a manner similar to the presentation in the bull of canonization. Thus the saint is frequently depicted gesturing upward with his right hand toward a vision of Christ in judgment, enclosed in a mandorla, seated on a rainbow and sometimes with a sword in his mouth (a reference to Rev. 1:16).[139] Typically, Vincent carries in his left hand an open book, in which is visible the inscription *Timete Deum et date illi honorem quia venit hora iudicii eius* (Fear God, and give him honor, for the hour of his judgment is at hand. Rev. 14:7, my translation). Occasionally, particularly in Valencian paintings, this inscription appears in a text scroll to which the preacher points with one hand.[140] This line, quoted by Vincent himself in his 1412 letter to Benedict XIII and echoed in the bull of canonization and the *Office* of the new saint, underscores Vincent's identification as the angel of the apocalypse.[141] Alberto Velasco Gonzàlez has plausibly suggested that this portrayal of Vincent, with the book and vision of Christ, represents a prototype circulated within the Dominican order immediately upon Vincent's canonization, explaining a remarkable uniformity among early portraits of the new saint; it seems equally likely that, as in other fifteenth-century examples, similar images were on display at the canonization ceremony itself in 1455.[142] Certainly it would have been difficult

---

139. This presentation mimics the Eastern-type *majestas domini*, a reference to the Last Judgment: See Klein 1992, 163–64; and Christe 1992, 237 and 251–55.

140. Velasco Gonzàlez 2008, esp. 252–63. I am grateful to the author for providing me with copies of his works.

141. General guides to iconography of the saints mentioning Vincent: Kaftal 1952, no. 314, col. 1021–26, figs. 1145–50; Kaftal 1965, no. 408, cols. 1133–48, figs. 1315–37; Kaftal and Bisogni 1978, no. 317, cols. 1065–84, figs. 1374–98; Kaftal and Bisogni 1985, no. 241, cols. 659–62, figs. 931–35; Kirschbaum and Braunfels 1968–76, vol. 8, cols. 561–65; Réau 1959, tome 3, vol. 3:1330–32; Cahier (1867–71) 1966, 1:26 (wings), 1:358 (saints with infants). See also the thorough collection of images on Domínicos Chile 2012.

142. Velasco Gonzàlez 2008, esp. 235–52, particularly noting examples from Aragon and Italy; Velasco Gonzàlez sees a separate tradition in Valencia, linked to a series of miracle-working images

for painters to avoid a reference to Vincent's preaching on the apocalypse, the topic contemporaries most frequently recalled when they spoke of his sermons. Yet rather than defend or explain away Vincent's failed predictions of Antichrist's advent (as Ranzano and Antoninus had done), artists, seemingly guided by instructions from the Order of Preachers or the curia itself, chose instead to ignore them and portray Vincent's apocalyptic pronouncements simply as a vague trumpet call to repentance.

In contrast to the striking similarity of early portraits of the new saint, a consideration of scenes from his life and miracles portrayed in fifteenth-century altarpieces shows a plethora of presentations in which one scarcely encounters the official vision of the saint articulated by Pietro Ranzano at the behest of the pope and the head of the Dominican order. Ranzano's influence is most apparent in two works: first, the altarpiece painted by the Neapolitan master Niccolò Antonio Colantonio—like Ranzano, a favorite of King Alfonso V and the royal family—for the Dominican church of San Pietro Martire in Naples around 1460[143] and second, a now-dismantled work painted in the late 1470s or 1480s by Bartolomeo and/or Angelo degli Erri for the church of San Domenico in Modena.[144] Even in these two cases, however, the artists or their patrons chose to illustrate a number of vignettes taken from Ranzano's text but did not adopt Ranzano's primary characterization of Vincent as healer of the Schism and converter of Jews and Muslims. Although both altarpieces include scenes of Vincent preaching, and the degli Erri brothers have a panel illustrating Vincent's baptism of converted Jews and Muslims, neither polyptych follows Ranzano in presenting Vincent as ending the Great Schism.

The prime subtext of the Colantonio altarpiece, rather, appears to be to link the holy Vincent Ferrer to the royal house of Naples. (See figure 5.) Immediately beneath the saint's portrait appears a kneeling Isabella of Chiaramonte, Alfonso's daughter-in-law, accompanied by her two children. Art historians have hypothesized that the panel was commissioned by Isabella, perhaps as an ex-voto, after a rebellion by Neapolitan barons trying to unseat her husband, Ferrante (r. 1458–94), which resulted in Ferrante's

---

from Vincent's own Dominican convent there. Woodcut canonization portraits: Cobianchi 2006, 53–54; 2007, esp. 209, 211, 213–14, 219.

143. Now in the Museo Nationale di Capodimonte, Naples. See Leone de Castris 1997, 62; Kaftal 1965, cols. 1134–48 (figs. 1316–19, 1322, 1325, 1330–31, 1333, 1336–37; Limentani Virdis 2001, 349–52; Natale 2001, 381, 388–90 (catalog no. 58a); and Molajoli 1960, 47–49 (catalog no. 9).

144. Now in Seminario Arcivescovale, Modena (portrait); Kunsthistorisches Museum, Vienna (twelve panels); and Ashmolean Museum, Oxford (preaching at Perpignan). See Kaftal and Bisogni 1978, cols. 1067–80 (figs. 1375–78, 1380–83, 1385–88, 1390); Benati 1988, 135–55; Chiodi 1951. Dates: 1480s (Benati 1996); 1474–79 (Chiodi 1951, 20).

humiliation at the Battle of Sarno in 1460.[145] The six panels flanking the imposing portrait of Vincent Ferrer emphasize exceptional signs of his sanctity detailed in Ranzano's *vita:* the bishop of Valencia's interpretation of unusual sounds emanating from Vincent's mother's womb; Vincent's preaching to an attentive and diverse crowd; the apparition of the Virgin to Vincent in his cell, promising to confirm him in his vow of chastity; the vision of Christ, who here blesses Vincent; and the saint working miracles. In one panel he emerges posthumously from the clouds to rescue a ship at sea, and in another he reassembles, through his prayers, the disarticulated limbs of the chopped-up baby. Below, to the left of the portrait of Isabella, Vincent is shown exorcising a female demoniac while a crippled man awaits his healing; to the right is depicted the holy friar's death in Vannes. In Colantonio's beautifully executed panels, the saint appears as a holy ascetic and a wonder worker with whom Christ and the Virgin converse. By extension, Isabella and Ferrante's family falls under his holy protection, and Ferrante's rule partakes thereby in a sacred legitimacy. Although Colantonio's work clearly depends upon Ranzano's text, his Vincent Ferrer is not the saint of the official *vita.*

The altarpiece painted by Bartolomeo and/or Angelo degli Erri for San Domenico in Modena similarly relies upon Ranzano as a source but does not follow his portrayal of the new saint. The altarpiece was part of a mid-fifteenth-century program of renewal of the altars dedicated to Dominican saints in San Domenico (that is, Dominic, Peter Martyr, Thomas Aquinas, and the newly canonized Vincent) and was thus likely commissioned by the Dominican friars themselves. If the terms of commission were like those stipulated for the Saint Dominic altarpiece completed in 1474, the painters were instructed to paint "in blue and other fine colors certain scenes [*ystoriali*] according to the direction of the friars."[146] In this case, the friars chose thirteen scenes from Ranzano's official *vita* to surround Vincent's portrait.[147] But far from presenting Vincent as a concerned healer of Schism, the Modena altarpiece unblinkingly displays the holy man's ties to the Avignon pope Benedict XIII. True, the degli Erri brothers' panels include the scene of Vincent's illness in Avignon and the healing vision of Christ that launched his preaching mission and departure from the papal city. But three of the twelve side panels show Vincent as clearly adhering to the Avignon pope: in one

---

145. Bologna 1977, 109–10; see also Strehlke 1998, 144 (who notes that San Pietro Martire had been loyal to Ferrante during the rebellion); Leone de Castris 1997, 62 (catalog no. 7); Limentari Virdis 2001, 351; Abulafia 1995, esp. 21 (on the battle of Sarno); Bentley 1987, 21–34 (on the reign of Ferrante), esp. 24–25 (on the barons' revolt).

146. Commission of 1467, quoted in Chiodi 1951, 21.

147. Identification of individual scenes: Kaftal and Bisogni 1978, cols. 1067–80.

**FIGURE 5.** Colantonio, Saint Vincent Ferrer altarpiece. Museo Nazionale di Capodimonte, Naples (originally in San Pietro Martire, Naples). Photo by Scala / Art Resource, NY. In the polyptych's central panel, Vincent holds open a book and gestures upward (both emblems of his apocalyptic preaching and part of the early established portraiture of the new saint). In the panel beneath his feet are depicted a kneeling Isabella of Chiaramonte, wife of Ferrante of Naples, with her two children. Six vignettes of Vincent's life and miracles flank the portrait, including, at the top right, the story of the chopped-up baby.

panel, he rides with the still cardinal Pedro de Luna; in another, he lectures to Pope Benedict and his cardinals; while in third, he carefully takes his leave from Benedict prior to quitting Avignon to evangelize the world. Furthermore, in the scene that, according to reconstructions, appeared directly beneath the saint's portrait, Vincent preaches in Perpignan before Benedict XIII and the emperor Sigismund.[148] Like Colantonio, the degli Erri brothers present a number of episodes from Ranzano's biography of Vincent, as well as examples of the saint's miraculous intercession. In one panel he diverts three devils in the form of horses who threaten to disrupt a sermon, while in another the artists narrate sequentially Ranzano's tale of the chopped-up baby, from the moment that the mother's cleaver hangs poised over the child's body to the ultimate reconstitution of the partially cooked infant.[149] (See figure 6.) But a viewer would be hard-pressed to read this lurid panel, or any other of the scenes from the Modena altarpiece, as a reminder that Vincent also worked, as Ranzano insisted, to restore a divided church.

Other fifteenth-century altarpieces stray even further from Ranzano's presentation of the new saint as healer of the Schism. In a work painted for the church of San Domenico del Maglio in Florence, Giovanni Francesco da Rimini (d. 1470) offers the standard pose of Vincent pointing to Christ in Judgment in the heavens and holding a book with the *Timete Deum* text from Revelation.[150] Beneath his feet are three vignettes. In the left scene, the saint expels a large, black, winged demon from a possessed woman. In the center, pilgrims kneel at Vincent's tomb in expectation of his miraculous intercession. And at the right, the saint baptizes a kneeling man. Vincent appears here as herald of the impending Last Judgment and as miracle-working converter of souls.

Another altarpiece, painted for the Dominican church in the Sicilian town of Castelvetrano in the late fifteenth century, largely emphasizes Vincent's thaumaturgic powers while nodding to his apocalyptic preaching

---

148. Reconstruction: Benati 1988, 143; the panel of Vincent preaching before the pope is Ashmolean Museum, Oxford, catalog no. A 93. Web reproduction: Ashmolean Museum 2012.

149. Daniele Benati identifies the scenes thus: (1) the bishop of Valencia announces to Vincent's mother the sanctity of the child in her womb; (2) Vincent enters the Dominican order; (3) Vincent rides with the cardinal legate Pedro de Luna; (4) Vincent, while flagellating himself, is tempted by a devil; the Virgin appears to him while he reads Jerome's treatise on virginity; the demon flees; (5) Christ heals Vincent by touching his jaw; (6) Vincent expounds on scripture before Pope Benedict XIII and cardinals; (7) Vincent takes his leave of Benedict XIII, who names him apostolic legate; (8) Vincent baptizes two converts in Granada; (9) a mother chops and cooks her baby and Vincent restores him; (10) Vincent orders Brother Gilbert to return to his own monastery to die there; (11) Vincent heals the woman killed by his follower who believed her to be the devil, and a baby is raised (Benati does not explain the small demon seen in the air above this latter miracle); and (12) in Murcia, three devils in the form of horses threaten to disrupt a sermon. All can be found in Ranzano's *vita*. Benati 1988, 144–55 (figs. 112–23). According to Roberto Rusconi, the altarpiece is strongly anti-Jewish. Rusconi 2004, 230–32.

150. Giovanni Francesco da Rimini, altarpiece and predella panels, Accademia, Florence (inventory no. 3461); reproduced in Kaftal and Bisogni 1978, fig. 1391, and Polo Museale Fiorentino 2012.

**FIGURE 6.**    Bartolomeo and/or Angelo degli Erri, Saint Vincent Ferrer altarpiece, detail, inv. no. GG 6696. Kunsthistorisches Museum, Vienna (originally in San Domenico, Modena). © Kunsthistorisches Museum, Vienna. In this depiction of the chopped-up baby miracle, which closely follows Ranzano's narration, to the left, the mother cuts up and cooks part of the child, leaving the remainder on the larder shelf. To the right, the cooked child is brought before the horrified saint and his companions. Vincent prays over the pieces and restores the child to his (presumably) grateful father.

and holy life.[151] The central portrait has Vincent gesturing toward a now-obliterated vision of Christ in judgment and, again, holding an open book with the text from Revelation 14 visible. At his feet, a cardinal's hat and a bishop's miter remind viewers of Vincent's rejection of worldly honors,

---

151. Anonymous, Vincent Ferrer altarpiece, Church of San Giovanni Battista, Castelvetrano (formerly at San Domenico); reproduction, Kaftal 1965, figs. 1315, 1318, 1320, 1321, 1324, 1326, 1327, 1328, 1329, 1332, 1334, 1335. See also Bottari 1954, fig. 118; Vigni and Carandente 1953, 73, no. 62, and fig. 72. Vigni and Carandente remark on the work's "peasant" character, a sentiment echoed in Velasco Gonzàlez 2008, 248–49, noting the painting's emphasis on the saint's thaumaturgic powers, appropriated here to respond to the needs of popular piety and devotion. According to Rusconi, the panel depicting the chopped-up baby contains an anti-Jewish Eucharist reference, explained by the nearness of the town of Trapani, where there was a Jewish community. Rusconi 2004, 230.

while an Annunciation scene above hints at Vincent's devotion to the Virgin. Six panels flank each side of the portrait. Two of these are preaching scenes, and the bottom right corner shows Vincent's death. The remainder are devoted to miracles, seven worked by the living saint and two after his death. The painter has perhaps been influenced by Colantonio's Naples altarpiece, for he repeats the miracle of the chopped-up baby (*in vita*) and that of the ship rescued at sea and also, like Colantonio, depicts the exorcism of a possessed woman. But there are several scenes here that do not appear in Colantonio's work or in Ranzano's biography, indicating that the artist or his patrons sought out additional miracle tales. Most notably, the Castelvetrano altarpiece portrays two miracles particularly highlighted by Antoninus of Florence: the pimps who sought to kill Vincent, only to be converted to a better life, and the multiplication of bread and wine to feed Vincent's followers. The effect of the whole is to emphasize Vincent's role as an effective intercessor. Though Ranzano's chopped-up baby numbers among the miracles here, it serves simply as one more example of the saint's intercessory powers and not as a reminder of his role in ending the Schism.

Another set of altarpieces shows artists again moving away from the depiction of Vincent in Ranzano's *Life* and now emphasizing his role as an intercessor effective against plague.[152] In Venice, in the great Dominican church of Santi Giovanni e Paolo, the *scuola* of Vincent Ferrer commissioned a polyptych to decorate the confraternity's chapel at the west end of the church's nave from an artist usually assumed to be Giovanni Bellini.[153] (See figure 7.) According to Peter Humfrey, the commission was a response to both a redecoration of the chapel belonging to the *scuola* of Saint Peter Martyr, just across the aisle, and a severe outbreak of plague in the summer of 1464.[154] Accordingly, Vincent appears, holding the usual open book and with Pentecost-like tongues of fire in his right hand, flanked by Saints Christopher, protector against sudden death, and Sebastian, the plague saint par excellence. Above him, an Annunciation scene frames an image of the dead Christ; below, three panels, typically attributed to another artist, illustrate

---

152. This depiction of Vincent as plague saint also can be seen in several fifteenth-century woodcuts, to the confusion of some art historians, e.g., Zucker 1992, 187–91; Saffrey 1982, 292–93. See chapter 3.

153. School of Giovanni Bellini, polyptych and predella panels, Church of Santi Giovanni e Paolo, Venice. Reproduction and identification of scenes in Kaftal and Bisogni 1978, figs. 1389, 1394, 1395, 1397, and 1398; see also Humfrey 1988, esp. 403–6, 410 (Bellini as artist). Augusto Gentili and Fabrizio Torella attribute the upper part of the altarpiece to Bellini and the predella panels to an unknown artist from the workshop of Bellini's father Jacopo. Gentili and Torella 1985. Rona Goffen attributes the main altarpiece to Bellini but disputes the dating to the mid-1460s, reading the records to conclude that the present altarpiece was in place already in the mid-1450s in anticipation of Vincent's canonization and suggesting that the style is consistent with Bellini's work at that time. Goffen 1985, 2:277–95, esp. 279, 281, 281–83. See also Goffen 1989, 274–76, suggesting that the predella panels are the work of Lauro Padovano in 1468–71.

154. Humfrey 1988, 405–6. Augusto Gentili dates the altarpiece to 1465–70. Gentili 1982, 2:566.

**FIGURE 7.** School of Giovanni Bellini, polyptych of Saint Vincent Ferrer. Santi Giovanni e Paolo, Venice. Photo by Cameraphoto Arte, Venice / Art Resource, NY. Vincent's portrait, in the center of the altarpiece, shows the saint holding an open book in his left hand (a reference to his apocalyptic preaching), while in his right hand flames remind viewers of Pentecost and the saint's own gift of tongues. Portraits of Saints Christopher and Sebastian flank Vincent. Scenes of the Annunciation and Christ's deposition from the cross are above, while three panels below illustrate scenes from Vincent's life and miracles.

Vincent's miracles and preaching. To the left, the saint's posthumous inter-cession rescues a drowning victim (probably Johannes Gueho, detailed in the Brittany inquest and in the *vitae* of Castiglione and Antoninus, where it numbers among the miracles in the letter of canonization) and a woman or young girl crushed under a building (perhaps Jameta Michart, related in the Brittany inquest).[155] To the right, the saint rescues an infant from a cradle surrounded by flames,[156] and a captive tied to a tree is freed by the saint's intercession. None of these scenes obviously derives from Ranzano's *vita,* nor are all detailed in the biography in Antoninus's *Chronicle,* the only other major life available in 1465.[157]

In fact, Bellini's employers appear to have requested at least one miracle tale that had circulated independently of Ranzano's or Antoninus's texts. In the center of the predella, Vincent is shown preaching before a large crowd, his arms outstretched in an inverted V. (See figure 8.) Two penitent figures, a man and a woman in thin, diaphanous white robes, kneel before his pulpit. A Dominican friar gestures toward the pair, drawing the viewer's attention to them, and a seemingly incredulous woman in the audience reaches gingerly toward the leg of the man kneeling on the left. On closer examination, the pair exhibits a curious feature: their torsos, upper bodies, and arms appear normal, while their legs are skeletally thin and in fact appear to be nothing but bone. The scene thus seems to illustrate not simply Vincent's preaching but also an odd miracle reported in Francesco Castiglione's 1470 *Brief Life of Vincent Ferrer,* in which two criminals about to be executed were reduced to nothing but bones by the vehemence of Vincent's preaching about their sins. Castiglione would draw many miracles from the canonization inquests for his *vita,* but for this one he specifically identified his source as an aged priest from Alessandria named Bartolomeo, who had numbered among Vincent's followers.[158] Augusto Gentili and Fabrizio Torella have suggested 1465–70 as the range of dates within which the altarpiece was executed,

---

155. The story can be found in the testimony of her father, Johannes Michart (*Procès,* witness 238; FPC, 197–98).

156. The Brittany inquest includes several examples of Vincent's being invoked in the case of a house fire (as Kaftal also notes); these do not appear in the fifteenth-century *vitae.*

157. Gentili and Torella interpret the scene of the freeing of the captive as one of the miracles recounted at length by Ranzano, a story in which a young follower of Vincent's kills a mute woman, believing her to be the devil. Vincent's intercession resuscitates the woman (restoring her speech also) for long enough to confess her sins; he also assures the young man's pardon. Gentili and Torella 1985, 25. They interpret the panel overall as presenting a reassuring message, avoiding the standard portrayal of Vincent announcing the impending Judgment and instead stressing that, through faith, his intercession had cured bodies and souls of the just and the unjust. The apocalyptic menace of the Turks is only a soft background noise in the altarpiece in this reading (28–30).

158. Castiglione 1496, fol. a4v. Augusto Gentili 1982 (2:568) also suggests this identification, as do Gentili and Torella 1985, 26–28.

**FIGURE 8.** School of Giovanni Bellini, polyptych of Saint Vincent Ferrer, predella, detail. Santi Giovanni e Paolo, Venice. Photo by Scala / Art Resource, NY. In this scene of Vincent's preaching, a man and a woman kneel before the pulpit in penitential garb. Their lower limbs appear to be nothing but charred bones, a reference to the miracle related by Francesco Castiglione, in which Vincent's ardent preaching so consumed the hearts of two criminals that they suffered purgatorial fires here on earth and were reduced to nothing but a pile of bones. The artist has rendered a moment partway through Vincent's sermon and, evidently, in the midst of the sinners' miraculous transformation.

and Rona Goffen has placed the predella panels between 1468 and 1471.[159] A later date of execution might possibly have allowed the work's planners to have seen Castiglione's *Brief Life*. Still, the presence of the miracle of the combusted criminals here confirms that the *scuola* of Vincent Ferrer and their Dominican hosts in Venice had access to a wide range of sources about

---

159. Gentili and Torella 1985, 1, 14; Goffen 1989, 276.

the new saint and suggests that they preferred these other texts to the official view promulgated in Ranzano's *vita* as they commissioned Bellini's portrayal of Vincent as a wonder-working plague saint.[160]

An altarpiece painted by Domenico Ghirlandaio and his assistants for the Malatesta chapel in the church of San Domenico in Rimini echoes this framing of Vincent Ferrer as a plague saint.[161] (See figure 9.) Everett Fahy has hypothesized that this altarpiece was commissioned by the Malatesta family after an assault and attempted assassination in the 1490s and noted that the four family members who were the subjects of the attack appeared as kneeling donors on the original altarpiece, later to be painted out of the picture.[162] Although the context of the commissioning of the altarpiece was thus a political crisis and not simply an epidemic, Vincent nonetheless appears in the company of the plague saints Sebastian and Roch.[163] He is portrayed in his usual guise, gesturing to Christ in a mandorla and holding an open book with the apocalyptic text *Timete Deum*. Beneath, a series of predella panels depicts Vincent's miraculous intercession. To the left, a child is revived after falling into a ditch; in the center, invalids cluster around Vincent's pulpit seeking to be healed; and to the right, the saint posthumously raises a dead person.[164] None of these miracles immediately derive from Ranzano's *vita,* nor does the painting depict either of Ranzano's two major themes: Vincent as healer of the Schism or Vincent as converter of Jews and Muslims. Rather, the effect is to associate Vincent with the Malatesta family and with saints already known to have power over plague.[165]

---

160. Not unlike the nearby reformed Dominican convent in Chioggia, the source of a *vita* utilizing a wide range of sources, written and oral. This *vita* also includes a version of the miracle of the combusted criminals, with slightly different details from Castiglione's. It is also possible that the date of the altarpiece is after 1470, the date of Castiglione's *vita,* but arguing against this possibility is the presumption that in 1470 Bellini was already at work on an altarpiece for the *scuola* of Catherine of Siena at Santi Giovanni e Paolo. Humfrey 1988, 406.

161. Discussion and reproduction in Pasini 1983, 92–96; Venturini 1996, 154–64; see also Kaftal 1952, figs. 1146 and 1148.

162. Fahy 1966, 456. The altarpiece is reproduced on 458, fig. 10.

163. Venturini 1996 (154) specifically mentions a plague in 1493.

164. Kaftal 1952, col. 1021, identifies the left scene as the reviving of a child who fell into a ditch near Saragossa, an event to which a monument was subsequently erected and to which Fages makes reference in his biography.

165. This association between Vincent and plague is apparent in other altarpieces, such as that painted by Andrea da Murano for San Pietro Martire, Murano, Venice, and now at the Accademia in Venice, which depicts Vincent and Roch together in the central panel, flanked by Sebastian to the left and Peter Martyr to the right. The altarpiece was commissioned by the *scuola* of San Pietro Martire, dating from 1477 to 1480. Humfrey 1988, 411 and 415, fig. 12. A panel from ca. 1495 by a follower of Ambrogio Borgognone, now in the possession of the Howard University Gallery of Art, Washington, D.C., depicts Vincent (with Pentecost-like flames atop his head, book in hand, and a cardinal's hat at his feet) together with Saint Roch (reproduction, Kress Foundation 2012). Vincent also appears in a plague context in a succession of seven saints in the chapel of Saint Sebastian in Saint-Étienne-de-Tinée. Kovalevsky 2002, 209–12. Kovalevsky asserts that this depiction of Vincent

**FIGURE 9.**    School of Domenico Ghirlandaio, Saint Vincent Ferrer altarpiece. Museo Civico Rimini (originally in Malatesta chapel, San Domenico, Rimini). Photo by Alfredo Dagli Orti / The Art Archive at Art Resource, NY. In the altarpiece's central panel, Vincent holds open a book with the *Timete Deum* text from Revelation 14:7 and gestures upward to a vision of Christ in judgment. To the left and right stand plague saints Sebastian and Roch, an indication of Vincent's configuration as a guardian against the pestilence. Below the trio of protectors against plague, appear donor portraits of four kneeling members of the Malatesta family, who had recently survived an assassination attempt.

Another polyptych that strays from Ranzano's official image of the new Dominican saint is an altarpiece by Francesco del Cossa and Ercole de' Roberti, now dismembered but originally installed in the Griffoni family

as a saint to invoke against the plague is specifically linked to the regions around Venice (211). However, an altarpiece painted by Vicente Macip (1475–1545) for the cathedral in the Valencian town of Segorbe and now in the Iglesia de Sangre there portrays Vincent Ferrer surrounded by Saints Christopher, Roch, Sebastian, and Lawrence (reproduction, Ono.com 2012), while an altarpiece painted by Macip's son Juan de Juanes (Joan Macip) for the Carthusian house of Valldecrist in 1540 shows Sebastian flanked by Saints Vincent Ferrer and the Carthusian Bruno. See Doménech 2000, 78–83 (reconstruction of the altarpiece at 79; Vincent's portrait, 83). Reproduction of portrait, Museu Nacional d'Art de Catalunya 2012.

**Figure 10.** Francesco del Cossa, *Saint Vincent Ferrer*. National Gallery, London (originally in Griffoni chapel, San Petronio, Bologna). © National Gallery, London / Art Resource, NY. In this portrait panel from the now-dismantled Griffoni altarpiece, Vincent appears as herald of the coming Last Judgment, holding open a book in his left hand and pointing upward toward a vision of Christ in judgment. The exotic landscape in the background mimics that in the predella portrayal of Vincent's miracles, with resonances that, it has been suggested, played into contemporary calls for a crusade against the Ottoman Turks.

chapel in the church of San Petronio in Bologna.[166] Cossa's striking portrait of Vincent, surmounted by a vision of Christ in judgment (now in the National Gallery in London), was originally surrounded by portraits of other saints. (See figure 10.) Peter and John the Baptist stood at the preacher's sides, and depictions above of Saints Floriano and Lucy acknowledged the presence of the donors, Floriano Griffoni and his first wife, Lucia—a fact that leads Fabrizio Torella to posit a date before 1472 (when Griffoni remarried after Lucia's death) for the painting of the altarpiece.[167] Griffoni was a member of a powerful Bologna family with close ties to the city's ruler, Giovanni II Bentivoglio (1462–1506). Not surprisingly, modern scholars have seen references to contemporary politics in the altarpiece Griffoni commissioned for the family chapel.

Key to this interpretation is the altarpiece's predella. Beneath the portraits of Vincent and the other saints, a long panel by Ercole de' Roberti, now in the Vatican Museums' Pinacoteca, portrays, in an eerie, exotic-looking setting, several of Vincent's miracles, drawn from a variety of sources beyond Ranzano's *vita*, perhaps even including the canonization inquests.[168] According to the most sensitive modern readings of the iconography (by Fabrizio Torella and Augusto Gentili), Ercole de Roberti's predella presents, foremost, a series of miracles that illustrate Vincent's intercession to heal bodies in order to save souls. For example, according to Torella and Gentili, the first miracle on the left shows a pregnant woman injured in a fall, whose child, thanks to Vincent's intercession was safely to be delivered and baptized.[169] The second scene shows the saint exorcising a woman possessed by a demon, while a third episode shows a boy saved by the saint's intercession from a deadly fall and from mortal sin.[170] The final episode depicts the tale of the chopped-up baby, in its postmortem version familiar through the works of Antoninus of Florence and Francesco Castiglione (and the canonization inquests). (See figure 11.) Both Torella and Gentili note that the architecture of the tomb on which the baby is resuscitated and the basin in which the reconstituted

---

166. Francesco del Cossa and Ercole de' Roberti, Griffoni altarpiece, National Gallery, London, and Pinacoteca, Vatican Museums, Vatican City. Reproductions in Kaftal and Bisogni 1978, figs. 1394, 1390, 1392, 1393, 1396; National Gallery [London] 2012; and Vatican Museums 2012. Modern reconstruction of the altarpiece: Longhi 1968, fig. 98, and 128–31; and Benati 1983–84, 2:156–74, figs. 185–205. See also Gentili 1982, 2:563–76; Torella 1985–87; Jaffé et al. 1999.

167. Torella 1985–87, 49.

168. Torella (ibid., 46–47) mentions *vitae* by Ranzano, Antoninus, and Castiglione, as well the short life in the Biblioteca comunale dell'Archiginnasio, MS B 2019. But he hypothesizes that the source for the predella scenes was a now-lost *vita* by the Bologna humanist Giovanni Garzoni, who had ties to both the Dominican community in Bologna and Floriano Griffoni. On Garzoni's abundant writings on the saints, see Frazier 2005, 169–219, 395–414, esp. 413 (lost life of Vincent Ferrer).

169. Torella 1985–87, 47; Gentili 1982, 568–69.

170. Torella 1985–87, 47–48; Gentili 1982, 569–71.

**FIGURE 11.**    Ercole de' Roberti, detail of predella panel, *The Miracles of Saint Vincent Ferrer*, no. 40286. Vatican Museums, Pinacoteca, Vatican City (originally in Griffoni chapel, San Petronio, Bologna). Photo by Scala / Art Resource, NY. In this detail from the predella of the Griffoni altarpiece, the artist has depicted the postmortem version of the miracle of the chopped-up baby. In the building to the left, the crazed mother leans on her elbow, while the pieces of the child sit on a table in the room to the rear. The father, dressed in a red tunic, carries the dismembered body to Vincent's tomb, crossing a small stream whose waters may echo the baptismal motif seen in the right-hand scene. There the resuscitated child stands in a basin atop what is presumably the saint's tomb, enclosed in an architectural space that resembles a baptistry.

baby stands are reminiscent of baptism scenes, again pointing to the healing of the body as prelude to the salvation of the soul.[171]

Alongside this theological message, Torella and Gentili have suggested two very different political allegories at work in the Griffoni altarpiece. In both cases the key to the allegory is the presence in the predella of numbers of exotic figures: Moors, Jews, Turks, and Arabs. For Gentili, the altarpiece, painted by two artists who had recently fled Ferrara, was a not-so-subtle dig—from safely anti-Ferrarese Bologna—at the Ferrarese ruler Borso d'Este, who was seen by critics as too tolerant of heretics and "infidels."[172] In Torella's reading, the political context at work was rather the call for a crusade after the 1453 fall of Constantinople, an event that inspired apocalyptic fears that appeared to echo prophecies attributed to Vincent Ferrer.

---

171. Torella 1985–87, 48; Gentili 1982, 571–72. In contrast, Rusconi sees a strong anti-Jewish cast to the painting. Rusconi 2004, 230. Another fifteenth-century panel depicting the postmortem version of this miracle lacks the baptismal overtones of the Griffoni altarpiece, simply showing, to the left, the mother cooking the child and, in the center, the father with the cut-up and recomposed child kneeling before a tomb, with Vincent in the air interceding. Photograph, *St. Vincent Ferrer Raising to Life a Child Killed by His Mother,* Biblioteca Berenson, Fototeca, Harvard University Library Visual Information Access.

172. Gentili 1982, 574–76; Gentili notes that Cossa had left Ferrara miffed at being so poorly paid by Borso d'Este for the Schifanoia frescoes.

According to Torella, the image of Vincent, canonized just on the heels of the Turkish defeat of the Byzantine Empire, was mobilized in calls for a crusade (and for contributions to fund one). The crusading impulse saw new urgency after the fall of Negroponte in 1470, prompting Sixtus IV to renew the call for the defense of Christendom late in 1471, just around the time (according to Torella) that Cossa and Roberti were painting the Griffoni altarpiece. Torella hypothesizes that the altarpiece forms part of Bolognese propaganda in favor of a crusade, calling for mobilization against the Turks and criticizing the indifference of those who did not heed the pope's call to arms.[173] Vincent, converter of Muslims and Jews, reminding viewers of an imminent apocalypse, loomed in the background. Whether Torella or Gentili is more correct about the work's political orientation, it seems clear that in the case of the Griffoni altarpiece, its patron and artists had little interest in Ranzano's framing of Vincent Ferrer as healer of the Great Schism.

Fifteenth-century altarpieces devoted to Vincent Ferrer thus provide a glimpse of artists and patrons who only sometimes relied on Pietro Ranzano's official *vita* for their portrayal of the saint and, even in those works that stayed close to Ranzano's narrations, largely ignored his attempt to present Vincent working tirelessly to end the Schism. Still, artists appear to have found Ranzano's favorite miracle tale irresistible. The resuscitation of the chopped-up baby appears on four of the altarpieces discussed above (making this story, along with the healing of demoniacs, the most frequently depicted scene on fifteenth-century altars to Vincent Ferrer). Similarly, the tale is found in other depictions of Vincent's life and miracles.

Two paintings illustrate the variety of ways in which artists could interpret the same subject. In one case, the artist stays fairly close to the horrific events narrated by Ranzano, with one crucial difference; in another case, the artist builds layers of symbolic resonances that would have made Pietro Ranzano happy. In the first instance, on the walls of a chapel in the church of San Domenico in the Umbrian hilltop town of Gubbio, a fresco by an unknown artist typically identified with the school of Ottaviano Nelli shows a woman thrusting a whole infant into a large cauldron set over a fire. To the right, the saint presides over the child's resuscitation. The child is cooked and, presumably in the now obliterated central portion of the fresco, dished up for a meal, but there is no indication that the baby was ever cut into pieces prior to being cooked.[174] (See figure 2.) The second instance, a panel (predella to an altarpiece?) attributed to the school of Ghirlandaio and now housed in Florence's Stibbert Museum, also portrays

---

173. Torella 1985–87, 49–51.
174. School of Ottaviano Nelli, fresco, San Domenico, Gubbio; reproduction, Kaftal 1965, fig. 1323; see also Giovagnoli 1922, 37–46.

the miracle of the chopped-up baby, but in a highly emblematic form.[175] (See figure 12.) Here, in contrast to the Griffoni altarpiece's references to the sacrament of baptism, the artist draws an explicit parallel to the Eucharist. Vincent, vested for Mass, stands before what appears to be an altar; an open book lies in front of him, as do a golden chalice and, directly in line with the chalice, a standing infant, his hands raised in a gesture of prayer. Lying on the table is a baby, eyes closed, the lower half of whose body is darker than the upper. This "before" view shows the chopped-up and partially cooked baby of the miracle tale. That this painting, at first glance, appears to depict a miraculous vision of the consecrated host as Christ child invites an identification of the chopped-up baby with the *corpus Christi,* emblematic of the body of the faithful or the church. Two other Italian Renaissance paintings portray the miracle in a similar Eucharistic setting, but whether contemporary viewers of such works grasped Ranzano's parallel between the chopped-up baby and the divided church is not at all clear.[176]

Other fifteenth-century images suggest that the chopped-up baby was becoming for artists simply another emblem for Vincent Ferrer, like the open book or the vision of Christ in judgment. For example, two copies of a 1487 edition of Vincent's sermons preserved in the municipal library in Colmar but originally belonging to the city's Dominican convent have illuminated initials that allude to this miracle. (It is not clear who produced or designed the illuminations.)[177] In the first, Vincent stands in his black-and-white robes, a closed book in his right hand and with his left pointing to Christ in judgment in the heavens. At his feet lies a naked child, with a clear line running vertically through his torso, reaching one hand toward

---

175. School of Domenico Ghirlandaio, panel, Stibbert Museum, Florence, no. 834; reproduction, Kaftal 1952, fig. 1149.

176. According to Federico Zeri, the first is by Bartolomeo Caporali (ca. 1467–68), part of a predella from an altarpiece by Caporali and Benedetto Bonfigli formerly at San Domenico in Perugia, now in the Galleria Nazionale dell'Umbria. Reproduction and attribution, Fondazione Federico Zeri 2012a. See Garibaldi 1996, 130–33, for a discussion of the altarpiece; and Todini 1989, 2:350, for reproductions of two scenes from the predella, identified by Todini as Benedetto Bonfigli, *Miracolo di San Paolo,* the chopped-up baby miracle, with the resuscitated child sitting up on the altar, hands joined in prayer; and Benedetto Bonfigli e Bartolomeo Caporali, *Miracolo di San Pietro Martire,* depicting, left to right, a drowning scene (Johannes Gueho?), a laden donkey being beaten (reference to the story of Vincent berating the colleague who cursed his humble mount?), and a kneeling Dominican friar presiding over the apparent resuscitation of a young girl. The second painting, by the early sixteenth-century painter Francesco Granacci—and, according to Everett Fahy, formerly at Florence's Dominican church of Santa Maria Novella—appeared in a Christie's auction catalog on April 18, 1980. *Important Old Master Pictures* 1980, 60 (lot 64, described as *Saint Zenobius Reviving a Child*). Reproduction, Fondazione Federico Zeri 2012b. It is possible, too, that viewers would have interpreted the scene along the lines of representations of Jewish host desecration tales.

177. Vincent Ferrer 1487. The relevant copies are in Bibliothèque Municipale, Colmar, shelf marks IV/8798, Pars III (initial D) and INC G 1614, t. I (initial B); reproductions and discussion in Heck 1978, 63–68, figs. 1 and 5.

**FIGURE 12.**   School of Domenico Ghirlandaio, panel, *Un Miracolo di San Francesco [sic] Ferrer*, detail. Museo Stibbert, Florence, no. 834. Courtesy Museo Stibbert, Florence. This portrayal of the chopped-up baby miracle has heavy Eucharistic overtones. Vincent is dressed in his pontifical robes for Mass and stands before an altar on which there sit a chalice and a crucifix. In place of the host, the artist has depicted the baby both "before" and "after": the dead child lies on the altar, with the lower half of his body discolored from having been cooked. The resuscitated infant stands facing Vincent, hands clasped as if in prayer. To either side, onlookers raise their hands in a gesture of wonder (not in this detail).

the saint. The left half of the infant's body and face is a pinkish, saffron hue, just as reported by a witness at the Naples canonization inquest who told the tale of the butchering mother who boiled the baby in broth and saffron. (See figure 3.) In this miniature, to the standard portrait of Vincent has been added a nod to his most famous miracle, the restoration of the chopped-up baby. An initial *D* in another copy of Vincent's sermons simply shows a baby seated in the grass, another reference, according to Christian Heck, to the same miracle.[178] As the baby became just one more emblem of the holy Dominican preacher, its meaning again appears to have drifted from Ranzano's spin. The baby now seems to be a nod to Vincent's thaumaturgic powers.

A German woodcut, now lost, provides a second example of the chopped-up baby's addition to the now-standard portrait of Vincent Ferrer. This woodcut, formerly in the Leipzig University library, survives only in a twentieth-century black-and-white reproduction.[179] (See figure 13.) Even without the original colors, it is an impressive piece. Headed in Latin *Saint Vincent, Doctor, of the Order of Preachers,* the woodcut features the preacher standing in the center of the page, pointing with his right hand to Christ in a mandorla above and holding a closed book in his left hand. A second Dominican stands behind Vincent, his hands joined in prayer (or wonder?). At Vincent's feet lie three corpses. Two are shrouded, but the third, directly in front of the preacher, is a naked child. A seam bisects his body vertically from head to toe, and the right side of the child's body is clearly darker than his left and bears the signs of having been sliced into many parts. He is unquestionably the chopped-up baby and, as in the Colmar miniature and in a fifteenth-century German panel painting, still displays the tint of the saffron in which he was cooked—a detail absent from Ranzano's telling of the story.[180] Again, in the presence of other corpses presumably also about to be resuscitated, the baby reminds viewers of the effectiveness of Vincent's intercession. Another fifteenth-century German woodcut now in the British Museum shows a similar composition, although the Dominican witness is absent. (See figure 14.) This time, however, the child, while still the only one of the three corpses not in a shroud, does not bear the scars of his dismemberment.[181] Given the frequency with which the story of the

---

178. Bibliothèque Municipale, Colmar, shelf mark IV/8798, Pars III (initial D); see Heck 1978, 66.

179. *Sanctus Vincentius doctor ordinis predicatorum* (formerly in Leipzig Universitätsbibliothek, missing since the Second World War); reproduction, W. Cohn 1935, no. 16. See also W. L. Schreiber (1926) 1969, 201, no. 1729; Falkenstein 1840, 64, no. 13.

180. The arrangement of the corpses in the lost woodcut is reminiscent of that in a fifteenth-century German panel painting by Friedrich Walther (ca. 1440–94) in the Cloisters Collection of the Metropolitan Museum of Art in New York (accession no. 64.215), although the saint is misidentified. Metropolitan Museum of Art 2000–2012. See Fries 1965 and, for the correct identification, Rusconi 2004, 230n15.

181. Anonymous, German, *St. Vincent Ferrer* (c. 1475), British Museum, London, 1895-1-22-19; W. L. Schreiber (1926) 1969, 201, no. 1730; Dodgson (1903) 1980, 1:104 (no. A 106). See also Heitz [1906]–42, vol. 54, no. 9 (Schreiber no. 1388a), identified by Heitz as Saint Dominic reviving Napoleon Orsini but that I think should also be identified as Vincent Ferrer. The saint holds a closed book and gestures toward Christ in a mandorla in the heavens (one of Vincent's emblems, not Dominic's). At his feet lies a naked child, his legs strangely askew, who perhaps reaches toward the saint in the manner of the child in the Colmar initial. No scars or lines of division are visible, but nonetheless, I see no reason not to read this, too, as a reference to the miracle of the chopped-up baby.

**Figure 13.** *Sanctus Vincentius doctor ordinis predicatorum.* From W. Cohn 1935, no. 16 (Schreiber no. 1729), formerly in Leipzig Universitätsbibliothek, missing since the Second World War. Print Collection, Miriam and Ira D. Wallach Division of Art, Prints and Photographs, The New York Public Library, Astor, Lenox and Tilden Foundations. Beneath the heading "Saint Vincent, doctor, of the Order of Preachers," Vincent gestures toward a vision of Christ in judgment. At his feet lie three corpses, two in burial shrouds and one, its right half differently colored from its left and marked with scars of having been butchered, clearly the chopped-up baby.

**FIGURE 14.** Anonymous, German, *Saint Vincent Ferrer* (c. 1475). British Museum, London, 1895-1-22-19.© The British Museum. In this beautifully colored woodcut, Vincent stands pointing to a vision of Christ in judgment. He holds in his left had a book open to the text of Revelation 14:7 ("Fear God, and give him honor, for the hour of his judgment is at hand.") At his feet lie three corpses. The middle one, not in a shroud, may represent the chopped-up baby.

chopped-up baby was depicted and recounted, however, the lines marking his division may not have been necessary for the identification.

To sum up, as artists sought to portray Vincent Ferrer in the first fifty years after his canonization, they fairly rapidly adopted a standard portraiture for the new saint, emphasizing his role as apocalyptic preacher through depicting the vision of Christ in Judgment and the book, frequently open to the text of Revelation 14:7. If this was indeed an image provided at or immediately after the canonization by the heads of the Dominican order or the curia itself, they must be credited with some success in standardizing the visual image of Vincent. But the evidence from narrative scenes included in altarpieces yields a far more complex situation. Patrons and artists did not always look to Pietro Ranzano's official *vita* as their source for depicting Vincent's life and miracles, and even when they did (as in the examples from Naples and Modena), they did not follow Ranzano's attempts to present Vincent as a healer of the Great Schism. Artists, just like Vincent's early hagiographers, used a variety of sources to mold Vincent to fit their own agendas or those of their powerful patrons. Where Pietro Ranzano did succeed, in art as in writing, was in associating Vincent with the miraculous restoration of the chopped-up baby. Artists, like hagiographers, delighted in the tale, making it emblematic of the new Dominican saint.

If, in recommencing canonizations after the Great Schism and the tense church councils of the early fifteenth century the papal curia had hoped to assert some greater degree of centralization and control over the meaning of sanctity, the case of Vincent Ferrer shows how messy a business the lived religion of the later fifteenth century was in reality. Was Vincent a healer of the Schism or a passionate partisan of Benedict XIII? Or did the division in the church simply not figure in his life? Fifteenth-century authors took all three positions. Nor are we simply dealing with an opposition between a learned interest in Vincent's ecclesiastical activities and a popular taste for the miraculous. For the learned and for the unlettered, this newly canonized saint remained largely a symbol awaiting definition. A saint could be a powerful conveyor of political legitimacy, as Vincent was for the rulers of Brittany and Naples, or could stand for a certain type of religious profession, as in Johannes Nider's and Johannes Meyer's use of Vincent to typify Dominican Observance. A saint could serve as an example of a pious life, as for Antoninus of Florence, or simply as the source of wonderful supernatural power, as for Francesco Castiglione. His life could be used to draw pilgrims to a single place, as for the friar from Chioggia, or to encourage the faithful to support a crusade, as in the Griffoni altarpiece. And if a single person could embody all these varied meanings, so too could a single tale told about that individual. In Vincent's case, the miraculous restoration of the chopped-up baby could nod to his healing of the Great Schism in the hands of Pietro Ranzano or simply signify his thaumaturgic powers in popular woodcuts.

Only two features remain near constant in early depictions of Vincent Ferrer: his presentation as an angel of the apocalypse, announcing the imminent Last Judgment and thereby bringing sinners to penitence, and the miracle of the chopped-up baby. As we shall see in the next chapter, only in the late seventeenth century would Pietro Ranzano's vision of Vincent Ferrer fully triumph, as Vincent's example would be mobilized in a Christendom again torn by schism and where apocalyptic expectations had guided mendicant missionaries to the unbelieving natives in the New World. And the chopped-up baby once again would form part of the evolving imagery of Saint Vincent Ferrer.

# APPENDIX

# The Lérida Inquest and the Letter of Canonization

Fifteenth- and early sixteenth-century authors had a variety of sources from which to draw information about Vincent's miraculous intercession. Some, such as Pietro Ranzano, Antoninus of Florence, and Francesco Castiglione, had direct access to the canonization inquests. For a number of his miracle tales, Ranzano appears also to have drawn upon an inquest conducted in Lérida, near Valencia, in 1451, probably in response to a call from the Dominican order to collect evidence of Vincent's miracles.[182] Others had to rely upon the accounts of Ranzano and later authors of lives of Vincent for a sampling of the 860 miracles that Ranzano says were approved by the pope.[183] But information about Vincent's intercessory powers could circulate in other, less formal ways as well, such as what Antoninus of Florence refers to as a letter of canonization.

## The Lérida Inquest

We know about the Lérida inquest through a Palermo manuscript from the fifteenth century that recounts, in Sicilian dialect, ten miracles worked by Vincent Ferrer.[184] Given that Ranzano, a Palermo native, served after Vincent's canonization as provincial of the Dominican order for Sicily, it is

---

182. Reichert 1900, 256 (chapter general of 1451).
183. RVV, 1:498.
184. Edited (and discussed) in Pagano 2000 (353–70); the manuscript is also discussed in Pagano 1999, 750–52.

tempting to connect him in some way with this manuscript or its contents. Nine of the ten tales that appear in the Palermo manuscript are also in Ranzano's *Life,* but the Palermo *Miracles* text does not seem to be derived from the work of the Sicilian humanist. First of all, the Palermo tales are longer and more elaborate than Ranzano's narratives, indicating a separate source for the stories. And second, the Sicilian miracle tales include specific references to the inquest held in Lérida in 1451, frequently indicating the name of the witness who related the miracle story and the fact that the testimony was given under oath and had been taken down by a notary.[185] Ranzano never so much as mentions the Lérida testimony, citing only the official canonization inquests held in 1453 and 1454 in Brittany, Avignon, Toulouse, and Naples. But none of the ten miracles in the Palermo manuscript appear in the records of the surviving canonization inquests from Brittany, Naples, and Toulouse. Nor does it seem likely that Palermo miracles reproduced by Ranzano were drawn from the missing Avignon inquest, given that witnesses from Aragon appear to have been funneled to the Naples inquest. Whether this Sicilian miracle compilation represents an independent circulation of the text of the Lérida inquest or whether it was excerpted from some larger list of approved miracles cannot be known. But clearly the material was available in some form to Ranzano as well as to the translator who rendered it in the Sicilian vernacular sometime in the half century after Vincent's canonization.

## The Letter of Canonization

More evidence for a separate circulation of information about Vincent's miracles comes from the biography of the saint in the *Chronicle* of Antoninus of Florence, composed sometime between 1456 and 1458.[186] There Antoninus lists six prophecies attributed to Vincent and twelve miracles worked in the saint's own lifetime.[187] He also includes what can only be considered two different groupings of postmortem miracles attributed to Vincent's intercession. In the first, Antoninus lists three resuscitations of dead persons. Two of these are tales that are recognizable from the Brittany inquest, that of an abbot's nephew who fell from a tree while gathering nuts and that of a youth who drowned while trying to learn to swim.[188] The third of these

---

185. E.g., Pagano 2000, 353, 356.

186. J. B. Walker 1933, 24.

187. Counting as both a prophecy and a miracle the story in which Vincent, during a sermon, knew prophetically to ask King Fernando to send two knights to fetch a crippled man (out of his range of vision) and then healed the man.

188. That is the abbot's nephew (recounted by Brittany witnesses 22–25) and Johannes Gueho (recounted by Brittany witnesses 41–44).

resuscitations (of a young boy whose birth as well had resulted from a vow to Vincent Ferrer) appears in the Sicilian miracle collection, the sole post-mortem miracle among the ten and the one story from that compilation that does not also feature in Ranzano's *Life*. Immediately following these three brief descriptions, Antoninus appends a lengthy list of the types of miracles worked by the saint's intercession.[189] At the end of his enumeration, the following mysterious line appears, bringing the paragraph to a close: "All of which aforesaid [miracles] have been extracted from the letter of his canonization [*epistola canonizationis eius*]."[190]

What was this letter of canonization?[191] It is clearly not the canonization bull issued by Pius II on October 1, 1458. That bull does not name any specific miracles and certainly not the three resuscitations just described by Antoninus, assuming his "aforesaid" was meant to include the entire paragraph listing the three miracles. But even if Antoninus drew from the letter only the typology of Vincent's miracles immediately preceding his reference, he still could not be referring to Pius's bull. There, too, one can find a generic list of miracles, but it is not the same as Antoninus's and in fact is rather shorter.[192] Nor can the letter of canonization be equated with a possible draft bull of canonization by Calixtus III dated June 29, 1455, and preserved in the library of the Dominicans in Vienna.[193] There Calixtus spins out the same typology of miracles that will appear in Pius's 1458 bull. Further, the fact that Antoninus speaks of a letter (*epistola*) and not a *bulla* must again point to a separate text, since the term "bull," deriving from the lead seal used by the popes to seal official documents, specifically referred to papal documents so marked.

So what was this text? It is likely that Antoninus was referring to a letter that circulated within the Dominican order itself, a letter probably written not by Calixtus (or Pius) but by some other witness to the canonization or even present at one of the two open consistories in which Vincent's miracles were read prior to his official canonization.[194] The same sort of letter had circulated among houses of the order after the canonizations of the two previously named Dominican saints, Peter Martyr (1253) and Thomas

---

189. Antoninus Florentinus 1484, fol. CCIX v.

190. Ibid.

191. I am indebted, in the discussion that follows, to wisdom shared in private e-mail correspondence by Thomas Wetzstein and Otfried Krafft in July 2007.

192. *Bullarum diplomatum* 1857–72, 5:147.

193. "Immensam dei nostri potentiam in eo," edited in Scheeben 1941, 219–24; see also Krafft 2005, 967–68.

194. Krafft 2005, 965, on the basis of the letter Calixtus sent to Duke Pierre II of Brittany on July 14, 1455, describing four closed and two open consistories. At the first of the two open consistories, an advocate read out the miracles. Pius's bull mentions only two closed and two open consistories; in these latter, the testimony gathered at the inquests was read out. Ibid., 971.

Aquinas (1323), and perhaps could be said to represent some sort of tradition among the Order of Preachers.[195] Since Vincent's bull of canonization did not appear until three years after his canonization and was read before assembled Dominicans only at the chapter general of May 1459, such an early, unofficial letter would have been a welcome way to spread the news of a new saint from the order.[196] Speculating, then, we can guess that the letter included—beyond the news of the canonization—a catalog of prophecies and miracles *in vita* and the three aforementioned postmortem resuscitation miracles, as well as the broader, unspecific list of miracles reported by Antoninus as having been worked at Vincent's invocation.

That at least the three resuscitations above came from some separate list is further supported by what follows in Antoninus's *Chronicle,* namely, a second set of eleven miracles worked after Vincent's death. These tales represent, according to Antoninus, "certain others [that] have been proven and collected [*testificata et recollecta*]."[197] Antoninus is not clear about his source here, but all the tales are immediately recognizable from the Brittany canonization inquest. The narrations are at times quite lengthy and contain names and locations, a feature lacking in the initial list of three postmortem miracles. Oddly, two of the stories in the second set are retellings of the miracles included in the initial three. Now, however, the tales include specific details of names and places missing in the previous brief recitations. Clearly, then, Antoninus is working now from yet another text, either the canonization inquest itself or a list of approved (*testificata*) miracles circulated around the time of Vincent's canonization.

---

195. Krafft, private e-mail of July 23, 2007, and letter of September 10, 2007; see also Krafft 2003, in which he discusses (and edits at 423–35) a letter written by the prior of the Dominican convent of San Eustorgio in Milan after the canonization of Peter Martyr but before the issuance of the bull of canonization, describing the elevation of Peter's relics. Krafft calls such letters "chain letters," meant to be circulated from one Dominican house to another.

196. Krafft 2005, 968. Another fifteenth-century life, that by the Chioggia friar, hints as well that letters publicized Vincent's canonization (presumably in the years between the canonization and the issuance of the bull): WBSA, MS 27, chap. 40, fol. 49v: "Sane venerationis illius inter sanctos *literis publicatis* ad ampliorem sue santitatis [*sic*] comendationem " (emphasis added).

197. Antoninus Florentinus 1484, fol. CCIX v.

CHAPTER 6

# The Afterlife of the Chopped-Up Baby

*The Sixteenth Century and Beyond*

On August 23, 1637, Sebastien de Rosmadec, bishop of Vannes, and an odd assortment of clerics, theologians, and local notables all stood breathlessly around a table in a chapel in the Vannes cathedral as two physicians and two surgeons examined a collection of bones. For starters, there was the saint's lower jawbone, removed from the silver reliquary in which it had long been housed. That jawbone and the meager contents of Vincent Ferrer's tomb in the cathedral—a vertebra and other small bones—were at the time the cathedral's only known authentic relics of the saint. What the assembled crowd awaited with some anxiety was to hear the medical experts' opinion about the rest of the bones: a skull lacking the mandible and numerous other skeletal remains. These bones, together with two coins from the reigns of the Breton dukes Jean V and François I, came from an ancient coffer closed with three locks, which had recently been discovered after two of the canons had mounted a diligent search for Vincent's relics.[1] The box in question had turned up in the cathedral's sacristy at the bottom of an armoire used to store ceremonial robes and staffs. A preliminary investigation several weeks prior by two of the medical men, the physician Jean Petit and the surgeon Claude Gossement, had yielded promising

---

1. The medical experts offered a full list of the contents of the coffer in their *procès-verbal* of August 7, 1637; reproduced in FND, 447–48. A microfilm of the original documents concerning the seventeenth-century authentication of Vincent's relics can be found in ADM, 1 Mi 293 ("Documents relatifs aux reliques de Saint-Vincent Ferrier, conservés au presbytère de la cathédrale de Vannes"), pièces 25–36. The originals are still preserved in the cathedral.

results. In the men's expert hands, the lower jawbone fit perfectly into the skull, with the upper and lower teeth coming into exact alignment. Still, as the bishop later reported, he had been advised to follow the procedure "established by holy Council of Trent for the recognition of newly discovered relics."[2] Hence the ceremonious gathering on August 23.

The next several days proved to be tense ones, however. As the clergy shuffled nervously in the freshly built Chapel of Our Lady and Saint Vincent, the additional physician and surgeon, Gilles Dubuisson and Nicollas Thomazo, expressed doubts about the authenticity of the new relics. Most disturbingly, they opined that when the skull bones were fitted together, the lower jaw did not move freely enough for them to believe that it was from the same body as the rest of the skull—despite the previous pronouncements of Petit and Gossement. The latter in response maintained that the mandible opened just as much as it should under the circumstances, noting that there was a world of difference between a living body and a corpse that had lain dead for a good two centuries or thereabouts and whose parts had been stored separately and in different places. Furthermore, Petit and Gossement argued, in a living body, "the movement of the two jaws is facilitated by a mobile, slippery, cartilaginous ligament, which entirely surrounds the mandibular condyles [*les apophises condiloïdes de la mantibule inférieure*]." The objection about the jaw's movement was thus, for a long-dead corpse, a moot point. It was enough, the two insisted, "that the aforesaid mandibular condyles [*apophises*] fit properly in their cavities, as was manifest." A hasty conference among the assembled theologians, dignitaries, and ecclesiastics resulted in a decision to seek the opinion of still more surgeons. A time was set some five days later. In the meantime, the clerics were to return to their respective posts and solicit from all their assistants fervent prayers for the recognition of these relics.[3]

Returning on the twenty-eighth, now in the presence of an additional five surgeons, the assembled clergy chanted the "Veni Creator Spiritus" to invoke the aid of the Holy Spirit, the same hymn sung at the opening of the canonization inquest for Vincent Ferrer so many years before. Their prayers were answered. The skeptical Dubuisson now said that, on further contemplation about the lower jaw, he attributed the difficulty in its movement to the fact that the skull had been stored in a more humid location than had the mandible, resulting in a restriction of the movement available to the jaw. He "avowed and confessed" that the said jaw was from the same head, but nevertheless, to make a perfect judgment about the relics, it would be necessary to see the vertebra from Vincent's tomb, to see if it fit with the

---

2. FND, 440–441 (bishop's report of September 10, 1637), quotation from 441.
3. FND, 442.

other vertebrae found in the coffer with three locks. The other medical experts agreed, and with the concurrence of the theologians and clergy, the next day was set for the examination of the vertebrae. The saint's tomb was opened, and the clerics drew out a small wooden box, which contained the precious vertebra wrapped in red taffeta, along with several small bones. The crowd assembled the following afternoon, its numbers swollen by the king of France's lieutenant and procurer and a number of nobles from the city. Once again, the clerics chanted the "Veni Creator." The bones again were laid on a table for examination by the physicians and surgeons, who declared that the vertebrae from the newly discovered box were without doubt from the same body as the vertebra from Vincent's tomb and thus that all the bones from the box were "true and certain relics of Saint Vincent Ferrer." Then it was the turn of the canons, religious, and theologians to affirm as well that the bones found in the three-keyed box were true relics of the saint that should be exposed for public veneration. With that, the bishop issued a formal declaration of the relics' authenticity, referring to the text on which Vincent himself had first preached in Vannes: *Colligite quae superaverunt fragmenta ne pereant* (Gather up the fragments that remain, lest they be lost. John 6:12, Douay-Rheims). With the grace of God, the bishop had indeed gathered up the precious fragments of Vincent's body. The entire crowd chanted the "Te Deum" in thanksgiving.[4] And on September 5 and 6, the newly found coffer was carried in procession throughout the city of Vannes.[5]

Thus were authenticated the long-lost relics of Vincent Ferrer. The divided remains of the saint who had restored the chopped-up baby were now themselves, after a long separation, reunited. The bishop explained only that the precious relics had been hidden "both to avoid the furor of heretical soldiers and to forbid that they should be stolen by the Spaniards who desire them."[6] But other sources relate a thrilling tale of intrigue and subterfuge behind the relics' loss. Namely, during the dark days of the French Wars of Religion, the Spanish monarch Felipe II had sent a number of troops to succor the Catholic League in Brittany. By 1592, Felipe—himself bent on amassing a collection of the relics of all of Spain's saints—was claiming what he saw as his just reward: the relics of Vincent Ferrer. In January 1592, using the duke de Mercoeur, the governor of Brittany, as his intermediary, the Spanish king respectfully made his request to the cathedral chapter in Vannes. In July, Felipe himself wrote to the canons, a little disingenuously perhaps, thanking them for their willingness to part with the sacred corpse.

---

4. FND, 443–45; the bishop's pronouncement of the long-lost relics' authenticity appears in FHSVF, 2:285–87.

5. FHSVF, 2:285, evidently drawing on the account in Le Mené 1888–89, 2:79.

6. The bishop's words are from his own report: FND, 439. Fages here reproduces only part of the bishop's text. Other parts of the report are in FHSVF, 2:285–86; AASS, Aprilis, 1:526–29.

The chapter wisely pleaded an inability to act in the absence of their bishop (conveniently away in Paris) and cited fifteenth-century papal bulls granting the relics to the cathedral in perpetuity. The Spanish were not to be dissuaded, however, and evidently began to plot to steal Vincent's relics. Fortunately, a certain Bourgerol, a citizen of Vannes living in Valencia, learned of the plot and alerted the chapter. The senior canon was instructed to hide the relics, and he kept the secret with him till his deathbed. Only then did he divulge the hiding place, after which the relics were transferred to the cathedral sacristy, where they remained in obscurity until their rediscovery in 1637.[7]

In many ways, this entire episode illustrates the major features of the backdrop against which the early modern treatment of Vincent Ferrer was painted: the division of Christendom between Protestant and Catholic (represented here by the Council of Trent and the Wars of Religion), the looming presence of the modern state (the French king's lieutenant, King Felipe II of Spain), the quest for authentication of religious phenomena (the physicians and surgeons), and the continuing pull of the miraculous (the prayers for God's intercession). But the saint whose body would be so carefully restored in Vannes in 1637 was fragmented again in texts, as sixteenth- and seventeenth-century authors composed fresh—and remarkably various—lives of Vincent Ferrer in response to the changed world around them. For some, what mattered was the saint's continuing thaumaturgic powers, a not-so-subtle answer to Protestant assertions of the cessation of miracles. Others, taking a cue from post-Tridentine concerns, took pains to present an accurate and authentic biography of the saint, steeped in archival sources and unafraid to confront head-on potential blemishes on Vincent's record. And still others depicted Vincent primarily as a local saint, whose sacred presence and patronage sanctified regional identities and liberties under increasing threat by the growing early modern state.

Lives of Vincent composed in the sixteenth and seventeenth centuries show hagiographers implicitly addressing Protestant criticisms about the cult of the saints and reacting to the growth of monarchical power. Perhaps thanks to its appearance in slightly abridged form in Laurentius Surius's monumental compilation of saints' lives, Pietro Ranzano's official *vita* provided one blueprint for the overall portrayal of Vincent Ferrer. But post-Tridentine hagiographers, aware of critiques like those of Erasmus ridiculing medieval saints' lives, moved beyond Ranzano's portrait, demonstrating a special concern for accuracy by citing sources, weighing evidence, and in

---

7. The source of this tale appears to be the account of an eyewitness, Bartholomaeus Vimont, S.J., forwarded to the Bollandists as they were compiling the *Acta Sanctorum:* AASS, Aprilis, 1:526. The story is related and elaborated in Le Mené 1888–89, 2:35–36, 38, 41–42; and FHSVF, 2:280–82 (reproducing the relevant letters).

places disputing with earlier authors. The outstanding example in Vincent's case was the Valencian author Vicente Justiniano Antist, whose work was rooted in local archives and the canonization inquests, as well as in the biographies of previous authors. As part of that commitment to historical accuracy, Antist and a number of other post-Tridentine authors tended to address directly the troublesome issue of Vincent's role during the Great Schism, in marked contrast to many late fifteenth-century compilers of saints' lives, who simply chose to ignore the problem. Hagiographers in the late sixteenth and seventeenth centuries also took delight in cataloging Vincent's miracles, particularly recent manifestations of the saint's intercession that sanctified the local and tied the present to a sacred past. The arrival of a relic of the saint in his native Valencia provided the occasion for a flowering of miracles, all carefully noted in Francisco Diago's *History of the Life, Miracles, Death, and Disciples of... Vincent Ferrer,* published in Barcelona in 1600. Hagiography could also offer a boost to a sagging local cult, as appears to have been the case in Vannes in the early seventeenth century, when a new tapestry and two new French lives of Vincent helped provide the stimulus for a revival of his cult at the site of his tomb, which resulted in the spectacular discovery of his missing relics. And whatever their commitment to historical accuracy and the publicizing of contemporary local miracles, sixteenth- and seventeenth-century authors—in a world plagued by a schism more bitter and intractable than that of Vincent's age—still could not resist the tale of saint and the chopped-up baby.

## Protestant Reform and the Cult of the Saints

Martin Luther and the other early Protestant reformers sought to base their religion on the principles of *sola fides* and *sola scriptura* as well as on the example of the primitive church. The question of the cult of the saints was thus not one of their chief concerns, and they frequently dismissed arguments about the veneration of saints as *adiaphora* (matters indifferent), "superfluous concerns" (Martin Luther), or "childish matter[s]" (Huldrich Zwingli).[8] Still, leaders of the Reformation denounced the cult of the saints on a number of grounds, while by and large admitting (as Luther did in a series of sermons preached in 1522) that images of saints were allowable, "although it would be better if we did not have them at all."[9] Saints, after all, were associated with religious orders discredited by Protestants and with the fruitless cultivation of good works as a substitute for true righteousness. For others,

---

8. Both quoted in Heming 2003, 1. See also (on Erasmus) Eire 1989, 36–45.

9. Quoted in Heming 2003, 7. A good, brief overview can be found in Soergel 1996. Still useful, although criticized for its overreliance simply on canonized saints, is Burke 1984.

the cult of the saints, strongly promoted by the mendicant orders, was rife with deplorable financial abuses. As had Erasmus, many reform-minded preachers saw the veneration of saints as shot through with superstitious pagan practices, while yet others lamented the link between popular festivals associated with saints' feast days and the potential for gluttony, drunkenness, and disorder.[10] Humanists like Erasmus also ridiculed the over-the-top wonders reported in many medieval saints' lives and lambasted their authors for a lack of attention to chronological precision.[11] In turn, some Catholic authors—such as George Witzel, who had briefly followed Luther in the 1520s—found it more palatable to focus on the saints as exemplary Christians and not as sources of supernatural miracles.[12] By century's end the fault line was clear: as Catholic apologist Robert Bellarmine observed in 1601, "There is nothing that they [the Protestants] shudder at and abhor more than the invocation of saints, the cult of relics and the veneration of images. For they consider that these things constitute manifest impiety and idolatry."[13]

By the late sixteenth century, it had also become a Protestant commonplace to insist that the age of miracles was over. The doctrine of the cessation of miracles grew out of hints in the writings of the major reformers. Luther, for example, had distinguished between miracles of the soul (that is, the transformation wrought by faith) and miracles of the body. This second, and lesser, type of miracle, according to Luther, had been necessary only to establish the new church and was no longer needed by a religion firmly grounded in scripture. Calvin, too, had insisted that such bodily miracles had been an affair of only a short time, such as was required to establish the Gospel, and that physical miracles were no longer to be expected.[14] In Protestant rhetoric, miracles were like baby food for the nascent church, whereas an adult, mature church such as theirs required only God's word for nourishment. The doctrine of the cessation of miracles reached a wide and often receptive audience. Evidence from Germany and the duchy of Bavaria suggests that the reformers were successful in discouraging the hope of modern-day miracles, with a dramatic decline in the reporting of miracles in the half century following 1520.[15] Even in the Iberian Peninsula, supposedly little touched by the evangelical movement, a Valencian author in the 1590s could lament the existence of "those who in these times reject miracles, nor accept anything

---

10. Heming 2003, chaps. 2 and 3.

11. See, especially, Frazier 2005; D. Collins 2008; and Heming 2003.

12. D. Collins 2008, 131–32.

13. Quoted in Ditchfield 1993, 283. On the cult of the saints as idolatry, particularly in Calvinist lands, see Eire 1989.

14. Cited in D. P. Walker 1988, 111–12. More recent scholarship has noted that Protestant dismissal of miracles, though widespread, was not as unanimous as Walker implies: see Walsham 2005; Shaw 2006, esp. chaps. 1–2.

15. Soergel 1996.

no matter how marvelous as a miracle, basing themselves on St. Paul saying that miracles are allowed by God for the conversion of unbelievers, and since we are all believers now there are no miracles."[16]

One reason that many Protestants in the late sixteenth and early seventeenth centuries were so adamant about the cessation of miracles was that Catholic missionaries and apologists used miracles to advertise the truth of their own religion, arguing that miracles constituted a better proof than scripture, which could be twisted or misinterpreted.[17] Miracle tales did not simply trumpet, in Alexandra Walsham's phrase, "Catholicism's superior thaumaturgic capabilities" but also could offer supernatural support to such disputed doctrines as purgatory and transubstantiation.[18] In the decades around 1600, the debate about miracles became particularly intense as Catholic apologists like Bellarmine and Justus Lipsius (a former Protestant) adduced contemporary miracles and theatrical public exorcisms as proofs of the Catholic faith and the cult of the saints.[19] Miracles and miracle tales flourished in border zones like the Spanish Netherlands, where Catholics and Protestants rubbed shoulders and frequently exchanged fire.[20] In turn, Protestants answered Catholic miracles with waves of pamphlets asserting that what papists alleged to be miracles were little more than impostures, fakes, and the "lying wonders" of Antichrist.

Catholic responses to the Protestant attack on the cult of the saints took their cue from the decrees of the twenty-fifth (final) session of the Council of Trent, just after an affirmation of the doctrine of purgatory. There the fathers of the council reiterated that it was "good and useful" to invoke the saints, whose prayers were helpful in "obtaining benefits from God, through His Son" (that is, miracles). The council also endorsed the veneration of relics and images, stipulating that in honoring images, the faithful were in fact adoring Christ and the saints whose likenesses were depicted in them. The fathers, however, also took some action against abuses in the veneration of saints. The council enjoined bishops to be watchful that "superstition," "filthy lucre," and "lasciviousness" be removed completely from the invocation of saints, veneration of relics, and sacred use of images. Bishops additionally were to keep a close guard over the growth of new cults and were required to approve any new images, relics, or miracles.[21] As in so many other

---

16. Jayme Prades, quoted in Kamen 1993, 89 (Kamen's translation).

17. Walsham 2005, 278, 280–81; D. P. Walker 1988, 112–13.

18. Walsham 2005, 278, 280 (quotation).

19. Ibid., 280–82; D. P. Walker 1988, 112–13, 119. See also, for an example in which the state played a guiding hand, Soergel 1993, 91–98.

20. See Harline 2003, esp. 5–7.

21. Decrees of the Council of Trent 1995. For evidence of the degree to which bishops took seriously the injunction to examine new miracle cases, see de Viguerie 1983, based on several declarations and inquests into miracles in France.

areas, Trent affirmed traditional Catholic beliefs and practices regarding the saints while attempting to curb abuses that had crept into the system.

As a number of scholars have noted, while the Council of Trent made few substantive changes to the traditional cult of the saints, it did tighten up the procedures for the creation of new saints and, through its actions, spurred a flurry of hagiographical writing, often composed with one ear cocked for the sound of Protestant derision.[22] In 1568, the liturgy was standardized throughout the Catholic Church with the publication of the revised Roman Breviary, which included new versions of the offices recited on the feast days of universally venerated saints. The year 1588 saw the creation of the Sacred Congregation of Rites and Ceremonies, most famously charged with the canonization of new saints but also with approving offices for local saints not venerated throughout all Catholic lands. A nineteenth-century scholar working in the Vatican Library found nearly two dozen Italian dioceses that had requested the congregation's approval for local saints' cults in the 1570s and '80s alone.[23] In a number of cases, authors were forced to rewrite older offices to meet the congregation's new standards of historical accuracy for saints' lives. Lessons on the saints in the new breviary showed careful attention to chronology, the current locations of relics, and citing precise sources for the readings.[24] As Simon Ditchfield has argued, modern historical method owes much to the post-Tridentine push for more accurate hagiographical materials.[25]

*Vitae* of Vincent Ferrer composed after the Council of Trent share in the general trends enumerated above. Although some fifteenth-century authors of lives of Vincent, as in the 1458 bull of canonization, had shown little interest in detailing the holy man's miracles, post-Tridentine authors delighted in laying out tales of Vincent's intercession, particularly those miracles that had happened recently and locally. Further, hagiographers in the late sixteenth and seventeenth centuries also took pains to present an accurate and well-documented picture to their readers.[26] Part of that attention to accuracy meant that it was difficult to ignore, as some fifteenth-century authors had, Vincent's long association with Benedict XIII, now widely reproved as an antipope. For some authors, scholarly rigor entailed taking an honest look at some other potential blemishes on Vincent's record, such as the band of flagellants who followed him from town to town (and for whom Jean Gerson

---

22. Most notably Ditchfield 1995, 1993; Soergel 1993, 1996; and Burke 1984.

23. Ditchfield 1995, 60.

24. On the transformations of the cult of the saints, liturgy, and hagiography, see especially Ditchfield 1995, esp. 36–38, on the interest in accuracy in the new breviary; and, for an excellent case study centered on Naples, Sallmann 1994.

25. Most forcefully in Ditchfield 1993, 284, 292–93.

26. See Smoller 2011a.

had rebuked him) or his assertions about the imminent reign of Antichrist. Lives of Vincent Ferrer from this period also show an interest in connecting the saint to the local, a concern that often centered on the site of Vincent's relics and continued to simmer long after his death and burial in the Vannes cathedral.

## Laurentius Surius: Saints as Miracle Workers

One of the most important Catholic hagiographers of the sixteenth century was the Carthusian Laurentius Surius (Lorenz Sauer, 1522–78).[27] Surius had come to the University of Cologne a young evangelical but under the guidance of Peter Canisius became a Catholic and joined the Carthusian order in 1542. In the years 1571–75, he produced his monumental *The Authenticated Stories of the Saints,* a collection of 699 saints' lives published in six volumes. Scholars have uniformly remarked on two aspects of Surius's collection: first, his "enormous enthusiasm" (in Philip Soergel's words) for recounting miracle tales and second, a commitment to precision and accuracy that makes him a forerunner of the Bollandists' project. Miracles certainly were an obsession for Surius. He adduces a dazzling array of miracle tales in his *Authenticated Stories,* some 6,538 in total, or nearly 100 miracles for every saint in the collection.[28] And prior to turning his hand to hagiography, Surius had composed a chronicle that recounted a number of contemporary miracles.[29]

But while Surius did adopt a scholarly stance in collecting the saints' lives that make up his *Authenticated Stories,* modern historians have noted that he sometimes sacrificed his critical principles in favor of his polemical goals. For the core of his collection, Surius relied on the hagiographical work of the Venetian humanist Aloisius Lippomanus, supplementing Lippomanus's texts with others drawn from humanist manuscripts and printed books. Yet, as David Collins has observed, he sometimes altered older texts without explanation, particularly to restore miracle tales that had been excised in earlier humanist revisions of a saint's *vita* or simply to insert new miracles. At other times, he slavishly followed texts in obvious need of correction.[30] Still, thanks to Surius's claims of authenticity, his collection offered testimony of the many miracles worked in the past by Catholic saints and accordingly

---

27. On Surius and his hagiographical enterprise, see Soergel 1993, 95–98; 1996; Ditchfield 1995, 124–26; D. Collins 2008, 133–34.

28. Soergel 1993, 97; D. Collins 2008, 134. The original edition of the *Authenticated Stories* is Surius 1570–75; I have consulted Surius 1875–80.

29. Soergel 1993, 95–96.

30. D. Collins 2008, 134.

found large numbers of largely clerical readers, who mined his collection for material for their sermons.

For the life of Vincent Ferrer, Surius closely based his own text on Pietro Ranzano's official *vita,* as a heading at the start of the biography makes clear, but he made some noteworthy changes to his model.[31] To begin, Surius offered a fairly literal transcription of Ranzano's books 1 and 2, the sections detailing Vincent's youth and adult career, with only a few brief omissions. His editorial hand was heavier when he turned to the saint's miraculous intercession. Rather than multiply Vincent's miracles as he did in other *vitae,* Surius actually omitted some of the ones that had been detailed by Ranzano. At the same time, he reworded and shortened the original narrations. Still, Surius took pains to give the impression that the miracle tales he offered formed only the tip of a very large iceberg. Thus, at the start of his book on Vincent's miracles, Surius penned a brief address to the reader. First, he noted that Ranzano, "in order to avoid excessive prolixity," had described only the fewest of the innumerable miracles worked by Vincent's merits. He also lamented that Ranzano "frequently used many words where a few would have sufficed." Consequently, Surius told the reader, he had attempted to remove unnecessary words without losing any of the substance of the narrations, at the same time omitting a few miracles for the sake of brevity.[32] One has the impression that a selective sampling follows. Surius ended the life with themes taken from Ranzano's book 4, on Vincent's final years in Brittany, death, burial, and postmortem miracles. Again, a note by the author alerts readers that Surius has truncated his material to a certain extent and has omitted some miracle tales from Ranzano's narration.[33]

At first glance, Surius's treatment of Vincent Ferrer is puzzling. His major deviations from his model involve a shortening of Ranzano's catalog of miracles, whereas, as modern scholars have all remarked, Surius was most concerned to portray saints as miracle workers and frequently added new stories of the saint's intercession to the texts from which he worked. Yet on closer observation, the only parts of Ranzano's *vita* on which Surius lavished any editorial care were the sections dealing with Vincent's miracles. The same prolix style that bothered Surius in Ranzano's miracle tales could be found throughout the *Life of Vincent.* Yet, as noted above, Surius transcribed Ranzano's first two books almost word for word. Only when he came to the section on miracles did he take the trouble and time to rephrase, tighten, "improve," and in a few instances rearrange Ranzano's presentations. It is

---

31. Surius 1875–80, 4:172–217. I am here assuming that he was working from a manuscript exemplar similar to the Utrecht manuscript edited by the Bollandists and the several other manuscripts I have examined.

32. Surius 1875–80, 4:202.

33. "Rursus lectori benevolo," ibid., 4:212.

hard to avoid the impression that this was the part of the *vita* about which Surius cared the most.

Surius's only other substantive change from Ranzano's text was the omission of several passages from books 1 and 2. Most notably, he skipped over a tale beloved by many of Vincent's other biographers, dating from the saint's days in Valencia. As Ranzano had told it, an elderly fellow Dominican, lascivious in temperament and deeds, grew tired of Vincent's constant rebukes and exhortations to a better life. To get back at the young upstart, the old friar brought a prostitute to his own cell one evening, enjoying a night full of illicit delights, and then in the morning gave her much less than the usual fee for such services. The woman, new to town, got a good look at the friar who had stiffed her and asked his name. "I am called," the wily old friar said, "Brother Vincent Ferrer, and I beg you to be careful not to tell anyone what we have done." The woman, of course, immediately told her pimp and many other people about the Brother Vincent who was happy to enjoy a night's worth of favors but unwilling to pay the price for it. Word spread throughout the city and came at last to the ears of Boniface, Vincent's brother, who was then serving as a municipal official. Boniface ordered a procession to be made with the city's clergy and religious and arranged that the prostitute should stand with the nobles and city fathers to watch the procession. When the real Vincent Ferrer passed by, he asked her if this was the friar who had so ill used her. No, she replied. She knew this one from having heard him preach several times, but the Brother Vincent she sought was an old man. At last the scheming older friar appeared, and the prostitute eagerly pointed him out. When the entire procession was finished, Boniface ordered the old friar to be brought before him, where he confessed his deception and libel and at last begged pardon of the real Vincent, which the latter graciously granted.[34]

It is easy to see the appeal of this tale, which demonstrates Vincent's patience in adversity as well as his merciful forgiveness of a sinner who had begged his pardon. The story appears at the very end of Ranzano's first book, and it is certainly possible that it simply did not appear in the manuscript from which Surius took the *vita*. But it seems more plausible that Surius chose to drop the tale from his own life of Vincent. After all, even though the events portrayed *Vincent* in a good light, such was not the case for the older Dominican friar, who was obviously well enough acquainted with prostitutes that he knew what a fair price for services rendered would be. He had evidently carried on his lascivious lifestyle for quite a number of years, and he had absolutely no hesitation about lying in order to injure a brother who tried to correct his behavior. Although Surius wrote from the

---

34. RVV (I.3.18), 1:489–90 (quotation, 490).

staunchly Catholic city of Cologne, Protestants had made some inroads there in the decades after 1550, particularly in the 1570s, the decade in which Surius was composing his *Authenticated Stories.*[35] It is not implausible that Surius, a convert back to the Catholic fold, preferred to leave out any story that might add fuel to Protestant anticlerical fires and diminish his work's polemical value for the Catholic cause.

Surius's collection of saints' lives was an instant hit; the duke of Bavaria ordered a vernacular translation in 1574 (before Surius had even completed all six volumes) and a second Latin edition was published in 1576 to 1581. One appeal was certainly Surius's care in citing evidence for his *Authenticated Stories* of saints' miraculous powers, and Jean van Bolland nodded to Surius as one of his sources in the first volume of the *Acta Sanctorum.* As Philip Soergel has observed, however, even in its German version, Surius's lengthy collection was probably beyond the means of most lay readers. But as fodder for many a Catholic sermon and source for later hagiographers, the *Authenticated Stories* spread widely the view of the Catholic Church as a space in which God was constantly active thanks to the intercession of saints like Vincent.[36]

## Vicente Justiniano Antist: Critical Hagiography

Whereas Laurentius Surius's biography of Vincent Ferrer most notably illustrates the post-Tridentine Catholic stress on miracles, the *Life and History of the Apostolic Preacher Vincent Ferrer, Valencian, of the Order of Saint Dominic* by Vicente Justiniano Antist fulfills the Catholic push toward more accurately written and completely documented hagiography.[37] Antist was born in 1543 into a noble Valencian family and entered the Dominican order there in 1559. A master of theology with extensive connections, he was also the author of a number of philosophical, historical, and theological works.[38] His 477-page *Life and History,* published in Castilian in 1575, demonstrates amply Antist's deep commitment to historical authenticity as well as his devotion to the local saint, whose biography he hoped would

35. Scribner 1996.

36. Soergel 1993, 97–98. Perhaps Surius deserves some of the credit for a thriving cult of Vincent Ferrer in German-speaking lands from the seventeenth century on, as detailed in G. Schreiber 1936, 289–99.

37. Antist 1956. The phrase "critical hagiography" is David Collins's, used to describe one of two directions taken by hagiography post 1520 (the other being "polemical hagiography"). D. Collins 2008, 133.

38. "Introducción," in Garganta and Forcada 1956, 91–93; see also Robles 1979; and, on Antist's biography of his former master Luis Bertrán, Vose 2011.

spur his fellow citizens to an imitation of Vincent's virtues.[39] (It is possible that Antist also hoped to revive devotion after a temporary suppression of the cult of Vincent in Valencia in 1565.)[40] Not content simply with reading previous *vitae* of the saint, Antist also sought out original sources—letters and other archival material in Valencia, as well as the canonization inquests—and weighed his sources for reliability with measured care. In fact, it is partly to Antist's diligence that we owe the survival of the Naples and Toulouse inquests into Vincent's sanctity. After a fruitless search in Rome for the manuscripts that, according to the bull of canonization, were deposited in the church of Santa Maria sopra Minerva, Valencian Dominicans located a copy in Palermo, a version of which Antist transcribed for his own use.[41]

Antist's commitment to critical, scholarly hagiography is evident throughout his biography of Vincent Ferrer. To each chapter heading in his work, Antist appends a footnote listing the sources on which he has relied for the material in that chapter. For example, Antist tells his readers that all the information in his first chapter, on Vincent's birth, childhood, and youth, was taken "from Ranzano, and from Bishop Robert [Roberto Caracciolo], and from Flamini; some, indeed, from Saint Antoninus, and from an ancient Valencian breviary, and from Ludovico Vivaldo in the book *On the Truth of Contrition*; and finally from Valencian records."[42] These footnotes are in Latin, as opposed to the Castilian of the text, perhaps as a nod to Latinate insiders or perhaps simply as a way to look more scholarly. Not simply does Antist provide many such footnotes (and references within his text), but he also devotes the entire final chapter of his *Life and History* to a discussion

---

39. Antist 1956, "Prologo y argumento de la obra al cristiano lector," 94–97. Antist explains his decision to write in Castilian and not Catalan in his prologue to part 2, 236–37.

40. FHSVF, 2:384. In 1565 the bishop of Valencia, Martin de Ayala, reformed the diocese's calendar, suppressing the obligation to celebrate the feast of Vincent Ferrer. The *jurados* of Valencia, however, petitioned Pope Pius V, who responded on May 24, 1567 ("Gloriosus in sanctis suis"), requiring that Vincent's feast be celebrated as a solemn feast in the city, diocese, and province and that the feast be restored to the calendar. In 1578, Antist's master Luis Bertrán (1526–81) preached a sermon in the house where Vincent was born (a structure that later became a church dedicated to the saint) in which he both lamented Valencia's lack of Vincentian relics and chided the city's inhabitants for their lack of gratitude to the saint. Ortuño Soriano 2005, 130, 134–35; Bertrán 1690, 201–2.

41. Antist 1956, 268; he provides much the same information in *Proceso,* fol. 2r. See also chapter 2, note 44, and accompanying text. For his life of Vincent, Antist worked from the now-lost copy of the Palermo manuscript ordered by Luis Bertrán. Ever the careful scholar, Antist in his own subsequent copy of the processes noted in the margins the folio numbers from the manuscript he had used and cited in the *vita*.

42. Antist 1956, pt. 1, chap. 1, p. 98n1. Aside from Pietro Ranzano and Giovanni Antonio Flamini (whose work relied heavily on Ranzano's), Antist thus has read Antoninus of Florence, a sermon by the Franciscan Roberto Caracciolo (Robertus Liciensis), the lessons in an older breviary in Valencia, and Giovanni Ludovico Vivaldi's *Aureum opus de veritate contritionis in quo mirifica documenta eterne salutis aperiuntur* (published several times, e.g., Paris: Jean Petit, 1530).

of his sources, thanking local archivists in a manner quite familiar to those who browse modern-day historians' prefaces and listing the major authors on whom he has relied. Here he also offers some comments about the value of these sources—for example, pointing out that Archbishop Antoninus of Florence was in a good position to be well informed about Vincent's life because of his familiarity with members of the papal curia who had seen Vincent preach but warning that there were some scribal errors in the life of Vincent in the archbishop's *Chronicle*.[43] Antist also notes that in working from papal bulls, the canonization process, and local archives unavailable to previous hagiographers, he had found it necessary at times to correct statements in earlier authors' works. For example, although many had said that Vincent's brother Boniface became general of the Carthusian order in his fourth year as a monk, Antist had direct proof from Boniface's own convent of Porta Coeli that the election happened in his sixth year as a Carthusian.[44] In other cases, foreign authors would say that a certain miracle had happened in one town in Spain, whereas Antist, always relying on his sources, places it in another. ("The reader can well believe," Antist reassures, "that I am not moving in the air.")[45] And with that sort of nitty-gritty detail, Antist brings his work to a rather abrupt end.

Antist's careful attention to precision appears throughout the *Life and History,* at times adding clarification and specificity to episodes that remain vague in earlier lives and at other moments rather tediously reinforcing the point that Antist's is a work of scholarly caliber and utmost reliability. In recounting some of the temptations that the young Vincent had overcome, for example, Antist is able to supply a name (Inés Hernández) and thus increased credibility to the tale of a previously anonymous Valencian woman who, smitten with love for the young preacher, feigned a mortal illness in order to lure him to her bedroom, ostensibly to hear her confession but really to attempt to seduce him.[46] At the same time, Antist follows this compelling and dramatic narration with a pedantic refutation of the contention that the story actually related to an older Dominican named Joan de Salerno, stacking up against a single writer's attribution the names of five authors who had told this story about Vincent Ferrer and carefully including the honorific titles of three of them ("*Bishop* Ranzano, *Bishop* Roberto de Licio, and *Master Friar* Joan López of Salamanca").[47]

---

43. Antist 1956, pt. 2, chap. 40, pp. 331–32. (The errors include misnamings of towns, such as Nitensi for Vicensi [Vic] and Tarraconensi for Dertosensi [Dertosa].)

44. Ibid., pt. 2, chap. 40, p. 333.

45. Ibid.

46. Ibid., pt. 1, chap. 4, p. 109 (the whole tale runs from 109 through 111); cf. RVV, I.3.16, 1: 488–89.

47. Antist 1956, pt. 1, chap. 4, p. 111 (emphasis added). According to Antist, Juan López de Salamanca wrote a life of Vincent for Leonor de Pimentel, countess of Plasencia, but there remains no trace of such a work today. See López de Salamanca 2004, 52–53.

Other examples of Antist's critical bent can be found in his obsessive references to the canonization inquests, his almost tedious citing of all the authors on a given topic, and his careful attention to details of language and usage in his sources. In discussing Vincent's time in Toulouse and Brittany, for example, Antist relies almost exclusively on the testimony in the canonization inquests, cited in his footnotes by specific folio numbers.[48] When he writes of Vincent's daily routine (what Latin authors often call his *ordo vivendi*), Antist makes the point that this information is particularly reliable because so many creditable authors had previously written on the topic. "[A]lthough everything that has been said up to this point is very authentic and researched," he gushes, "that which is said in this chapter is that much more so, because such learned and creditable men have attested to it that there could not be anything for a sane person to doubt from it."[49] After warning that he therefore will have to repeat himself several times in the chapter, Antist proceeds to present Vincent's customs as described first by Pius II in the bull of canonization and then by Antoninus of Florence, Juan Luis Vivaldo (Giovanni Lodovico Vivaldi), and Flamini, citing along the way Pietro Ranzano and Roberto Caracciolo.[50] Antist also frequently includes transcriptions of major source documents, such as a letter Vincent wrote to King Fernando of Aragon after the monarch had asked him to explain the meaning of a miraculous apparition of a cross in the heavens in the city of Guadalajara. In this case Antist actually expresses some hesitation about the source, cautioning the reader that "in the letters I have seen in the Saint's own hand, he calls himself 'Sinner' [*Peccator*] and not 'Preacher' [*Praedicator*]," whereas this letter was signed "F. Vincentius Ferrer Praedicator."[51] In similar fashion throughout the *Life,* Antist conveys such an air of (slightly pedantic) scholarly thoroughness.

Antist also takes pains to present a biography that is chronologically accurate in every possible respect.[52] He departs, accordingly, from the thematic approach taken in Ranzano's *vita,* presenting the saint's adult career almost exclusively in strict chronological order. Antist also inserts several digressions on the dating of key events in Vincent's biography, most notably on the exact year of Vincent's death, whether in the year 1418 or 1419. Here he offers the type of technical discussion that a modern historian might relegate to a footnote or an appendix, for after stating that Vincent died on the Wednesday before Palm Sunday, April 5, 1418, he begins to

---

48. Toulouse: Antist 1956, pt. 1, chap. 28, p. 207n1. Brittany: ibid., pt. 2, chap. 3, p. 246n1.

49. Ibid., pt. 1, chap. 6, p. 118.

50. Ibid., 118–26; he follows this up with a chapter titled "What is found in the process on the same topic," citing folio numbers and also the sermon of Gabriel Barletta (126).

51. Ibid., pt. 1, chap. 22, pp. 183–85 (quotation, 184–85). He also notes that the letter was not in Madrid when he was there, so he had to content himself with a transcription (*traslado*).

52. Simon Ditchfield sees a similar trend in the revision of saints' lessons in the new Roman Breviary of 1568. Ditchfield 1995, 37–38.

question that date. The canonization inquests, for example, several times mention that Vincent died in the week in which is recited *Iudica me,* the week before Holy Week. But, says Antist, the *computus* (or art of reckoning Easter dates) shows that in 1418, Easter fell on March 27, whereas the saint is said to have died on April 5, which would have fallen after Easter in 1418. Furthermore, according to the canonization inquests and Antoninus of Florence, Vincent died on a Wednesday. But in 1418, April 5 fell on a Tuesday. Therefore, Antist says, Vincent must have died in 1419, when April 5 fell on the Wednesday of the week before Easter Week. For those not yet entirely convinced, Antist continues in this vein for another page and a half before concluding that those authors who put Vincent's death in 1418 were simply wrong.[53]

Antist is particularly attentive to accuracy in his treatment of Vincent's miracles. He recounts tales of Vincent's intercession throughout his biography but also devotes the bulk of part 2 of the *Life* (chapters 7–32) specifically to the saint's miracles, arranged here by category, such as resuscitations of the dead, rescues from grave danger, restoring sight to the blind, and helping pregnant women. Antist appears to have taken special pains to present as authenticated the stories of Vincent's miracles. The bulk of the miracles related in part 2, for example, come directly from the canonization inquests and not from later biographers, and here Antist is careful to note dates, locations, and the number and social status of witnesses to each miracle. For example, when he relates the tale of the resuscitation of the blaspheming Breton archer Johannes Guerre, Antist remarks that this miracle was attested by six eyewitnesses in the canonization process, including a master of arts and a cleric.[54] The resuscitation of an abbot's nephew, he notes, had four witnesses, of whom three were Cistercian friars.[55] The story of the miraculous multiplication of bread and wine in a monastery where Vincent and his followers had stayed came to Antist by letter from the monks of the monastery itself.[56] Antist even weighs carefully discrepancies in the records, such as Antoninus's assertion that there were twenty-eight resuscitations from the dead in Vincent's canonization process, as opposed to his own finding of sixteen resuscitations in the Brittany inquest. It could be that the saint had performed more resuscitations in Brittany, acknowledges Antist,

---

53. Antist 1956, pt. 2, chap. 5, pp. 257–60.

54. Ibid., pt. 2, chap. 9, pp. 275–76.

55. Ibid., 277–78.

56. The Carthusian house of Scala Dei. Ibid., pt. 1, chap. 27, pp. 202–3. In the same chapter (206), Antist reassures his readers that "when we write that a certain miracle happened in a certain place, if [the reader] should find that another foreign author says that it was in another place, he should think that we depart from his with a purpose, even though we do not always give the reason why in order to avoid prolixity."

"since the copy of the Brittany canonization process that we have is missing some folios."[57]

One wonders whether, as he carefully laid out his evidence for Vincent's miracles, Antist had in the back of his mind those Protestant-inspired critics (even in Valencia) who asserted that the age of miracles was over. He devoted three chapters of the biography, for example, specifically to miracles worked after Vincent's canonization, including an entire chapter on miracles that occurred in Valencia between the years 1511 and 1527. Even though his source for the latter was a book whose author he reproved for his "minimal diligence," Antist found it trustworthy because the miracle tales related there "had been examined by persons who could easily verify their truth."[58] Antist's trust here may be a bit overplayed in comparison with the rigor he exhibits elsewhere, but clearly it was important to him to be able to include stories of miracles that had happened in his own town and within the lives "of our fathers and grandfathers."[59]

Similarly, Antist appears to have hoped that his *Life and History* could answer other Protestant criticisms of Catholic doctrine. He frames several miracle tales, for example, in such a way as to stress the place of Catholic sacraments in the events. Take, for example, the story of Johannes Guerre, archer to the duke of Brittany, mortally wounded in a fight and resuscitated after a vow to Vincent Ferrer. In the version of the tale reported by Antoninus of Florence, one of the most disturbing aspects of Guerre's death was that, without having confessed his sins, he would have to be buried outside sacred ground. In fact, in Antoninus's redaction, after trying unsuccessfully to administer last rites to Guerre, the priest Oliverius leaves to prepare for this unfortunate burial.[60] In Antist's version, the focus is much more upon the salvific benefit of the church's last rites. After Guerre's death, according to Antist, "everyone [was] sorrowful about his damnation (because before he was wounded and also during his convalescence he had been a blasphemer and curser, and it seemed that he had died without any sign of repentance)."[61] One of the women who testified at the canonization inquest had supplied this information about Guerre's bad character.[62] The archer's blasphemies do not appear in Antoninus's version of the tale, but Antist evidently chose to include this detail because it strengthened his point about the necessity of the sacrament of penance. Antist's narration diverges in one other crucial

---

57. Or better, quires (*cuadernos*). Ibid., pt. 2, chap. 9, p. 280.

58. Ibid., pt. 2, chap. 37, pp. 322–23.

59. Ibid., 322.

60. Antoninus Florentinus 1484, Pars III, titulus xxiii, chap. viii, sec. 9, fol. CCXr.

61. Antist 1956, pt. 2, chap. 9, p. 275.

62. Britanny witness Richarda, wife of Johannes Lefichant, *Procès,* witness 51; FPC, 91. See Smoller 1998, 443–54.

respect from Antoninus's telling. In Antist's version, the priest does not leave the scene but is present during the vow to Vincent Ferrer and Guerre's subsequent miraculous resuscitation.[63] Whereas, as I have suggested elsewhere, the divergent stories of witnesses to this tale during the fifteenth-century canonization inquest had pointed to some tension between lay and priestly authority,[64] in Antist's telling, the sacraments—and the Catholic priest who alone can administer them—retain a central role.

Through Antist's carefully authenticated biography of Vincent Ferrer, readers received assurance that the Catholic Church offered its faithful a continuing stream of miracles as well as the spiritual gifts of its sacraments. His *Life and History* did not find the same widespread audience as Laurentius Surius's massive collection of saints' lives, although Antist's choice to compose his work in Castilian did at least assure a broader circulation on the Iberian Peninsula. Still, his work was influential on a number of Spanish authors in the sixteenth and seventeenth centuries and must be seen as part of a move to reinvigorate the cult of Vincent Ferrer in his native Valencia in the decades following the Council of Trent.[65]

## Francisco Diago: A Valencian Saint Chronicled

The Valencian Dominican Francisco Diago (ca. 1560–1615) was an enthusiastic champion of the history of his own religious order and his native region. Sharing Antist's commitment to archival documentation and historical rigor, Diago composed, in addition to his life of Vincent Ferrer, histories of the Dominican order in Aragon (1598), the counts of Barcelona (1603), and the kingdom of Valencia (1613), as well as *vitae* of the thirteenth-century Catalan Dominican Raymond of Peñafort (canonized in 1601), the sixteenth-century Dominican Luis of Granada (1505–88), and the fourteenth-century Avignon cardinal Peter of Luxembourg (beatified in 1527).[66] His skills as a

---

63. Antist 1956, pt. 2, chap. 9, pp. 275–76.

64. See Smoller 1998. The women's tales give them a central role in Guerre's resuscitation and spiritual rebirth; male witnesses (including the priest) discount the women's role and assign the most crucial place to the priest.

65. Antist's influence: Garganta and Forcado 1956, 89–90. The *vida* was translated into Italian and published in Palermo (in 1600) and Naples (in 1613). Robles 1979, 205.

66. Diago 1598 (Order of Preachers in Aragon); *Historia de los victoriosissimos antiguos Condes de Barcelona* (Barcelona: Sebastian de Cormellas, 1603); Diago 1613 (kingdom of Valencia); *Historia del B. cathalan barcelones S. Raymundo de Peñafort* (Barcelona: Sebastian de Cormellas, 1601); *Historia de la vida exemplar, libros, y muerte, del insigne padre maestro F. Luys de Granada de buena memoria de la Orden de los predicadores* (Barcelona: Sebastian de Cormellas, 1605); *Historia del bienauenturado cardenal San Pedro de Lucemburgo* (Barcelona: Sebastian de Cormellas, 1605). A biography of Vincent Ferrer appears in Diago 1598, bk. 2, chaps. 50–72, fol. 165r–219r. For a discussion of the sixteenth-century Dominican order's relative lack of interest in missionary activity, as highlighted in Diago's *Historia de la provincia de Aragon,* see Vose 2011.

historian also won Diago royal recognition when Felipe III (r. 1598–1621) named him official chronicler (*cronista general*) of the kingdom of Aragon.[67] Diago's 1600 *History of the Life, Miracles, Death, and Disciples of the Blessed Valencian Apostolic Preacher Saint Vincent Ferrer* shows the Dominican author striving to outdo previous biographers, most notably Antist, in historical and chronological accuracy. More strikingly, however, Diago's work, dedicated to the *señores jurados de Valencia* (the city council of Valencia), presents Vincent as a local, Valencian saint, using fresh archival research to highlight not simply the holy preacher's ties to his native city but also a thriving cult and intercessory presence stretching from Vincent's childhood to the present.

In many ways Diago's attention to archival sources and chronological accuracy makes his *History* of Vincent Ferrer even more tedious to read than Vicente Justiniano Antist's. Reporting on research in the canonization process, manuscript and printed books, and various archives throughout Aragon, Diago devotes a considerable amount of space simply to correcting his predecessors' errors. In the first chapter of the first book of his *History,* for example, Diago spends two and a half pages listing five reasons why Antist's dating of Vincent's birth was wrong and his own date of 1350 was correct.[68] Antist's chronology comes under scrutiny again when Diago debates the date of Vincent's entry into the Dominican Order, basing his argument on a spate of archival documents that provided him, again, with five reasons why Antist was wrong.[69] Another lengthy discussion, again with copious citations of archival records, has Diago disputing the conclusion of Antist and others that Vincent received the title of master in theology in the year 1368.[70] Just as Antist had, with good reason, prided himself on the discovery of new archival sources for Vincent's life, so too did Diago. He took particular delight in quoting from the volume of Vincent's sermons preserved in the Colegia de El Patriarca in Valencia,[71] as well as in meticulously citing letters from the Archivo Real in Barcelona.[72] In several places, Diago's text conveys all the bibliographical detail, and all the narrative excitement, of a modern footnote.

When he is not busy citing his sources or criticizing previous authors, however, Diago expends a considerable amount of effort to portray Vincent as a Valencian saint whose heavenly virtues could be felt in the city from the time of his birth to the present. To that end, Diago adds to the history

---

67. Martí Ferrando 2012; Pérez Vilatela 2004; Esponero Cerdán 2009, esp. 305–9 on Diago's biographies of Vincent Ferrer.

68. Diago 2001, bk. 1, chap. 1, pp. 5–7.

69. Ibid., bk. 1, chap. 3, pp. 33–34.

70. Ibid., bk. 1, chap. 4, pp. 54–63.

71. E.g., ibid., bk. 1, chap. 7, p. 94.

72. E.g., ibid., bk. 1, chap. 16, p. 203: "Las quales se pueden ver en el Archivo real de Barcelona en el registro sexto de diversas cosas del mismo rey del dicho año en el folio ciento y noventa y dos."

of Vincent's early years a number of episodes not found in previous *vitae,* details frequently drawn from his own archival research. For example, when describing Vincent's baptism, Diago does not simply supply the names of Vincent's godparents but also cites archival records indicating that three of them had also served the city as *jurados.*[73] Just as in the dedication of his work to the *señores jurados* of Valencia, Diago here draws a connection between the corporate expression of the city and its saintly citizen son, who was, though baptism, made a member of the *jurados'* spiritual family. And, Diago notes, in his own day, one can see devotion to the very font in which Vincent was baptized in Valencia.[74] Diago's second book, devoted to the careers of Vincent's disciples, establishes a chain of holiness running outward from Vincent and, through his followers, touching people throughout Valencia, Catalonia, and Majorca.[75]

Another of Diago's additions to the saint's biography establishes a miraculous presence for Vincent in Valencia from his earliest childhood days. According to Diago, at the moment of his baptism, Vincent was infused with the grace to work miracles, an ability that had already begun to show itself by the age of nine years. Citing a memoir translated from Limousin into Castilian, Diago recounts the tale of five-year-old Antonio Garrigues, son of the Valencian spice merchant Miquel Garrigues. When little Antonio lay languishing with "apostemes" (probably meaning plague buboes), Miquel, having heard of the "sanctity and the marvelous things that the son of Guillermo Ferrer was said to do," arranged to have Vincent come and touch his son. Vincent was, evidently, all too happy to comply and not only touched the aposteme but also licked it. At once Antonio was restored to health, and afterwards all the mothers in the neighborhood would send their sick or injured children to be touched and prayed over by Guillermo Ferrer's son. The family preserved the memory of the miracle, not simply in the memoir Diago cited, written for Antonio's son Juan Garrigues, but also through an image of the saint placed in the corner of the family house by Juan in 1461, after Vincent's canonization.[76]

More details bolster Diago's presentation of Vincent's unbroken sacred presence in Valencia from his childhood on. For example, in discussing Vincent's entry into the Dominican order, not simply does Diago rectify the issue of its date (1367 instead of Antist's 1357), but he also makes the event more concrete by adding a local anecdote. When Vincent had completed

---

73. Ibid., bk. 1, chap. 2, pp. 17–19.

74. Ibid., bk. 1, chap. 2, p. 21.

75. Ibid., bk. 2, chaps. 2–3, esp. pp. 504–17.

76. Ibid., bk. 1, chap. 2, pp. 23–25 (quotation, 24). The family thus capitalized on the fame of the new saint and took pains to publicly associate themselves with Vincent by erecting the statue in memory of the miracle worked on their ancestor.

his novitiate and taken the habit of the Order of Preachers, Diago relates, his mother came away from the ceremony upset and in tears. A wise man she encountered on the way home, however, rebuked her. It turned out that this stranger was in fact an angel.[77] Further, the moment of Vincent's becoming a Dominican friar continued to be marked out as sacred. Diago adds that Valencian Dominicans hold a special celebration each year on the Feast of Saint Agatha (February 5), the day on which Vincent is said to have taken the habit.[78] Even Vincent's cell remained a holy space in Diago's telling. Not simply had the Virgin appeared to him there, as related by Ranzano and many other hagiographers, but also Vincent's own activities had turned the chamber into a sort of relic. As Diago relates, when the Dominicans in Valencia wanted to rebuild the convent's dormitory, they chose to leave Vincent's cell intact because its floor was stained with the saint's own blood, the result of his vigorous self-flagellations every night for the eighteen years he resided in the convent. Endowed with an image in 1552, the cell is visited devoutly by all great prelates who come to Valencia, Diago notes, and continues to manifest the saint's presence through the numerous visions and miracles experienced by those who make a pilgrimage there.[79]

Although, as Diago was well aware, Vincent's holy corpse lay in Brittany and not in Valencia, he is careful to lay out for his readers many manifestations of Vincent's continuing intercession in his hometown. For example, Diago notes that while the city prepared to turn out for a grand procession after the publication of the bull of canonization in 1458, the saint's merits brought an end to a bitter drought—with the precipitation conveniently falling on the day *before* the saint's feast day.[80] Vincent knew better than to rain on his own parade. Further, Diago chronicles a number of miracles that had been granted to Valencians during the course of the previous century, carefully providing dates and the names of the beneficiaries of Vincent's intercession. Several of these miracles concerned members of high-ranking families: a woman named Doña Angela, healed from the wounds of a brutal attack following an apparition of the saint in 1574; a *donzella* named Isabel Iuan Camora, cured by a relic of Saint Vincent in 1588; and Doña Beatriz de Çanoguera, wife of a *cavallero* and current *jurado* of Valencia, whose difficult childbirth was eased by touching Vincent's shoe to her belly.[81] And while Valencia did not possess Vincent's body, the Dominican convent had been able to acquire several important relics. Most notably for Diago—he makes this tale the last chapter of his first book—the city had just taken possession

---

77. Ibid., bk. 1, chap. 3, pp. 42–44.
78. Ibid., bk. 1, chap. 3, p. 41.
79. Ibid., bk. 1, chap. 6, pp. 85–92.
80. Ibid., bk. 1, chap. 37, pp. 434–35.
81. Ibid., bk. 1, chaps. 38–39, pp. 443–59.

of a new relic in 1600, thanks to the efforts of a Castilian *cavallero* named Don Juan de Aguila, who had persuaded the cathedral chapter in Vannes to part with one of the saint's ribs. The relic's arrival was celebrated with a grand procession, complete with the miraculous cure of a paralyzed woman and a deaf-mute boy.[82] While Diago does recount some contemporary miracles from outside Aragon—including a charming tale of a Portuguese woman freed from the shame of ugliness by the saint's intercession—he keeps his reader's focus on Valencia.[83] From his baptism through to the moment of Diago's writing, Diago's Vincent Ferrer graced the city of his birth with his miraculous intercession and—with the arrival of glorious relics—his physical presence, while the work of his disciples continued to spread the saint's teaching and charisma in the region.

Francisco Diago's presentation of Vincent Ferrer's unbroken sacred presence in the city of Valencia fits well with the friar's larger program of producing a sacred history for the region of Aragon. As a number of scholars have noted, one of the goals of Catholic historiography following the Council of Trent was to demonstrate that the church was unchanged since apostolic times (*semper eadem* or "always the same," as Cesare Baronio put it in his *Ecclesiastical Annals*), marked continually by miracles that gave witness to the church's divine presence.[84] Diago's catalog of works reveals a man bent on showing this unbroken chain of holiness in Valencia and Aragon (despite the medieval centuries of Muslim rule there). His hagiographical writings reveal a preference for local saints,[85] while his historical efforts centered exclusively on Valencia, Barcelona, and Aragon. Diago's *History of the Province of Aragon of the Order of Preachers* (1598) emphasized the order's missionary work from the time of its founding to the present.[86] But he would most obviously link Aragon's sacred history to apostolic days in his *Annals of the Kingdom of Valencia* (1613). Writing in response to Gaspar Escolano's 1610 *General History of Valencia,* Diago in his *Annals* defended the mythic history of Spain laid out in the fabricated chronicle of Berosus—supposedly "edited" by fellow Dominican Annius de Viterbo in 1498—which Escolano had derided in his work.[87]

---

82. Ibid., bk. 1, chap. 40–[41] ("cap. ultimo"), 459–92. Diago devotes several pages to describing how Charles V in 1532 had been promised either the whole body or a major relic but received a much lesser relic; the fight went all the way to Pope Clement VII. For more on the struggles of Valencians to acquire Vincent's relics, see FHSVF, 2:280–84, 301–8.

83. Diago 2001, bk. 1, chap. 39, pp. 458–59. Diago says his source is Christoual de Fonseca's *Tratado del amor de Dios,* chap. 41. The miracle, he explains, is the reason all women in Portugal are devoted to Vincent Ferrer.

84. Ditchfield 1993, 287; Soergel 1993, 171; 1996; Sallmann 1994, 337, 370–71.

85. The exception to this pattern, Diago's life of Peter of Luxembourg, may have been a deliberate attempt to show the affiliation of saints with the Avignon papacy, to which Vincent Ferrer and the crown of Aragon long adhered.

86. Vose 2009, 8.

87. Pérez Vilatela 2004, 389–413.

But, although he differed with Escolano by tracing the region's history to Noah's grandson Tubal, Diago eagerly seized upon Escolano's presentation of another manifestation of Valencia's sacred past and present: the Holy Grail. In his *General History,* Escolano had devoted several pages to the Holy Grail, "now preserved in the main church in Valencia." According to Escolano, the third-century martyr Saint Lawrence—a native of Valencia in his account—had arranged before his martyrdom that the Grail would come to his native Spain. After the Muslim conquest, the Grail was preserved in the remote mountain monastery of San Juan de la Peña, from which in turn it came into the hands of King Martí (the Humane) of Aragon. That the cup displayed in the cathedral was indeed the chalice used at the Last Supper Escolano demonstrated by explaining that the so-called Grail in Jerusalem was rather the platter from the same meal.[88] Despite his distaste for Escolano's work, Diago closely followed Escolano's tale about the Holy Grail and his arguments in favor of Lawrence's Valencian birth.[89] His *Annals* thus traced a history of Valencia that included Noah's grandson, a servant of Solomon,[90] the early Christian martyrs Lawrence and Vincent, and finally the Holy Grail itself, still resplendent in the Valencia cathedral. Given the devotion of the Hapsburg king Felipe II to Saint Lawrence (his massive palace-monastery complex the Escorial was dedicated to the Spanish martyr),[91] Diago's appropriation of the Lawrence-Grail story could serve both to hitch Valencia to the monarchy's sacred mission and to highlight the smaller kingdom's own sacred past and present. And like the Grail, the Vincent Ferrer of Diago's *vita* functioned as a clear sign of the unfailing presence of the divine in the city of Valencia.

## Bernard Guyard and Albert Le Grand: A Breton Saint for a Breton Public

While Diago's writings emphasized the sacred character of the place of Vincent Ferrer's birth, the city that saw his death and tomb received a similar

---

88. Escolano 1610, bk. 2, chap. 6, cols. 259–67 (discusses the reasons for holding Lawrence to be a native of Valencia, not Huesca; says that Lawrence and Vincent are "relatives" [*deudos*]); bk. 5, chap. 2, cols. 895–901 (on the Grail), translating a letter from King Martí describing his acquisition of the chalice from San Juan de la Peña. See also Beltrán 1960, 24–25; Mira 2002; Barber 2004, 169–70; and (with extreme caution) Bennett 2004. I discuss several sixteenth- and seventeenth-century treatments of the Valencian Grail in Smoller 2011b.

89. Diago 1613, bk. 4, chap. 19, fol. 164r–166r (reasons for holding Lawrence's birthplace to be Valencia), chap. 20, fol. 166v–168r; Beltrán 1960, 26.

90. Pérez Vilatela 2004, 407–9. Diago was here following another apocryphal history from the twelfth century, the *División de los Obispados, hecha por el Rey godo Wamba (Hitación de Wamba).*

91. See, especially, Lazure 2007; Kamen 2010. Richard L. Kagan has also noted the tension between interests of center and periphery in Spanish historiography of the sixteenth and seventeenth centuries. Kagan 1995.

panegyric several decades later in fellow Dominican Bernard Guyard's 1634 *Life of Saint Vincent Ferrer,* dedicated to the bishop and "messieurs de Vennes." Occasioned by the long-awaited opening of a Dominican house in Vannes, Guyard's lengthy and flowery biography is divided into two sections: a first part, dealing with Vincent's life and *in vita* miracles and based in part on the *vitae* of Ranzano and Antoninus of Florence, and a second part, treating the saint's time and miracles in the duchy and largely based on the Brittany canonization inquest.[92] While the second part, cataloging Vincent's miracles according to their locations in Brittany, demonstrates the saint's intercessory presence throughout the duchy, Guyard's effusive ending makes clear that the saint's real passion was for "Vannes, my dear Vannes." In fact, according to Guyard, Vincent's intercession had showered the city with "special graces," preserving its inhabitants from plague, enemy siege, shipwreck, and sterility and leading mothers to bring their children to kiss the saint's tomb, as the saint "stretches out his hand to drive away pestiferous winds" from the city. So great a boon was the presence of Vannes's special protector that from the moment of his canonization, people spoke only of the city, which Guyard calls "the baptismal font of France."[93] It is hard to avoid the conclusion that Vincent's presence had emphatically marked Vannes as a center of spiritual gifts.

Although Guyard's biography lavished praise on the city of Vannes, the more pressing issue for sixteenth- and seventeenth-century Bretons was the status of the duchy itself. Thus the entry on Saint Vincent Ferrer in the Dominican Albert Le Grand's 1636 *Lives of the Saints of Armorican Brittany* presents the Valencian preacher as a *Breton* saint for an unabashedly patriotic Breton audience. Drawing in part on Guyard's biography of the saint, Le Grand crafted a portrait of Vincent Ferrer that appealed to the region's self-identification as an area whose Catholic faith had remained pure and strong for over a millennium, untainted by Protestant heresy.[94] That religious orientation overlapped with Brittany's insistent assertion, particularly after the duchy's union with the French crown in 1532, that a common

---

92. Guyard 1634. The two dedicatory letters to Bishop Sebastien de Rosmadec and to "messieurs de Vennes" are unpaginated. Guyard reproduces Antoninus's arguments about the schism (82–84) and Vincent's apocalyptic pronouncements (112–17), all the while following Ranzano's basic order of narration for the biography. His omissions and elaborations, however, make the work quite different in character from Ranzano's or Antoninus's work. He also mentions other earlier biographies, including those by Leandro Alberti, Antist, and Surius, as well as "une authentique coppie tirée sur l'original de l'information de sa vie & de sa mort faite à Vennes" ("Au lecteur," unpaginated). A list of miracles extracted from Guyard's work appears in AASS, Aprilis, 1:514–23.

93. Guyard 1634, 390–96. Quotations: 391, 395, 390. Vincent is called "Apostre de la Bretagne, & Protecteur de Vennes" in the unpaginated prefatory letter "Au lecteur."

94. Tingle 2005, 237–39. "The Bretons were thus," in the words of Tingle, "a chosen people of God" (239). See also Nice 2009, esp. chap. 5. On the relative weakness of the Protestant movement in Brittany, see Croix 1993, esp. 391–400.

historical bond united the area culturally as well, setting the Bretons apart from the rest of France, a difference enshrined in a number of particular political concessions made to the duchy.[95] While still faithful to the conventions of Counter-Reformation writing about the saints, Le Grand made of the Valencian Vincent Ferrer an emblem of Breton religious and political particularism.

Albert Le Grand's own life put him at the intersection of Catholic reform and regional patriotism in Brittany. He was born in the heart of Breton-speaking Basse-Bretagne, as he later would tell his readers as an excuse for his inelegant French,[96] and entered the Dominican order in his hometown of Morlaix (in a convent reformed in 1629). As a young preaching friar, Le Grand soon began researching the lives of the saints of the diocese to provide material for his sermons. In 1628 Noël des Landes, vicar of the minister general of the Gallican Congregation of the Order, commissioned Le Grand to travel throughout the duchy to collect archival materials to write lives for the full panoply of Breton saints. The resulting collection received the vicar general's approval on July 12, 1634.[97] The same years in which Le Grand was conducting his research witnessed a dramatic alteration in Brittany's relationship with the crown of France. Although Breton elites in the last decades of the sixteenth century had managed to exercise considerable influence through the institution of the Estates—Brittany was one of a handful of so-called *pays d'États*—that "cozy little relationship," as one historian has put it, was beginning to change in Le Grand's lifetime. In the late 1620s, as Albert Le Grand was making his religious profession, Louis XIII's chief minister, Cardinal Richelieu, moved to increase his patronage in and control of the region, eventually assuming the title of governor of Brittany in 1631. The Estates and the crown squared off over the issues of nonnative appointments to Breton bishoprics and increasing royal financial demands.[98] In response to the challenge to regional identity posed by French absolutism, the Breton Estates sponsored a number of historical works in the late sixteenth and seventeenth centuries, underscoring the region's distinctiveness over the span of time. Le Grand's collection of saints' lives from "Armorican Brittany" (his title deliberately reaching back to the area's Roman past), offered a religious complement to those histories, and

---

95. Most notably, Brittany was one of the few areas in France to retain an Estates, which both approved financial payments to the crown and sought redress for various local grievances. J. Collins 1994, 154, 158. In addition, the Treaty of Union of 1532 stipulated that Brittany was exempt from the Concordat of Bologna of 1516 and that only natives were to be appointed to Breton bishoprics: Tingle 2005, 239; Nice 2009, 11–15, 99.

96. Le Grand 1901, xii (1st ed., Nantes: Pierre Doriou, 1636 or 1637).

97. A.-M. Thomas, "Albert Le Grand," in Le Grand 1901, ii–iii.

98. J. Collins 1994, 175 ("cozy little relationship"), 187–92; Nice 2009, 99–106.

he was rewarded for his efforts by a payment of one thousand livres from the Estates.[99]

Prefacing the entire volume, Le Grand's dedicatory epistle "to *Messeigneurs* of the Estates of Brittany" and his "Warning to the Reader" make clear the patriotic character of his writing on Breton saints. To the Estates, Le Grand writes of the "sincere affections that the Author has dedicated to the service of his land [*Pays*]" in composing his volume.[100] He claims as inspiration "the honor and glory" of what he calls "our Patriot Saints," who had "given luster to this Province by their sanctity."[101] And he informs *Messeigneurs* that in appending a chronology of prelates from the province "from the first century of grace up to this year" he has offered, in effect, "an Epitome of the history of our land."[102] In his address to the reader, Le Grand similarly calls attention to the work's orientation as a brief history of Brittany, noting his concluding "chronological and genealogical catalog of kings, queens, dukes, and duchesses of Brittany, their alliances, children, arms, some of their Chancellors and the governors of the Most Christian kings in the said land."[103] (The word "France," strikingly, appears in neither of Le Grand's prefaces.)

Le Grand's opening letters also make clear that he envisions his work as furthering the aims of a post-Tridentine Catholic Church. His stated goals, as he tells his readers, are "the honor of God, the glory of his Saints, your utility and edification, and the confusion of enemies of the Church."[104] Thus he promises the reader that his compilation will serve as "an arsenal well stocked with arms…to silence the enemies of the truth:…a highly effective antidote against the poison of heresies with which this century has been corrupted," by demonstrating, among other things, the unbroken succession of bishops and celebration of Mass in Brittany for more than fifteen centuries, as well as "the truth of miracles."[105] He "forbid[s] absolutely," Le Grand informs the reader, any "atheists, libertines, indifferents, [or] heretics" to read his book, as well as "those stuck-up persons who, measuring the power of God by their own deranged heads, scoff at the marvels that he has worked through his servants."[106] Furthermore, Le Grand specifically links the defense

---

99. Tingle 2005, 239 (mentioning Bertrand d'Argentré's *History*). On d'Argentré's "patriotisme provincial," see Balcou and Le Gallo 1987, 257–59. See also Nice 2009, 9, 33, 101–3 (payment to Le Grand, 102), 111. Nice, however, does not view Le Grand as a "Breton nationalist," noting that his saints' lives often insist upon the province's responsibilities toward the larger kingdom (109).

100. Le Grand 1901, "A Messeigneurs des Estats de Bretagne," ix.

101. Ibid.

102. Ibid.

103. Le Grand 1901, "Avertissement au Lecteur," xi.

104. Ibid, xiii.

105. Ibid.

106. Ibid., xii–xiii.

of Catholicism with Breton patriotism, anticipating critiques by skeptical Protestant readers. "I will glory," he writes, "to be persecuted by such libertines and Anti-Bretons, rendering this service to the Church and to my fatherland [*patrie*], to the confusion of the enemies of both the one and the other."[107] To attack the Catholic saints was thus to attack Brittany.

In turning to "The Conversation of Saint Vincent Ferrer," Le Grand explicitly centers his biography on the saint's time in and ties to Brittany. In fact, only five lines out of thirteen printed pages of text are devoted to Vincent's Valencian origins and travels prior to arriving in the duchy.[108] Le Grand expends considerable space, however, in tracing Vincent's itinerary in Brittany during his final years, as well as his death, canonization, and cult in the duchy. To emphasize that divine providence had made Vincent into a *Breton* saint, for example, Le Grand repeats the familiar miracle tale in which, persuaded by his companions, he tried to leave the duchy under the cloak of night, only to travel in circles and return to the gates of Vannes. In Le Grand's telling, the futile attempt at escape served as proof to Vincent that "it is God's will that I die in this land."[109] Similarly, Le Grand has the saint on his deathbed promising "to be a perpetual advocate and intercessor" for the people of Vannes, "provided, always, that you do not distance yourself from my teaching."[110] The only postmortem miracles that Le Grand reports—all found in Antoninus of Florence's *vita*—take place in Brittany, including the resuscitations of the abbot of Lanvaux's nephew and of the archer Johannes Guerre, the cure of the raving Perrinus Hervei, and the restoration of the chopped-up baby.[111] And at the end of his biography, Le Grand details Vincent's continued sacred presence in Brittany, noting that there were few parishes in which his image had not been erected.[112]

---

107. Ibid., xii.

108. Le Grand 1901, "La conversation de S. Vincent Ferrier, de l'Ordre des Frères Predicateurs en Bretagne; sa Mort, Canonization, et aucuns Miracles, le 5. Avril," 123, para. 1.

109. Ibid., 126, para. 8. Although this tale appears in Ranzano's *vita*, as well as in the canonization inquests that informed Guyard's biography mentioned by Le Grand in his first paragraph, his citation here is to "F. Abraham Bzovius, Annal. Eccles. post Baron, tom, 15. sub. A. C. 1419 num 3." Le Grand is referring to the continuation of Cesare Baronio's *Annales Ecclesiastici* by the Polish Dominican Abraham Bzovius (Abraham Bzowski, 1567–1637), Baronio 1616–40, 15:582 (the eight volumes of Bzovius's continuation are numbered 13–20, after the twelve volumes authored by Baronio). Bzovius's life of Vincent, although he claims to follow Ranzano, is more an amalgamation of Ranzano's and Surius's biographies, with the addition of a set of postmortem miracles drawn from Antoninus's *vita*.

110. Le Grand 1901, 127, para. 12, again citing Bzovius (closely following Baronio 1616–40, 15:582–83).

111. Le Grand 1901, 129–30, paras. 19–25. Given that Bzovius also draws on Antoninus for his postmortem miracles, Bzovius may well be Le Grand's source here.

112. Ibid., 135, para. 32.

As in the Brittany canonization inquest, Le Grand's narrative particularly stresses the ties between the holy preacher and the ducal family, from Duke Jean V's triple invitation to Vincent to preach in the duchy through Duchess Jeanne's attendance at his deathbed to the Breton dukes' role in Vincent's canonization.[113] For example, Le Grand specifically calls Duchess Jeanne Vincent's "spiritual daughter" (*fille spirituelle*) and, citing Alain Bouchart's 1514 *Annales de Bretagne,* has the saint prophesy the birth and subsequent murder of her son Gilles de Bretagne (1420–50) at the hands of his own brother, François.[114] Furthermore, Le Grand stretches the truth to make "the duke and duchess of Brittany" number among the witnesses who testified at the Brittany canonization inquest.[115] Le Grand is, in fact, so insistent on Vincent's closeness to the ducal family that he feels compelled to excuse Duke Jean V's *absence* from the scenes of Vincent's 1419 death and burial, explaining that "several authors" had written that the duke was held prisoner by Margot de Clisson, countess of Penthièvre, from February 13, 1419 until May 1420.[116]

Nowhere do the dukes of Brittany figure more prominently in Le Grand's Vincent biography than in the sections dealing with the holy preacher's canonization. Duke Jean V, he records, commanded all nine bishops in Brittany to record Vincent's miracles and report them to the Breton *parlement*. Those reports formed the basis of an ineffectual petition to Pope Eugenius IV to open canonization proceedings. Thus the real force behind the canonization in Le Grand's telling was Duke Pierre II, at whose insistence and expense the Dominican chapter general of 1543 was celebrated in Nantes with an eye to planning for Vincent's canonization. Le Grand paints a dramatic picture of "the duke and duchess and all their court" kneeling in prayer while the assembled friars elected a new master general, Martial Auribelli, with Pierre II then rushing to greet him. By dinner that night, Le Grand relates, the duke was importuning Auribelli to procure Vincent's canonization—and offering "to furnish all the necessary costs."[117]

Le Grand also presents a detailed description of the June 1456 ceremony held in Vannes at Duke Pierre II's request, at which a papal legate (the Breton Alain de Coativi, cardinal of Avignon) solemnly elevated the holy

---

113. Ibid., 123, para. 1 (invitation of Duke Jean V); 123–25, paras. 2–6 (itinerary); 126–28, paras. 10–18 (final illness, death, and burial); 130–32, paras. 26–27 (canonization).

114. Ibid., 125, para. 7, citing "Allain Bouchard és Annal. de Bret. l. 4. fol. 153." On Alain Bouchart (Bouchard), Balcou and Le Gallo 1987, 261–62.

115. Ibid., 131, para. 27.

116. Ibid., 128, para. 16. Jean's captivity was actually from February 1420 until May 1420 (Le Grand is perhaps confused—or counts on his readers' being confused—by the old-style dating, in which the year did not commence on January 1). See chapter 1.

117. Ibid., 131, para. 26. Cf. Ranzano, who has Auribelli importuning the duke: BC, MS 112, fol. 62v.

corpse and announced the news of Vincent's canonization.[118] According to Le Grand's manuscript sources, in order to offset the costs of the ceremony, the grand council of Brittany had imposed a subsidy of five deniers on each household, "a sum that all gladly paid and that the majority paid double, on account of the devotion that they held toward the saint."[119] A long list of bishops, abbots, and nobles from Brittany and surrounding regions was in attendance. On the papal legate's arrival in Vannes, the duke feted him with a magnificent reception in the palace of La Motte. Two days later, the legate Coativi and an entourage of prelates processed to the cathedral for vespers, to be met by the duke and his great nobles and officers coming from the ducal castle l'Hermine. The crowds returned to the cathedral at midnight for the elevation of Vincent's body and Mass, during which the announcement of Vincent's canonization was read out in three languages—Latin, Breton, and French—reflecting the unique linguistic makeup of the saint's resting place.[120]

Le Grand closes his biography with a reminder of Vincent's continuing physical and spiritual presence in Brittany. After Vincent's canonization, Le Grand notes, five different Dominican master generals made the pilgrimage to Vannes to visit his tomb, most recently in 1632. That last visit by the Order of Preachers' head resulted in the founding of a Dominican house in the city of Vannes itself, guaranteeing its citizens perpetual access to the same sort of spiritual teaching Vincent had long ago brought there and, as we have seen, inspiring Bernard Guyard's enthusiastic praise of the town. Le Grand also describes the numerous relics (both corporal relics and items Vincent had used) preserved in churches in both Brittany and France, through whose touch "many miracles are worked" for those "armed with strong faith and devout invocation of the saint's intercession."[121] And, "in the last few years," he adds, the people of Vannes, who proclaim Vincent their "patron and protector," had erected a magnificent city gate bearing a statue of Vincent and "recognizing him as their tutelary angel in this world, as well as their advocate in the other."[122] The saint who had been "one of the apostles of this province"[123] two centuries previously was thus still watching over the people of Brittany.

Le Grand's treatment of Vincent Ferrer fit well with the general program of Catholic hagiography after the Council of Trent. Although his

---

118. No earlier source offers such a detailed description of this ceremony, for which Le Grand cites Du Pas, *Geneal. d'Espinay;* D'Argentré; Alain Bouchart; and "mes mémoirs manuscrits." Ibid., 132nn1 and 2; 133n2).

119. Ibid., 132, para. 28.

120. Ibid., 133, para. 29–30.

121. Ibid., 135, para. 32.

122. Ibid., 136, para. 32.

123. Ibid., 123, para. 1.

citations of sources are nowhere near as tedious as those found in Antist's or Diago's works, Le Grand does include occasional source annotations, as well as a final bibliographical paragraph. Like Antist and Diago, Le Grand also avails himself of local archival sources, including "ancient manuscript legendaries and old printed breviaries from all the bishoprics in Brittany," manuscript chronicles from various Dominican convents in Brittany, and "handwritten memoirs of Messire Yves Le Grand…, who was present at the elevation of the holy corpse at Vannes."[124] Further, in addition to Le Grand's more pointed remarks in the letters prefacing his entire collection, it is possible to see the occasional subtle dig at Protestant heretics in his life of Vincent. When he mentions the numbers of images of Vincent Ferrer to be found in Breton parishes, for example, he adds, "and they may still be seen in those places where the new sham iconoclasts have not exercised their furor."[125] It is hard to know exactly what to make of this statement, which seems to imply that Protestant iconoclasm had indeed been a problem in Brittany (which prided itself on its firm Catholicism). Le Grand, probably wisely, moves on without comment. It is also possible to read an affirmation of Catholic doctrine in Le Grand's description of the people of Vannes honoring Vincent as patron and tutelary angel. After all, a number of Protestant reformers had attacked the belief in guardian angels along with the cult of the saints.[126] Furthermore, the practice of choosing a patron saint for a town or village was becoming increasingly popular after the Council of Trent. As Jean-Michel Sallmann has nicely demonstrated for the case of Naples, vast numbers of communities elected new patron saints in the years after 1630, when such elections were officially placed under papal reserve.[127] Finally, Le Grand's concluding section on the current veneration of Vincent

---

124. Ibid., 136. Interestingly, although Le Grand mentions in a note at the beginning of his biography of Vincent (123n1) the *vitae* by Ranzano, Antoninus, Flamini, Alberti, Casseta, Antist, Diago, Bzovius (all Dominicans), as well as those of Surius, Ribadeneira, "and others," in his concluding paragraph he names as his sources only the Roman Martyrology (with Baronius's annotations), Razius's *Vies des Saints de l'Ordre des Freres Predicateurs,* Antoninus of Florence's *Chronicon,* legendaries by Guillaume Gazet and René Benoist, Alain Bouchart's *Annales de Bretagne,* Robert Caenalis's *De re Gallica,* and Bzovius's continuation of Baronio (in addition to the manuscript and early printed sources mentioned above). In other words, although he was aware of Ranzano's official *vita* of Vincent Ferrer, he either did not have access to it or chose to ignore it. Either option shows the limits of the fifteenth-century effort to shape the image of Vincent Ferrer on the part of the papacy and the Dominican order (although Ranzano's *Office* likely lay behind the lessons in the breviaries consulted by Le Grand). Le Grand's reference to "Ribadeneira" is to the *vita* of Vincent by Jesuit Pedro de Ribadeneyra (1526–1611), as found in Ribadeneyra 1734, 1:475–86. (The work was originally published in Madrid in 1599–1601). See Bilinkoff 1999.

125. Le Grand 1901, 135, para. 32. Le Grand's mention of iconoclasm may be a reference to Jansenism (a Catholic movement that adhered to an Augustinian position on grace and predestination), as anti-Jansenists sometimes referred to their opponents as Protestants and iconoclasts.

126. See Marshall and Walsham 2006, 13–31.

127. Sallmann 1994, 25, 111, and esp. 66–68.

Ferrer in Vannes could be viewed as part of his larger effort to demonstrate an unbroken chain of sanctity and Catholic practice in the region from the time of the apostles to his own day.

Although Le Grand attempts to trace a continuous cult of Vincent Ferrer in Brittany from the fifteenth century through the present, it is hard to avoid concluding from his text that Vincent's cult in fact was undergoing a process of deliberate revivification in the early seventeenth century. After all, of the five Dominican masters general Le Grand says visited Vincent's tomb, the first four had made their journeys to the duchy before its 1532 union with France. Over a hundred years had intervened before the visit of Nicolas Rodulphius in 1632, resulting in the new Dominican convent in Vannes.[128] Other evidence supports the conclusion that the saint's cult in Brittany received a jump start in the early seventeenth century. For example, Bishop Jacques Martin de Belleassise, perhaps spurred by the Spanish king Felipe II's attempts to acquire Vincent's body in the 1590s, commissioned a set of tapestries illustrating Vincent's miracles, which were hung in the Vannes cathedral in 1615.[129] In 1632, the cathedral chapter provided a new silver reliquary at the cost of 2,623 livres, followed by the completion of a new chapel to house Vincent's relics in 1634.[130] And as we have seen, in 1637, the year following the publication of Le Grand's *Lives of the Saints of Armorican Brittany,* a commission of theologians and physicians solemnly authenticated Vincent's relics in Vannes prior to a formal ceremonial translation.[131]

As with other Catholic regions, Brittany in the early seventeenth century felt the intensified pull of Catholic reform. Bishops began an attempt to modify the religious life of the laity, focusing on such outward manifestations of "impiety" as the frequenting of taverns and dances on Sundays and feast days or the holding of meetings and social gatherings in churches. Some parishes undertook the rebuilding of their churches, enlarging the space and removing rood screens that hindered lay participation in the Mass.[132] Missionaries crisscrossed the region, preaching and offering catechism lessons in fields and roadsides.[133] The saints—held up as models to imitate and examples of God's intervention in daily life—formed an integral part of Breton Catholic renewal.[134] Hagiographical texts such as Le Grand's, aimed at a

---

128. Le Grand 1901, 134–35, para. 31.

129. FHSVF, 2:280–84; Thomas 1901, 137–39; Le Mené 1882.

130. Thomas 1901, 139.

131. Ibid., 139–40; FHSVF, 2:284–86.

132. Tingle 2005, 242–43; Croix 1981, 2:1183–95; Châtellier 1997, 34–35, 39, 45–46, 101–3.

133. Tingle 2005, 247.

134. Ibid., 248–52; Croix 1981, 2:1112–16. As Croix notes, Catholic reformers were much more successful promoting the cult of older Breton saints than they were in stirring up fervor for newer saints. Jean-Christophe Cassard observes that devotion to the Valencian Vincent Ferrer in Brittany could be seen as a little "cool" when compared with that given to Saint Yves or Saint Anne d'Auray

lay audience, complemented more direct demonstrations of saints' presence such as the ceremonial translation of Vincent's relics in Vannes in 1637.

But hagiography also supported the cause of Breton patriotism, as the once-separate duchy increasingly felt the presence of French royal authority. Le Grand's Vincent Ferrer inhabits an exclusively Breton context; no contemporary events save Breton ones appear in the pages of Le Grand's biography. He breathes not a word, for example, about the Great Schism that dominated Vincent's career but is careful to note the specific details of the duke of Brittany's captivity at the time of Vincent's death. In Le Grand's hands, Vincent Ferrer, although born in Aragon, becomes a Breton saint working miracles for the Breton people, who see him as patron and "tutelary angel." As Le Grand's example makes clear, in Brittany as in Aragon, writing about the saints could serve to assert local identity as well as to defend the truth of Catholicism. Le Grand's vision of Brittany was that of a region long and deeply steeped in the Catholic faith; in his writing, Vincent Ferrer formed part of an unbroken chain of sanctity linking the present to the duchy's ancient apostolic past.

## Andrés Ferrer de Valdecebro: Hero of the Schism, Converter of Muslims and Jews

Le Grand's presentation of the saint as both intercessor and role model is echoed in a final influential biography from the seventeenth century, Andrés Ferrer de Valdecebro's *History of the Marvelous and Admirable Life of the Second Paul, Apostle of Valencia, Saint Vincent Ferrer*, originally published in 1682.[135] A Dominican friar best known today for his book of animal emblems, Andrés Ferrer de Valdecebro (1620–80) spent time in the New World and later served as confessor to a number of women and nobles in the royal court in Madrid. Professor of moral theology in Alcalá in the early 1660s, he also composed works of natural philosophy, moral theology, and hagiography.[136] Trumpeting neither the vehement anti-Protestantism nor the passionate patriotism of other sixteenth- and seventeenth-century authors of Vincentian *vitae*, Ferrer de Valdecebro rather sought, through his *History*

---

(who had appeared to a peasant not far from Vannes in 1624–25). Cassard 2000, 199–201. Similarly, in Spain, Marian devotion easily trumped that of other saints. Christian 1981, 73–89, 102–3, 121–25.

135. My references are to Ferrer de Valdecebro 1781; the original edition was Madrid: Matheo de Llanos, 1682.

136. There is a brief biography in Roig Condomina 1985, 81. See also "Introducción," in Ferrer de Valdecebro 2007, 17–49 (biographical sketch at 19–22). The emblemata book is *Govierno general, moral, y politico, hallando en las fieras y animales sylvestres*, first published in 1658. In addition to his life of Vincent Ferrer, Ferrer de Valdecebro also composed lives of Saint Dominic, the Portuguese Dominican friar João de Vasconcelos (ca. 1588–1652), and the Dominican tertiary Rosa de Santa Maria (Rosa of Lima, canonized 1671).

*of the Marvelous and Admirable Life* of the man he claimed as kinsman,[137] to inculcate proper Catholic belief and behavior in his readers, holding out the promise of Vincent's intercession on behalf of the truly faithful. Accordingly, while still cataloging Vincent's many past miracles, Ferrer de Valdecebro also stressed Vincent's holy life, his effectiveness as a preacher, and his labors on behalf of the church in ending the Schism. The resulting image of Vincent—one of which the fifteenth-century Pietro Ranzano would have gladly approved—portrays him as healer of the Schism and converter of sinners, Muslims, and Jews, enlarging Catholic orthodoxy through his peacemaking and his preaching.

The arrangement of Ferrer de Valdecebro's book makes clear his orientation in holding up Vincent as both role model and intercessor. The work is divided into five books. The first two and the final book point to Vincent's exemplary life, treating his exterior life (or deeds), internal life (his virtues), and his correspondence with those in power ("Letters that different individuals, especially kings, wrote to Saint Vincent").[138] The third and fourth books cover Vincent's supernatural capabilities, highlighting his miracles as well as his prophetic gifts. As the "second Paul" of the book's title, Ferrer de Valdecebro's Vincent shared both the apostle's spiritual powers and his mission to spread the Christian life.

Similarly, Ferrer de Valdecebro's three prefaces to the life proper also present Vincent as one to be both imitated and invoked. For example, his introductory letter "To the Reader" begins by touting the moral value of hagiography. "Reading the life of the saints," he writes, "is an activity that teaches men to detest vices and embrace virtues."[139] Still, Ferrer de Valdecebro also dwells on Vincent's miracles in this letter, despite the fact that "the most Excellent Señor Conde de Oropesa" had urged him to write Vincent's life without any miracles.[140] According to the good count, "the life is to imitate, [whereas] the miracles are to admire; and from admiration no benefit is obtained, from imitation, many."[141] Still, the Excellent Señor's suggestion notwithstanding, Ferrer de Valdecebro noted that even though he had tried to tease out the life from the miracles, some of Vincent's miracles were interwoven with his biography and could not be separated from it. Furthermore, he mentioned specifically in the "Letter to the Reader" the many miracles

---

137. "Mi Santo Pariente": Ferrer de Valdecebro 1781, "Al que leyere" (not paginated).

138. Ibid., 231.

139. Ibid., "Al que leyere."

140. Ibid. "El excelentisimo Señor Conde de Oropesa" is probably Manuel Joaquín Álvarez de Toledo y Portugal, conde de Oropesa (d. 1707), an important political figure and doubtless one Ferrer de Valdecebro would have known at court. At the time of Ferrer de Valdecebro's death in 1680, he was Consejero de Estado (1680). He would become president of the Consejo de Castilla in 1684 and first minister under Carlos II from 1685. Biografías y Vidas, 2004–12.

141. Ferrer de Valdecebro 1781, "Al que leyere."

associated with a relic of the saint in Florence and an image of Vincent in Majorca. Clearly, to Ferrer de Valdecebro, Vincent's wonder working was not just a source of empty admiration but had also boosted the saint's wide veneration, which in turn would spur imitation on the part of the faithful.[142]

A second prefatory item further demonstrates the way in which Ferrer de Valdecebro links Vincent's intercessory powers with a call to proper Catholic doctrine and devotion. After the "Letter to the Reader" Ferrer de Valdecebro appends a "Holy and devout prescription [*receta*], which Saint Vincent Ferrer left so that those women who are sterile might have the fruit of blessing."[143] At first this "prescription" appears to have been little more than an advertisement of Vincent's thaumaturgic powers. Thus, Ferrer de Valdecebro exults that Vincent had "worked innumerable miracles for sterile women" while he was alive and also had performed a similar miracle last year on "the Most Excellent Señora Condesa de Oropesa" (wife of his adviser in the "Letter to the Reader"), a fact now known throughout Spain. The countess had been cured of fourteen years of barrenness, as Ferrer de Valdecebro relates, after fulfilling what Vincent commanded in "this prescription." Vincent's prescription was at closer glance, however, a recipe for the good Catholic life. According to Ferrer de Valdecebro, Vincent had commanded sterile women to live well, try not to sin, and not deny paying the conjugal debt to their husbands. In addition, they were to offer up prayers to God, reciting the creed in the mornings and the rosary in the evenings. Those who could were to read Psalm 127 (*Beati omnes qui timent Dominum*); those who could not were to listen attentively as another read it.[144] Ferrer de Valdecebro's prescription thus held out the promise of Vincent's miraculous intercession—but only for good Catholic wives.

A third prefatory section, "Exordium," again juxtaposes the ideas of moral exhortation and supernatural remedies. After lamenting the difficulty of reducing a life so richly adorned with virtues to such a short volume,

---

142. Ibid. He mentions Vincent's cult in Italy, Valencia, Sicily, and Majorca, specifically naming the cities of Palermo, Messina, and Florence and adding, "To a Florentine gentleman a Bishop of Armenia said that it was constant that in the Greek Church no saint among the Latin confessors was more celebrated and venerated than Saint Vincent Ferrer."

143. Ibid., "Santa y devota receta, que dejo San Vicente Ferrer, para que las que son esteriles tengan fruto de benedicion" (not paginated).

144. Ibid. As Ferrer de Valcedbro notes, the Psalm promises that those who fear the Lord will be rewarded: "Thy wife as a fruitful vine, on the sides of thy house" (Ps. 127:3, Douay-Rheims translation). This recommendation appears in the testimony of Naples witness Fernandus, bishop of Telesia (*Proceso,* fol. 283v; FPC, 422, witness 9): "Item dixit idem testis quod vidit plures mulieres que non poterant habere proles et data eis regula a dicto Magistro bene vivendi et orandi et inter cetera imponebat eis quod mane et sero dicerent credo in Deum, Ave Maria, pater noster et quod dicerent seu dicere facerent psalmum Beati omnes, et quod uterentur suo matrimonio, et quod unusquisque redderet debitum alteri. Et cum Dei benedictione plures postea habuerunt filios." The same advice appears in the brief *vita* by Francesco Castiglione in Vincent Ferrer 1496, fol. a3v.

Ferrer de Valdecebro offers a few paragraphs setting the context of Vincent's life. The salient historical reference is *not,* surprisingly, the Great Schism that dominated Vincent's adult career but rather the Black Death, whose ravages colored the years just prior to his birth in 1350. In colorful language Ferrer de Valdecebro depicts the misery of men and women "clamoring for a remedy for a pain for which there was no remedy."[145] Like medieval chroniclers, he describes parents abandoning children and children left without a father to help them. But from that "gloomy dark cloud," writes Ferrer de Valdecebro, was born "the sun" of Saint Vincent, "to repair the cracks that threatened greater ruins in souls."[146] Ferrer de Valdecebro does not explicitly mention here Vincent's many miraculous cures of plague, but he probably did not have to do so for his audience. His readers presumably already had an image of Vincent as plague saint, as did Miguel Parets, a seventeenth-century Barcelona tanner and diarist, whose wife had requested a Mass in honor of Vincent Ferrer to be said after her death from plague in 1651.[147] Rather, the author emphasizes the need for *moral* healing after the ravages of plague, a spiritual cure that was produced by the rays of Vincent's preaching.

Many passages in Ferrer de Valdecebro's *History* underscore the divine nature of Vincent's preaching mission. In describing Vincent's baptism, for example, and the providential choice of the name Vincent for him, Ferrer de Valdecebro does not simply nod to Valencia's ancient martyr-patron but also explains that from the same city this other Vincent would "be victorious [*venciese*] and triumph over innumerable infidels, Jews, heretics, and reprobates."[148] And although Ferrer de Valdecebro goes on to cite Laurentius Surius's figure of some 160,000 souls converted by Vincent, his account here does not at all mirror Surius's description of the saint's baptism. While both authors agree that the name Vincent was imposed by the priest after the family could not agree on one, Surius comments on bystanders' wonder at this choice, since none among the family or friends had the name Vincent.[149] Ferrer de Valdecebro's linking of the name to Vincent's later preaching triumph is his own addition. Further, like many previous authors, Ferrer de Valdecebro also underscores the heavenly mandate behind Vincent's evangelization. Thus, in recounting the vision that inaugurated the holy friar's mission to "reform the world," Ferrer de Valdecebro has Jesus specifically

---

145. Ferrer de Valdecebro 1781, "Exordio" (not paginated). He is relying in part here on Diago 2001, bk. 1, chap. 1, which sets Vincent's birth in the context of the jubilee year of 1350 and the previous plague.

146. Ferrer de Valdecebro 1781, "Exordio."

147. Parets 1991, 68.

148. Ferrer de Valdecebro 1781, bk. 1, chap. 3, p. 4.

149. Surius 1875–80, 4:175.

charging Vincent with "the office of Apostle."[150] When Benedict XIII offers him a cardinal's hat to try to persuade him to stay in Avignon, Vincent replies, "I have another [office] of higher consequence, since the supreme and eternal Pontiff has made me his Apostle so that I might preach his gospel to all creatures."[151] Finally, as did Antist, Ferrer de Valdecebro portrays Vincent in the midst of an apocalyptic sermon proclaiming himself to be the angel of the apocalypse, then resuscitating a woman who had recently died so that she might confirm his pronouncement.[152] Ferrer de Valdecebro's Vincent was an apostolic preacher sent and supported by God's miraculous presence and works.

To further his goal of presenting Vincent as a role model for the faithful, Ferrer de Valdecebro also devotes a considerable amount of space to enumerating Vincent's heroic virtues, the subject of his book 2, which runs to some thirty-five pages. Most remarkably, however, Ferrer de Valdecebro uses the backdrop of the Great Schism to highlight Vincent's admirable qualities, at one point even inventing incidents in the saint's life that *must* have happened because of his devotion to the church and obedience to his superiors. Clearly the bad taste left by the memory of the Avignon pope Benedict XIII's stubbornness remained to some degree, for in treating Vincent's prophetic gifts in book 4, Ferrer de Valdecebro interrupts his narrative to excuse Vincent's adherence to the Avignon papacy. Citing Antoninus of Florence's similar assertion, he interjects that "to this point the Church [still] has not determined which of the parties [in the Great Schism] suffered fraud."[153] In addition, like some fifteenth-century authors before him, Ferrer de Valdecebro vastly compresses the time that Vincent spent with the stubborn Avignon pontiff Benedict XIII to a mere two years. Further, he insists that after the French subtraction of obedience in 1398, Vincent declared to Benedict that "he was of the opinion that he was not [pope]," anticipating by more than a decade Vincent's public withdrawal of allegiance from Benedict.[154]

Even more pointedly, however, Ferrer de Valdecebro insists that Vincent Ferrer was present at the Council of Constance that ended the Schism, an event for which there is absolutely no contemporary textual support. Our author realizes that he is in the minority on this point. In a blatant understatement, Ferrer de Valdecebro admits, "Some authors of the life of Saint Vincent conclude that he was not at the Council."[155] In fact, the only

---

150. Ferrer de Valdecebro 1781, bk. 1, chap. 20, 37.
151. Ibid., 38.
152. Ibid., bk. 1, chap. 32, p. 62.
153. Ibid., book 4, chap. 43, p. 230.
154. Ibid., book 1, chap. 20, p. 36.
155. Ibid., book 1, chap. 48, p. 102.

previous writer Ferrer de Valdecebro can find to back up his assertion is "Abbot Trithemius, who says that he was [there]." His source is a mere three-line entry in Johannes Trithemius's 1494 *Catalog of Ecclesiastical Writings*.[156] Indeed, Ferrer de Valdecebro employs an almost circular reasoning in support of his contention that Vincent was present, insisting that such a great saint could not have failed to attend this crucial gathering. Given that King Fernando of Aragon, the emperor Sigismund, and the council itself repeatedly wrote Vincent that "his assistance at [the council] was important, for the greater service of God and his Church," Ferrer de Valdecebro concludes, "I have no reason to doubt that he would have obeyed."[157] "It is not to be believed," he continues, "that a man of such constant virtue and sanctity and who yearned with such anxiety for the union of the church would have been absent, called by the same Church which the Council represented, to achieve the peace that it achieved."[158] When faced with the facts that the fathers of the council had been forced to send messengers to consult Vincent on a difficult point of theology and that Pierre d'Ailly and Jean Gerson had written specifically requesting Vincent's presence at Constance, Ferrer de Valdecebro simply opines that it is "far outside the paths of reason" that if a cardinal had written him, Vincent would not have gone to the council. For Ferrer de Valdecebro, it was simply implausible "that a Saint would not have obeyed the Church."[159] In this author's eyes, a saint would have attended the Council of Constance when asked, and therefore, since Vincent was a indeed a saint, he must have been there.

Andrés Ferrer de Valdecebro's *History of the Marvelous and Admirable Life* aimed to present a constant and coherent image of Vincent Ferrer as a saint whose virtues served as a model for good Catholics and whose intercessory powers would reward the faithful and pious. Separate books devoted to Vincent's virtues, miracles, and prophecies helped underscore Ferrer de Valdecebro's message, as did his emphasis within the biography proper (the *Vida exterior* of book 1) on Vincent's preaching and labors to end the Schism, a point to which the author returned again in the final chapter of book 4. Comparison with the Spanish-language biographies by Antist and Diago, both cited by Ferrer de Valdecebro, reinforces this picture. There are striking absences in Ferrer de Valdecebro's work when read side by side with two of his major sources. He does not stress Vincent's Valencian origins or his

---

156. Ibid., 102, 104. Ferrer de Valdecebro would have found a dismissive reference to Trithemius's assertion in Antist's biography, Antist 1956, pt. 1, chap. 30, p. 231. The relevant source is Trithemius (1601) 1966, 349–50 (entry on Vincent Ferrer), esp. the brief notice following the list of works on 350.

157. Ferrer de Valdecebro 1781, bk. 1, chap. 48, p. 102.

158. Ibid.

159. Ibid., bk. 1, chap. 49, p. 104.

continuing intercessory presence in the city. He is not interested in tracing the presence of Vincentian relics in Spain. Beyond the mention of the countess of Oropesa's cure from infertility, he recounts scarcely any contemporary miracles worked by the saint and none with the level of detail found in Antist's or Diago's works.[160] Although he mentions the work of other authors, Ferrer de Valdecebro refrains from the obsessive citation of sources seen in Antist and Diago. In short, his work lacks both the patriotic and the vehemently anti-Protestant orientation of the lives of the first half of the seventeenth century, offering instead a model of the good Catholic life. Given that fact, it is perhaps significant that, of all the lives of Vincent Ferrer, Ferrer de Valdecebro's most extensively quotes Vincent's own *Treatise on the Spiritual Life*.[161]

Although Vicente Justiniano Antist set the standard for a carefully authenticated treatment of Vincent's life, and Francisco Diago carried on and extended Antist's work, oddly enough, it was Ferrer de Valdecebro's *Life* of Vincent Ferrer that saw the greatest future success. After its initial printing in Madrid in 1682, the *History of the Marvelous and Admirable Life of the Second Paul, Apostle of Valencia, Saint Vincent Ferrer* went through seven additional editions in the course of the eighteenth century.[162] At least one of these made its way to Spain's New World colonies and rests today in the Chilean National Library.[163] For Spanish-speaking audiences, then, Ferrer de Valdecebro's treatment solidified a portrait of Vincent Ferrer as a divinely inspired preacher; converter of sinners, Jews, and Muslims; and healer—through his presence at the Council of Constance—of the Great Schism. Ferrer de Valdecebro's vision of Vincent's major works conforms to the image put forth in Pietro Ranzano's official post-canonization *vita* from 1456, but Ranzano's example can hardly have been the deciding influence on Ferrer de Valdecebro, who scarcely mentions the fifteenth-century Dominican's *Life*.[164] Still, like Ranzano before him, Ferrer de Valdecebro decided that to highlight Vincent's saintly life, he must present him not simply as the inspired preacher of the bull of canonization but also as a major force in the healing of the Great Schism. Ferrer de Valdecebro's depiction of Vincent as mending the Schism would prove to be a lasting one. A prayer

---

160. Aside from the countess of Oropesa, the only named recipient of a contemporary miracle is King Felipe IV, on whose behalf Vincent's intercession helped in the "miraculous restoration" of Naples to royal obedience. Ferrer de Valdecebro 1781, bk. 3, chap. 48, p. 215. There follow two chapters about a miraculous image of Vincent in the Balearic Islands, but no specific details emerge.

161. Particularly in Ferrer de Valdecebro 1781, bk. 2.

162. Enumerated in Robles Sierra 1999, xx.

163. Brown University possesses a microfilm of an exemplar from the Chilean National Library (Madrid: Antonio Perez do Soto, 1760).

164. Ranzano's *vita* would, however, appear in an edition of Vincent's works printed in Valencia a decade later. Vincent Ferrer 1693, [25]–[40].

on the devotional card one can buy in the Valencia cathedral today reads, "Your love for the Church made you apostle of its unity."[165]

## A Catholic Saint in a Divided Christendom

Sixteenth- and seventeenth-century hagiographers who composed lives of Vincent Ferrer each did so with a purpose in mind, whether it was Laurentius Surius's aim to prove the reality of miracles or the goal of a Francisco Diago or Albert Le Grand to further the cause of regional patriotism. Still, writing in the light of Protestant challenges to the cult of the saints and a reinvigorated post-Tridentine Catholicism, the authors examined above shared certain concerns. For many of them, faced with a Christendom torn by a far greater division than that of Vincent's years, highlighting the saint's role during the Great Schism of 1378–1414 was a primary concern. In addition, several of these authors were concerned to defend Vincent's reputation in areas that had come under attack in his own lifetime: his sponsorship of a group of penitential flagellants and his preaching about the imminent Last Judgment. Finally, whatever particular spin each of these hagiographers put on Vincent's life, they all found irresistible the tale of the saint and the chopped-up baby, which increasingly became Vincent's emblematic miracle.

It fell to the Spanish authors to greatly elaborate Vincent's role as a healer of the Schism. Laurentius Surius's life, closely based on Pietro Ranzano's official *vita,* merely echoed Ranzano's telling of the events of the Schism, a narration, as we have seen in chapter 4, in which Ranzano manipulated his chronology in order to magnify Vincent's role in mending the Schism and to downplay his adherence to the Avignon pope Benedict XIII.[166] Albert Le Grand, focused on Vincent's time in Brittany, paid no attention whatsoever to the Schism. But Vicente Justiniano Antist, committed both to historical accuracy and to lionizing his hero, confronted the issue more directly. For example, in Antist's telling, the 1398 vision of Christ that inaugurated Vincent's preaching mission came not simply in order that Jesus might heal Vincent's illness but also directly as a result of the saint's earnest prayers for a remedy to the Schism.[167] Furthermore, in a lengthy two-chapter digression, Antist took head-on those "who have expressed astonishment" that Saint Vincent took the side of Clement VII and Benedict XIII, "who, according to

---

165. "Tu amor a la Iglesia te hizo apóstol de su unidad." The biographical notice on the card (Dep. Leg. B-30.360–90; S-59/1) adds, "La Iglesia sufría el doloroso Cisma de Occidente, y él fué el gran apóstol de la Iglesia Una, Santa, Católica y Apostólica...y pudo ver la reunificación Pontificia en la persona del Papa Martin V."

166. Surius 1875–80, 4:186–89 (omitting Ranzano's description of the Council of Constance in II.1.7).

167. Antist 1956, pt. 1, chap. 5, p. 116.

the most common opinion, were schismatic popes and intruders."[168] Relating the entire history of the Schism from its start to its completion, Antist noted that God had often allowed such persecutions for the greater glory of the church (including "in our own times" that of "the terrible beast of Luther").[169] In some of these cases, it was not clear to observers who were the true popes and who were the antipopes. "Such is in my judgment," opined Antist, "the schism between Urban VI and Clement VII," adding that to his day "the Holy Mother Church does not hold it certainly determined which of the two was deceived." Accordingly, even though Antist was of the opinion that Urban's party had a better case for legitimacy, he concluded that "Saint Vincent did not sin in taking the side of Clement."[170] Furthermore, in his narration of the Schism's end, Antist made of Vincent's preaching against Benedict at Perpignan the pivotal moment, "something worthy of eternal memory," as he wrote.[171] Only those ignorant of the full story of the Schism would lay any blame on Vincent Ferrer, he concluded.[172]

Francisco Diago and Andrés Ferrer de Valdecebro, as in many other instances, followed Antist's example, adding their own elaborations. Diago echoed Antist's assertion that it was not certain which was the true pope, explaining that thus "they did not sin mortally" who followed one side or the other. But he also added a possibly disturbing quotation from a sermon Vincent preached in 1411, in which the saint informed his hearers, "And if you seek to know which be the true Pope of the three [including the Pisan line after 1409], I say that the Pope Benedict de Luna [is], which I know through the grace of God." Diago explained, however, that "this revelation was particular and does not obligate others to follow it and embrace it, to quit the obedience of the other two who held themselves for popes and to give it to Benedict."[173] In fact, since the church could not judge among the three contenders, each was obliged to resign the papacy for the good of Christianity. When Benedict refused, Vincent "showed himself to be truly a saint," by preaching against him in Perpignan.[174]

Ferrer de Valdecebro, as we have seen, went even further than Antist or Diago in defending Vincent's actions during the Schism years, most notably by insisting on his presence at the Council of Constance that ended the division. In so doing, he may have been following some directive from the center of the Dominican order. In the years after 1570, in the Dominican church of

---

168. Ibid., pt. 1, chap. 24, 187. The entire discussion is found in chaps. 24–25, pp. 187–97.
169. Ibid., 187–88 (quotation, 188).
170. Ibid., 189–90.
171. Ibid., pt. 1, chap. 25, pp. 194–95 (quotation, 194).
172. Ibid., 197.
173. Diago 2001, pt. 1, chap. 7, pp. 93–95 (quotations, 94, 95).
174. Ibid., 95–96 (quotation, 96).

Santa Maria sopra Minerva, the order's master general, Vincenzo Giustiniani, commissioned a chapel dedicated to Vincent Ferrer. The chapel's altarpiece, painted by Bernardo Castello some time around 1584, depicts Saint Vincent Ferrer at the Council of Constance.[175] (See figure 15.) Closer to Ferrer de Valdecebro's time, in 1675, the Dominican scholar and prior of the Minerva Vincentio Maria Fontana published his *Monuments of the Dominican Order,* in which the saint also was said to have played a defining role at the Council of Constance.[176] The notion of Vincent Ferrer's assisting at the council can also be found in some modern hagiography, perhaps a testament to the wide and lasting influence of Ferrer de Valdecebro's biography.[177]

If Vincent's adherence to the "wrong" side in the Great Schism was the most glaring problem addressed by sixteenth- and seventeenth-century authors of his *vitae,* a number of these authors also felt compelled to defend his sponsorship of a band of flagellants that followed him on his preaching tour. Antist, again, set the tone for the later authors, since Le Grand had ignored the topic and Surius, following Pietro Ranzano's lead, had done little more than to mention approvingly the extreme penitence Vincent inspired in his followers and to note that he had instructed that the crowd should be arranged in an orderly fashion, with men and women and clerics and laypeople kept separate.[178] The more honest and thorough Antist admitted, however, that Jean Gerson had written a letter to Vincent reproving him for his band of flagellants. But, Antist explained, "while Pope Gregory X ruled the Church, a good hundred and forty years before the Council of Constance," there had arisen in Italy a heretical sect "who publicly flagellated themselves." Since Vincent had a number of flagellants among his followers, "some people," including Gerson, suspected that they were of the same heretical bent. Not so, said Antist. Those former heretical flagellants despised the sacraments of the church, whereas Vincent's flagellants partook of the sacraments as frequently as possible and hastened to obey their prelates and bishops.[179] Francisco Diago echoed Antist's line of defense and added that in an Advent sermon preached in Castile, Vincent had proclaimed that one who reprehended this "discipline" was a minister of Antichrist.[180] Ferrer de Valdecebro, in his own elaboration, asserted that the

---

175. See Galassi 1996.

176. Fontana 1675, pt. 2, chap. 12, anno 1417, 301. Fontana's other entries on Vincent Ferrer, scattered throughout his annals, stress Vincent's conversions of Jews, Muslims, and sinners, his work to end the Schism, and his role in the Compromise of Caspe. On Fontana, see Busolini 1997.

177. E.g., *The Book of Saints* 1994, 568.

178. Surius 1875–80, 4:192–93 (following RVV, 1:494).

179. Antist 1956, pt. 1, chap. 30, p. 231.

180. Diago 2001, bk. 1, chap. 9, pp. 129–31 (quotation, 130–31). He continues to quote from another Advent sermon in which Vincent says that the great penitence of the flagellants was a sign that the Day of Judgment and end of the world were not far off (131). He adds a comment on the

**Figure 15.**    Bernardo Castello, *Saint Vincent Ferrer Assisting at the Council of Constance*. Guistiniani chapel, Santa Maria sopra Minerva, Rome. Photo courtesy Jason G. Smoller. This ca. 1584 painting depicting Vincent at the Council of Constance illustrates a line of interpretation pushed by Pietro Ranzano, which viewed Vincent as instrumental in healing the Great Schism, resolved by the council's actions. Although Vincent never attended the council, Johannes Trithemius in 1494 had written that the preacher had been there.

public penitence Vincent urged on sinners, far from representing a dangerous novelty, was "reviving the ancient style of the Church…in the manner that today is done in all Christendom during Holy Week, Lent, and some other days in the year such as the feasts of the Holy Cross."[181] In fact, the

flagellants in book 2, chapter 1, page 500, stressing, as had Antist, that the members of the flagellant band took frequent communion.

181. Ferrer de Valdecebro 1781, bk. 1, chap. 22, p. 40.

baseless attack on Vincent's flagellants was caused by "the ardor of envy" and the work of "the devil," which inspired the envious to tell the Council of Constance that Vincent had revived the heretical flagellant sect of old.[182]

Post-Tridentine authors also devoted their attention to defending Vincent's apocalyptic preaching, for although Pietro Ranzano and Antoninus of Florence had mentioned the suspicion of Vincent's disseminating "novelties," the bull of canonization, iconography, and other hagiographical traditions had stressed his self-identification as the angel of the apocalypse. Ranzano and other fifteenth-century authors had excused Vincent in part by pointing to the authorizing vision in which Christ had commanded him to go forth and preach the imminence of the Last Judgment. In a lengthy defense of Vincent's apocalyptic preaching, Antist pointed as well to that vision but also admitted that Vincent's pronouncement that the apocalypse would come "soon and very soon" could seem a little suspect when more than 150 years later "we still have not seen the birth of Antichrist."[183] Seventeenth-century authors also added a second supernatural confirmation to Vincent's apocalyptic preaching. In Antist's rendition, when Vincent was preaching at the Dominican convent of St. Stephen in Salamanca, he announced that he was that angel from the Book of Revelation who proclaims, "Fear God and give him honor, for the hour of his judgment is at hand" (Rev. 14:7). In proof, he resuscitated a dead woman at the portal of Saint Paul.[184] Francisco Diago repeated this miracle tale and explicitly mentioned it as well in the context of his defense of Vincent's role as "ambassador or herald of the Judgment."[185] Ferrer de Valdecebro elaborated even further, adding vivid dialogue between the saint and the resurrected woman of Salamanca.[186]

One area in which all the major post-Tridentine authors of Vincent's biography agreed was in the primacy accorded to the miraculous restoration of the chopped-up baby. Yet with their commitment to historical authenticity and the discovery of new sources for Vincent's life, the authors

---

182. Ibid., bk. 1, chap. 23, p. 42. Interestingly, Matthieu-Maxime Gorce lists two sixteenth-century editions (1545 in Castilian and 1547 in Catalan), now lost, of a "rule for the *disciplinati*" attributed to Vincent Ferrer, perhaps also evidence of a move to exonerate Vincent's reputation on this sore point. Gorce 1923, 11.

183. Antist 1956, pt. 1, chap. 28, 213–16 (quotations, 213 and 214). Antist's defense rested on the meaning of "soon," when measured against the standard of eternity, as well as the distinction between "definitive" and "denunciatory" (conditional) pronouncements.

184. Ibid., pt. 1, chap. 19, pp. 172–73; the story is also briefly mentioned in a 1578 sermon for the Feast of Vincent Ferrer preached at the saint's birthplace by Antist's master Luis Bertrán. Ortuño Soriano 2005, 143; Bertrán 1690, 206–7.

185. Diago 2001, bk. 1, chap. 9, pp. 114–15; chap. 22, pp. 267–68.

186. Ferrer de Valdecebro 1781, bk. 1, chap. 32, pp. 64–65. The newly founded Jesuit order, interestingly, also seized upon the notion of Vincent as apocalyptic prophet, interpreting as a reference to the Jesuit order his prediction (in the letter to Benedict XIII as well as in *On the Spiritual Life*) of the appearance of new evangelical men who would preach the Gospel throughout the world prior to the Second Coming. Reeves 1969, 275–80.

we have examined offered very different takes on the story. Although, as we have seen, the tale had appeared in the canonization inquests as a post-mortem miracle, with the central scenes taking place at Vincent's tomb in Brittany, Pietro Ranzano had shifted the miracle to the saint's own lifetime and to an unnamed location in Languedoc.[187] Surius, basing his text on Ranzano's *Life of Vincent,* followed the Sicilian Dominican in making the miracle one worked by the living Vincent Ferrer. But he placed the miracle neither in Ranzano's Languedoc nor in the Brittany of the canonization inquests. Rather, for Surius, the miracle had happened in the Spanish town of Morella ("not a great distance from Valencia"), where today one can still visit the house in which the gruesome events are said to have occurred. (See Figure 16.)[188]

Both Vicente Justiniano Antist, working from his copy of the canonization inquests, and Albert Le Grand, following the narration in Antoninus of Florence's biography of Vincent, present the miracle as one effected in Brittany after the saint's death. Antist's telling would have a great influence on later Spanish authors. Antist notes that the tale of the chopped-up baby could be found three times in the canonization process and repeats the basic narrative from the inquests: a tale of a crazed pregnant woman, craving human flesh, who butchered and cooked her own infant son. Antist also expands upon a detail found in the inquests[189]—namely, that in thanks for such a great miracle, the father later dedicated his son to the service of the church in which Vincent's tomb lay.[190] As Antist much later informs his readers, the son went on to become a Dominican friar and preached extensively in Sicily, promoting the cult of Vincent Ferrer. His words were reinforced by the "colored signs of his division" that he exhibited to his audience in confirmation of the saint's miraculous powers.[191] Still, Antist, ever the careful scholar, also acknowledges the competing versions of the story, citing Flamini, Surius, and Claudius Rota as all describing a miracle worked *during* Vincent's life that is "very similar." But Antist raises some doubts about this version by noting that there are some contradictions among these three authors (who place the miracle in Languedoc, Morella, and Toulouse, respectively). Perhaps, he opines, the carelessness of printers can explain these discrepancies, but the reader is also left with some doubts about the veracity of the *in vita* narration of the tale. And, whether by choice or out of ignorance, Antist fails to include Pietro Ranzano as presenting a similar miracle in the saint's own life.[192]

---

187. See chapter 4.
188. Surius 1875–80, 4:207.
189. *Proceso,* fol. 260r–260v; FPC, 442 (witness 18).
190. Antist 1956, pt. 2, chap. 9, p. 275.
191. Ibid., pt. 2, chap. 36, p. 322.
192. Ibid., pt. 2, chap. 9, p. 275.

**FIGURE 16.** Mosaic over doorway commemorating the miracle of the chopped-up baby. Casa della Rovira, Morella. Photo courtesy Jason G. Smoller. The caption of this mosaic reads, "In this house, Saint Vincent Ferrer worked the prodigious miracle of the resurrection of a child whose insane mother cut him up and cooked him to present to the saint. (1414)." In keeping with the claim, as attested in Laurentius Surius's life of Vincent, that the miracle had happened in Morella, members of a local family were identified as the protagonists of the tale.

Francisco Diago and Andrés Ferrer de Valdecebro largely follow Antist's telling of the chopped-up baby story. For Diago, this tale represents "the most principal of the miracles worked in restoring life to the dead" by Saint Vincent after his death, and he, too, completes the miracle story with the tale of the boy's career as a Dominican preacher in Sicily.[193] Ferrer de Valdecebro also sets the story after Vincent's death. Simultaneously acknowledging and

---

193. Diago 2001, bk. 1, chap. 38, pp. 436–37.

dismissing the alternate version of the tale, Ferrer de Valdecebro states, "Some with intelligence say that Saint Vincent worked [this miracle] while alive, but without good reasons."[194] As with Antist and Diago, the boy goes on to become a Dominican preacher in Sicily, but now in Ferrer de Valdecebro's telling, his wounds continue miraculously to bleed as a sign of the saint's power.[195] This equation of the chopped-up baby with a Sicilian Dominican evidently was known beyond Spanish circles, for in Fontana's *Monuments of the Dominican Order*, an entry for the year 1466 highlights "Vincentius Pistoya" in Sicily, a preacher and disciple of Vincent Ferrer, who "was that little boy who was divided through the middle, roasted, and put on the table for a meal by an insane mother; by Saint Vincent at once he was resuscitated."[196] It is possible that Fontana, Antist, and his followers were thinking of the fifteenth-century Dominican Giovanni da Pistoia, to whom Pietro Ranzano sent an abridged version of his life of Vincent to aid in his preaching. But there is no evidence that this Giovanni was in truth the chopped-up baby, and it seems unlikely that Ranzano would have failed to mention such a fact in his letter to Giovanni.[197]

By far the most lurid version of the chopped-up baby miracle appears in Bernard Guyard's 1634 *Life of Saint Vincent Ferrer*, where the narration takes up seven pages of text, heading a chapter "On the dead that he resuscitated."[198] After promising his readers a story that would engender "horror, pity, and admiration," Guyard proceeded to lay out an elaborated version of Surius's tale of the insane mother in Morella and the ghastly meal she prepared for the saint. Once again, the mother seized—"Oh! thing of horror," exclaims Guyard—her young son to butcher. But in Guyard's telling, the mother now deftly cut off the baby's "head, hands, and feet," placing them in a pot to boil, threading the remaining trunk onto a spit to roast. Once again, she proudly offered the saint "very choice and delicate meat," and, once again, her husband berated her for forgetting that the preacher ate only fish, subsequently bursting into the kitchen to spy "his son roasting on the spit" and the babe's discolored hair and "a leg half sticking out of the kettle." The saint, calling for all the pieces of the boy to be brought to him, was presented with "one boiled part, and the other roasted." At the saint's prayers, again, the parts marvelously reunited themselves, and "everyone stood admiring"

---

194. Ferrer de Valdecebro 1781, bk. 4, chap. 44, pp. 205–6 (quotation, 205).

195. Ibid., 205.

196. Fontana 1675, pt. 3, chap. 6, anno 1466, 361. Fontana implies that the miracle was worked during the saint's lifetime.

197. See chapter 4 for details on Ranzano's letter to Giovanni. For a modern author's reporting this tradition, see Barilaro 1977–78, 44n143. Giovanni's identification with the chopped-up baby is not mentioned in Longo 2000. Fages (FHSVF, 2:424–25), like Fontana, equates the chopped-up baby with a "Vincent Pistoia" (who he appears to believe was a different person from Giovanni da Pistoia), disciple of Vincent Ferrer, apostolic preacher to Sicily, and converter of many Jews.

198. Guyard 1634, 148. The tale appears at 149–55.

at the miracle. "You should not expect, nor can I present you with a greater [miracle]," Guyard assured his readers. This time, however, no residual scars marked the baby for life; nor did Guyard allude to his future career. The restored baby stood, simply, as an emblem of Vincent's powerful intercession, "the touchstone and miracle of miracles."[199]

Despite the differences in their narrations, hagiographers of the Counter-Reformation era were unanimous in viewing the restoration of the chopped-up baby as one of Vincent Ferrer's most important miracles. Artistic representations of the saint confirm the central place of this miracle in the lore of Vincent Ferrer. Although most sixteenth- and seventeenth-century authors insisted that the baby's restoration was, as in the canonization inquests, a postmortem miracle, artists could not resist depicting the saint himself with the chopped-up baby. So, for example, in a now-lost painting formerly in the Musée du Hiéron and attributed to Lucas de Leyde (1494–1533), an anxious mother and father kneel as the saint prays over a platter holding the once-cooked child. (See figure 1.)[200] A canvas by the Valencian Gaspar de la Huerta (1645–1714) depicts the moment just after the child's resuscitation; as onlookers clearly marvel at the great miracle they have just witnessed, the boy stands facing the saint, arms folded, his feet still on the platter on which he had been served.[201] In later paintings and engravings, the baby serves simply as an emblem of the saint—as, for example, in a pair of baroque engravings preserved in the Bibliothèque nationale de France, where a child with Guyard's cooking spit crouches next to the saint (figure 17);[202] in an eighteenth-century engraving by the Augsburg workshop of Joseph and Johannes Klauber (figure 18); and in a painting in San Sisto Vecchio in Rome, where a child kneels at Vincent's feet beside a platter full of baby parts.[203]

---

199. Ibid., 149, 150, 152, 153, 148 (resuscitation of the dead as touchstone). In the second part of his biography (337–38), containing a listing of miracles from Brittany, Guyard does mention the postmortem version of the tale as related in the Brittany canonization inquest, but he does not draw any connection between the two miracles.

200. I am grateful to the staff of the Musée du Hiéron for providing me with a photograph of the lost painting.

201. *San Vicente Ferrer en el milagro del niño de Morella,* Museo de Bellas Artes de Valencia. Similarly, a painting by Sebastiano Ricci (1678–1734) depicts the reconstituted child on a serving platter, the saint bending over him in blessing. Fondazione Federico Zeri 2012c. The composition was evidently picked up by Gasparo Diziani (1689–1767) for a similar canvas, now in a private collection. Bridgeman Art Library Limited 1972–2013.

202. I. De Schoore, after A. Sallaerts, *S. Vincentius Ferrerius,* engraving. BNF, Département des estampes et de la photographie, microfilm no. H 181632; Pierre Mariette I, *Sanctus Ferrerius,* Typis P. Mariette, via Iacobea sub sig. Spei, engraving, microfilm no. H 181630, derived from Schoore's work. The engravings have texts in French and Flemish. Schoore was active in the seventeenth century, Sallaerts around 1620; Mariette died in 1657 and was active at the via Iacobea address in Paris after 1632. Strutt 1785–86, 1:293, 296, 308; British Museum 2013.

203. Reproduced at Domínicos Chile 2012, http://www.dominicos.net/santos/san_vicente_ferrer/215_san_vincenzo_ferreris_san_sisto_pala_d'altare.html.

**FIGURE 17.** I. De Schoore, after A. Sallaerts, *S. Vincentius Ferrerius*. Bibliothèque nationale de France, Département des estampes et de la photographie (microfilm no. H 181632). Paris. Courtesy of Bibliothèque nationale de France. In this seventeenth-century engraving, Vincent is portrayed with apocalyptic imagery (a vision showing the Last Trumpet and Christ in judgment; the text from Revelation 14:7) and with a nod to the miracle of the chopped-up baby. Here the child kneels holding the cooking spit on which he was roasted, just as described in Bernard Guyard's narration.

**FIGURE 18.** Workshop of Joseph and Johannes Klauber, *S. Vincentius Fererius*. Augsburg. From G. Schreiber 1936, no. 112. In this eighteenth-century engraving, Vincent is said to be resplendent in virtues, doctrine, and prodigies. A flagellant's whip serves as emblem of the saint's virtues. Exotic figures underneath the heading *Doctrina* point to Vincent's apostolic teaching, his gift of tongues, and his conversion of thousands to the Christian faith. Illustrating Vincent's prodigies, an angel holds a platter on which are stacked the dismembered parts of the chopped-up baby.

The popularity of this arresting miracle tale perhaps requires no explanation. Authors clearly enjoyed retelling and embellishing the story with
details that pulled at the reader's emotions. In Ferrer de Valdecebro's narration, for example, when the father returned home to find his partially
cooked son, "he went cold and stiff as an icicle from grief."[204] Guyard invited
his readers to imagine "the head of a little innocent with blond hair, boiling in hot cauldron" and to feel the horror of seeing "a delicate little body
chopped up and put on a spit, spilling its grease into a drip-pan like a roast
of lamb."[205] To add such flights was almost irresistible to many writers. But
it seems equally possible that the appeal of the miracle of the chopped-up
baby also spoke to the specific aims of Counter-Reformation hagiography.
If their Protestant neighbors could scoff that the age of miracles was over,
faithful Catholics could boast of the divine intercession that had restored the
butchered and stewed flesh of a human infant—one who went on to preach
the virtues of the saint who had resuscitated him. And if, in Pietro Ranzano's day, Vincent's recomposition of the chopped-up baby could symbolize
his role in healing a church divided, Catholic readers and viewers in the sixteenth and seventeenth centuries yearned even more to see a united Christendom miraculously restored to its pristine wholeness. And as the various
geographical permutations of the story indicate, the addition or alteration
of a detail here or there could associate the saint's most famous miracle with
communities as far-flung as Brittany, Spain, and Sicily.

Interestingly enough, aside from Laurentius Surius, most sixteenth- and
seventeenth-century authors did not base their tellings of this miracle tale
or their biographies of Vincent Ferrer on the official life penned by Pietro
Ranzano and commissioned by the pope and the head of the Dominican
order after Vincent's canonization. Nonetheless, by the end of the seventeenth century, the major outlines of Vincent's hagiography echoed the
themes emphasized by the fifteenth-century Dominican: his extraordinarily
effective preaching, his ability to move sinners to penitence by pointing to
the imminent Last Judgment, his success in converting Muslims and Jews, his
dramatic intercessory powers, and his key role in healing the Great Schism.
Ranzano's image of Vincent Ferrer in some respects triumphed in spite of
its patrons' intentions, as Ranzano's *vita* of the saint was not printed in full
until the Bollandists made it the standard life of Vincent by incorporating
it into the *Acta Sanctorum* in 1675.[206] Still, as post-Tridentine authors sought
to rewrite the life of Vincent in accordance with new, tighter standards for

---

204. Ferrer de Valdecebro 1781, bk. 4, chap. 44, p. 205.

205. Guyard 1634, 151.

206. The AASS was issued starting in 1643. The volume containing Vincent's dossier (Aprilis,
vol. 1) was published in Antwerp in 1675. Ranzano's *vita* was also published with a volume of
Vincent's works in 1693. See note 164.

hagiography, they found themselves drawn to the same areas highlighted in Ranzano's *vita*. Scrupulous hagiographers like Antist and his followers offered even fuller defenses than had fifteenth-century authors of Vincent's apocalyptic pronouncements, his encouragement of flagellant processions, and his actions in the matter of the Schism. By the end of the seventeenth century, an author like Ferrer de Valdecebro could emphatically assert that Vincent *had* to have participated in the Council of Constance.[207]

Still, just as the newly canonized Vincent represented a symbol still to be defined in the late fifteenth century, post-Tridentine authors also managed to put their own stamps on the saint's image. As in so many other Catholic regions, Vincent Ferrer became for his native Valencia as well as for his resting place of Brittany an emblem of an unbroken chain of local sanctity stretching from the days of the primitive church through to the present. Key to these demonstrations was the continued presence of the saint's miraculous activity, in some instances fanned by the arrival of a new relic, the erection of a new chapel, or a ceremonial authentication of the saint's relics. The tale of the chopped-up baby remained a key component in this advertising of Vincent's intercessory abilities. Yet the imposition of Counter-Reformation ideals was far from the top-down operation historians once envisioned.[208] Although hagiographers brought new critical rigor to the writing of saints' lives, they were still able to press Vincent's story into the service of local assertions of identity, as once-independent regions like Aragon and Brittany were subsumed into the powerful monarchical states of the early modern world. Even as the historical Vincent Ferrer gradually became the Saint Vincent Ferrer that one might find on a modern devotional card, the saint remained a powerful symbol with which individuals, cities, and regions could make claims about their own identities.

---

207. In 1555, at the Valencian festivities celebrating the hundredth anniversary of Vincent's canonization, banners depicted his preaching to "Moors and Jews, and to others who were listening to him." Antist 1956, pt. 2, chap. 34, p. 313. But at the bicentennial in 1655, the altar at the Valencian church of St. Martin displayed three images: in the middle, John on the island of Patmos, clearly a reference to Vincent's role as angel of the apocalypse; on the right, the miraculous conversion of the synagogue at Salamanca, a nod to his role in converting thousands of Jews; and on the left, the restoration of the chopped-up baby. FHSVF, 2:401. See also Escartí 1997.

208. For critiques of that older view, see, e.g., Tingle 2005, Harline and Put 2002.

# Epilogue

# Saint Vincent Ferrer
# in the Spanish Americas

As Iberian explorers sailed westward across the Atlantic Ocean, they brought their Catholic faith with them. The sails of Columbus's vessels were painted with religious images, while millennial dreams fired the imagination of the admiral who came to see himself as *Christo-ferens,* Christ-bearer. By papal decree, the claims of Portugal and Spain to lands in the New World rested upon their acceptance of the charge to bring Christianity to the peoples they found there. In turn, the church functioned in many ways as an arm of the state in Spanish colonies. Still, if the oft-cited triad "gold, God, and glory" lays bare the mercenary motives behind many of the Spanish conquistadors, it also acknowledges the sense of mission, often tinged with apocalyptic fervor, that inspired the clergy who accompanied them.[1] Among the numerous cargoes of books that arrived in Latin American ports to support the clergy's task were the lives of saints: saints who inspired and served as role models for both missionaries and their converts, saints who mediated between native and European religious traditions, saints whose examples became fodder in political conflicts, and saints whose intercession offered hope and succor to the faithful.[2]

Although the Franciscans and Jesuits were the most prominently represented among the religious orders who served as New World missionaries,

---

1. Nice overview in Bakewell and Holler 2010, 97–108, 171–94. On Columbus: Watts 1985, 74, 95–102.

2. Greer and Bilinkoff 2003. E.g., Saint Anne, mother of the Virgin, was equated with the Aztec goddess Toci, "Our Grandmother." Black 2003, 22–24.

Vincent's own Order of Preachers played a major role—and in some regions constituted the dominant presence—in the Americas. Dominican friars, naturally, looked to and promoted the example of their brother saint, particularly since Vincent was known as a new apostle whose effective preaching had converted tens of thousands of souls to the Christian faith in Europe. As Dominicans established missions and provinces in the Americas, the sainted Valencian preacher was not forgotten. But while in Europe, by the eighteenth century, biographies of Vincent Ferrer had come to echo Pietro Ranzano's portrait of the saint as healer of the Schism and converter of Jews and Muslims, the predominant view of him in colonial Latin America was as a miracle worker and the angel of the apocalypse. True, works that issued from presses in New Spain and Peru demonstrate that Vincent served to inspire fellow Dominicans as they worked to Christianize indigenous populations, but more important, they indicate his significance as an intercessor and miracle worker for the Catholic faithful. In Latin American art, Vincent Ferrer is typically associated with his apocalyptic preaching, but a handful of paintings survive that also allude to his many miracles. Among them, predictably, numbers the tale of the saint and the chopped-up baby.

## Dominican Implantation in the Spanish Colonies

The first Dominican missionaries in the New World arrived on the island of Hispaniola in 1510. They almost immediately set themselves up as advocates for and protectors of the indigenous peoples whom they sought to convert, a position that often put the friars at odds with Spanish settlers and the crown. Antonio de Montesinos, for example, was compelled to return to Spain to answer for a sermon he preached on December 21, 1511, pointing out the abuses of the Spanish forced labor system on the island and asserting the basic humanity and rights of the natives.[3] Bartolomé de las Casas, who later would become the best known "protector of the Indians," took inspiration from Montesinos's words, entering the Dominican order in 1523. The Dominican convent established in Santo Domingo, Hispaniola, became the basis of and staging point for the order's expansion into other Spanish possessions. Most notably, a group of twelve friars—a number chosen for its apostolic resonance—arrived in the newly conquered territory of Mexico on June 24, 1526, to announce the advent of Christ, just as had John the Baptist, the saint on whose feast day they had landed.[4]

---

3. M. A. Medina 1992, 15–17; Schwaller 2008, 2:848; Gibson 1966, 75–76.

4. As pointed out by Lara 2004, 67. The group did not fare well; five died within the year and four returned to Spain by the year's end. See Schwaller 2008, 2:848; and Ricard 1974, 22, who places the friars' arrival on July 2. The first Franciscan mission also consisted of twelve friars.

Although evangelization of the natives was the primary motivation for Dominican expansion in the Spanish colonies, the friars were also aware of their more traditional roles vis-à-vis the Spanish and eventually the Creole population there, creating networks of schools and universities and serving the pastoral needs of their flocks in the absence of a developed parochial system. By 1530, the first Dominican province in the New World had been created, that of Santa Cruz de las Indias. Large numbers of Spanish friars emigrated to Spain's possessions in the Americas, as well as to the Philippines, inspired by examples such as that of the Valencian saint Luis Bertrán (1526–81, canonized 1671), considered a relative of Vincent Ferrer and possessed, like his progenitor, of the gift of tongues. Bertrán spent a number of years as a missionary in South America and in 1690 was proclaimed principal patron of New Granada.[5] By the early eighteenth century the number of Dominican provinces in the Spanish colonies would swell to ten, with an eleventh carved out in 1807. The fourth of these provinces, founded in 1551, was the province of San Vicente Ferrer de Chiapa y Guatemala,[6] one of only three provinces named in honor of Dominican saints (the other two honored Antoninus of Florence and Catherine of Siena). It is difficult to know exactly what guided the Dominicans in choosing the names of their American provinces, but it is tempting to think that Vincent's apostolic preaching, along with his Spanish origins, recommended him for this honor.[7]

The Dominicans' presence was particularly strong in the region of the diocese of Oaxaca, in the southeast of Mexico, where they constituted the sole religious order serving as missionaries to the Mixteca and Zapoteca peoples there.[8] By 1569 a string of Dominican houses and convents, each a day's journey distant from the next, linked the route from Mexico City to Oaxaca. As in every place they went, the friars worked to learn the natives' languages. By the mid-sixteenth century, Dominican authors were publishing bilingual books containing the elements of the Christian faith, guides for confession, and compendia of sermons; Dominican friars also composed introductions to the rosary, songs, and plays on saints' lives in indigenous

---

5. Robles Sierra 1991, 269–70; J. T. Medina 1919, 49–55. Antist, one of Vincent Ferrer's sixteenth-century biographers, also wrote a life of Luis Bertrán.

6. Arenas Frutos and Cebrian Gonzalez 1991, 7. The eighteenth-century Dominican Francisco Ximénez wrote a history of the province. Ximénez 1999.

7. Two of the provinces were named after other Spanish saints: Santiago de Mexico and San Lorenzo Mártir de Chile. Other names point toward the conversion of non-Christians, the announcing of Christ, or the refuting of heretics: San Hipólito Mártir de Oaxaca, San Juan Bautista del Perú, and San Augustín de Buenos Aires. Augustine was also important to the order because the Order of Preachers followed the Rule of Saint Augustine.

8. M. A. Medina 1992, 74–75.

vernaculars.[9] In the province of San Vicente, regulations specified that no Dominican friar arriving from Spain, however mature or learned he might be, would be allowed to preach to or to hear the confessions of the natives until he had learned their language. In 1646, the provincial could boast that friars in the province of San Vicente were working in as many as seventeen different indigenous tongues.[10] Perhaps their patron's apostolic gift of tongues inspired the Dominicans of New Spain as they sought to master strange new languages. A number of churches and Dominican houses in the region, including foundations in Chimalhuacán and Juchitán, were dedicated to Vincent Ferrer.[11]

A second area of relative strength was in the lands of the former Inca Empire. A Dominican friar, Vicente de Valverde, accompanied Pizarro in the conquest of Cuzco, the Inca capital; in turn, he became the capital's first bishop. The order's formal establishment in the region came in 1540, with the creation of the province of San Juan Bautista del Perú. By the time of the province's first chapter general in 1544, there were forty-seven friars in the province, with key convents in Lima, Cuzco, and Arequipa, and the Dominicans were busily sharing little primers (*cartillas*) on the Quechua language. In 1560, Domingo de Santo Tomás published, in Vallodolid, the first Quechua grammar, of which he imported 1,500 copies to Peru for the friars' use.[12] In Cuzco, the order received the Qorikancha, the Inca Temple of the Sun, on which to build their convent of Santo Domingo, prompting one seventeenth-century chronicler to exult, "[Pizarro] handed over the famous Temple of the Sun of the Indians to the sacred Order of Preachers. [This] occur[red] happily, so advantageously; the gold of the sun of Lucifer, [became] the diamond of the star of Domingo."[13] Farther south, the Dominicans were the first religious order established in Chile, with the 1557 foundation of Nuestra Señora del Rosario in Santiago. On the city's outskirts in Apoquindo, the former convent and Iglesia de

---

9. Ibid., 98–105.

10. Ibid., 158.

11. Ibid., 73 (Chimalhuacán); López Sanmartín 2005. Juchitán was part of the province of San Vicente Ferrer from 1551 through 1555, after which it came under the sway of the province of Santiago; according to López Sanmartín, Vincent Ferrer was designated as the town's patron in 1551 (35). Today, the town is known, among other things, for its festival celebrating the town's *muxes* (a Zapotec word for a man who dresses as a woman or adopts feminine roles). Local legend has it that God gave Saint Vincent Ferrer a bag of *muxes* to distribute throughout Mexico, but when he arrived in Juchitán, the *muxes* exuberantly burst forth from the bag and settled in the town. Vrana 2007–8 and Gage 2005. (López Sanmartín 2005, 96, is somewhat troubled by this legend.) See also Stephen 2002, esp. 42–44 on the *muxes* of Juchitán.

12. M. A. Medina 1992, 233. That is, his *Grammatica o Arte de la lengua general de los Indios de los Reynos del Peru*.

13. J. Mogrovejo de la Cerda, quoted in Redden 2008, 19 (Redden's translation).

San Vicente Ferrer is now a national landmark.[14] The Dominicans particularly distinguished themselves in seventeenth-century Lima. The first canonized saint from the Americas, Rosa de Lima, was a Dominican tertiary, and three other seventeenth-century Dominicans from the city eventually received papal canonization or beatification.[15] By the mid-sixteenth century, friars from the Order of Preachers were also present in the territory of modern Argentina, a region that formed the heart of the province of San Augustín de Buenos Aires created in 1724.[16]

With the passage of time, the friars' emphasis shifted from missionary work proper to the pastoral care of Spaniards and Creoles in the cities, along with the task of effectively Christianizing indigenous converts whose covert adherence to traditional religious practices was constantly suspected. Only the frontiers remained centers of true missionary activity, and after the expulsion of the Jesuits from Spanish lands in 1767, the Dominicans played an important role in these regions. The order took over Jesuit establishments and built new missions in Baja California in the late eighteenth century. The largest of these was that of San Vicente Ferrer, established in 1780.[17] Wherever Dominican missionaries went, the memory of Vincent Ferrer was not far behind.

## The Evidence from Print

But which Vincent Ferrer did colonial Latin Americans venerate? Of the many visions of the saint presented in lives from the fifteenth through the seventeenth centuries, which ones caught on in Spain's American colonies? What little evidence survives regarding the holdings of colonial libraries offers at least a glimpse of the variety of portrayals of the saint available to readers in the New World: Dominican breviaries, likely containing some version of Ranzano's lessons on Vincent's life;[18] a smattering of Vincent's own writings;[19] the 1599 compendium of saints' lives, including Vincent's, penned by the Jesuit Pedro de Ribadeneyra;[20] Andrés Ferrer de Valdecebro's

---

14. Ramirez 1979, 17, 158.

15. On Rosa of Lima, see Myers 2003. Dominican saints from Lima: Schwaller 2008, 2:849 (Martín de Porres, 1579–1639, canonized 1962; Juan Macias, 1585–1645, beatified 1837; and Mariana de Jesús Paredes, 1618–1645, canonized 1950).

16. M. A. Medina 1992, 294. The new province included convents from Buenos Aires, Tucumán, and Paraguay.

17. Rodríguez 1992; Nieser 1998; Barrón Escamillo 1980.

18. M. A. Medina 1992, 53, attests to breviaries' being brought over from Spain for the friars' use.

19. In Argentina, in the Dominican house in Córdoba. Llamosas and Tagle de Cuenca 2004, 187: Vicentius Ferrer, *Epitome cursus theologici ad mente D. Thomae Doctoris Angelici* (Valencia: Antonius Bordazar, 1720); and another edition of the same (Valencia: Antonio Badle, 1725).

20. The following entry in the catalog of the Biblioteca Nacional de Chile lists as its provenence the Colegio de San Miguel de la Compañia de Jesús: *Flos sanctorum, o, libro de las vidas de los santos / escrito por el padre de Ribadeneyra…* (Barcelona: Vicente Suria, 1688). I have consulted

1682 biography of the saint;[21] and a 1724 life of Vincent composed by Dominican Ignacio Catoyra.[22] There were doubtless other biographies of the saint available to Latin American clergy, who imported vast numbers of books from Europe to assist them in their duties.[23] From the *vitae* known to have been in Latin American libraries, one could glean a portrait of Vincent Ferrer as a dynamic preacher who, as the angel of the apocalypse, announced the imminence of the Last Judgment and whose fiery rhetoric converted thousands of Muslims and Jews to the Christian faith. Readers would also have learned that Vincent played an active role in healing the Great Schism, particularly as described in the biography by Andrés Ferrer de Valdecebro, who had insisted that the holy friar had attended the Council of Constance. And they would have encountered abundant tales of Vincent's miraculous intercession, among them the tale of the chopped-up baby, recounted both as a postmortem miracle and as a miracle worked by the living saint. This prodigy is in fact the sole miracle related by Pedro de Ribadeneyra, whose narration closely follows that of Laurentius Surius, naming Morella as the location in which Vincent restored the partially cooked infant prepared for his own repast.[24]

The titles and colophons of books printed by colonial Latin American presses shed further light on the ways in which Catholics in the Spanish colonies understood and related to Vincent Ferrer.[25] The earliest of these to which I have found reference is a Latin edition of the *Office for the Feast of Saint Vincent Ferrer,* printed in Mexico City in 1670. The copy of this book in the Biblioteca Nacional de Chile is bound together with the Latin *Office of Saint Canute* (King Canute IV of Denmark, d. 1086) from the same press, issued two years later.[26] The Latin text and the unusual pairing suggest a work aimed at the clergy, although tradition dictated that the laity attend at least matins on a saint's feast day, at which the saint's biography would

Ribadeneyra 1734, 1:475–86. Ribadeneyra's life roughly follows, in its first sections, the sort of presentation found in Ranzano's and Surius's *vitae,* but it is his own composition.

21. There are five seventeenth- and eighteenth-century editions of this work in the collection of the Biblioteca Nacional de Chile in Santiago (1682, 1729, 1760, 1771, and 1791), perhaps all originating in colonial libraries.

22. In Argentina, in the Dominican house in Córdoba. Llamosas and Tagle de Cuenca 2004, 182: Ignacio Catroya, *Ilustraciones a las maravillas del apóstol de Valencia S. Vicente de Ferrer,* 2 vols. (Seville: Francisco Sánchez Reciente, 1724).

23. M. A. Medina 1992, 53–54, 130–32.

24. Ribadeneyra 1734, 1:481.

25. I am relying here primarily on the not yet complete CCILA (Catálogo Colectivo de Impresos Latinoamericanos), http://ccila.ucr.edu, supplemented by entries from the Biblioteca Nacional de Chile and the World Cat, and other printed bibliographies, such as Olivera López and Meza Oliver 2006. Many thanks to Adan Benavides at the Benson Collection at the University of Texas, Austin, for his assistance in this matter.

26. *Officium S. Vincentii Ferrerii, confessoris, Ordinis Praedicatiorum* [sic], *Semiduplex, et ad libitum Sanctissumus D. N. Clemens Nonus, sub die 29 novembris 1667 ad preces serenissime Hispaniarum Regina…* (Mexico City: Officina Viduae Bernardi Calderon, 1670).

be read out. A major theme of the biographical lessons in the *Office* was Vincent's identification as the angel of the apocalypse and his vigorous preaching about the Last Judgment.[27]

An early eighteenth-century confessor's manual in the Mixe language confirms the notion that Vincent's abundant conversions of non-Christians and apostolic gift of tongues served to inspire Dominican missionaries in the Spanish colonies. The volume, authored by the Dominican friar Augustín de Quintana and including Mixe prayers, lessons in the faith, vocabulary, and a pronunciation guide, was dedicated to "the glorious apostle of Europe, Saint Vincent Ferrer."[28] Quintana's prefatory remarks, addressed to Vincent, offered his *Confessonario* as a humble gift to "my most saintly father," specifically praising the saint for the numerous conversions effected by his apostolic preaching, citing Antoninus of Florence's figures of one hundred thousand penitent sinners, as well as twenty-five thousand Jews and eight thousand Muslims brought to the Christian faith.[29] The Mixe language was spoken in the southeastern Oaxaca region, the Dominicans' particular stronghold. Even as the early conversion efforts of the first generation of missionaries had turned to the harder work of inculcating proper Christian behavior and doctrine, Quintana's example shows that Dominicans in the field continued to look to Vincent Ferrer as a model for their actions.

By far the most frequent New World publication relating to Vincent Ferrer was the text of a novena, to the performance of which innumerable miracles were attributed. I have located more than two dozen different editions of this novena issued by Latin American printers from the years 1710 to 1850, attesting to the saint's reputation as a source of supernatural aid in the eighteenth-century colonies, as well as to the wide range of this devotion. Copies of the novena—a matter of a couple of dozen pages or less—survive from presses in Mexico City, Lima, Puebla, Guatemala, and Buenos Aires.[30] A few editions were accompanied by a brief narration of some of Vincent's miracles.[31] Even when a list of miracles was missing, the title

---

27. E.g., *Breviarium juxta ritum* 1909, 1: 1054–78.

28. Original: Augustín de Quintana, *Confessonario en Lengua Mixe*…([Puebla de los Angeles]: Vidua de Miguel de Ortega, 1733). My citations are from Quintana 1890.

29. Quintana 1890, 3–4 (quotation, 3).

30. Through CCILA and the online catalog of the Biblioteca Nacional de Chile. There is, in addition, one septena among the listings, by a nun from Mexico City: Madre María Bernarda de San José, *Septena devota que el afecto agradecido de la R. M. Maria Bernarda de San Joseph, Religiosa Professa de el Maximo Convento de la Purissima Concepción de esta Ciudad de Mexico, consagrammante á el esclarecido Angel Predicador S. Vicente Ferrer* (Mexico City: Francisco Xavier Zanchez, 1743). The novena was also frequently printed in the Philippines (and still today). The first two Dominican friars arrived there in 1581, one of them having already been named the first bishop of Manila in 1579 (Fray Domingo de Salazar). Sitoy 1985, 238–45.

31. E.g., *Novena sagrada, del Glorioso San Vicente Ferrer Angel del Apocalipsis, Apostol de la Europa, Gloria de Valencia, y honra del Sagrado orden de Predicadores.—Para que sus devotos alcancen del Santo, todo*

page often alerted the reader to Vincent's intercessory powers, particularly when solicited by means of the novena.[32] According to one version from Guatemala, Vincent's aid was particularly effective against epilepsy and earthquakes, the latter, at least, a problem of known local concern.[33] The practice of performing a novena to Vincent Ferrer had originated in Europe and was widespread in Catholic lands there by the early eighteenth century. According to the Valencian Francisco Vidal y Micó's 1735 *History of the Portentous Life and Miracles of the Valencian Apostle of Europe Saint Vincent Ferrer*, which also contained the text of the novena, it was regularly recited throughout Spain and as far as Germany, generating everywhere a train of miracles for the saint's devotees. (A 1777 edition of the same specified that the novena could be found in Rome, Naples, Saragossa, Turin, and Sardinia.)[34] At least one of the New World imprints was aimed at confraternities of the saint, "wherever they are found," suggesting the role of the novena in sustaining lay devotion to him and in turn inculcating good Catholic behavior.[35]

Other offerings from Latin American presses provided yet more ways in which the faithful might solicit the intercession of Vincent Ferrer, at times in imitation of practices performed at local Dominican convents. For example, in 1731, Domingo Veguellina, a bachelor in theology, offered readers a *devocionario* to obtain divine grace through the intercession of Vincent Ferrer.[36]

---

consuelo, assi en lo temporal, como en espiritual (Guatemala City: Ioachín de Arévalo, c. 1760). An introduction relates several of the saint's miracles. J. T. Medina (1919) 1960, 2:644–45.

32. E.g., Damían Veguilina Burdel, *Viva Jesús. Novena para alcanzar de Dios nuestro Señor, la Divina gracia, por medio del glorioso Apostol de Valencia S. Vicente Ferrer* (Puebla: Viuda de Miguel de Ortega, 1746); *Novena del Ilustre, y Esclarecido Apostol Valenciano S. Vicente Ferrer, Angel del Apocalysis, Apostol de Christo, Honra de la Catholica Iglesia Luz del mundo, Astro resplandecie[n]te del Cielo Dominicano, segundo S. Pablo en la Predicacion, y sin segundo en su Admirable Vida, y prodigiosos Milagros* (Mexico City: D. Nicolas Paglo de Torres, 1754); *Novena del ilustre y esclarecido Apostol Valenciano San Vicente Ferrer, Angel del Apocalypsi. Apostol de Christo, Honra de la Iglesia Católica, Luz del Mundo, Astro resplandeciente del Cielo Dominicano, segundo San Pablo en su Predicacion, y Sinsegundo en su admirable Vida, y prodigiosos Milagros* ([Puebla]: Oficina de D. Pedro de la Rosa, 1782); *Novena de el Angel de el Apocalipsis, Apostol de la Europa, y gloria de la Religión Guzmana el Esclarecido S. Vicente Ferrer milagro de los Milagros, y universal consuelo de todos los necesitados y afligidos* ([Lima]: Con licencia, 1724).

33. *Novena sagrada*. Vincent's power to protect against earthquakes had been advertised in Vidal y Micó 1735, bk. 4, chap. 10, pp. 345–47, in which the author availed himself of a juridical inquest held in the kingdom of Naples in 1733. There the archbishop authenticated the miraculous sparing of lives in an earthquake of November 21, 1732.

34. Vidal y Micó 1735, 446; Vidal y Micó 1777, 401.

35. *Novena del Ilustre, y Esclarecido Apostol Valenciano S. Vicente Ferrer, Angel del Apocalysis, Apostol de Christo, Honra de la Catholica Iglesia ... Dispuesta por un Religioso Sacerdote del mismo Orden a Devocion de la Cofradia del Santo, donde se hallarán* ([Mexico City]: D. Nicolas Pablo de Torres, 1754). Establishing confraternities was part of the arsenal of conversion techniques used by the Dominicans in Latin America. M. A. Medina 1992, 49.

36. Domingo Veguellina, *Devocionario para alcanzar la Divina Gracia por la intercesion del Apostol de Valencia, S. Vicente Ferrer. Por don Domingo Veguellina, bachiller, teólogo. Reimpreso* (Puebla: Morales, 1731). (The first edition is unknown).

Similarly, a Guatemalan press in 1777 presented its readers an *exercicio devoto* to be performed each Monday in honor of the saint, "mediator between God and men, and the most prodigious in working miracles."[37] Finally, five different editions from Mexico City instructed the faithful in the *Means of Praying on Mondays or Fridays to the Angel of the Apocalypse…Saint Vincent Ferrer.* The offerings were specifically designed to solicit Vincent's patronage, "especially at the hour of death." And readers learned that the same prayers were offered up "each Monday in the Imperial Convent of Our Father Saint Dominic" in Mexico City.[38] In imitating the friars' Monday prayers to Saint Vincent Ferrer, lay Christians could obtain an intercessor who might spare them some of the pains of purgatory.

A single-leaf imprint from Buenos Aires in 1783 affords a glimpse of popular practices associated with devotion to Saint Vincent Ferrer. (See figure 19.) The text, a "Prayer, which the glorious Saint Vincent Ferrer made against the plague," invokes the merits of the Virgin, all the holy martyrs and confessor saints, and Saints Fabian, Sebastian, Cosmos and Damian, Athanasius, Marianus, Roch, and Dominic, in beseeching Christ to preserve the speaker from "all illness and plague." Instructions on the sheet specify that the prayer (that is, presumably, the sheet on which the prayer is printed) is to be applied to the afflicted part of the body while a person recites the prayer and makes the sign of the cross at the places indicated in the text.[39] This practice is reminiscent of the remarks made by Vicente Justiniano Antist regarding the Sicilian exemplar of Vincent's canonization inquests. The manuscript, according to Antist, had been rendered incomplete by the locals' habit of taking leaves from the volume to lay on the sick.[40] A similar ritual is still attested to today among Filipino American Catholics,

---

37. *Exercicio devoto para todos los lunes del Año. Dedicado este dia en cada Semana al glorioso S. Vicente Ferrer, Angel del Apocalypsis, Apostol de la Europa, Clarín sonoro del Evangelio, Trueno espantoso del dia del Juicio, Medianero entre Dios, y los hombres, y el mas prodigioso en hacer milagros. Para que consigan sus devotos el alivio que desean en sus necesidades* ([Guatemala City]: Reimpreso en la Nueva Guatemala por D. Antonio Cubillas, 1777).

38. Juan Palmero, *Modo de ofrecer los lunes ó viernes al Angel del Apocalypsi, Apostol de la Europa Clarin del Juicio San Vicente Ferrer, Para alcanzar su patrocinio con especialidad á la hora de la muerte, como se practica todos los Lunes en el Imperial Convento de Nuestro Padre Santo Domingo de esta Ciudad de Mexico. Por el P. Predicador Fr. Juan Palmero, del Orden de Predicadores* ([Mexico City]: Reimpresso in la Imprenta de la Biblioteca Mexicana, 1761); also ([Mexico City]: Oficina de D. María Fernández de Jáuregui, 1816), ([Mexico City]: Viuda de D. Joseph Bernando de Hogal, 1748), (Mexico City: Calle de Santo Domingo [Jauregui], 1816), and (Mexico City: Herederos del Lic. D. Joseph de Jaurequi, 1790?). These last two are entries from the WorldCat (but there are no libraries listed as holding them).

39. *Oracion que hizo el glorioso San Vicente Ferrer contra la peste* (Buenos Aires: Niños expositos, 1783). Reproduced in J. T. Medina (1892) 2002, following the notice of the publication at 27. Medina notes that it is evident that the print run was at least 2,650.

40. *Proceso,* fol. 2r; FPC, 269. See chapter 2.

# ORACION
## QUE HIZO EL GLORIOSO
# SAN VICENTE FERRER
### CONTRA LA PESTE.

Esta Oracion se aplica à la     parte doliente rezandola,

y haciendo las Cruzes que     en ella van puestas.

CHRISTO vence ✠ Christo manda ✠ Christo reyna ✠ Christo de todo mal, y peste me defienda ✠ Jesus Nazareno Rey de los Judios ✠ compadeceos de nosotros ✠ por la señal de la Santa Cruz ✠ y por los meritos de la gloriosísima Virgen Maria Madre tuya, y Señora nuestra, y de tus Santos Màrtires, y Confesores, Fabian, y Sebaftian, Cosme, y Damian, Atanacio, y Mariano, Roque, y Domingo, libranos Señor de todos nueftros enemigos. Santo Dios, Santo fuerte, Santo inmortal que encarnò en la Virgen Maria tened piedad de nosotros. Amen.

    La bendicion de efta Oracion se darà en el Convento de Predicadores hecha por el mismo Santo.

Buenos-Ayres: En la Imprenta de los Niños expositos: Año de 1783.

**FIGURE 19.** "Oracion que hizo el glorioso San Vicente Ferrer contra la peste." Buenos Aires: Niños expositos, 1783. Reproduced in J. T. Medina (1892) 2002. Courtesy Martino Publishing. This "Prayer, which the glorious Saint Vincent Ferrer made against the plague," promised the faithful protection against all sickness when they uttered it while making the sign of the cross as indicated and touching the sheet to the afflicted body part. The text was known as early as 1510, when Miquel Peres repeated it in his life of the saint, noting that Vincent had taught this prayer to his followers in Brittany.

who believe that a statue of Vincent Ferrer, placed on a person's head, has miraculous healing powers.[41]

The plague prayer attributed to Vincent was known as early as 1510, when it appears in the Valencian Miquel Peres's vernacular *Life of Saint Vincent Ferrer,* and it can also be found in Vidal y Micó's 1735 biography of the saint. The ritual practice prescribed in Peres's *Life* is similar, as well. According to Peres, when his followers wished to flee from a Breton city stricken with plague, Vincent had instead given them a "brief prayer, with a cross with seven knobs [*poms*]" that would protect those who wore it against the plague. He instructed his disciples as well, every morning when they rose, to make the sign of the cross on each part of the body where one typically would get a bubo, saying "Jesus, Virgin Mary."[42] Not simply did the printed prayer from Buenos Aires provide hope of Vincent's intercession against the plague, however. It also funneled the faithful into the local Dominican house, the fine italic print at the bottom of the leaf noting, "Blessing of this prayer can be obtained in the Convent of Preachers dedicated to the same Saint."[43] The bishop of Buenos Aires had created several new rural parishes in 1780, including one dedicated to San Vicente Ferrer.[44] Perhaps this new foundation also thought to increase its offerings and attendance by its blessing of the prayer against plague.

Written evidence regarding the cult of Vincent Ferrer in Latin America thus indicates that while Vincent's example as an apostolic preacher fired the imagination of New World missionaries, his most enduring image in offerings from colonial presses—particularly in the eighteenth century— was as a worker of miracles, whether by the recitation of the oft-printed novena to the saint or by the use of the saint's own prayer against the plague. A closer observation, however, hints at the ways in which the clergy channeled the appetite for supernatural intercession into a means of inculcating proper Catholic practice, whether those who sought Vincent's aid were instructed to make the sign of the cross, invoke the Virgin and other saints, join a confraternity, or emulate the devotions carried out in nearby Dominican houses. Other aspects of the saint's image in European hagiography were seemingly squeezed out of the colonial print portrayal of the saint. Vincent's vigorous preaching about the Last Judgment—a focus,

41. E.g., in a 2010 celebration of the Feast of Saint Vincent Ferrer among Filipino immigrants outside Chicago. Frasco 2010. See also mention in an online auction selling an antique Philippine statue of Vincent Ferrer at http://www.worthpoint.com/worthopedia/old-winged-santo-san-vicente-ferrer-st-vincent.

42. Peres 2007, at fol. [12r]. The text of the prayer (in Latin) appears at [12v]. The prayer also appears in Vidal y Micó 1735, bk. 4, chap. 6, 334, where the author cites (333) the edition in Vicente Justiniano Antist's 1591 *Opusculos de San Vicente.*

43. *Oracion* in J. T. Medina (1892) 2002, after 27.

44. Ciudad de San Vicente Buenos Aires 2013.

for example, of the bull of canonization and of the lessons of the saint's *Office*—appears to have been compressed into the simple and ubiquitous shorthand epithet "angel of the apocalypse." And the notion of Vincent as peacemaker and healer of the Schism nearly disappeared in the Latin American printed record.

A single eighteenth-century publication suggests, however, that—when the occasion demanded—Vincent's role in settling divisions and in healing a divided church still had resonance with audiences, or at least with ecclesiastical authorities. The pamphlet in question reproduces a "panegyric oration" delivered by Fray Manuel López de Aragón in the Imperial Convent of Santo Domingo in Mexico City on May 1, 1772, on the occasion of a solemn feast in Vincent Ferrer's honor celebrated by the confraternity dedicated to the saint. The sermon's title was "The Apostle of Peace."[45] The oration portrayed Vincent as a hero invested with apostolic ardor, establishing in his time "divine and human peace" through his preaching and miracles. After a brief biographical sketch, Fray Manuel described Vincent's efforts to end the Great Schism through his indefatigable labors to persuade Christian kings and prelates to celebrate a council in Constance, resulting in the election of Martin V as a single, legitimate pope. Similarly, Fray Manuel insisted, Vincent brought peace to humans through his prodigies and miracles, some of which he recounted for his audience.[46] Although the sermon delivered up a set of miracle tales for eager listeners, the main focus was on Vincent's role as bringer of peace—peace in a time of ecclesiastical and political turmoil.

Since the Confraternity of Saint Vincent Ferrer associated with the convent of Santo Domingo presumably celebrated the feast of its patron every year, it is a little puzzling that the members chose to publish only this particular oration on the merits of Vincent Ferrer. But given the sermon's emphasis on Vincent's role as apostle of peace, it seems plausible to conclude that Fray Manuel's words must have touched on tensions and divisions in the air in Mexico City in 1772. One likely source of conflict was the 1771 Fourth Mexican Provincial Council, a reforming council whose clerical elite leaders

---

45. López de Aragón [1772]. I cite the edition from the Bancroft Library, University of California, Berkeley. A copy also exists in the Biblioteca Nacional de Chile. The University in Puebla also possessed a copy in its library: Olivera López and Meza Oliver 2006, 99–100, where the authors give a lengthy summary of the text. A few sketchy biographical details about Manuel López de Aragon appear in Beuchot 1987, namely that this Dominican friar taught a course in arts at the Colegio de Porta Coeli in 1757–59, and that he was a Thomist.

46. López de Aragón [1772], 5–16 (biography, including 11–16 on the Schism), 16–20 (miracles, largely in the form of generic lists but relating at greater length at 19 one "de aquella erudita obra, intitulada *Acta Sanctorum*," namely, a tale of the ship in distress in which the Breton Jacobus Parvus was paralyzed after speaking out against Vincent's merits; quotation, 5). See also the summary in Olivera López and Meza Oliver 2006, 99–100.

sought to weed out the excesses of the baroque Catholicism of the laity.[47] For example, participation in flagellant processions during Holy Week, a staple of Hispanic piety since at least the sixteenth century, was now condemned as "a cause of mockery and laughter," and the *penitentes* who participated in the processions were associated with *castas* (persons of mixed blood) and drunkenness.[48] Penitential self-flagellation frequently numbered among the practices of confraternities such as the one devoted to Saint Vincent Ferrer, and the saint was known to have sponsored similar penitential groups during his lifetime. In addition, the council's decrees now prohibited priests from celebrating certain Mass cycles, including the trental known as the Masses of Saint Vincent, celebrated over the course of thirty days following a person's death and presumed to be effective in freeing the deceased's soul from purgatory.[49]

The council's decrees were not universally accepted, however. According to one study of wills from Mexico City, this clampdown on lay devotional behavior was not particularly effective, pointing to a sharp division between clerical elites bent on the reform of lay practice and the ordinary faithful, for whom traditional exercises continued to have meaning.[50] Given the rift between the dictates of the council and the preferences of lay Christians like the members of the Confraternity of Saint Vincent Ferrer, it is possible that the learned Fray Manuel's presentation of Vincent Ferrer as an agent of peace was a plea to the members of the confraternity to reconcile themselves to the reforming decrees of the Fourth Provincial Council and thus was seen as worthy of publication. The string of names of clerics offering their stamp of approval to the publication of the sermon adds weight to this hypothesis, for among the names listed appears that of the Augustinian maestro Fray Gregorio Bauza, "*definidor* of the Provincia del Santísmo Nombre de Jesús, *adviser of the Fourth Mexican Council,* and synodal examiner of the Archbishopric [of Mexico]."[51] Bauza's

---

47. On the reforms of the eighteenth-century, see Larkin 2004; and Luque Alcaide 2005.

48. Larkin 2004, 510–11.

49. Ibid., 514–15. On the Masses of Saint Vincent, as well as similar traditions such as the Masses of Saint Amador and Masses of Saint Gregory, see Martínez Romero 2006; and Martínez Gil 1993, 213–40, 545–46.

50. Larkin 2004, 516–18. One could also argue that the prayer against plague printed in Buenos Aires in 1783 confirms that the dictates of the eighteenth-century reforming councils were not always heeded. For discontent with the reform decrees, see also W. B. Taylor 1996.

51. López de Aragón [1772], "Dictamen del R. P. Mro. Fr. Gregorio Bauza, del Orden de N. P. S. Augustin, Difinidor actual de la Provincia del Smo. Nombre de Jesus, Consultor del IV. Concilio Mexicano, y Exâminador Synodal de este Arzobispado de México," unpaginated. Bauza offered his "dictamen" on May 20, 1772 (emphasis added). (A *definidor* was a member of the Augustinian order's provincial governing body.) An older interpretation of the eighteenth-century ecclesiastical reforms saw provincial councils as a means of subjecting the church in the Spanish colonies to the

endorsement of the publication hints that those who favored the council's reform program saw Fray Manuel's sermon on Vincent Ferrer as furthering their goals.

## Artistic Representations of Saint Vincent Ferrer

By far the most common representation of Vincent Ferrer in colonial Latin American art was as the angel of the apocalypse. Typically in such portraits, whether they be signed canvases executed for major churches or small private *retablos* on tin by folk artists, Vincent is winged and gestures upward with his right index finger, both indicators of his self-identification as the angel of Revelation 14:6.[52] In fifteenth-century European depictions, Vincent's extended index finger typically points upward to a vision of Christ in judgment or to a banner inscribed with the text of Revelation 14:7, "Fear God and give him honor, for the hour of his judgment is at hand" (my translation). Often in colonial portraits, however, he holds or is accompanied by a trumpet, another nod toward Vincent's role in announcing the Last Judgment. (See figure 20.) This vision of Vincent as the angel of the apocalypse must have had particular appeal in colonial Latin America not simply because of the millennial fervor of the early missionary friars whose orders would have established the iconography of the saint in their convents but also because the angel in Revelation 14:6 is specifically said to bring the Gospel to "every nation, and tribe, and tongue, and people." Further, the image of angels may have had resonance for indigenous viewers, for whom hawks, condors, hummingbirds, and other winged creatures traditionally had religious and mythological significance. Powerful angels abound in colonial art, particularly in Peru, where artists were in the habit of depicting angels carrying guns.[53]

---

Bourbon monarchy. Luque Alcaide 2005, 743–44. Given Fray Manuel's emphasis on Vincent's role in persuading *monarchs* (and prelates) to call the Council of Constance (López de Aragón [1772], 13), the sermon could also be read as subtly advocating royal control of the clergy.

52. Schenone 1992–98, 2:773–79, esp. 773–74 (at 2:775, Schenone reproduces a portrait of a winged Vincent Ferrer by an anonymous seventeenth-century painter from Cuzco, Peru, in the convent of Santo Domingo in Cuzco). A marvelously comprehensive collection of images of Saint Vincent Ferrer can be found at Domínicos Chile 2012. For other images of the winged Vincent Ferrer see Barbieri 2004, 104, illus. 36 (from the church of Santo Domingo in Córdoba, by an eighteenth-century artist from Cuzco, Peru); Cossio del Pomar 1964, 107 (*A Winged Saint,* Mercedes Gallagher de Park Collection). There are also a number of Philippine statues of a winged Vincent Ferrer (see, e.g., note 41). Saint Francis of Assisi also typically appears with wings in Latin American art. See Lara 2005.

53. Cossio del Pomar 1964, 147. See also Mo 1992, 38–39 (angels with guns).

**FIGURE 20.** Cuzco School, *San Vicente Ferrer*. New Orleans Museum of Art. Courtesy of New Orleans. The New Orleans Museum of Art. Museum purchase through the Ella West Freeman Foundation Matching Fund, 67.17. As is typical in Latin American portraits of the saint, Vincent appears here with wings and a trumpet, both references to his identification as angel of the apocalypse. The gesture with his right hand and the book at his side are also emblems of Vincent's announcing the Last Judgment.

There are occasional variations to this standard iconography of Vincent Ferrer. The saint's wings are not always present. At times, as in some European paintings, a bishop's miter and a cardinal's hat lie at Vincent's feet, a reference to the honors Vincent refused in his own lifetime.[54] In a few portraits, Vincent holds or rests his hand on a book.[55] In some, flames play over Vincent's head, alluding to the descent of the Holy Spirit at Pentecost and the saint's apostolic gift of tongues.[56] In one early nineteenth-century portrait in Buenos Aires, Vincent is wingless, but a caption beneath the figure of the saint reads, "I am the angel of the Apocalypse," as the saint is alleged to have said at a sermon in Salamanca.[57] Despite small variations in iconography, the overwhelming image of Vincent supplied by Latin American portraits of the saint is in agreement with that self-identification.

Aside from portraits, few narrative cycles survive comparable to those seen in the great fifteenth-century European altarpieces dedicated to Vincent Ferrer. Héctor Schenone, in his study of the iconography of the saints in colonial Latin American art, describes only one, attributed to the eighteenth-century Cuzco painter Marcos Zapata, executed for the church of Santo Domingo in the important artistic center of Cuzco. In addition, a handful of other paintings of Vincent move beyond the standard portraiture to illustrate the deeds of the saint.[58] In all these portrayals the predominant image of Vincent, as in works issuing from colonial presses, is as a miracle worker.[59] Some of the miracles depicted in Zapata's Cuzco appear to be more or less contemporary; that is to say, they do not appear in fifteenth- to seventeenth-century biographies of the saint. In fact, in the case of the Cuzco cycle, the scenes are set in a cityscape reflecting eighteenth-century Cuzco life, inviting viewers to picture themselves among the recipients

---

54. E.g., figure 20 and the Cuzco portrait reproduced in Schenone 1992–98, 2:775.

55. Often with a verse from Mark 13:37 ("And what I say to you, I say to all: Watch." Douay Rheims translation). Schenone 1992–98, 2:774.

56. Several examples at Domínicos Chile 2012.

57. Painting by Angel María Camponeschi (1803), Museo Isaac Fernández Blanco, Buenos Aires. Reproduction at Domínicos Chile 2012, http://www.dominicos.net/santos/san_vicente_ferrer/021_San_Vicente_Ferrer_(Angel_Maria_Camponesqui_1803_Museo_Isaac_Fernandez_Blanco).html.

58. Schenone 1992–98, 2:774–79, offering descriptions of the scenes Zapata depicted. The paintings occupy the spaces over the arches that hold up the raised choir. Schenone, 2:774, also mentions a smaller cycle, which surrounded a canvas in the collection of Anita Fernandini de Naranjo (mayor of Lima, Peru, 1963–64), but does not describe any of the scenes depicted there. He also notes two other paintings illustrating scenes from Vincent's life and miracles, one in Santo Domingo in Quito (2:776) and one in the Museu Isaac Fernández Blanco in Buenos Aires (2:778). On Zapata, see Mesa and Gisbert 1982, 1:209–15; 2: figs. 323–25 (reproductions of three scenes from the Cuzco cycle).

59. Out of sixteen scenes from Cuzco described by Schenone, only two (the saint with penitential flagellants and the saint being received under a canopy) make no reference to Vincent's miracles or prophecies.

of Vincent's intercession. Accompanying captions ensure that the viewer grasps the episodes being illustrated. Although eighteenth-century reforms such as those enacted by the Fourth Mexican Provincial Council sought to discourage the demonstrative baroque Catholicism of many laypeople, the evidence from paintings suggests a degree of toleration, or even encouragement, of such practices in the name of fostering devotion to the saint and his church.

Three examples illustrate the ways in which artistic representations could help to reinforce the baroque religious practices that worried eighteenth-century reformers. Two of these paintings, for example, associate Vincent Ferrer with penitential self-flagellation, such as occurred in the Holy Week processions frowned upon by the Fourth Provincial Mexican Council. An eighteenth-century painting in the church of Santo Domingo in Quito, Ecuador, depicts a bloodied Vincent in the act of disciplining himself, caught unawares by an admiring female observer. One of Zapata's scenes in Cuzco shows Vincent leading in public procession a band of penitential flagellants like those who accompanied him throughout his years of itinerant preaching.[60] In both works, the artist portrays in a positive fashion the sort of penitential discipline that allowed participants to identify with Christ and his saints—and that reformers abhorred in favor of a more internalized, spiritual piety. Another vignette in the Cuzco group depicts Vincent's miraculous saving of a city in Brittany from plague. The saint stands, holding a large card on which is written his own prayer against the pestilence. The art historians José de Mesa and Teresa Gisbert speculate that at the time Zapata was painting, memory was still fresh of a 1719–20 epidemic in the Andes region.[61] Given the painting's setting in an unnamed city in Brittany, just as in Peres's 1510 recounting of the origins of the plague prayer, it seems likely that this is the same prayer printed in Buenos Aires in 1783. Whether viewers in Cuzco were encouraged to place the text of the prayer on ailing body parts, as were the faithful in Buenos Aires, is not clear, but it seems unlikely that this practice was confined to one parish in Buenos Aires, especially since the Andes region was not immune to epidemic disease.

Most of the other scenes in Zapata's Cuzco cycle underscore Vincent's miraculous powers. In one appear miracles Vincent worked while still a young boy; another shows a shoe miraculously ejected from a well into which it fell. Vincent resuscitates the dead, cures the blind and deaf, and detects cases of fraud: the faked death of a student and a winemaker trying to pass off poor-quality wine. Here the saint prophesies to the mother of Pope Calixtus III about her son's future. There the ugly Portuguese woman

---

60. Schenone 1992–98, 2:776 (Quito), 777 (Cuzco).

61. Ibid., 2:777; Mesa and Gisbert 1982, 1:215, also mention a mural depicting this plague in the church in Catca. See Stavig and Schmidt 2008, 12–13.

is miraculously made beautiful. In one scene the saint orders some men not to cut the cypress tree growing in a house; years later the tree is made into a statue of the saint. In another scene the duchess of Plascencia is upset that she has not hired a preacher to preach for the Feast of Saint Vincent Ferrer; the saint himself miraculously appears in the vacant pulpit. In yet another vignette, a statue of Vincent in Majorca itself begins to preach, moving Christians to penitence and Jews to conversion. Even when Zapata presents Vincent as the angel of the apocalypse, he works in a miracle story, in this case, that of the dead woman in Salamanca resuscitated in order to confirm Vincent's proclamation, "I am the angel of the apocalypse."[62] And, of course, Zapata paints the miracle of the chopped-up baby.

As the long list of miracles depicted by Zapata suggests, the Dominican friars in Cuzco had access to a number of early modern biographies of Vincent Ferrer from which to draw the material for the wall paintings. Interestingly, in the case of the chopped-up baby, rather than decide between the two competing versions of the tale as *in vita* and as a postmortem miracle that could be found in these *vitae,* Zapata (or his employer) chose simply to depict both. (See figure 21.) On the right of one archway, the viewer sees Vincent presiding over a serving basin, making a gesture of blessing; the reconstituted baby stands in the midst of the stew before him. Bread, wine, and silverware on the table show how close to disaster the situation had come, while a well-dressed crowd of onlookers marvels at the miracle. In the background, the postmortem variation appears. A pregnant mother wishing to eat human flesh has her own child butchered; the father takes the body parts and places them on the saint's tomb. As he exits the church, the father feels a tug at his cape. It is the restored baby, the sign of his division remaining etched in his flesh. Years later, the grown child enters the Dominican order (an allusion to the tradition in which the chopped-up baby went on to become a famous Dominican preacher in Sicily).[63]

Although I have not located other colonial portrayals of the gruesome chain of events leading to Vincent's celebrated miracle, at least one portrait survives in which the restored baby serves as an emblem of the saint. The painting is the work of the celebrated artist Cristóbal de Villalpando (ca. 1649–1714) and dates from the period in which the artist was active in Mexico City and Puebla in the 1680s.[64] (See figure 22.) In this striking

---

62. All described in Schenone 1992–98, 2:776–78. Schenone (2:778) also identifies another painting of the miraculous transformation of the ugly woman, by an anonymous eighteenth-century Cuzco painter, now in the Museo Isaac Fernández Blanco, Buenos Aires, Argentina.

63. My description is based on photographs of the painting graciously sent me by Anne Pushkal and Vera Tyuleneva; the reproduction in Mesa and Gisbert 1982, 2, fig. 324; and Schenone 1992–98, 2:778, which latter I am presuming summarizes the explanatory texts that feature in the paintings.

64. Gutiérrez Haces et al. 1997, 380 (illus. no. 53): *La visión de San Vicente Ferrer,* Templo de San Felipe Neri, La Profesa, Mexico City. (According to the authors, there is no information about the

**FIGURE 21.** Marcos Zapata, *Milagro de San Vicente Ferrer durante la comida*. Santo Domingo, Cuzco, Peru. Photo: Danita Delimont / Gallo Images / Getty Images. In the foreground of this striking wall painting from the Dominican priory in the former Inca capital, Vincent raises the chopped-up baby from the bowl of stew in which he has just been cooked. Onlookers gaze in amazement at the miracle. In the background, a well-dressed mother presides as servants butcher the child.

presentation, a winged and kneeling Vincent Ferrer turns from his desk to glimpse, over his right shoulder, a vision of Christ with an interceding figure of Mary. A cityscape (Mexico City or Puebla?) sits just below the image of Christ. To the right, over the saint's left shoulder, angels sound the trumpets of the Last Judgment. And kneeling before the saint, a small child turns to gaze at the viewer. With his left hand, he reaches toward Vincent; his right hand grasps the cooking spit that featured in Bernard Guyard's exuberant rendering of the tale. The depiction of the baby with the cooking spit follows the emblematic portrayal of the same miracle in two seventeenth-century engravings in the Bibliothèque nationale de France. But the composition is unique to Villalpando. In a neat diagonal, the formerly chopped-up baby draws the viewer's eye to Vincent, who in turn reminds the viewer of the imminence of the Last Judgment. The kneeling virgin, immediately above the saint's head, points to Vincent's role as intercessor. In striking fashion, Villalpando's canvas acknowledges the importance of miracles to the faithful but also demonstrates the ways in

painting's provenance.) See also *Arte y Mística* 1994, 274 (commentary by Rogelio Ruiz Gomar) and 275 (illustration).

**FIGURE 22.** Cristóbal de Villalpando, *San Vicente Ferrer*. Templo de San Felipe Neri, La Profesa, Mexico City. Reproduction in *Arte y mística* 1994. Vincent is portrayed here with wings as angel of the apocalypse. He interrupts his reading to peer over his right shoulder, glimpsing a vision of Christ in judgment. Above, Mary intercedes with her son as angels sound the Last Trumpet. Directly in front of the saint kneels a small child holding a cooking spit, just as in some seventeenth-century engravings referring to the miracle of the chopped-up baby.

which tales of the miraculous can be worked into a point about doctrine. In this appealing painting, Vincent is both miracle worker and angel of the apocalypse, and the viewer is invited both to turn to heavenly intercessors like Vincent and the Virgin *and* to repent before the Day of Judgment.

As Dominican missionaries brought the cult of Saint Vincent Ferrer to their churches in Latin America, they translated the image of the saint found in European art and hagiography into a form seemingly more suited to the colonial context. With a single exception, Fray Manuel's 1772 panegyric oration in Mexico City, Latin American artists and authors paid little heed to the careful construction of Vincent Ferrer as a committed healer of the Schism in the church, although the biographies they carried with them gave ample credit to Vincent for ending the division. His role as a new apostle, converter of thousands of Jews and Muslims, served more as model for fellow Spanish Dominican missionaries—who erected missions, churches, convents, and provinces in his honor—than as inspiration held out to the faithful. Vincent's apocalyptic preaching—subject of some discomfort for biographers from Ranzano and Antoninus in the fifteenth to Antist, Diago, and Ferrer de Valdecebro in the sixteenth and seventeenth centuries—was transformed into the near-ubiquitous portrayal of the saint as the winged angel of the apocalypse. Although this depiction had its roots in Vincent's own words and in the 1458 bull of canonization, colonial audiences may have understood Vincent as a powerful archangel like Michael just as much as the harsh herald of Judgment Day. For the Vincent Ferrer of colonial Latin America was primarily a source of supernatural aid against real, pressing problems like plagues and earthquakes, an intercessor at the hour of death. While it is true that, as visual and printed evidence indicates, petitioners were guided into proper Catholic devotions as they sought Vincent's intercession, the Vincent Ferrer known and beloved in Latin America was a worker of miracles. And no miracle more epitomized the saint's power than that of the restoration of the chopped-up baby.

Meanwhile, in Europe, while Vincent continued to be invoked as a spiritual patron, in hagiography his image increasingly came to stabilize along the lines laid out by Pietro Ranzano and enshrined in the *Acta Sanctorum*: as a charismatic preacher and converter of souls and as the untiring peacemaker whose efforts ended the Great Schism, the very task Ranzano must have hoped to neatly symbolize in highlighting and elaborating on the nearly folkloric miracle tale of the chopped-up baby. By our own times, Ranzano's portrayal of the saint was thoroughly established. For according to Donald Attwater's *A New Dictionary of Saints* (published in 1994), Vincent Ferrer's two great works were his preaching, which "convert[ed] thousands," and "the mending of the…Great Schism."[65] But Ranzano's signature miracle appears nowhere in Attwater's dictionary entry. And although the author of a contemporary devotional website does offer up Ranzano's version of the tale, he hastens to add a bit of an apology for the prodigy's apparent "sensationalism."[66] Although lurid miracles like Ranzano's favored one are no longer quite to the taste of all hagiographers, the story's relative absence in current writings on the saint makes little difference. The chopped-up baby had done his job.

Or had he?

———

December 20, 2011. As I do every time I am in New York, I stop in to visit the lovely gothic revival church of Saint Vincent Ferrer at Sixty-Sixth and Lexington. It is a grand old building, popular for weddings and first communions, and, decorated for Christmas, it appears at its resplendent best. Entering the nave, I head to the right toward the little chapel devoted to the church's namesake. A statue portrays Vincent, gesturing upward with one hand while the other holds a book bearing in Latin the familiar words of Revelation 14:7 ("Fear God and give him honor"), a text repeated on the wall to Vincent's left. To my right, on a column, hangs "the miracle bell." Rows of gleaming candles just beyond testify to the saint's continued relevance in twenty-first-century America. The framed text of a novena instructs viewers to invoke the intercession of Vincent and his "inexhaustible treasure of grace": "St. Vincent Ferrer pray for me. St. Vincent Ferrer aid me. St. Vincent Ferrer relieve me. St. Vincent Ferrer cure me." Although the church's website describes its patron saint primarily as a preacher of Judgment and healer of the Schism, he appears here—just blocks away from the

---

65. Attwater and Cumming 1994, 318. Although his comment is more measured, J. B. Walker (2003) in *The New Catholic Encyclopedia* implies as much in his entry devoted to Vincent Ferrer. Under the boldface heading "The Schism," Walker writes, "But it was not as professor he was to do his most distinguished work." Similarly, the author of an 1878 biography explicitly based on Ranzano's *vita* in the AASS discusses Vincent's efforts to end the Schism but skips over the miracle of the chopped-up baby in favor of other prodigies related by Ranzano. Allies 1878.

66. JeevanJal Ministries 2012. The author observes, "Of course, one cannot be credulous and believe everything one hears." Still, again in a somewhat apologetic vein, he adds a reference (through Henri Ghéon) to Fages's biography of the saint, noting that Fages himself ("a patient researcher") had visited the house and kitchen in which the miracle had been played out. The author or his source here attributes to Fages personally what the author repeats from "Segura, *Hist. de Morella*" (probably José Segura Barreda, *Morella y sus aldeas* [1868]): FHSVF, 2:54. Similarly, in his 1939 biography of the saint, Henri Ghéon observes, regarding the tale of the chopped-up baby, "One is tempted to think that some unscrupulous biographer made the whole thing up.…But the house still exists—not that that proves it, of course." Ghéon 1939, 182–83.

**FIGURE 23.** Representation of Manuel Sánchez Navarrete, *Un ànima rescatada*. Asociación Pila Bautismal de San Vicente Ferrer, Valencia. Photo courtesy Robin Vose. As has been the custom since the seventeenth century, Valencian schoolchildren here act out scenes from Vincent's life and miracles on the occasion of his annual feast day.

commercial world of Bloomingdale's and Urban Outfitters—less as a hard-working ascetic than as a fount of miracles.[67]

But that is only one of the many Vincent Ferrers I have encountered. Once—but only once—in New York, a plaque appeared at Vincent's shrine that had the saint thinking primarily of "my poor motherland!"—promising *Valencians* that "my constant assistance and that my continuous prayers, up in heaven, will be for them."[68] And certainly Valencians retain a firm affection for their native son. Anyone lucky enough to be there for the annual celebration of the Feast of Saint Vincent Ferrer can witness—aside

67. Church of Saint Vincent Ferrer 2012. The biography also includes the interesting statement, "Of special interest to New York is St. Vincent's great love for the Jews."

68. "Oh My poor motherland!" Signed "New York and Valencia United by the Kindness of Saint Vincent Ferrer, Francesco Camps i Ortiz, January 27, 2010." (I saw it on March 25, 2010.)

from the processions and ceremonial masses—schoolchildren acting out his miracles on outdoor stages throughout the city, just as they have done since the seventeenth century.[69] (See figure 23.) Across the Atlantic, in Juchitán, Mexico, a noisy and festive Vela de San Vicente Ferrer—complete with processions, music, dancing, and plenty of food and drink—celebrates a beloved local patron who has also been co-opted by the town's gender-bending *muxe* population.[70] At Vincent's tomb in Vannes, I am more often struck by an aura of respectful near oblivion. Vincent's shrine, in a quiet semicircular chapel ringed by the seventeenth-century tapestry of his miracles, is almost overshadowed by the blazing rows of candles set before the image of the Virgin farther up the nave.

While hagiographers, aided by the literal and figurative weight of the *Acta Sanctorum,* may eventually have settled on a fixed image of Vincent Ferrer, religion lives among places and people as well as in books and words. What was difficult for the fifteenth-century papacy—to stabilize the meaning of a saint as a model for pious emulation—remains equally hard among the faithful today. Scholars turn to the Bollandists' volumes (or, more likely, to their digital version) not simply out of convenience but because they see them as authoritative, as presenting a standard narrative that would have been known to Christian audiences from the saint's own lifetime to the present. "Ah, here," we think with naive relief, "is *the* life of Vincent Ferrer." And so Ranzano's vision wins. But only in print. The historians, it turns out, are more easily persuaded than has been the cacophonous world of lived religion.

Having paid my respects to Vincent, I step out of the church into the bustle of last-minute shoppers on Lexington Avenue. I blink in the bright December sun and head uptown. But long after I have left the church, I am haunted by the memory of the miracle bell—and of all those candles. My mind runs back to the fifteenth century and the words of the men and women who so proudly related to the papal commissioners their tales of encounters with the holy: how one might subtly praise Breton dukes or Aragonese kings, another might get in a dig at a rival religious order, and yet another might assert her own worthiness as a holy woman. And I think again of the candles on Lexington Avenue, each one sheltering one person's vision of Vincent Ferrer and one individual's story of despair, faith, and hope.

---

69. Pierre-Henri Fages photographed a group portraying the miracle of the chopped-up baby in the late 1800s: FHSVF 1:18.

70. E.g., in a 2010 YouTube video of the festival. Guzmán 2010. Aside from the festival in his honor, as mentioned above (in note 11), Vincent Ferrer has also become something of a patron for the abundant *muxe* population, praised with gusto at the annual Vela de las Auténticas Intrépidas Buscadoras del Peligro (Festival of the Authentic, Intrepid Danger Seekers). Gage 2005.

# Bibliography

## Manuscripts

Bologna: Biblioteca comunale dell'Archiginnasio, MS B 2019.
Bologna: Biblioteca Universitaria, MS 1999.
Colmar: Bibliothèque Municipale de Colmar, MS CPC 280.
Innsbruck: Servitenkloster Innsbruck, Codex I.b.29 (Hill Monastic Manuscript Library 28950).
London: British Library, MS additional 32,579.
Nantes: Archives municipales de Nantes, CC 244, II 120.
Novara: Archivio Storico Diocesano, Codex XXVII.
Paris: Archives nationales, LL 1529.
Paris: Bibliothèque nationale de France MS lat. 1159, MS lat. 1324, MS lat. 1369, MS lat. 3303, MS lat. 14669.
Rome: Biblioteca Casanatense, MS 112.
Toulouse: Bibliothèque municipale, MS 486.
Trier: Stadtbibliothek, MS 1168/470.
Valencia: Universidad de Valencia, Biblioteca, G.C. 1869, M. 690.
Vannes: Archives Départementales du Morbihan, MS 87 G 11, 49 H 2, 1 Mi 293 (microfilm of "Documents relatifs aux reliques de Saint-Vincent Ferrier, conservés au presbytère de la cathédrale de Vannes").
Vatican City: Biblioteca Apostolica Vaticana, MS Chigi F. IV. 91.
Walberberg (Germany): Bibliothek St. Albert, MS 27 (Hill Monastic Manuscript Library 35238).

## Printed Primary Sources

*Acta Sanctorum: The Full-Text Database.* Cambridge: Chadwyck-Healey, 2000–.
Alberti, Leandro. 1517. *De viris illustribus ordinis praedicatorum libri sex.* Bologna: Hieronymus Plato.
Antist, Vicente Justiniano. 1956. "La vida e historia del apostólico predicador Sant Vicente Ferrer, Valenciano, de la Orden de Santo Domingo." In *Biografía y escritos de San Vicente Ferrer,* edited by José de Garganta and Vicente Forcada, 94–334. Madrid: Biblioteca de Autores Cristianos.
Antoninus Florentinus. 1484. *Chronicon seu opus historiarum.* Nuremberg: Koberger.
Augustine of Hippo. 1950. *St. Augustine's Confessions with an English Translation by William Watts.* 2 vols. Loeb Classical Library. Cambridge, MA: Harvard University Press.

Barletta, Gabriel. 1521. *Barlete Sermones exactissime impressi et per F. Benedictum Britannicum ad unguem castigati additis multis quae aliis omnibus inpressionibus defuere.* Bound with *Sanctuarium Barlete summa diligentia revisum et emendatum: Necnon multis adiunctis prologis: Sermonibus ac notabilibus illustratum.* Brescia, It.: D. Ludovicus Britannicus.

Baronio, Cesare. 1616–40. *Annalium ecclesiasticorum post illustriss. et reverendiss. Caesarem Baronium...auctore R. P. Fr. Abrahamo Bzovio...*8 vols. Cologne: Apud Antonium Boëtzerum.

Bertrán, Luis. 1690. *Tomo segundo de las obras y sermones que predicò, y dexò escritos el glorioso padre, y apostolico varon San Luis Bertran de la sagrada Orden de Predicadores.* Edited by Joan Thomas de Rocaberti. Valencia: Iayme de Bordazar.

*Biblia sacra cum glossis interlineari et ordinaria, Nicolai Lyrani postilla et moralitatibus, Burgensis additionibus et Thoringi replici.* 1545. Lyon.

Blanchard, René. 1890. *Lettres et mandements de Jean V, duc de Bretagne.* 5 vols. Archives de Bretagne 4–8. Nantes: Société des Bibliophiles Bretons.

Bouchart, Alain. 1986. *Grandes croniques de Bretaigne.* Edited by Marie-Louise Auger, Gustave Jeanneau, and Bernard Guenée. 2 vols. Paris: Centre National de la Recherche Scientifique.

*Breviarium juxta ritum S. Ordinis Praedicatorum.* 1909. 2 vols. Rome: In Hospitio Reverendissimi Magistri Ordinis.

*Breviarium secundum ordinem sancti Dominici.* 1481. Venice: Joannes de Solonia and Nicolai Jenson.

*Bullarum diplomatum et privilegiorum sanctorum romanorum pontificum taurinensis editio.* 1857–72. Edited by Francisco Gaude. 25 vols. Turin: Seb. Franco et Henrico Dalmazzo.

Caracciolo, Roberto [Robertus Liciensis]. 1490. *Sermones de laudibus sanctorum.* Basel: Nicolaus Kesler.

Castiglione, Francesco. 1496. "Vita beati Vincentii abbreviata." In Vincent Ferrer, *Sermones de tempore et de sanctis pars hyemalis,* fols. a1v–a5r. Venice: Jacobus Pentius de Leuco, for Lazarus de Soardis.

Decrees of the Council of Trent. 1995. http://history.hanover.edu/texts/trent/ct25.html.

Diago, Francisco. 1598. *Historia de la provincia de Aragon de la orden de predicadores.* Barcelona: Sebastian de Cormellas.

——. 1613. *Anales del Reyno de Valencia...despues del Diluuio hasta la muerte del Rey Don Iayme el Conquistador.* Valencia: Pere Patrici Mey.

——. 2001. *Historia de la vida, milagros, muerte y discípulos del bienaventurado Predicador Apostólico valenciano S. Vicente Ferrer.* Barcelona: Gabriel Graells y Giraldo Dotil, 1600; facsimile, Valencia: Paris-Valencia S.L.

Dykmans, Marc, S.J. 1980. *L'oeuvre de Patrizi Piccolomini ou le cérémonial papal de la première Renaissance.* 2 vols. Vatican City: Biblioteca Apostolica Vaticana.

——. 1985. *Le cérémonial papal de la fin du Moyen Âge à la Renaissance.* 4 vols. Brussels: Institut Historique Belge de Rome.

Escolano, Gaspar. 1610. *Decada primera de la historia de la insigne y Coronada ciudad y Reyno de Valencia.* Valencia: Pedro Patricio Mey.

Ferrer de Valdecebro, Andrés. 1781. *Historia de la vida maravillosa y admirable del segundo Pablo apostol de Valencia S. Vicente Ferrer.* Madrid: Manuel de Sancha.

———. 2007. *El porqué de todas las cosas*. Edited by Antonio Bernat Vistarini and John T. Cull. Palma de Mallorca, Sp.: José J. de Olañeta.

Flamini, Giovanni Antonio. 1529. *Vitae patrum inclyti ordinis praedicatorum*. Bologna: Haeredes Hieronymi de Benedictis.

Fontana, Vincentio Maria. 1675. *Monumenta Dominicana*. Rome: Nicolai Angelo Tinassio.

Gerson, Jean. 1960–73. *Oeuvres complètes*. Edited by Palémon Glorieux. 10 vols. Paris: Desclée & Cie.

*Grandes croniques de Bretaigne*. 1986. Edited by Marie-Louise Auger and Gustave Jeanneau, under the direction of Bernard Guenée. 2 vols. Paris: Éditions du Centre National de la Recherche Scientifique.

Guyard, Bernard. 1634. *La vie de S. Vincent Ferrier religieux de l'Ordre des Freres Prescheurs diuisée en deux parties*. Paris: Denis Moreau.

Head, Thomas. 2000. *Medieval Hagiography: An Anthology*. New York: Garland.

Henricus de Herpf. 1509. *Sermones de tempore et de sanctis*. Hagenau: Henricus Gran for Joannes Rynman.

*Historiae plurimorum sanctorum noviter et laboriose ex diversis libris in unum collecte*. 1483. Cologne: [Ulrich Zell].

Horrox, Rosemary. 1994. *The Black Death*. Manchester Medieval Sources. Manchester, UK: Manchester University Press.

Jacobus de Voragine. 1555. *Legenda, auria ut vocant, seu Sanctorum sanctarumque vitae, ex variis historiis quam diligentissime collectae, ac sedundum anni progressum opera Claudii a Rota digestae*. Lyon: Godefridus Gailliandus.

———. 1993. *The Golden Legend: Readings on the Saints*. Translated by William Granger Ryan. 2 vols. Princeton: Princeton University Press.

Josephus, Flavius. 1981. *The Jewish War*. Translated by G. A. Williamson. Revised ed. by E. Mary Smallwood. Harmondsworth, UK: Penguin.

Kramer, Heinrich. 1501. *Sancte Romane ecclesie fidei defensionis clippeum adversus waldensium seu Pickardorum heresim*. Olomouc: Konrad Baumgarten.

Le Grand, Albert. 1901. *Les vies des Saints de la Bretagne Armorique*. Quimper: J. Salaun.

López de Aragón, Manuel. [1772]. *El Apostol de la paz. Oracion panegyrica, que en la solemne fiesta, que hace su ilustre cofradía al glorioso San Vicente Ferrer, dixo en la Iglesia del Imperial Convento de N. P. Santo Domingo, de México, dia 1 de Mayo de 1772*. Mexico City: Josef de Jáuregui.

López de Salamanca, Juan. 2004. *Evangelios moralizados*. Edited by Arturo Jiménez Moreno. Salamanca: Ediciones Universidad de Salamanca.

Malden, A. R. 1901. *The Canonization of St. Osmund from the Manuscript Records in the Muniment Room of Salisbury Cathedral*. Salisbury, UK: Bennett.

Mansi, Joannes Dominicus. 1759–98. *Sacrorum conciliorum nova, et amplissima collectio*, ed. novissima. 31 vols. Florence: Antonius Zatta.

Martinez Ferrando, J. E., and F. Solsona Climent. 1953. "San Vicente Ferrer y la Casa real de Aragón. Documentación conservada en el Archivo Real de Barcelona." *Analecta sacra Tarraconensia: Revista de ciencias histórico-eclesiásticas* 26:1–143.

Meyer, Johannes. 1918. *Liber de Viris Illustribus Ordinis Praedicatorum*. Edited by Fr. Paulus Loë. Quellen und Forschungen zur Geschichte des Dominikanerordens in Deutschland 12. Leipzig: Otto Harrassowitz.

———. 1933. *Cronica brevis Ordinis Praedicatorum*. Edited by Heribert C. Scheeben. Quellen und Forschungen zur Geschichte des Dominikanerordens in Deutschland 29. Leipzig: Albertus Magnus Verlag.

Mirk, John. 1905. *Mirk's Festial: A Collection of Homilies by Johannes Mirkus (John Mirk), Part 1*. Edited by Theodor Erbe. London: Published for the Early English Text Society by Keegan Paul, Trench, Trübner & Co.

*Missale Romanum ex decreto SS. Concilii tridentini restitutum, S. Pii V., pontificis maximi, jussu editum Clementis VIII, Urbain VIII et Leonis XIII auctoritate recognitum*. 1911. Rome: Societas S. Joannis Evang.

Muratori, L. A. 1900–[75]. *Rerum italicarum scriptores: Raccolta degli storici italiani dal cinquecento al millecinquecento*. 26 vols. Città di Castello, It.: S. Lapi.

Ostrero, Martine, Agostino Paravicini Bagliani, Kathrin Utz Tremp, and Catherine Chène. 1999. *L'imaginaire du sabbat: Édition critique des textes les plus anciens (1430 c.–1440 c.)*. Lausanne: Université de Lausanne.

Ovid. 1972. *Ovid's Metamorphoses*. Edited by William S. Anderson. 2 vols. Norman: University of Oklahoma Press.

Parets, Miquel. 1991. *A Journal of the Plague Year: The Diary of the Barcelona Tanner Miquel Parets, 1651*. Edited and translated by James Amelang. New York: Oxford University Press.

*Patrologia Latina: The Full Text Database*. 1996–. Cambridge: Chadwyck-Healey.

Peres, Miquel. 2007. *La vida de sant Vicent Ferrer*. Edited by Carme Arronis i Llopis. Text based on the same title published in Valencia by Joan Jofré in 1510. Valenciana prosa. Biblioteca. http://tintadellamp.ua.es/biblioteca/santvicentfitxa.htm.

Petrus de Natalibus. 1519. *Catalogus sanctorum [et] gestorum eorum ex diversis voluminibus collectus*. Lyon: Jacobus Saccon.

Pio, Michele. 1620. *Delle vite degli huomini illustri di S. Domenico*. Bologna: Sebastiano Bonomi.

Plaine, François. 1921. *Monuments du procès de canonisation du bienheureux Charles de Blois, duc de Bretagne, 1320–1364*. Saint-Brieuc, Fr.: R. Prud'homme.

Pseudo-Albertus Magnus. 1992. *Women's Secrets: A Translation of Pseudo-Albertus Magnus's* De Secretis Mulierum *with Commentaries*. Translated by Helen Rodnite Lemay. Albany: SUNY Press.

Quintana, Augustín de. 1890. *Confessonario en Lengua Mixe … Publié par le Comte de Charancey*. Alençon, Fr.: E. Renaut-De Broise, Imp.

Ranzano, Pietro [Petrus Ransanus]. 2000–. *Vita Vincentii*. In *Acta sanctorum: The Full-Text Database*. Aprilis, 1:482–512. Cambridge: Chadwyck-Healey.

Reichert, Benedictus Maria. 1900. *Monumenta ordinis fratrum praedicatorum historica, 8. Acta capitulorum generalium, 3: Ab anno 1380 usque ad annum 1498*. Rome: Domo Generalitia.

Ribadeneyra, Pedro de. 1734. *Flos sanctorum, de las vidas de los santos*. 2 vols. Barcelona: Juan Piferrer.

Rolevinck, Werner. 1479. *Fasciculus temporum omnes antiquorum chronicas complectus*. Cologne: Heinrich Quentell.

Rölleke, Heinz. 1985. *Kinder- und Hausmärchen gesammelt durch die Brüder Grimm. Vollständige Ausgabe auf der Grundlage der dritten Auflage (1837)*. Frankfurt am Main: Deutscher Klassiker Verlag.

"Solemnia Canonizationis S. Nicolai de Tolentino (An. 1446)." 1909. *Analecta Augustiniana* 3 (10): 236–37.

Surius, Laurentius. 1570–75. *De probatis sanctorum historiis.* 6 vols. Cologne: Geruinus Calenius & Haeredes Quntelii.

——. 1875–80. *Historiae seu vitae sanctorum juxta optimam coloniensem editionem.* 13 vols. Turin: Marietti.

Tatar, Maria. 2002. *The Annotated Classic Fairy Tales.* New York: Norton.

Teixidor, José. 1999. *Vida de San Vicente Ferrer. Apóstol de Europa.* Edited by Alfonso Esponera Cerdán. 2 vols. Valencia: Ajuntament de Valencia.

Teoli, Antonio. 1735. *Storia della vita, e del culto di S. Vincenzo Ferrerio dell'Ordine de' Predicatori.* Rome: Giovanni Battista de Caporali.

Thomas Aquinas. 2012. *Summa theologiae.* http://www.corpusthomisticum.org/iopera.html.

Thomas de Cantimpré. 1986. *Life of Christina Mirabilis.* Translated by Margot King. Toronto: Peregrina Publishing.

Torquemada, Juan de [Johannes de Turrecremata]. 1477. *Quaestiones evangeliorum de tempore quam de sanctis.* Rome: Johannes Schurener de Bopardia.

Trithemius, Johannes. (1601) 1966. *Opera historica, quotquot hactenus reperiri potuerunt, omnia.* Frankfurt: Typis Wechelianis apud Claudium. Reprint, Frankfurt: Minerva.

Vaucelle, E.-R. 1908. *Catalogue des lettres de Nicolas V concernant la province ecclésiastique de Tours d'après les registres des Archives Vaticanes.* Paris: Alphonse Picard.

Vidal y Micó, Francisco. 1735. *Historia de la portentosa vida, y milagros del Valenciano apostol de Europa S. Vicente Ferrer.* Valencia, Joseph Estevan Dolz.

——. 1777. *Portentosa vida de el apostol de la Europa S. Vicente Ferrer.* Barcelona: Eulalia Piferrer Viuda.

Vincent Ferrer. 1487. *Sermones de tempore et de sanctis.* Cologne: [Heinrich Quentell].

——. 1496. *Sermones de tempore et de sanctis pars hyemalis.* Venice: Jacobus Pentius de Leuco, for Lazarus de Soardis.

——. 1693. *Sancti Vincentii Ferrarii Hispani, patria Valentini Ordinis Praedicatorum ... Opera omnia: Tomus primus.* Valencia: Iacobus de Bordazer & Artazú.

Zanacchi, Simone. 2010. "Life of the Blessed Ursulina of Parma." In *Two Women of the Great Schism,* 75–119. Edited and translated by Bruce L. Venarde and Renate Blumenfeld-Kosinski. Toronto: Iter Inc.

## Secondary Works

Abulafia, David. 1995. "Ferrante of Naples: The Statecraft of a Renaissance Prince." *History Today* 45 (2): 19–25.

——. 2004. "The South." In *Italy in the Age of the Renaissance, 1300–1550,* edited by John M. Najemy, 208–25. Oxford: Oxford University Press.

Aguzzi-Barbagli, Danilo. 2003. "Roberto Caracciolo of Lecce, c. 1425–6 May 1495." In *Contemporaries of Erasmus: A Biographical Register of the Renaissance and Reformation.* Vols. 1–3, edited by Peter G. Bietenholz and Thomas Brian Deutscher, 265–66. Toronto: University of Toronto Press.

Alecci, Antonio. 1964. "Barletta, Gabriele." In *Dizionario Biografico degli Italiani.* http://www.treccani.it/enciclopedia/gabriele-barletta_(Dizionario-Biografico)/.

Allies, Mary H. 1878. *Three Catholic Reformers of the Fifteenth Century.* London: Burns and Oates.

Ames, Christine Caldwell. 2009. *Righteous Persecution: Inquisition, Dominicans, and Christianity in the Middle Ages.* Philadelphia: University of Pennsylvania Press.

Andrić, Stanko. 2000. *The Miracles of St. John Capistran.* Budapest: Central European University Press.

Areford, David S. 2010. *The Viewer and the Printed Image in Late Medieval Europe.* Farnham, UK, and Burlington, VT: Ashgate.

Arenas Frutos, Isabel, and Carmen Cebrian Gonzalez. 1991. "La orden dominicana en el mapa americano del siglo XVII." In *Los dominicos y el nuevo mundo. Actas del III Congreso Internacional (Granada, 10–14 de septiembre de 1990),* 1–33. Madrid: Deimos.

Arnau-García, Ramón. 1987. *San Vicente Ferrer y las eclesiologías del cisma.* Valencia: Facultad de teología San Vicente Ferrer.

Arnold, John H. 2001. *Inquisition and Power: Catharism and the Confessing Subject in Medieval Languedoc.* Philadelphia: University of Pennsylvania Press.

Arnoux, Mathieu. 2002. "Oath." In *Encyclopedia of the Middle Ages,* edited by André Vauchez. London: James Clarke. http://www.oxfordreference.com.

*Arte y mística del barroco. Catálogo de exposición, marzo-junio 1994.* 1994. Mexico City: Departamento del Distrito Federal, Universidad Autónoma de México, and Consejo Nacional para la Cultura y las Artes.

Ashley, Benedict M. 1990. *The Dominicans.* Collegeville, MN: Liturgical Press.

Ashmolean Museum. 2012. "Bartolommeo degli Erri: *St Vincent Ferrer Preaching before a Pope.*" http://www.ashmolean.org/ash/objects/objectviews/WA1850.18.html.

Attwater, Donald, and John Cumming. 1994. *A New Dictionary of Saints.* Collegeville, MN: Liturgical Press.

Aupest-Conduché, Dominique, and Guy Devailly. 1980. *Histoire religieuse de la Bretagne.* Chambray, Fr.: C.L.D.

Bäärnhielm, Güran, and Janken Myrdal. 2004. "Miracles and Medieval Life: Canonization Proceedings as a Source for Medieval Social History." In *Procès de canonisation au Moyen Âge: Aspects juridiques et religieux,* edited by Gábor Klaniczay, 101–16. Collection de l'École française de Rome 340. Rome: École française de Rome.

Bailey, Michael D. 2003. *Battling Demons: Witchcraft, Heresy, and Reform in the Late Middle Ages.* University Park: Pennsylvania State University Press.

Bakewell, Peter, and Jacqueline Holler. 2010. *A History of Latin America to 1825.* 3rd ed. Chichester, UK: Wiley-Blackwell.

Balcou, Jean, and Yves Le Gallo, eds. 1987. *Histoire littéraire et culturelle de la Bretagne.* Paris: Champion.

Barber, Richard W. 2004. *The Holy Grail: Imagination and Belief.* Cambridge, MA: Harvard University Press.

Barbieri, Sergio. 2004. "Patrimonio Artistico." In *La Orden de Santo Domingo en Córdoba. Historia y patrimonio,* edited by Rubén González, Alberto Saguier Fonrouge, Esteban F. Llamosas, Sergio Barbieri, Javier Correa, and Matilde Tagle, 59–134. Córdoba, Argen.: Gráficos Pugliese Siena.

Barcellona, Valentino. 1761. *Memorie della vita letteraria, e de' viaggi di Pietro Ranzano.* Opuscoli di autori siciliani 6. Catania: Gioachimo Pulejo.

Barilaro, Antonio. 1977–78. "Pietro Ranzano, vescovo di Lucera, umanista domenicano di Palermo." *Memorie Domenicane,* n.s., 8–9:1–197.

Barrón Escamillo, Martin. 1980. *San Vicente Ferrer 1780–1980: Historia de un pueblo.* N.p.: Talleres de litoformas Muñoz.

Bartlett, Robert J. 2004. *The Hanged Man: A Story of Miracle, Memory, and Colonialism in the Middle Ages.* Princeton: Princeton University Press.

Bausi, Francesco. 1991. "Francesco da Castiglione fra umanesimo e teologia." *Interpres* 11:112–81.

Bayón, Damián, and Murillo Marx. 1992. *History of South American Colonial Art and Architecture: Spanish South America and Brazil.* Translated by Jennifer F. Blankley, Angela P. Hall, and Richard Rees. New York: Rizzoli.

Beltrán, Antonio. 1960. *Estudio sobre el Santo Cáliz de la catedral de Valencia.* Valencia: Instituto Diocesano Valentino.

Benati, Daniele. 1983–84. "La pittura rinascimentale." In *La Basilica di San Petronio in Bologna,* edited by Luciano Bellosi, 2:143–94. Milan: Silvana Editoriale.

———. 1988. *La bottega degli Erri e la pittura del Renascimento a Modena.* Modena: Artioli Editore.

———. 1996. "Erri." In *The Dictionary of Art,* edited by Jane Turner, 10:489–90. New York: Grove.

Bennett, Janice. 2004. *St. Laurence and the Holy Grail: The Story of the Holy Chalice of Valencia.* San Francisco: Ignatius Press.

Ben-Shalom, Ram. 2004. "A Minority Looks at the Mendicants: Isaac Nathan the Jew and Thomas Connecte the Carmelite." *Journal of Medieval History* 30:213–43.

Bentley, Jerry H. 1987. *Politics and Culture in Renaissance Naples.* Princeton: Princeton University Press.

Benvenuti, Anna, Elena Giannarelli, and Chiara Battigelli Baldasseroni. 1998. *Il diacono Lorenzo tra storia e leggenda.* Florence: Edizioni della Meridiana.

Bertolotti, Maurizio. 1991. "The Ox's Bones and the Ox's Hide: A Popular Myth, Part Hagiography and Part Witchcraft." In *Microhistory and the Lost Peoples of Europe,* edited by Edward Muir and Guido Ruggiero and translated by Eren Branch, 42–70. Baltimore: Johns Hopkins University Press.

Bertucci, Sadoc M. 1969. "Vincenzo Ferrer, santo." In *Bibliotheca Sanctorum,* 12:1171–72. Rome: Istituto Giovanni XXIII.

Beuchot, Mauricio. 1987. "La cosmovisión filosófica de Manuel López de Aragón." *Omnia* 3 (7): 9–15.

*Biblioteca agiografica italiana (BAI): Repertorio di testi e manoscritti, secoli XIII–XV.* 2003. Edited by Jacques Dalarun, Lino Leonardi et al. 2 vols. and CD-rom. Florence: Edizioni del Galluzzo.

*Bibliotheca hagiographica latina antiquae et mediae aetatis.* 1900–1901. 2 vols. Brussels: Société des Bollandistes.

*Bibliotheca hagiographica latina antiquae et mediae aetatis. Supplementi.* 1911. Brussels: Société des Bollandistes.

Bilinkoff, Jodi. 1999. "The Many 'Lives' of Pedro de Ribadeneyra." *Renaissance Quarterly* 52 (1): 180–96.

Biografías y Vidas. 2004–12. "Conde de Oropesa." http://www.biografiasyvidas. com/biografia/o/oropesa.htm.

Biraben, Jean-Noel. 1975–76. *Les hommes et la peste en France et dans les pays européens et méditerranéens,* 2 vols. Civilisations et Sociétés 35–36. Paris: Mouton.

Bisson, Thomas N. 1986. *The Medieval Crown of Aragon: A Short History.* Oxford: Clarendon Press.

Black, Charlene Villaseñor. 2003. "St. Anne Imagery and Maternal Archetypes in Spain and Mexico." In *Colonial Saints: Discovering the Holy in the Americas,* edited by Allan Greer and Jodi Bilinkoff, 3–29. New York: Routledge.

Blumenfeld-Kosinski, Renate. 2006. *Poets, Saints, and Visionaries of the Great Schism, 1378–1417.* University Park: Pennsylvania State University Press.

——. 2007. "Dramatic Troubles of *Ecclesia:* Gendered Performances of the Divided Church." In *Cultural Performances in Medieval France,* edited by Eglal Doss-Quinby, Roberta L. Krueger, and E. Jane Burns, 181–194. Rochester, NY: D. S. Brewer.

——. 2009. "The Conceptualization and Imagery of the Great Schism." In *A Companion to the Great Western Schism, 1378–1417,* edited by Joëlle Rollo-Koster and Thomas Izbicki, 123–58. Leiden, Neth.: Brill.

Boiteux, Martine. 2004. "Le rituel romain de canonisation et ses représentations à l'époque moderne." In *Procès de canonisation au Moyen Âge: aspects juridiques et religieux,* edited by Gábor Klaniczay, 327–55. Collection de l'École française de Rome 340. Rome: École française de Rome.

Bologna, Ferdinando. 1977. *Napoli e le rotte Mediterranee della pittura da Alfonso il Magnanimo a Ferdinando il Cattolico.* Naples: Società napoletana di storia patria.

Bolte, Johannes, and Georg Polívka. (1913–32) 1963. *Anmerkungen zu den Kinder- und Hausmärchen der Brüder Grimm.* 5 vols. Leipzig: Dieterich. Reprint, Hildesheim: Georg Olms.

*The Book of Saints: A Dictionary of Servants of God Canonized by the Catholic Church Compiled by the Benedictine Monks of St Augustine's Abbey, Ramsgate.* 1994. 6th ed. London: Cassell.

Bottari, Stefano. 1954. *La pittura del Quattrocento in Sicilia.* Messina: G. d'Anna.

Boureau, Alain. 2004. "Saints et démons dans les procès de canonisation du début du XIV siècle." In *Procès de canonisation au Moyen Âge: Aspects juridiques et religieux,* edited by Gábor Klaniczay, 199–221. Collection de l'École française de Rome 340. Rome: École française de Rome.

Bozóky, Edina. 2007. *La politique des reliques de Constantin à Saint Louis: Protection collective et légitimation du pouvoir.* Paris: Beauchesne.

Brettle, P. Sigismond. 1924. *San Vicente Ferrer und sein literarischer Nachlass.* Vorreformationsgeschichtliche Forschungen 10. Münster, Ger.: Aschendorff.

Bridgeman Art Library Limited. 1972–2013. "St. Vincent Ferrer Performing a Miracle." http://www.bridgemanart.com/asset/59675/Diziani-Gasparo-1689–1767/St.-Vincent-Ferrer-performing-a-miracle.

British Museum. 2013. "Pierre Mariette I (Biographical details)." http:// www.britishmuseum.org/research/search_the_collection_database/term_ details.aspx?bioId=93848.

Britnell, Jennifer, and Derek Stubbs. 1986. "The *Mirabilis Liber:* Its Compilation and Influence." *Journal of the Warburg and Courtauld Institutes* 49:126–49.

Brown, Peter. 1981. *The Cult of the Saints: Its Rise and Function in Latin Christianity.* Chicago: University of Chicago Press.

Brunvand, Jan Harold. 1989. *Curses! Broiled Again! The Hottest Urban Legends Going.* New York: Norton.

Burke, Peter. 1984. "How to Be a Counter-Reformation Saint." In *Religion and Society in Early Modern Europe, 1500–1800,* edited by Kaspar von Greyerz, 45–55. London: George Allen & Unwin.

Burrow, John Anthony. 2004. *Gestures and Looks in Medieval Narrative.* Cambridge: Cambridge University Press.

Busolini, Dario. 1997. "Fontana, Vincenzo Maria." In *Dizionario Biografico degli Italiani.* http://www.treccani.it/enciclopedia/vincenzo-maria-fontana_(Dizionario-Biografico)/.

Butler, Alban. 1963. "April 5: St. Vincent Ferrer (A.D. 1419)." In *Butler's Lives of the Saints,* edited by Herbert Thurston and Donald Attwater, 2:31–34. New York: Kenedy.

Bynum, Caroline Walker. 1982. *Jesus as Mother: Studies in the Spirituality of the High Middle Ages.* Berkeley: University of California Press.

———. 1999. Review of *Sainthood in the Later Middle Ages,* by André Vauchez, translated by Jean Birrell. *Journal of Social History* 32(4):991-93.

———. 2001. "Wonder." In *Metamorphosis and Identity,* 37–75. Brooklyn: Zone Books.

———. 2007. *Wonderful Blood: Theology and Practice in Late Medieval Northern Germany and Beyond.* Philadelphia: University of Pennsylvania Press.

Caby, Cécile. 2004. "L'humanisme au service de l'observance: Quelques pistes de recherche." In *Humanisme et Église en Italie et en France méridionale (XVe siècle–milieu du XVIe siècle),* edited by Patrick Gilli, 115–48. Collection de l'École française de Rome 330. Rome: École française de Rome.

Caby, Cécile, and R. M. Dessi, eds. 2012. *Les humanistes et l'église: pratiques culturelles et échanges entre les litterati ecclésiastiques et laïcs dans les villes italiennes, XIIIe–début XVIe siècle.* Turnhout, Belg.: Brepols, 2012.

Cahier, Charles. (1867–71) 1966. *Charactéristiques des Saints dans l'art populaire.* 2 vols. Paris: Librairie Poussielgue Frères. Reprint, Brussels: Culture et Civilisation.

Cameron, Euan. 2010. *Enchanted Europe: Superstition, Reason, and Religion, 1250–1750.* Oxford: Oxford University Press.

Camporeale, Salvatore I. 2000. "Rhetoric, Freedom, and the Crisis of Christian Tradition: Valla's *Oratio* on the Pseudo Donation of Constantine." In *Innovation and Tradition: Essays on Renaissance Art and Culture,* edited by Dag Andersson and Roy Eriksen, 17–25. Rome: Kappa.

Cassard, Jean-Christophe. 1995. "Propagande partisane et miracles engagés dans la guerre de Succession de Bretagne." *Annales de Bretagne et des pays de l'Ouest* 102 (2): 7–24.

———. 1996. "Vincent Ferrier, le Breton et les Sahraouis." *Bulletin de la société archéologique du Finistère* 125:341–43.

———. 1998. "Le légat catéchiste. Vincent Ferrier en Bretagne (1418–1419)." *Revue historique* 298 (2): 323–43.

——. 2000. "La carrière posthume de Vicente Ferrer en Bretagne." In *Miscellanées de langues et cultures romanes et celtiques: en homage à Robert Omnès,* edited by Philippe Cahuzac and Yvon Cousquer, 193–201. Brest, Fr.: Université de Bretagne Occident.

——. 2006. "Vincent Ferrier en Bretagne: Un tournée triomphale, prélude à une riche carrière posthume." In *Mirificus praedicator:À l'occasion du sixième centenaire du passage de Saint Vincent Ferrier en pays romand: Actes du colloque d'Estavayer-le-Lac, 7–9 octobre 2004,* edited by Paul-Bernard Hodel and Franco Morenzoni, 77–104. Rome: Istituto storico domenicano.

*Catalogue général des manuscrits des bibliothèques publiques des départements.* 1849–85. 7 vols. Paris: Imprimerie Nationale.

Châtellier, Louis. 1997. *The Religion of the Poor: Rural Missions in Europe and the Formation of Modern Catholicism, c.1500–c.1800.* Translated by Brian Pearce. Cambridge: Cambridge University Press.

Chène, Catherine. 2006. "La plus ancienne vie de Vincent Ferrier racontée par le Dominicain allemand Jean Nider (ca. 1380–1438)." In *Mirificus praedicator: À l'occasion du sixième centenaire du passage de Saint Vincent Ferrier en pays romand: Actes du colloque d'Estavayer-le-Lac, 7–9 octobre 2004,* edited by Paul-Bernard Hodel and Franco Morenzoni, 121–66. Rome: Istituto storico domenicano.

Chiodi, Alberto Mario. 1951. "Bartolomeo degli Erri e i polittici Domenicani." *Commentari: Rivista di critica e storia dell'arte* 2:17–25.

Church of Saint Vincent Ferrer. 2012. "Saint Vincent Ferrer." http://www.csvf.org/stvincentofferrer.html.

Christe, Yves. 1992. "The Apocalypse in Monumental Art." In *The Apocalypse in the Middle Ages,* edited by Richard K. Emmerson and Bernard McGinn, 234–58. Ithaca: Cornell University Press.

Christian, Wiliam A. 1981. *Local Religion in Sixteenth-Century Spain.* Princeton: Princeton University Press.

Ciudad de San Vicente Buenos Aires. 2013. "Ciudad. Historia. Primeras iglesias. Iglesia San Vicente." http://www.websanvicente.com.ar.

Coakley, John Wayland. 1980. "The representation of Sanctity in Late Medieval Hagiography: Evidence from *Lives* of Saints of the Dominican Order." ThD diss., Harvard Divinity School, Harvard University.

Cobianchi, Roberto. 2006. "The Use of Woodcuts in Fifteenth-Century Italy." *Print Quarterly* 23:47–54.

——. 2007. "Raphael, Ceremonial Banners and Devotional Prints: New Light on the Città di Castello's Nicholas of Tolentino Altarpiece." In *Art and the Augustinian Order in Early Renaissance Italy,* edited by Louise Bourdua and Anne Dunlop, 205–28. Aldershot, UK: Ashgate.

Cochrane, Eric. 1981. *Historians and Historiography in the Italian Renaissance.* Chicago: University of Chicago Press.

Cohn, Norm. 1975. *Europe's Inner Demons: An Enquiry Inspired by the Great Witch-Hunt.* New York: New American Library.

Cohn, Werner. 1935. *Holz- und Metallschnitte aus öffentlichen Sammlungen und Bibliotheken in Hannover, Koblenz, Köln, Leipzig, und Lüneberg.* Strasbourg: J. H. E.

Heitz. (Vol. 86 of Paul Heitz. [1906]–42. *Einblattdrucke des fünfzehnten Jahrhunderts,* 100 vols. Strasbourg: Heitz.)

Collins, David J. 2008. *Reforming Saints: Saints' Lives and Their Authors in Germany, 1470–1530.* New York: Oxford University Press.

Collins, James. 1994. *Classes, Estates, and Order in Early Modern Brittany.* Cambridge: Cambridge University Press.

Cooper, Kate, and Jeremy Gregory, eds. 2005. *Signs, Wonders, Miracles: Representations of Divine Power in the Life of the Church.* Studies in Church History 41. Woodbridge, UK: Boydell Press.

Cossio del Pomar, Felipe. 1964. *Peruvian Colonial Art: The Cuzco School of Painting.* Translated by Genaro Arbaiza. New York: Wittenborn.

Creytens, Raymond. 1975. "La déposition de maître Martial Auribelli O.P. par Pie II (1462)," *Archivum fratrum praedicatorum* 45:147–200.

Croix, Alain. 1981. *La Bretagne aux 16e et 17e siècles: La vie—La mort—La foi.* 2 vols. Paris: Maloine.

———. 1993. *L'âge d'or de la Bretagne 1532–1675.* Rennes: Éditions Ouest-France.

Darnton, Robert. 1984. *The Great Cat Massacre and Other Episodes in French Cultural History.* New York: Vintage Books.

Daston, Lorraine. 1991. "Marvelous Facts and Miraculous Evidence in Early Modern Europe," *Critical Inquiry* 18 (1): 93–124.

d'Avray, David L. 2005. *Medieval Marriage: Symbolism and Society.* Oxford: Oxford University Press.

Debby, Nirit Ben-Aryeh. 2001. *Renaissance Florence in the Rhetoric of Two Popular Preachers: Giovanni Dominici (1356–1419) and Bernardino da Siena (1380–1444).* Late Medieval and Early Modern Studies [formerly Binghamton Medieval and Early Modern Studies], 4. Turnhout, Belg.: Brepols.

Delaruelle, Étienne. 1975. "L'Antéchrist chez S. Vincent Ferrier, S. Bernardin de Sienne, et autour de Jeanne d'Arc." In *La piété populaire au Moyen Âge,* 39–64. Turin: Bottega d'Erasmo.

Delooz, Pierre. 1969. *Sociologie et canonisations.* Collection scientifique de la Faculté de droit du l'Université de Liège 30. Liège, Belg.: Faculté de droit.

de Viguerie, Jean. 1983. "Le miracle dans la France du XVIIe siècle." *Dix-septième siècle* 35:313–31.

di Macco, M. 1979. "Dux Aymo, 1429." In *Giacomo Jacquerio e il gotico internazionale,* edited by Enrico Castelnuovo and Giovanni Romano, 398–403. Turin: Museo Civico.

Ditchfield, Simon. 1993. "Martyrs on the Move: Relics as Vindicators of Local Diversity in the Tridentine Church." In *Martyrs and Martyrologies: Papers Read at the 1992 Summer Meeting and the 1993 Winter Meeting of the Ecclesiastical History Society,* 283–94. Studies in Church History 30. Oxford: Blackwell.

———. 1995. *Liturgy, Sanctity and History in Tridentine Italy: Pietro Maria Campi and the Preservation of the Particular.* Cambridge: Cambridge University Press.

Dodgson, Campbell. (1903) 1980. *Catalogue of Early German and Flemish Woodcuts Preserved in the Department of Prints and Drawings in the British Museum.* 2 vols. London: British Museum. Reprint, Vadus, Liechtenstein: Quarto Press.

Doménech, Fernando Benito. 2000. *Joan de Joanes: Un maestro del Renacimiento. Fundación Santander Central Hispano, del 3 de octubre al 26 de noviembre de 2000.* Valencia: BSCH Fundación, Generalitat Valenciana.

Domínicos Chile. 2012. "Iconografía di San Vicente Ferrer." http://www.dominicos. net/santos/san_vicente_ferrer/san_vicente_ferrer_iconos1.html.

Duffy, Eamon. 1992. *The Stripping of the Altars: Traditional Religion in England c. 1400–c. 1580.* New Haven: Yale University Press.

Eire, Carlos N. 1989. *War against the Idols: The Reformation of Worship from Erasmus to Calvin.* Cambridge: Cambridge University Press.

Enders, Jody. 2002. *Death by Drama and Other Medieval Urban Legends.* Chicago: University of Chicago Press.

Escartí, Vicent Josep. 1997. "Els centenaris de la canonització de sant Vicent: Testimonis en Valencià dels segles XVI i XVII." In *Paradigmes de la Història, I. Actes del Congrés "Sant Vicent Ferrer i el seu temps" (València, 13–16 maig, 1996),* 135–53. Valencia: Biblioteca "Josep Giner."

Esponera Cerdán, Alfonso. 2005. "Cronología de San Vicente Ferrer." *Escritos del Vedat* 35:209–14.

——. 2007. *El oficio de predicar: Los postulados teológicos de los sermones de San Vicente Ferrer.* Monumenta histórica iberoamericana de la Orden de Predicadores 30. Salamanca: Editorial San Esteban.

——. 2008 "El Dominico San Vicente Ferrer y los Judios." *Escritos del Vedat,* 38:223–64.

——. 2009. "El historiador Francisco Diago, O.P. (1561–1615)." *Escritos del Vedat* 39:281–319.

Fages, Pierre-Henri. 1901. *Histoire de Saint Vincent Ferrier.* 2 vols. Paris: Picard.

——. 1904. *Procès de la canonisation de Saint Vincent Ferrier pour faire suite à l'histoire du même saint.* Paris: Picard.

——. 1905. *Notes et documents de l'histoire de Saint Vincent Ferrier.* Paris: Picard.

Fahy, Everett. 1966. "The Beginnings of Fra Bartolommeo." *Burlington Magazine* 108 (762): 456–63.

Falkenstein, Karl. 1840. *Geschichte der Buchdruckerkunst.* Leipzig: Teubner.

Farmer, Sharon. 2002. *Surviving Poverty in Medieval Paris: Gender, Ideology, and the Daily Lives of the Poor.* Ithaca: Cornell University Press.

Feige, P. 1989. "Ferrer, Vicent[e]." In *Lexikon des Mittelalters,* vol. 4, cols. 395–97. Stuttgart: Metzler. *Brepolis Medieval Encyclopedias—Lexikon des Mittelalters Online.* http://www.brepolis.net/bme.

Fentress, James, and Chris Wickham. 1992. *Social Memory.* Oxford: Blackwell.

Ferri Chulio, Andrés de Sales. 1995. *Iconografía de San Vicente Ferrer.* Valencia: Federico Domenech.

Field, Sean L. 2006. *Isabelle of France: Capetian Sanctity and Franciscan Identity in the Thirteenth Century.* Notre Dame, IN: University of Notre Dame Press.

Figliuolo, Bruno. 1997. *La cultura a Napoli nel secondo Quattrocento. Ritratti di protagonisti.* Udine, It.: Forum.

Finucane, Ronald C. 1995. *Miracles and Pilgrims: Popular Beliefs in Medieval England.* 2nd ed. New York: St. Martin's.

——. 1997. *The Rescue of the Innocents: Endangered Children in Medieval Miracles.* New York: St. Martin's.

Foa, Anna. 1978. "Cassetta (Casseta, Caseta), Salvo." In *Dizionario Biografico degli Italiani.* http://www.treccani.it/enciclopedia/salvo-cassetta_(Dizionario-Biografico)/.

Fondazione Federico Zeri. 2012a. "Caporali Bartolomeo, San Vincenzo Ferrer riporta alla vita un bambino." http://fe.fondazionezeri.unibo.it/catalogo/scheda.jsp?decorator=layout&apply=true&tipo_scheda=OA&id=19795&tito lo=Caporali+Bartolomeo+%2c+San+Vincenzo+Ferrer+riporta+alla+vita+un +bambino.

———. 2012b. "Granacci Francesco, San Vincenzo Ferrer riporta alla vita un bambino." http://fe.fondazionezeri.unibo.it/catalogo/scheda.jsp?decorator=layout&app ly=true&tipo_scheda=OA&id=39465&titolo=Granacci+Francesco+%2c+San +Vincenzo+Ferrer+riporta+alla+vita+un+bambino.

———. 2012c. "Ricci Sebastiano, San Vincenzo Ferrer riporta alla vita un bambino." http://fe.fondazionezeri.unibo.it/catalogo/scheda.jsp?decorator=layout&app ly=true&tipo_scheda=OA&id=68311&titolo=Ricci+Sebastiano+%2c+San+ Vincenzo+Ferrer+riporta+alla+vita+un+bambino.

Frasco, Armand B. 2010. "'Tugtorogtog': The 2010 Fiesta of San Vicente Ferrer in Chicago." http://www.flickr.com/photos/ambibo/sets/72157623996859865/.

Frazier, Alison Knowles. 2005. *Possible Lives: Authors and Saints in Renaissance Italy.* New York: Columbia University Press.

———. 2010. "A Layman's *Life of St. Augustine* in Late Medieval Italy: Patronage and Polemic." *Traditio* 65:231–86.

Frenken, Ansgar. [2002]. "Vinzenz (Vincent) Ferrer OP." In *Biographisch-Bibliographisches Kirchenlexikon.* Herzberg: Traugott Bautz. http://www.bautz.de/bbkl/v/vinzenz_ferrer.shtml.

Fries, Albert. 1965. "Albertus Magnus auf des Kanzel: Ein Andachtsbild." *Archivum fratrum praedicatorum* 35:249–54.

Fros, Henryk. 1986. *Bibliotheca hagiographica latina antiquae et mediae aetatis. Novum supplementum.* Brussels: Société des Bollandistes.

Fubini, Riccardo. 1996. "Humanism and Truth: Valla Writes against the Donation of Constantine." *Journal of the History of Ideas* 57 (1): 79–86.

Gage, Eleni N. 2005. "Oaxaca's Alternate Lifestyle Scene." *Travel and Leisure,* November. http://www.travelandleisure.com/articles/stepping-out.

Galassi, Maria Clelia. 1996. "Bernardo Castello." In *The Dictionary of Art,* edited by Jane Turner, 6:25–26. New York: Grove.

Galliou, Patrick, and Michael Jones. 1991. *The Bretons.* The Peoples of Europe. Oxford: Blackwell.

Gaposhkin, M. Cecilia. 2008. *The Making of Saint Louis: Kingship, Sanctity, and Crusade in the Later Middle Ages.* Ithaca: Cornell University Press.

Garganta, José M. de, and Vicente Forcada. 1956. *Biografía y escritos de San Vicente Ferrer.* Madrid: Biblioteca de Autores Christianos.

Garibaldi, Vittoria. 1996. *Un pittore e la sua città: Benedetto Bonfigli e Perugia.* Milan: Electa.

Gecser, Ottó Sándor. 2003. "Itinerant Preaching in Late Medieval Central Europe: St John Capistran in Wrocław." *Medieval Sermon Studies* 47:5–20.

———. 2010. "Preaching and Publicness: St John of Capestrano and the Making of His Charisma North of the Alps." In *Charisma and Religious Authority: Jewish,*

*Christian, and Muslim Preaching, 1200–1500,* edited by Katherine L. Jansen and Miri Rubin, 145–59. Europa sacra 4. Turnhout, Belg.: Brepols.

Gentili, Augusto. 1982. "Mito cristiano e storia ferrarese nel *Polittico Griffoni.*" In *La corte e lo spazio: Ferrara estense,* edited by Guiseppe Papagno and Amedeo Quondam, 2: 563–76. Centro studi "Europa delle Corti," Biblioteca del Cinquecento 17. Rome: Bulzoni.

Gentili, Augusto, and Fabrizio Torella. 1985. *Giovanni Bellini. Il polittico di San Vincenzo Ferrer.* Venice: Arsenale.

Ghéon, Henri. 1939. *St. Vincent Ferrer.* Translated by F. J. Sheed. New York: Sheed & Ward.

Gibson, Charles. 1966. *Spain in America.* New York: Harper, 1966.

Ginzburg, Carlo. 1991. *Ecstasies: Deciphering the Witches' Sabbath.* Translated by Raymond Rosenthal. Harmondsworth, UK: Penguin.

———. 1999. "Lorenzo Valla on the 'Donation of Constantine.'" In *History, Rhetoric, and Proof,* 54–70. Hanover, NH: University Press of New England.

Giovagnoli, Enrico. 1922. *Le origini della pittura Umbra: Gli affreschi recentemente scoperti nell'alta Umbria.* Città di Castello, It.: Il "Solco" casa editrice.

Given, James B. 1997. *Inquisition and Society: Power, Discipline, and Resistance in Languedoc.* Ithaca: Cornell University Press.

Gneuhs, Geoffrey B. 1989. "Vincent Ferrer, St. (1350–1419)." In *Dictionary of the Middle Ages,* edited by Joseph R. Strayer, 12:452–53. New York: Scribner's.

Goffen, Rona. 1985. "Giovanni Bellini and the Altarpiece of St. Vincent Ferrer." In *Renaissance Studies in Honor of Craig Hugh Smyth,* edited by Andrew Morrogh et al., 2:277–95. Florence: Giunti Barbèra.

———. 1989. *Giovanni Bellini.* New Haven: Yale University Press.

González, Rubén, Alberto Saguier Fonrouge, Esteban F. Llamosas, Sergio Barbieri, Javier Correa, and Matilde Tagle. 2004. *La Orden de Santo Domingo en Córdoba. Historia y patrimonio.* Córdoba, Argen.: Gráficos Pugliese Siena.

Goodich, Michael. 1995. *Violence and Miracle in the Fourteenth Century: Private Grief and Public Salvation.* Chicago: University of Chicago Press.

———. 2001. "Liturgy and the Foundation of Cults in the Thirteenth and Fourteenth Centuries." In *De Sion exibet lex et verbum domini de Hierusalem. Essays on Medieval Law, Liturgy, and Literature in Honour of Amnon Linder,* edited by Yitzhak Hen, 145–57. Cultural Encounters in Late Antiquity and the Middle Ages 1. Turnhout, Belg.: Brepols.

———. 2005. *Lives and Miracles of the Saints: Studies in Medieval Latin Hagiography.* Aldershot, UK: Ashgate Variorum.

———. 2006a. "The Multiple Miseries of Dulcia of St. Chartier (1266) and Cristina of Wellington (1294)." In *Voices from the Bench: The Narratives of Lesser Folk in Medieval Trials,* edited by Michael Goodich, 99–126. New York: Palgrave-Macmillan.

———, ed. 2006b. *Voices from the Bench: The Narratives of Lesser Folk in Medieval Trials.* New York: Palgrave-Macmillan.

Gorce, Matthieu–Maxime. 1923. *Les bases de l'étude historique de Saint Vincent Ferrier.* Paris: Plon-Nourrit.

———. 1924. *Saint Vincent Ferrier (1350–1419).* Paris: Plon-Nourrit.

Greer, Allan, and Jodi Bilinkoff, eds. 2003. *Colonial Saints: Discovering the Holy in the Americas.* New York: Routledge.

Grohe, Johannes. 1993. "Ferrer, 1) Vinzenz (Vicent)." In *Lexikon für Theologie und Kirche,* 3rd ed., edited by Michael Buchberger, col. 1245. Freiburg im Breisgau, Ger.: Herder.

Gutiérrez Haces, Juana, Pedro Ángeles, Clara Bargellini, and Rogelio Ruiz Gomar. 1997. *Cristóbal de Villalpando, ca. 1649–1714: Catálogo razonado.* Mexico City: Fomento Cultural Banamex.

Guzmán, Rodrigo Rhema. 2010. "Vela San Vicente Ferrer, 2010." http://www.youtube.com/watch?v=jSOUuhHYeCk.

Harline, Craig. 2003. *Miracles at the Jesus Oak: Histories of the Supernatural in Reformation Europe.* New York: Doubleday.

Harline, Craig, and Eddy Put. 2002. *The Bishop's Tale: Mathias Hovius among His Flock in Seventeenth-Century Flanders.* New Haven: Yale University Press.

Harvey, Margaret. 1993. *England, Rome, and the Papacy, 1417–1464: The Study of a Relationship.* Manchester, UK: Manchester University Press.

Heck, Christian. 1978. "Saint Vincent Ferrier dans des miniatures et un manuscrit inédits du XVe siècle." *Annuaire de la Société d'Histoire et d'Archéologie de Colmar* 27:63–68.

Heitz, Paul. [1906]–42. *Einblattdrucke des fünfzehnten Jahrhunderts.* 100 vols. Strasbourg: Heitz.

Heming, Carol Piper. 2003. *Protestants and the Cult of the Saints in German-Speaking Europe, 1517–1531.* Kirksville, MO: Truman State University Press.

Heng, Geraldine. 1998. "Cannibalism, the First Crusade, and the Genesis of Medieval Romance." *Differences* 10:98–174.

Herlihy, David. 1984. Review of *La sainteté en Occident aux derniers siècles du Moyen Age d'après les procès de canonisation et les documents hagiographiques,* by André Vauchez. *Catholic Historical Review* 70:173–74.

Herzig, Tamar. 2006. "Witches, Saints, and Heretics: Heinrich Kramer's Ties with Italian Women Mystics." *Magic, Ritual, and Witchcraft* 1:24–55.

Hinnebusch, William A., O.P. 1965. *The History of the Dominican Order: Origins and Growth to 1500.* 2 vols. Staten Island, NY: Alba House.

———. 1984. "Dominicans." In *Dictionary of the Middle Ages,* edited by Joseph R. Strayer, 4:242–55. New York: Scribner's.

Hobbins, Daniel. 2013. "Hearsay, Belief, and Doubt: The Arrival of Antichrist in Fifteenth-Century Italy." Unpublished manuscript.

Hodel, Paul-Bernard. 2006. "D'une édition à l'autre: La lettre de Saint Vincent Ferrier à Jean de Puynoix du 17 décembre 1403." In *Mirificus praedicator: À l'occasion du sixième centenaire du passage de saint Vincent Ferrier en pays romand: Actes du colloque d'Estavayer-le-Lac, 7–9 octobre 2004,* edited by Paul-Bernard Hodel and Franco Morenzoni, 189–204. Dissertationes Historicae 32. Rome: Istituto storico domenicano.

———. 2008. *Le Tractatus de moderno ecclesie scismate de saint Vincent Ferrier (1380). Édition et étude.* Studia Friburgensia 104. Fribourg: Academic Press Fribourg.

Hodel, Paul-Bernard, and Franco Morenzoni, eds. 2006. *Mirificus praedicator: À l'occasion du sixième centenaire du passage de Saint Vincent Ferrier en pays romand: Actes du colloque d'Estavayer-le-Lac, 7–9 octobre 2004.* Dissertationes Historicae 32. Rome: Istituto storico domenicano.

Howard, Peter Francis. 1995. *Beyond the Written Word: Preaching and Theology in the Florence of Archbishop Antoninus, 1427–1459.* Quaderni di "Rinascimento" 28. Florence: Olschki.

——. 2005. "The Fear of Schism." In *Rituals, Images, and Words: Varieties of Cultural Expression in Late Medieval and Early Modern Europe,* edited by F. W. Kent and Charles Zika, 297–323. Late Medieval and Early Modern Studies 3. Turnhout, Belg.: Brepols.

——. 2008. "Preaching Magnificence in Renaissance Florence." *Renaissance Quarterly* 61:325–69.

Hsia, R. Po-Chia. 1992. *Trent 1475: Stories of a Ritual Murder Trial.* New Haven: Yale University Press, in cooperation with Yeshiva University Library.

Huerga, Alvaro. 1994. "Vincent Ferrer." In *Dictionnaire de spiritualité ascétique et mystique. Doctrine et histoire,* vol. 16, cols. 813–22. Paris: Beauchesne.

Humfrey, Peter. 1988. "Competitive Devotions: The Venetian *Scuole Piccole* as Donors of Altarpieces in the Years around 1500." *Art Bulletin* 70:401–23.

*Important Old Master Pictures: The Properties of Mrs. James Hasson … and from Various Sources, Which Will Be Sold at Christie's Great Rooms on Friday, April 18, 1980.* 1980. London: Christie, Manson & Woods.

Jacqueline, Bernard. 1979. "Trois scènes de la vie de saint Vincent Ferrier dans un vitrail de Notre-Dame de Saint-Lô (XVe siècle)." *Archivum fratrum praedicatorum* 49:133–44.

Jaffé, David, Luke Syson, Denise Allen, and Jennifer Helvey. 1999. "Ercole de' Roberti: The Renaissance in Ferrara." *Burlington Magazine* 141 (1153): i–xl.

JeevanJal Ministries. 2012. "Resurrection Miracles." http://www.jeevanjal.org/jeevanjal/rm6.html.

Jones, Michael. 1981. "The Breton Civil War." In *Froissart, Historian,* edited by J. J. N. Palmer, 64–81, 169–72. Woodbridge, UK: Boydell Press, 1981.

——. 1988a. "The Chancery of the Duchy of Brittany from Peter Mauclerc to Duchess Anne, 1213–1514." In Jones, *The Creation of Brittany,* 111–58.

——. 1988b. *The Creation of Brittany: A Late Medieval State.* London: Hambledon Press.

——. 1988c. "The Duchy of Brittany in the Middle Ages." In Jones, *The Creation of Brittany,* 1–12.

——. 1988d. "Les manuscrits d'Anne de Bretagne, Reine de France, Duchesse de Bretagne." In Jones, *The Creation of Brittany,* 371–409.

——. 2003a. *Between France and England: Politics, Power and Society in Late Medieval Brittany.* Variorum Collected Studies Series CS769. Aldershot, UK: Ashgate.

——. 2003b. "'En son habit royal': Le duc de Bretagne et son image vers la fin du Moyen Âge." In Jones, *Between France and England,* 253–78.

——. 2003c. "Notaries and Notarial Practices in Medieval Brittany." In Jones, *Between France and England,* 773–815.

——. 2003d. "Politics, Sanctity and the Breton State: The Case of the Blessed Charles de Blois, Duke of Brittany (d. 1364)." In Jones, *Between France and England,* 215–32.

Jordan, Weseley D. 1992. "An Assessment of a Fifteenth-Century Manuscript Fragment in the Hone Collection Containing Part of a Rhymed Office for St. Vincent Ferrer." *Studies in Music* 26:1–33.

Kaeppeli, Thomas, and Emilio Panella. 1970–93. *Scriptores Ordinis Praedicatorum Medii Aevi.* 4 vols. Rome: Istituto storico domenicano.

Kaftal, George. 1952. *Iconography of the Saints in Tuscan Painting.* Saints in Italian Art 1. Florence: Sansoni.

———. 1965. *Iconography of the Saints in Central and South Italian Schools of Painting.* Saints in Italian Art 2. Florence: Sansoni.

Kaftal, George, and Fabio Bisogni. 1978. *Iconography of the Saints in the Painting of North East Italy,* Saints in Italian Art 3. Florence: Sansoni.

———. 1985. *Iconography of the Saints in the Painting of North West Italy.* Saints in Italian Art 4. Florence: Le Lettere.

Kagan, Richard L. 1995. "Clio and the Crown: Writing History in Habsburg Spain." In *Spain, Europe, and the Atlantic World: Essays in Honour of John H. Elliott,* edited by Richard L. Kagan and Geoffrey Parker, 73–99. Cambridge: Cambridge University Press.

Kamen, Henry. 1993. *The Phoenix and the Flame: Catalonia and the Counter Reformation.* New Haven: Yale University Press.

———. 2010. *The Escorial: Art and Power in the Renaissance.* New Haven: Yale University Press.

Kaminsky, Howard 1971. "The Politics of France's Subtraction of Obedience from Pope Benedict XIII, 27 July 1398." *Proceedings of the American Philosophical Society* 115:366–97.

Katajala-Peltomaa, Sari. 2009. *Gender, Miracles, and Daily Life: The Evidence of Fourteenth-Century Canonization Processes.* Turnhout, Belg.: Brepols.

———. 2010. "Recent Trends in the Study of Medieval Canonizations." *History Compass* 8–9:1083–92.

Kelemen, Pál. 1971. *Peruvian Colonial Painting: A Special Exhibition. The Collection of the Stern Fund and Mr. and Mrs. Arthur Q. Davis with an Additional Selection from the Brooklyn Museum.* [New York]: [Brooklyn Museum].

Kemp, Eric Waldram. 1948. *Canonization and Authority in the Western Church.* Oxford: Oxford University Press.

Kerhervé, Jean. 1987. *L'État Breton aux 14e et 15e siècles: Les ducs, l'argent et les hommes.* 2 vols. Paris: Maloine.

———. 1996. "Nantes. Capitale des Ducs de Bretagne?" In *Nantes et la Bretagne,* edited by Jean Guiffan, 63–78. Nantes-Histoire. Morlaix, Fr.: Éditions Skol Vreich.

Keuffer, Max, and Gottfried Kentenich. (1914) 1973. *Beschreibendes Verzeichnis der Handschriften der Stadtbibliothek zu Trier. VIII. Verzeichnis der Handschriften des historischen Archivs.* Trier, Ger.: Fr. Lintzschen Buchhandlung Friedr. Val. Lintz. Reprint, Wiesbaden: Otto Harrassowitz.

Kieckhefer, Richard. 1984. *Unquiet Souls: Fourteenth-Century Saints and Their Religious Milieu.* Chicago: University of Chicago Press.

———. 1989. *Magic in the Middle Ages.* Cambridge: Cambridge University Press.

Kirschbaum, Engelbert, and Wolfgang Braunfels. 1968–76. *Lexikon der christlichen Ikonographie.* 8 vols. Rome: Herder.

Klaniczay, Gábor, ed. 2004. *Procès de canonisation au Moyen Âge: Aspects juridiques et religieux.* Collection de l'École française de Rome 340. Rome: École française de Rome.

Klein, Peter K. 1992. "Introduction: The Apocalypse in Medieval Art." In *The Apocalypse in the Middle Ages,* edited by Richard K. Emmerson and Bernard McGinn, 159–99. Ithaca: Cornell University Press.

Kleinberg, Aviad M. 1989. "Proving Sanctity: Selection and Authentication of Saints in the Later Middle Ages." *Viator* 20:183–205.

——. 1992. *Prophets in Their Own Country: Living Saints and the Making of Sainthood in the Later Middle Ages.* Chicago: University of Chicago Press.

Knowlson, George Akenhead. 1964. *Jean V, duc de Bretagne et l'Angleterre (1399–1442).* Archives Historiques de Bretagne 2. Cambridge: W. Heffer and Sons.

Koopmans, Rachel. 2011. *Wonderful to Relate: Miracle Stories and Miracle Collecting in High Medieval England.* Philadelphia: University of Pennsylvania Press.

Kovalevsky, Sophie. 2002. "Iconographie de Vincent Ferrier dans les Alpes méridionales." In *D'une montagne à l'autre: Études comparées,* edited by Dominique Rigaux, 197–219. Les cahiers du CRHIPA 6. Grenoble, Fr: CRHIPA.

Krafft, Otfried. 2003. "Ein Brief des Mailänder Dominikanerpriors Lambert von S. Eustorgio zu Kanonisation, Elevation and Kultanfängen des Petrus Martyr (1235)." *Sonderdruck aus Quellen und Forschungen aus Italienischen Archiven und Bibliotheken* 83:403–25.

——. 2005. *Papsturkunde und Heiligsprechung: Die päpstlichen Kanonisationen vom Mittelalter bis zur Reformation: Ein Handbuch.* Cologne: Böhlau.

Kress Foundation. 2012. "Saints Roch and Vincent Ferrer. Ambrogio Borgognone, follower of, Italian." http://www.kressfoundation.org/collection/ViewCollection.aspx?id=72&collectionID=27278.

Krötzl, Christian. 1994. *Pilger, Mirakel und Alltag: Formen des Verhaltens im skandinavischen Mittelalter (12.–15. Jahrhundert).* Helsinki: SHS.

——. 1998. "Prokuratoren, Notare und Dolmetscher: Zur Gestaltung und Ablauf der Zeugeneinvernahmen bei spätmittelalterlichen Kanonisationsprozessen." *Hagiographica* 5:119–40.

——. 1999. "Kanonisationsprozess, Sozialgeschichte und Kanonisches Recht im Spätmittelalter." In *Nordic Perspectives on Medieval Canon Law,* edited by Mia Korpiola, 19–39. Publications of Matthias Calonius Society 2. Helsinki: Matthias Calonius Society.

Künstle, Karl. 1926. *Ikonographie der Heiligen.* Freiburg im Breisgau, Ger.: Herder.

La Borderie, Arthur Le Moyne de. 1895. *Étude historique sur les neuf barons de Bretagne.* Rennes: Plihon et Hervé.

——. 1900. "La Mission de Saint Vincent Ferrier en Bretagne (1418–1419)." *Revue de Bretagne, de Vendée et d'Anjou* 23:245–59.

*La Bretagne au temps des ducs [1491–1991]: Abbaye de Daoulas, 15 juin 1991–6 octobre 1991, Musée Dobrée, Nantes, 9 novembre 1991–9 février 1992.* 1991. Daoulas, Fr.: Centre culturel Abbaye de Daoulas.

Labalme, Patricia H. 1996. "Holy Patronage, Holy Promotion: The Cult of Saints in Fifteenth-Century Venice." In *Saints: Studies in Hagiography,* edited by Sandro

Sticca, 223–49. Medieval and Renaissance Texts and Studies 141. Binghamton, NY: Medieval and Renaissance Texts and Studies.

Langmuir, Gavin. 1990. *History, Religion, and Antisemitism.* Berkeley: University of California Press.

Lara, Jaime. 2004. *City, Temple, Stage: Eschatological Architecture and Liturgical Theatrics in New Spain.* Notre Dame, IN: University of Notre Dame Press.

———. 2005. "A Vulcanological Joachim of Fiore and an Aerodynamic Francis of Assisi in Colonial Latin America." In *Signs, Wonders, Miracles: Representations of Divine Power in the Life of the Church,* edited by Kate Cooper and Jeremy Gregory, 249–72. Studies in Church History 41. Woodbridge, UK: Boydell Press.

Larkin, Brian. 2004. "Liturgy, Devotion, and Religious Reform in Eighteenth-Century Mexico City." *The Americas* 60 (4):493–518.

Lazure, Guy. 2007. "Possessing the Sacred: Monarchy and Identity in Philip II's Relic Collection at the Escorial." *Renaissance Quarterly* 60:58–93.

Le Goff, Jacques. 1980. "Merchant's Time and Church's Time in the Middle Ages." In *Time, Work, and Culture in the Middle Ages,* edited by Jacques Le Goff, translated by Arthur Goldhammer, 29–42. Chicago: University of Chicago Press.

Le Mené, Joseph-Marie. 1881. "Tapisserie de Saint Vincent Ferrier." *Bulletin de la société polymathique du Morbihan,* 115–20.

———. 1888–89. *Histoire du diocèse de Vannes,* 2 vols. Vannes: Lafolye.

———. 1895. "Les Carmes du Bondon." *Bulletin de la société polymathique du Morbihan,* 4–33.

Leguay, Jean-Pierre. 1975. "Vannes au XVe siècle: Étude de topographie urbaine [1ère partie]." *Annales de Bretagne et des pays de l'Ouest* 82:115–32.

———. 1981. *Un réseau urbain au Moyen Âge: Les villes du duché de Bretagne au XIVème et XVème siècles.* Paris: Maloine S. A. Editeur.

Leguay, Jean-Pierre, and Hervé Martin. 1982. *Fastes et malheurs de la Bretagne ducale 1213–1532.* Rennes: Ouest France.

Lehmijoki-Gardner, Maiju. 1998. Review of *Sainthood in the Later Middle Ages,* by André Vauchez, translated by Jean Birrell. *Church History* 67 (3):578–79.

Leone de Castris, Pierluigi. 1997. *Quattrocento Aragonese: La pittura a Napoli al tempo di Alfonso e Ferrante d'Aragona.* Naples: Electa.

Lerner, Robert. 1976. "Refreshment of the Saints: The Time after Antichrist as a Station for Earthly Progress in Medieval Thought." *Traditio* 32:97–144.

L'Estrange, Elizabeth. 2008. *Holy Motherhood: Gender, Dynasty and Visual Culture in the Later Middle Ages.* Manchester, UK: Manchester University Press.

Lett, Didier. 2008. *Un procès de canonisation au Moyen Âge: Essai d'histoire sociale. Nicolas de Tolentino, 1325.* Paris: Presses Universitaires de France.

———. 2009. "La langue du témoin sous la plume du notaire: Témoignages oraux et rédaction de procès de canonisation au début du XIVe siècle." In *L'autorité de l'écrit au Moyen Âge (Orient—Occident): XXXIXe congrès de la SHMESP (Le Caire, 30 avril—5 mai 2008),* 89–106. Paris: Publications de la Sorbonne.

Leveleux, Corinne. 2001. *La parole interdite: Le blasphème dans la France médiévale (XIIIe–XVe siècles): Du péché au crime.* Romanité et Modernité de Droit. Paris: De Boccard.

Levesque, Jean-Donatien. 2000. *Les imprimeurs lyonnais des Sermons de Saint Vincent Ferrier aux XVe et XVIe siècles.* Lyon: Dominicains.

Levot, Prosper-Jean. (1852–57) 1971. "Conecte ou Connecte (Thomas)." In *Biographie Bretonne,* 1:437–39. Vannes: Cauderan. Reprint, Geneva: Slatkine.

Limentani Virdis, Caterina. 2001. *Polittici.* San Giovanni Lupatoto, Italy: Arsenale.

Llamosas, Esteban F., and Matilde Tagle de Cuenca. 2004. "Librería de Predicadores de Córdoba." In *La Orden de Santo Domingo en Córdoba. Historia y patrimonio,* edited by Rubén González, Alberto Saguier Fonrouge, Esteban F. Llamosas, Sergio Barbieri, Javier Correa, and Matilde Tagle, 165–203. Córdoba, Argen.: Gráficos Pugliese Siena.

Longhi, Roberto. 1968. *Officina ferrarese 1934, seguíta dagli Ampliamenti 1940 e dai Nuovi Ampliamenti 1940–55.* Florence: Sansoni.

Longo, Carlo. 2000. "Jean de Pistoie." In *Dictionnaire d'histoire et de géographie ecclésiastiques,* vol. 27, cols. 451–53. Paris: Letouzey et Ané.

López Sanmartín, Germán. 2005. *San Vicente Ferrer en Juchitán Oaxaca.* Tlaxpana, Mex.: Ediciones Quinto Sol.

*Los dominicos y el nuevo mundo. Actas del III Congreso Internacional (Granada, 10–14 de septiembre de 1990).* 1991. Madrid: Deimos.

Luque Alcaide, Elisa. 2005. "Reformist Currents in the Spanish-American Councils of the Eighteenth Century." *Catholic Historical Review* 91 (4): 743–60.

Marshall, Louise. 1994. "Manipulating the Sacred: Image and Plague in Renaissance Italy." *Renaissance Quarterly* 47:485–532.

Marshall, Peter, and Alexandra Walsham. 2006. "Migrations of Angels in the Early Modern World." In *Angels in the Early Modern World,* edited by Peter Marshall and Alexandra Walsham, 1–40. Cambridge: Cambridge University Press.

Martí Ferrando, Josep. 2012. "Francisco Diago." http://bv2.gva.es/catalogo_imagenes/grupo.cmd?path=1001347&responsabilidad_civil=on.

Martin, Dennis D. 2004. "Carthusians, Canonization, and the Universal Call to Sanctity." In *San Bruno di Colonia: Un eremita tra Oriente e Occidente,* edited by Pietro De Leo, 131–50. Soveria Mannelli, It.: Rubbetino.

Martin, Hervé. 1975. *Les ordres mendiants en Bretagne vers 1230–vers 1530. Pauvreté volontaire et prédication à la fin du Moyen-Âge.* Paris: C. Kincksieck.

———. 1988. *Le métier de prédicateur en France septentrionale à la fin du Moyen Âge (1350–1520).* Paris: Cerf.

———. 1997. "La mission de saint Vincent Ferrier en Bretagne (1418–1419): Un exercice mesuré de la violence prophétique." *Comptes rendus, procès-verbaux, mémoires—Association bretonne et union régionaliste bretonne* 106:127–41.

Martínez Gil, Fernando. 1993. *Muerte y sociedad en la España de los austrias.* Madrid: Siglo XXI de España Editores.

Martínez Romero, Tomàs. 2006. "De les *Misses de sant Gregori* a les *Misses de sant Vicent Ferrer.* Un breu recorregut per l'hagiografia vicentina." *Afers* 21:353–66.

Mateu y Llopis, Felipe. 1955. "La iconografía tipográfica de San Vicente Ferrer de los siglos XV y XVI." *Archivo de Arte Valenciano* 26:33–49.

Matz, Jean-Michel. 1991. "Rumeur publique et diffusion d'un nouveau culte à la fin du Moyen Âge: Les miracles de Jean Michel, Évêque d'Angers (1439–†1447)." *Revue d'histoire de l'Église de France* 77 (198): 83–100.

Mazzatinti, Giuseppe. 1957. *Inventari dei manoscritti delle biblioteche d'Italia. LXXXII: Bologna, Biblioteca comunale dell'Archiginnasio, Serie B, continuazione.* Florence: Olschki.

Medina, José Toribio. 1919. *Ensayo de una bibliografía extranjera de santos y venerables americanos.* Santiago de Chile: Elzeviriana.

——. (1910) 1960. *La imprenta en Guatemala (1660–1821).* 2nd ed. 2 vols. Santiago de Chile: En casa del autor. Reprint, Guatemala City: Tipografía Nacional de Guatemala.

——. (1892) 2002. *Historia y bibliografía de la imprenta en el antiguo Vireinato del Rio de la Plata.* La Plata, Argen.: Taller de publicaciones del Museo. Reprint, Mansfield Center, CT: Martino Publishing.

Medina, Miguel Ángel. 1992. *Los dominicos en América. Presencia y actuación de los dominicos en la América colonial española de los siglos XVI–XIX.* Madrid: Editorial MAPFRE.

Meersseman, Gilles. 1947. "La bibliothèque des Frères Prêcheurs de la Minerve à la fin du XVe siècle." In *Mélanges Auguste Pelzer: Études d'histoire littéraire et doctrinale de la Scolastique médiévale offertes à Monseigneur Auguste Pelzer, scriptor de la Bibliothèque Vaticane, à l'occasion de son soixante-dixième anniversaire,* 605–34. Louvain, Belg.: Bibliothèque de l'Université, Éditions de l'Institut Supérieur de Philosophie.

Mesa, José de, and Teresa Gisbert. 1982. *Historia de la pintura cuzqueña.* 2 vols. Lima: Fundación Augusto N. Wiese.

Metropolitan Museum of Art. 2000–2012. "Sermon of Saint Albertus Magnus." http://www.metmuseum.org/Collections/search-the-collections/70012479.

Mira, Eduardo. 2002. "El Santo Grial de Valencia." In *Il Santo Graal: Un mito senza tempo dal Medioevo al cinema. Atti del Convegno Internazionale di studi su "Le reliquie tra storia e mito: il Sacro Catino di Genova e il Santo Graal,"* edited by Massimiliano Macconi and Marina Montesano, 89–104. Genoa: De Ferrari.

Mo, Charles L. 1992. *Splendors of the New World: Spanish Colonial Masterworks from the Viceroyalty of Peru.* Charlotte, NC: Mint Museum of Art.

Molajoli, Bruno. 1960. *IV. Mostra di Restauri: Catalogo.* Naples: Palazzo Reale.

Molinier, A. 1893. *Catalogue général des manuscrits des bibliothèques publiques de France. Départements, tome XXII.* Paris: Plon.

Monetti, Franco. 1978a. "Preziosi affreschi a La Stella. Il primo ciclo pittorico su S. Vincenzo Ferreri." *Piemonte vivo* 1:41–45.

——. 1978b. "Una documentazione della presenza di Vincenzo Ferreri nel Pinerolese." *Studi piemontesi* 8:386–92.

Monetti, Franco, and Arabella Cifani. 1985. *Percorsi periferici: Studi e ricerche di storia dell'arte in Piemonte (secc. XV–XVIII).* Turin: Centro Studi Piemontesi.

Monroe, William S. 2008. "The Scribe, Iacobus Laurentianus, and the Copying of Printed Books in the Fifteenth Century." Presentation at the annual meeting of the Medieval Academy of America, Vancouver, April 3–5.

Montagnes, Bernard. 1980. "Saint Vincent Ferrier devant le schisme." In *Genèse et débuts du grand schisme d'occident,* 607–13. Colloques internationaux du C.N.R.S. No. 586. Avignon, September 25–28, 1978. Paris: Éditions du Centre National de la Recherche Scientifique.

——. 1988. "La guérison miraculeuse et l'investiture prophétique de Vincent Ferrier au couvent des prêcheurs d'Avignon (3 octobre 1398)." In *Avignon au Moyen Âge: Textes et documents,* 193–98. Avignon: Aubanel.

——. 1992. "Prophétisme et eschatologie dans la prédication méridionale de saint Vincent Ferrier." In *Fin du monde et signes des temps: Visionnaires et prophètes en France méridionale ( fin 13e-début 14e siècle),* 331–49. Cahiers de Fanjeaux 27. Fanjeaux: Centre d'Études historiques de Fanjeaux.

——. 2002. "Vincent Ferrer." In *Encyclopedia of the Middle Ages,* edited by André Vauchez. Cambridge: James Clarke & Co. http://0-www.oxfordreference.com. iii-server.ualr.edu/view/10.1093/acref/9780227679319.001.0001/acref-9780227679319-e-2982.

Moore, R. I. 1987. *The Formation of a Persecuting Society: Power and Deviance in Western Europe, 950–1250.* Oxford: Blackwell.

Morçay, Raoul. 1913. *Chroniques de Saint Antonin: Fragments originaux du titre XXII (1378–1459).* Paris: Librairie Gabalda.

Mortier, Daniel-Antonin. 1903–13. *Histoire des maitres généraux de l'ordre des Frères Prêcheurs,* 7 vols. Paris: Alphonse Picard.

Museu Nacional d'Art de Catalunya. 2012. "Sant Vicenç Ferrer." http://art.mnac. cat/fitxatecnica.html;jsessionid=c2019ab134152a6c1ea699f2c0f0557dac641c ffaca6e5e647545a230a8eacce?inventoryNumber=015942–000.

Myers, Kathleen Ann. 2003. "'Redeemer of America': Rosa de Lima (1586–1617), the Dynamics of Identity, and Canonization." In *Colonial Saints: Discovering the Holy in the Americas,* edited by Allan Greer and Jodi Bilinkoff, 251–75. New York: Routledge.

Natale, Mauro. 2001. *El Renacimiento Mediterráneo: Viajes de artistas e itinerarios de obras entre Italia, Francia y España en el siglo XV.* Madrid: Fundación Colección Thyssen-Bornemisza.

National Gallery [London]. 2012. "Saint Vincent Ferrer." http://www.nationalgallery. org.uk/paintings/francesco-del-cossa-saint-vincent-ferrer.

Naughton, Joan Margaret. 1995. "Manuscripts from the Dominican Monastery of Saint-Louis de Poissy." PhD diss., University of Melbourne.

Netanyahu, B. 1995. *The Origins of the Inquisition in Fifteenth Century Spain.* New York: Random House.

Nice, Jason. 2009. *Sacred History and National Identity: Comparisons between Early Modern Wales and Brittany.* London: Pickering & Chatto.

Niederlender, Philippe. 1986–88. "Vincent Ferrier." In *Histoire des saints et de la sainteté chrétienne.* Vol. 7, *Une église éclatée 1275–1545,* edited by André Vauchez, 248. Paris: Hachette.

——. 1993. "Vincent Ferrier: Prédicateur du jugement et thaumaturge." In *2000 ans d'histoire de Vannes,* 71–94. Vannes: Archives municipales de Vannes.

Nieser, Albert B. 1998. *Las fundaciones misionales dominicas en Baja California, 1769–1822.* Translated by Esteban Arroyo G. and Carlos Amado L. Mexicali: Universidad Antónoma de Baja California.

Nirenberg, David. 2002. "Conversion, Sex, and Segregation: Jews and Christians in Medieval Spain." *American Historical Review* 107:1065–93.

O'Callaghan, Joseph F. 1975. *A History of Medieval Spain.* Ithaca: Cornell University Press.

Olivera López, Luis, and Rocío Meza Oliver. 2006. *Catálogo de la colección Lafragua de la Benemérita Universidad Autónoma de Puebla, 1616–1873.* Mexico City: UNAM.

O'Malley, John W. 1979. *Praise and Blame in Renaissance Rome: Rhetoric, Doctrine, and Reform in the Sacred Orators of the Papal Court, c. 1450–1521.* Durham, NC: Duke University Press.

O'Malley, Michelle. 2005. *The Business of Art: Contracts and the Commissioning Process in Renaissance Italy.* New Haven:Yale University Press.

Ono.com. 2012. "La Génesis y procedencia del retablo de SanVicente Ferrer (Iglesia de la Sangre)." http://webs.ono.com/mabacam/Retablo de SanVicente.htm.

Orsi, Robert. 2003. "Is the Study of Lived Religion Irrelevant to the World We Live in?" *Journal for the Scientific Study of Religion* 42 (2): 169–74.

Ortuño Soriano, Roberto. 2005. "Sermón de San Luis Bertrán en la fiesta de San Vicente Ferrer," *Escritos del Vedat* 35:127–44.

Paciocco, Roberto. 1996. *"Sublimia negotia": Le canonizzazioni dei santi nella curia papale e il nuovo ordine dei frati minori.* Padua: Centro Studi Antoniani.

Pagano, Mario. 1999. "Un inedito volgarizzamento siciliano dalla *Legenda Aurea:* La *Vita di S. Cristina."* *Siculorum gymnasium* 52:747–66.

———. 2000. "I 'Miracoli' inediti di S. Vincenzo Ferrer in volgare siciliano." *Siculorum gymnasium* 53:345–90.

Pane, Roberto. 1975. *Il Rinascimento nell'Italia meridionale.* 2 vols. Milan: Edizioni di Comunità.

Paravy, Pierette. 1984. "Remarques sur les passages de saint Vincent Ferrier dans les vallées vaudoises." In *Croyances religieuses et sociétés alpines: Actes du Colloque de Freissinières, 15, 16 et 17 octobre 1981,* 143–55. Gap, Fr.: Société d'études des Hautes-Alpes.

———. 1993. *De la Chrétienté Romaine à la réforme en Dauphiné: Évêques, fidèles et déviants (vers 1340–vers 1530).* 2 vols. Rome: École française de Rome.

Parsons, Gerald. 2008. *The Cult of Saint Catherine of Siena: A Study in Civil Religion.* Aldershot, UK: Ashgate.

Pasini, Pier Giorgio. 1983. *La pinacoteca di Rimini.* Milan: Silvana.

Paul, Jacques. 1983. "Expression et perception du temps d'après l'enquête sur les miracles de Louis d'Anjou." In *Temps, mémoire, tradition au Moyen Âge: Actes du XIIIe congrès de la Société des historiens médiévistes de l'enseignement supérieur public, Aix-en-Provence, 4–5 juin 1982,* 19–41. Aix-en-Provence: Université de Provence.

Pegg, Mark. 2001. *The Corruption of Angels: The Great Inquisition of 1245–46.* Princeton: Princeton University Press.

Pellegrini, Letizia. 2004. "La sainteté au XVe siècle entre procès et droit canonique: Avant et après Bernardin de Sienne." In *Procès de canonisation au Moyen Âge: Aspects juridiques et religieux,* edited by Gábor Klaniczay, 309–26. Collection de l'École française de Rome 340. Rome: École française de Rome.

———. 2009. *Il processo di canonizzazione di Bernardino da Siena, 1445–1450.* Analecta Franciscana 16. Grottaferrata, It.: Frati editori di Quaracchi.

Pérez Vilatela, Luciano. 2004. "Francisco Diago O.P. y sus *Anales* (1613): Ecos de Viterbo y otras mixtificaciones." *Estudi general: Revista de la Facultat de Lietres de la Universitat de Girona* 23–24:389–413.

Polo Museale Fiorentino. 2012. "Inventario 1890." http://www.polomuseale.firenze. it/inv1890/.

Poncelet, Albert. 1925. "Catalogus Codicum hagiographicorum latinorum Bibliothecae Capituli Novariensis," *Analecta Bollandiana* 43:330–77.

Prudlo, Donald. 2008. *The Martyred Inquisitor: The Life and Cult of Peter of Verona (†1252)*. Church, Faith and Culture in the Medieval West. Aldershot, UK: Ashgate.

Rabotti, Giuseppe. 1960. "Albertucci de' Borselli, Girolamo." *Dizionario Biografico degli Italiani*. http://www.treccani.it/enciclopedia/albertucci-de-borselli-girolamo_(Dizionario-Biografico)/.

Ramirez, Ramón. 1979. *Los dominicos en Chile y la primera universidad*. Santiago: Universidad Técnica del Estado.

Réau, Louis. 1959. *Iconographie de l'art chrétien*. 3 vols. in 6. Paris: Presses Universitaires de France.

Redden, Andrew. 2008. *Diabolism in Colonial Peru, 1560–1750*. London: Pickering & Chatto.

Reeves, Marjorie. 1969. *The Influence of Prophecy in the Later Middle Ages: A Study in Joachimism*. Oxford: Clarendon Press.

Reilly, Bernard F. 1993. *The Medieval Spains*. Cambridge: Cambridge University Press.

Resta, Gianvito. 1978. "Cassarino, Antonio." *Dizionario Biografico degli Italiani*. http://www.treccani.it/enciclopedia/antonio-cassarino_(Dizionario-Biografico)/.

Ricard, Robert. 1974. *The Spiritual Conquest of Mexico*. Translated by Lesly Byrd Simpson. Berkeley: University of California Press.

Ricci, Giovanni. 1982. "Donzelle in pericolo e fanciulli in salamoia. Una immagine indisciplinata e la sua normalizzazione." *Annali dell'Istituto storico italo-germanico in Trento* 8:373–406.

Rice, Eugene F., Jr. 1985. *Saint Jerome in the Renaissance*. Johns Hopkins Symposia in Comparative History 13. Baltimore: Johns Hopkins University Press.

Robles, Laureano. 1979. "Vicente J. Antist, O.P., y su opúsculo 'De viris illustribus.'" *Revista Española de Teología* 39–40 (154–61): 199–242.

Robles Sierra, Adolfo. 1984. "Manuscritos del Archivo del Real Convento de Predicadores de Valencia," *Escritos del Vedat* 14:349–402.

——. 1991. "Misioneros dominicos valencianos del siglo XVII." In *Los dominicos y el nuevo mundo. Actas del III Congreso Internacional (Granada, 10–14 de septiembre de 1990)*, 267–319. Madrid: Deimos.

——. 1999. "Algunos problemas que plantea la historiografía de San Vicente." In José Teixidor, *Vida de San Vicente Ferrer. Apóstol de Europa*. 1:i–xxviii. Valencia: Ajuntament de Valencia.

Rodríguez, Santiago. 1992. "Listas de misioneros dominicos en Baja California." In *Dominicos en Mesoamérica: 500 años*, 487–548. Mexico City: Provincia Santiago de México; Provincia de Teutonia.

Roig Condomina, Vicente María. 1985. "Los emblemas animalísticos de fray Andrés Ferrer de Valdecebro." *Goya: Revista de arte* 187–88:81–86.

Rollo-Koster, Joëlle. 2001. "Vincent Ferrer, Saint (1350–1419)." In *The Late Medieval Age of Crisis and Renewal, 1300–1500: A Biographical Dictionary*, edited by Clayton J. Drees, 490–91. Westport, CT: Greenwood Press.

——. 2003. "The Politics of Body Parts: Contested Topographies in Late-Medieval Avignon." *Speculum* 78:66–98.

Rollo-Koster, Joëlle, and Thomas Izbicki, eds. 2009. *A Companion to the Great Western Schism, 1378–1417.* Leiden, Neth.: Brill.

Roy, Bruno. 1966. "Les sources de l'Office de S. Vincent Ferrier." *Sciences ecclésiastiques* 18:283–304.

Rubin, Miri 1999. *Gentile Tales: The Narrative Assault on Late Medieval Jews.* New Haven: Yale University Press.

Ruiz, Teofilo F. 2007. *Spain's Centuries of Crisis, 1300–1474.* Malden, MA: Blackwell.

Rusconi, Roberto. 1979. *L'attesa della fine: Crisi della società, profezia ed Apocalisse in Italia al tempo del grande scisma d'Occidente (1378–1417).* Rome: Istituto Storico Italiano per il Medio Evo.

——. 1990. "Vicent Ferrer e Pedro de Luna: Sull'iconografia di un predicatore fra due obbedienze." In *Conciliarismo, stati nazionali, inizi dell'umanesimo: Atti del XXV Convegno storico internazionale, Todi, 9–12 ottobre 1988,* 213–34. Spoleto: Accademia Tudertina.

——. 2004. "Anti-Jewish Preaching in the Fifteenth Century and Images of Preachers in Italian Renaissance Art." In *Friars and Jews in the Middle Ages and Renaissance,* edited by Susan E. Meyers and Steven J. McMichael, 225–37. Medieval Franciscans 2. Leiden, Neth.: Brill.

Ryder, Alan. 1990. *Alfonso the Magnanimous: King of Aragon, Naples and Sicily, 1396–1458.* Oxford: Clarendon Press.

Saffrey, Henri D. 1982. "Les images populaires de saints dominicains à Venise au XVe siècle et l'édition par Alde Manuce des 'Epistole' de Sainte Cathérine de Sienne." *Italia medioevale e umanistica* 25:241–312.

Sallmann, Jean-Michel. 1994. *Naples et ses saints à l'âge baroque (1540–1750).* Paris: Presses Universitaires de France.

Scheeben, Heribert Christian. 1941. "Handschriften III." *Archiv der deutschen Dominikaner* 3:201–26.

Schenone, Héctor H. 1992–98. *Iconografía del arte colonial.* Vols. 1–2, *Los santos.* Vol. 3, *Jesucristo.* Buenos Aires: Fundación Tarea.

Schimmelpfennig, Bernhard. 2004. "Die Berücksichtigung von Kanonisationen in den kurialen Zeremonienbüchern des 14. und 15. Jahrhunderts." In *Procès de canonisation au Moyen Âge: Aspects juridiques et religieux,* edited by Gábor Klaniczay, 245–57. Collection de l'École française de Rome 340. Rome: École française de Rome.

Schmitt, Jean-Claude. 1990. *La raison des gestes dans l'Occident médiévale.* Paris: Gallimard.

Schreiber, Georg. 1936. *Deutschland und Spanien: Volkskundliche und kulturkundliche Beziehung. Zusammenhänge abendländischer und Ibero-amerikanischer Sakralkultur.* Düsseldorf: L. Schwann.

Schreiber, W. L. (1926) 1969. *Handbuch der Holz- und Metallschnitte des XV. Jahrhunderts. 3: Holzschnitte mit Darstellungen der männlichen und weiblichen Heiligen, nr. 1174–1782a.* Stuttgart: Anton Hiersemann. Reprint, Nendeln, Liechtenstein: Kraus.

Scribner, Robert W. 1996. "Cologne." In *The Oxford Encyclopedia of the Reformation,* edited by Hans J. Hillebrand. Oxford: Oxford University Press.

http://0-www.oxfordreference.com.iii-server.ualr.edu/view/10.1093/acref/9780195064933.001.0001/acref-9780195064933-e-0309.

Schwaller, John F. 2008. "Dominicans." In *Encyclopedia of Latin American History and Culture,* 2nd ed., edited by Jay Kinsbruner and Erick D. Langer, 2:848–50. Detroit: Scribner's. Retrieved from http://0-go.galegroup.com.iii-server.ualr.edu/ps/i.do?id=GALE%7CCX3078901951&v=2.1&u=uofa_lr&it=r&p=GVRL&sw=w.

Sébillot, Paul. 1880. *Contes populaires de la Haute-Bretagne.* Paris: G. Charpentier.

———. 1881. *Contes des paysans et des pêcheurs.* Contes Populaires de la Haute-Bretagne 2. Paris: G. Charpentier.

———. 1882. *Contes des marins.* Contes Populaires de la Haute-Bretagne 3. Paris: G. Charpentier.

———. 1892. *Les incidents des contes populaires de la Haut-Bretagne.* Vannes: La Foyle.

Shaw, Jane. 2006. *Miracles in Enlightenment England.* New Haven: Yale University Press.

Sigal, Pierre-André. 1985. *L'homme et le miracle dans la France médiévale (XIe–XIIe siècle).* Paris: Cerf.

Sitoy, T. Valentino, Jr. 1985. *A History of Christianity in the Philippines.* Vol. 1, *The Initial Encounter.* Quezon City, Philip.: New Day.

Smith, Alistair, Anthony Reeve, and Ashok Roy. 1981. "Francesco del Cossa's 'S. Vincent Ferrer.'" *National Gallery Technical Bulletin* 5:44–57.

Smoller, Laura Ackerman. 1994. *History, Prophecy, and the Stars: The Christian Astrology of Pierre d'Ailly, 1350–1420.* Princeton: Princeton University Press.

———. 1997. "Defining the Boundaries of the Natural in Fifteenth-Century Brittany: The Inquest into the Miracles of Saint Vincent Ferrer, d. 1419." *Viator* 28:333–59.

———. 1998. "Memory, Miracle, and Meaning in the Canonization of Vincent Ferrer, 1453–54." *Speculum* 73:429–54.

———. 2004a. "Northern and Southern Sanctity in the Canonization of Vincent Ferrer: The Effects of Procedural Differences on the Image of the Saint." In *Procès de canonisation au Moyen Âge: Aspects juridiques et religieux,* edited by Gábor Klaniczay, 289–308. Collection de l'École française de Rome 340. Rome: École française de Rome.

———. 2004b. "Two-Headed Monsters and Chopped-Up Babies: Re-Imagining the Schism after the Council of Constance." Presentation at the annual meeting of the Medieval Academy of America, Seattle, April 1–3.

———. 2005. "Holy Mothers: The History of a Designation of Spiritual Status." In *Piety and Family in Early Modern Europe: Essays in Honour of Steven Ozment,* edited by Marc R. Forster and Benjamin J. Kaplan, 178–200. Aldershot, UK: Ashgate.

———. 2006. "A Case of Demonic Possession in Fifteenth-Century Brittany: Perrin Hervé and the Nascent Cult of Vincent Ferrer." In *Voices from the Bench: The Narratives of Lesser Folk in Medieval Trials,* edited by Michael Goodich, 149–76. New York: Palgrave-Macmillan.

———. 2009. "Vincent Ferrer, the Heretics of Valpute, and the Origins of the Witches' Sabbath." Presentation at the annual meeting of the Medieval Academy of America, Chicago, March 27.

——. 2011a. "From Authentic Miracles to a Rhetoric of Authenticity: Examples from the Canonization and Cult of St. Vincent Ferrer." *Church History* 80 (4):773–97.

——. 2011b. "How the Holy Grail Came to Valencia: Sacred History in Post-Tridentine Aragon." Presentation at the annual meeting of the American Historical Association, Boston, January 7.

Soergel, Philip M. 1993. *Wondrous in His Saints: Counter-Reformation Propaganda in Bavaria.* Berkeley: University of California Press.

——. 1996. "Miracles." In *The Oxford Encyclopedia of the Reformation.* Oxford: Oxford University Press. http://0-www.oxfordreference.com.iii-server.ualr.edu/view/10.1093/acref/9780195064933.001.0001/acref-9780195064933-e-0941.

Sorbelli, Albano. 1922. "Una raccolta poco nota d'antiche vite di santi e religiosi domenicani." *Rendiconto delle sessioni della R. Accademia delle Scienze dell'Istituto di Bologna, Classe di scienze morali,* 2nd ser., 6:79–108.

Spano, S. 1998. "Vincenzo Ferrer." In *Il grande libro dei santi: Dizionario enciclopedico,* edited by Elio Guerriero, Tonino Tuniz, Claudio Leonardi, Andrea Riccardi, and Gabriella Zarri, 3:1936–39. Turin: San Paolo.

Stadler, Johann Evangelist, Franz Joseph Heim, and J. N. Ginal. 1858–82. *Vollständiges Heiligen-Lexikon oder Lebensgeschichten aller Heiligen,* 5 vols. Augsburg: G. Schmid.

Stavig, Ward, and Ella Schmidt. 2008. *The Tupac Amaru and Catarista Rebellions: An Anthology of Sources.* Indianapolis: Hackett.

Stephen, Lynn. 2002. "Sexualities and Genders in Zapotec Oaxaca." *Latin American Perspectives* 29 (2): 41–59.

Strehlke, Carl Brandon. 1998. "Review: Naples. Quattrocento Aragonese." *Burlington Magazine* 140 (1139): 144–45.

Strnad, Alfred A. 1978. "Salvo Cassetta: Verfasser einer Vita des Hl. Vinzenz Ferrer?" In *Xenia Medii Aevi Historiam Illustrantia oblata Thomae Kaeppeli O.P.,* edited by Raymundus Creytens, and Pius Künzle, 2:519–45. Rome: Edizioni di Storia e Letteratura.

Strutt, Joseph. 1785–86. *A Biographical Dictionary Containing a Historical Account of All the Engravers.* 2 vols. London: J. Davis for R. Faulder.

"Supplementum ad vitam Beati Iacobi Veneti." 1893. *Analecta bollandiana* 12:367–70.

Taylor, Anna. 2013. "Hagiography and Early Medieval History." *Religion Compass* 7 (1): 1–14. Doi:10.1111/rec3.12023.

Taylor, William B. 1996. *Magistrates of the Sacred: Priests and Parishioners in Eighteenth-Century Mexico.* Stanford, CA: Stanford University Press.

Termini, F. A. 1915. *Pietro Ransano, umanista palermitano del sec. XV.* Palermo: Libreria editrice Ant. Trimarchi.

——. 1916. "Ricostruzione cronologica della biografia di Pietro Ransano." *Archivio storico siciliano,* n.s., 41:81–104.

Thomas, A.-M. 1901. "Annotations. Les reliques de Saint Vincent Ferrier." In Albert Le Grand, *Les vies des Saints de la Bretagne Armorique,* 136–41. Quimper, Fr.: J. Salaun.

Thomas-Lacroix, Pierre. 1954. *Saint Vincent Ferrier, 1350–1419, canonisé en 1455.* Vannes: Galles.

Thompson, Augustine. 2005. *Cities of God: The Religion of the Italian Communes, 1125–1325.* University Park: Pennsylvania State University Press.

Thompson, Stith. 1966. *Motif-index of Folk-literature: A Classification of Narrative Elements in Folktales, Ballads, Myths, Fables, Medieval Romance, Exempla, Fabliaux, Jest-books, and Local Legends.* Rev. ed. Bloomington: Indiana University Press.

Tingle, Elizabeth. 2005. "The Sacred Space of Julien Maunoir: The Re-Christianising of the Landscape in Seventeenth-Century Brittany." In *Sacred Space in Early Modern Europe,* edited by Will Coster and Andrew Spicer, 237–58. Cambridge: Cambridge University Press.

Todini, Filippo. 1989. *La pittura umbra: Dal Duecento al primo Cinquecento.* 2 vols. Milan: Longanesi.

Toldrà, Albert. 2004. "Sant Vicent Ferrer. Debats historiogràfics." *Afers* 19:157–73.

Torella, Fabrizio. 1985–87. "L'ombra della mezzaluna sull'arte italiana. Il polittico Griffoni." *Musei ferraresi: Bollettino annuale* 15:43–60.

Touchard, Henri. 1969. "Le Moyen-Age Breton (XIIe–XVIe siècles)." In *Histoire de la Bretagne,* edited by Jean Delumeau, 153–215. Univers de la France et des pays francophones, Histoire des provinces. Toulouse: Privat.

Toynbee, Margaret. 1929. *S. Louis of Toulouse and the Process of Canonisation in the Fourteenth Century.* Manchester, UK: Manchester University Press.

Trachtenberg, Joshua. (1943) 1983. *The Devil and the Jews: The Medieval Conception of the Jew and Its Relation to Modern Anti-Semitism.* New Haven: Yale University Press. Reprint, Philadelphia: Jewish Publication Society of America.

Tresvaux, M. l'Abbé. 1839. *L'Église de Bretagne, depuis ses commencements jusqu'à nos jours, ou Histoire des sièges épiscopaux, séminaires et collégiales, abbayes et autres communautés régulières et séculières de cette province: Publié d'après les matériaux de Dom Hyacinthe Morice de Beaubois, Religieux bénédictin de la Congrégation de Saint-Maur.* Paris: Méquignon Junior.

Valois, Noël. (1896–1902) 1967. *La France et le Grand Schisme d'occident.* 4 vols. Paris: A. Picard, 1896–1902. Reprint, Hildesheim: Georg Olms.

Vatican Museums. 2012. "The Miracles of St Vincent Ferrer." http://mv.vatican.va/3_EN/pages/x-Schede/PINs/PINs_Sala05_04_022.html.

Vauchez, André. 1978. "Canonisation et politique au XIVe siècle. Documents inédits des Archives du Vatican relatifs au procès de canonisation de Charles de Blois, duc de Bretagne (†1364)." In *Miscellanea in onore di Monsignor Martini Guisti,* 2:381–404. Collectanea Archivi Vaticani 5–6. Vatican City: Archivio Vaticano.

——. 1988. *La sainteté en Occident aux derniers siècles du Moyen Âge d'après les procès de canonisation et les documents hagiographiques.* Rev. ed. Bibliothèque des écoles françaises d'Athènes et de Rome 241. Rome: École française de Rome.

——. 1997. *Sainthood in the Later Middle Ages.* Translated by Jean Birrell. Cambridge: Cambridge University Press. (Translation is based on 1988 French edition.)

Velasco Gonzàlez, Alberto. 2008. "Dos arquetips iconogràfics i dos models de difusió en la iconografia primerenca de sant Vicent Ferrer." In *Hagiografia peninsular en els segles medievals,* edited by Francesca Español Bertran and Francesc Fité Llevot, 235–64. Lérida, Sp.: Edicions de la Universitat de Lleida.

——. 2008–9. "El periple de Sant Vicent Ferrer per les terres de Lleida i la Franza." In *Arrels cristianes: Presència i significació del cristianisme en la història i la societat de Lleida,* edited by Romà Sol Clot, Carme Torres Graell, Ximo Company Climent, and Joan-Ramon González, 267–86. Lérida, Sp.: Bisbat de Lleida, Pagès.

Venturini, Lisa. 1996. "Riflessioni sulla pala ghirlandaiesca di Rimini." In *Domenico Ghirlandaio, 1449–1494: Atti del Covegno Internazionale, Firenze, 16 –18 ottobre 1994,* edited by Wolfram Prinz and Max Seidel, 154–64. Florence: Centro DI.

Vigni, Giorgio, and Giovanni Carandente. 1953. *Antonello da Messina e la pittura del '400 in Sicilia: Catalogo della Mostra.* Venice: Alfieri Editore.

Vose, Robin. 2009. *Dominicans, Muslims, and Jews in the Medieval Crown of Aragon.* Cambridge: Cambridge University Press.

———. 2011. "Christian Missionary Ideals among the Dominicans of Valencia: Memories of San Luis Bertrán." In *Francisco de Borja y su tiempo: Política, religión y cultura en la edad moderna,* edited by Enrique García Hernán and María del Pilar Ryan, 255–68. Valencia: Albatros/Institutum Historicum Societatis Iesu.

Vrana, Heather. 2007–8. "An 'Other' Woman? Juchitec *Muxes* in *Marie Claire* and Documentary." *Michigan Feminist Studies,* 21 (1): 1–23. http://hdl.handle. net/2027/spo.ark5583.0021.101.

Walker, D. P. 1988. "The Cessation of Miracles." In *Hermeticism and the Renaissance: Intellectual History and the Occult in Early Modern Europe,* edited by Ingrid Merkel and Allen G. Debus, 111–24. Folger Institute Symposia. Washington, DC: Folger Shakespeare Library.

Walker, J. B. 2003. "Vincent Ferrer." In *The New Catholic Encyclopedia,* 2nd ed., 14:520–21. Washington, DC: Thomson/Gale.

Walker, James Bernard. 1933. *The "Chronicles" of Saint Antoninus: A Study in Historiography.* Washington, DC: Catholic University of America.

Wallet, Marc, and Martine Demartres. 1975. "Le Cuzco, triomphe d'un empire colonial." *L'architecture d'aujourd'hui* 179:105–14.

Walsham, Alexandra. 2005. "Miracles in Post-Reformation England." In *Signs, Wonders, Miracles: Representations of Divine Power in the Life of the Church,* edited by Kate Cooper and Jeremy Gregory, 273–306. Woodbridge, UK: Boydell Press.

Ward, Benedicta. 1987. *Miracles and the Medieval Mind: Theory, Record, and Event, 1000–1215.* Rev. ed. Philadelphia: University of Pennsylvania Press.

Watts, Pauline Moffitt. 1985. "Prophecy and Discovery: On the Spiritual Origins of Christopher Columbus's 'Enterprise of the Indies.'" *American Historical Review* 90:73–102.

Webster, Jill Rosemary. 2003. "Ferrer, Vicente, St." In *Medieval Iberia: An Encyclopedia,* edited by E. Michael Gerli, Samuel G. Armistead et al., 332–33. New York: Routledge.

Wetzstein, Thomas. 1999. "Vom 'Volksheiligen' zum 'Fürstenheiligen.' Die Wiederbelebung des Wernerkults im 15. Jahrhundert." *Archiv für mittelrheinische Kirchengeschichte* 51:11–68.

———. 2002. "*Virtus morum et virtus signorum?* Zur Bedeutung der Mirakel in den Kanonisationsprozessen des 15. Jahrhunderts." In *Mirakel im Mittelalter: Konzeption, Erscheinungsformen, Deutungen,* edited by Martin Heinzelmann, Klaus Herbers, and Dieter R. Bauer, 351–76. Beiträge zur Hagiographie 3. Stuttgart: Franz Steiner Verlag.

———. 2004a. *Heilige vor Gericht: Das Kanonisationsverfahren im europäischen Spätmittel-alter.* Forschungen zur kirchlichen Rechtsgeschichte und zum Kirchenrecht 28. Cologne: Böhlau Verlag.

———. 2004b. "Proving the Supranatural: Miracles, Sanctity, and Law of Evidence in Medieval and Early Modern Canonization." Presentation at the conference "Miracles as Epistemic Things," Max Planck Institute for the History of Science, Berlin, October 29–30.

Wittlin, Curt. 1986. "El Padre Juan Meyer de Zuric, traductor y divulgador de la 'Vita Sancti Vincentii Ferrer' de Ranzano." *Escritos del Vedat* 16:217–23.

———. 1987. "La première traduction allemande de la 'Vie de Saint Vincent Ferrier,' de Ranzano, attribuable au dominicain Jean Meyer, dans un manuscrit inédit de Colmar (1457–62). Le miracle de l'enfant découpé." *Archives de l'Église d'Alsace* 46:53–62.

———. 1994. "Sobre les Vides de sant Vicent Ferrer compilades per Ranzano, Antonino, i Miquel Peres; amb una edició de la *Vita Sancti Vincentii* de Francesc de Castiglione." *Anuari de l'Agrupació Borrianenca de Cultura* 5:5–27.

Woodward, Kenneth L. 1996. *Making Saints: How the Catholic Church Determines Who Becomes a Saint, Who Doesn't, and Why.* New York: Simon and Schuster.

Wurster, Wolfgang. 2000. "Cuzco in zwei Welten: Hauptstadt der Inka und spanische Kolonialstadt." *Antike Welt* 31 (2): 141–55.

Ximénez, Francisco. 1999. *Historia de la provincia de San Vicente de Chiapa y Guatemala de la orden de predicadores.* Edited by Carmelo Sáenz de Santa María. 2 vols. Mexico City: Consejo Estatal para la Cultura y las Artes de Chiapas.

Zafarana, Zelina. 1976. "Caracciolo, Roberto (Roberto da Lecce)." In *Dizionario Biografico degli Italiani.* http://www.treccani.it/enciclopedia/roberto-caracciolo_(Dizionario-Biografico)/.

Zeldes, Nadia. 2006. "The Last Multi-Cultural Encounter in Medieval Sicily: A Dominican Scholar, an Arabic Inscription, and Jewish Legend." *Mediterranean Historical Review* 21 (2): 159–91.

Ziegler, Joseph. 1999. "Practitioners and Saints: Medical Men in Canonization Processes in the Thirteenth to Fifteenth Centuries." *Social History of Medicine* 12 (2): 191–225.

Zucker, Mark J. 1992. "Problems in Dominican Iconography: The Case of St. Vincent Ferrer." *Artibus et historiae: An Art Anthology* 13 (25): 181–93.

# INDEX

2 Thessalonians 2:3, 136, 143

*Acta Sanctorum,* 15, 234, 272, 294, 297
Alanou, Alieta, 16n3, 92, 96
Alanus (cardinal of Santa Prassede).
    *See* Coativi, Alain de
Alberti, Leandro, 188–90
Alfonso V of Aragon
    association with miracle, 45
    Calixtus III and, 46, 131n45
    canonization process and, 30, 46, 50,
        61, 62, 82, 83
    cost of canonization to, 34, 44
    father of, 43
    inquests, canonization, 31, 44, 46
    Nicholas V and, 131n45
    Ranzano, Pietro, and, 47, 124
    represented at canonization, 35,
        44, 47
    territory of, 123
    *See also* Trastámara dynasty
Alfonsus (cardinal of the Four Crowned
        Martyrs). *See* Borja (Borgia), Alfonso
        de; Calixtus III
altarpieces. *See* artworks
Americas, Spanish, 274–97
    angel of the apocalypse in, 15, 279,
        282, 284–85, 294
    artworks, 287–95, 288 fig. 20
    baby, chopped-up, in, 291–92
    conversions in, 275, 278, 280, 294
    Dominican province names in, 276,
        276n7, 277
    *History of the Marvelous and Admirable
        Life* ... (Ferrer de Valdecebro), 260
    languages in, 276–77
    miracles in, 282–84, 289–91
    overview, 274–75
    popular practices in, 280–84
    publications in, 275, 276, 278–87,
        283 fig. 19

angel of the apocalypse, 122–23
    in Americas, Spanish, 15, 279, 282,
        284–85, 294
    in artworks, 196, 218, 287–89, 288
        fig. 20
    described as, 9, 94, 95, 99
    self-description as, 8, 94–95, 136
    *See also* preaching, apocalyptic
Angers inquest, 28, 69
*Annales omnium temporum (Annals of All
        Times)* (Ranzano), 125, 126, 127, 170,
        171, 172–73, 187
Annunciation, 196, 202, 203 fig. 7
*Anthill, The* (Nider), 161, 162, 165–69,
        174, 191
Anthony of Rivoli, Saint, 126, 127
Antichrist
    2 Thessalonians 2:3, 136, 143
    Antist, Vicente Justiniano, on, 265
    early modern approaches to, 230
    flagellation and, 263
    mission to preach against, 133–34, 142,
        162, 164
    popes as, 135, 178
    preaching on, 1, 7–8, 136–38, 172, 178
    prediction of, 136–37, 158, 165, 170,
        177, 180, 231
    Protestants on, 229
    Schism as preamble to, 5, 133, 136, 143
    *See also* Great Schism; Last Judgment;
        preaching, apocalyptic
antisemitism, 7, 132, 154–55, 157–58,
        201n151
    *See also* Jews
Antist, Vicente Justiniano
    baby, chopped-up, 266
    Diago, Francisco, and, 241
    Great Schism, 262, 263
    *Life and History* ..., 234–40
    on preaching, apocalyptic, 265
    sources, 60, 138, 227